Essentials *of* Business Communication

SIXTH EDITION

Mary Ellen Guffey

Professor of Business Emeritus
Los Angeles Pierce College

THOMSON

SOUTH-WESTERN

Australia · Canada · Mexico · Singapore · Spain · United Kingdom · United States

THOMSON

SOUTH-WESTERN

Essentials of Business Communication, 6th Edition

Mary Ellen Guffey

Publisher:
Melissa Acuña

Acquisitions Editor:
Jennifer Codner

Developmental Editor:
Mary Draper

Marketing Manager:
Larry Qualls

Sr. Production Editor:
Deanna Quinn

Manufacturing Coordinator:
Diane Lohman

Media Technology Editor:
Jim Rice

Media Developmental Editor:
Josh Fendley

Media Production Editor:
Kelly Reid

Photography Manager:
Deanna Ettinger

Photo Researcher:
Susan Van Etten

Sr. Design Project Manager:
Michelle Kunkler

Internal and Cover Designer:
Jennifer Lambert/Jen2Design

Cover Illustration:
© Armen Kojoyian

Production House:
WordCrafters Editorial Services, Inc

Compositor:
GGS Information Services, Inc.

Printer:
Cadmus

Library of Congress Control
Number: 2002116498

ISBN: 0-324-23364-7 (Student Edition InfoTrac Package)

ISBN: 0-324-19154-5 (Student Edition Text)

ISBN: 0-324-23365-5 (Student CD)

ISBN: 0-534-55853-4 (InfoTrac Card)

ISBN: 0-324-23366-3 (Annotated Instructor's Edition Package)

ISBN: 0-324-19150-2 (Annotated Instructor's Edition Text)

About the Author

A dedicated professional, Mary Ellen Guffey has taught business communication and business English topics for over thirty years. She received a bachelor's degree, *summa cum laude*, in business education from Bowling Green State University; a master's degree in business education from the University of Illinois, where she held a fellowship; and a doctorate in business and economic education from the University of California, Los Angeles (UCLA). She has taught at the University of Illinois, Santa Monica College, and Los Angeles Pierce College.

She is the author of many books in the field of business communication. *Business Communication: Process and Product*, the leading textbook in its field, recently won the top award in the field of communication from the Text and Academic Authors Association. The Canadian version of *Business Communication: Process and Product* was named Book of the Year by Nelson Publishing. Dr. Guffey's *Business English*, 7e, which serves more students than any other book in its field, was honored by the Text and Academic Authors Association for its excellence and longevity in the field. *Business English* and portions of *Essentials of Business Communication* have been translated into Chinese for overseas audiences. With Carolyn M. Seefer, Dr. Guffey has written *Essentials of College English*, 2e. Dr. Guffey also serves on the review boards of *The Delta Pi Epsilon Journal* and *The Business Communication Quarterly* of the Association for Business Communication.

A teacher's teacher and leader in the field, Dr. Guffey acts as a partner and mentor to hundreds of business communication instructors across the country. Her workshops, seminars, newsletters, articles, teaching materials, and Web sites help novice and veteran business communication instructors achieve effective results in their courses. She privately maintains comprehensive Web sites for students and instructors. Her print and online newsletters are used by thousands of instructors in this country and abroad.

Brief Contents

Contents

4 Revising and Proofreading Business Messages   80

Unit 3   Corresponding at Work   99

5 E-Mail and Memorandums   100

Contents

Contents

Preface

Welcome to the sixth edition of *Essentials of Business Communication* by Mary Ellen Guffey. This text/workbook has soared to a leadership position in the business communication market because of its time-tested, interactive learning system that prepares students to excel in today's digital workplace. In the following pages, you will find a description of the features and abundant resources for students and instructors that set the bar for the next generation of business communication education.

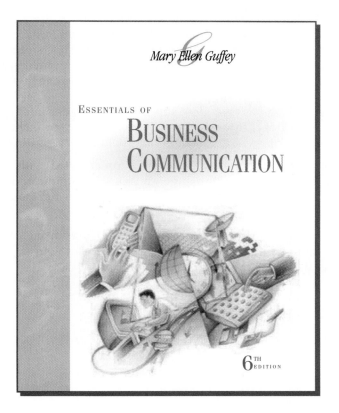

G

Dr. Mary Ellen Guffey
Thomson/South-Western Publishing

E-mail: meguffey@westwords.com
Student Web site: http://www.westwords.com/guffey/students.html
Instructor's Web site: http://www.westwords.com/instructor.html

Dear Friends and Colleagues:

Thanks to the overwhelming support of students and instructors, *Essentials of Business Communication* continues to be the leading text/workbook in the field of business communication. The first five editions have been adopted in over 700 four-year, two-year, and career schools across the U.S. and Canada, as well as in many schools around the world. Because of its concise, efficient coverage, it has been especially appealing to students in a hurry to develop marketable skills.

The following features, illustrated in the Preface, describe some of the improvements in *Essentials of Business Communication*, Sixth Edition:

- **New Chapter on Interpersonal Skills** provides in-depth coverage to equip students with the soft skills employers demand.
- **Enhanced Coverage of E-Mail** in completely revised Chapter 5 includes new discussion of e-mail dangers, effective techniques, and timely case studies.
- **Expanded Oral Presentation Chapter** enlarges PowerPoint® coverage.
- **New "Before" and "After" Documents** help students visualize the process and effect of revision.
- **New Four-Color Design and More Cartoons** maximize reader interest.
- **"Bridging the Gap" Video Case Studies** integrate videos in many chapters.
- **Free InfoTrac® Online Library** helps students build knowledge and research skills.
- **Fresh Case Studies** (more than 60 to 80 percent new problems) enliven writing exercises with many topics from current events.
- **WebTutor™ Advantage**, a Web-based student supplement, includes interactive learning tools that build student competence. Features of WebTutor™ Advantage include author-narrated PowerPoint® slides, chapter quizzes, demonstration problems, and writing exercises.

Most important, *Essentials of Business Communication* is supplemented with the most extensive publisher ancillaries and the best student Web site in business communications. I regularly hear from instructors and students from around the country with praises for the abundant resources offered with this text.

Please continue to share your comments and recommendations with me. As one of the most accessible and responsive authors in the field, I am eager to receive your suggestions regarding this book, our Web site, and your business communication course.

Cordially,

Mary Ellen Guffey

Maintaining Essentials —

EFFECTIVE FEATURES AND RESOURCES REMAIN UNCHANGED

Since its first edition, *Essentials of Business Communication* featured a practical teaching/learning program that helped students build employment skills quickly. *Essentials* has been especially successful in developing communication skills for students with outdated, inadequate, or weak language arts training. Writing skills receive special emphasis because these skills are increasingly important and because such skills require special training to develop.

Although the Sixth Edition represents a substantial revision, it retains the powerful foundation features that moved the first five editions to the head of the market in this country and abroad. The following major features, resources, and effective strategies have helped thousands of students improve their communication skills.

- **Text/Workbook Format.** The convenient text/workbook format presents an all-in-one teaching-learning package that includes concepts, workbook application exercises, writing problems, and a combination handbook/reference manual. Students purchase and work with only one resource for efficient, economical instruction.

- **Comprehensive Yet Concise Coverage.** An important reason for the enormous success of *Essentials of Business Communication* is that it practices what it preaches. The Sixth Edition follows the same strategy, concentrating on essential concepts presented without wasted words. The Sixth Edition still contains only 14 chapters, making it possible to cover the entire text easily in one quarter or semester.

- **Writing Plans and Writing Improvement Exercises.** Clear step-by-step writing plans structure the assignments so that novice writers can get started quickly and stay focused on the writing experience—without struggling to provide unknown details to unfamiliar, hypothetical cases. Ample revision exercises build confidence and skills.

> "The writing exercises presented are a blessing for any teacher. The clarity of the writing sections of the text permits students to learn proper business writing and grammar. The clear examples and exercises provide the student with ample writing practice. Overall, an excellent text that will teach students proper business writing."
>
> *Sandie Idziak*
> *University of Texas, Arlington*

WRITING PLAN FOR A PERSUASIVE REQUEST

- *Opening:* **Obtain the reader's attention and interest.** Describe a problem, state something unexpected, suggest reader benefits, offer praise or compliments, or ask a stimulating question.
- *Body:* **Build interest.** Explain logically and concisely the purpose of the request. Prove its merit. Use facts, statistics, expert opinion, examples, specific details, and direct and indirect benefits.
- *Body:* **Reduce resistance.** Anticipate objections, offer counterarguments, establish credibility, demonstrate competence, and show the value of your proposal.
- *Closing:* **Motivate action.** Ask for a particular action. Make the action easy to take. Show courtesy and respect.

- **Wide Coverage of Communication Technology.** All relevant chapters build technology skills by including discussions and applications involving e-mail, Web research, contemporary software, online employment, and electronic presentations.

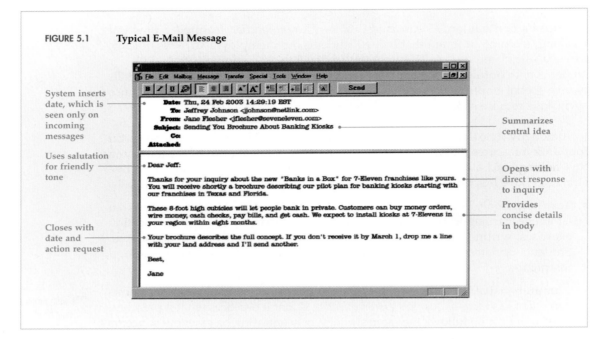

FIGURE 5.1   Typical E-Mail Message

System inserts date, which is seen only on incoming messages

Uses salutation for friendly tone

Closes with date and action request

Summarizes central idea

Opens with direct response to inquiry

Provides concise details in body

- **Grammar/Mechanics Emphasis.** Each chapter features a systematic review of the Grammar/Mechanics Handbook that is included at the end of the text. Readers take a short quiz to review specific concepts and proofread business documents that provide a cumulative review of all concepts previously presented.

- **Premier Web Sites.** No other textbook supplies both students and instructors with such comprehensive resources immediately available on the Internet. Interactive student exercises promote learning and retention, while exceptional instructional modules and classroom aids ease a teacher's load. Students can visit http://www.westwords.com/guffey/students.html for instructional support and career information. Instructors will find a wealth of resources at http://www.westwords.com/instructor.html.

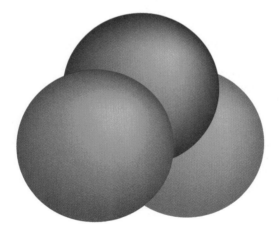

"I've taught Business Communication since 1999 at Los Medanos College, and every semester the students comment on how much they like *Essentials of Business Communication* and especially the Web site. As an instructor I particularly enjoy the number of supplemental items that make my job easier, more interesting, and fun for the students and myself, and, most importantly, educational. Dr. Guffey is a dedicated and passionate professional, and instructors and students both benefit greatly from her textbooks."

Courtney Knauer
Los Medanos College

Exceeding Expectations—

REVISIONS FOR MORE EFFECTIVE TEACHING AND LEARNING

The following pedagogical features update and enhance the Sixth Edition:

- **New "Before" and "After" Documents.** To help students visualize the process and effect of revision, many chapters now show side-by-side versions of before-and-after messages.

- **Enhanced Coverage of E-Mail.** A completely revised Chapter 5 includes new coverage of e-mail dangers, such as when to use e-mail and when to send hard-copy memos, and extensive new problems on timely topics such as car phone safety, workplace violence, unwanted e-mail, time management, and smoking bans.

SMART E-MAIL PRACTICES

✓ Quick Check

Because e-mail is now a main-stream communication channel, messages should be well-organized, carefully composed, and grammatically correct.

Despite its dangers and limitations, however, e-mail is increasingly the preferred choice for sending many business messages. Because e-mail has become a main-stream channel of communication, it's important to take the time to organize your thoughts, compose carefully, and be concerned with correct grammar and punctuation.

Getting Started.   The following pointers will help you get off to a good start in using e-mail safely and effectively.

- **New Chapter on Interpersonal Skills.** Chapter 11, "Communicating in Person, by Telephone, and in Meetings," provides in-depth coverage of key interpersonal skills so that students are equipped with the soft skills employers demand.

- **Expanded Oral Presentation Chapter.** An amplified Chapter 12 now provides helpful suggestions regarding audience types, gaining and keeping attention, achieving audience rapport, concluding a talk, and adapting to international and cross-cultural audiences.

- **Enhanced PowerPoint® Preparation Instruction.** In addition to updated how-to coverage for PowerPoint presentations, students now learn how to convert statements into bullet points and how to avoid being upstaged by their slides.

- **New Four-Color Design.** To maximize reader interest and illustrate concepts with greater emphasis, a new four-color design enhances the Sixth Edition.

"I'm impressed with the creativity of the Web-based activities. They're great because they show students new ways to use the Internet interactively. I've been to Web sites for other courses and haven't seen one that was as thorough or as useful or that had such a wide variety of activities."

Karin Jacobson, Student
University of Montana, Helena

- **Timely Communication Workshops.** Communication Workshops provide insight into special business communication topics and skills not discussed in the chapters. These topics cover ethics, technology, career skills, and collaboration. Each workshop includes a career application with a case study or problem to help students develop important skills. New workshops cover topics such as "Dr. Guffey's Guide to Business Etiquette and Workplace Manners" (an interactive Web module) and "How to Deal with Difficult People at Work."

COMMUNICATION WORKSHOP: ETHICS

Whose Computer Is It Anyway?

More and more companies today provide their employees with computers and Internet access. Should employees be able to use those computers for online shopping, personal messages, personal work, and listening to music or playing games?

But It's Harmless

The Wall Street Journal reports that many office workers have discovered that it's far easier to do their shopping online than racing to malls and waiting in line. To justify her Web shopping at work, one employee, a recent graduate, says, "Instead of standing at the water cooler gossiping, I shop online." She went on to say, "I'm not sapping company resources by doing this."

Some online office shoppers say that what they're doing is similar to making personal phone calls. So long as they don't abuse the practice, they see no harm. And besides, shopping at the office is far faster than shopping from most dial-up home computer connections. Marketing director David Krane justifies his online shopping by explaining that his employer benefits because he is more productive when he takes minibreaks. "When I need a break, I just pull up a Web page and just browse," he says. "Ten minutes later, I'm all refreshed, and I can go back to business-plan writing."

Companies Urged to Crack Down

Employers are less happy about increasing use of bandwidth for personal online discovered an empl ing a personal business of

COMMUNICATION WORKSHOP: CAREER SKILLS

Dr. Guffey's Guide to Business Etiquette and Workplace Manners

Etiquette, civility, and goodwill efforts may seem out of place in today's fast-paced, high-tech offices. Yet, etiquette and courtesy are more important than ever if diverse employees are to be able to work cooperatively and maximize productivity and workflow. Many organizations recognize that good manners are good for business. Some colleges and universities offer management programs that include a short course in manners. Companies are also conducting manners seminars for trainee and veteran managers. Why is politeness regaining legitimacy as a leadership tool? Primarily because courtesy works.

Good manners convey a positive image of an organization. People like to do business with people who show respect and treat others civilly. People also like to work in an environment that is pleasant. Considering how much time is spent at work, doesn't it make sense to prefer an agreeable environment to one that is rude and uncivil?

Etiquette is more about attitude than about formal rules of behavior. That attitude is a desire to show others consideration and respect. It includes a desire to make others feel comfortable. You don't have to become a "sissy" or an etiquette nut, but you might need to polish your social competencies a little to be an effective businessperson today.

up your workpl kills online at "Dr. G

- **"Bridging the Gap" Integrated Video Case Studies.** New "Bridging the Gap" video case studies are incorporated into end-of-chapter activities so that students have discussion questions and key points immediately available.

- **Free InfoTrac® Online Library.** To help students build knowledge and research skills, the sixth edition carries a free subscription to InfoTrac®. Many chapter activities incorporate InfoTrac® assignments to expand students' access to newspaper, journal, and magazine articles.

VIDEO CASE

Designing and Delivering Oral Presentations at Burke Marketing

Burke Marketing Research is one of the premier international marketing research and consulting firms in the industry. It is the world's seventh largest research company, and a large part of its business revolves around presenting research findings to clients. In the video a Burke vice president says that to be most meaningful, research results should be explained in person. This is usually done in an oral presentation accompanied by a written report. In this video Burke consultants discuss how to plan, organize, and deliver an effective presentation. They also present tips regarding dress, honesty, repetition, animation, and brevity.

Your Task. After watching the video, be prepared to answer these questions:

- What are the four main steps that Burke consultants follow in creating an effective oral presentation?
- What tips do Burke consultants mention for improving the delivery of a presentation?
- How can unfavorable results be successfully presented?
- ___ the worst error a present___ ___ make?

- **New APA Documentation Formats.** In addition to MLA documentation formats, the Sixth Edition now provides APA formats as well.

"Guffey seems to have her hands on the pulse of not only what is currently needed by students and instructors, but is looking toward what might be needed in the future. I think this is what has always made her textbooks seem more current than some of the other texts out there."

Sheryl E. C. Joshua
University of North Carolina

- **Fresh Case Studies.** In the writing chapters, 60 to 80 percent of the case studies are new, thus avoiding carry-over from previous editions. Adapted from current events, many case studies feature high-profile companies that students recognize such as Coca-Cola, McDonald's, and Starbucks.

> **5.6 PROCEDURE E-MAIL OR MEMO: RULES FOR WIRELESS PHONE USE IN SALES REPS' CARS.** As one of the managers of LaReve, a hair care and skin products company, you are alarmed at a newspaper article you just saw. A stockbroker for Smith Barney was making cold calls on his personal phone while driving. His car hit and killed a motorcyclist. The brokerage firm was sued and accused of contributing to an accident by encouraging employees to use cellular telephones while driving. To avoid the risk of paying huge damages awarded by an emotional jury, the brokerage firm offered the victim's family a $500,000 settlement.

> **8.14 BAD NEWS FOR CUSTOMERS: STARBUCKS CHARGES WORLD TRADE CENTER RESCUE WORKERS.** Immediately after the September 11 attack in New York, rescue workers rushed to a Starbucks coffee shop near the World Trade Center to get water to treat shock victims. Starbucks employees demanded $130 for three cases of bottled water. Ambulance workers shelled out the cash from their own pockets. But they weren't happy about it.

- **New Test Bank Questions.** Totally revised test banks offer from 50 to 100 percent new questions.

- **More Cartoons!** Lightening the learning load and sharpening chapter concepts are many new cartoons centered on workplace communication.

- **Greater Use of Guffey Web Site.** To provide meaningful Web practice, this edition promotes the rich resources of the Guffey Student Web site at http://www.westwords.com/guffey/students.html. Assignments using the Guffey Web site are particularly effective for distance-learning classes and for intact classes with limited lecture time.

Enhancing Education—

RESOURCES FOR TEACHERS AND STUDENTS

Unparalleled Instructor Support

The Sixth Edition of *Essentials of Business Communication* continues to set the standard for business communication support. Classroom success is easy to achieve because of the many practical ancillary items that supplement Guffey textbooks. No other author matches her level of support. Professor Melanie Young, Clark College, Vancouver, Washington, wrote,

> "*Essentials* is a big hit with my students. While they are working through all the exercises and sharing their completed case problems with each other, I'm enjoying the ease provided the instructor. The instructor's manual, electronic test bank, transparencies, and annotated teacher's text are wonderful tools. I'm amazed at the total number of items available to help me!"

"The end-of-chapter activities are superb and key to the text's success. I like the number, variety, and difficulty range of the activities and cases. With the gradual deterioration of basic English skills of college students and greater numbers of international students, the grammar exercises are valuable additions to the text."

Kenneth Mayer
Cleveland State University

The following timesaving ancillaries and resources accompany the Sixth Edition of *Essentials*:

- **Annotated Instructor's Edition.** The Instructor's Edition includes an answer key so that teachers have an easy-to-read, all-in-one manual from which to teach. In-text answers to the end-of-chapter review questions, writing improvement exercises, grammar/mechanics checkups, and the diagnostic test ensure classroom efficiency. Places where supplementary lectures may be presented are marked in the text. (ISBN: 0-324-19152-9)

- **Leading Web Site for Instructors.** The password-protected Web site for instructors http://www.westwords.com/instructor.html supplies an extensive collection of practical teaching materials such as download-able modules on listening, peer editing, and report-writing projects. Instructors will also find discussion guides, bonus exercises, and sample syllabi for online courses.

- **Instructor's Manual With Test Banks and Solution Masters.** The IM supplies general suggestions for teaching business communication, lesson plans for each chapter, test banks with 50 questions for each chapter, three unit tests, transparency master solutions for all memo- and letter-writing cases, and keys for all cumulative editing quizzes. In addition to ideas for course organization and evaluation, the IM provides many supplementary lectures on relevant topics not covered in the text. (ISBN: 0-324-19153-7)

- **Instructor Resource CD.** The Instructors' Manual and other teaching supports are also available in digital form on CD-ROM. The Instructor Resource CD includes transparency masters, PowerPoint slides, test banks, unit tests, and the instructor's manual in one handy, compact tool with documents that can be customized to fit specific class and student needs. Most of the supplements are formatted in MS Word so that they can be easily revised and printed. (ISBN: 0-324-19157-X)

- **Transparencies.** Compiled by Mary Ellen Guffey, nearly 200 acetates and masters summarize, supplement, and highlight course concepts. They offer lecture summaries, additional examples, effective/ineffective documents, enrichment ideas, and interactive quizzes. With nearly 150 additional solution masters in the Instructor's Manual, *Essentials*, 6e, provides a remarkable total of nearly 350 pages of transparency support—the biggest and best transparency support package in the field. The transparency masters may also be downloaded from the Web site for instructors at http://www.westwords.com/instructor.html. (ISBN: 0-324-19155-3)

- **PowerPoint® Slides.** Summaries of important chapter concepts are rendered professionally in PowerPoint. Instructors can use the chapter presentations as is, or alter them for custom lectures. This unique interactive program not only introduces concepts but also engages students in a dialogue that reviews and reinforces what they are learning. The PowerPoint program for this edition captures attention, creates lively lectures, and, most important, improves learning and retention. Students receive a simplified version of the PowerPoint slides on the Student CD. Instructors receive an enhanced version of the PowerPoint slides on the Instructor's Resource CD. (ISBN: 0-324-19157-X)

"This book is great! It will be going to work with me as a reference book. The interactive quizzes are wonderful. What a great way to review for tests! I also enjoy the 'fun stuff.' My instructor recommended your site, and I'm very glad she did."

Deanna Jokinen, Student
Dakota County Technical College

- **Printed Testing Materials.** The Instructor's Manual for the Sixth Edition supplies totally revised test banks with 50 questions for each chapter. These test banks contain 20 multiple-choice, 20 true-false, and 10 fill-in questions. In this edition more than 50 percent of the multiple-choice and true-false questions are new; in some chapters 100 percent of the questions are new. Instructors may also have tests created and printed by calling the **Academic Resource Center at Thomson/South-Western at 1-800-423-0563 between 8:30 a.m. and 6 p.m. EST.**

- **ExamView Testing Software.** All items from the printed test banks are available electronically on ExamView Testing Software. This automated testing program allows instructors to easily create customized exams by selecting provided questions, modifying existing questions, and adding questions. It is included on the Instructor's Resource CD and is provided free to instructors at educational institutions that adopt *Essentials of Business Communication*, 6e.

- **"Bridging the Gap" Video Library.** Featuring real companies with real communication issues that managers and employees face, nine videos (all about eight to ten minutes long) require student analysis, problem-solving skills, and application of communication concepts from the text. Students complete practical applications for each video.

- **Newsletters.** *Business Communication News,* a twice-yearly print newsletter, brings relevant business communication news, teaching tips, and announcements of new free materials. *The Online Guffey Report* is a monthly electronic newsletter sent directly to instructors' e-mail boxes. This electronic newsletter provides relevant news nuggets, classroom teaching and management tips, lecture ideas, and bonus case-study problems.

- **Distance Learning Resources.** Numerous distance learning instructors have made *Essentials* their textbook choice because of its comprehensive learning/testing system, its technologically savvy approach, and its many online resources. At the author's Web site, distance learning students have direct access to chapter review questions, interactive skill builders, electronic citation formats, and many other student-oriented electronic resources. At the WebTutor™ site, students will find many additional resources and tutorials for developing writing skills.

"Dr. Guffey's support materials enable me to keep my courses interesting and up-to-date without doing it all from scratch."

Susan Dunn
College of the Siskiyous

"Guffey's exceptional supplementary materials make my teaching much easier and very entertaining, and I get GREAT reactions from students!"

Jo-Ann Swanson
University of Great Falls
Great Falls, Montana

- **WebTutor™ Advantage for Blackboard® or WebCT™.** This interactive, Web-based supplement, rich with text-specific materials, is available in two platforms and can be packaged with the textbook. WebTutor™ Advantage extends the classroom with the power of the Internet: instructors can incorporate it as an integral part of the course, or students can use it on their own as a study aid. WebTutor™ Advantage for *Essentials* includes the following features:

✓ Chapter highlights by Dr. Guffey
✓ Chapter review tutorials, multiple-choice, and true-false quizzes
✓ Writing improvement tutorials
✓ Model document demonstration problems
✓ Flashcards of key vocabulary
✓ Critical thinking case tutorials
✓ Online testing and scoring
✓ Threaded discussion questions
✓ Video cases and video segments

Dr. Mary Ellen Guffey

Distance-learning instructors will find the WebTutor™ supplement particularly helpful in designing and customizing online activities. To see a demonstration and learn more about WebTutor™, visit http://webtutor.thomsonlearning.com. To view the demonstration, choose a platform (WebCT™ or Blackboard®). Click "Available Products"; on the next screen click "Search" and type "Guffey." From the list choose *Essentials*.

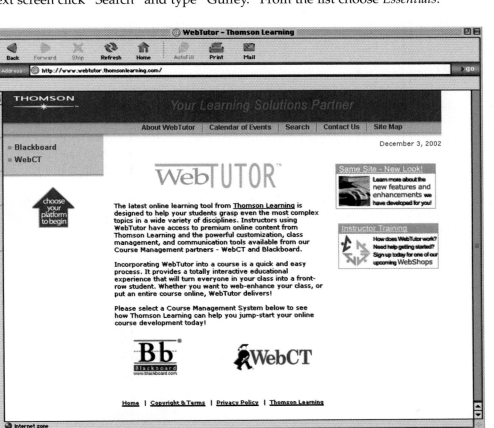

Exceptional Student Resources

- **FREE Student CD.** Every new textbook is packaged with a complimentary Student CD that contains valuable resources to reinforce language concepts and to improve student learning and retention. Comprehensive PowerPoint slides review important chapter concepts. Advanced grammar/mechanics worksheets help students review grammar, punctuation, capitalization, number style, spelling, and word use. All of the Documents for Revision are provided as Word documents so that students do not have to rekey them before revising and correcting them.

- **Premier Web Site for Students.** Because of the heavy demand, identical versions of the Guffey student Web site are available. For *Essentials of Business Communication*, the primary Web site is located at http://www.westwords.com/guffey/students.html. A mirror site is located at http://www.meguffey.com. At either of these locations, students can test their

  knowledge of chapter concepts with interactive review exercises that provide immediate feedback electronically. To expand their vocabulary, spelling, and sentence competency skills, students can use many self-paced skill-building drills written by the author. In addition to the text-specific items, students are offered links to the best search engines, employment and internship information sites, Web-site creation information, writing labs, electronic citation formats, online newspapers and magazines from around the world, and many other online resources of significance to business communication students. There are more than 2,000 student-oriented pages. No other Web site sponsored by an author matches this breadth of materials and speed of service!

- **Free InfoTrac® College Edition.** Students receive an entire library for the price of one textbook. With InfoTrac College Edition, they are given complete, 24-hour-a-day access to over 10 million full-text articles from over 4,000 journals, popular periodicals, and newspapers such as *Newsweek*, *Time*, and *USA Today*. The database is updated daily with full-length, substantive articles representing over 20 years of content. Because InfoTrac is accessible from any computer with Internet access, it is perfect for all students, from dorm-dwellers to commuters and distance learners. *Essentials of Business Communication*, 6e, includes InfoTrac activities that help students learn how to use this vast resource.

Connecting
with the Real World—

CRITICAL TOPICS AND LEARNING TOOLS

Although the Sixth Edition of *Essentials of Business Communication* packs considerable information into a small space, it covers all of the critical topics necessary in a comprehensive business communication course. It also features many teaching-learning devices to facilitate instruction, application, and retention.

- **Focus on Writing Skills.** Most students need a great deal of instruction and practice in developing basic and advanced writing techniques, particularly in view of today's increased emphasis on communication by e-mail. Writing skills have returned to the forefront since so much of today's business is transacted through written messages. *Essentials* is the premier text/workbook in its focus on grammar and writing techniques.

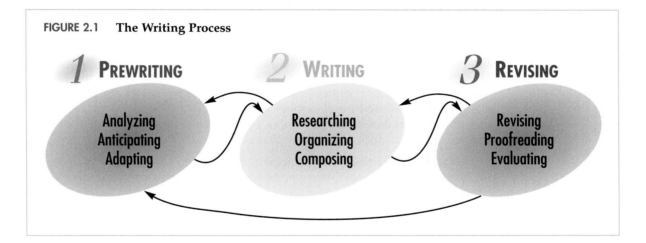

FIGURE 2.1 The Writing Process

1 PREWRITING — Analyzing Anticipating Adapting

2 WRITING — Researching Organizing Composing

3 REVISING — Revising Proofreading Evaluating

- **E-Mail and Memo Emphasis.** *Essentials* is the only text/workbook that devotes an entire chapter to the writing of e-mail and memos, which have become the most used communication channels in the business world.

- **Listening, Speaking, and Nonverbal Skills.** Employers are increasingly seeking well-rounded individuals who can interact with fellow employees as well as represent the organization effectively. *Essentials* provides professional tips for managing nonverbal cues, overcoming listening barriers, developing speaking skills, planning and participating in meetings, and making productive telephone calls.

- **Coverage of Informal and Formal Reports.** Two chapters develop functional report-writing skills. Chapter 9 provides detailed instruction in the preparation of six types of informal reports, while Chapter 10 covers proposals and formal reports. For quick comprehension, all reports contain marginal notes that pinpoint writing strategies.

"After checking several texts for Business Communication, I chose *Essentials of Business Communication* not only because it was so thorough in explaining communication, but also because it contained the grammar sections that help my students in their writing exercises."

Joan Moore
Community College of Denver

- **Employment Communication Skills.** Successful résumés, letters of application, and other employment documents are among the most important topics in a good business communication course. *Essentials* provides the most realistic and up-to-date résumés in the field. The models show chronological, functional, combination, and computer-friendly résumés.

- **Employment Interviewing.** *Essentials* devotes an entire chapter to effective interviewing techniques, including a discussion of screening interviews and hiring interviews. Chapter 14 also teaches techniques for fighting fear, answering questions, and following up.

- **Models Comparing Effective and Ineffective Documents.** To facilitate speedy recognition of good and bad writing techniques and strategies, *Essentials* presents many before-and-after documents. Marginal notes spotlight targeted strategies and effective writing.

- **Variety in End-of-Chapter Activities.** An amazing array of review questions, critical-thinking questions, writing improvement exercises, revision exercises, activities, and case problems hold student attention and help them apply chapter concepts meaningfully.

- **Diagnostic Test.** An optional grammar/mechanics diagnostic test helps students and instructors systematically determine specific student writing weaknesses. Students may be directed to the Grammar/Mechanics Handbook for remediation.

- **Grammar/Mechanics Handbook.** A comprehensive Grammar/Mechanics Handbook, included within the text, supplies a thorough review of English grammar, punctuation, capitalization style, and number usage. Its self-teaching exercises may be used for classroom instruction or for supplementary assignments. The handbook also serves as a convenient reference throughout the course and afterwards.

- **Textbook Coordination.** The principles of grammar and usage incorporated in *Essentials of Business Communication* coordinate with and reinforce those presented in Guffey's *Business English*, Guffey's *Essentials of College English*, and Clark and Clark's *Handbook for Office Workers*. This coordination means that students can move from one book to another without experiencing contradictory usage or style guidelines.

> "*Essentials of Business Communication* is the most comprehensive, yet easy-to-understand, book I've ever used in our business communication course. The organization of the material — from the introduction of the grammar and mechanics material through the writing stages — with the help of practical transparencies and examples, facilitates a realistic approach to the teaching/learning process. It's great!"
>
> Lois Wootton
> Tidewater Community College

FIGURE 7.1   Persuasive Favor Request BEFORE and AFTER Revision

BEFORE Revision

Dear Mr. Hoffman:

Would you be willing to speak to the members of the Dallas-Fort Worth chapter of the American Marketing Association? We hate to ask such a busy person, but we hoped you might be free on March 19.

You would address our members on the topic of how to succeed in marketing in Japan. As you know, few American companies have been able to make it in Japan. You may not want to consider this invitation because we can offer you only a $300 honorarium. We'll throw in dinner, of course.

Our group is informal, but I'm sure they would be interested in a 45-minute speech. Please let me know if you can join us at the Cattleman's Inn in Grand Prairie at 7 p.m.

- Fails to pique interest; provides easy excuse
- Does not promote direct and indirect benefits
- Does not anticipate objections; fails to make it easy to respond

AFTER Revision

American Marketing Association

Dallas-Fort Worth Chapter
P.O. Box 3598, Dallas, TX 74209   www.dallasama.com
(817) 469-8274

January 28, 200x

Mr. Bryant Hoffman
Marketing Manager, Western Division
Toys "R" Us, Inc.
Dallas, TX 75323

Dear Mr. Hoffman:

One company is legendary for marketing American products successfully in Japan.

That company, of course, is Toys "R" Us. The triumph of your thriving toy store in Amimachi, Japan, has given other American marketers hope. But this success story has also raised numerous questions. Specifically, how did Toys "R" Us circumvent local trade restrictions? How did you solve the complex distribution system? And how did you negotiate with all the levels of Japanese bureaucracy?

The members of the Dallas-Fort Worth chapter of the American Marketing Association asked me to invite you to speak at our March 19 dinner meeting on the topic of "How Toys 'R' Us Unlocked the Door to Japanese Trade." By describing your winning effort, Mr. Hoffman, you can help launch other American companies who face the same quagmire of Japanese restrictions and red tape that your organization overcame. Although we can offer you only a small honorarium of $300, we can assure you of a big audience of enthusiastic marketing professionals eager to hear your war story.

Our relaxed group doesn't expect a formal address; they are most interested in what steps Toys "R" Us took to open its Japanese toy outlet. To make your talk easy to organize, I've enclosed a list of questions our members submitted. Most talks are about 45 minutes long.

Can we count on you to join us for dinner at 7 p.m. March 19 at the Cattleman's Inn in Grand Prairie? Just call me at (214) 860-4320 by February 15 to make arrangements.

Sincerely,

Judy Wagner

Judy Wagner
Program Chair, AMA

JW:grw
Enclosure

- Piques reader's curiosity
- Notes indirect benefit
- Notes direct benefit
- Offsets reluctance by making the talk informal and easy to organize
- Makes acceptance as simple as a telephone call
- Gains attention
- Builds interest
- Reduces resistance
- Motivates action

Acknowledgments

I gratefully acknowledge the following reviewers whose excellent advice and constructive suggestions helped shape the Sixth Edition of *Essentials of Business Communication:*

Sandie Idziak
University of Texas, Arlington

Debra Hawhee
University of Illinois

Bruce E. Guttman
Katharine Gibbs School, Melville, New York

Sheryl E. C. Joshua
University of North Carolina, Greensboro

Elaine Lux
Nyack College

Kenneth R. Mayer
Cleveland State University

Catherine Peck
Chippewa Valley Technical College

Karin Jacobson
University of Montana

Marilyn St. Clair
Weatherford College

For their contributions to previous editions, I warmly thank the following professionals:

Joyce M. Barnes
Texas A & M University – Corpus Christi

Patricia Beagle
Bryant & Stratton Business Institute

Nancy C. Bell
Wayne Community College

Ray D. Bernardi
Morehead State University

Karen Bounds
Boise State University

Jean Bush-Bacelis
Eastern Michigan University

Dee Anne Dill
Dekalb Technical Institute

Jeanette Dostourian
Cypress College

Nancy J. Dubino
Greenfield Community College

Cecile Earle
Heald College

Valerie Evans
Cuesta College

Pat Fountain
Coastal Carolina Community College

Marlene Friederich
New Mexico State University – Carlsbad

Christine Foster
Grand Rapids Community College

Nanette Clinch Gilson
San Jose State University

Margaret E. Gorman
Cayuga Community College

Judith Graham
Holyoke Community College

Tracey M. Harrison
Mississippi College

L. P. Helstrom
Rochester Community College

Jack Hensen
Morehead State University

Rovena L. Hillsman
California State University, Sacramento

Karen A. Holtkamp
Xavier University

Michael Hricik
Westmoreland County Community College

Edna Jellesed
Lane Community College

Edwina Jordan
Illinois Central College

Diana K. Kanoy
Central Florida Community College

Ron Kapper
College of DuPage

Lydia Keuser
San Jose City College

Linda Kissler
Westmoreland County Community College

Keith Kroll
Kalamazoo Valley Community College

Richard B. Larsen
Francis Marion University

Mary E. Leslie
Grossmont College

Nedra Lowe
Marshall University

Margarita Maestas-Flores
Evergreen Valley College

Jane Mangrum
Miami-Dade Community College

Maria Manninen
Delta College

Karen McFarland
Salt Lake Community College

Bonnie Miller
Los Medanos College

Mary C. Miller
Ashland University

Willie Minor
Phoenix College

Nancy Moody
Sinclair Community College

Nancy Mulder
Grand Rapids Junior College

Paul W. Murphey
Southwest Wisconsin Technical College

Jackie Ohlson
University of Alaska – Anchorage

Carol Pemberton
Normandale Community College

Carl Perrin
Casco Bay College

Jan Peterson
Anoka-Hennepin Technical College

Jeanette Purdy
Mercer County College

Carolyn A. Quantrille
Spokane Falls Community College

Susan Randles
Vatterott College

Ruth D. Richardson
University of North Alabama

Carlita Robertson
Northern Oklahoma College

Vilera Rood
Concordia College

Rose Ann Scala
Data Institute School of Business

Joseph Schaffner
SUNY College of Technology, Alfred

James Calvert Scott
Utah State University

Laurie Shapero
Miami-Dade Community College

Lance Shaw
Blake Business School

Cinda Skelton
Central Texas College

Estelle Slootmaker
Aquinas College

Clara Smith
North Seattle Community College

Judy Sunayama
Los Medanos College

Dana H. Swensen
Utah State University

David A. Tajerstein
SYRIT College

Marilyn Theissman
Rochester Community College

Lois A. Wagner
Southwest Wisconsin Technical College

Linda Weavil
Elan College

William Wells
Lima Technical College

Beverly Wickersham
Central Texas College

Leopold Wilkins
Anson Community College

Gerard Weykamp
Grand Rapids Community College

Almeda Wilmarth
State University of New York – Delhi

Barbara Young
Skyline College

In addition to honoring these friends and colleagues, I extend my warmest thanks to the many skillful professionals at Thomson/South-Western, including Bob Lynch, Jack Calhoun, Melissa Acuna, Jennifer Codner, Larry Qualls, and Deanna Quinn. Special gratitude goes to my developmental editor, Mary Draper. For preparing excellent new test questions, I salute Carolyn Seefer, Diablo Valley College.

Finally, I express deep gratitude to my husband, Dr. George R. Guffey, professor emeritus of English, University of California, Los Angeles, for the creation and maintenance of our exceptional Web sites, for his development of an exciting PowerPoint program for Essentials, for his incredible technical and editorial skills, and, most of all, for his love, strength, and wisdom.

Laying Communication Foundations

1

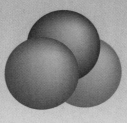

Facing Today's Communication Challenges

If I went back to college again, I'd concentrate on two areas: learning to write and to speak before an audience. Nothing in life is more important than the ability to communicate effectively.

GERALD R. FORD, 38th President of the United States

LEARNING OBJECTIVES

1. Understand the importance of becoming an effective business communicator in today's changing workplace.
2. Examine the process of communication.
3. Discuss how to become an effective listener.
4. Analyze nonverbal communication and explain techniques for improving nonverbal communication skills.
5. Explain how culture affects communication and describe methods for improving cross-cultural communication.
6. Identify specific techniques that improve effective communication among diverse workplace audiences.

THE IMPORTANCE OF COMMUNICATION SKILLS TO YOU

N early three decades ago when he was president, Gerald Ford spoke about the importance of communication skills. If he had a second chance at college, he said, he'd concentrate on learning to write and learning to speak before an audience. Today, communication is even more important and more challenging than when President Ford spoke. We live in an information age that revolves around communication.

Developing excellent communication skills is extremely important to your future. Surveys of employers often show that communication skills are critical to effective job placement, performance, career advancement, and organizational success.[1] In making hiring decisions, employers often rank communication skills among the most-requested competencies.[2] In fact, many job advertisements specifically ask for excellent oral and written communication skills. In a recent poll of recruiters, oral and written communication skills were far and away the top skill set sought in applicants.[3] Another survey of managers and executives ranked the skills most lacking in job candidates, and writing skills topped that list.[4]

✓ *Quick Check*

The information revolution has made writing skills extremely important.

Communication skills consistently rank near the top of competencies sought by recruiters. Because more and more messages are being sent, writing skills are particularly important to succeed in first jobs and to be promoted into management.
© Mark Richards/ PhotoEdit

Writing skills are particularly important today because we are transmitting messages more rapidly, more often, and to greater numbers of people than ever before.[5] "One of the most surprising features of the information revolution," said one Internet executive, "is that the momentum has turned back to the written word."[6]

This book focuses on developing basic writing skills. But you will also learn to improve your listening, nonverbal, and speaking skills. The abilities to read, listen, speak, and write effectively, of course, are not inborn. When it comes to communication, it's more *nurture* than *nature*. Good communicators are not born; they are made. Thriving in the dynamic and demanding new world of work will depend on many factors, some of which you cannot control. One factor that you *do* control, however, is how well you communicate.

✓ Quick Check

Because communication skills are learned, you control how well you communicate.

The goals of this book are to teach you basic business communication skills. These include learning how to write an e-mail or a letter and how to make a presentation. Anyone can learn these skills with the help of instructional materials and good model documents, all of which you'll find in this book. You also need practice—with meaningful feedback. You need someone such as your instructor to tell you how to modify your responses so that you can improve.

✓ Quick Check

Developing good communication skills requires instruction, practice, and feedback from a specialist.

We've designed this book, its supplements, and our Web site (http://www. westwords.com/guffey/students.html) to provide you and your instructor with everything necessary to make you a successful business communicator in today's dynamic workplace. Given the increasing emphasis on communication, many corporations are paying thousands of dollars to communication coaches and trainers to teach employees the very skills that you are learning in this course. Your coach is your instructor. Get your money's worth! Pick your instructor's brains.

With this book as your guide and your instructor as your coach, you may find this course to be the most important in your entire college curriculum. To get started, this first chapter presents an overview. You'll take a look at (1) the changing workplace, (2) the communication process, (3) listening, (4) nonverbal communication, (5) culture and communication, and (6) workplace diversity. The remainder of the book is devoted to developing specific writing and speaking skills.

✓ Quick Check

This book and this course might well be the most important in your entire college career.

SUCCEEDING IN THE CHANGING WORLD OF WORK

Quick Check

Trends in the new world of work emphasize the importance of communication skills.

The world of work is changing dramatically. The kind of work you'll do, the tools you'll use, the form of management you'll work under, the environment in which you'll work, the people with whom you'll interact—all are undergoing a pronounced transformation. Many of the changes in this dynamic workplace revolve around processing and communicating information. As a result, the most successful players in this new world of work will be those with highly developed communication skills. The following business trends illustrate the importance of excellent communication skills.

- **Flattened management hierarchies.** To better compete and to reduce expenses, businesses have for years been trimming layers of management. This means that as a frontline employee, you will have fewer managers. You will be making decisions and communicating them to customers, to fellow employees, and to executives.

Quick Check

Today's employees must contribute to improving productivity and profitability.

- **More participatory management.** Gone are the days of command-and-control management. Now, even new employees like you will be expected to understand and contribute to the big picture. Improving productivity and profitability will be everyone's job, not just management's.
- **Increased emphasis on self-directed work and project teams.** Businesses today are often run by cross-functional teams of peers. You can expect to work with a team in gathering information, finding and sharing solutions, implementing decisions, and managing conflict. Good communication skills are extremely important in working together successfully in a team environment.

Quick Check

Increasing global competition and revolutionary technologies demand cultural and communication skills.

- **Heightened global competition.** Because American companies are moving beyond local markets, you may be interacting with people from many different cultures. As a successful business communicator, you will want to learn about other cultures. You'll also need to develop multicultural skills including sensitivity, flexibility, patience, and tolerance.
- **Innovative communication technologies.** E-mail, fax, the Web, mobile technologies, audio and video conferencing—all these technologies mean that you will be communicating more often and more rapidly than ever before. Your writing and speaking skills will be showcased as never before.
- **New work environments.** Mobile technologies and the desire for a better balance between work and family have resulted in flexible working arrangements. You may become part of an increasing number of workers engaged in full- or part-time telecommuting.[7] Working away from the office requires even more communication, since staying connected means exchanging more messages.
- **Focus on information and knowledge as corporate assets.** Corporate America is increasingly aware that information is the key to better products and increased profitability. You will be expected to gather, sort, store, and disseminate data in a timely and accurate fashion. This is the new way of business life.[8]

EXAMINING THE COMMUNICATION PROCESS

As you can see, you can expect to be communicating more rapidly, more often, and with greater numbers of people than ever before. The most successful players in this new world of work will be those with highly developed communication skills. Since good communication skills are essential to your success, we need to take a closer look at the communication process.

Just what is *communication*? For our purposes communication is the *transmission of information and meaning from one individual or group to another*. The crucial element in this definition is *meaning*. Communication has as its central objective the transmission of meaning. The process of communication is successful only when the receiver understands an idea as the sender intended it. This process generally involves five steps, discussed here and shown in Figure 1.1.

✓ *Quick Check*

Communication is the transmission of information and meaning from one individual or group to another.

1. **Sender has an idea.** The form of the idea may be influenced by the sender's mood, frame of reference, background, culture, and physical makeup, as well as the context of the situation.
2. **Sender encodes the idea in a message.** *Encoding* means converting the idea into words or gestures that will convey meaning. A major problem in communicating any message verbally is that words have different meanings for different people. That's why skilled communicators try to choose familiar words with concrete meanings on which both senders and receivers agree.
3. **Message travels over a channel.** The medium over which the message is transmitted is the *channel*. Messages may be sent by computer, telephone, letter, or memorandum. They may also be sent by means of a report, announcement, picture, spoken word, fax, or other channel. Because both verbal and nonverbal messages are carried, senders must choose channels carefully. Anything that disrupts the transmission of a message in the communication process is called *noise*. Channel noise ranges from static that disrupts a telephone conversation to spelling errors in an e-mail message. Such errors damage the credibility of the sender.
4. **Receiver decodes message.** The person for whom a message is intended is the *receiver*. Translating the message from its symbol form into meaning involves *decoding*. Successful communication takes place only when a receiver understands the meaning intended by the sender. Such success is often hard to

✓ *Quick Check*

The communication process has five steps: idea formation, message encoding, message transmission, message decoding, and feedback.

FIGURE 1.1 Communication Process
Communication barriers and noise may cause the communication process to break down.

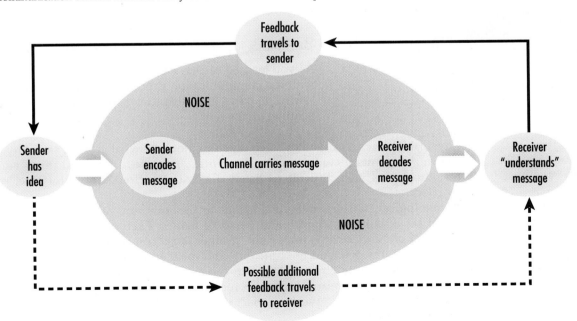

achieve because no two people share the same backgrounds. Success is further limited because barriers and noise may disrupt the process.

5. **Feedback travels to sender.** The verbal and nonverbal responses of the receiver create *feedback*, a vital part of the entire communication process. Feedback helps the sender know that the message was received and understood. Senders can encourage feedback by asking questions such as *Am I making myself clear?* and *Is there anything you don't understand?* Senders can further improve feedback by delivering the message at a time when receivers can respond. Senders should provide only as much information as a receiver can handle. Receivers can improve the process by paraphrasing the sender's message. They might say, *Let me try to explain that in my own words,* or *My understanding of your comment is. . . .*

DEVELOPING BETTER LISTENING SKILLS

An important part of the communication process is listening. By all accounts, however, most of us are not very good listeners. Do you ever pretend to be listening when you're not? Do you know how to look attentive in class when your mind wanders far away? How about "tuning out" people when their ideas are boring or complex? Do you find it hard to focus on ideas when a speaker's clothing or mannerisms are unusual?

Quick Check

Most individuals listen at only 25 percent efficiency.

© Ted Goff (www.tedgoff.com)

You probably answered *yes* to one or more of these questions because many of us have developed poor listening habits. In fact, some researchers suggest that we listen at only 25 percent efficiency. Such poor listening habits are costly in business. Letters must be rewritten, shipments reshipped, appointments rescheduled, contracts renegotiated, and directions restated.

To improve listening skills, we must first recognize barriers that prevent effective listening. Then we need to focus on specific techniques that are effective in improving listening skills.

BARRIERS TO EFFECTIVE LISTENING

As you learned earlier, barriers and noise can interfere with the communication process. Have any of the following barriers and distractions prevented you from hearing what's said?

Quick Check

Barriers to listening may be physical, psychological, verbal, or nonverbal.

- **Physical barriers.** You cannot listen if you cannot hear what is being said. Physical impediments include hearing disabilities, poor acoustics, and noisy surroundings. It's also difficult to listen if you're ill, tired, uncomfortable, or worried.
- **Psychological barriers.** Everyone brings to the communication process a different set of cultural, ethical, and personal values. Each of us has an idea of what is right and what is important. If other ideas run counter to our preconceived thoughts, we tend to "tune out" the speaker and thus fail to hear.
- **Language problems.** Unfamiliar words can destroy the communication process because they lack meaning for the receiver. In addition, emotion-laden or "charged" words can adversely affect listening. If the mention of words such

The better a businessperson listens to a customer, the better she or he will be at fulfilling expectations, resolving disputes, reducing uncertainty, and projecting goodwill. Any employee listening to a customer should learn to defer judgment, pay attention to content rather than surface issues, focus on main ideas, and avoid replying to sidetracking issues.
© PhotoDisc, Inc./Getty Images

as *abortion* or *overdose* has an intense emotional impact, a listener may be unable to think about the words that follow.

- **Nonverbal distractions.** Many of us find it hard to listen if a speaker is different from what we view as normal. Unusual clothing, speech mannerisms, body twitches, or a radical hairstyle can cause enough distraction to prevent us from hearing what the speaker has to say.
- **Thought speed.** Because we can process thoughts more than three times faster than speakers can say them, we can become bored and allow our minds to wander.
- **Faking attention.** Most of us have learned to look as if we are listening even when we're not. Such behavior was perhaps necessary as part of our socialization. Faked attention, however, seriously threatens effective listening because it encourages the mind to engage in flights of unchecked fancy. Those who practice faked attention often find it hard to concentrate even when they want to.
- **Grandstanding.** Would you rather talk or listen? Naturally, most of us would rather talk. Since our own experiences and thoughts are most important to us, we grab the limelight in conversations. We sometimes fail to listen carefully because we're just waiting politely for the next pause so that we can have our turn to speak.

TIPS FOR BECOMING AN ACTIVE LISTENER

You can reverse the harmful effects of poor habits by making a conscious effort to become an active listener. This means becoming involved. You can't sit back and hear whatever a lazy mind happens to receive. The following techniques will help you become an active and effective listener.

- **Stop talking.** The first step to becoming a good listener is to stop talking. Let others explain their views. Learn to concentrate on what the speaker is saying, not on what your next comment will be.

Quick Check
Most North Americans speak at about 125 words per minute. The human brain can process information at least three times as fast.

Quick Check
To become an active listener, stop talking, control your surroundings, develop a positive mind-set, listen for main points, and capitalize on lag time.

- **Control your surroundings.** Whenever possible, remove competing sounds. Close windows or doors, turn off radios and noisy appliances, and move away from loud people or engines. Choose a quiet time and place for listening.
- **Establish a receptive mind-set.** Expect to learn something by listening. Strive for a positive and receptive frame of mind. If the message is complex, think of it as mental gymnastics. It's hard work but good exercise to stretch and expand the limits of your mind.
- **Keep an open mind.** We all sift and filter information through our own biases and values. For improved listening, discipline yourself to listen objectively. Be fair to the speaker. Hear what is really being said, not what you want to hear.
- **Listen for main points.** Concentration is enhanced and satisfaction is heightened when you look for and recognize the speaker's central themes.
- **Capitalize on lag time.** Make use of the quickness of your mind by reviewing the speaker's points. Anticipate what's coming next. Evaluate evidence the speaker has presented. Don't allow yourself to daydream.
- **Listen between the lines.** Focus both on what is spoken and what is unspoken. Listen for feelings as well as for facts.
- **Judge ideas, not appearances.** Concentrate on the content of the message, not on its delivery. Avoid being distracted by the speaker's looks, voice, or mannerisms.
- **Hold your fire.** Force yourself to listen to the speaker's entire argument or message before reacting. Such restraint may enable you to understand the speaker's reasons and logic before you jump to false conclusions.
- **Take selective notes.** For some situations thoughtful notetaking may be necessary to record important facts that must be recalled later. Select only the most important points so that the note-taking process does not interfere with your concentration on the speaker's total message.
- **Provide feedback.** Let the speaker know that you are listening. Nod your head and maintain eye contact. Ask relevant questions at appropriate times. Getting involved improves the communication process for both the speaker and the listener.

© Ted Goff (www.tedgoff.com)

"How can I listen to you if you don't say the things I want to hear?"

Quick Check

Listening actively may mean taking notes and providing feedback.

IMPROVING YOUR NONVERBAL COMMUNICATION SKILLS

Understanding messages often involves more than merely listening to spoken words. Nonverbal cues, in fact, can speak louder than words. These cues include eye contact, facial expression, body movements, space, time, distance, and appearance. All these nonverbal cues affect how a message is interpreted, or decoded, by the receiver.

Quick Check

Nonverbal communication includes all unwritten and unspoken messages, intended or not.

Just what is nonverbal communication? It includes all unwritten and unspoken messages, whether intended or not. These silent signals have a strong effect on receivers. But understanding them is not simple. Does a downward glance indicate modesty? Fatigue? Does a constant stare reflect coldness? Dullness? Do crossed arms mean defensiveness? Withdrawal? Or do crossed arms just mean that a person is shivering?

Messages are even harder to decipher when the verbal codes and nonverbal cues do not agree. What will you think if Scott says he's not angry, but he slams the door when he leaves? What if Alicia assures the hostess that the meal is excellent, but she eats very little? The nonverbal messages in these situations speak more loudly than the words.

When verbal and nonverbal messages conflict, receivers put more faith in nonverbal cues. In one study speakers sent a positive message but averted their eyes as they spoke. Listeners perceived the total message to be negative. Moreover, they thought that averted eyes suggested lack of affection, superficiality, lack of trust, and nonreceptivity.[9]

Successful communicators recognize the power of nonverbal messages. Although it's unwise to attach specific meanings to gestures or actions, some cues broadcast by body language are helpful in understanding the feelings and attitudes of senders.

✓ *Quick Check*

When verbal and nonverbal messages clash, listeners tend to believe the nonverbal message.

HOW THE EYES, FACE, AND BODY SEND SILENT MESSAGES

Words seldom tell the whole story. Indeed, some messages are sent with no words at all. The eyes, face, and body can convey a world of meaning without a single syllable being spoken.

Eye Contact. The eyes have been called the "windows to the soul." Even if they don't reveal the soul, the eyes are often the best predictor of a speaker's true feelings. Most of us cannot look another person straight in the eyes and lie. As a result, in American culture we tend to believe people who look directly at us. Sustained eye contact suggests trust and admiration; brief eye contact signals fear or stress. Good eye contact enables the message sender to see whether a receiver is paying attention, showing respect, responding favorably, or feeling distress. From the receiver's viewpoint, good eye contact, in North American culture, reveals the speaker's sincerity, confidence, and truthfulness.

✓ *Quick Check*

The eyes are thought to be the best predictor of a speaker's true feelings.

Facial Expression. The expression on a person's face can be almost as revealing of emotion as the eyes. Experts estimate that the human face can display over 250,000 expressions.[10] To hide their feelings, some people can control these expressions and maintain "poker faces." Most of us, however, display our emotions openly. Raising or lowering the eyebrows, squinting the eyes, swallowing nervously, clenching the jaw, smiling broadly—these voluntary and involuntary facial expressions can add to or entirely replace verbal messages.

Posture and Gestures. A person's posture can convey anything from high status and self-confidence to shyness and submissiveness. Leaning toward a speaker suggests attraction and interest; pulling away or shrinking back denotes fear, distrust, anxiety, or disgust. Similarly, gestures can communicate entire thoughts via simple movements. However, the meanings of some of these movements differ in other cultures. Unless you know local customs, they can get you into trouble. In the United States and Canada, for example, forming the thumb and forefinger in a circle means everything's OK. But in Germany and parts of South America, the OK sign is obscene.

What does your own body language say about you? To take stock of the kinds of messages being sent

© Ted Goff (www.tedgoff.com)

"I know you're saying no, but I think your body language is saying maybe."

by your body, ask a classmate to critique your use of eye contact, facial expression, and body movements. Another way to analyze your nonverbal style is to videotape yourself making a presentation. Then study your performance. This way you can make sure your nonverbal cues send the same message as your words.

How Time, Space, and Territory Send Silent Messages

In addition to nonverbal messages transmitted by your body, three external elements convey information in the communication process: time, space, and distance.

Time.   How we structure and use time tells observers about our personality and attitudes. For example, when Ellen Kwan, a banking executive, gives a visitor a prolonged interview, she signals her respect for, interest in, and approval of the visitor or the topic to be discussed.

Space.   How we order the space around us tells something about ourselves and our objectives. Whether the space is a bedroom, a dorm room, an office, or a department, people reveal themselves in the design and grouping of their furniture. Generally, the more formal the arrangement, the more formal and closed the communication. The way office furniture is arranged sends cues on how communication is to take place. Former FBI director J. Edgar Hoover used to make his visitors sit at a small table below his large, elevated desk. Clearly, he did not want office visitors to feel equal to him.[11]

Territory.   Each of us has a certain area that we feel is our own territory, whether it's a specific spot or just the space around us. Your father may have a favorite chair in which he is most comfortable, a cook might not tolerate intruders in his or her kitchen, and veteran employees may feel that certain work areas and tools belong to them.

We all maintain zones of privacy in which we feel comfortable. Figure 1.2 categorizes the four zones of social interaction among Americans, as formulated by anthropologist Edward T. Hall.[12] Notice that Americans are a bit standoffish; only intimate friends and family may stand closer than about $1\frac{1}{2}$ feet. If someone violates that territory, Americans feel uncomfortable and defensive and may step back to reestablish their space.

"Sorry, Ridgely, but this area is my personal space."

© 2003 Sidney Harris.

How Appearance Sends Silent Messages

The physical appearance of a business document, as well as the personal appearance of an individual, transmits immediate and important nonverbal messages.

Appearance of Business Documents.   The way a letter, memo, or report looks can have either a positive or a negative effect on the receiver. Sloppy e-mail messages send a nonverbal message that says you are in a terrific hurry or that the receiver is not important enough for you to care. Envelopes— through their postage, stationery, and printing— can suggest routine, important, or junk mail. Letters

FIGURE 1.2 Four Space Zones for Social Interaction

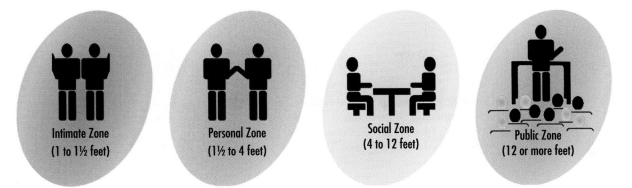

Intimate Zone
(1 to 1½ feet)

Personal Zone
(1½ to 4 feet)

Social Zone
(4 to 12 feet)

Public Zone
(12 or more feet)

and reports can look neat, professional, well-organized, and attractive—or just the opposite. In succeeding chapters you'll learn how to create documents that send positive nonverbal messages through their appearance, format, organization, readability, and correctness.

Personal Appearance.   The way you look—your clothing, grooming, and posture—telegraphs an instant nonverbal message about you. Based on what they see, viewers make quick judgments about your status, credibility, personality, and potential. Because appearance is such a powerful force in business, some aspiring professionals are turning for help to image consultants (who charge up to $500 an hour!). As one human relations specialist observes, "If you don't look and act the part, you will probably be denied opportunities."[13]

✓ *Quick Check*

The appearance of a message and of an individual can convey positive or negative nonverbal messages.

TIPS FOR IMPROVING YOUR NONVERBAL SKILLS

Nonverbal communication can outweigh words in the way it influences how others perceive us. You can harness the power of silent messages by reviewing the following tips for improving nonverbal communication skills:

✓ *Quick Check*

Because nonverbal cues can mean more than spoken words, learn to use nonverbal communication positively.

- **Establish and maintain eye contact.** Remember that in the United States and Canada appropriate eye contact signals interest, attentiveness, strength, and credibility.
- **Use posture to show interest.** Encourage communication interaction by leaning forward, sitting or standing erect, and looking alert.
- **Improve your decoding skills.** Watch facial expressions and body language to understand the complete verbal and nonverbal message being communicated.
- **Probe for more information.** When you perceive nonverbal cues that contradict verbal meanings, politely seek additional cues (*I'm not sure I understand, Please tell me more about . . .,* or *Do you mean that . . .*).
- **Avoid assigning nonverbal meanings out of context.** Don't interpret nonverbal behavior unless you understand a situation or a culture.
- **Associate with people from diverse cultures.** Learn about other cultures to widen your knowledge and tolerance of intercultural nonverbal messages.
- **Appreciate the power of appearance.** Keep in mind that the appearance of your business documents, your business space, and yourself sends immediate positive or negative messages to receivers.
- **Observe yourself on videotape.** Ensure that your verbal and nonverbal messages are in sync by taping and evaluating yourself making a presentation.

- **Enlist friends and family.** Ask them to monitor your conscious and unconscious body movements and gestures to help you become a more effective communicator.

UNDERSTANDING HOW CULTURE AFFECTS COMMUNICATION

Verbal and nonverbal meanings are even more difficult to interpret when people are from different cultures.

Comprehending the verbal and nonverbal meanings of a message is difficult even when communicators are from the same culture. But when they are from different cultures, special sensitivity and skills are necessary.

Negotiators for a North American company learned this lesson when they were in Japan looking for a trading partner. The North Americans were pleased after their first meeting with representatives of a major Japanese firm. The Japanese had nodded assent throughout the meeting and had not objected to a single proposal. The next day, however, the North Americans were stunned to learn that the Japanese had rejected the entire plan. In interpreting the nonverbal behavioral messages, the North Americans made a typical mistake. They assumed the Japanese were nodding in agreement as fellow North Americans would. In this case, however, the nods of assent indicated comprehension—not approval.

Every country has a unique culture or common heritage, joint experience, and shared learning that produce its culture. Their common experience gives members of that culture a complex system of shared values and customs. It teaches them how to behave; it conditions their reactions. Comparing traditional North American values with those in other cultures will broaden your world view. This comparison should also help you recognize some of the values that shape your actions and judgments of others.

COMPARING KEY CULTURAL VALUES

Until relatively recently, typical North Americans shared the same broad cultural values. Some experts identified them as "Anglo" or "mainstream" values.[14] These values largely represented white, male, Northern European views. Women and many minorities now entering the workforce may eventually modify these values. However, a majority of North Americans are still governed by these mainstream values.

Although North American culture is complex, we'll focus on four dimensions to help you better understand some of the values that shape your actions and judgments of others. These four dimensions are individualism, formality, communication style, and time orientation.

✓ Quick Check

While North Americans value individualism and personal responsibility, other cultures emphasize group- and team-oriented values.

Individualism.   One of the most identifiable characteristics of North Americans is their *individualism*. This is an attitude of independence and freedom from control. They think that initiative and self-assertion result in personal achievement. They believe in individual action, self-reliance, and personal responsibility; and they desire a large degree of freedom in their personal lives. Other cultures emphasize membership in organizations, groups, and teams; they encourage acceptance of group values, duties, and decisions. Members of these cultures typically resist independence because it fosters competition and confrontation instead of consensus.

✓ Quick Check

While North Americans value informality and directness, other cultures may value tradition and indirectness.

Formality.   A second significant dimension of North American culture is our attitude toward *formality*. Americans place less emphasis on tradition, ceremony, and social rules than do people in some other cultures. They dress casually and are soon on a first-name basis with others. Their lack of formality is often characterized by directness. In business dealings North Americans tend to come to the point immediately; indirectness, they feel, wastes time, a valuable commodity.

Communication Style. A third important dimension of our culture relates to *communication style*. North Americans value straightforwardness, are suspicious of evasiveness, and distrust people who might have a "hidden agenda" or who "play their cards too close to the chest."[15] North Americans also tend to be uncomfortable with silence and impatient with delays. Moreover, they tend to use and understand words literally. Latins, on the other hand, enjoy plays on words; Arabs and South Americans sometimes speak with extravagant or poetic figures of speech (such as "the Mother of all battles").

Time Orientation. A fourth dimension of our culture relates to *time orientation*. North Americans consider time a precious commodity to be conserved. They correlate time with productivity, efficiency, and money. Keeping people waiting for business appointments wastes time and is also rude. In other cultures, time may be perceived as an unlimited and never-ending resource to be enjoyed.

Figure 1.3 compares a number of cultural values for U.S. Americans, Japanese, and Arabs. Notice that belonging, group harmony, and collectiveness are very important to Japanese people, while family matters rank highest with Arabs. As we become aware of the vast differences in cultural values illustrated in Figure 1.3, we can better understand why communication barriers develop and how misunderstandings occur in cross-cultural interactions.

CONTROLLING ETHNOCENTRISM AND STEREOTYPING

The process of understanding and accepting people from other cultures is often hampered by two barriers: ethnocentrism and stereotyping. These two barriers, however, can be overcome by developing tolerance, a powerful and effective aid to communication.

Ethnocentrism. The belief in the superiority of one's own culture is known as *ethnocentrism*. This natural attitude is found in all cultures. Ethnocentrism causes us to judge others by our own values. If you were raised in North America, the values just described probably seem "right" to you, and you may wonder why the rest of the world doesn't function in the same sensible fashion. A North American businessperson in an Arab or Asian country might be upset at time spent over coffee or other social rituals before any "real" business is transacted. In these cultures, however, personal relationships must be established and nurtured before earnest talks may proceed.

FIGURE 1.3 Comparison of Cultural Values Ranked by Priority*

U.S. AMERICANS	JAPANESE	ARABS
1. Freedom	1. Belonging	1. Family security
2. Independence	2. Group harmony	2. Family harmony
3. Self-reliance	3. Collectiveness	3. Parental guidance
4. Equality	4. Age/Seniority	4. Age
5. Individualism	5. Group consensus	5. Authority
6. Competition	6. Cooperation	6. Compromise
7. Efficiency	7. Quality	7. Devotion
8. Time	8. Patience	8. Patience
9. Directness	9. Indirectness	9. Indirectness
10. Openness	10. Go-between	10. Hospitality

*1 represents the most important value.
Source: Reprinted from *Multicultural Management*, F. Elashmawi and P. R. Harris, p. 72, © 2000 with permission of Elsevier Science.

Stereotypes.   Our perceptions of other cultures sometimes cause us to form stereotypes about groups of people. A *stereotype* is an oversimplified perception of a behavioral pattern or characteristic applied to entire groups. For example, the Swiss are hard-working, efficient, and neat; Germans are formal, reserved, and blunt; Americans are loud, friendly, and impatient; Canadians are polite, trusting, and tolerant; Asians are gracious, humble, and inscrutable. These attitudes may or may not accurately describe cultural norms. But when applied to individual business communicators, such stereotypes may create misconceptions and misunderstandings. Look beneath surface stereotypes and labels to discover individual personal qualities.

Tolerance.   Working among people from other cultures demands tolerance and flexible attitudes. As global markets expand and as our society becomes increasingly multiethnic, tolerance becomes critical. *Tolerance*, here, does not mean "putting up with" or "enduring," which is one part of its definition. Instead, we use *tolerance* in a broader sense. It means having sympathy for and appreciating beliefs and practices different from our own.

One of the best ways to develop tolerance is by practicing *empathy*. This means trying to see the world through another's eyes. It means being nonjudgmental, recognizing things as they are rather than as they "should be." It includes the ability to accept others' contributions in solving problems in a culturally appropriate manner. When Kal Kan Foods began courting the pet owners of Japan, for example, an Asian advisor suggested that the meat chunks in its Pedigree dog food be cut into perfect little squares. Why? Japanese pet owners feed their dogs piece by piece with chopsticks. Instead of insisting on what "should be" (feeding dogs chunky meat morsels), Kal Kan solved the problem by looking at it from another cultural point of view (providing neat small squares).[16]

The following tips provide specific suggestions for preventing miscommunication in oral and written transactions across cultures.

TIPS FOR MINIMIZING ORAL MISCOMMUNICATION AMONG CROSS-CULTURAL AUDIENCES

"He doesn't understand you. Try shouting a little louder."

BERRY'S WORLD reprinted by permission of Newspaper Enterprise Association, Inc.

When you have a conversation with someone from another culture, you can reduce misunderstandings by following these suggestions:

- **Use simple English.** Speak in short sentences (under 15 words) with familiar, short words. Eliminate puns, sports and military references, slang, and jargon (special business terms). Be especially alert to idiomatic expressions that can't be translated, such as *burn the midnight oil* and *under the weather*.
- **Speak slowly and enunciate clearly.** Avoid fast speech, but don't raise your voice. Overpunctuate with pauses and full stops. Always write numbers for all to see.
- **Encourage accurate feedback.** Ask probing questions, and encourage the listener to paraphrase what you say. Don't assume that a *yes*, a nod, or a smile indicates comprehension or assent.
- **Check frequently for comprehension.** Avoid waiting until you finish a long explanation to request feedback. Instead, make one point at a time, pausing to check for comprehension. Don't proceed to B until A has been grasped.
- **Observe eye messages.** Be alert to a glazed expression or wandering eyes. These tell you the listener is lost.
- **Accept blame.** If a misunderstanding results, graciously accept the blame for not making your meaning clear.

- **Listen without interrupting.** Curb your desire to finish sentences or to fill out ideas for the speaker. Keep in mind that North Americans abroad are often accused of listening too little and talking too much.
- **Remember to smile!** Roger Axtell, international behavior expert, calls the smile the single most understood and most useful form of communication in either personal or business transactions.
- **Follow up in writing.** After conversations or oral negotiations, confirm the results and agreements with follow-up letters. For proposals and contracts, engage a translator to prepare copies in the local language.

TIPS FOR MINIMIZING WRITTEN MISCOMMUNICATION AMONG CROSS-CULTURAL AUDIENCES

When you write to someone from a different culture, you can improve your chances of being understood by following these suggestions:

- **Adopt local styles.** Learn how documents are formatted and how letters are addressed and developed in the intended reader's country. Use local formats and styles.
- **Consider hiring a translator.** Engage a translator if (1) your document is important, (2) your document will be distributed to many readers, or (3) you must be persuasive.
- **Use short sentences and short paragraphs.** Sentences with fewer than 15 words and paragraphs with fewer than 5 lines are most readable.
- **Avoid ambiguous wording.** Include relative pronouns (*that, which, who*) for clarity in introducing clauses. Stay away from contractions (especially ones like *Here's the problem*). Avoid idioms (*once in a blue moon*), slang (*my presentation really bombed*), acronyms (*ASAP* for *as soon as possible*), abbreviations (*DBA* for *doing business as*), and jargon (*input, output, bottom line*). Use action-specific verbs (*purchase a printer* rather than *get a printer*)
- **Cite numbers carefully.** For international trade it's a good idea to learn and use the metric system. In citing numbers, use figures (*15*) instead of spelling them out (*fifteen*). Always convert dollar figures into local currency. Avoid using figures to express the month of the year. In North America, for example, March 5, 2003, might be written as 3/5/03, while in Europe the same date might appear as 5.3.03. For clarity, always spell the month out.

CAPITALIZING ON WORKFORCE DIVERSITY

As global competition opens world markets, North American businesspeople will increasingly interact with customers and colleagues from around the world. At the same time, the North American workforce is also becoming more diverse—in race, ethnicity, age, gender, national origin, physical ability, and countless other characteristics.

No longer, say the experts, will the workplace be predominantly male or Anglo-oriented. Nearly 85 percent of the new entrants to the workforce will be women, minorities, and immigrants, according to estimates from the U.S. Bureau of Labor Statistics. By the year 2005, groups now considered minorities (African Americans, Hispanics, Asians, Native Americans, and others) will make up 27 percent of the workforce.[17] Women will make up 48 percent of the workforce. And more than 22 million workers will be 55 years or older.[18]

While the workforce is becoming more diverse, the structure of many businesses in North America is also changing. As you learned earlier, workers are now organized by teams. Organizations are flatter, and rank-and-file workers are increasingly making decisions among themselves. What does all this mean for you as a future business communicator? Simply put, your job may require you to interact with colleagues and customers from around the world. Your work environment will probably demand that you cooperate effectively with small groups of coworkers. And these coworkers may differ from you in race, ethnicity, gender, age, and other ways.

A diverse work environment has many benefits. Consumers want to deal with companies that respect their values and create products and services tailored to their needs. Organizations that hire employees with different experiences and backgrounds are better able to create the different products that these consumers desire. In addition, businesses with diverse workforces suffer fewer discrimination lawsuits, fewer union clashes, and less government regulatory action. That's why a growing number of companies view today's diversity movement as a critical bottom-line business strategy. They are convinced that it improves employee relationships and increases productivity.[19]

© Grantland Enterprises; http://www.grantland.net

TIPS FOR EFFECTIVE COMMUNICATION WITH DIVERSE WORKPLACE AUDIENCES

Capitalizing on workplace diversity is an enormous challenge for most organizations and individuals. Harmony and acceptance do not happen automatically when people who are dissimilar work together. The following suggestions can help you become a more effective communicator as you enter a rapidly evolving workplace with ethnically diverse colleagues and clients.

- **Understand the value of differences.** Diversity makes an organization innovative and creative. Sameness fosters "groupthink," an absence of critical thinking sometimes found in homogeneous groups. Case studies, for example, of the Kennedy administration's decision to invade Cuba and of the *Challenger* missile disaster suggest that groupthink prevented alternatives from being considered.[20] Diversity in problem-solving groups encourages independent and creative thinking.
- **Don't expect conformity.** Gone are the days when businesses could say, "This is our culture. Conform or leave."[21] The CEO of athletic shoemaker Reebok stressed seeking people who have new and different stories to tell. "It accomplishes next to nothing to employ those who are different from us if the condition of their employment is that they become the same as us. For it is their differences that enrich us, expand us, provide us the competitive edge."[22]
- **Create zero tolerance for bias and stereotypes.** Cultural patterns exist in every identity group, but applying these patterns to individuals results in stereotyp-

ing. Assuming that African Americans are good athletes, that women are poor at math, that French Canadians excel at hockey, or that European American men are insensitive fails to admit the immense differences in people in each group. Check your own use of stereotypes and labels. Don't tell sexist or ethnic jokes at meetings. Avoid slang, abbreviations, and jargon that imply stereotypes. Challenge others' stereotypes politely but firmly.

- **Practice focused, thoughtful, and open-minded listening.** Much misunderstanding can be avoided by attentive listening. Listen for main points; take notes if necessary to remember important details. The most important part of listening, especially among diverse communicators, is judging ideas, not appearances or accents.

- **Invite, use, and give feedback.** As you learned earlier, a critical element in successful communication is feedback. You can encourage it by asking questions such as *Is there anything you don't understand?* When a listener or receiver responds, use that feedback to adjust your delivery of information. Does the receiver need more details? A different example? Slower delivery? As a good listener, you should also be prepared to give feedback. For example, summarize your understanding of what was said or agreed on.

- **Make fewer assumptions.** Be careful of seemingly insignificant, innocent workplace assumptions. For example, don't assume that everyone wants to observe the holidays with a Christmas party and a decorated tree. Celebrating only Christian holidays in December and January excludes those who honor Hanukkah, Kwanza, and the Chinese New Year. Moreover, in workplace discussions don't assume that everyone is married or wants to be or is even heterosexual, for that matter. For invitations, avoid phrases such as "managers and their *wives*." *Spouses* or *partners* is more inclusive. Valuing diversity means making fewer assumptions that everyone is like you or wants to be like you.

- **Learn about your cultural self.** Knowing your own cultural biases helps you become more objective and adaptable. Begin to recognize the stock reactions and thought patterns that are automatic to you as a result of your upbringing. Become more aware of your own values and beliefs. That way you can see them at work when you are confronted by differing values.

- **Learn about other cultures and identity groups.** People are naturally threatened by the unknown. Consider the following proverb: "I saw in the distance what I took to be a beast, but when I came close, I saw it was my brother and my sister." The same error occurs in communities and work groups. From a distance an unknown person may appear to be threatening. But when the person is recognized or better known, our reactions change. Learning more about diverse groups and individuals helps you reduce the threat of the unknown.

- **Seek common ground.** Look for areas where you and others not like you can agree or share opinions. Be prepared to consider issues from many perspectives, all of which may be valid. Accept that there is room for different points of view to coexist peacefully. Although you can always find differences, it's much harder to find similarities. Look for common ground in shared experiences, mutual goals, and similar values. Concentrate on your objective even when you may disagree on how to reach it.[23]

SUMMING UP AND LOOKING FORWARD

This chapter described the importance of becoming an effective business communicator in this information economy. Many of the changes in today's dynamic workplace revolve around processing and communicating information. Flattened management hierarchies, participatory management, increased emphasis on work teams, heightened global competition, and innovative communication technologies

Summing Up and Looking Forward

are all trends that increase the need for good communication skills. To improve your skills, you should understand the communication process. Communication doesn't take place unless senders encode meaningful messages that can be decoded and understood by receivers.

One important part of the communication process is listening. You can become a more active listener by keeping an open mind, listening for main points, capitalizing on lag time, judging ideas and not appearances, taking selective notes, and providing feedback. The chapter also described ways to help you improve your nonverbal communication skills.

You learned the powerful effect that culture has on communication, and you became more aware of key cultural values for North Americans. Finally, the chapter discussed ways that businesses and individuals can capitalize on workforce diversity.

The following chapters present the writing process. You will learn specific techniques to help you improve your written and oral expression. Remember, communication skills are not inherited. They are learned. John Bryan, the highly respected CEO of Sara Lee, recognized this when he said that communication skills are "about 99 percent developed." Bryan contends that "the ability to construct a succinct memo, one that concentrates on the right issues, and the ability to make a presentation to an audience—these are skills that can be taught to almost anyone."[24]

Interactive Learning @ http://www.westwords.com/guffey/students.html
Prepare for tests and reinforce your chapter knowledge with interactive quizzes and crossword puzzles.

CRITICAL THINKING

1. Why should business and professional students strive to improve their communication skills, and why is it difficult or impossible to do without help?
2. Recall a time when you experienced a problem as result of poor communication. What were the causes of and possible remedies for the problem?
3. How are listening skills important to employees, supervisors, and executives? Who should have the best listening skills?
4. What arguments could you give for or against the idea that body language is a science with principles that can be interpreted accurately by specialists?
5. Since English is becoming the world's language and since the United States is a dominant military and trading force, why should Americans bother to learn about other cultures?

CHAPTER REVIEW

6. Are communication skills acquired by *nature* or by *nurture*? Explain.

7. List seven trends in the workplace that affect business communicators. Be prepared to discuss how they might affect you in your future career.

8. Give a brief definition of the following words:
   a. Encode
   b. Channel
   c. Decode

9. List 11 techniques for improving your listening skills. Be prepared to discuss each.

10. What is nonverbal communication? Give several examples.

11. Why is good eye contact important for North American communicators?

12. Describe the concept of North American individualism. How does this concept set North Americans apart from people in some other cultures?

13. What is ethnocentrism, and how can it be reduced?

14. List seven suggestions for enhancing comprehension when you are talking with people for whom English is a second language. Be prepared to discuss each.

15. List at least eight suggestions for becoming a more effective communicator in a diverse workplace. Be prepared to discuss each.

ACTIVITIES AND CASES

INFOTRAC

INFOTRAC COLLEGE EDITION

BUILDING KNOWLEDGE AND RESEARCH SKILLS

To excel as a knowledge worker in today's digital workplace, you must know how to find and evaluate information on the Internet. As a student purchasing a new copy of Guffey's *Essentials of Business Communication*, 6e, you have an extraordinary opportunity to develop these research skills. For four months you have special access to InfoTrac College Edition, a comprehensive Web-based collection of over 1 million journal, magazine, encyclopedia, and newspaper articles. You'll find many activities and study questions in this text that help you build knowledge and develop research skills using InfoTrac. Watch for the InfoTrac icons.

HOW TO USE INFOTRAC

1. With your Web browser on your computer screen, key the URL for InfoTrac, **http://www.infotrac-college.com**.
2. Learn about using InfoTrac by clicking **Demonstration** (left side of screen).
3. To begin searching, enter the **Passcode Login** that came with your new textbook. Click **InfoTrac Login**. On the search page, click **Keywords**. Enter your search term. Click **Search**. (Use the **Subject** search for more general terms.)
4. Browse the listed citations by using the scroll bar at the right side of your browser.
5. Study the description for each citation. Use full-text articles, which will be most helpful to you.
6. Click one citation to view. Scroll down to read the article.
7. To return to your citation list, scroll to the top of the page and click **Return to: Easy-Trac**. This is more efficient than using the browser Back button, which takes you through all previous browser screens.
8. To start a new search, click **New Search**.
9. To search by author, journal, or title, click **PowerTrac**. From **Select index** click your category (author, title, etc.). Insert the author's name or other search expression in the entry box. A symbol (such as *au*) will appear in the search box. Click in the box and insert the author's name. Click **Search**. Be sure to click **View** to see the citation list.

1.1 GETTING TO KNOW YOU. Since today's work and class environments often involve cooperating in teams or small groups, getting to know your fellow classmates is important. To learn something about the people in this class and to give you practice in developing your communication skills, your instructor may choose one of the following activities:

Your Task

a. For larger classes, divide into groups of four or five. Take one minute to introduce yourself briefly (name, major interest, hobbies, goals) within your group. Spend five minutes in the first group session. Record the first name of each individual you meet. Then informally regroup. In new groups again spend five minutes on introductions. After three or four sessions, study your name list. How many names can you associate with faces?

b. For smaller classes introduce yourself in a two-minute oral presentation while standing before the class at the rostrum. Where are you from? What are your educational goals? What are your interests? This informal presentation may serve as the first of two or three oral presentations correlated with Chapters 11 and 12.

1.2 CLASS LISTENING. Have you ever consciously observed the listening habits of others?

Your Task. In one of your classes, study student listening habits for a week. What barriers to effective listening did you observe? How many of the suggestions described in this chapter are being implemented by listeners in the class? Write a memo or an e-mail message to your instructor briefly describing your observations. (See Chapter 5 to learn more about memos.)

1.3 YOUR OWN LISTENING. Focusing on your own listening can reveal a number of good and bad habits.

Your Task. Analyze your own listening habits. What are your strengths and weaknesses? Decide on a plan for improving your listening skills. Write a memo or e-mail message to your instructor including your analysis and your improvement plan. (See Chapter 5 to learn more about memos.)

1.4 HOW GOOD ARE YOUR LISTENING SKILLS? SELF-CHECKED RATING QUIZ. WEB
You can learn whether you are a poor, fair, good, or excellent listener by completing a listening quiz.

Your Task. Take the quiz at this Web site: http:www.oxyfresh.ww.com/grow_listeningquiz.asp. What two listening behaviors do you think you need to work on the most? Remember to check the updated URLs at the student Web site in case any URL doesn't work.

1.5 FINDING RELEVANT LISTENING ADVICE. Your manager, Alex Evans, has been INFOTRAC
asked to be part of a panel discussion at a management conference. The topic is "Workplace Communication Challenges," and his area of expertise is listening. He asks you to help him prepare for the discussion by doing some research.

Your Task. Using an InfoTrac subject search, locate at least three articles with suggestions for improving workplace listening skills. Use full-text articles, not abstracts. In a memo to Alex Evans, present a two- to three-sentence summary explaining why each article is helpful. Include the author's name, publication, date of publication, and page number. Then list at least ten listening suggestions. See Chapter 5 for memo format. Begin your memo with a sentence such as, "As you requested, I found three articles on listening techniques. After discussing the articles, I will present a list with the most helpful suggestions."

1.6 SILENT MESSAGES. Becoming more aware of the silent messages you send helps you make them more accurate.

Your Task. Analyze the kinds of silent messages you send your instructor, your classmates, and your employer. How do you send these messages? Group them into categories, as suggested by what you learned in this chapter. What do these messages mean? Be prepared to discuss them in small groups or in a memo to your instructor.

1.7 BODY LANGUAGE. Can body language be accurately interpreted?

Your Task. What attitudes do the following body movements suggest to you? Do these movements always mean the same thing? What part does context play in your interpretations?

a. Whistling, wringing hands
b. Bowed posture, twiddling thumbs
c. Steepled hands, sprawling sitting position
d. Rubbing hand through hair
e. Open hands, unbuttoned coat
f. Wringing hands, tugging ears

CRITICAL THINKING TEAM

1.8 UNIVERSAL SIGN FOR "I GOOFED." In an effort to promote peace and tranquillity on the highways, motorists submitted the following suggestions to a newspaper columnist.[25]

Your Task. In small groups consider the pros and cons for each of the following gestures intended as an apology when a driver makes a mistake. Why would some fail?

a. Lower your head slightly and bonk yourself on the forehead with the side of your closed fist. The message is clear: "I'm stupid. I shouldn't have done that."
b. Make a temple with your hands, as if you were praying.
c. Move the index finger of your right hand back and forth across your neck—as if you were cutting your throat.
d. Flash the well-known peace sign. Hold up the index and middle fingers of one hand, making a *V*, as in Victory.
e. Place the flat of your hands against your cheeks, as children do when they've made a mistake.
f. Clasp your hand over your mouth, raise your brows, and shrug your shoulders.
g. Use your knuckles to knock on the side of your head. Translation: "Oops! Engage brain."
h. Place your right hand high on your chest and pat a few times, like a basketball player who drops a pass or a football player who makes a bad throw. This says, "I'll take the blame."
i. Place your right fist over the middle of your chest and move it in a circular motion. This is universal sign language for "I'm sorry."
j. Open your window and tap the top of your car roof with your hand.
k. Smile and raise both arms, palms outward, which is a universal gesture for surrender or forgiveness.
l. Use the military salute, which is simple and shows respect.
m. Flash your biggest smile, point at yourself with your right thumb and move your head from left to right, as if to say, "I can't believe I did that."

1.9 ALICE IN WONDERLAND TRAVELS TO TOKYO. Jeff Davis is the leader of a creative team representing a large American theme park company. The owners of a Japanese park rely on the American company to develop new attractions for their Tokyo park. But the Japanese own their park and must approve any new addition. Jeff and his team recently traveled to Japan to make an important presentation to the owners. His team had worked for the past year developing the concept of an outdoor garden maze with a network of hedge passageways for children to wander through. The concept was based on *Alice in Wonderland*.

The jobs of his entire team depended on selling the idea of this new attraction (including restaurants and gift shops) to the owners of the Tokyo park. Because the Japanese smiled and nodded throughout the presentation, Jeff assumed they liked the idea. When he pushed for final approval, the Japanese smiled and said that an outdoor garden attraction might be difficult in their climate. Jeff explained away that argument. Then, he asked for a straightforward yes or no, but the Japanese answered, "We will have to study it very carefully." Thinking he had not made himself clear, Jeff began to review the strong points of the presentation.

Your Task. Analyze the preceding cross-cultural incident. What cultural elements may be interfering with communication in this exchange?

1.10 SOUP'S ON.

As a junior manager of Campbell Soup Company, you have been sent to Hong Kong to work on the development of new regional soup varieties to appeal to 2 billion Asian consumers. The Chinese are among the highest per capita soup eaters in the world, consuming an average of one bowl a day. In the Hong Kong taste kitchen, you are currently working on cabbage soup, scallop broth, and a special soup that combines watercress and duck gizzards. You've even tested exotic ingredients such as shark's fin and snake.[26] The supervisor of the taste kitchen understands English, but sometimes her eyes glaze over when you discuss procedures with her.

Your Task. What could you do to improve comprehension and minimize misunderstandings?

1.11 TRANSLATING IDIOMS.

Many languages have idiomatic expressions that do not always make sense to outsiders.

Your Task. Explain in simple English what the following idiomatic expressions mean. Assume that you are explaining them to people for whom English is a second language.

a. let the cat out of the bag
b. take the bull by the horns
c. he is a tightwad
d. putting the cart before the horse
e. to be on the road
f. lend someone a hand
g. with flying colors
h. turn over a new leaf

1.12 ANALYZING DIVERSITY AT REEBOK.

Reebok grew from a $12 million a year sport shoe company into a $3 billion footwear powerhouse without giving much thought to the hiring of employees. "When we were growing very, very fast, all we did was bring another friend into work the next day," recalled Sharon Cohen, Reebok vice president. "Everybody hired nine of their friends. Well, it happened that nine white people hired nine of their friends, so guess what? They were white, all about the same age. And then we looked up and said, 'Wait a minute. We don't like the way it looks here.' That's the kind of thing that can happen when you are growing very fast and thoughtlessly."[27]

E-MAIL

Your Task. In what ways would Reebok benefit by diversifying its staff? What competitive advantages might it gain? Outline your reasoning in an e-mail message to your instructor.

1.13 VIDEO CASE STUDY: DIVERSITY IN BUSINESS AT DAYTON HUDSON DE-PARTMENT STORES. Ask your instructor to show the VHS video describing Hudson's commitment to diversity. Stop the tape at the designated spot and break into small groups to analyze the pictures of potential customers No. 1 and No. 12.

Your Task. In your group speculate about the person whose picture you have been assigned.

- What are that person's profession, interests and hobbies, family life, buying habits, and personal characteristics? Make lists of your group's profile of the targeted person.
- When the tape resumes, watch the profile developed by the Hudson's trainee group.
- How did your profile compare with that of the Hudson's trainee group?
- How close were you to describing the actual individual?
- What stereotypes were at work here?
- Why is it important to look beyond stereotypes in judging individuals? Your instructor may ask your group to submit its profile list.

GRAMMAR/MECHANICS CHECKUP—1

These checkups are designed to improve your control of grammar and mechanics. They systematically review all sections of the Grammar/Mechanics Handbook. Answers are provided near the end of the book.

NOUNS

Review Sections 1.01–1.06 in the Grammar/Mechanics Handbook. Then study each of the following statements. Underscore any inappropriate form, and write a correction in the space provided. Also record the appropriate G/M section and letter to illustrate the principle involved. If a sentence is correct, write C. When you finish, compare your responses with those provided. If your answers differ, study carefully the principles shown in parentheses.

companies (1.05e) **Example**   Two surveys revealed that many companys will move to the new industrial park.

_____   1. Several attornies worked on the three cases simultaneously.
_____   2. Counter business is higher on Saturday's, but telephone business is greater on Sundays.
_____   3. Some of the citys in Kevin's report offer excellent opportunities.
_____   4. Frozen chickens and turkies are kept in the company's lockers.
_____   5. All secretaries were asked to check supplies and other inventorys.
_____   6. Only the Nashs and the Lopezes brought their entire families.
_____   7. In the 1980s profits grew slowly; in the 1990's investments soared.
_____   8. Both editor in chiefs instituted strict proofreading policies.
_____   9. Luxury residential complexs are part of the architect's plan.
_____   10. Voters in three countys are likely to approve new gas taxes.
_____   11. The instructor was surprised to find three Jennifer's in one class.
_____   12. André sent descriptions of two valleys in France to us via the Internet.
_____   13. How many copies of the statements showing your assets and liabilitys did you make?
_____   14. My monitor makes it difficult to distinguish between *o*'s and *a*'s.
_____   15. Both runner-ups complained about the winner's behavior.

Your instructor may assign the Advanced Grammar/Mechanics Checkup, which is on your student CD.

DOCUMENT FOR REVISION

The following memo has many faults in grammar, spelling, punctuation, capitalization, word use, and number form. Use standard proofreading marks (see Appendix B) to correct the errors. Study the guidelines in the Grammar/Mechanics Handbook to sharpen your skills. When you finish, your instructor can show you the revised version of this memo.

TO: Tran Nguyen

FROM: Rachel Stivers, Manager

DATE: May 14, 200X

SUBJECT: WORK AT HOME GUIDELINES

Since you will be completeing most of your work at home for the next 4 months. Follow these guidelines;

1. Check your message bored daily and respond promptly, to those who are trying to reach you.

2. Call the office at least twice a day to pick up any telephone messages, return these calls promly.

3. Transmit any work you do, on the computer to Jerry Gonzalez in our computer services department, he will analyze each weeks accounts, and send it to the proper Departments.

4. Provide me with monthly reports' of your progress.

In prepareing your work space you should make sure you have adequate space for your computer printer fax and storage. For Security reasons you're workingarea should be off limits to your family and friends.

We will continue to hold once a week staff meetings on Friday at 10 a.m. in the morning. Do you think it would be possible for you to attend 1 or 2 of these meeting. The next one is Friday May 17th.

I know you will work satisfactory at home Tran. Following these basic guidelines should help you accomplish your work, and provide the office with adequate contact with you.

Communication Workshops (such as the one on the next page) provide insight into special business communication topics and skills not discussed in the chapters. These topics cover ethics, technology, career skills, and collaboration. Each workshop includes a career application with a case study or problem to help you develop skills relevant to the workshop topic.

Using Job Boards to Check Out Employment Possibilities

This communication workshop will help you use the Web to study job openings in your field. Nearly everyone looking for a job today starts with the Web. Using the Web to locate a job or an internship has distinct advantages. For many job seekers, the Web leads to bigger salaries, wider opportunities, and faster hiring. The Web, however, can devour huge chunks of time and produce slim results unless you know what you are doing.

In terms of actually finding a job, the Web seems to work best for professionals looking for similar work in their current fields and for those who are totally flexible about location. Yet the Web is an excellent place for any job seeker to learn what's available, what qualifications are necessary, and what salaries are being offered. Thousands of "job boards" with many job listings for employers across the United States and abroad are available on the Web.

Career Application. Assume that you are about to finish your degree or certification program, and you are now looking for a job. The easiest way to job search today is on the Web. A terrific selection of Web job-search sites is available to students at the Guffey Web site for students. At the direction of your instructor, conduct a survey of electronic job advertisements in your field. What's available? How much is the salary? What are the requirements?

Your Task

- **Go to http://www.westwords.com/guffey/students.html** and click "Job Search." Scroll down to "Job Resources." You'll see many excellent job sites. To get you started, click "Monster.com," one of the most popular job boards.
- **Study the opening page.** Confusing, eh? Remember that all the free services on the Web are supported by advertisements. Try to ignore the clutter. Notice that you can post your résumé, search for jobs, or read articles in the career center. Click "Search Jobs."
- **Read "Tips on Searching."** This may take a few minutes, but it's well worth the time. Notice that you can limit your search to specific locations and categories. Under "Keyword Search," you can further pinpoint your search with the title of the position you seek or terms that describe technical or professional experience. Close this box by clicking the X in the top right corner.
- **Conduct a practice search.** On the search page, scroll down the "Location Search" box. Then highlight a geographical area. Just for fun, try "Hawaii, Hawaii." In the "Job Category Search" box, select "Administrative/Clerical." Leave the "Keyword Search" box empty. Then press Enter in the "Search Jobs" box. You should see many current job ads.
- **Conduct a real search.** Now conduct a job search in your career area and in geographical areas of your choice. If you don't find suitable jobs at Monster.com, use one of the other job sites. Select five ads and print them. If you cannot print, make notes on what you find.
- **Analyze the skills required.** How often do the ads mention communication, teamwork, and computer skills? What tasks do the ads mention? What is the salary range identified in these ads for this position? Your instructor may ask you to submit your findings and/or report to the class.

The Writing Process

Chapter 2

Writing for Business Audiences

I wanted to know where they came from, what their interests were, and what I could talk to them about.

JOHN H. JOHNSON, founder of *Ebony* and *Jet* magazines and
Fashion Fair cosmetics, talking about customers

LEARNING OBJECTIVES

1. Understand that business writing should be audience-oriented, purposeful, and economical.
2. Identify and implement the three phases of the writing process.
3. Appreciate the importance of analyzing the task and profiling the audience for business messages.
4. Create messages that spotlight audience benefits and cultivate a "you" view.
5. Develop a conversational tone and use positive language.
6. Explain the need for inclusive language, plain expression, and familiar words.
7. List seven ways in which technology helps improve business writing.

BASICS OF BUSINESS WRITING

*I*n communicating with others, newspaper founder and businessman John H. Johnson always concentrated on what *they* wanted rather than what *he* wanted. An exceedingly successful entrepreneur, Johnson was born in a tin-roof shack in Arkansas. Despite the odds, he became the first black on the *Forbes* magazine list of the 400 richest people in America. "Being poor made me run scared," he confessed. It also motivated him to find ways to succeed in publishing and in life. What is his greatest success secret? Focusing totally on his audience. With prospective advertisers, he always talked about what he could do for them. How could he help them improve their bottom line? How could he help them increase their sales? How could he make their lives easier?[1]

Audience awareness is one of the basics of business communication. This chapter focuses on writing for business audiences. Business writing may be different from other writing you have done. High school or college compositions and term papers may have required you to describe your feelings, display your knowledge, and meet a minimum word count. Business writing, however, has different goals. In preparing business messages and oral presentations, you'll find that your writing needs to be:

- **Audience-oriented.** Like publisher John Johnson, you will concentrate on looking at a problem from the receiver's perspective instead of seeing it from your own.
- **Purposeful.** You will be writing to solve problems and convey information. You will have a definite purpose to fulfill in each message.
- **Economical.** You will try to present ideas clearly but concisely. Length is not rewarded.

✓ *Quick Check*

Business writing is audience-oriented, purposeful, and economical.

These distinctions actually ease the writer's task. You won't be searching your imagination for creative topic ideas. You won't be stretching your ideas to make them appear longer. One writing consultant complained that "most college graduates entering industry have at least a subliminal perception that in technical and business writing, quantity enhances quality."[2] Wrong! Get over the notion that longer is better. Conciseness is what counts in business.

The ability to prepare concise, audience-centered, and purposeful messages does not come naturally. Very few people, especially beginners, can sit down and compose a terrific letter or report without training. But following a systematic process, studying model messages, and practicing the craft can make nearly anyone a successful business writer or speaker.

✓ *Quick Check*

Following a systematic process helps beginning writers create effective messages and presentations.

THE WRITING PROCESS FOR BUSINESS MESSAGES AND ORAL PRESENTATIONS

Whether you are preparing an e-mail message, memo, letter, or oral presentation, the process will be easier if you follow a systematic plan. Our plan breaks the entire task into three separate phases: prewriting, writing, and revising. As you can see in Figure 2.1, however, the process is not always linear.

To illustrate the writing process, let's say that you own a popular local McDonald's franchise. At rush times, you've got a big problem. Customers complain about the chaotic multiple waiting lines to approach the service counter. You once saw two customers nearly get into a fistfight over cutting into a line. And customers often are so intent on looking for ways to improve their positions in line that they fail to examine the menu. Then they are undecided when their turn arrives. You want to convince other franchise owners that a single-line (serpentine)

✓ *Quick Check*

The writing process has three parts: prewriting, writing, and revising.

FIGURE 2.1 The Writing Process

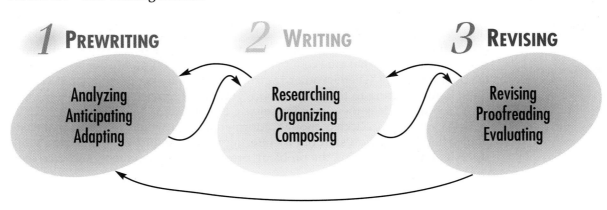

1 **PREWRITING**
Analyzing
Anticipating
Adapting

2 **WRITING**
Researching
Organizing
Composing

3 **REVISING**
Revising
Proofreading
Evaluating

The first phase of the writing process involves analyzing information currently available, deciding what the purpose of your message is, anticipating the reaction of the receiver, and thinking of ways to adapt your message for the best reception. Spending adequate time on this first phase results in less pain in the writing and revising phases as well as in more successful messages.
© PhotoDisc, Inc./Getty Images

system would work better. You could telephone everyone. But you want to present a serious argument with good points that owners will remember and be willing to act on when they gather for their next district meeting. You decide to write a letter that you hope will win their support.

PREWRITING

The first phase of the writing process prepares you to write. It involves *analyzing* the audience and your purpose for writing. The audience for your letter will be other franchise owners, some of whom are highly educated and some of whom are not. Your purpose in writing is to convince them that a change in policy would improve customer service. You are convinced that a single-line system, such as that used in banks, would reduce chaos and make customers happier because they would not have to worry about where they are in line.

Prewriting also involves *anticipating* how your audience will react to your message. You're sure that some of the other owners will agree with you, but others might fear that customers seeing a long single line might go elsewhere. In *adapting* your message to the audience, you try to think of the right words and the right tone that will win approval.

WRITING

The second phase involves researching, organizing, and then composing the message. In *researching* information for this letter, you would probably investigate other kinds of businesses that use single lines for customers. You might check out your competitors. What are Wendy's and Burger King doing? You might do some telephoning to see whether other franchise owners are concerned about chaotic lines. Before writing to the entire group, you might brainstorm with a few owners to see what ideas they have for solving the problem.

Once you have collected enough information, you would focus on *organizing* your letter. Should you start out by offering your solution? Or should you work up to it slowly, describing the problem, presenting your evidence, and then ending with the solution? The final step in the second phase of the writing process is actually *composing* the letter. Naturally, you'll do it at your computer so that you can make revisions easily.

REVISING

The third phase of the process involves revising, proofreading, and evaluating your letter. After writing the first draft, you'll spend a lot of time *revising* the message for clarity, conciseness, tone, and readability. Could parts of it be rearranged to make your point more effectively? This is the time when you look for ways to improve the organization and sound of your message. Next, you'll spend time *proofreading* carefully to ensure correct spelling, grammar, punctuation, and format. The final phase involves *evaluating* your message to decide whether it accomplishes your goal.

Quick Check
The third phase of the writing process includes revising for clarity and readability, proofreading for errors, and evaluating for effectiveness.

SCHEDULING THE WRITING PROCESS

Although Figure 2.1 shows the three phases of the writing equally, the time you spend on each varies depending on the complexity of the problem, the purpose, the audience, and your schedule. One expert gives these rough estimates for scheduling a project:

* Prewriting—25 percent (planning and worrying)
* Writing—25 percent (organizing and composing)
* Revising—50 percent (45 percent revising and 5 percent proofreading)

Quick Check
Because revising is the most important part of the writing process, it takes the most time.

These are rough guides, yet you can see that good writers spend most of their time on the final phase of revising and proofreading. Much depends, of course, on your project, its importance, and your familiarity with it. What's critical to remember, though, is that revising is a major component of the writing process.

It may appear that you perform one step and progress to the next, always following the same order. Most business writing, however, is not that rigid. Although writers perform the tasks described, the steps may be rearranged, abbreviated, or repeated. Some writers revise every sentence and paragraph as they go. Many find that new ideas occur after they've begun to write, causing them to back up, alter the organization, and rethink their plan.

ANALYZING THE PURPOSE FOR WRITING AND THE AUDIENCE

We've just taken a look at the total writing process. As you begin to develop your business writing skills, you should expect to follow this process closely. With experience, though, you'll become like other good writers and presenters who alter, compress, and rearrange the steps as needed. But following a plan is very helpful at first. The remainder of this chapter covers the first phase of the writing process. You'll learn to analyze the purpose for writing, anticipate how your audience will react, and adapt your message to the audience.

IDENTIFYING YOUR PURPOSE

As you begin to compose a message, ask yourself two important questions: (1) Why am I sending this message? (2) What do I hope to achieve? Your responses will determine how you organize and present your information.

Quick Check
The primary purpose of most business messages is to inform or to persuade; the secondary purpose is to promote goodwill.

Your message may have primary and secondary purposes. For college work your primary purpose may be merely to complete the assignment; secondary purposes might be to make yourself look good and to get a good grade. The primary purposes for sending business messages are typically to inform and to persuade. A secondary purpose is to promote goodwill: you and your organization want to look good in the eyes of your audience.

SELECTING THE BEST CHANNEL

After identifying the purpose of your message, you need to select the most appropriate communication channel. Some information is most efficiently and effectively delivered orally. Other messages should be written, and still others are best delivered electronically. Whether to set up a meeting, send a message by e-mail, or write a report depends on some of the following factors:

* Importance of the message
* Amount and speed of feedback required

FIGURE 2.2   Choosing Communication Channels

CHANNEL	BEST USE
Face-to-face conversation	When you want to be persuasive, deliver bad news, or share a personal message.
Telephone call	When you need to deliver or gather information quickly, when nonverbal cues are unimportant, and when you cannot meet in person.
Voice mail message	When you wish to leave important or routine information that the receiver can respond to when convenient.
Fax	When your message must cross time zones or international boundaries, when a written record is significant, or when speed is important.
E-mail	When you need feedback but not immediately. Insecurity makes it problematic for personal, emotional, or private messages. Effective for communicating with a large, dispersed audience.
Face-to-face group meeting	When group decisions and consensus are important. Inefficient for merely distributing information.
Video or teleconference	When group consensus and interaction are important but members are geographically dispersed.
Memo	When you want a written record to explain policies clearly, discuss procedures, or collect information within an organization.
Letter	When you need a written record of correspondence with customers, the government, suppliers, or others outside an organization.
Report or proposal	When you are delivering considerable data internally or externally.

- Necessity of a permanent record
- Cost of the channel
- Degree of formality desired

These five factors will help you decide which of the channels shown in Figure 2.2 is most appropriate for delivering a message.

SWITCHING TO FASTER CHANNELS

Technology and competition continue to accelerate the pace of business today. As a result, communicators are switching to ever-faster means of exchanging information. In the past business messages within organizations were delivered largely by hard-copy memos. Responses would typically take a couple of days. But that's too slow for today's communicators. They want answers and action now! Cell phones, faxes, Web sites, and especially e-mail can deliver that information much faster than can traditional channels of communication.

Within many organizations, hard-copy memos are still written, especially for messages that require persuasion, permanence, or formality. But the channel of choice for corporate communicators today is clearly e-mail. It's fast, cheap, and easy. Thus, fewer hard-copy memos are being written. Fewer letters are also being written. That's because many customer service functions can now be served through Web sites or by e-mail.

Whether your channel choice is e-mail, a hard-copy memo, or a report, you'll be a more effective writer if you spend sufficient time in the prewriting phase.

ANTICIPATING THE AUDIENCE

A good writer anticipates the audience for a message: What is the reader like? How will that reader react to the message? Although you can't always know exactly who the reader is, you can imagine some of the reader's characteristics. Even writers of direct mail sales letters have a general idea of the audience they wish

Messages and advertisements aimed at visitors to theme parks such as Universal Studios focus on the thrills and excitement that visitors expect. Anticipating the audience for a message helps the writer decide what to include and what to emphasize. In profiling the audience, good writers visualize the reader or listener and develop an appropriate communication strategy based on the anticipated audience. © Jeff Greenberg/PhotoEdit, Inc.

to target. Picturing a typical reader is important in guiding what you write. One copywriter at Lands' End, the catalog company, pictures his sister-in-law whenever he writes product descriptions for the catalog. By profiling your audience and shaping a message to respond to that profile, you are more likely to achieve your communication goals.

PROFILING THE AUDIENCE

Visualizing your audience is a pivotal step in the writing process. The questions in Figure 2.3 will help you profile your audience. How much time you devote to answering these questions depends greatly on your message and its context. An analytical report that you compose for management or an oral presentation before a big group would, of course, demand considerable audience anticipation. On the other hand, an e-mail message to a coworker or a letter to a familiar supplier might require only a few moments of planning. No matter how short your message, though, spend some time thinking about the audience so that you can tailor your words to your readers or listeners. "The most often unasked question in business and professional communication," claims a writing expert, "is as simple as it is important: *Have I thought enough about my audience?*"[3]

RESPONDING TO THE PROFILE

Profiling your audience helps you make decisions about shaping the message. You'll discover what kind of language is appropriate, whether you're free to use specialized technical terms, whether you should explain everything, and so on. You'll decide whether your tone should be formal or informal, and you'll select the most desirable channel. Imagining whether the receiver is likely to be neutral, positive, or negative will help you determine how to organize your message.

Another advantage of profiling your audience is considering the possibility of a secondary audience. For instance, you might write a report that persuades your boss to launch a Web site for customers. Your boss is the primary reader, and she

FIGURE 2.3 Asking the Right Questions to Profile Your Audience

PRIMARY AUDIENCE	SECONDARY AUDIENCE
Who is my primary reader or listener?	Who might see or hear this message in addition to the primary audience?
What is my personal and professional relationship with that person?	How do these people differ from the primary audience?
What position does the individual hold in the organization?	
How much does that person know about the subject?	
What do I now about that person's education, beliefs, culture, and attitudes?	
Should I expect a neutral, positive, or negative response to my message?	

is familiar with many of the details of your project. But she will need to secure approval from her boss, and that person is probably unfamiliar with the project details. Because your report will be passed along to secondary readers, it must include more background information and more extensive explanations than you included for the primary reader, your boss. Analyzing the task and anticipating the audience assists you in adapting your message so that it will accomplish what you intend.

ADAPTING TO THE TASK AND AUDIENCE

After analyzing your purpose and anticipating your audience, you must convey your purpose to that audience. Adaptation is the process of creating a message that suits your audience.

One important aspect of adaptation is *tone*. Conveyed largely by the words in a message, tone reflects how a receiver feels upon reading or hearing a message. Skilled communicators create a positive tone in their messages by using a number of adaptive techniques, some of which are unconscious. These include spotlighting audience benefits, cultivating a "you" attitude, sounding conversational, and using inclusive language. Additional adaptive techniques include using positive expression and preferring plain language with familiar words.

© Ted Goff (www.tedgoff.com)

AUDIENCE BENEFITS

Focusing on the audience sounds like a modern idea, but actually one of America's early statesmen and authors recognized this fundamental writing principle over 200 years ago. In describing effective writing, Ben Franklin observed, "To be good, it ought to have a tendency to benefit the reader."[4] These wise words have become a fundamental guideline for today's business communicators. Expanding on Franklin's counsel, a contemporary communication consultant gives this solid advice to his business clients: "Always stress the benefit to the readers of whatever it is you're

"You haven't been listening. I keep telling you that I don't want a product fit for a king."

trying to get them to do. If you can show them how you're going to save *them* frustration or help them meet their goals, you have the makings of a powerful message."[5]

Adapting your message to the receiver's needs means putting yourself in that person's shoes. It's called *empathy*. Empathic senders think about how a receiver will decode a message. They try to give something to the receiver, solve the receiver's problems, save the receiver's money, or just understand the feelings and position of that person. Which of the following messages is more appealing to the audience?

Sender focus	To enable us to update our stockholder records, we ask that the enclosed card be returned.
Audience focus	So that you may promptly receive dividend checks and information related to your shares, please return the enclosed card.

Sender focus	Our warranty becomes effective only when we receive an owner's registration.
Audience focus	Your warranty begins working for you as soon as you return your owner's registration.
Sender focus	We offer a CD-ROM language course that we have complete faith in.
Audience focus	The sooner you order the CD-ROM language program, the sooner the rewards will be yours.
Sender focus	The Human Resources Department requires that the enclosed questionnaire be completed immediately so that we can allocate our training resource funds.
Audience focus	By filling out the enclosed questionnaire, you can be one of the first employees to sign up for the new career development program.

"YOU" VIEW

Quick Check

Because receivers are most interested in themselves, emphasize the word *you* whenever possible.

Notice how many of the previous audience-focused messages included the word *you*. In concentrating on receiver benefits, skilled communicators naturally develop the "you" view. They emphasize second-person pronouns (*you, your*) instead of first-person pronouns (*I/we, us, our*). Whether your goal is to inform, persuade, or promote goodwill, the catchiest words you can use are *you* and *your*. Compare the following examples.

"I/We" View	I have scheduled your vacation to begin May 1.
"You" View	You may begin your vacation May 1.
"I/We" View	We have shipped your order by UPS, and we are sure it will arrive in time for the sales promotion January 15.
"You" View	Your order will be delivered by UPS in time for your sales promotion January 15.
"I/We" View	I'm asking all employees to respond to the attached survey regarding working conditions.
"You" View	Because your ideas count, please complete the attached survey regarding working conditions.

Emphasis on the "you" view, however, can result in stilted expression. Readers resent obvious attempts at manipulation. Some sales messages, for example, are guilty of overkill when they include *you* dozens of times in a direct mail promotion. Furthermore, the word can sometimes create the wrong impression. Consider this statement: *You cannot return merchandise until you receive written approval.* *You* appears twice, but the reader feels singled out for criticism. In the following version the message is less personal and more positive: *Customers may return merchandise with written approval.* Another difficulty in emphasizing the "you" view and deemphasizing *we/I* is that it may result in overuse of the passive voice. For example, to avoid *We will give you* (active voice), you might write *You will be given* (passive voice). The active voice in writing is generally preferred because it identifies who is doing the acting. You'll learn more about active and passive voice in Chapter 3.

In recognizing the value of the "you" *attitude*, writers do not have to sterilize their writing and totally avoid any first-person pronouns or words that show their feelings. Skilled communicators are able to convey sincerity, warmth, and enthusiasm by the words they choose. Don't be afraid to use phrases such as *I'm happy* or *We're delighted*, if you truly are. When speaking face to face, communicators show sincerity and warmth with nonverbal cues such as a smile and a pleasant voice tone. In letters, memos, and e-mail messages, however, only ex-

Quick Check

Emphasize *you* but don't eliminate all *I* and *we* statements.

pressive words and phrases can show these feelings. These phrases suggest hidden messages that say to readers and customers *You are important, I hear you, and I'm honestly trying to please you.*

CONVERSATIONAL BUT PROFESSIONAL

Most e-mail messages, business letters, memos, and reports replace conversation. Thus, they are most effective when they convey an informal, conversational tone instead of a formal, pretentious tone. But messages should not become so casual that they sound low-level and unprofessional. With the increasing use of e-mail, a major problem has developed. Sloppy, unprofessional expression appears in many e-mail messages. You'll learn more about e-mail in Chapter 5. At this point, though, we urge you to strive for a warm, conversational tone that does not include slang or low-level diction. Levels of diction, as shown in Figure 2.4, range from unprofessional through formal.

✓ *Quick Check*
Strive for conversational expression, but also remember to be professional.

Your goal is a warm, friendly tone that sounds professional. Talk to the reader with words that are comfortable to you. Avoid long and complex sentences. Use familiar pronouns such as *I, we,* and *you* and an occasional contraction, such as *we're* or *I'll.* Stay away from third-person constructions such as *the undersigned, the writer,* and *the affected party.* Also avoid legal terminology and technical words. Your writing will be easier to read and understand if it sounds like the following conversational examples:

Formal	All employees are herewith instructed to return the appropriately designated contracts to the undersigned.
Conversational	Please return your contracts to me.
Formal	Pertaining to your order, we must verify the sizes that your organization requires prior to consignment of your order to our shipper.
Conversational	We'll send your order as soon as we confirm the sizes you need.
Formal	The writer wishes to inform the above-referenced individual that subsequent payments may henceforth be sent to the address cited below.
Conversational	Your payments should now be sent to us in Lakewood.
Formal	To facilitate ratification of this agreement, your negotiators urge that the membership respond in the affirmative.
Conversational	We urge you to approve the agreement by voting yes.

FIGURE 2.4 Levels of Diction

UNPROFESSIONAL (LOW-LEVEL DICTION)	CONVERSATIONAL (MID-LEVEL DICTION)	FORMAL (HIGH-LEVEL DICTION)
badmouth	criticize	denigrate
guts	nerve	courage
pecking order	line of command	dominance hierarchy
ticked off	upset	provoked
rat on	inform	betray
rip off	steal	expropriate

Examples:

Unprofessional	If we just hang in there, we can snag the contract.
Conversational	If we don't get discouraged, we can win the contract.
Formal	If the principals persevere, they can secure the contract.

POSITIVE LANGUAGE

Positive language creates goodwill and gives more options to receivers.

The clarity and tone of a message are considerably improved if you use positive rather than negative language. Positive language generally conveys more information than negative language does. Moreover, positive messages are uplifting and pleasant to read. Positive wording tells what *is* and what *can be done* rather than what *isn't* and what *can't be done*. For example, *Your order cannot be shipped by January 10,* is not nearly as informative as *Your order will be shipped January 20*. Notice in the following examples how you can revise the negative tone to reflect a more positive impression.

Negative We are unable to send your shipment until we receive proof of your payment.
Positive We look forward to sending your shipment as soon as we receive your payment.

Negative We are sorry that we must reject your application for credit at this time.
Positive At this time we can serve you on a cash basis only.

Negative You will never regret opening a charge account with us.
Positive Your new charge account enables you to purchase executive suits at reasonable prices.

Negative If you fail to pass the exam, you will not qualify.
Positive You'll qualify if you pass the exam.

Negative Although I've never had a paid position before, I have worked as an intern in an attorney's office while completing my degree requirements.
Positive My experience in an attorney's office and my recent training in legal procedures and computer applications can be assets to your organization.

INCLUSIVE LANGUAGE

Sensitive communicators avoid language that excludes people.

A business writer who is alert and empathic will strive to use words that include rather than exclude people. Some words have been called *sexist* because they seem to exclude females. Notice the use of the masculine pronouns *he* and *his* in the following sentences:

If a physician is needed, *he* will be called.
Every homeowner must read *his* insurance policy carefully.

These sentences illustrate an age-old grammatical rule called "common gender." When a speaker or writer did not know the gender (sex) of an individual, masculine pronouns (such as *he* or *his*) were used. Masculine pronouns were understood to indicate both men and women. Today, however, sensitive writers and speakers replace common-gender pronouns with alternate inclusive constructions. You can use any of four alternatives.

Sexist Every attorney has ten minutes for *his* summation.

Alternative 1 All *attorneys* have ten minutes for *their* summations. (Use a plural noun and plural pronoun.)

Alternative 2 Attorneys have ten minutes for summations. (Omit the pronoun entirely.)

Alternative 3 Every attorney has ten minutes for *a* summation. (Use an article instead of a pronoun.)

Alternative 4 Every attorney has ten minutes for *his or her* summation. (Use both a masculine and a feminine pronoun.)

Note that the last alternative, which includes a masculine and a feminine pronoun, is wordy and awkward. Don't use it too frequently.

Other words are considered sexist because they suggest stereotypes. For example, the nouns *fireman* and *mailman* suggest that only men hold these positions.

You can avoid offending your listener or reader by using neutral job titles or functions. Consider the following: *firefighter, letter carrier, salesperson, flight attendant, department head, committee chair, technician,* and *police officer.*

DILBERT By Scott Adams

PLAIN ENGLISH

Business communicators who are conscious of their audience try to use plain language that expresses clear meaning. They avoid showy words, long sentences, and confusing expression. Some business, legal, and government documents, however, are written in an inflated style that obscures meaning. This style of writing has been given various terms such as *legalese, federalese, bureaucratese, doublespeak,* and the *official style.*

Over the past 30 years, consumer groups and the government have joined forces in the Plain English movement. It encourages businesses, professional organizations, and government bodies to write any official document—such as a contract, warranty, insurance policy, or lease—in clear, concise language.[6] As a result of the Plain English movement, numerous states have passed laws requiring that business contracts and public documents be written in plain language. One branch of the government, the Securities and Exchange Commission, has even written "A Plain English Handbook." This booklet illustrates many of the principles of good writing, some of which are shown in Figure 2.5. Throughout this textbook we will be practicing these principles to help you improve your writing skills.

Don't be impressed by high-sounding language and legalese, such as *herein, thereafter, hereinafter, whereas,* and similar expressions. Your writing will be better understood if you use plain English.

✓ *Quick Check*

Inflated, unnatural writing that is intended to impress readers often confuses them.

FIGURE 2.5 **Selected Principles of Plain English**

- Use the active voice with strong verbs (instead of *the stock was acquired by the investor* write *the investor bought the stock*).
- Don't be afraid of personal pronouns (e.g., *I, we,* and *you*).
- Bring abstractions down to earth (instead of *asset,* write *one share of IBM common stock*).
- Omit superfluous words (instead of *in the event that,* write *if*).
- Use positive expression (instead of *it is not unlike,* write *it is similar*).
- Prefer short sentences.
- Remove jargon and legalese.
- Keep the subject, verb, and object close together.
- Keep sentence structure parallel.

Source: U.S. Securities and Exchange Commission, "A Plain English Handbook" (http://www.sec.gov/investor/pubs/englishhndbk.htm).

FIGURE 2.6 E-Mail Message
(illustrating lack of reader benefits, lack of "you" attitude, negative language, and lack of plain English)

BEFORE Revision

Fails to use conversational language

Presents idea negatively instead of positively

Fails to use inclusive language

Does not use plain English

Emphasizes viewpoint of sender rather than that of audience

Fails to use familiar language

Uses negative language and fails to focus on "you" view

Presents idea negatively instead of positively

Includes legalese and other expressions that do not sound conversational

---

To: All Employees
From: Samantha Evers
Subject: Company Desire to Reduce Employee Driving Trips to Office
Cc:
Bcc:

This is to inform you that our company faces harsh governmental penalties if we fail to comply with the Air Quality Management District's program to reduce the number of automobile trips made by employees.

The aforementioned program stipulates that we offer incentives to entice employees to discontinue driving their vehicles as a means of transportation to and from this place of employment. So that you will not regret leaving your cars at home, the following incentives are offered:

* **Full Day Off Without Penalty.** Any employee who doesn't drive to work and maintains a 75 percent participation rate in our ride-share program for a six-month period will be given one day off with pay.

* **Van Pool Subsidy.** Assistance will be provided in obtaining a van, and a monthly $100 subsidy will be given as well. Each van-pool driver will also not be limited in the personal use he can make of the vehicle on his own time.

* **Preferential Parking.** Employees coming to work in car pools will not be forced to park in outlying lots. Reserved spaces will be made available.

Pertaining to our need to have you leave your cars at home, all employees are herewith instructed to communicate with Taylor Adams, who will be facilitating our program. Contact her for more information about the program or to sign up for any of the above-referenced incentives.

Samantha Evers
Human Resources Coordinator

FAMILIAR WORDS

Clear messages contain words that are familiar and meaningful to the receiver. How can we know what is meaningful to a given receiver? Although we can't know with certainty, we can avoid long or unfamiliar words that have simpler synonyms. Whenever possible in business communication, substitute short, common, simple words. Don't, however, give up a precise word if it says exactly what you mean.

DILBERT   By Scott Adams

FIGURE 2.7 E-Mail Message

AFTER Revision

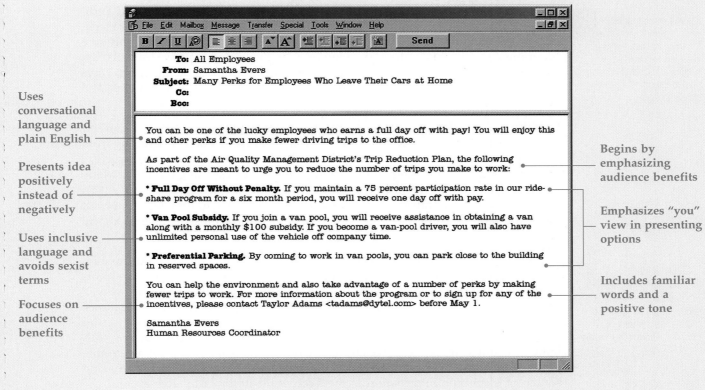

Uses conversational language and plain English

Presents idea positively instead of negatively

Uses inclusive language and avoids sexist terms

Focuses on audience benefits

Begins by emphasizing audience benefits

Emphasizes "you" view in presenting options

Includes familiar words and a positive tone

To: All Employees
From: Samantha Evers
Subject: Many Perks for Employees Who Leave Their Cars at Home
Cc:
Bcc:

You can be one of the lucky employees who earns a full day off with pay! You will enjoy this and other perks if you make fewer driving trips to the office.

As part of the Air Quality Management District's Trip Reduction Plan, the following incentives are meant to urge you to reduce the number of trips you make to work:

* **Full Day Off Without Penalty.** If you maintain a 75 percent participation rate in our ride-share program for a six month period, you will receive one day off with pay.

* **Van Pool Subsidy.** If you join a van pool, you will receive assistance in obtaining a van along with a monthly $100 subsidy. If you become a van-pool driver, you will also have unlimited personal use of the vehicle off company time.

* **Preferential Parking.** By coming to work in van pools, you can park close to the building in reserved spaces.

You can help the environment and also take advantage of a number of perks by making fewer trips to work. For more information about the program or to sign up for any of the incentives, please contact Taylor Adams <tadams@dytel.com> before May 1.

Samantha Evers
Human Resources Coordinator

Although you yourself may not use some of the words in the following list of unfamiliar words, you may see them in business documents. Remember that the simple alternatives shown here will make messages more readable for most people.

Less Familiar Words	Simple Alternatives	Less Familiar Words	Simple Alternatives
ascertain	find out	perpetuate	continue
compensate	pay	perplexing	troubling
conceptualize	see	reciprocate	return
encompass	include	stipulate	require
hypothesize	guess	terminate	end
monitor	check	utilize	use
operational	working		

As you revise a message, you will have a chance to correct any writing problems. Notice in Figures 2.6 and 2.7 what a difference revision makes. Before revision, the message failed to use familiar language. Many negative ideas could have been expressed positively. After revision the message is shorter, more conversational, and emphasizes the viewpoint of the reader rather than that of the sender. Which message do you think will be more likely to achieve its goal?

Adapting to the Task and Audience

TECHNOLOGY IMPROVES YOUR BUSINESS WRITING

✓ **Quick Check**

Powerful writing tools can help you fight writer's block, collect information, outline and organize ideas, improve correctness and precision, add graphics, and design professional-looking documents.

Thus far, we've concentrated on the basics of business writing, especially the prewriting phase of analyzing, anticipating, and adapting to the intended audience. Another basic for beginning business communicators is learning to use technology to enhance their writing efforts. Although computers and software programs cannot actually do the writing for you, they provide powerful tools that make the process easier and the results more professional. Here are seven ways your computer can help you improve written documents, oral presentations, and even Web pages.

Fighting writer's block.   Because word processors enable ideas to flow almost effortlessly from your brain to a screen, you can expect fewer delays resulting from writer's block. You can compose rapidly, and you can experiment with structure and phrasing, later retaining and polishing your most promising thoughts. Many authors "sprint write," recording unedited ideas quickly, to start the composition process and also to brainstorm for ideas on a project. Then, they tag important ideas and use computer outlining programs to organize those ideas into logical sequences.

✓ **Quick Check**

The most valuable employees are able to find accurate information quickly and cheaply by using commercial databases (such as ABI, Lexis, or InfoTrac) or by searching the Web.

Collecting information electronically.   As a knowledge worker in an information economy, you will need to find information quickly. Much of the world's information is now accessible by computer. You can locate the titles of books, as well as full-text articles from magazines, newspapers, and government publications. Massive amounts of information are available from the Internet, CD-ROMs, and online services. Through specialized information-retrieval services (such as ABI-INFORM, InfoTrac, or Lexis-Nexis), you can have at your fingertips up-to-the-minute legal, scientific, scholarly, and business information. The most amazing source of electronic information is the Web, with its links to sites around the world—some incredibly helpful and others worthless.

Outlining and organizing ideas.   Most high-end word processors include some form of "outliner," a feature that enables you to divide a topic into a hierarchical order with main points and subpoints. Your computer keeps track of the levels of ideas automatically so that you can easily add, cut, or rearrange points in the outline. This feature is particularly handy when you're preparing a report or organizing a presentation. Some programs even enable you to transfer your outline directly to slide frames to be used as visual aids in a talk.

✓ **Quick Check**

Savvy business communicators rely heavily on their word processing programs to correct spelling, typographical, and even grammatical errors.

Improving correctness and precision.   Nearly all word processing programs today provide features that catch and correct spelling and typographical errors. Poor spellers and weak typists universally bless their spell checkers for repeatedly saving them from humiliation. Most high-end word processing programs today also provide grammar checkers that are markedly improved over earlier versions. They now detect many errors in capitalization, word use (such as *it's, its*), double negatives, verb use, subject–verb agreement, sentence structure, number agreement, number style, and other writing faults. However, most grammar programs don't actually correct the errors they detect. You must know how to do that. Still, grammar checkers can be very helpful. In addition to spelling and grammar programs, thesaurus programs help you choose precise words that say exactly what you intend.

Adding graphics for emphasis.   Your letters, memos, and reports may be improved by the addition of graphs and artwork to clarify and illustrate data. You can import charts, diagrams, and illustrations created in database, spreadsheet, graphics, or draw-and-paint programs. Moreover, ready-made pictures, called *clip art*, can be used to symbolize or illustrate ideas.

Designing and producing professional-looking documents, presentations, and Web pages.   Most high-end word processing programs today include a large selection of scalable fonts (for different character sizes and styles), italics, boldface, symbols, and styling techniques to aid you in producing consistent formatting and professional-looking results. Moreover, today's presentation software enables you to incorporate showy slide effects, color, sound, pictures, and even movies into your talks for management or customers. Web document builders also help you design and construct Web pages.

Using collaborative software for team writing.   Assume you are part of a group preparing a lengthy proposal to secure a government contract. You expect to write one segment of the proposal yourself and help revise parts written by others. Special word processing programs with commenting and strikeout features allow you to revise easily and to identify each team member's editing. Some collaborative programs, called *groupware*, also include decision-support tools to help groups generate, organize, and analyze ideas more efficiently than in traditional meetings.

SUMMING UP AND LOOKING FORWARD

In this chapter you learned that good business writing is audience centered, purposeful, and economical. To achieve these results, business communicators typically follow a systematic writing process. This process includes three phases: prewriting, writing, and revising. In the prewriting phase, communicators analyze the task and the audience. They select an appropriate channel to deliver the message, and they consider ways to adapt their message to the task and the audience. Effective techniques include spotlighting audience benefits, cultivating the "you" view, striving to use conversational language, and expressing ideas positively. Good communicators also use inclusive language, plain English, and familiar words. Today's computer software provides wonderful assistance for business communicators. Technological tools help you fight writer's block, collect information, outline and organize ideas, improve correctness and precision, add graphics, design professional-looking documents and presentations, and collaborate on team writing projects.

The next chapter continues to examine the writing process. It presents additional techniques to help you become a better writer. You'll learn how to eliminate repetitious and redundant wording, as well as how to avoid wordy prepositional phrases, long lead-ins, needless adverbs, and misplaced modifiers. You'll also take a closer look at spell checkers and grammar checkers.

Interactive Learning @ http://www.westwords.com/guffey/students.html

Prepare for tests and reinforce your chapter knowledge with interactive quizzes and crossword puzzles.

CRITICAL THINKING

1. As a business communicator, you are encouraged to profile or "visualize" the audience for your messages. How is this possible if you don't really know the people who will receive a sales letter or who will hear your business presentation?
2. If adapting your tone to the receiving audience and developing reader benefits are so important, why do we see so much writing that fails to reflect these suggestions?
3. Discuss the following statement: "The English language is a landmine—it is filled with terms that are easily misinterpreted as derogatory and others that are blatantly insulting. . . . Being fair and objective is not enough; employers must also appear to be so."
4. Why is writing in a natural, conversational tone difficult for many people?
5. If computer software is increasingly able to detect writing errors, can business communicators stop studying writing techniques? Why?

CHAPTER REVIEW

6. Name three ways in which business writing differs from other writing.

7. List the three phases of the writing process and summarize what happens in each phase. Which phase requires the most time?

8. What five factors are important in selecting an appropriate channel to deliver a message?

9. How does profiling the audience help a business communicator prepare a message?

10. What is meant by *audience benefit*? Give an original example.

11. List three specific techniques for developing a warm, friendly, and conversational tone in business messages.

12. Why does positive language usually tell more than negative language? Give an original example.

13. List five examples of sexist pronouns and nouns.

14. List at least five principles of the Plain English movement.

15. Name seven ways your computer can help you improve written documents.

Check your skill!

To review the chapter and check your comprehension, take the interactive chapter review quiz at the Guffey Web site for students: http://www.westwords.com/guffey/students.html. With its pop-up feedback, this quiz helps you retain what you have learned and also prepares you for chapter tests. Your instructor may ask you to send an e-mail certificate of completion.

You can also increase your chapter knowledge and vocabulary by completing the interactive crossword puzzles.

SELECTING COMMUNICATION CHANNELS. Using Figure 2.2, suggest the best communication channels for the following messages. Assume that all channels shown are available. Be prepared to explain your choices.

1. As a project manager, you wish to inform three fellow employees of a meeting scheduled for three weeks from now.

2. As assistant to the vice president, you are to investigate the possibility of developing internship programs with several nearby colleges and universities.

3. You wish to send price quotes for a number of your products in response to a request from a potential customer in Taiwan.

4. You must respond to a notice from the Internal Revenue Service insisting that you did not pay the correct amount for last quarter's employer's taxes.

5. As a manager, you must inform an employee that continued tardiness is jeopardizing her job.

6. Members of your task force must meet to discuss ways to improve communication among 5,000 employees at 32 branches of your large company. Task force members are from Los Angeles, Orlando, San Antonio, White Plains, and Columbus (Ohio).

7. You need to know whether Paula in Printing can produce a special pamphlet for you within two days.

AUDIENCE BENEFITS AND THE "YOU" VIEW. Revise the following sentences to emphasize the perspective of the audience and the "you" view.

8. To help us process your purchase order, we must require that you fill out another requisition.

9. To prevent us from possibly losing large sums of money, our bank now requires verification of any large check presented for immediate payment.

10. So that we may bring our customer records up to date and eliminate the expense of duplicate mailings, we are asking you to complete the enclosed card.

11. For just $300 per person, we have arranged a three-day trip to Las Vegas that includes deluxe accommodations, the "City Lights" show, and selected meals.

12. I give my permission for you to attend the two-day workshop.

13. We're requesting all employees to complete the enclosed questionnaire so that we may develop a master schedule for summer vacations.

14. I think my background and my education match the description of the manager trainee position you advertised.

15. We are offering an in-house training program for employees who want to improve their writing skills.

16. We are pleased to announce an arrangement with Compaq that allows us to offer discounted computers in the student bookstore.

17. We have approved your application for credit, and the account may be used immediately.

18. We are pleased to announce that we have selected you to join our trainee program.

19. Our safety policy forbids us from renting power equipment to anyone who cannot demonstrate proficiency in its use.

20. We will reimburse you for all travel expenses.

Writing Improvement Exercises

21. To enable us to continue our policy of selling name brands at discount prices, we cannot give cash refunds on returned merchandise.

CONVERSATIONAL, PROFESSIONAL TONE.   Revise the following sentences to make the tone conversational yet professional.

Example   Kindly inform the undersigned whether or not your representative will be making a visitation in the near future.

Revision   Please tell me whether your representative will be visiting before June 1.

22. As per your recent request, the undersigned is happy to inform you that we are sending you forthwith the brochures you requested.

23. Pursuant to your letter of the 12th, please be advised that your shipment was sent 9 June 2003.

24. She was pretty ticked off because the manager accused her of ripping off office supplies.

25. Kindly be informed that your vehicle has been determined to require corrective work.

26. He didn't have the guts to badmouth her to her face.

27. The undersigned respectfully reminds affected individuals that employees desirous of changing their health plans must do so before December 30.

POSITIVE EXPRESSION.   Revise the following statements to make them more positive.

28. We will withhold payment until you complete the job satisfactorily.

29. In the message you left at our Web site, you claim that you returned a defective headset.

30. We can't process your application because you neglected to insert your social security number.

31. Construction cannot begin until the building plans are approved.

32. It is impossible to move forward without community support.

33. Customers are ineligible for the 10 percent discount unless they show their membership cards.

34. Titan Insurance Company will not process any claim not accompanied by documented proof from a physician showing that the injuries were treated.

INCLUSIVE LANGUAGE. Revise the following sentences to eliminate terms that are considered sexist or that suggest stereotypes.

35. Any applicant for the position of fireman must submit a medical report signed by his physician.

36. Every employee is entitled to see his personnel file.

37. All conference participants and their wives are invited to the banquet.

38. At most hospitals in the area, a nurse must provide her own uniform.

39. Representing the community are a businessman, a lady attorney, and a female doctor.

40. A salesman would have to use all his skills to sell those condos.

PLAIN ENGLISH AND FAMILIAR WORDS. Revise the following sentences to use plain expression and more familiar words.

41. Please ascertain whether we must perpetuate our current contract despite perplexing profits.

42. He hypothesized that the vehicle was not operational because of a malfunctioning gasket.

43. Because we cannot monitor all cash payments, we must terminate the contract.

44. The contract stipulates that management must perpetuate the retirement plan.

PLAIN, POSITIVE LANGUAGE. The following excerpt is from a Veterans Benefits Administration letter. Can you make it understandable? (*Evidence*, by the way, means "documents.")

45. If your evidence is not received before June 18, 2000, which is one year from the date of our first letter, your claim, if entitlement is established, cannot be processed before the date of the receipt of the evidence.

INFOTRAC

2.1 UNDERSTANDING PLAIN ENGLISH. You work in a small financial services organization. Your boss is new to her job, and she wants to learn more about plain English in relation to investments and prospectus information. She doesn't have the time or expertise to do much research. She asks you to help her.

Your Task. Using InfoTrac, find an article that explains how the Securities and Exchange Commission (SEC) wants writers to use plain English. (Hint: You might read an article by Rick Lowry, published in 2000 in the *Sacramento Business Journal.* Or you might locate something more recent.) In a memo to Eileen Fowler, summarize the article, listing at least five rules for text and five for graphics. See Chapter 5 for format suggestions. You could begin your memo with, "As you suggested, I am submitting the following information about. . . ." Be sure to identify the author and article you summarize.

GRAMMAR/MECHANICS CHECKUP—2

PRONOUNS

Review Sections 1.07–1.09 in the Grammar Review section of the Grammar/Mechanics Handbook. Then study each of the following statements. In the space provided, write the word that completes the statement correctly and the number of the G/M principle illustrated. When you finish, compare your responses with those provided near the end of the book. If your responses differ, study carefully the principles in parentheses.

<u>its</u>   (1.09d)   Example   The Recreation and Benefits Committee will be submitting (*its, their*) report soon.

_____ 1. I was expecting the manager to call. Was it (*he, him*) who left the message?

_____ 2. Every one of the members of the men's soccer team had to move (*his car, their cars*) before the game could begin.

_____ 3. A serious disagreement between management and (*he, him*) caused his resignation.

_____ 4. Does anyone in the office know for (*who, whom*) this stationery was ordered?

_____ 5. It looks as if (*her's, hers*) is the only report that cites electronic sources.

_____ 6. Mrs. Simmons asked my friend and (*I, me, myself*) to help her complete the work.

_____ 7. My friend and (*I, me, myself*) were also asked to work on Saturday.

_____ 8. Both printers were sent for repairs, but (*yours, your's*) will be returned shortly.

_____ 9. Give the budget figures to (*whoever, whomever*) asked for them.

_____ 10. Everyone except the broker and (*I, me, myself*) claimed a share of the commission.

_____ 11. No one knows that problem better than (*he, him, himself*).

_____ 12. Investment brochures and information were sent to (*we, us*) shareholders.

_____ 13. If any one of the women tourists has lost (*their, her*) scarf, she should see the driver.

_____ 14. Neither the glamour nor the excitement of the position had lost (*its, it's, their*) appeal.

_____ 15. Any new subscriber may cancel (*their, his or her*) subscription within the first month.

GRAMMAR/MECHANICS CHALLENGE—2

The following e-mail message has many faults in grammar, spelling, punctuation, capitalization, word use, and number form. Pay attention to developing a conversational but professional tone, using familiar words, and striving for positive expression. Use standard proofreading marks (see Appendix B) to correct the errors. When you finish, your instructor can show you the revised version of this e-mail.

```
File  Edit  Mailbox  Message  Transfer  Special  Tools  Window  Help

B  I  U              A  A                        Send

From:  Richard.Randolph@crestline.com
Date:  Thu, 28 Sept 2003 10:00:43 EDT
  To:  Erin.Powers@crestline.com
  Cc:
Subject:  USE OF WEB IN HOSPITALITY INDUSTRY
```

Dear Erin:

Pertaining to your request I finalized some research on the utilization of the Web in hospitality operations. Perhaps the most extrordinary things that I learned are that the internet is considered the major driver of change in the lodging industry! Its allready changing the way we offer services, reshaping organizational structures and altaring the relationships between our guests and us.

In a survey of two thousand mangers the Hospitality information technology association uncovered some really weird findings. Hereinafter is a quick rundown of the survey results.

- Internet service is rapidly becoming the most sought-after amenity in Hotel Rooms

- Two thirds of the respondents worked at propertys that had Web cites.

- A large majority said that a outside party had created there Web site.

- The average cost for creating a Web site was estimated at two thousand dollars and the cost of maintinance is two hundred and fifty dollars a month (requiring five man hours).

- 56% of the respondents said that there guests could make reservations using their Web site.

If we fail to develop our own Web cite, in my opinion I don't see how we can hope to compete in the rapidly-changing hospitality industry. Please advice me if you want me to begin preliminary plans for developing such a site.

Communication Workshops (such as the one on the next page) provide insight into special business communication topics and skills not discussed in the chapters. These topics cover ethics, technology, career skills, and collaboration. Each workshop includes a career application with a case study or problem to help you develop skills relevant to the workshop topic.

Sharpening Your Skills for Critical Thinking, Problem Solving, and Decision Making

Gone are the days when management expected workers to check their brains at the door and do only as told. Today, you'll be expected to use your brains in thinking critically. You'll be solving problems and making decisions. Much of this book is devoted to helping you solve problems and communicate those decisions to management, fellow workers, clients, the government, and the public. Faced with a problem or an issue, most of us do a lot of worrying before separating the issues or making a decision. You can change all that worrying to directed thinking by channeling it into the following procedure.

1. **Identify and clarify the problem.** Your first task is to recognize that a problem exists. Some problems are big and unmistakable, such as failure of an air-freight delivery service to get packages to customers on time. Other problems may be continuing annoyances, such as regularly running out of toner for an office copy machine. The first step in reaching a solution is pinpointing the problem area.

2. **Gather information.** Learn more about the problem situation. Look for possible causes and solutions. This step may mean checking files, calling suppliers, or brainstorming with fellow workers. For example, the air-freight delivery service would investigate the tracking systems of the commercial airlines carrying its packages to determine what is going wrong.

3. **Evaluate the evidence.** Where did the information come from? Does it represent various points of view? What biases could be expected from each source? How accurate is the information gathered? Is it fact or opinion? For example, it is a fact that packages are missing; it is an opinion that they are merely lost and will turn up eventually.

4. **Consider alternatives and implications.** Draw conclusions from the gathered evidence and pose solutions. Then weigh the advantages and disadvantages of each alternative. What are the costs, benefits, and consequences? What are the obstacles, and how can they be handled? Most important, what solution best serves your goals and those of your organization? Here's where your creativity is especially important.

5. **Choose and implement the best alternative.** Select an alternative and put it into action. Then, follow through on your decision by monitoring the results of implementing your plan. The freight company decided to give its unhappy customers free delivery service to make up for the lost packages and downtime. Be sure to continue monitoring and adjusting the solution to ensure its effectiveness over time.

Career Application. Let's return to the McDonald's problem (discussed on page 29) in which some franchise owners are unhappy with the multiple lines for service. Customers don't seem to know where to stand to be the next served. Tempers flare when aggressive customers cut in line, and other customers spend so much time protecting their places in line that they fail to study the menu. Then they don't know what to order when they approach the counter. As a franchise owner, you would like to find a solution to this problem. Any changes in procedures, however, must be approved by all the McDonald's owners in a district. That means you'll have to get a majority to agree. You know that McDonald's management feels that the multiline system accommodates higher volumes of customers more quickly than a single-line system. Moreover, the problem of perception is important. What happens when customers open the door to a restaurant and see a long, long single line? Do they stick around to learn how fast the line is moving?

Your Task

- Individually or with a team, use the critical thinking steps outlined here. Begin by clarifying the problem.
- Where could you gather information to help you solve this problem? Would it be wise to see what your competitors are doing? How do banks handle customer lines? Airlines? Sports arenas?
- Evaluate your findings and consider alternatives. What are the pros and cons of each alternative?
- Within your team choose the best alternative. Present your recommendation to your class and give your reasons for choosing it.

Related Web Site: Visit the McDonald's Web site at www.mcdonalds.com to learn about its people policy and its commitment to its employees.

Chapter 3

Improving Writing Techniques

Writing skills . . . are no longer simply an advantage—they are a necessity.

MAX MESSMER, chairman and CEO of Robert Half International[1]

LEARNING OBJECTIVES

1. Contrast formal and informal methods of researching data and generating ideas for messages.
2. Specify how to organize information into outlines.
3. Compare direct and indirect patterns for organizing ideas.
4. Distinguish components of complete and effective sentences.
5. Emphasize important ideas and deemphasize unimportant ones.
6. Use active voice, passive voice, and parallelism effectively in messages.
7. Develop sentence unity by avoiding zigzag writing, mixed constructions, and misplaced modifiers.
8. Identify strategies for achieving paragraph coherence and composing the first draft of a message.

*E*ven in an age filled with technological advances, says author and CEO Max Messmer, proficiency in written communication is highly valued. Developing that proficiency takes instruction and practice. You've already learned some techniques for writing effectively (using a conversational tone, positive language, plain expression, and familiar words). This chapter presents additional writing tips that help you gather information, organize it into outlines, and compose sentences.

In Chapter 2 we focused on the prewriting stage of the writing process. Figure 3.1 reviews the entire process. This chapter addresses the second stage, which includes researching, organizing, and composing.

RESEARCHING

No smart businessperson would begin writing a message before collecting the needed information. We call this collection process *research*, a rather formal-sounding term. For simple documents, though, the process can be quite informal. Research is necessary before beginning to write because the information you collect

FIGURE 3.1 The Writing Process

helps shape the message. Discovering significant data after a message is completed often means starting over and reorganizing. To avoid frustration and inaccurate messages, collect information that answers this primary question:

- What does the receiver need to know about this topic?

When the message involves action, search for answers to secondary questions:

- What is the receiver to do?
- How is the receiver to do it?
- When must the receiver do it?
- What will happen if the receiver doesn't do it?

Whenever your communication problem requires more information than you have in your head or at your fingertips, you must conduct research. This research may be formal or informal.

FORMAL RESEARCH METHODS

Long reports and complex business problems generally require some use of formal research methods. Let's say you are a market specialist for Coca-Cola, and your boss asks you to evaluate the impact on Coke sales of private-label or generic soft drinks (the bargain-basement-brand knockoffs sold at Kmart and other outlets). Or, let's assume you must write a term paper for a college class. Both tasks require more data than you have in your head or at your fingertips. To conduct formal research, you could:

- **Search manually.** You'll find helpful background and supplementary information through manual searching of resources in public and college libraries. These traditional sources include books and newspaper, magazine, and journal articles. Other sources are encyclopedias, reference books, handbooks, dictionaries, directories, and almanacs.
- **Access electronically.** Much of the printed material just described is now available from the Internet, databases, or compact discs that can be accessed by computer. College and public libraries subscribe to retrieval services that permit you to access most periodic literature. You can also find extraordinary amounts of information by searching the Web. You'll learn more about using electronic sources in Chapters 10 and 11.
- **Go to the source.** For firsthand information, go directly to the source. For the Coca-Cola report, for example, you could find out what consumers really think

Quick Check

The second stage of the writing process involves research, which means collecting the necessary information to prepare a message.

Quick Check

Formal research may include searching libraries and electronic databases or investigating primary sources (interviews, surveys, and experimentation).

Most routine business messages require informal research to gather background information. These methods include talking with your boss, looking in the files, interviewing the target audience, conducting an informal survey, and brainstorming.
© Michael Newman/PhotoEdit

by conducting interviews or surveys, by putting together questionnaires, or by organizing focus groups. Formal research includes structured sampling and controls that enable investigators to make accurate judgments and valid predictions.

- **Conduct scientific experiments.** Instead of merely asking for the target audience's opinion, scientific researchers present choices with controlled variables. Let's say, for example, that Coca-Cola wants to determine at what price and under what circumstances consumers would switch from Coca-Cola to a generic brand. The results of such experimentation would provide valuable data for managerial decision making.

Because formal research techniques are particularly necessary for reports, you'll study resources and techniques more extensively in Chapters 10 and 11.

INFORMAL RESEARCH AND IDEA GENERATION

Most routine tasks—such as composing e-mail messages, memos, letters, informational reports, and oral presentations—require data that you can collect informally. Here are some techniques for collecting informal data and for generating ideas:

- **Look in the files.** If you are responding to an inquiry, you often can find the answer to the inquiry by investigating the company files or by consulting colleagues.
- **Talk with your boss.** Get information from the individual making the assignment. What does that person know about the topic? What slant should be taken? What other sources would he or she suggest?

Quick Check

Good sources of primary information are interviews, surveys, questionnaires, and focus groups.

Quick Check

Informal research may include looking in the files, talking with your boss, interviewing the target audience, conducting an informal survey, and brainstorming.

- **Interview the target audience.** Consider talking with individuals at whom the message is aimed. They can provide clarifying information that tells you what they want to know and how you should shape your remarks.
- **Conduct an informal survey.** Gather unscientific but helpful information via questionnaires or telephone surveys. In preparing a memo report predicting the success of a proposed fitness center, for example, circulate a questionnaire asking for employee reactions.
- **Brainstorm for ideas.** Alone or with others, discuss ideas for the writing task at hand, and record at least a dozen ideas without judging them. Small groups are especially fruitful in brainstorming because people spin ideas off one another.

ORGANIZING DATA

Once you've collected data, you must find some way to organize it. Organizing includes two processes: grouping and patterning. Well-organized messages group similar items; ideas follow a sequence that helps the reader understand relationships and accept the writer's views. Unorganized messages proceed free-form, jumping from one thought to another. Such messages fail to emphasize important points. Puzzled readers can't see how the pieces fit together, and they become frustrated and irritated. Many communication experts regard poor organization as the greatest failing of business writers. Two simple techniques can help you organize data: the scratch list and the outline.

Quick Check

Writers of well-organized messages group similar ideas so that readers can see relationships and follow arguments.

OUTLINING

In developing simple messages, some writers make a quick scratch list of the topics they wish to cover. They then compose a message at their computers directly from the scratch list. Most writers, though, need to organize their ideas—especially if the project is complex—into a hierarchy, such as an outline. The beauty of preparing an outline is that it gives you a chance to organize your thinking before you get bogged down in word choice and sentence structure. Figure 3.2 shows a format for an outline.

Quick Check

Two simple ways to organize data are the scratch list and the outline.

FIGURE 3.2   Format for an Outline

Title: Major Idea or Purpose
I. First major component
   A. First subpoint
      1. Detail, illustration, evidence
      2. Detail, illustration, evidence
   B. Second subpoint
      1.
      2.
II. Second major component
   A. First subpoint
      1.
      2.
   B. Second subpoint
      1.
      2.

TIPS FOR MAKING OUTLINES

- Define the main topic in the title.
- Divide the topic into main points, preferably three to five.
- Break the components into subpoints.
- Don't put a single item under a major component if you have only one subpoint; integrate it with the main item above it or reorganize.
- Strive to make each component exclusive (no overlapping).
- Use details, illustrations, and evidence to support subpoints.

THE DIRECT PATTERN

After developing an outline, you will need to decide where in the message you will place the main idea. Placing the main idea at the beginning of the message is called the *direct pattern*. In the direct pattern the main idea comes first, followed by details, explanation, or evidence. Placing the main idea later in the message (after the details, explanation, or evidence) is called the *indirect pattern*. The pattern you select is determined by how you expect the audience to react to the message, as shown in Figure 3.3.

In preparing to write any message, you need to anticipate the audience's reaction to your ideas and frame your message accordingly. When you expect the reader to be pleased, mildly interested, or, at worst, neutral—use the direct pattern. That is, put your main point—the purpose of your message—in the first or second sentence. Compare the direct and indirect patterns in the following memo openings. Notice how long it takes to get to the main idea in the indirect opening.

Indirect Opening
Our company has been concerned with attracting better-qualified prospective job candidates. For this reason, the Management Council has been gathering information about an internship program for college students. After considerable investigation, we have voted to begin a pilot program starting next fall.

Direct Opening
The Management Council voted to begin a college internship pilot program next fall.

FIGURE 3.3 **Audience Response Determines Pattern of Organization**

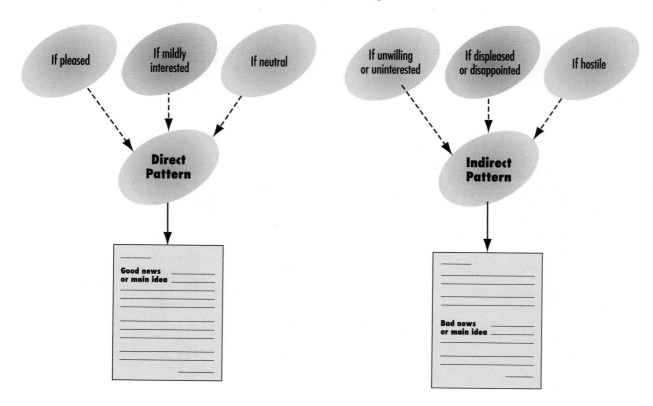

Explanations and details should follow the direct opening. What's important is getting to the main idea quickly. This direct method, also called *frontloading*, has at least three advantages:

- **Saves the reader's time.** Many of today's businesspeople can devote only a few moments to each message. Messages that take too long to get to the point may lose their readers along the way.
- **Sets a proper frame of mind.** Learning the purpose up front helps the reader put the subsequent details and explanations in perspective. Without a clear opening, the reader may be thinking, *Why am I being told this?*
- **Prevents frustration.** Readers forced to struggle through excessive verbiage before reaching the main idea become frustrated. They resent the writer. Poorly organized messages create a negative impression of the writer.

This frontloading technique works best with audiences who are likely to be receptive to or at least not likely to disagree with what you have to say. Typical business messages that follow the direct pattern include routine requests and responses, orders and acknowledgments, nonsensitive memos, e-mail messages, informational reports, and informational oral presentations. All these tasks have one element in common: none has a sensitive subject that will upset the reader.

THE INDIRECT PATTERN

When you expect the audience to be uninterested, unwilling, displeased, or perhaps even hostile, the indirect pattern is more appropriate. In this pattern you don't reveal the main idea until after you have offered explanation and evidence. This approach works well with three kinds of messages: (1) bad news, (2) ideas that require persuasion, and (3) sensitive news, especially when being transmitted to superiors. The indirect pattern has these benefits:

- **Respects the feelings of the audience.** Bad news is always painful, but the trauma can be lessened when the receiver is prepared for it.
- **Encourages a fair hearing.** Messages that may upset the reader are more likely to be read when the main idea is delayed. Beginning immediately with a piece of bad news or a persuasive request, for example, may cause the receiver to stop reading or listening.
- **Minimizes a negative reaction.** A reader's overall reaction to a negative message is generally improved if the news is delivered gently.

Typical business messages that could be developed indirectly include letters and memos that refuse requests, deny claims, and disapprove credit. Persuasive requests, sales letters, sensitive messages, and some reports and oral presentations also benefit from the indirect strategy. You'll learn more about how to use the indirect pattern in Chapters 7 and 8.

In summary, business messages may be organized directly, with the main idea first, or indirectly, with the main idea delayed. Although these two patterns cover many communication problems, they should be considered neither universal nor inviolate. Every business transaction is distinct. Some messages are mixed: part good news, part bad; part goodwill, part persuasion. In upcoming chapters you'll practice applying the direct and indirect patterns in typical situations. Then, you'll have the skills and confidence to evaluate communication problems and vary these patterns depending on the goals you wish to achieve.

✓ *Quick Check*

Sentences must have subjects and verbs and must make sense.

After deciding how to organize your message, you are ready to begin composing it. As you create your first draft, you'll be working at the sentence level of composition. Although you've used sentences all your life, you may be unaware of how they can be shaped and arranged to express your ideas most effectively. First, let's review some basic sentence elements.

Complete sentences have subjects and verbs and make sense.

SUBJECT VERB   SUBJECT   VERB
This report is clear and concise. Our employees write many reports.

✓ *Quick Check*

Clauses have subjects and verbs, but phrases do not.

Clauses and phrases, the key building blocks of sentences, are related groups of words. Clauses have subjects and verbs; phrases do not.

PHRASE   PHRASE
The CEO of that organization sent a message to our staff.

PHRASE   PHRASE
By reading carefully, we learned about the merger.

CLAUSE   CLAUSE
Because she writes well, Tracy answers most customer letters.

CLAUSE   CLAUSE
If you are going away, you should redirect your e-mail messages.

✓ *Quick Check*

Independent clauses may stand alone; dependent clauses may not.

Clauses may be divided into two groups: independent and dependent. Independent clauses are grammatically complete. Dependent clauses depend for their meaning on independent clauses. In the two preceding examples, the clauses beginning with *If* and *Because* are dependent. Dependent clauses are often introduced by words such as *if, when, because,* and *as.*

INDEPENDENT CLAUSE
Tracy uses simple language.

DEPENDENT CLAUSE   INDEPENDENT CLAUSE
When she writes to customers, Tracy uses simple language.

By learning to distinguish phrases, independent clauses, and dependent clauses, you'll be able to punctuate sentences correctly and avoid three basic sentence faults: the fragment, the run-on sentence, and the comma splice.

SENTENCE FRAGMENT

✓ *Quick Check*

Fragments are broken-off parts of sentences and should not be punctuated as sentences.

One of the most serious errors a writer can make is punctuating a fragment as if it were a complete sentence. A fragment is a broken-off part of a sentence.

Fragment   Because most transactions require a permanent record. Good writing skills are critical.

Revision   Because most transactions require a permanent record, good writing skills are critical.

Fragment	The recruiter requested a writing sample. Even though the candidate seemed to communicate well.
Revision	The recruiter requested a writing sample, even though the candidate seemed to communicate well.

Fragments often can be identified by the words that introduce them—words such as *although, as, because, even, except, for example, if, instead of, since, so, such as, that, which,* and *when.* These words introduce dependent clauses. Make sure such clauses always connect to independent clauses.

RUN-ON (FUSED) SENTENCE

A sentence with two independent clauses must be joined by a coordinating conjunction (*and, or, nor, but*) or by a semicolon (;). Without a conjunction or a semicolon, a run-on sentence results.

✓ *Quick Check*

When two independent clauses are run together without punctuation or a coordinating conjunction, a run-on (fused) sentence results.

Run-on	Most job seekers present a printed résumé some are also using Web sites as electronic portfolios.
Revision	Most job seekers present a printed résumé, but some are also using Web sites as electronic portfolios.
Improved	Most job seekers present a printed résumé; some are also using Web sites as electronic portfolios.

COMMA-SPLICE SENTENCE

A comma splice results when a writer joins (splices together) two independent clauses with a comma. Independent clauses may be joined with a coordinating conjunction (*and, or, nor, but*) or a conjunctive adverb (*however, consequently, therefore,* and others). Notice that clauses joined by coordinating conjunctions require only a comma. Clauses joined by a coordinating adverb require a semicolon. Here are three ways to rectify a comma splice:

© Randy Glasbergen.
www.glasbergen.com

"Sentence fragments, comma splices, run-ons — who cares?
I know what I meant!"

Comma Splice	Some employees responded by e-mail, others picked up the telephone.
Revision 1	Some employees responded by e-mail, and others picked up the telephone.
Revision 2	Some employees responded by e-mail; however, others picked up the telephone.
Revision 3	Some employees responded by e-mail; others picked up the telephone.

✓ *Quick Check*

When two independent clauses are joined by a comma without a conjunction, a comma splice results.

SENTENCE LENGTH

Because your goal is to communicate clearly, you're better off limiting your sentences to about 20 or fewer words. The American Press Institute reports that reader comprehension drops off markedly as sentences become longer.[2] Thus, in crafting your sentences, think about the relationship between sentence length and comprehension:

✓ *Quick Check*

Sentences of 20 or fewer words have the most impact.

Sentence Length	Comprehension Rate
8 words	100%
15 words	90%
19 words	80%
28 words	50%

Instead of stringing together clauses with *and, but,* and *however,* break some of those complex sentences into separate segments. Business readers want to grasp ideas immediately. They can do that best when thoughts are separated into short sentences. On the other hand, too many monotonous short sentences will sound "grammar schoolish" and may bore or even annoy the reader. Strive for a balance between longer sentences and shorter ones.

Speakers can emphasize their words with nonverbal gestures, such as a thumbs-up. They can also add emphasis by a raised or lowered voice. Writers do not have these options. Instead, writers emphasize important parts of a message (1) mechanically, such as using underlining, boldface, or all caps, or (2) stylistically, such as using vivid words or placing ideas strategically.
© Mark Scott/taxi

EMPHASIS

When you are talking with someone, you can emphasize your main ideas by saying them loudly or by repeating them slowly. You could even pound the table if you want to show real emphasis! Another way you could signal the relative importance of an idea is by raising your eyebrows or by shaking your head or whispering in a low voice. But when you write, you must rely on other means to tell your readers which ideas are more important than others. Emphasis in writing can be achieved primarily in two ways: mechanically or stylistically.

EMPHASIS THROUGH MECHANICS

To emphasize an idea in print, a writer may use any of the following devices:

Underlining	<u>Underlining</u> draws the eye to a word.
Italics and boldface	Using *italics* or **boldface** can convey special meaning and provide emphasis.
Font changes	Changing from a large font to a small font or to a different font adds interest and emphasis.
All caps	Printing words in ALL CAPS is like shouting them.
Dashes	Dashes—if used sparingly—can be effective in capturing attention.
Tabulation	Listing items vertically makes them stand out: 1. First item 2. Second item 3. Third item

Other means of achieving mechanical emphasis include the arrangement of space, color, lines, boxes, columns, titles, headings, and subheadings. Today's software and color printers provide a wonderful array of capabilities for setting off ideas.

EMPHASIS THROUGH STYLE

Although mechanical means are occasionally appropriate, more often a writer achieves emphasis stylistically. That is, the writer chooses words carefully and constructs sentences skillfully to emphasize main ideas and deemphasize minor or negative ideas. Here are four suggestions for emphasizing ideas stylistically:

Quick Check

You can emphasize ideas stylistically by using vivid words, labeling the main idea, and positioning the main idea strategically.

- **Use vivid words.** Vivid words are emphatic because the reader can picture ideas clearly.

General	One business uses personal selling techniques.
Vivid	Avon uses face-to-face selling techniques.

General	A customer said that he wanted the contract returned soon.
Vivid	Mr. Le Clerc insisted that the contract be returned by July 1.

- **Label the main idea.** If an idea is significant, tell the reader.

Unlabeled	Explore the possibility of leasing a site, but also hire a consultant.
Labeled	Explore the possibility of leasing a site; but most important, hire a consultant.

- **Place the important idea first or last in the sentence.** Ideas have less competition from surrounding words when they appear first or last in a sentence. Observe how the concept of productivity is emphasized in the first and second examples:

Emphatic	Productivity is more likely to be increased when profit-sharing plans are linked to individual performance rather than to group performance.
Emphatic	Profit-sharing plans linked to individual performance rather than to group performance are more effective in increasing productivity.
Unemphatic	Profit-sharing plans are more effective in increasing productivity when they are linked to individual performance rather than to group performance.

- **Place the important idea in a simple sentence or in an independent clause.** Don't dilute the effect of the idea by making it share the spotlight with other words and clauses.

Emphatic	You are the first trainee that we have hired for this program. (Use a simple sentence for emphasis.)
Emphatic	Although we considered many candidates, you are the first trainee that we have hired for this program. (Independent clause contains main idea.)
Unemphatic	Although you are the first trainee that we have hired for this program, we had many candidates and expect to expand the program in the future. (Main idea is lost in a dependent clause.)

DEEMPHASIS

To deemphasize an idea, such as bad news, try one of the following stylistic devices:

Quick Check

You can deemphasize ideas by using general words and placing the ideas in dependent clauses.

- **Use general words.**

Vivid	Our records indicate that you were recently fired.
General	Our records indicate that your employment status has changed recently.

- **Place the bad news in a dependent clause connected to an independent clause with something positive.** In sentences with dependent clauses, the main emphasis is always on the independent clause.

| Emphasizes bad news | We cannot issue you credit at this time, but we do have a plan that will allow you to fill your immediate needs on a cash basis. |
| Deemphasizes bad news | We have a plan that will allow you to fill your immediate needs on a cash basis since we cannot issue credit at this time. |

ACTIVE AND PASSIVE VOICE

Quick Check

Active-voice sentences are preferred because the subject is the doer of the action.

In sentences with active-voice verbs, the subject is the doer of the action. In passive-voice sentences, the subject is acted upon.

| **Active verb** | Mr. Johnson *completed* the tax return before the April 15 deadline. (The subject, *Mr. Johnson*, is the doer of the action.) |
| **Passive verb** | The tax return *was completed* before the April 15 deadline. (The subject, *tax return*, is acted upon.) |

In the first sentence, the active-voice verb emphasizes Mr. Johnson. In the second sentence, the passive-voice verb emphasizes the tax return. In sentences with passive-voice verbs, the doer of the action may be revealed or left unknown. In business writing, as well as in personal interactions, some situations demand tact and sensitivity. Instead of using a direct approach with active verbs, we may prefer the indirectness that passive verbs allow. Rather than making a blunt announcement with an active verb (*Tyler made a major error in the estimate*), we can soften the sentence with a passive construction (*A major error was made in the estimate*).

Quick Check

Although active-voice verbs are preferred in business writing, passive-voice verbs perform useful functions.

Here's a summary of the best use of active- and passive-voice verbs:

- **Use the active voice for most business writing.** It clearly tells what the action is and who is performing that action.
- **Use the passive voice to emphasize an action or the recipient of the action.** *You have been selected to represent us.*
- **Use the passive voice to deemphasize negative news.** *Your printer has not yet been repaired.*
- **Use the passive voice to conceal the doer of an action.** *A major error was made in the estimate.*

How can you tell if a verb is active or passive? Identify the subject of the sentence and decide whether the subject is doing the acting or it is being acted upon. For example, in the sentence *An appointment was made for January 1*, the subject is *appointment*. The subject is being acted upon; therefore, the verb (*was made*) is passive. Another clue in identifying passive-voice verbs is that they generally include a *to be* helping verb, such as *is, are, was, were, being,* or *been*.

PARALLELISM

Parallelism is a skillful writing technique that involves balanced writing. Sentences written so that their parts are balanced or parallel are easy to read and understand. To achieve parallel construction, use similar structures to express similar ideas. For example, the words *computing, coding, recording,* and *storing* are parallel because the words all end in *-ing.* To express the list as *computing, coding, recording,* and *storage* is disturbing because the last item is not what the reader expects. Try to match nouns with nouns, verbs with verbs, and clauses with clauses. Avoid mixing active-voice verbs with passive-voice verbs. Your goal is to keep the wording balanced in expressing similar ideas.

© Ted Goff (www.tedgoff.com)

"To make this easy to read, I have divided it into three parts: A, B, and 3."

Lacks parallelism	The market for industrial goods includes manufacturers, contractors, wholesalers, and *those concerned with the retail function.*
Revision	The market for industrial goods includes manufacturers, contractors, wholesalers, and *retailers.* (Parallel construction matches nouns.)
Lacks parallelism	Our primary goals are to increase productivity, reduce costs, and *the improvement of product quality.*
Revision	Our primary goals are to increase productivity, reduce costs, and *improve product quality.* (Parallel construction matches verbs.)
Lacks parallelism	We are scheduled to meet in Dallas on January 5, *we are meeting in Montreal on the 15th of March,* and in Chicago on June 3.
Revision	We are scheduled to meet in Dallas on January 5, *in Montreal on March 15,* and in Chicago on June 3. (Parallel construction matches phrases.)
Lacks parallelism	Mrs. Horne audits all accounts lettered A through L; accounts lettered M through Z are audited by Mr. Shapiro.
Revision	Mrs. Horne audits all accounts lettered A through L; Mr. Shapiro audits accounts lettered M through Z. (Parallel construction matches active-voice verbs in balanced clauses.)

✓ **Quick Check**

Balanced wording helps the reader anticipate and comprehend your meaning.

In presenting lists of data, whether shown horizontally or tabulated vertically, be certain to express all the items in parallel form.

Parallelism in vertical list	Three primary objectives of advertising are as follows: 1. Increase the frequency of product use. 2. Introduce complementary products. 3. Enhance the corporate image.

✓ **Quick Check**

All items in a list should be expressed in balanced constructions.

Unity

Unified sentences contain thoughts that are related to only one main idea. The following sentence lacks unity because the first clause has little or no relationship to the second clause:

✓ **Quick Check**

Unified sentences contain only related ideas.

Lacks unity	Our insurance plan is available in all the states and provinces, and you may name anyone as a beneficiary for your coverage.
Revision	Our insurance plan is available in all the states and provinces. What's more, you may name anyone as a beneficiary for your coverage.

The ideas are better expressed by separating the two dissimilar clauses and by adding a connecting phrase, as shown above. Other writing faults that destroy sentence unity are (a) zigzag writing, (b) mixed constructions, and (c) misplaced modifiers.

ZIGZAG WRITING

Quick Check

Zigzag sentences often should be broken into two sentences.

Sentences that twist or turn unexpectedly away from the main thought are examples of zigzag writing. Such confusing writing may result when too many thoughts are included in one sentence or when one thought does not relate to another. To rectify a zigzag sentence, revise it so that the reader understands the relationship between the thoughts. If that is impossible, move the unrelated thoughts to a new sentence.

Zigzag writing	I appreciate the time you spent with me last week, and I have purchased a computer and software that generate graphics.
Revision	I appreciate the time you spent with me last week. As a result of your advice, I have purchased a computer and software that generate graphics.
Zigzag writing	The stockholders of a corporation elect a board of directors, although the chief executive officer is appointed by the board and the CEO is not directly responsible to the stockholders.
Revision	The stockholders of a corporation elect a board of directors, who in turn appoints the chief executive officer. The CEO is not directly responsible to the stockholders.

MIXED CONSTRUCTIONS

Quick Check

Mixed grammatical constructions confuse readers.

Writers who fuse two different grammatical constructions destroy sentence unity and meaning.

Mixed construction	The reason I am late is *because* my car battery is dead.
Revision	The reason I am late is *that* my car battery is dead. (The construction introduced by *the reason is* should be a noun clause beginning with *that*, not an adverbial clause beginning with *because*.)
Mixed construction	When the stock market index rose five points was our signal to sell.
Revision	When the stock market index rose five points, we were prepared to sell. *OR:* Our signal to sell was an increase of five points in the stock market index.

DANGLING AND MISPLACED MODIFIERS

Quick Check

Modifiers must be close to the words they describe or limit.

For clarity, modifiers must be close to the words they describe or limit. A modifier dangles when the word or phrase it describes is missing from its sentence. A modifier is misplaced when the word or phrase it describes is not close enough to be clear. In both instances, the solution is to position the modifier closer to the word(s) it describes or limits. Introductory verbal phrases are particularly dangerous; be sure to follow them immediately with the words they logically describe or modify.

Dangling Modifier	To win the lottery, a ticket must be purchased. (The introductory verbal phrase must be followed by a logical subject.)
Revision	To win the lottery, you must purchase a ticket.
Dangling Modifier	Driving through Malibu Canyon, the ocean suddenly came into view. (Is the ocean driving through Malibu Canyon?)
Revision	Driving through Malibu Canyon, we saw the ocean suddenly come into view.

Try this trick for detecting and remedying these dangling modifiers. Ask the question *who?* or *what?* after any introductory phrase. The words immediately following should tell the reader who or what is performing the action. Try the *who?* test on the previous danglers.

Misplaced Modifier	Seeing his error too late, the envelope was immediately resealed by Matt. (Did the envelope see the error?)
Revision	Seeing his error too late, Matt immediately resealed the envelope.
Misplaced Modifier	A wart appeared on my left hand that I want removed. (Is the left hand to be removed?)
Revision	A wart that I want removed appeared on my left hand.
Misplaced Modifier	The busy personnel director interviewed only candidates who had excellent computer skills in the morning. (Were the candidates skilled only in the morning?)
Revision	In the morning the busy personnel director interviewed only candidates who had excellent computer skills.

PARAGRAPH COHERENCE

A paragraph is a group of sentences with a controlling idea, usually stated first. Paragraphs package similar ideas into meaningful groups for readers. Effective paragraphs are coherent; that is, they hold together. But coherence does not happen accidentally. It is achieved through effective organization and (1) repetition of key ideas, (2) use of pronouns, and (3) use of transitional expressions.

✓ *Quick Check*

Three ways to create paragraph coherence are (1) repetition of key ideas, (2) use of pronouns, and (3) use of transitional expressions.

- **Repetition of key ideas or key words.** Repeating a word or key thought from a preceding sentence helps guide a reader from one thought to the next. This redundancy is necessary to build cohesiveness into writing.

Effective repetition	*Quality* problems in production are often the result of inferior raw materials. Some companies have strong programs for ensuring the *quality* of incoming production materials and supplies.

The second sentence of the preceding paragraph repeats the key idea of *quality*. Moreover, the words *incoming production materials and supplies* refer to *raw materials* mentioned in the preceding sentence. Good writers find similar words to describe the same idea, thus using repetition to clarify a topic for the reader.

- **Use of pronouns.** Pronouns such as *this, that, they, these,* and *those* promote coherence by connecting the thoughts in one sentence to the thoughts in a previous sentence. To make sure that the pronoun reference is clear, consider joining the pronoun with the word to which it refers, thus making the pronoun into an adjective.

Pronoun repetition   Xerox has a four-point program to assist suppliers. *This program* includes written specifications for production materials and components.

Be very careful, though, in using pronouns. A pronoun without a clear antecedent can be most annoying. That's because the reader doesn't know precisely to what the pronoun refers.

Faulty   When company profits increased, employees were given either a cash payment or company stock. *This* became a real incentive to employees.

Revision   When company profits increased, employees were given either a cash payment or company stock. *This profit-sharing plan* became a real incentive to employees.

- **Use of transitional expressions.** One of the most effective ways to achieve paragraph coherence is through the use of transitional expressions. These expressions act as road signs: they indicate where the message is headed, and they help the reader anticipate what is coming. Here are some of the most effective transitional expressions. They are grouped according to uses.

Time Association	**Contrast**	**Illustration**
before, after	although	for example
first, second	but	in this way
meanwhile	however	
next	instead	
until	nevertheless	
when, whenever	on the other hand	

Cause, Effect	**Additional Idea**
consequently	furthermore
for this reason	in addition
hence	likewise
therefore	moreover

PARAGRAPH LENGTH

Although no rule regulates the length of paragraphs, business writers recognize the value of short paragraphs. Paragraphs with eight or fewer printed lines look inviting and readable. Long, solid chunks of print appear formidable. If a topic can't be covered in eight or fewer printed lines (not sentences), consider breaking it into smaller segments.

COMPOSING THE FIRST DRAFT

Once you've researched your topic, organized the data, and selected a pattern of organization, you're ready to begin composing. Communicators who haven't completed the preparatory work often suffer from "writer's block" and sit staring at a piece of paper or at the computer screen. It's easier to get started if you have organized your ideas and established a plan. Composition is also easier if you have a quiet environment in which to concentrate. Businesspeople with messages to compose set aside a given time and allow no calls, visitors, or other interruptions. This is a good technique for students as well.

As you begin composing, keep in mind that you are writing the first draft, not the final copy. Experts suggest that you write quickly (*sprint writing*). Get your thoughts down now and refine them in later versions.[3] As you take up each idea, imagine that you are talking to the reader. Don't let yourself get bogged down. If you can't think of the right word, insert a substitute or type "find perfect word later."[4] Sprint writing works especially well for those composing on a computer because it's simple to make changes at any point of the composition process. If you are handwriting the first draft, double-space so that you have room for changes.

 Quick Check

Create a quiet place in which to write. Experts recommend "sprint writing" for first drafts.

SUMMING UP AND LOOKING FORWARD

This chapter explained the second phase of the writing process, including researching, organizing, and composing. Before beginning a message, every writer collects data, either formally or informally. For most simple messages, you would look in the files, talk with your boss, interview the target audience, or possibly conduct an informal survey. Information for a message is then organized into a list or an outline. Depending on the expected reaction of the receiver, the message can be organized directly (for positive reactions) or indirectly (for negative reactions or when persuasion is necessary).

In composing the first draft, writers must be sure that sentences are complete. Emphasis can be achieved through mechanics (underlining, italics, font changes, all caps, and so forth) or through style (using vivid words, labeling the main idea, and positioning the important ideas). Important writing techniques include skillful use of active- and passive-voice verbs, developing parallelism, and achieving unity while avoiding zigzag writing, mixed constructions, and misplaced modifiers. Coherent paragraphs result from planned repetition of key ideas, proper use of pronouns, and inclusion of transitional expressions.

In the next chapter you'll learn helpful techniques for the third phase of the writing process, which includes revising and proofreading.

Interactive Learning @ http://www.westwords.com/guffey/students.html
Prepare for tests and reinforce your chapter knowledge with interactive quizzes and crossword puzzles.

CRITICAL THINKING

1. Why is audience analysis so important in choosing the direct or indirect pattern of organization for a business message?
2. In what ways do you imagine that writing on the job differs from the writing you do in your academic studies?
3. How are speakers different from writers in the manner in which they emphasize ideas?

4. Why are short sentences and short paragraphs appropriate for business communication?

5. When might it be unethical to use the indirect method of organizing a message?

CHAPTER REVIEW

6. What three steps are included in the second phase of the writing process?

7. Distinguish between formal and informal methods of researching data for a business message.

8. What is the difference between a list and an outline?

9. What is *frontloading* and what are its advantages?

10. When is the indirect method appropriate, and what are the benefits of using it?

11. List five techniques for achieving emphasis through mechanics.

12. List four techniques for achieving emphasis through style.

13. What is parallelism? Give an original example.

14. List three techniques for developing paragraph coherence.

15. What environment should you establish if you have something to write?

WRITING IMPROVEMENT EXERCISES

REVISING SENTENCES.   Revise the following sentences to remedy sentence fragments, run-on sentences, and comma splices.

16. Because they wanted to take advantage of the law of supply and demand. Major soft-drink companies tested vending machines that raise prices in hot weather.

17. Thirsty consumers may think that variable pricing is unfair they may also refuse to use the machine.

18. Aggressive advertisements can backfire that's why marketing directors consider them carefully.

19. Although Pizza Hut is the country's number one pizza chain. Domino's Pizza leads in deliveries.

20. About half of Pizza Hut's 6,600 outlets make deliveries, the others concentrate on walk-in customers.

EMPHASIS.   For each of the following sentences, circle (a) or (b). Be prepared to justify your choice.

21. Which is more emphatic?
    a. Our dress code is good.
    b. Our dress code reflects common sense and good taste.

22. Which is more emphatic?
    a. Increased advertising would improve sales.
    b. Adding $50,000 in advertising would double our sales.

23. Which is more emphatic?
    a. The committee was powerless to act.
    b. The committee was unable to take action.

24. Which sentence places more emphasis on *product loyalty*?
    a. Product loyalty is the primary motivation for advertising.
    b. The primary motivation for advertising is loyalty to the product, although other purposes are also served.

25. Which sentence places more emphasis on the seminar?
    a. An executive training seminar that starts June 1 will include four candidates.
    b. Four candidates will be able to participate in an executive training seminar that we feel will provide a valuable learning experience.

26. Which sentence places more emphasis on the date?
    a. The deadline is December 30 for applications for overseas assignments.
    b. December 30 is the deadline for applications for overseas assignments.

27. Which is *less* emphatic?
    a. Our company profits decreased last quarter.
    b. Our company's profits fell 15 percent last quarter.

28. Which sentence *deemphasizes* the credit refusal?
    a. We are unable to grant you credit at this time, but we will reconsider your application later.
    b. Although we welcome your cash business, we are unable to offer you credit at this time; but we will be happy to reconsider your application later.

29. Which sentence gives more emphasis to *judgment*?
    a. He has many admirable qualities, but most important is his good judgment.
    b. He has many admirable qualities, including good judgment and patience.

30. Which is more emphatic?
    a. Three departments are involved: (1) Legal, (2) Accounting, and (3) Distribution.
    b. Three departments are involved:
       1. Legal
       2. Accounting
       3. Distribution

ACTIVE-VOICE VERBS.   Business writing is more forceful if it uses active-voice verbs. Revise the following sentences so that verbs are in the active voice. Put the emphasis on the doer of the action. Add subjects if necessary.

   Example   The computers were powered up each day at 7 a.m.
   Revision   Kevin powered up the computers each day at 7 a.m.

31. Employees were given their checks at 4 p.m. every Friday by the manager.

32. New spices and cooking techniques were tried by McDonald's to improve its hamburgers.

33. Substantial sums of money were earned by employees who enrolled early in our stock option plan.

34. A significant financial commitment has been made by us to ensure that our customers take advantage of our discount pricing.

PASSIVE-VOICE VERBS. When indirectness or tact is required, use passive-voice verbs. fRevise the following sentences so that they are in the passive voice.

Example Stacy did not submit the accounting statement on time.
Revision The accounting statement was not submitted on time.

35. Bill made a computational error in the report.

36. We cannot ship your order for 10 monitors until June 15.

37. The government first issued a warning regarding the use of this pesticide more than 15 months ago.

38. We will notify you immediately if we make any changes in your travel arrangements.

39. We cannot allow a cash refund unless you provide a register receipt.

PARALLELISM. Revise the following sentences so that their parts are balanced.

40. (Hint: Match verbs.) Some guidelines for improving security at food facilities include inspecting incoming and outgoing vehicles, restriction of access to laboratories, preventing workers from bringing personal items into food-handling areas, and inspection of packaging for signs of tampering.

41. (Hint: Match active voice of verbs.) Wendy Johnston, of the Red River office, will now supervise our Western Division; the Eastern Division will be supervised by our Ottawa office manager, David Haskins.

Writing Improvement Exercises

42. (Hint: Match nouns.) Word processing software is used extensively in the fields of health care, by attorneys, by secretaries in insurance firms, for scripts in the entertainment industry, and in the banking field.

43. If you have decided to cancel our service, please cut your credit card in half, and the card pieces should be returned to us.

44. We need more laboratory space, additional personnel is required, and we also need much more capital.

45. The application for a grant asks for this information: funds required for employee salaries, how much we expect to spend on equipment, and what is the length of the project.

46. To lease an automobile is more expensive than buying one.

47. To use the copier, insert your meter, the paper trays must be loaded, indicate the number of copies needed, and your original sheet should be inserted through the feeder.

SENTENCE UNITY.   The following sentences lack unity. Rewrite, correcting the identified fault.

Example   (Dangling modifier) By advertising extensively, all the open jobs were filled quickly.
Revision   By advertising extensively, we were able to fill all the open jobs quickly.

48. (Dangling modifier) To apply for early admission, applications must be received by October 1.

49. (Mixed construction) The reason why Mrs. Harris is unable to travel extensively is because she has family responsibilities.

50. (Misplaced modifier) Identification passes must be worn at all times in offices and production facilities showing the employee's picture.

51. (Misplaced modifier) The editor in chief's rules were to be observed by all staff members, no matter how silly they seemed.

52. (Zigzag sentence) The business was started by two engineers, and these owners worked in a garage, which eventually grew into a million-dollar operation.

COHERENCE. Revise the following paragraphs to improve coherence. Study the example and review the chapter. But be aware that the transitional expressions and key words selected depend largely on the emphasis desired. Many possible revisions exist.

> **Example** Computer style checkers rank somewhere between artificial intelligence and artificial ignorance. Style checkers are like clever children: smart but not wise. Business writers should be cautious. They should be aware of the usefulness of style checkers. They should know their limitations.
>
> **Revision** Computer style checkers rank somewhere between artificial intelligence and artificial ignorance. *For example,* they are like clever children: smart but not wise. *For this reason,* business writers should be cautious. *Although* they should be aware of the usefulness of these software programs, business writers should *also* know their limitations.

53. Our computerized file includes all customer data. It provides space for name, address, and other vital information. It has an area for comments. The area for comments comes in handy. It requires more time and careful keyboarding though.

54. No one likes to turn out poor products. We began highlighting recurring problems. Employees make a special effort to be more careful in doing their work right the first time. It doesn't have to be returned to them for corrections.

55. Service was less than perfect for many months. We lacked certain intangibles. We didn't have the customer-specific data that we needed. We made the mistake of removing all localized, person-to-person coverage. We are returning to decentralized customer contacts.

ACTIVITY

3.1 HOW DO SUPERVISORS IMPROVE THEIR WRITING?   Nearly everyone who goes to college will eventually be promoted into some kind of supervisory position. In that role you will be writing memos, letters, instructions, reports, and other business documents.

`INFOTRAC`

Your Task. Using InfoTrac, find an article that describes how supervisors can improve their writing skills. We recommend "Writing Clearly and Forcefully" by W. H. Weiss, which appeared in the December 2001 issue of *Supervision.* However, you may find a more recent article that is equally helpful. Read the article carefully, and make a list of eight to ten suggestions that you think would be most helpful to you in improving your own writing. Discuss your list in small groups or submit it to your instructor.

VERBS

Review Sections 1.10–1.15 in the Grammar Review section of the Grammar/ Mechanics Handbook. Then study each of the following statements. Underline any verbs that are used incorrectly. In the space provided write the correct form (or *C* if correct) and the number of the G/M principle illustrated. When you finish, compare your responses with those provided near the end of the book. If your responses differ, study carefully the principles in parentheses.

| was _____ (1.10c) | **Example** | Our inventory of raw materials <u>were</u> presented as collateral for a short-term loan. |

1. In the company's next annual report is a summary of our environmental audit and a list of charitable donations.
2. Only one of the top-ranking executives have been insured.
3. CitiCorp Bank, along with 20 other large national banks, offer a variety of savings plans.
4. Neither the plans that this bank offers nor the service just rendered by the teller are impressive.
5. Finding a good bank and selecting a savings/checking plan often require considerable research and study.
6. The budget analyst wants to know whether the Equipment Committee are ready to recommend a printer.
7. Either of the printers that the committee selects is acceptable to the budget analyst.
8. If Mr. Davis had chose the Maximizer Plus savings plan, his money would have earned maximum interest.
9. Although the applications have laid there for two weeks, they may still be submitted.
10. Jessica acts as if she was the manager.
11. One of the reasons that our Alaskan sales branches have been so costly are the high cost of living.

In the space provided write the letter of the sentence that illustrates consistency in subject, voice, and mood.

12.a. If you will read the instructions, the answer can be found.
   b. If you will read the instructions, you will find the answer.
13.a. All employees must fill out application forms; only then will you be insured.
   b. All employees must fill out application forms; only then will they be insured.
14.a. First, take an inventory of equipment; then, order supplies.
   b. First, take an inventory of equipment; then, supplies must be ordered.
15.a. Select a savings plan that suits your needs; deposits may be made immediately.
   b. Select a savings plan that suits your needs; begin making deposits immediately.

DOCUMENT FOR REVISION

The following memo has many faults in grammar, spelling, punctuation, capitalization, word use, and number form. Use standard proofreading marks (see Appendix B) to correct the errors. Study the guidelines in the Grammar/Mechanics Handbook to sharpen your skills. When you finish, your instructor can show you the revised version of this memo.

Signal Products, Inc.
Interoffice Memo

DATE: October 2, 200X

TO: Garth Johnson, Vice President

FROM: Nicole Holloway, Manager, Payroll

SUBJECT: Departmental Error

This is to inform you that last month our central accounting department changed it's computer program for payroll processing. When this computer change was operationalized some of the stored information was not transfered to the new information database. As a consequence of this maneuver several errors occured in employee paychecks (1) medical benifits were not deducted (2) annuity deductions were not made and (3) errors occured in Federal witholding calculations.

Each and every one of the employees effected have been contacted; and this problem has been elucidated. My staff and myself has been working overtime to replace all the missing data; so that corrections can be made by the November 3rd payroll run.

Had I made a verification of the true facts before the paychecks were ran this slip-up would not have materialized. To prevent such an error in the future I decided to take the bull by the horns. At this point in time I have implemented a rigorous new verification system. I am of the firm opinion that utilization of the new system will definitely prevent this perplexing event from reoccuring.

> Communication Workshops provide insight into special business communication topics and skills not discussed in the chapters. These topics cover ethics, technology, career skills, and collaboration. Each workshop includes a career application with a case study or problem to help you develop skills relevant to the workshop topic.

COMMUNICATION WORKSHOP: ETHICS

Using Ethical Tools to Help You Do the Right Thing

In your career you will doubtless face times when you are torn by conflicting loyalties. Should you tell the truth and risk your job? Should you be loyal to your friends even if it means bending the rules? Should you be tactful or totally honest? Is it your duty to help your company make a profit, or should you be socially responsible?

Being ethical, according to the experts, means doing the right thing *given the circumstances*. Each set of circumstances requires analyzing issues, evaluating choices, and acting responsibly. Resolving ethical issues is never easy, but the task can be made less difficult if you know how to identify key issues. The following questions may be helpful.

- **Is the action you are considering legal?** No matter who asks you to do it or how important you feel the result will be, avoid anything that is prohibited by law. Giving a kickback to a buyer for a large order is illegal, even if you suspect that others in your field do it and you know that without the kickback you will lose the sale.
- **How would you see the problem if you were on the opposite side?** Looking at all sides of an issue helps you gain perspective. Consider the issue of mandatory drug testing among employees. From management's viewpoint such testing could stop drug abuse, improve job performance, and lower health insurance premiums. From the employees' viewpoint mandatory testing reflects a lack of trust of employees and constitutes an invasion of privacy. By weighing both sides of an issue, you can arrive at a more equitable solution.
- **What are the alternate solutions?** Consider all dimensions of other options. Would the alternative be more ethical? Under the circumstances, is the alternative feasible? Can an alternate solution be implemented with a minimum of disruption and with a high degree of probable success?
- **Can you discuss the problem with someone whose opinion you value?** Suppose you feel ethically bound to report accurate information to a client—even though your boss has ordered you not to do so. Talking about your dilemma with a coworker or with a colleague in your field might give you helpful insights and lead to possible alternatives.
- **How would you feel if your family, friends, employer, or coworkers learned of your action?** If the thought of revealing your action publicly produces cold sweats, your choice is probably not a wise one. Losing the faith of your friends or the confidence of your customers is not worth whatever short-term gains might be realized.

Career Application. One of the Big Five accounting firms uses an ethical awareness survey that includes some of the following situations. You may face similar situations with ethical issues on the job or in employment testing.

Your Task. In teams or individually, decide whether the ethical issue is (a) very important, (b) moderately important, or (c) unimportant. Then decide whether you (a) strongly approve, (b) are undecided, or (c) strongly disapprove of the action taken.[5] Apply the ethical tools presented here in determining whether the course of action is ethical. What alternatives might you suggest?

1. **Recruiting.** You are a recruiter for your company. Although you know company morale is low, the turnover rate is high, and the work environment in many departments is deplorable, you tell job candidates that it's "a great place to work."
2. **Training Program.** Your company is offering an exciting training program in Hawaii. Although you haven't told anyone, you plan to get another job shortly. You decide to participate in the program anyway because you've never been to Hawaii. One of the program requirements is that participants must have "long-term career potential" with the firm.
3. **Thievery.** As a supervisor, you suspect that one of your employees is stealing. You check with a company attorney and find that a lie detector test cannot be legally used. Then you decide to scrutinize the employee's records. Finally, you find an inconsistency in the employee's records. You decide to fire the employee, although this inconsistency would not normally have been discovered.
4. **Downsizing.** As part of the management team of a company that makes potato chips, you are faced with rising prices for potatoes. Rather than increase the cost of your chips, you decide to decrease slightly the size of the bag. Consumers are less likely to notice a smaller bag than a higher price.

Related Web Site: To see a concise ethics test developed by Texas Instruments, visit http://www.ti.com/corp/docs/company/citizen/ethics/quicktest.shtml. If this URL fails, use a search engine to look for "TI Ethics Quick Test."

WEB

Chapter 4

Revising and Proofreading Business Messages

Vigorous writing is concise. A sentence should contain no unnecessary words . . . for the same reason that a drawing should have no unnecessary lines and a machine no unnecessary parts.

STRUNK AND WHITE, *The Elements of Style*

LEARNING OBJECTIVES

1. Understand the third phase of the writing process, revision.
2. Revise messages to achieve concise wording by eliminating wordy prepositional phrases, long lead-ins, outdated expressions, and needless adverbs.
3. Revise messages to eliminate fillers, repetitious words, and redundancies.
4. Revise messages to use jargon sparingly and avoid slang and clichés.
5. Revise messages to include precise verbs, concrete nouns, and vivid adjectives.
6. Describe effective techniques for proofreading routine and complex documents.

UNDERSTANDING THE PROCESS OF REVISION

✓ Quick Check

The third phase of the writing process includes revision, proofreading, and evaluating.

The best business writing is concise, clear, and vigorous. In this chapter you'll concentrate on techniques to achieve those qualities. These techniques are part of the third phase of the writing process, which centers on revising and proofreading. Revising means improving the content and sentence structure of your message. It may include adding, cutting, and recasting what you've written. Proofreading involves correcting the grammar, spelling, punctuation, format, and mechanics of your messages.

Both revising and proofreading require a little practice to develop your skills. That's what you will be learning in this chapter. Take a look at Figure 4.1. Notice how the revised version of this memo is clearer, more concise, and more vigorous because we removed much dead wood. Major ideas stand out when they are not lost in a forest of words.

FIGURE 4.1   Memo Revised for Conciseness

MEMO

DATE: September 5, 200x

TO: Ryan Rhodes

FROM: Courtney James

SUBJECT: Comparison of ~~A~~ Web Sites ~~of Some of Our Competitors~~   [*Competitors'* inserted above; *Our* circled]

~~This is just a short note to inform you that~~ as you requested, I have ~~made an examination of~~ *examined*
several of our competitors' Web sites. Attached ~~hereto~~ is a summary of my findings ~~of my~~
~~investigation~~. I was ~~really~~ most interested in ~~making a comparison of the~~ *comparing* navigational
graphics or cues that ~~were used to~~ guide visitors through the sites. ~~In view of the fact that~~ *Since* we
will be building our own Web site ~~in the near future~~ *soon*, I was ~~extremely~~ intrigued by the
organization, ~~kind of~~ content, and navigation at each ~~and every~~ site I visited.
~~In the event that~~ *If* you would like to discuss this information with me, please ~~feel free to~~ call
me.

Rarely is the first or even the second version of a message satisfactory. One expert says, "Only amateurs expect writing perfection on the first try."[1] The revision stage is your chance to make sure your message is clear, forceful, and says what you mean.[2] It's also your chance to project a good image of yourself.

Many professional writers compose the first draft quickly without worrying about language, precision, or correctness. Then they revise and polish extensively. Other writers, however, prefer to revise as they go—particularly for shorter business documents. Whether you revise as you go or do it when you finish a document, you'll want to focus on concise wording. This includes eliminating wordy prepositional phrases, long lead-ins, outdated expressions, needless adverbs, fillers, and repetitious and redundant words. You'll also decide whether to include jargon, slang, and clichés. And you'll be looking for precise words that say exactly what you mean.

✓ **Quick Check**
Some communicators write the first draft quickly; others revise and polish as they go.

CONCISE WORDING

In business, time is indeed money. Translated into writing, this means that concise messages save reading time and, thus, money. In addition, messages that are written directly and efficiently are easier to read and comprehend. In the revision process look for shorter ways to say what you mean. Examine every sentence that you write. Could the thought be conveyed in fewer words? Notice how the following flabby expressions could be said more concisely.

✓ **Quick Check**
Main points are easier to understand in concise messages.

✓ Quick Check

Flabby phrases can often be reduced to a single word.

Flabby	Concise	Flabby	Concise
at a later date	later	fully cognizant of	aware of
at this point in time	now	in addition to the above	also
afford an opportunity	allow	in spite of the fact that	even though
are of the opinion that	believe, think that	in the event that	if
at the present time	now, presently	in the amount of	for
despite the fact that	although	in the near future	soon
due to the fact that	because, since	in view of the fact that	because
during the time	while	inasmuch as	since
feel free to	please	more or less	about
for the period of	for	until such time as	until

WORDY PREPOSITIONAL PHRASES

✓ Quick Check

Replace wordy prepositional phrases with adverbs whenever possible.

Some wordy prepositional phrases may be replaced by single adverbs. For example, *in the normal course of events* becomes *normally* and *as a general rule* becomes *generally*.

Wordy MCI approached the merger *in a careful manner*.
Concise MCI approached the merger *carefully*.

Wordy The merger will *in all probability* be effected.
Concise The merger will *probably* be effected.

Wordy We have taken this action *in very few cases*.
Concise We have *seldom* taken this action.

LONG LEAD-INS

✓ Quick Check

Avoid long lead-ins that delay the reader from the reaching the meaning of the sentence.

Delete unnecessary introductory words. The meat of the sentence often follows the words *that* or *because*.

Wordy *I am sending you this announcement to let you all know that* the office will be closed Monday.
Concise The office will be closed Monday.

Wordy *You will be interested to learn that* you can now be served at our Web site.
Concise You can now be served at our Web site.

Wordy *I am writing this letter because* Dr. Steven Hunt suggested that your organization was hiring trainees.
Concise Dr. Steven Hunt suggested that your organization was hiring trainees.

OUTDATED EXPRESSIONS

The world of business has changed greatly in the past century or two. Yet, some business writers continue to use antiquated phrases and expressions borrowed from a period when the "language of business" was exceedingly formal and flowery. In the 1800s, letter writers "begged to state" and "trusted to be favored with" and assured their readers that they "remained their humble ser-

It's hard to imagine in today's modern business offices that anyone would use a quill pen and sealing wax to send messages. Yet some writers persist in using outdated expressions such as *as per your request* and *enclosed please find*. Smart communicators make sure their vocabularies are as contemporary as the equipment used in offices like this one.

© PhotoDisc, Inc./Getty Images

vants." Such language suggests quill pens, sealing wax, green eyeshades, and sleeve guards. Avoid using time-worn, stale expressions that linger from the past. Replace outdated expressions such as those shown here with more modern phrasing:

Don't try to sound businesslike by using outdated expressions.

Outdated Expressions	Modern Phrasing
are in receipt of	have received
as per your request	at your request
attached hereto	attached
enclosed please find	enclosed is/are
pursuant to your request	at your request
thanking you in advance	thank you
I trust that	I think, I believe
under separate cover	separately

NEEDLESS ADVERBS

Eliminating adverbs such as *very, definitely, quite, completely, extremely, really, actually, somewhat,* and *rather* streamlines your writing. Omitting these intensifiers generally makes you sound more credible and businesslike. Writers who wish to sound sincere and conversational often include some intensifiers, but they guard against excessive use.

Avoid excessive use of adverb intensifiers.

Wordy We *actually* did not *really* give his plan a *very* fair trial.
Concise We did not give his plan a fair trial.

Wordy Professor Susan Fagan offers an *extremely* fine course that students *definitely* appreciate.
Concise Professor Susan Fagan offers a fine course that students appreciate.

FILLERS

Avoid fillers that fatten sentences with excess words. Beginning an idea with *There is* usually indicates that writers are spinning their wheels until they decide where the sentence is going. Used correctly, *there* indicates a specific place (*I placed the box there*). Used as fillers, *there* and occasionally *it* merely take up space. Most, but not all, sentences can be revised so that these fillers are unnecessary.

Wordy *There are* three vice presidents *who* report directly to the president.
Concise Three vice presidents report directly to the president.

Wordy *It is* the client *who* should *make application* for licensing.
Concise The client should apply for licensing.

REPETITIOUS WORDS

Quick Check
Avoid the monotony of unintentionally repeated words.

Good communicators vary their words to avoid unintentional repetition. Not only does this shorten a message, but it also improves vigor and readability. Variety of expression can be achieved by searching for appropriate synonyms and by substituting pronouns. Compare the following wordy paragraph with the more concise version. Notice in the concise version that synonyms (*representatives, members*) replace the overused *employee*.

Wordy
Employees will be able to elect an additional six employees to serve with the four previously elected employees who currently comprise the employees' board of directors.

Concise
Employees may vote for six additional representatives to serve with the previously elected members of their board of directors.

Good writers are also alert to the overuse of the articles *a, an,* and particularly *the*. Often the word *the* can simply be omitted, particularly with plural nouns.

Wordy The committee members agreed on many of the rule changes.
Improved Committee members agreed on many rule changes.

REDUNDANT WORDS

Quick Check
Redundancies convey a meaning more than once.

Repetition of words to achieve emphasis or effective transition is an important writing technique discussed in the previous chapter. The needless repetition, however, of words whose meanings are clearly implied by other words is a writing fault called *redundancy*. For example, in the expression *final outcome*, the word *final* is redundant and should be omitted, since *outcome* implies finality. Learn to avoid redundant expressions such as the following:

absolutely essential   *grateful* thanks
adequate *enough*   *mutual* cooperation
advance warning   *necessary* prerequisite

basic fundamentals	*new* beginning
big *in size*	*passing* fad
combined *together*	*past* history
consensus *of opinion*	reason *why*
continue *on*	red *in color*
each *and every*	refer *back*
exactly identical	repeat *again*
few *in number*	*true* facts

✓ **Quick Check**

Don't use words that repeat meaning. Which words could be omitted?

JARGON

Except in certain specialized contexts, you should avoid jargon and unnecessary technical terms. Jargon is special terminology that is peculiar to a particular activity or profession. For example, geologists speak knowingly of *exfoliation, calcareous ooze,* and *siliceous particles.* Engineers are familiar with phrases such as *infrared processing flags, output latches,* and *movable symbology.* Telecommunication experts use such words and phrases as *protocols, clickstream,* and *asynchronous transmission.*

Every field has its own special vocabulary. Using that vocabulary within the field is acceptable and even necessary for accurate, efficient communication. Don't use specialized terms, however, if you have reason to believe that your reader may misunderstand them.

✓ **Quick Check**

Jargon, which is terminology unique to a certain profession, should be reserved for individuals who understand it.

SLANG

Slang is composed of informal words with arbitrary and extravagantly changed meanings. Slang words quickly go out of fashion because they are no longer appealing when everyone begins to understand them. Consider the following statement of a government official who had been asked why his department was dropping a proposal to lease offshore oil lands: "The Administration has an awful lot of other things in the pipeline, and this has more wiggle room so they just moved it down the totem pole." He added, however, that the proposal might be offered again since "there is no pulling back because of hot-potato factors."

The meaning here, if the speaker really intended to impart any, is considerably obscured by the use of slang. Good communicators, of course, aim at clarity and avoid unintelligible slang.

✓ **Quick Check**

Slang sounds fashionable, but it lacks precise meaning and should be avoided in business writing.

DILBERT **By Scott Adams**

CLICHÉS

✓ **Quick Check**

Clichés are dull and sometimes ambiguous.

Clichés are expressions that have become exhausted by overuse. These expressions lack not only freshness but also clarity. Some have no meaning for people who are new to our culture. The following partial list contains clichés you should avoid in business writing.

below the belt	keep your nose to the grindstone
better than new	last but not least
beyond the shadow of a doubt	make a bundle
easier said than done	pass with flying colors
exception to the rule	quick as a flash
fill the bill	shoot from the hip
first and foremost	stand your ground
hard facts	true to form

PRECISE VERBS

✓ **Quick Check**

Precise verbs make your writing forceful, clear, and lively.

Effective writing creates meaningful images in the mind of the reader. Such writing is sparked by robust, concrete, and descriptive words. Ineffective writing is often dulled by insipid, abstract, and generalized words. The most direct way to improve lifeless writing is through effective use of verbs. Verbs not only indicate the action of the subject but also deliver the force of the sentence. Select verbs carefully so that the reader can visualize precisely what is happening.

General Our salesperson will *contact* you next week.
Precise Our salesperson will (*telephone, fax, e-mail, visit*) you next week.

General The CEO *said* that we should contribute.
Precise The CEO (*urged, pleaded, demanded*) that we contribute.

General We must *consider* this problem.
Precise We must (*clarify, remedy, rectify*) this problem.

General The newspaper was *affected* by the strike.
Precise The newspaper was (*crippled, silenced, demoralized*) by the strike.

The power of a verb is diminished when it is needlessly converted to a noun. This happens when verbs such as *acquire, establish,* and *develop* are made into nouns (*acquisition, establishment,* and *development*). These nouns then receive the central emphasis in the sentence. In the following pairs of sentences, observe how forceful the original verbs are as compared with their noun forms.

Weak *Acquisition* of park lands was made recently by the city. (Noun-centered)
Strong The city *acquired* park lands recently. (Verb-centered)

Weak The webmaster and the designer had a *discussion* concerning graphics. (Noun-centered)
Strong The webmaster and the designer *discussed* graphics. (Verb-centered)

Weak Both companies must grant *approval* of the merger. (Noun-centered)
Strong Both companies must *approve* the merger. (Verb-centered)

CONCRETE NOUNS

Nouns name persons, places, and things. Abstract nouns name concepts that are difficult to visualize, such as *automation, function, justice, institution, integrity, form, judgment,* and *environment.* Concrete nouns name objects that are more easily imagined, such as *desk, car,* and *lightbulb.* Nouns describing a given object can range from the very abstract to the very concrete—for example, *object, motor vehicle, car, convertible, Mustang.* All of these words or phrases can be used to describe a Mustang convertible. However, a reader would have difficulty envisioning a Mustang convertible when given just the word *object* or even *motor vehicle* or *car.*

In business writing, help your reader "see" what you mean by using concrete language.

General	a *change* in our budget
Concrete	a *10 percent reduction* in our budget
General	*that company's* new *product*
Concrete	*Nokia's* new *cell phone-music player combo*
General	*a person* called
Concrete	*Mrs. Swain, the administrative assistant,* called
General	we *improved* the assembly line
Concrete	we *installed 26 advanced Unimate robots* on the assembly line

✓ **Quick Check**
Concrete nouns help readers visualize the meanings of words.

VIVID ADJECTIVES

Including highly descriptive, dynamic adjectives makes writing more vivid and concrete. Be careful, though, neither to overuse them nor to lose objectivity in selecting them.

General	Jon submitted his report on time.
Vivid	Jon submitted his *detailed 12-page* report on time.
General	Rick needs a better truck.
Vivid	Rick needs a *rugged, four-wheel-drive Dodge* truck.
General	We enjoyed the movie.
Vivid	We enjoyed the *entertaining* and *absorbing* movie.
Overkill	We enjoyed the *gutsy, exciting, captivating,* and *thoroughly marvelous* movie.

✓ **Quick Check**
A thesaurus (computer or printed) helps you select precise words and increase your vocabulary.

UNDERSTANDING THE PROCESS OF PROOFREADING

Once you have the message in its final form, it's time to proofread. Don't proofread earlier because you may waste time checking items that eventually are changed or omitted.

✓ **Quick Check**
Proofreading before a document is completed is generally a waste of time.

WHAT TO WATCH FOR IN PROOFREADING

Careful proofreaders check for problems in these areas:

- **Spelling.** Now's the time to consult the dictionary. Is *recommend* spelled with one or two *c*'s? Do you mean *affect* or *effect*? Use your computer spell checker,

When fans wanted to protest a baseball player, they made their own sign. No one seems to notice the misspelling, but you can be sure it would be noticed in a business document. Proofreading involves checking spelling, grammar, punctuation, names and numbers, and format.
© Reuters NewMedia, Inc./CORBIS

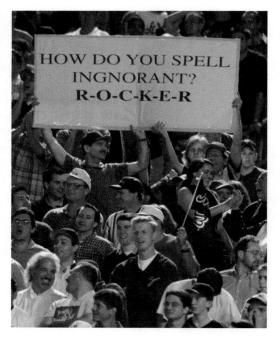

but don't rely on it totally. See the accompanying Communication Workshop to learn more about the benefits and hazards of computer spell checkers.

- **Grammar.** Locate sentence subjects; do their verbs agree with them? Do pronouns agree with their antecedents? Review the .principles in the Grammar/Mechanics Handbook if necessary. Use your computer's grammar checker, but be suspicious. The Communication Workshop discusses grammar checkers more extensively.
- **Punctuation.** Make sure that introductory clauses are followed by commas. In compound sentences put commas before coordinating conjunctions (*and, or, but, nor*). Double-check your use of semicolons and colons.
- **Names and numbers.** Compare all names and numbers with their sources because inaccuracies are not immediately visible. Especially verify the spelling of the names of individuals receiving the message. Most of us immediately dislike someone who misspells our name.
- **Format.** Be sure that letters, printed memos, and reports are balanced on the page. Compare their parts and format with those of standard documents shown in Appendix A. If you indent paragraphs, be certain that all are indented.

How to Proofread Routine Documents

Most routine messages, including e-mails, require a light proofreading. Use the down arrow to reveal one line at a time, thus focusing your attention at the bottom of the screen. Read carefully for faults such as omitted or doubled words. Use the spell checker, if available.

For routine messages such as printed letters or memos, a safer proofreading method is reading from a printed copy. You're more likely to find errors and to observe the tone. "Things really look different on paper," observes veteran writer Louise Lague at *People* magazine. "Don't just pull a letter out of the printer and stick it in an envelope. Read every sentence again. You'll catch bad line endings, strange page breaks, and weird spacing. You can also get a totally different feeling about what you've said when you see it in print. Sometimes you can say something with a smile on your face; but if you put the same thing in print, it won't work."[3] Use standard proofreading marks, shown in Figure 4.2, to indicate changes.

FIGURE 4.2 Proofreading Marks

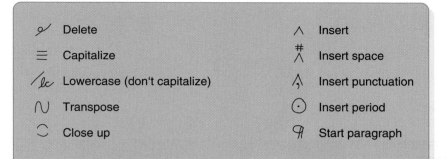

	Delete		Insert
	Capitalize		Insert space
	Lowercase (don't capitalize)		Insert punctuation
	Transpose		Insert period
	Close up		Start paragraph

Marked Copy

~~This is to inform you that~~ beginning september 1, the doors
leading to the West side of the building will have alarms.
Because ~~of the fact that~~ these ~~exits~~ doors also function as fire exits,
they can not ~~actually~~ be locked, consequently, we are installing
alarms. Please ~~utilize~~ use the east side exists to avoid setting off
the ear-piercing alarms.

✓ **Quick Check**

Most proofreaders use these standard marks to indicate revisions.

How to Proofread Complex Documents

Long, complex, or important documents demand more careful proofreading using the following techniques:

✓ **Quick Check**

For both routine and complex documents, it's best to proofread from a printed copy, not on a computer screen.

- Print a copy, preferably double-spaced, and set it aside for at least a day. You'll be more alert after a breather.
- Allow adequate time to proofread carefully. A common excuse for sloppy proofreading is lack of time.
- Be prepared to find errors. One student confessed, "I can find other people's errors, but I can't seem to locate my own." Psychologically, we don't expect to find errors, and we don't want to find them. You can overcome this obstacle by anticipating errors and congratulating, not criticizing, yourself each time you find one.
- Read the message at least twice—once for word meanings and once for grammar/mechanics. For very long documents (book chapters and long articles or reports), read a third time to verify consistency in formatting.
- Reduce your reading speed. Concentrate on individual words rather than ideas.
- For documents that must be perfect, have someone read the message aloud. Spell names and difficult words, note capitalization, and read punctuation.
- Use standard proofreading marks, shown in Figure 4.2, to indicate changes.

Your computer word processing program may include a style or grammar checker. These programs generally analyze aspects of your writing style, including readability level and use of passive voice, trite expressions, split infinitives, and wordy expressions. Most programs use sophisticated technology (and a lot of computer memory) to identify significant errors. In addition to finding spelling

© Randy Glasbergen
www.glasbergen.com

GLASBERGEN

**"But there can't be any errors. My grammar
and spell checkers found nothing wrong!"**

and typographical errors, grammar checkers can find subject–verb lack of agreement, word misuse, spacing irregularities, punctuation problems, and many other faults. But they won't find everything, as you will see in the accompanying Communication Workshop. While grammar and spell checkers can help you a great deal, you are the final proofreader.

SUMMING UP AND LOOKING FORWARD

Revision is the most important part of the writing process. To revise for clarity and conciseness, look for flabby phrases that can be shortened (such as *more or less*). Eliminate wordy prepositional phrases (*in all probability*), long lead-ins (*This is to inform you that*), outdated expressions (*pursuant to your request*), needless adverbs (*definitely, very*), and fillers (*There are*). Also watch for repetitious words and redundancies (*combined together*). Use jargon only when it is clear to receivers, and avoid slang and clichés altogether. The best writing includes precise verbs, concrete nouns, and vivid adjectives. After revising a message, you're ready for the last step in the writing process: proofreading. Watch for irregularities in spelling, grammar, punctuation, names and numbers, and format. Although routine messages may be proofread on the screen, you will have better results if you proofread from a printed copy. Complex documents should be printed, put away for a day or so, and then proofread several times.

In these opening chapters you've studied the writing process. You've also learned many practical techniques for becoming an effective business communicator. Now it's time for you to put these techniques to work. Chapter 5 introduces you to writing e-mail messages and memorandums, the most frequently used forms of communication for most businesspeople. Later chapters present letters and reports.

CRITICAL THINKING

1. "A real writer can sit down at a computer and create a perfect document the first time." Do you agree or disagree? Why?
2. Carefully written short messages often take longer to write than longer messages. Do you agree or disagree? Why?
3. Because clichés are familiar and have stood the test of time, do they help clarify writing?
4. If your boss writes in a flowery, formal tone and relies on outdated expressions, should you follow that style also?
5. Is it unethical to help a friend revise a report when you know that the friend will be turning that report in for a grade?

CHAPTER REVIEW

6. How is revising different from proofreading?

7. Why is conciseness especially important in business?

8. What is a long lead-in? Give an original example.

9. What's wrong with using adverbs such as *very, really,* and *actually*?

10. What is a redundancy? Give an example.

11. What is jargon? When can it be used? What are examples in your field?

12. What happens when a verb (such as *describe*) is converted to a noun expression (*to make a description*)? Give an original example.

13. Should you proofread when you are writing or after you finish? Why?

14. What five areas should you especially pay attention to when you proofread?

15. How does the proofreading of routine and complex documents differ?

WRITING IMPROVEMENT EXERCISES

WORDINESS. Revise the following sentences to eliminate flabby phrases, wordy prepositional phrases, outdated expressions, and long lead-ins.

Example This is to notify you that meetings held on a weekly basis are most effective.
Revision Meetings held weekly are most effective.

16. It is our opinion that you should not attempt to move forward until such time as you seek and obtain approval of the plan from the team leader prior to beginning this project.

17. This is to advise you that beginning with the date of April 1 all charges made after that date will be charged to your new credit card number.

18. Pursuant to your request, enclosed please find a copy of your August statement.

19. In view of the fact that our sales are increasing in a gradual manner, we must secure a loan in the amount of $50,000.

20. This is to let you know that you should feel free to use your credit card for the purpose of purchasing household items for a period of 60 days.

NEEDLESS ADVERBS, FILLERS, REPETITIOUS WORDS. Revise the following sentences to eliminate needless adverbs, fillers (such as *there is* and *it is*), and unintentional repetition.

21. There are many businesses that can benefit from totally improving the customer service they provide for online customers.

22. It is certainly clear that there are many younger managers who are very eager but who are actually unprepared to assume management or leadership roles.

23. There are four employees who definitely spend more time in Internet recreational uses on the Internet than they spend on business-related Internet work.

24. There are definitely five advantages that computers have over a human decision maker.

REDUNDANCIES, JARGON, SLANG, CLICHÉS. Revise the following sentences to eliminate redundancies, jargon, slang, clichés, and any other wordiness.

Example First and foremost, we plan to emphasize an instructional training program.
Revision First, we plan to emphasize an instructional [or training] program.

25. Last but not least, Troy collected together as much support material as possible to avoid getting burned in cash losses or bottom-line profits.

26. It was the consensus of opinion of members of the committee that the committee should meet at 11 a.m. in the morning.

27. If you will refer back to the contract, you will definitely find that there are specific specifications that prevent anyone from blowing the budget.

28. This memorandum serves as an advance warning that all books and magazines borrowed from the library must be taken back to the library by June 1.

29. In view of the fact that our last presentation bombed, we are at this point in time convinced that we must include only the most absolutely essential selling points this time.

30. In the normal course of events, we would wait until such time as we had adequate enough credit reports.

PRECISE VERBS. Revise these sentences, centering the action in the verbs.

Example The webmaster made a description of the project.
Revision The webmaster described the project.

31. Mr. Thomas gave an appraisal of the home's value.

32. Can you bring about a change in our company travel policy?

33. Web-based customer service will produce the effect of reduction in overall costs.

34. In writing this proposal, we must make application of new government regulations.

35. The board of directors made a recommendation affirming abandonment of the pilot project.

36. An investigator made a determination of the fire damages.

37. We hope to have production of our new line of products by January.

38. The duty of the comptroller is verification of departmental budgets.

39. Please make a correction in my account to reflect my late payment.

VIVID WORDS.   Revise the following sentences to include vivid and concrete language. Add appropriate words.

Example   They said it was a long way off.
Revision   Management officials announced that the merger would not take place for two years.

40. Soon we will be at our new location.

41. An employee from that company notified us about the change in date.

42. Please contact them soon.

43. They said that the movie they saw was good.

44. Workers improved when they saw the big picture.

45. The report was weak.

ACTIVITY

4.1 WHAT'S NEW IN GRAMMAR AND SPELL CHECKERS? Your boss thinks that you know more about Internet research than she does. She saw an article in the newspaper complaining that nothing new had been developed in grammar technology for many years. She wants you to check to see whether any new grammar or spell checking programs have been developed for general business writers. INFOTRAC

Your Task. You know that if you searched the Web, you would probably be overwhelmed with commercial Web sites selling products. You would prefer to find an article that reviews new software. Use InfoTrac to locate at least one article describing a new grammar or spell checking program for general use. In a brief memo addressed to your boss, Terry Broderick, summarize the article. See Chapter 5 to learn about memo formats.

GRAMMAR/MECHANICS CHECKUP—4

ADJECTIVES AND ADVERBS

Review Sections 1.16 and 1.17 of the Grammar/Mechanics Handbook. Then study each of the following statements. Underscore any inappropriate forms. In the space provided write the correct form (or *C* if correct) and the number of the G/M principle illustrated. You may need to consult your dictionary for current practice regarding some compound adjectives. When you finish, compare your responses with those provided at the end of the book. If your answers differ, carefully study the principles in parentheses.

Example He was one of those individuals with a live and let live attitude.   <u>live-and-let-live(1.17e)</u>

1. The newly reorganized magazine tried to retain its long time customers. _____
2. Many subscribers considered the $50 per year charge to be a bargain. _____
3. Other subscribers complained that $50 per year was exorbitant. _____
4. The Internet supplied the answer so quick that we were all amazed. _____
5. He only had $1 in his pocket. _____
6. Some experts predict that double digit inflation may return. _____
7. Jeremy found a once in a lifetime opportunity. _____

8. Although the car was four years old, it was in good condition. _____
9. Of the two colors, which is best for a Web background? _____
10. Dr. Elaine Lux is well known in her field. _____
11. Channel 12 presents up to the minute news broadcasts. _____

12. Lower tax brackets would lessen the after tax yield of some bonds. _____
13. The conclusion drawn from the statistics couldn't have been more clearer. _____

14. This new investment fund has a better than fifty fifty chance of outperforming the older fund. _____
15. If you feel badly about the transaction, contact your portfolio manager. _____

DOCUMENT FOR REVISION

The following letter has faults in grammar, punctuation, conversational language, outdated expressions, sexist language, concise wording, long lead-ins, and many other problems. Use standard proofreading marks (see Appendix B) to correct the errors. Study the guidelines in the Grammar/Mechanics Handbook to sharpen your skills. When you finish, your instructor may show you the revised version of this letter.

June 9, 200x

Ms. Kay Bradley

Title Guaranty & Abstract Company

2430 Providence Avenue

Anchorage, AK 99508

Dear Kay:

Pursuant to our telephone conversation this morning, this is to advise that two (2) agent's packages will be delivered to you next week. Due to the fact that new forms had to be printed; we do not have them immediately available.

Although we cannot offer a 50/50 commission split, we are able to offer new agents a 60/40 commission split. There are two new agreement forms that show this commission ratio. When you get ready to sign up a new agent have her fill in these up to date forms.

When you send me an executed agency agreement please make every effort to tell me what agency package was assigned to the agent. On the last form that you sent you overlooked this information. We need this data to distribute commissions in an expeditious manner.

If you have any questions, don't hesitate to call on me.

Yours very truly,

Brian Simpson

Brian Simpson

Sales Manager

Grammar and Spell Checkers: They've Come a Long Way, Baby!

Nearly all high-end word processing programs now include sophisticated grammar and spell checkers to help writers with their proofreading chores.

Grammar Checkers

When first introduced, grammar and style checkers were not too helpful. They were limited in scope, awkward to use, and identified many questionable "errors." But today's grammar checkers detect an amazing number of legitimate writing lapses. Microsoft Word finds faults in word use (such as *there, their*) capitalization, punctuation, subject–verb agreement, sentence structure, singular and plural endings, repeated words, wordy expressions, gender-specific expressions, and many other problems.

How does a grammar checker work? Let's say you typed the sentence, *The office and its equipment is for sale*. You would see a wavy green line appear under *is*. When you point your cursor at *Tools* in the tool bar and click *Spelling and Grammar*, a box opens up. It identifies the subject–verb agreement error and suggests the verb *are* as a correction. When you click *Change*, the error is corrected.

Does a grammar checker find all errors? Hardly! When an English professor tested the grammar-checking features in Word 2000, he found that it failed to identify the most common errors.[4] Moreover, many "errors" were falsely marked. That's why you should not make any change unless you know the grammar rule that applies.

Spell Checkers

Spell checkers compare your typed words with those in the computer's memory. Microsoft Word uses a wavy red line to underline misspelled words caught "on the fly." Although some writers dismiss spell checkers as an annoyance, most of us are happy to have our typos and misspelled words detected. What's annoying is that spell checkers don't find all the problems. In the following poem, for example, only two problems were detected (*your* and *it's*).

> I have a spell checkers
>   That came with my PC.
> It plainly marks four my review
>   Mistakes I cannot sea.
> I've run this poem threw it,
>   I'm sure your pleased too no.
> Its letter perfect in it's weigh
>   My checker tolled me sew.
>   —Anonymous

The lesson to be learned here is that you can't rely totally on any spell checker. Misused words may not be highlighted because the spell checker doesn't know what meaning you have in mind. A wise practice is to print out important messages and proofread them word by word.

Career Application. Your boss, Serena Johnson, is developing an in-service training program on word processing. She wants you to analyze the effectiveness of your computer's grammar and spell checkers. Your brief report will become part of a presentation to new employees.

Your Task

- You decide to try out your software with a set of test sentences. At a computer that has grammar and spell checking software, type the following four sentences, including all the errors. Print the sentences.
    1. Is the companys office located on riverside drive in new york city.
    2. The manger adviced her to make a consciensous effort to improve.
    3. There house and it's furniture was allready sold before they moved to miami.
    4. My friend and me was going to apply for the job in june but we were to late.
- For each sentence, underline the errors the software identified. Then circle the errors that the software missed. (A word may contain only one error.) Total your underlines and circles. Make notes on the kinds of errors identified and the kinds missed. Tip: You should find 20 errors.
- Based on your findings, how would you rate the usefulness of your computer's grammar and spell checkers? What are the strengths and weaknesses?
- What advice would you give to employees about relying on these programs for proofreading?
- In class discussion or in a memo, convey your findings and your advice to your boss, Serena Johnson.

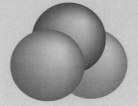

Corresponding at Work

Chapter 5

E-Mail and Memorandums

E-mail is changing our behavior, our way of interacting with people, our institutions. And it is happening incredibly fast. . . . Because it's spread so fast, it has raced ahead of our abilities to fully adapt to this new form of communication.

MICHAEL EISNER, CEO, Walt Disney Company[1]

LEARNING OBJECTIVES

1. Explain the importance of internal communication.
2. Analyze the characteristics of and writing process for successful e-mail messages and memos.
3. Understand how to use e-mail safely and effectively.
4. Explain and demonstrate a writing plan for memos and e-mail messages.
5. Write procedure, instruction, and information e-mail messages and memos.
6. Write e-mail messages and memos that make requests.
7. Write e-mail messages and memos that respond.

THE IMPORTANCE OF INTERNAL COMMUNICATION

As Michael Eisner recognizes, revolutionary changes are taking place in business communication and especially in internal communication. In the past, written messages from insiders took the form of hard-copy memorandums. But recently e-mail has become the communication channel of choice. Estimates suggest that more than 90 percent of U.S. companies and more than 70 percent of foreign companies use e-mail.[2]

A primary function of e-mail is exchanging messages within organizations. Such internal communication is increasingly important today. Organizations are downsizing, flattening chains of command, forming work teams, and empowering rank-and-file employees. Given more power in making decisions, employees find that they need more information. They must collect, exchange, and evaluate information about the products and services they offer. Management also needs input from employees to respond rapidly to local and global market actions. This growing demand for information means increasing use of e-mail, although hard-copy memos are still written.

Developing skill in writing e-mails and memos brings you two important benefits. First, well-written documents are likely to achieve their goals. They create goodwill by being cautious, caring, and clear. They do not intentionally or unintentionally foment ill feelings. Second, well-written documents enhance your image within the organization. Individuals identified as competent, professional writers are noticed and rewarded; most often, they are the ones promoted into management positions.

Quick Check
Well-written e-mail messages and memos achieve their goals and reward their writers.

This chapter concentrates on routine e-mail messages and memos. These straightforward messages open with the main idea because their topics are not sensitive and require little persuasion. You'll study characteristics, the writing process, and organization for e-mail messages and memos. Because e-mail is such a new and powerful channel of communication, we'll devote special attention to using it safely and effectively. Finally, you'll learn to write procedure, information, request, reply, and confirmation e-mail messages and memos.

Characteristics of Successful E-Mail Messages and Memos

E-mail messages and memos are standard forms of communication within most organizations. They will probably become your most common business communication medium. These indispensable messages inform employees, request data, supply responses, confirm decisions, and give directions. Good e-mail messages and memos generally share certain characteristics.

Quick Check
Effective e-mail messages and memos contain guide-word headings, focus on a single topic, are concise and conversational, and often use graphic highlighting.

To, From, Date, Subject Headings. E-mails and memos contain guide-word headings as shown in Figure 5.1. These headings help readers immediately identify the date, origin, destination, and purpose of a message. Please note that outgoing e-mail messages will not show a dateline because it is inserted automatically by your computer. The position of the dateline in incoming e-mail messages varies

FIGURE 5.1 Typical E-Mail Message

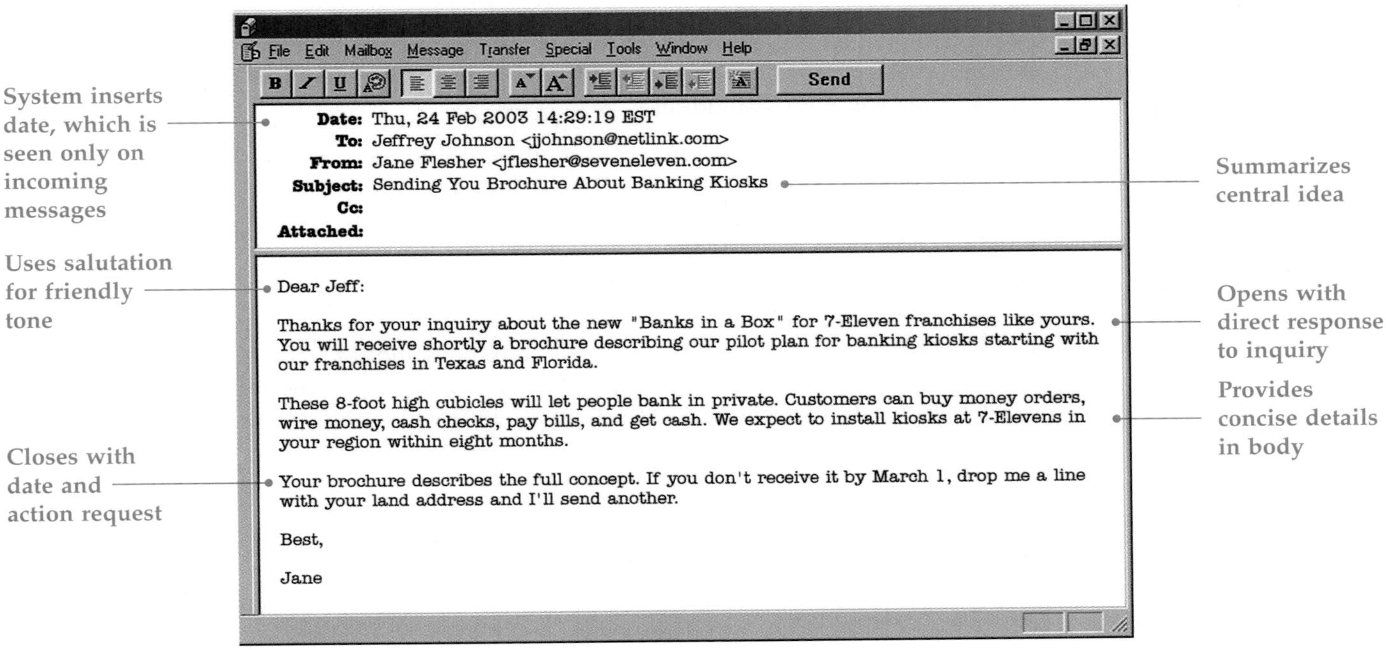
File Edit Mailbox Message Transfer Special Tools Window Help

Send

Date: Thu, 24 Feb 2003 14:29:19 EST
To: Jeffrey Johnson <jjohnson@netlink.com>
From: Jane Flesher <jflesher@seveneleven.com>
Subject: Sending You Brochure About Banking Kiosks
Cc:
Attached:

Dear Jeff:

Thanks for your inquiry about the new "Banks in a Box" for 7-Eleven franchises like yours. You will receive shortly a brochure describing our pilot plan for banking kiosks starting with our franchises in Texas and Florida.

These 8-foot high cubicles will let people bank in private. Customers can buy money orders, wire money, cash checks, pay bills, and get cash. We expect to install kiosks at 7-Elevens in your region within eight months.

Your brochure describes the full concept. If you don't receive it by March 1, drop me a line with your land address and I'll send another.

Best,

Jane
System inserts date, which is seen only on incoming messages
Uses salutation for friendly tone
Closes with date and action request
Summarizes central idea
Opens with direct response to inquiry
Provides concise details in body

E-mail messages can be warm and friendly without being emotional, gushy, or intimate. Your goals should be maintaining a conversational yet professional tone. And remember that e-mail messages are not telephone conversations. E-mails produce a permanent record.
© PhotoDisc/Getty Images

depending on your program. The position of the dateline in hard-copy memos also is flexible.

Single Topic.   Good e-mail messages and memos generally discuss only one topic. Notice that Figure 5.1 considers only one topic. Limiting the topic helps the receiver act on the subject and file it appropriately. A memo writer who, for example, describes a computer printer problem and also requests permission to attend a conference runs a 50 percent failure risk. The reader may respond to the printer problem but forget about the conference request.

Conversational Tone.   The tone of e-mail messages and memos is expected to be conversational because the communicators are usually familiar with one another. This means using occasional contractions (*I'm, you'll*), ordinary words, and first-person pronouns (*I/we*). Yet, the tone should also be professional. E-mail is so fast and so easy to use that some writers have been seduced into an "astonishing lack of professionalism."[3] Although warm and friendly, e-mail messages should not be emotional or sarcastic. They should never include remarks that would not be said to the face of an individual.

Conciseness.   As functional forms of communication, e-mails and memos contain only what's necessary to convey meaning and be courteous. Often, they require less background explanation and less attention to goodwill efforts than do letters to outsiders. Be particularly alert to eliminating wordiness. Avoid opening fillers (*there is, it is*), long lead-ins (*I am writing this memo to inform you that*), and wordy phrases (*because of the fact that*).

Graphic Highlighting.   E-mail messages and memos should be designed for quick reading and comprehension. One of the best ways to improve readability is through graphic highlighting techniques. Spotlight important items by setting them off with

- Letters, such as (a), (b), and (c), within the text
- Numerals, such as 1, 2, and 3, listed vertically
- Bullets—asterisks, black squares, raised periods, or other figures
- Headings
- Capital letters, underscores, boldface, and italics

In e-mail messages you should change your bullets to keyboard characters such as asterisks or plus signs (+) to be sure they transmit properly.

Ideas formerly buried within sentences or paragraphs stand out when targeted with graphic highlighting. Readers not only understand your message more rapidly and easily but also consider you efficient and well organized. In the following sentence notice how highlighting with letters makes the three items more visible and emphatic.

Without Highlighting
Nordstrom attracts upscale customers by featuring quality fashions, personalized service, and a generous return policy.

Highlighted With Letters
Nordstrom attracts upscale customers by featuring (a) quality fashions, (b) personalized service, and (c) a generous return policy.

If you have the space and wish to create even greater visual impact, you can list items vertically. Capitalize the word at the beginning of each line. Don't add end punctuation unless the statements are complete sentences. And be sure to use parallel construction whenever you itemize ideas. In the following examples, each item in the bulleted list follows an adjective/noun sequence. In the bulleted list, each item begins with a verb. Notice, too, that we use bullets when items have no particular order or importance. Numbers, however, are better to show a sequence or to identify items for reference. Bulleted or numbered lists may be flush left or indented 2 to 5 spaces.

✓ **Quick Check**
Lists that are offset from the text and introduced with bullets or numbers have a strong visual impact.

Highlighted With Bullets
Nordstrom attracts upscale customers by featuring the following:
- Quality fashions
- Personalized service
- Generous return policy

Highlighted With Numbers
Nordstrom advises recruiters to follow these steps in hiring applicants:
1. Examine application
2. Interview applicant
3. Check references

Headings are another choice for highlighting information. They force the writer to organize carefully so that similar data are grouped together. And they help the reader separate major ideas from details. Moreover, headings enable a busy reader to skim familiar or less important information. They also provide a quick preview or review. Although headings appear more often in reports, they are equally helpful in complex letters and memos. Here, they informally summarize items within a message:

✓ **Quick Check**
Headings help writers to organize information and enable readers to absorb important ideas quickly.

Highlighted With Headings
Nordstrom focuses on the following areas in the employment process:
- **Attracting applicants.** We advertise for qualified applicants, and we also encourage current employees to recommend good people.
- **Interviewing applicants.** Our specialized interviews include simulated customer encounters as well as scrutiny by supervisors.
- **Checking references.** We investigate every applicant thoroughly, including conversations with former employers and all listed references.

To highlight individual words in hard-copy memos, use CAPITAL letters, underlining, **bold** type, or *italics*. Be careful with these techniques, though, in e-mail messages. Words written in all caps seem to SHOUT at the reader; and italics, bold type, and underlining may not transmit properly.

"One of the most amazing features of the information revolution," says one technology vice president, is that the "momentum has turned back to the written word."[4] Businesspeople are writing more messages than ever before, and many of them are e-mail messages and memos. Although routine, memos and e-mail messages require preparation because they may travel farther than you expect. A novice market researcher in Illinois, for example, was eager to please her boss. When asked to report on the progress of her project, she e-mailed a quick summary of her work. Later that week a vice president asked her boss how the project was progressing. Her boss forwarded the market researcher's hurried memo. Unfortunately, the resulting poor impression was difficult for the new employee to overcome.

Careful writing takes time—especially at first. By following a systematic plan and practicing your skill, however, you can speed up your efforts and greatly improve the product. The effort you make to improve your communication skills can pay big dividends. Frequently, your speaking and writing abilities determine how much influence you'll have in your organization. To make the best impression and to write the most effective messages, follow the three-phase writing process.

PHASE 1: ANALYSIS, ANTICIPATION, AND ADAPTATION

In Phase 1 (prewriting) you'll need to spend some time analyzing your task. It's amazing how many of us are ready to put our pens or computers into gear before engaging our minds. Ask yourself several important questions:

- **Do I really need to write this e-mail or memo?** A phone call or a quick visit to a nearby coworker might solve the problem—and save the time and expense of a written message. On the other hand, some written messages are needed to provide a permanent record. Should you write a hard-copy memo or send an

Quick Check

A systematic plan helps you write faster and more effectively.

Quick Check

The first phase of the writing process focuses on prewriting: analyzing, anticipating, and adapting.

Disney CEO Michael Eisner thinks long and hard before dashing off e-mail messages, especially when he's angry. "I learned early in the hard paper world of the '70s that when I was annoyed with someone, I should write it down in a memo. I would then put the memo in my desk drawer and leave it there until the next day." By the next morning, his anger had passed; and he realized that telephoning or seeing the other person was a better way to respond. © AP/Wide World Photos, Inc.

e-mail? If a message must be sent quickly, if formality is not required, and if the content is not complex, send an e-mail. Otherwise, send a hard-copy memo.

- **Why am I writing?** Know why you are writing and what you hope to achieve. This will help you recognize what the important points are and where to place them.
- **How will the reader react?** Visualize the reader and the effect your message will have. Consider ways to shape the message to benefit the reader.

PHASE 2: RESEARCH, ORGANIZATION, AND COMPOSITION

In Phase 2 (writing) you'll first want to check the files, gather documentation, and prepare your message. Make an outline of the points you wish to cover. For short messages you can jot down notes on the document you are answering. Be sure to prepare for revision, because excellence is rarely achieved on the first effort.

✓ *Quick Check*

The second phase of the writing process involves gathering background information, organizing ideas, and composing the first draft.

PHASE 3: REVISION, PROOFREADING, AND EVALUATION

Careful and caring writers revise their messages, proofread the final copy, and make an effort to evaluate the success of their communication by planning for feedback.

- **Revise for clarity.** Viewed from the receiver's perspective, are the ideas clear? Do they need more explanation? If the memo is passed on to others, will they need further explanation? Consider having a colleague critique your message if it is an important one.
- **Proofread for correctness.** Are the sentences complete and punctuated properly? Did you overlook any typos or misspelled words? Remember to use your spell checker and grammar checker to proofread your message before sending it.
- **Plan for feedback.** How will you know whether this message is successful? You can improve feedback by asking questions (such as *Do you agree with these suggestions?*) and by making it easy for the receiver to respond.

✓ *Quick Check*

The third phase of the writing process involves revising for clarity, proofreading for accuracy, and evaluating for effectiveness.

© Grantland Enterprises; http://www.grantland.net

USING E-MAIL SAFELY AND EFFECTIVELY

Early e-mail users were encouraged to ignore style and grammar. They thought that "words on the fly," as e-mail messages were considered, required little editing or proofing. Correspondents used emoticons (such as sideways happy faces) to express their emotions. And some e-mail today is still quick and dirty. But as this communication channel matures, messages are becoming more proper and more professional.

Wise e-mail business communicators, such as Michael Eisner at Disney, are aware not only of the benefits of e-mail but also of its dangers. They know that thoughtless messages can cause irreparable harm. They know that their messages can travel (intentionally or unintentionally) long distances. A quickly drafted note may end up in the boss's mailbox or be forwarded to an adversary's box. "It's as if people put their brains on hold when they write e-mail," said one expert. They think that e-mail "is a substitute for a phone call, and that's the danger."[5] Making matters worse, computers—like elephants and spurned lovers—never forget.[6] Even erased messages can remain on disk drives. Monica Lewinsky learned this in relation to "deleted files" extracted from her home computer.[7] Microsoft founder Bill Gates also got burned when his old e-mail files were subpoenaed in the Microsoft monopoly trial. Careless and casual e-mail messages have become "smoking guns" in workplace lawsuits.[8] That is, e-mail messages with damaging statements have been introduced as evidence in trials.

SMART E-MAIL PRACTICES

Despite its dangers and limitations, however, e-mail is increasingly the preferred choice for sending many business messages. Because e-mail has become a mainstream channel of communication, it's important to take the time to organize your thoughts, compose carefully, and be concerned with correct grammar and punctuation.

Getting Started.   The following pointers will help you get off to a good start in using e-mail safely and effectively.

- **Compose offline.** Instead of dashing off hasty messages, consider using your word processing program to write offline. Then upload your message to the e-mail network. This avoids "self destructing" (losing all your writing through some glitch or pressing the wrong key) when working online.
- **Get the address right.** E-mail addresses are sometimes complex, often illogical, and always unforgiving. Omit one character or misread the letter *l* for the number *1*, and your message bounces. Solution: Use your electronic address book for people you write frequently. And double-check every address that you key in manually. Also be sure that you don't reply to a group of receivers when you intend to answer only one.

© Grantland Enterprises; http://www.grantland.net

The normally tranquil beachside town of Clearwater, Florida, is still reeling from e-mail misuse by local officials. In separate incidents, officials lost their jobs over sexually provocative, discriminatory, or private-use messages. Clearwater's struggle with e-mail policy is not unique. Many organizations need to develop a computer-use policy and train employees in its application.
© Carl & Ann F. Purcell/CORBIS

- **Avoid misleading subject lines.** With an abundance of "spam" (unwanted commercial e-mail) clogging most inboxes, make sure your subject line is relevant and helpful. Generic tags such as *Hello, Important,* and *Great Deal* may cause your message to be deleted before it is opened.

Content, Tone, and Correctness.   Although e-mail seems as casual as a telephone call, it's not. Because it produces a permanent record, think carefully about what you say and how you say it.

✓ *Quick Check*

Avoid wordiness and don't send confidential, inflammatory, angry, sloppy, or "tongue-in-cheek" messages.

- **Be concise.** Don't burden readers with unnecessary information. Remember that monitors are small and typefaces are often difficult to read. Organize your ideas tightly.
- **Don't send anything you wouldn't want published.** Because e-mail seems like a telephone call or a person-to-person conversation, writers sometimes send sensitive, confidential, inflammatory, or potentially embarrassing messages. Beware! E-mail creates a permanent record that often does not go away even when deleted. And every message is a corporate communication that can be used against you or your employer. Don't write anything that you wouldn't want your boss, your family, or a judge to read.
- **Don't use e-mail to avoid contact.** E-mail is inappropriate for breaking bad news or for resolving arguments. For example, it's improper to fire a person by e-mail. It's also not a good channel for dealing with conflict with supervisors, subordinates, or others. If there's any possibility of hurt feelings, pick up the telephone or pay the person a visit.
- **Never respond when you're angry.** Always allow some time to cool off before shooting off a response to an upsetting message. You often come up with different and better alternatives after thinking about what was said. If possible, iron out differences in person.
- **Care about correctness.** People are still judged by their writing, whether electronic or paper-based. Sloppy e-mail messages (with missing apostrophes, haphazard spelling, and stream-of-consciousness writing) make readers work too hard. They resent not only the information but also the writer.

Using E-Mail Safely and Effectively

- **Resist humor and tongue-in-cheek comments.** Without the nonverbal cues conveyed by your face and your voice, humor can easily be misunderstood.

Netiquette.   Although e-mail is a new communication channel, a number of rules of polite online interaction are emerging.

- **Limit any tendency to send blanket copies.** Send copies only to people who really need to see a message. It is unnecessary to document every business decision and action with an electronic paper trail.
- **Never send spam.** Most businesspeople detest receiving unsolicited advertisements (*spam*) either by fax or e-mail. Legislation is pending to prohibit unsolicited e-mail.
- **Consider using identifying labels.** When appropriate, add one of the following labels to the subject line: ACTION (action required, please respond); FYI (for your information, no response needed); RE (this is a reply to another message); URGENT (please respond immediately).
- **Use capital letters only for emphasis or for titles.** Avoid writing entire messages in all caps, which is like SHOUTING.
- **Announce attachments.** If you're sending a lengthy attachment, tell your receiver. You might also ask what format is preferred.
- **Don't forward without permission.** Obtain approval before forwarding a message.

Replying to E-Mail.   The following tips can save you time and frustration when answering messages.

- **Scan all messages in your inbox before replying to each individually.** Because subsequent messages often affect the way you respond, read them all first (especially all those from the same individual).
- **Don't automatically return the sender's message.** When replying, cut and paste the relevant parts. Avoid irritating your recipients by returning the entire "thread" (sequence of messages) on a topic.
- **Revise the subject line if the topic changes.** When replying or continuing an e-mail exchange, revise the subject line as the topic changes.

Personal Use.   Remember that office computers are meant for work-related communication.

- **Don't use company computers for personal matters.** Unless your company specifically allows it, never use your employer's computers for personal messages, personal shopping, or entertainment.
- **Assume that all e-mail is monitored.** Employers legally have the right to monitor e-mail, and many do.

Cathy

CATHY © Cathy Guisewite. Reprinted with permission of Universal Press Syndicate. All rights reserved.

Other Smart E-Mail Practices. Depending on your messages and audience, the following tips promote effective electronic communication.

- **Use design to improve the readability of longer messages.** When a message requires several screens, help the reader with headings, bulleted listings, side headings, and perhaps an introductory summary that describes what will follow. Although these techniques lengthen a message, they shorten reading time.
- **Consider cultural differences.** When using this borderless tool, be especially clear and precise in your language. Remember that figurative clichés (*pull up stakes, playing second fiddle*), sports references (*hit a home run, play by the rules*), and slang (*cool, stoked*) cause confusion abroad.
- **Double-check before hitting the *Send* button.** Have you included everything? Avoid the necessity of sending a second message, which makes you look careless. Use spell-check and reread for fluency before sending.

FORMATTING E-MAIL MESSAGES

Since e-mail is a developing communication channel, its formatting and usage conventions are still fluid. Users and authorities, for instance, do not always agree on what's appropriate for salutations and closings. The following suggestions, however, can guide you in formatting most e-mail messages, but always check with your organization to observe its practices.

Guide Words.   Following the guide word *To*, some writers insert just the recipient's electronic address, such as *<hgrattan@accountpro.com>*. Other writers prefer to include the receiver's full name plus the electronic address, as shown in Figure 5.2. By including full names in the *To* and *From* slots, both receivers and senders are better able to identify the message. By the way, the order of *Date, To, From, Subject,* and other guide words varies depending on your e-mail program and whether you are sending or receiving the message.

Most e-mail programs automatically add the current date after *Date*. On the *Cc* line (which stands for *carbon* or *courtesy copy*) you can type the address of anyone who is to receive a copy of the message. Remember, though, to send copies only to those people directly involved with the message. Most e-mail programs also include a line for *Bcc* (*blind carbon copy*). This sends a copy without the addressee's knowledge. Many savvy writers today use *Bcc* for the names and addresses of a list of receivers, a technique that avoids revealing the addresses to the entire group. On the subject line, identify the subject of the memo. Be sure to include enough information to be clear and compelling.

Salutation.   What to do about a salutation is tricky. Many writers omit a salutation because they consider the message a memo. In the past, hard-copy memos were sent only to company insiders, and salutations were omitted. However, when e-mail messages travel to outsiders, omitting a salutation seems curt and unfriendly. Because the message is more like a letter, a salutation is appropriate (such as *Dear Helen; Hi, Helen; Greetings;* or just *Helen*). Including a salutation is also a visual cue to where the message begins. Many messages are transmitted or forwarded with such long headers that finding the beginning of the message can be difficult. A salutation helps, as shown in Figure 5.2. Other writers do not use a salutation; instead, they use the name of the recipient in the first sentence.

Body.   The body of an e-mail message should be typed with uppercase and lowercase characters—never in all uppercase or all lowercase characters. Cover just one topic, and try to keep the total message under three screens in length. To assist you, many e-mail programs have basic text-editing features, such as cut, copy, paste, and word-wrap. However, avoid boldface and italics because they may cre-

FIGURE 5.2 E-Mail Message Illustrating Formatting

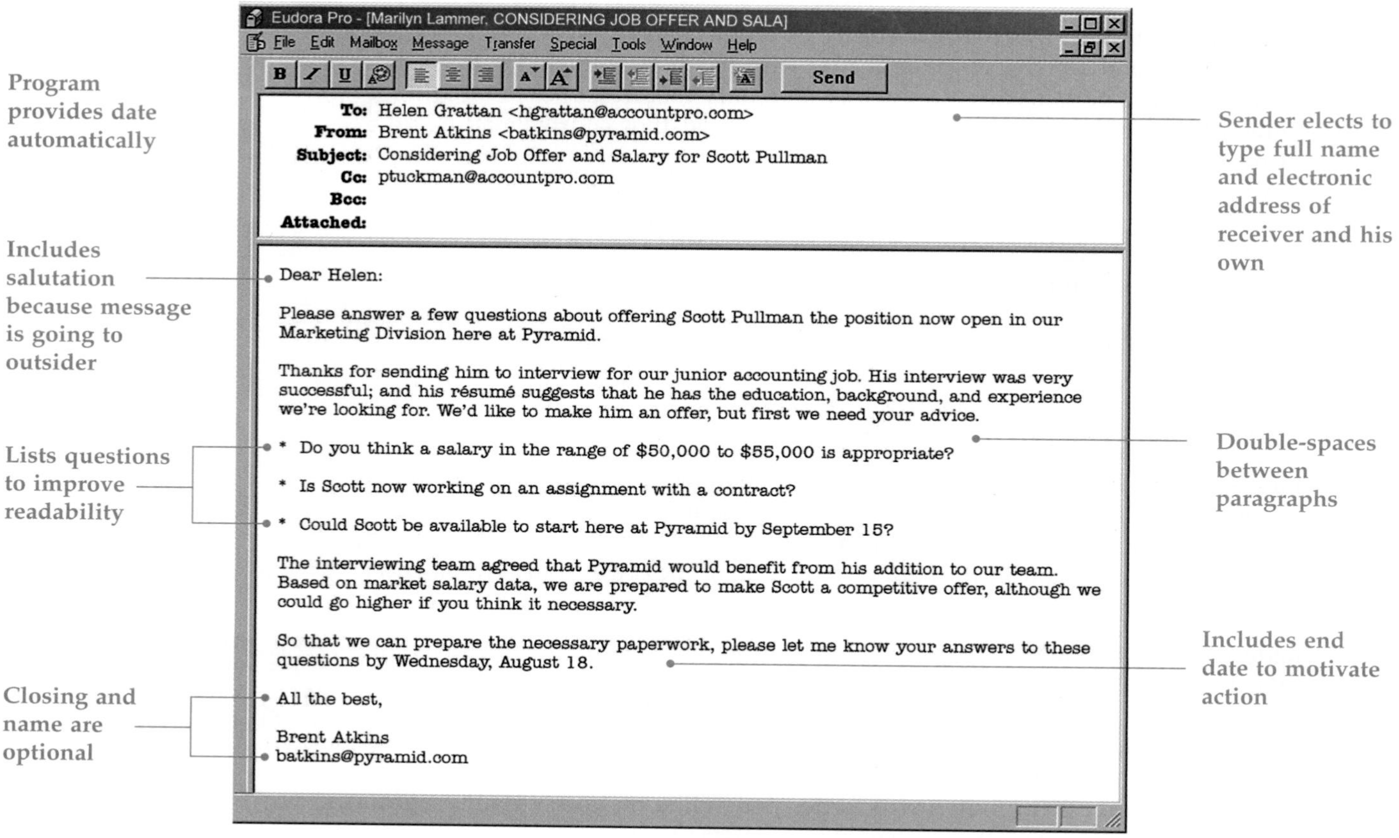

Program provides date automatically

Includes salutation because message is going to outsider

Lists questions to improve readability

Closing and name are optional

Sender elects to type full name and electronic address of receiver and his own

Double-spaces between paragraphs

Includes end date to motivate action

```
Eudora Pro - [Marilyn Lammer, CONSIDERING JOB OFFER AND SALA]    [_][□][X]
File  Edit  Mailbox  Message  Transfer  Special  Tools  Window  Help    [_][β][X]

B  I  U  🌐  ☰ ☰ ☰  A˅ A˄  *≣ ≣ ≣ ≣  ⓐ      Send

       To:  Helen Grattan <hgrattan@accountpro.com>
     From:  Brent Atkins <batkins@pyramid.com>
  Subject:  Considering Job Offer and Salary for Scott Pullman
       Cc:  ptuckman@accountpro.com
      Bcc:
  Attached:

Dear Helen:

Please answer a few questions about offering Scott Pullman the position now open in our
Marketing Division here at Pyramid.

Thanks for sending him to interview for our junior accounting job. His interview was very
successful; and his résumé suggests that he has the education, background, and experience
we're looking for. We'd like to make him an offer, but first we need your advice.

*  Do you think a salary in the range of $50,000 to $55,000 is appropriate?

*  Is Scott now working on an assignment with a contract?

*  Could Scott be available to start here at Pyramid by September 15?

The interviewing team agreed that Pyramid would benefit from his addition to our team.
Based on market salary data, we are prepared to make Scott a competitive offer, although we
could go higher if you think it necessary.

So that we can prepare the necessary paperwork, please let me know your answers to these
questions by Wednesday, August 18.

All the best,

Brent Atkins
batkins@pyramid.com
```

TIPS FOR FORMATTING E-MAIL MESSAGES

- After *To,* type the receiver's electronic address. If you include the receiver's name, enclose the address in angle brackets.
- After *From,* type your name and electronic address, if your program does not insert it automatically.
- After *Subject,* provide a clear description of your message.
- Insert the addresses of anyone receiving carbon or blind copies.
- Include a salutation (such as *Dear Helen, Hi Helen, Greetings*) or weave the receiver's name into the first line (see Figure 5.5). Some writers omit a salutation.
- Use a line length of no more than 60 characters if you expect your message to be forwarded.
- Generally use word wrap rather than pressing *Enter* at line ends.
- Double-space (press *Enter*) between paragraphs.
- Do not type in all caps or in all lowercase letters.
- Include a complimentary close, your name, and your address if you wish.

ate a string of control characters that may cause chaos on the recipient's computer.

Closing Lines.   Writers of e-mail messages sent within organizations may omit closings and even skip their names at the end of messages. They can omit these items because receivers recognize them from identification in the opening lines. But for outside messages, a writer might include a closing such as *Cheers* or *All the best* followed by the writer's name and e-mail address (because some systems do not transmit your address automatically). If the recipient is unlikely to know you, it's wise to include your title and organization. Some veteran e-mail users include a *signature file* with identifying information embellished with keyboard art. Use restraint, however, because signature files take up precious bandwidth (Internet capacity).

DEVELOPING A WRITING PLAN FOR E-MAIL MESSAGES AND MEMOS

Quick Check
A writing plan helps you organize a complete message.

In this book you will be shown a number of writing plans appropriate for different messages. These plans provide a skeleton; they are the bones of a message. Writers provide the flesh. Simply plugging in phrases or someone else's words won't work. Good writers provide details and link their ideas with transitions to create fluent and meaningful messages. However, a writing plan helps you get started and gives you ideas about what to include. At first, you will probably rely on these plans considerably. As you progress, they will become less important. Later in the book no plans are provided.

Here is a general writing plan for a routine e-mail message or memo that is not expected to create displeasure or resistance. You can see how this writing plan is implemented in the fully formatted hard-copy memo shown in Figure 5.3.

WRITING PLAN FOR ROUTINE E-MAIL MESSAGES AND MEMOS

- *Subject line:* Summarize memo contents.
- *Opening:* State the main idea.
- *Body:* Provide background data and explain the main idea.
- *Closing:* Request action, summarize the message, or present a closing thought.

WRITING THE SUBJECT LINE

Quick Check
A subject line must be concise but meaningful.

Probably the most important part of an e-mail message or memo is the subject line. It should summarize the central idea and provide quick identification. It is usually written in an abbreviated style, often without articles (*a, an, the*). It need not be a complete sentence, and it does not end with a period. E-mail subject lines are particularly important, since meaningless ones may cause readers to delete a message without ever opening it. Good subject lines, such as the following, are specific, eye-catching, and talking (that is, they often contain a verb form):

Effective Subject Lines
Three Promotional Items to Showcase at Our Next Trade Show
Beefing Up Our Messaging Capabilities
Staff Meeting to Discuss Summer Vacation Schedules

Ineffective Subject Lines
Trade Show
New Software
Meeting

BEGINNING WITH THE MAIN IDEA

Quick Check
Frontloading means revealing the main idea immediately.

Most e-mails and memos cover routine, nonsensitive information that can be handled in a straightforward manner. Begin by frontloading; that is, reveal the main idea immediately. Even though the purpose of a memo or e-mail is summarized in the subject line, that purpose should be restated—and amplified—in the first sentence. Some readers skip the subject line and plunge right into the first sentence. Notice how the following indirect openers can be improved by frontloading.

FIGURE 5.3   Hard-Copy Memo Illustrating Writing Plan and Formatting

Guide words: Align all information after the longest item

Subject Line: Summarizes purpose and gains attention

Opening: Grabs attention and introduces purpose

Body: Explains purpose and uses list for readability

Closing: Includes action request, deadline, and reasons

2 inches

MEMO

DATE: November 8, 200x

1 blank line

TO: All Staff Members

FROM: Pamela Brune, Manager *PB*
            Human Resources Department

SUBJECT: Recommended Options for Child-Care Benefits

2 blank lines

We need your input! Members of your employee council and representatives from management recommend the following four options for child-care benefits. However, your feedback will determine the final choice.

- **On-site day-care centers.** This option accommodates employees' children on the premises. Weekly rates would be competitive with local day-care facilities. Although this option is most costly, it is worth pursuing if local facilities are deficient.

- **Off-site centers in conjunction with other local employers.** We are looking into the possibility of developing central facilities to be shared with nearby firms.

- **Neighborhood child-care centers.** We would contract with local centers to buy open slots for employees' children, perhaps at a discount.

- **Sick-child services.** This plan would provide employees with alternatives to missing work when children are ill. We are investigating sick-child programs at local hospitals, as well as services that send workers to employees' homes to look after sick children.

Before December 15 let your employee council representative know how you feel about these options. Once we have cost estimates and once we have your feedback, we can make a better decision. In January our benefits package will be negotiated.

TIPS FOR FORMATTING HARD-COPY MEMOS
- Leave a 2-inch top margin.
- Set side margins at 1 to 1¼ inches.
- Leave a blank line between the heading guide words.
- Align the information following the headings.
- For the subject line use (1) initial capital letters for the main words or (2) all capital letters.
- Leave two blank lines between *Subject* and the first line of the memo.
- Single-space within the memo and double-space between paragraphs.
- Sign your initials after your name on the *From* line.

Indirect Opening

This is to inform you that for the past six months we have been examining benefits as part of our negotiation package under a contract that expires soon.

As you may know, employees in Accounting have been complaining about eye fatigue as a result of the overhead fluorescent lighting.

Direct Opening

Please review the following four changes in our benefit package and let us know your preference by January 1.

To improve lighting in Accounting, I recommend that we purchase high-intensity desk lamps.

EXPLAINING CLEARLY IN THE BODY

In the body of the message, explain the main idea. If you are asking for detailed information, arrange your questions in logical order. If you are providing information, group similar information together. The body of a letter may consist of more than one paragraph. It may consist of a list. When considerable data are involved, use a separate paragraph for each topic. Work for effective transitions between paragraphs.

Design your data for easy comprehension by using graphic highlighting techniques you learned about earlier. All these techniques make readers understand important points quickly. Compare the following two versions of the same message. Notice how the graphic devices of bullets, columns, headings, and white space make the main points easier to comprehend.

Hard-to-Read Paragraph
Effective immediately are the following air travel guidelines. Between now and December 31, only account executives may take company-approved trips. These individuals will be allowed to take a maximum of two trips per year, and they are to travel economy or budget class only.

Improved With Graphic Highlighting
Effective immediately are the following air travel guidelines:
- Who may travel: Account executives only
- How many trips: A maximum of two trips yearly
- By when: Between now and December 31
- Air class: Economy or budget class only

In addition to highlighting important information, pay attention to the tone of your message. Although e-mail messages and memos are generally informal, they should also be professional. Remember that e-mail messages are not telephone conversations. Don't be overly casual, jocular, or blunt. Do attempt to establish a conversational tone by using occasional contractions (*won't, didn't, couldn't*) and personal pronouns (*I, me, we*).

CLOSING WITH ACTION INFORMATION

Generally, end an e-mail message or memo with (1) action information, dates, or deadlines; (2) a summary of the message; or (3) a closing thought. Here again the value of thinking through the message before actually writing it becomes apparent. The closing is where readers look for deadlines and action language. An effective closing might be, *Please submit your report by June 15 so that we can have your data before our July planning session.*

In more complex messages a summary of main points may be an appropriate closing. If no action request is made and a closing summary is unnecessary, you might end with a simple concluding thought (*I'm glad to answer your questions* or *This sounds like a useful project*). Although you needn't close messages to coworkers with goodwill statements such as those found in letters to customers or clients, some closing thought is often necessary to prevent a feeling of abruptness.

Closings can show gratitude or encourage feedback with remarks such as *I sincerely appreciate your cooperation* or *What are your ideas on this proposal?* Other closings look forward to what's next, such as *How would you like to proceed?* Avoid trite expressions, such as *Please let me know if I may be of further assistance.*

Whenever possible, the closing paragraph of a request should be *end dated*. An end date sets a deadline for the requested action and gives a reason for this action to be completed by the deadline. Such end dating prevents procrastination

Quick Check
Organize the message logically, keeping similar information grouped together.

Quick Check
Graphic highlighting (bullets, numbered lists, headings) makes information easier to read and review.

Quick Check
The end of a memo should include action information (such as a deadline), a summarizing statement, or a closing thought.

FIGURE 5.4   Procedure E-Mail BEFORE Revision

BEFORE Revision

Uses vague, negative subject line ———

Fails to pinpoint main idea in opening ———

Uses negative expression and fails to explain new procedure clearly ———

Uses threats instead of showing benefits to reader ———

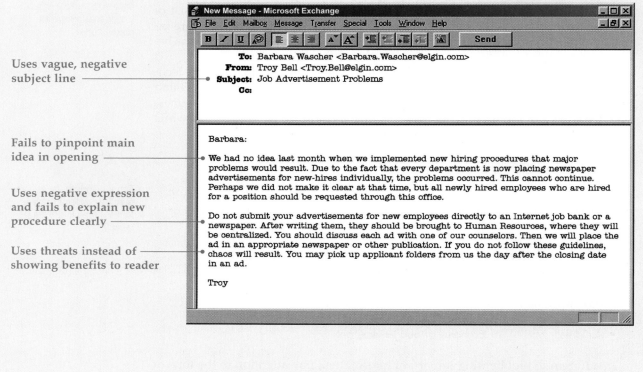

> New Message - Microsoft Exchange
>
> File Edit Mailbox Message Transfer Special Tools Window Help
>
> B *I* U ... Send
>
> **To:** Barbara Wascher <Barbara.Wascher@elgin.com>
> **From:** Troy Bell <Troy.Bell@elgin.com>
> **Subject:** Job Advertisement Problems
> **Cc:**
>
> Barbara:
>
> We had no idea last month when we implemented new hiring procedures that major problems would result. Due to the fact that every department is now placing newspaper advertisements for new-hires individually, the problems occurred. This cannot continue. Perhaps we did not make it clear at that time, but all newly hired employees who are hired for a position should be requested through this office.
>
> Do not submit your advertisements for new employees directly to an Internet job bank or a newspaper. After writing them, they should be brought to Human Resources, where they will be centralized. You should discuss each ad with one of our counselors. Then we will place the ad in an appropriate newspaper or other publication. If you do not follow these guidelines, chaos will result. You may pick up applicant folders from us the day after the closing date in an ad.
>
> Troy

and allows the reader to plan a course of action to ensure completion by the date given. Giving a reason adds credibility to a deadline. For example, *Please submit your order by December 1 so that sufficient labels will be on hand for mailing the year-end reports January 15.*

You've studied a basic plan for writing e-mail messages and memos, and you've learned how to highlight ideas with listing techniques. Now you'll apply these techniques to three specific kinds of e-mails and memos: (1) messages that send information, including procedures and instruction, (2) messages that make requests, and (3) messages that reply.

E-MAILS AND MEMOS THAT RELATE INFORMATION, PROCEDURES, AND INSTRUCTIONS

✓ **Quick Check**

Information and procedure memos must be so clear that further correspondence is unnecessary.

Many e-mail messages and memos distribute information, describe procedures, and deliver instructions. These messages typically flow downward from management to employees and relate to the daily operation of an organization. They have one primary function: conveying your idea so clearly that no further explanation (return message, telephone call, or personal visit) is necessary.

Messages that explain procedures have to be particularly clear. One way to improve clarity is to discuss what *can* be done rather than what *can't* be done. Figure 5.4 shows a procedure memo that describes a new procedure for submitting job advertisements. Notice in the "before" draft that the writer dwells on telling

FIGURE 5.4 Procedure E-Mail AFTER Revision

AFTER Revision

New Message - Microsoft Exchange

File Edit Mailbox Message Transfer Special Tools Window Help

[B] [I] [U] [✎] [≡ ≡ ≡] [A⌄ A⌃] [⊞ ⊞ ⊞ ⊞ ⊠]   **Send**

To: Barbara Wascher <Barbara.Wascher@elgin.com>
From: Troy Bell <Troy.Bell@elgin.com>
Subject: New Procedure for Placing Job Advertisements ●————— Provides informative, upbeat subject line
Cc:

Barbara:

Effective today, all advertisements for departmental job openings should be routed ●————— Summarizes main idea concisely
through the Human Resources Department.

A major problem resulted from the change in hiring procedures implemented last month.
Each department began placing advertisements for new-hires individually, when all such ●————— Explains why change in procedures is necessary
requests should be centralized in this office. To process applications more efficiently,
please follow this procedure:

1. Write an advertisement for a position in your department. ●

2. Bring the ad to Human Resources and discuss it with one of our counselors.   Starts each listed item with a verb

3. Let Human Resources place the ad with an appropriate newspaper or Web agency.

4. Pick up applicant folders from Human Resources the day following the closing date ●
   provided in the ad.

Following these guidelines will save you work and will also enable Human Resources to help
you fill your openings more quickly. Call Ms. Conniff at Ext. 2505 if you have questions ●————— Closes by reinforcing benefits to reader
about this procedure.

Troy

---

readers what not to do (*Do not submit advertisements for new employees directly to an Internet job bank or a newspaper.*) In the "after" version, the writer emphasizes what can be done, making the message more helpful and more positive.

Another way to enhance clarity is to break the procedure or instructions down into numbered steps. List the steps in chronological order. Begin each step with an active verb in the command mode. Notice in the "after" version of Figure 5.4 that numbered items begin with *Write, Bring, Let,* and *Pick up.* It's not always easy to force all the steps into this kind of command language. But if you try out different wording, you can usually find a verb that works. Why go to so much trouble to make lists and achieve parallelism? Because readers can comprehend what you have said much more quickly. And it makes you look professional and efficient.

In writing procedure and information messages, be careful of tone. Today's managers and team leaders seek employee participation and cooperation. These goals can't be achieved, though, if the writer sounds like a dictator or an autocrat. Avoid making accusations and fixing blame. Rather, explain changes, give reasons, and suggest benefits to the reader. Assume that employees want to contribute to the success of the organization and to their own achievement. Notice in the revised e-mail message in Figure 5.4 that the writer tells readers that they will save time and have their open positions filled more quickly if they follow the new procedures.

For more examples, links, and information on how to write instructions, go to the Guffey Web site (http://www.westwords.com/guffey/students.html) and click "Book Support" and "Supplement: How to Write Instructions."

Quick Check
Procedures and instructions often include numbered steps that are parallel and written in "command" language (*Do this; don't do that*).

Quick Check
The tone of a request message should encourage cooperation.

In requesting routine information or action within an organization, the direct approach works best. Generally, this means asking for information or making the request without first providing elaborate explanations and justifications. Remember that readers are usually thinking, "Why me? Why am I receiving this?" Readers can understand the explanation better once they know what you are requesting.

If you are seeking answers to questions, you have two options for opening the message: (1) ask the most important question first, followed by an explanation and then the other questions, or (2) use a polite command, such as *Please answer the following questions regarding. . . .* In the body of the memo, explain and justify your request. When you must ask many questions, list them, being careful to phrase them similarly.

Requests should be courteous and respectful, as illustrated in Figure 5.5. Charles Hipps, vice president of Employee Relations at PowerData, asks his managers whether they would like to implement a casual dress day. Notice that his e-mail opens with an immediate description of his request. The body explains the reasoning behind his request, and a list asks specific questions to be answered. He closes by asking that the responses be made before May 5 because the information will be used for a Management Council meeting May 8. Providing an end date helps the reader know how to plan a response so that action is completed by the date given. Expressions such as *do it whenever you can* or *complete it as soon as possible* make little impression on procrastinators or very busy people. It's always wise to provide a specific date for completion. Dates can be entered into calendars to serve as reminders.

> ✓ **Quick Check**
>
> In messages that ask questions, open with the most important question or with a polite command (*Please answer the following . . .*).

FIGURE 5.5   E-Mail Message That Requests

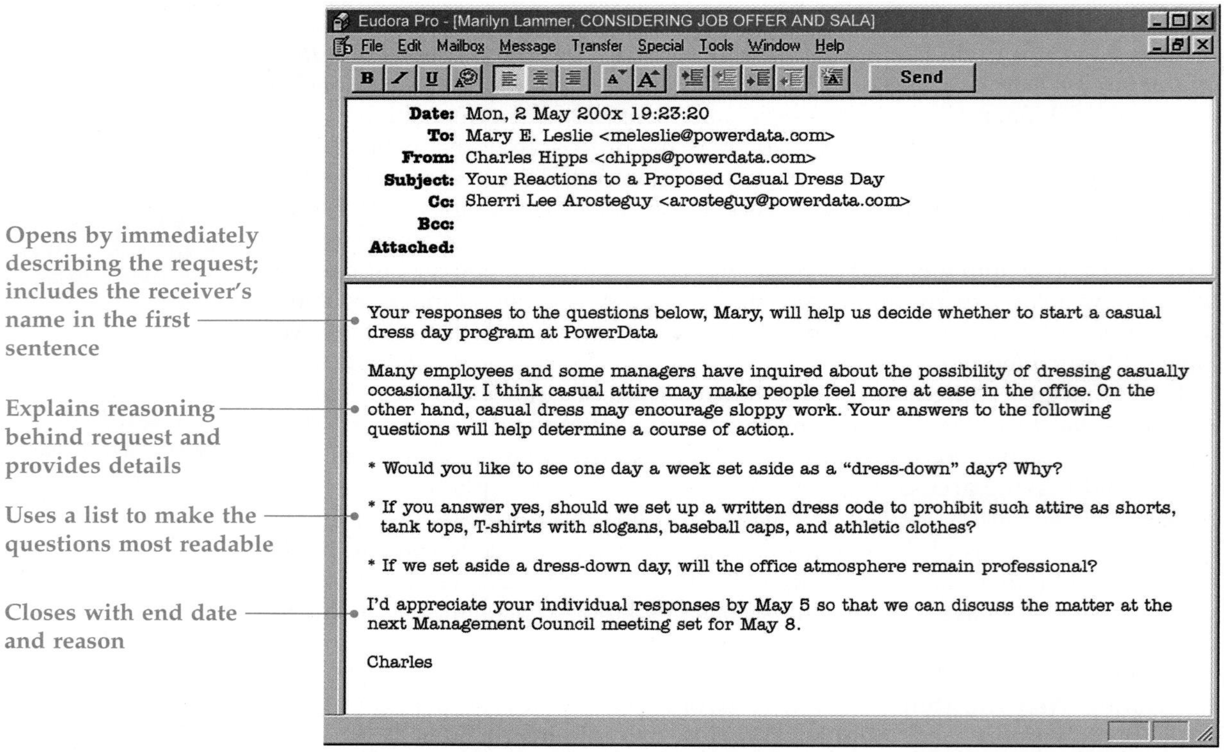

Opens by immediately describing the request; includes the receiver's name in the first sentence

Explains reasoning behind request and provides details

Uses a list to make the questions most readable

Closes with end date and reason

Much office correspondence reacts or responds to e-mail messages, memos, and other documents. When responding to a document, follow these preparatory steps:

1. Collect whatever information is necessary.
2. Organize your thoughts.
3. Make a brief outline of the points you plan to cover.

Quick Check

In responding to messages, gather background information and organize your ideas in a brief outline.

Begin the memo with a clear statement of the main idea, which often is a summary of the contents of the memo. Avoid wordy and dated openings such as *Pursuant to your request of January 20, I am herewith including the information you wanted.* Although many business messages actually sound like the preceding, they waste time and say little.

Notice in Figure 5.6 that Mary Leslie, manager of Legal Support Services, uses a straightforward opening in responding to her boss's request for information.

FIGURE 5.6   Memo That Responds

PowerData Associates
Interoffice Memo

DATE: May 4, 200x

TO: Charles Hipps, Vice President, Employee Relations

FROM: Mary E. Leslie, Manager, Legal Support Services   *MEL*

SUBJECT: Reactions to Proposed Casual Dress Day Program

Here are my reactions, Charles, to your inquiry about a casual dress day program made in your e-mail message of May 2.

- **Establish a dress-down day?** Yes, I would like to see such a day. In my department we now have a number of employees with flex schedules. They perform part of their work at home, where they can be as casual as they wish. Employees confined here in the office are a little resentful. I think a dress-down day could offer some compensation to those who come to the office daily.

- **Implement a dress code?** By all means! We definitely need a written dress code not only to establish standards but also to protect the company from frivolous lawsuits.

- **Professional office atmosphere?** I would hope that casual dress would not promote casual work attitudes as well. We must establish that professionalism is nonnegotiable. For example, we can't allow two-hour lunches or entire afternoons spent gossiping instead of working. Moreover, I think we should be careful in allowing casual dress only on the designated day, once a week.

A casual attire program can be beneficial and improve morale. But we definitely need a dress code in place at the beginning of the program. Let me know if I may assist in implementing a casual dress day program.

Right-margin annotations:
- Announces main idea
- Summarizes main idea and refers to previous message
- Arranges responses in order of original request and uses boldface headings to emphasize and clarify groupings
- Closes with reassuring remark and offer of further assistance

---

She refers to his request, announces the information to follow, and identifies the date of the original message. Mary decides to answer with a standard hard-copy memo because she considers her reactions private and because she thinks that Vice President Hipps would like to have a permanent record of each manager's reactions to take to the Management Council meeting. She also knows that she is well within the deadline set for a response.

The body of a response memo provides the information requested. Its organization generally follows the sequence of the request. In Mary's memo she answers the questions as her boss presented them. However, she further clarifies the information by providing summarizing headings in bold type. These headings emphasize the groupings and help the reader see immediately what information is covered. The memo closes with a reassuring summary.

SUMMING UP AND LOOKING FORWARD

✓ **Quick Check**

In response messages, the use of paragraph headings helps readers grasp content more quickly.

Memorandums and e-mail messages serve as vital channels of information within business offices. They use a standardized format to request and deliver information. Because e-mail messages are increasingly a preferred channel choice, this chapter presented many techniques for sending safe and effective e-mail messages. You learned to apply the direct strategy in writing messages that inform, request, and respond. You also learned to use bullets, numbers, and parallel form for listing information so that main points stand out. In the next chapter you will extend the direct strategy to writing letters that make requests and respond to requests.

Interactive Learning @ http://www.westwords.com/guffey/students.html
Prepare for tests and reinforce your chapter knowledge with interactive quizzes and crossword puzzles.

CRITICAL THINKING

1. How can the writer of a business memo or an e-mail message develop a conversational tone and still be professional? Why do e-mail writers sometimes forget to be professional?
2. What factors would help you decide whether to write a memo, send an e-mail, make a telephone call, leave a voice mail message, or deliver a message in person?
3. Why are lawyers and technology experts warning companies to store, organize, and manage computer data, including e-mail, with sharper diligence?
4. Discuss the ramifications of the following statement: *Once a memo or any other document leaves your hands, you have essentially published it.*
5. Ethical Issue: Should managers have the right to monitor the e-mail messages of employees? Why or why not? What if employees are warned that e-mail could be monitored? If a company sets up an e-mail policy, should only in-house transmissions be monitored? Only outside transmissions?

6. What questions should a writer ask before beginning a memo or e-mail message?

7. Why are subject lines such as "Hello" or "Meeting" inappropriate?

8. Since e-mail messages are almost like telephone calls, why should one bother about correct spelling, grammar, punctuation, and expression?

9. In formatting e-mail messages, when should you include a salutation (*Dear Mark*)?

10. Should writers of e-mail messages include their names at the ends of messages?

11. What are the four parts of the writing plan for a routine memo or an e-mail message? What is included in each?

12. How can listed items improve memos and e-mail messages?

13. When are numbers appropriate for listing items? Bullets? Asterisks?

14. What are three kinds of e-mail messages and memos frequently used for business messages?

15. What is *end dating*?

WRITING IMPROVEMENT EXERCISES

MESSAGE OPENERS.   Compare the following sets of message openers. Circle the letter of the opener that illustrates a direct opening. Be prepared to discuss the weaknesses and strengths of each.

16. An e-mail message inquiring about Web hosting:
    a. We are considering launching our own Web site because we feel it is the only way to keep up with our competition and make our product more visible in a crowded market. We need some information about Web hosting.
    b. Please answer the following questions about hosting our new Web site, which we hope to launch to increase our product visibility in a crowded market.

17. An e-mail message announcing an in-service program:
    a. Employees interested in improving their writing and communication skills are invited to an in-service training program beginning October 4.
    b. For the past year we have been investigating the possibility of developing an in-service training program for some of our employees.

18. An e-mail message announcing a study:
    a. We have noticed recently a gradual but steady decline in the number of customer checking accounts. We are disturbed by this trend, and for this reason I am asking our Customer Relations Department to conduct a study and make recommendations regarding this important problem.
    b. Our Customer Relations Department will conduct a study and make recommendations regarding the gradual but steady decline of customer checking accounts.

19. A memo announcing a new procedure:
    a. Some customer representatives in the field have suggested that they would like to key their reports from the field instead of coming back to the office to enter them in their computers. That's why we have made a number of changes. We would like you to use the following procedures.
    b. Customer representatives may now key their field reports using the following procedures.

OPENING PARAGRAPHS.   The following opening paragraphs to memos are wordy and indirect. After reading each paragraph, identify the main idea. Then, write an opening sentence that illustrates a more direct opening. Use a separate sheet if necessary.

20. Several staff members came to me and announced their interest in learning more about severance policies and separation benefits. As most of you know, these areas of concern are increasingly important for most Human Resources professionals. A seminar entitled "Severance & Separation Benefits" is being conducted February 11. I am allowing the following employees to attend the seminar: Terence Curran, Cindy Thompson, and Darlene McClure.

21. Your Intel Employees Association has secured for you discounts on auto repair, carpet purchases, travel arrangements, and many other services. These services are available to you if you have a Buying Power Card. All Intel employees are eligible for their own private Buying Power Cards.

LISTS.   Write lists as indicated below.

22. Use the following information to compose a single sentence that includes an introductory statement and a list with letters (*a, b, c*). Do not list the items vertically.
    The front page of a Web site should orient readers. This front page should tell them what the site is about. It should also tell about the organization of the site. Finally, it should tell them how to navigate the site.

23. Use the following instructions to compose a bulleted vertical list with an introductory statement.
    To use the conventional Rollerblade heel brake, you should do these things. First, you should move one leg slightly forward. Then the ball of your foot should be lifted. Finally, the heel should be dragged to complete the braking action.

24. Use the following information to compose a sentence containing a list.
    Your equipment lease will mature in a month. When it does, you must make a decision. Three options are available to you. If you like, you may purchase the equipment at fair market value. Or the existing lease may be extended, again at fair market value. Finally, if neither of these options is appealing, the equipment could be sent back to the lessor.

25. Use the following hard-to-read paragraph to write a set of instructions with a title.
    We are concerned about your safety in using our automated teller machines (ATMs) at night, so we think you should consider the following tips. Users of ATMs are encouraged to look around—especially at night—before using the service. If you notice anything suspicious, the use of another ATM is recommended. Or you could come back later. Another suggestion that we give our customers involves counting your cash. Be sure that the cash you receive is put away quickly. Don't count it as soon as you get it. It's better to check it in the safety of your car or at home. Also, why not take a friend with you if you must use an ATM at night? Parking in a well-lighted area close to the actual location of the ATM is also wise.

Writing Improvement Exercises

5.1 PROCEDURE MEMO OR E-MAIL: FLYING CHEAPER AND BETTER.

As assistant to the executive director of the American Statistical Association, you've been asked to draft a memo to ASA directors and committee members. In talking with the executive director, Dr. Gary Wishniewsky, you learn that when directors and committee members travel to meetings for the ASA, they generally make their own arrangements and then expect ASA to reimburse them. Sometimes the submitted expenses have been way beyond normal living expenses, and the paperwork involved was chaotic. Dr. W., as everyone calls him, decided that the ASA could save money, reduce chaos, and get better travel packages if arrangements were channeled through a travel agency. He also wants directors and others who travel for ASA to use a new Travel/Expense Reimbursement Form. This form will itemize travel expenses and should be submitted to ASA after anyone travels. It can be downloaded from the ASA Web site.

Your memo should tell people who travel on ASA business that they must now make all arrangements through McKay Travel Services (1-800-433-9782) or at www.mckaytravel. com. Dr. W. wants to encourage travelers to make their ticket reservations at least fourteen days in advance. Every effort should be made to book tickets even further in advance if possible. For car rentals, ASA travelers must seek prior approval. Because meals have been a problem in the past, the ASA is putting a maximum on the amount it will reimburse: $9 for breakfast, $16 for lunch, and $30 for dinner.

Dr. W. says that working with an agency should result in lower prices and better travel arrangements. He's also excited about the new travel expense form, which should reduce paperwork, produce consistent reporting, and result in faster reimbursement.

Your Task. For Dr. Wishniewsky's signature, draft a memo to ASA directors and committee members describing the change in travel policy. You know that your message is a draft and that Dr. W. will revise it later, but you want to do your best. Think through the process involved in creating a memo announcing these changes. To help you apply the principles you have learned in this chapter, read the options suggested here. Circle the most appropriate response for each question. If your instructor directs, compose the message as a memo addressed to all ASA directors and committee members.

DEVELOPING THE MEMO

1. What is the main idea in this memo?
   a. ASA will no longer tolerate outrageous travel expenses.
   b. Travel expenses must now be submitted on a special form, and car rentals must receive prior authorization.
   c. ASA-related travel will have limits on meal reimbursement.
   d. Travel plans must now be made through a travel agency, and expenses must be submitted on a new form.
2. Which of the following is the best opening sentence for your memo?
   a. This is to inform you that effective immediately ASA is instituting a new policy in regard to making travel reservations and reporting expenses.
   b. Because of unrealistic expense requests in the past, ASA finds it necessary to implement a new travel policy for directors and committee members.
   c. Effective immediately all travel reservations for ASA-related business should be made through McKay Travel Services.
   d. Because in the past ASA has had difficulty controlling travel expenses and reimbursements, we have been considering ways to reduce our paperwork and improve our procedures.

3. Which of the following should the body of the memo accomplish?
   a. Explain the benefits of the new system and list bulleted steps in following it.
   b. Recount the highlights of your conversation with Dr. Wishniewsky.
   c. Identify the worst travel expense reports from the past to explain why a new policy is necessary.
   d. Praise McKay Travel Services and tell why it was selected to process all ASA travel plans.
4. In explaining the new procedure, you will probably want to list each step. Which of the following statements illustrates the best form?
   a. You should make airlines reservations at least fourteen days in advance.
   b. Airlines reservations must be made at least fourteen days in advance.
   c. Book airlines tickets at least fourteen days in advance and earlier whenever possible.
   d. When you need to fly, you must book your reservations fourteen days in advance and earlier if possible.
5. Which of the following would make an appropriate closing?
   a. Thank you for your cooperation in this matter.
   b. If we may be of further service, do not hesitate to call on us.
   c. We appreciate your following this new procedure, which we believe will lower costs and provide you with better service and faster reimbursement.
   d. Travel requests and expenses will no longer be approved or reimbursed if you fail to follow these procedures.

5.2 Information E-Mail or Memo: Reducing Workplace Violence.

In the following e-mail message, Avianca Harper intends to inform her boss, Todd Shimoyama, about a conference she attended on the topic of workplace violence. This first draft of her information memo needs work.

Your Task. Analyze Avianca's first draft. It suffers from wordiness and lack of graphic highlighting techniques to improve readability. List its weaknesses and outline an appropriate writing plan. If your instructor directs, revise it.

DATE: April 2, 200x
TO: Todd Shimoyama <tshimoyama@chemco.com>
FROM: Avianca Harper <aharper@chemco.com>
SUBJECT: Violence Conference

Todd:

I went to the OfficePro conference on May 2. The topic was how to prevent workplace violence, and I found it very fascinating. Although we have been fortunate to avoid serious incidents at our company, it's better to be safe than sorry. Since I was the representative from our company, I thought you would like me to report about some suggestions for preventing workplace violence. Robert Mather was the presenter, and he made suggestions in three categories, which I will summarize here.

Mr. Mather cautioned organizations to prescreen job applicants. As a matter of fact, wise companies do not offer employment until after a candidate's background has been checked. Just the mention of a background check is enough to make some candidates withdraw. These candidates, of course, are the ones with something to hide.

A second suggestion was that companies should prepare a good employee handbook that outlines what employees should do when they suspect potential workplace violence. This handbook should include a way for informers to be anonymous.

A third recommendation had to do with recognizing red-flag behavior. This involves having companies train managers to recognize signs of potential workplace violence. What are some of the red flags? One sign is an increasing number of arguments (most of them petty) with coworkers. Another sign is extreme changes in behavior or statements indicating depression over family or financial problems. Another sign is bullying or harassing behavior. Bringing a firearm to work or displaying an extreme fascination with firearms is another sign.

By the way, the next OfficePro conference is in September, and the topic is the new OSHA standards.

I think that the best recommendation is prescreening job candidates. This is because it is most feasible. If you want me to do more research on prescreening techniques, do not hesitate to let me know. Let me know by May 7 if you want me to make a report at our management meeting, which is scheduled for June.

Avianca

1. List at least five weaknesses in the preceding information e-mail.

2. Outline a general writing plan for this memo.

   Subject line:

   Opening:

   Body:

   Closing:

5.3 REQUEST E-MAIL OR MEMO: FLOATING HOLIDAY. The following memo requests a response from staff members. But it is so poorly written that they may not know what to do.

Your Task. Analyze the message. List its weaknesses and outline an appropriate writing plan. If your instructor directs, revise it.

DATE:	Current
TO:	All Employees
FROM:	Elizabeth Mendoza, Human Resources
SUBJECT:	New Holiday Plan

In the past we've offered all employees 11 holidays (starting with New Year's Day in January and proceeding through Christmas Day the following December). Other companies offer similar holiday schedules.

In addition, we've given all employees one floating holiday. As you know, we've determined that day by a companywide vote. As a result, all employees had the same day off. Now, however, management is considering a new plan that we feel would be better. This new plan involves a floating holiday that each individual employee may decide for herself or himself. We've given it considerable thought and decided that such a plan could definitely work. We would allow each employee to choose a day that he or she wants. Of course, we would have to issue certain restrictions. Selections would have to be subject to our staffing needs within individual departments. For example, if everyone wanted the same day, we could not allow everyone to take it. In that case, we would allow the employee with the most seniority to have the day off.

Before we institute the new plan, though, we wanted to see what employees thought about this. Is it better to continue our current companywide uniform floating holiday? Or should we try an individual floating holiday? Please let us know what you think as soon as possible.

1. List at least five faults in this message.

2. Outline a general writing plan for this message.

Subject line:

Opening:

Body:

Closing:

ACTIVITIES AND CASES

5.4 INFORMATION E-MAIL OR MEMO: WHAT I DO ON THE JOB. Some employees have remarked to the boss that they are working more than other employees. Your boss has decided to study the matter by asking all employees to describe exactly what they are doing. If some jobs are found to be overly demanding, your boss may redistribute job tasks or hire additional employees.

Your Task. Write a well-organized memo describing your duties, the time you spend on each task, and the skills needed for what you do. Provide enough details to make a clear record of your job. Use actual names and describe actual tasks. Describe a current or previous job. If you have not worked, report to the head of an organization to which you belong. Describe the duties of an officer or of a committee. Your boss or organization head appreciates brevity. Keep your memo under one page.

5.5 INFORMATION E-MAIL OR MEMO: PARTY TIME! Staff members in your office were disappointed that no holiday party was given last year. They don't care what kind of party it is, but they do want some kind of celebration this year.

Your Task. You have been asked to draft a memo to the office staff about a December holiday party. Decide what kind of party you would like. Include information about where the party will be held, when it is, what the cost will be, a description of the food to be served, whether guests are allowed, and whom to make reservations with.

5.6 Procedure E-Mail or Memo: Rules for Wireless Phone Use in Sales Reps' Cars.

As one of the managers of LaReve, a hair care and skin products company, you are alarmed at a newspaper article you just saw. A stockbroker for Smith Barney was making cold calls on his personal phone while driving. His car hit and killed a motorcyclist. The brokerage firm was sued and accused of contributing to an accident by encouraging employees to use cellular telephones while driving. To avoid the risk of paying huge damages awarded by an emotional jury, the brokerage firm offered the victim's family a $500,000 settlement.

You begin to worry, knowing that your company has provided its 75 sales representatives with wireless phones to help them keep in touch with home base while they are in the field. At the next management meeting, other members agreed that you should draft a memo detailing some wireless phone safety rules for your sales reps. On the Web you learned that anyone with a wireless phone should get to know its features, including speed dial, automatic memory, and redial. Another suggestion involved using a hands-free device. Management members decided to purchase these for every sales rep and have the devices available within one month. In positioning the wireless phone in a car, it should be within easy reach. It should be where you can grab it without removing your eyes from the road. If you get an incoming call at an inconvenient time, your voice mail should be allowed to pick up the call. You should never talk, of course, during hazardous driving conditions, such as rain, sleet, snow, and ice.

Taking notes or looking up phone numbers is dangerous when driving. You want to warn sales reps not to get into dangerous situations by reading (such as an address book) or writing (such as taking notes) while driving.

The more you think about it, the more you think that sales reps should not use their wireless phones while the car is moving. They really should pull over. But you know that would be hard to enforce.

Your Task. Individually or in teams write a memo to LaReve sales reps outlining company suggestions (or should they be rules?) for safe wireless phone use in cars. You may wish to check the Web for additional safety ideas. Try to suggest receiver benefits in this message. How is safety beneficial to the reader? The memo is from you acting as Operations Manager.

5.7 Information Memo or E-Mail: Sick and Tired of Spam.

Your boss wants to do something about all the spam (unwanted commercial e-mail messages) being delivered to her computer and other computers in your company. She's sick and tired of wading through mortgage offers, work-at-home schemes, get-rich offers, and porno announcements. She asks you to use the Internet to learn about techniques for avoiding unsolicited e-mail.

Your Task. Using an InfoTrac subject or keyword search, read several articles on fighting spam. A good article is Helen Bradley's "Fight Back Against Spam!" in *Home Office Computing*, April 2001, Article No. A72790790. After looking at several articles, prepare an information memo or e-mail message to send to your boss, Cheryl Lopez. In your own words describe ten techniques for reducing the amount of incoming spam in your office. Be sure to include an appropriate opening and closing, along with listing techniques for your tips. Do you think items should be bulleted or numbered?

5.8 Procedure Memo: Managing Your Time More Wisely.

You work with a group of engineers who are constantly putting in 60- and 70-hour workweeks. The vice president worries that major burnout will occur. Personally, he believes that some of the engineers simply manage their time poorly. He asks you to look into the topic of time management and put together a list of procedures that might help these professionals use their time more wisely. Your suggestions may become the basis for an in-service training program.

Your Task. Using InfoTrac, conduct a keyword search for articles about time management. Read several articles. Summarize five or six procedures that might be helpful to employees. Write a memo to Thomas Sawicky, vice president, with your suggestions.

5.9 REQUEST E-MAIL OR MEMO: SMOKERS VS. NONSMOKERS.

The city of Milwaukee has mandated that employers "shall adopt, implement, and maintain a written smoking policy which shall contain a prohibition against smoking in restrooms and infirmaries." Employers must also "maintain a nonsmoking area of not less than two thirds of the seating capacity in cafeterias, lunchrooms, and employee lounges, and make efforts to work out disputes between smokers and nonsmokers."

Your Task. As the director of human resources, write a memo to all department managers of National General, a large foods company. Announce the new restriction, and tell the managers that you want them to set up departmental committees to mediate any smoking conflicts before the complaints surface. Explain why this is a good policy.

5.10 REPLY MEMO OR E-MAIL: ENFORCING SMOKING BAN.

As manager of accounting services for National General, you must respond to the director's memo described in Activity 5.9. You could have made a telephone call and explained your response. But you prefer to have a permanent record of this message. Here's your problem. You are having difficulty enforcing the smoking ban in restrooms. Only one men's room serves your floor, and 9 of your 27 male employees are smokers. You have already received complaints, and you see no way to enforce the ban in the restrooms. You have also noticed that smokers are taking longer breaks than other employees. Smokers complain that they need more time because they must walk to an outside area. Smokers are especially unhappy when the weather is cold, rainy, or snowy. Moreover, smokers huddle near the building entrances, thus creating a negative impression for customers and visitors. Your committee members can find no solutions; in fact, they have become polarized in their meetings to date. You need help from a higher authority.

Your Task. Write an e-mail or memo to the director of human resources appealing for solutions. Perhaps the director should visit your department.

5.11 REQUEST E-MAIL OR MEMO: PROTECTING THE CEO FROM PRYING EYES.

As an experienced executive assistant, you really never had any problems with the confidentiality aspect of your job. Your boss, however, was recently promoted to CEO of your company. Now it seems that both your office and his have become Grand Central Station. Company officers float in and out because the CEO has an open-door policy. They have a barrage of questions about projects, budgets, and problems. When the CEO is out of town, they inquire about his travel schedule and what he's doing. Some of them even enter his office and go through papers on his desk.

Because your boss and you are increasingly processing a huge amount of sophisticated, confidential information, you are afraid that the wrong person is going to lay hands on company information. And if something confidential ever leaks, you worry that you will be held responsible and "hung out to dry."[9]

Your Task. You decide to write to your boss, Sebastian Watts, to gain some understanding about managing sensitive information. You wonder about his open-door policy. You don't know whether to stop company officers when he is on the telephone and they walk right in. When he's away, the open-door policy becomes even more problematic. You would like to clarify what documents are strictly confidential—for your eyes and your boss's eyes only. When packages or mail arrive with items marked "Personal" or "Confidential," you don't know whether to open them or not. What should you do, for example, when his paycheck arrives in an envelope? You're concerned about who should have access to what information and under what circumstances. You worry about sharing materials related to current projects. When a department head asks for documents related to her department and the CEO is gone, what should you do? Should anyone be allowed to use the boss's computer? Who? Under what circumstances should you be allowed to talk to the media? Think of other matters of confidentiality. Spell them out in a request memo to Sebastian Watts. You prefer to have his response in writing so that you can use it to back up enforcement. Because he's leaving on another trip next week, you want his written response before he leaves. You know how busy he is. How could you make it easy for him to respond?

WEB **5.12 REPLY MEMO: WHAT IS THIS USPS ELECTRONIC POSTMARK?** You work in a law firm that sends out many documents by "snail mail" because the time and date of mailing can be certified. Often your firm uses FedEx and UPS for faster delivery, but the rates are expensive. The attorneys in your office are looking for a way to send confidential documents electronically, and they heard about the U.S. Postal Service's Electronic Postmark (EPM) service. Your manager asks you to research this service. And while you're at it, she wants you to find out the current rate for sending Priority Mail flat-rate envelopes.

Your Task. Visit the USPS Web site at http://www.usps.gov. Use the keyword/search function to locate Electronic Postmark (EPM). In a memo or e-mail to your manager, Charlotte Richardson, answer these questions: What is EPM? What kind of documents might require EPM? Why would EPM be helpful to your attorneys? Whom should your manager contact for pricing information? At the USPS Web site, also check out the current price and specifications for sending Priority Mail flat-rate envelopes. In the closing, include your reaction to the information you report. The manager values your opinion.

WEB **5.13 REPLY MEMO: WHAT IS A FICO CREDIT RATING SCORE?** For years the credit industry hushed up a consumer's credit score. Credit bureaus would reveal a consumer's credit rating only to a lender when an applicant wanted a loan. Customers could not learn their scores unless credit was denied. Now, all that has changed. Using the Internet, consumers can check their credit files and even obtain specific credit scores, which are key factors in obtaining loans, renting property, and protecting against identity theft. Although the three national credit bureaus (Equifax, Experian, and TransUnion) may use different scoring systems, many lenders now mention FICO scores as the favored ranking to estimate the risk involved in an individual's loan application.

Your Task. As an intern in architect Eric Larson's office, you must do some Internet research. Mr. Larson recently had to reject two potentially lucrative house construction jobs because the clients received low FICO scores from their credit bureaus. They could not qualify for construction loans. He wants you to learn exactly what "FICO" means and how this score is determined. Mr. Larson also wants to know how consumers can raise their FICO scores. Go to http://www.myfico.com and study its information. (Use a search engine with the term "My Fico" if this URL fails.) Summarize your findings in your own words in a well-organized, concise memo or e-mail addressed to Eric Larson elarson@arnet.com. Use bulleted lists for some of the information.

WEB **5.14 WRITING INSTRUCTIONS.** At the student Web site for this book, you will find a supplement devoted to writing instructions. It includes colorful examples and hot links to Web sites with relevant examples of real sets of instructions from business Web sites.

Your Task. At your student Web site, click "Book Support" and "Bonus Supplement: How to Write Instructions." Study all of the sections of this supplement. Then choose one of the following application activities: A-5, Revising the Instructions for an Imported Fax Machine; A-6, Evaluation: Catnix Basic Cat Playground; or A-7, Instructions for Dealing With Car Emergencies. Complete the assignment and submit it to your instructor.

Innovation, Learning, and Communication at Yahoo

Ask your instructor to show the VHS video describing the Internet company Yahoo. Assume you are an assistant to John Briggs, senior producer, who appeared in the video. John has just received a letter asking for permission from another film company to use Yahoo offices and personnel in an educational video, similar to the one you just saw. John wants you to draft an e-mail message for him to send to the operations manager, Ceci Lang, asking for permission for VX Studios to film. VX says it needs about 15 hours of filming time and would like to interview four or five managers as well as founders David Filo and Jerry Yang. VX would need to set up its mobile studio van in the parking lot and would need permission to use advertising film clips.

Although VX hopes to film in May, it is flexible about the date. John Briggs reminds you that Yahoo has participated in a number of films in the past two years, and some managers are complaining that they can't get their work done.

Your Task. Write a persuasive memo or e-mail message to Ceci Lang, Operations Manager, asking her to allow VX Studios to film at Yahoo. Your request memo should probably emphasize the value of these projects in enhancing Yahoo's image among future users. Provide any other details you think are necessary to create a convincing request memo that will win authorization from Ceci Lang to schedule this filming.

GRAMMAR/MECHANICS CHECKUP—5

PREPOSITIONS AND CONJUNCTIONS

Review Sections 1.18 and 1.19 in the Grammar Review section of the Grammar/Mechanics Handbook. Then study each of the following statements. Write *a* or *b* to indicate the sentence in which the idea is expressed more effectively. Also record the number of the G/M principle illustrated. When you finish, compare your responses with those provided. If your answers differ, study carefully the principles shown in parentheses.

Example   a. Tiffany will graduate college this spring.   b_____   (1.18a)
             b. Tiffany will graduate from college this spring.

1.a. Our new Web site is much better then the previous one.   _____
   b. Our new Web site is much better than the previous one.

2.a. Don't you hate it when the e-mail system is down?   _____
   b. Don't you hate when the e-mail system is down?

3.a. Salaries for temporary positions seem to be higher than permanent positions.   _____
   b. Salaries for temporary positions seem to be higher than for permanent positions.

4.a. Gross profit is where you compute the difference between total sales and the cost of goods sold.   _____
   b. Gross profit is computed by finding the difference between total sales and the cost of goods sold.

_____ 5.a. We advertise to increase the frequency of product use, to introduce complementary products, and to enhance our corporate image.

b. We advertise to have our products used more often, when we have complementary products to introduce, and we are interested in making our corporation look better to the public.

_____ 6.a. What type online service do you use?

b. What type of online service do you use?

_____ 7.a. Where are you going to?

b. Where are you going?

_____ 8.a. The sale of our San Antonio branch office last year should improve this year's profits.

b. The sale of our branch office in San Antonio during last year should improve the profits for this year.

_____ 9.a. Do you know where the meeting is at?

b. Do you know where the meeting is?

_____ 10.a. The cooling-off rule is an FTC rule that protects consumers from making unwise purchases at home.

b. The cooling-off rule is where the FTC has made a rule that protects consumers from making unwise purchases at home.

_____ 11.a. Meetings can be more meaningful if the agenda is stuck to, the time frame is followed, and if someone keeps follow-up notes.

b. Meetings can be more meaningful if you stick to the agenda, follow the time frame, and keep follow-up notes.

_____ 12.a. They printed the newsletter on yellow paper like we asked them to do.

b. They printed the newsletter on yellow paper as we asked them to do.

_____ 13.a. A code of ethics is a set of rules spelling out appropriate standards of behavior.

b. A code of ethics is where a set of rules spells out appropriate standards of behavior.

_____ 14.a. We need an individual with an understanding and serious interest in black-and-white photography.

b. We need an individual with an understanding of and serious interest in black-and-white photography.

_____ 15.a. The most dangerous situation is when employees ignore the safety rules.

b. The most dangerous situation occurs when employees ignore the safety rules.

DOCUMENT FOR REVISION

The following memo has faults in grammar, punctuation, spelling, capitalization, number form, repetition, wordiness, and other areas. Use standard proofreading marks (see Appendix B) to correct the errors. When you finish, your instructor may show you one possible revised version of this memo.

DATE: March 2, 200x

TO: Department Heads, Managers, and Supervisors

FROM: James Robbins, Director, Human Resources

SUBJECT: Submitting Appraisals of Performance by April 15th

Please be informed that performance appraisals for all you're employees' are due, before April 15th . These appraisal are esspecially important and essential this year. Because of job changes, new technologys and because of office re-organization.

To complete your performance appraisals in the most effective way, you should follow the procedures described in our employee handbook, let me briefly make a review of those procedures;

1. Be sure each and every employee has a performance plan with 3 or 4 main objective.

2. For each objective make an assessment of the employee on a scale of 5 (consistently excedes requirements) to 0 (does not meet requirements at all.

3. You should identify 3 strengths that he brings to the job.

4. Name 3 skills that he can improve. These should pertain to skills such as Time Management rather then to behaviors such as habitual lateness.

5. The employee should be met with to discuss his appraisal.

6. Finish the appraisal and send the completed appraisal to this office.

We look upon appraisals like a tool for helping each worker assess his performance. And enhance his output. If you would like to discuss this farther, please do not hessitate to call me.

Whose Computer Is It Anyway?

More and more companies today provide their employees with computers and Internet access. Should employees be able to use those computers for online shopping, personal messages, personal work, and listening to music or playing games?

But It's Harmless

The Wall Street Journal reports that many office workers have discovered that it's far easier to do their shopping online than racing to malls and waiting in line. To justify her Web shopping at work, one employee, a recent graduate, says, "Instead of standing at the water cooler gossiping, I shop online." She went on to say, "I'm not sapping company resources by doing this."

Some online office shoppers say that what they're doing is similar to making personal phone calls. So long as they don't abuse the practice, they see no harm. And besides, shopping at the office is far faster than shopping from most dial-up home computer connections. Marketing director David Krane justifies his online shopping by explaining that his employer benefits because he is more productive when he takes minibreaks. "When I need a break, I just pull up a Web page and just browse," he says. "Ten minutes later, I'm all refreshed, and I can go back to business-plan writing."

Companies Urged to Crack Down

Employers are less happy about increasing use of bandwidth for personal online activities. UPS discovered an employee running a personal business from his office computer. And Lockheed Martin fired an employee who disabled its entire company network for six hours because of an e-mail message heralding a holiday event that the worker sent to 60,000 employees. One company found that people were downloading music from broadcast.com, using up 4 percent of the company's bandwidth.

Attorney Carole O'Blenes thinks that companies should begin cracking down. Online shopping generates junk e-mail that could cause the company's server to crash. And what about productivity? "Whether they're checking their stocks, shopping, or doing research for their upcoming trip to Spain," she says, "that's time diverted from doing business."[10]

What's Reasonable?

Some companies try to enforce a "zero tolerance" policy, prohibiting any personal use of company equipment. Ameritech Corporation specifically tells employees that "computers and other company equipment are to be used only to provide service to customers and for other business purposes." Companies such as Boeing, however, allow employees to use faxes, e-mail, and the Internet for personal reasons. But Boeing sets guidelines. Use has to be of "reasonable duration and frequency" and can't cause "embarrassment to the company."[11] Strictly prohibited are chain letters, obscenity, and political and religious solicitation.

Career Application. As an administrative assistant at Texas Technologies in Fort Worth, you have just received an e-mail from your boss asking for your opinion. It seems that many employees have been shopping online; one person actually received four personal packages from UPS in one morning. Although reluctant to do so, management is considering installing monitoring software that not only tracks Internet use but also allows extensive blocking of Web sites such as porno, hate, and game sites.

Your Task

- In teams or as a class, discuss the problem of workplace abuse of e-mail and the Internet. Should full personal use be allowed?
- Are computers and their links to the Internet similar to other equipment such as telephones?
- Should employees be allowed to access the Internet for personal use if they use their own private e-mail accounts?
- Should management be allowed to monitor all Internet use?
- Should employees be warned if e-mail is to be monitored?
- What specific reasons can you give to support an Internet crackdown by management?
- What specific reasons can you give to oppose a crackdown?

Decide whether you support or oppose the crackdown. Explain your views in an e-mail or a memo to your boss, Arthur W. Rose <awrose@txtech.com>.

Chapter

6

Routine Letters and Goodwill Messages

A good business letter can get you a job interview, get you off the hook, or get you money. It's totally asinine to blow your chances of getting whatever you want—with a business letter that turns people off instead of turning them on.[1]

MALCOLM FORBES, **Publisher and Founder,** *Forbes* Magazine

LEARNING OBJECTIVES

1. Write letters requesting information and action.
2. Write letters ordering merchandise.
3. Write letters making claims.
4. Write letters responding to information requests.
5. Write letters responding to customer orders.
6. Write letters granting claims.
7. Write letters of recommendation.
8. Write goodwill messages.

WRITING EVERYDAY BUSINESS LETTERS

✓ *Quick Check*

Letters communicate with outsiders and produce a formal record.

Publisher Malcolm Forbes understood the power of business letters. They can get you anything you want if you can write letters that turn people on instead of off. This chapter teaches you how to turn readers on with effective business letters and goodwill messages. Most of these messages travel outside an organization. Although many businesspeople today are writing fewer letters and more e-mail messages, you will still find many occasions when letters are required. When you need a formal record of an inquiry, response, or complaint, letters are the best communication channel.

Most business correspondence consists of routine letters. These everyday messages go to suppliers, government agencies, other businesses, and, most important, customers. Customer letters receive a high priority because these messages encourage product feedback, project a favorable image of the company, and promote future business. In this chapter you'll learn to write information and action requests, order requests, simple claim requests, information responses, customer claim responses, letters of recommendation, and goodwill messages.

Like memos, letters are easiest to write when you have a plan to follow. The plan for letters, just as for memos, is fixed by the content of the message and its expected effect on the receiver. Letters delivering bad news require an indirect approach, which you will learn about in Chapter 7. Most letters, however, carry good or neutral news. These letters should follow the direct strategy. You will recall that the main idea comes first in the direct strategy.

INFORMATION AND ACTION REQUEST

Many business messages are written to request information or action. Although the specific subject of each inquiry may differ, the similarity of purpose in routine requests enables writers to use the following writing plan.

 ## WRITING PLAN FOR AN INFORMATION OR ACTION REQUEST

- *Opening:* Ask the most important question first or express a polite command.
- *Body:* Explain the request logically and courteously. Ask other questions if necessary.
- *Closing:* Request a specific action with an end date, if appropriate, and show appreciation.

OPENING DIRECTLY

The most emphatic positions in a letter are the openings and closings. Readers tend to look at them first. The writer, then, should capitalize on this tendency by putting the most significant statement first. The first sentence of an information request is usually a question or a polite command. It should not be an explanation or justification, unless resistance to the request is expected. When the information requested is likely to be forthcoming, immediately tell the reader what you want. This saves the reader's time and may ensure that the message is read. A busy executive who skims the mail, quickly reading subject lines and first sentences only, may grasp your request rapidly and act on it. A request that follows a lengthy explanation, on the other hand, may never be found.

A letter inquiring about hotel accommodations, shown in Figure 6.1, begins immediately with the most important idea. Can the hotel provide meeting rooms and accommodations for 250 people? Instead of opening with an explanation of who the writer is or how the writer happens to be writing this letter, the letter begins more directly.

If several questions must be asked, you have two choices. You can ask the most important question first, as shown in Figure 6.1. An alternate opening begins with a summary statement, such as *Will you please answer the following questions about providing meeting rooms and accommodations for 250 people from May 25 through May 29.* Notice that the summarizing statement sounds like a question but has no question mark. That's because it's really a command disguised as a question. Rather than bluntly demanding information (*Answer the following questions*), we often prefer to soften commands by posing them as questions. Such statements, called rhetorical questions, should not be punctuated as questions because they do not require answers.

DETAILS IN THE BODY

The body of a letter that requests information should provide necessary details. Remember that the quality of the information obtained from a request letter depends

FIGURE 6.1 **Letter That Requests Information**

Letterhead ———————————

Dateline ———————————

Inside address ———————————

Salutation ———————————

Body ———————————

Complimentary close ———————————

Author's name and
identification ———————————

Reference initials ———————————

DCC 958 Alum Creek Drive Columbus, OH 43208 PHONE: (614) 455-3201
FAX: (614) 455-6621 WEB: www.dcs.com
Digital Communication Corporation

October 14, 200x

Mr. Dennis Purdy, Manager
MGM Grand Hotel and Casino
3799 Las Vegas Boulevard South
Las Vegas, NV 89109

Dear Mr. Purdy:

Can the MGM Grand Hotel provide meeting rooms and accommodations for
about 250 DCC sales representatives from May 25 through May 29?

Your hotel received strong recommendations because of its excellent resort and
conference facilities. Our spring sales conference is scheduled for next May, and
I am collecting information for our planning committee. Will you please answer
these additional questions regarding the MGM Grand:

•Does the hotel have a banquet room that can seat 250?

•Do you have at least four smaller meeting rooms, each to accommodate a
  maximum of 75?

•What kind of computer facilities are available for electronic presentations?

•What is the nearest airport, and do you provide transportation to and from it?

Answers to these questions and any other information you can provide will help
us decide which conference facility to choose. Your response before November 15
would be most appreciated since our planning committee meets November 19.

Sincerely yours,

Carol A. Allen

Carol A. Allen
Corporate Travel Department

CAA:gdr

TIPS FOR FORMATTING LETTERS
- Start the date on line 13 or 1 blank line below
  the letterhead.
- For block style, begin all lines at the left margin.
- Leave side margins of 1 to 1½ inches
  depending on the length of the letter.
- Single-space the body and double-space
  between paragraphs.

✓ *Quick Check*

The body of a request letter may
contain an explanation or a list of
questions.

on the clarity of the inquiry. If you analyze your needs, organize your ideas, and
frame your request logically, you are likely to receive a meaningful answer that
doesn't require a follow-up message. Whenever possible, itemize the information
to improve readability. Notice that the questions in Figure 6.1 are bulleted, and
they are parallel. That is, they use the same balanced construction.

CLOSING WITH AN ACTION REQUEST

Use the final paragraph to ask for specific action, to set an end date if appropriate, and to express appreciation. As you learned in working with memos, a request for action is most effective when an end date and reason for that date are
supplied, as shown in Figure 6.1.

It's always appropriate to end a request letter with appreciation for the action taken. However, don't fall into a cliché trap, such as *Thanking you in advance, I remain . . .* or the familiar *Thank you for your cooperation.* Your appreciation will sound most sincere if you avoid mechanical, tired expressions.

✓ **Quick Check**

The ending of a request letter should tell the reader what you want done and when.

ORDER REQUEST

Customers generally order merchandise by telephone, catalog order form, fax, or Web page. Sometimes, though, you may not have a telephone number, order form, or Web address—only a street address. Other times you may wish to have a written record of the date and content of your order. When you must write a letter to order merchandise, use the direct strategy, beginning with the main idea.

✓ **Quick Check**

To order merchandise, you may occasionally have to write a letter.

 ### WRITING PLAN FOR AN ORDER REQUEST

- *Opening:* Authorize purchase and suggest method of shipping.
- *Body:* List items vertically; provide quantity, order number, description, and unit price; and show total price of order.
- *Closing:* Request shipment by a specific date, tell method of payment, and express appreciation.

The following letter from the human resources department of a business illustrates the pattern of an order letter.

Greetings:

Please send by express mail the following items from your summer catalog.

Quantity	Catalog Number	Description	Price
250	OG44-18	Payroll greeting cards	$102.50
250	OG31-22	Payroll card envelopes	21.95
100	OM22-01	Performance greeting cards	80.00
	Subtotal		$204.45
	Tax at 7%		14.31
	Shipping		24.00
	Total		$242.76

My company would appreciate receiving these cards immediately since we are starting an employee recognition program February 12. Enclosed is our check for $242.76. If additional charges are necessary, please bill my company.

Sincerely,

Opens directly with authorization for purchase, method of delivery, and catalog source.

Uses columns to make quantity, catalog number, description, and price stand out.

Calculates totals to prevent possible mistakes.

Expresses appreciation and tells when items are expected; identifies method of payment.

To order items by letter, supply the same information that an order blank would require. In the opening let the reader know immediately that this is a purchase authorization and not merely an information inquiry. Instead of *I saw a number of interesting items in your catalog,* begin directly with order language such as *Please send me by UPS the following items from your fall merchandise catalog.*

If you're ordering many items, list them vertically in the body of your letter. Include as much specific data as possible: quantity, order number, complete description, unit price, and total price. Show the total amount, and figure the tax and shipping costs if possible. The more information you provide, the less likely it is that a mistake will be made.

In the closing tell how you plan to pay for the merchandise. Enclose a check, provide a credit card number, or ask to be billed. Many business organizations have credit agreements with their regular suppliers that enable them to send goods without prior payment. In addition to payment information, tell when the merchandise should be sent and express appreciation.

SIMPLE CLAIM REQUEST

✓ Quick Check

Claim letters register complaints and usually seek correction of a wrong.

In business many things can go wrong—promised shipments are late, warranted goods fail, or service is disappointing. When a customer must write to identify or correct a wrong, the letter is called a *claim*. Straightforward claims are those to which you expect the receiver to agree readily. But even these claims often require a letter. While your first action may be a telephone call or a visit to submit your claim, you may not get the results you seek. Written claims are often taken more seriously, and they also establish a record of what happened. Claims that require persuasion are presented in Chapter 7. In this chapter you'll learn to apply the following writing plan for a straightforward claim that uses a direct approach.

WRITING PLAN FOR A SIMPLE CLAIM

- *Opening:* Describe clearly the desired action.
- *Body:* Explain the nature of the claim, tell why the claim is justified, and provide details regarding the action requested.
- *Closing:* End pleasantly with a goodwill statement and include an end date if appropriate.

When an unhappy customer launches a complaint, 7 out of 10 will do business with the company again so long as their complaint is handled properly. A staggering 19 out of 20 will do business with the company again if the grievance is dealt with swiftly.
© Eyewire

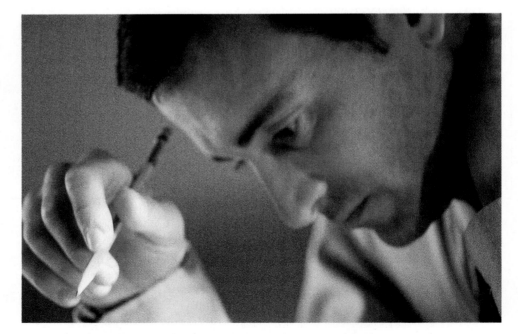

OPENING WITH ACTION

If you have a legitimate claim, you can expect a positive response from a company. Smart businesses today want to hear from their customers. That's why you should open a claim letter with a clear statement of the problem or with the action you want the receiver to take. You might expect a replacement, a refund, a new order, credit to your account, correction of a billing error, free repairs, free inspection, or cancellation of an order.

When the remedy is obvious, state it immediately (*Please send us 24 Royal hot-air popcorn poppers to replace the 24 hot-oil poppers sent in error with our order shipped January 4*). When the remedy is less obvious, you might ask for a change in policy or procedure or simply for an explanation (*Because three of our employees with confirmed reservations were refused rooms September 16 in your hotel, would you please clarify your policy regarding reservations and late arrivals*).

EXPLAINING IN THE BODY

In the body of a claim letter, explain the problem and justify your request. Provide the necessary details so that the difficulty can be corrected without further correspondence. Avoid becoming angry or trying to fix blame. Bear in mind that the person reading your letter is seldom responsible for the problem. Instead, state the facts logically, objectively, and unemotionally; let the reader decide on the causes.

Include copies of all pertinent documents such as invoices, sales slips, catalog descriptions, and repair records. (By the way, be sure to send copies and *not* your originals, which could be lost.) When service is involved, cite names of individuals spoken to and dates of calls. Assume that a company honestly wants to satisfy its customers—because most do. When an alternative remedy exists, spell it out (*If you are unable to send 24 Royal hot-air popcorn poppers immediately, please credit our account now and notify us when they become available*).

CLOSING PLEASANTLY

Conclude a claim letter with a courteous statement that promotes goodwill and expresses a desire for continued relations. If appropriate, include an end date (*We realize that mistakes in ordering and shipping sometimes occur. Because we've enjoyed your prompt service in the past, we hope that you will be able to send us the hot-air poppers by January 15*).

Finally, in making claims, act promptly. Delaying claims makes them appear less important. Delayed claims are also more difficult to verify. By taking the time to put your claim in writing, you indicate your seriousness. A written claim also starts a record of the problem, should later action be necessary. Be sure to keep a copy of your letter.

PUTTING IT ALL TOGETHER

Figure 6.2 shows a first draft of a hostile claim that vents the writer's anger but accomplishes little else. Its tone is belligerent, and it assumes that the company intentionally mischarged the customer. Furthermore, it fails to tell the reader how to remedy the problem. The revision tempers the tone, describes the problem objectively, and provides facts and figures. Most important, it specifies exactly what the customer wants done.

Notice that the letter in Figure 6.2 is shown with the return address typed above the date. This personal business style may be used when typing on paper without a printed letterhead. Notice, too, that this letter uses modified block style. The return address, date, and closing lines start at the center.

Simple Claim Request

FIGURE 6.2 Direct Claim Letter BEFORE and AFTER Revision

Sounds angry; jumps to conclusions

Forgets that mistakes happen

Fails to suggest solution

Dear Good Vibes:

You call yourselves Good Vibes, but all I'm getting from your service is bad vibes! I'm furious that you have your salespeople slip in unwanted service warranties to boost your sales.

When I bought my Panatronic VCR from Good Vibes, Inc., in August, I specifically told the salesperson that I did NOT want a three-year service warranty. But there it is on my VISA statement this month! You people have obviously billed me for a service I did not authorize. I refuse to pay this charge.

How can you hope to stay in business with such fraudulent practices? I was expecting to return this month and look at CD players, but you can be sure I'll find an honest dealer this time.

Sincerely,

Keith Cortez

AFTER Revision

1201 Lantana Court
Lake Worth, FL 33461
September 3, 200x

Mr. Sam Lee, Customer Service
Good Vibes, Inc.
2003 53rd Street
West Palm Beach, FL 33407

Dear Mr. Lee:

Please credit my VISA account, No. 0000-0046-2198-9421, to correct an erroneous charge of $299.

On August 8 I purchased a Panatronic VCR from Good Vibes, Inc. Although the salesperson discussed a three-year extended warranty with me, I decided against purchasing that service for $299. However, when my credit card statement arrived this month, I noticed an extra $299 charge from Good Vibes, Inc. I suspect that this charge represents the warranty I declined.

Enclosed is a copy of my sales invoice along with my VISA statement on which I circled the charge. Please authorize a credit immediately and send a copy of the transaction to me at the above address.

I'm enjoying all the features of my Panatronic VCR and would like to be shopping at Good Vibes for a CD player shortly.

Sincerely,

Keith Cortez

Keith Cortez

Enclosure

Personal business letter style

States simply and clearly what to do

Explains objectively what went wrong

Documents facts

Uses friendly tone and suggests continued business once problem is resolved

INFORMATION RESPONSE LETTER

Often, your messages will respond favorably to requests for information or action. A customer wants information about a product. A supplier asks to arrange a meeting. Another business inquires about one of your procedures. But before responding to any inquiry, be sure to check your facts and figures carefully. Any letter written on company stationery is considered a legally binding contract. If a policy or procedure needs authorization, seek approval from a supervisor or executive before writing the letter. In complying with requests, you'll want to apply the same direct pattern you used in making requests.

WRITING PLAN FOR AN INFORMATION RESPONSE LETTER

- *Subject line:* Identify previous correspondence and/or refer to the main idea.
- *Opening:* Deliver the most important information first.
- *Body:* Arrange information logically, explain and clarify it, provide additional information if appropriate, and build goodwill.
- *Closing:* End pleasantly.

SUBJECT LINE EFFICIENCY

An information response letter might contain a subject line, which helps the reader recognize the topic immediately. Knowledgeable business communicators use a subject line to refer to earlier correspondence or to summarize the main idea. Notice in Figure 6.3 that the subject line identifies the subject completely. The subject line may be in all capital letters or a combination of upper- and lowercase.

OPENING DIRECTLY

In the first sentence of an information response, deliver the information the reader wants. Avoid wordy, drawn-out openings (*I have before me your letter of February 6, in which you request information about . . .*). More forceful and more efficient is an opener that answers the inquiry (*Here is the information you wanted about . . .*). When agreeing to a request for action, announce the good news promptly (*Yes, I will be happy to speak to your business communication class on the topic of . . .*).

ARRANGING INFORMATION LOGICALLY

When answering a group of questions or providing considerable data, arrange the information logically and make it readable by using lists, tables, headings, boldface, italics, or other graphic devices. When customers or prospective customers inquire about products or services, your response should do more than merely supply answers. You'll also want to promote your organization and products. Be sure to present the promotional material with attention to the "you" view and to reader benefits (*You can use our standardized tests to free you from time-consuming employment screening*). You'll learn more about special techniques for developing sales and persuasive messages in Chapter 7.

CLOSING PLEASANTLY

To avoid abruptness, include a pleasant closing remark that shows your willingness to help the reader. Provide extra information if appropriate. Tailor your remarks to fit this letter and this reader. Since everyone appreciates being recognized as an individual, avoid form-letter closings such as *If we may be of further assistance, . . .*

FIGURE 6.3 Information Response Letter

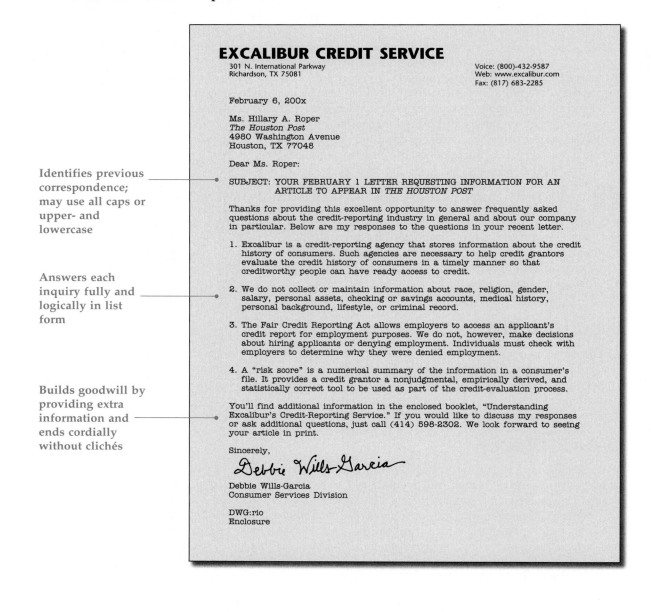

Identifies previous correspondence; may use all caps or upper- and lowercase

Answers each inquiry fully and logically in list form

Builds goodwill by providing extra information and ends cordially without clichés

---

EXCALIBUR CREDIT SERVICE

301 N. International Parkway
Richardson, TX 75081

Voice: (800)-432-9587
Web: www.excalibur.com
Fax: (817) 683-2285

February 6, 200x

Ms. Hillary A. Roper
The Houston Post
4980 Washington Avenue
Houston, TX 77048

Dear Ms. Roper:

SUBJECT: YOUR FEBRUARY 1 LETTER REQUESTING INFORMATION FOR AN ARTICLE TO APPEAR IN *THE HOUSTON POST*

Thanks for providing this excellent opportunity to answer frequently asked questions about the credit-reporting industry in general and about our company in particular. Below are my responses to the questions in your recent letter.

1. Excalibur is a credit-reporting agency that stores information about the credit history of consumers. Such agencies are necessary to help credit grantors evaluate the credit history of consumers in a timely manner so that creditworthy people can have ready access to credit.

2. We do not collect or maintain information about race, religion, gender, salary, personal assets, checking or savings accounts, medical history, personal background, lifestyle, or criminal record.

3. The Fair Credit Reporting Act allows employers to access an applicant's credit report for employment purposes. We do not, however, make decisions about hiring applicants or denying employment. Individuals must check with employers to determine why they were denied employment.

4. A "risk score" is a numerical summary of the information in a consumer's file. It provides a credit grantor a nonjudgmental, empirically derived, and statistically correct tool to be used as part of the credit-evaluation process.

You'll find additional information in the enclosed booklet, "Understanding Excalibur's Credit-Reporting Service." If you would like to discuss my responses or ask additional questions, just call (414) 598-2302. We look forward to seeing your article in print.

Sincerely,

Debbie Wills-Garcia

Debbie Wills-Garcia
Consumer Services Division

DWG:rio
Enclosure

CUSTOMER ORDER RESPONSE

✓ *Quick Check*

Letters that follow up orders create excellent opportunities to improve the company image and to sell products.

Many companies acknowledge orders by sending a printed postcard that merely informs the customer that the order has been received. Other companies take advantage of this opportunity to build goodwill and to promote new products and services. A personalized letter responding to an order is good business, particularly for new accounts, large accounts, and customers who haven't placed orders recently. An individualized letter is also necessary if the order involves irregularities, such as delivery delays, back-ordered items, or missing items. Letters that respond to orders should deliver the news immediately; therefore, the direct strategy is most effective. Here's a writing plan that will achieve the results you want in acknowledging orders.

Gateway Computer not only encourages in-store business with its Kids Zone, but it also promotes repeat business with its order response letters. New computer owners are offered 24-hour technical support and 12 months of free service with American Online. Smart companies use the order response letter to build goodwill through resale information as well as to introduce new products and services.
© Spencer Grant/ PhotoEdit, Inc.

 ## WRITING PLAN FOR AN ORDER RESPONSE

- *Opening:* Tell when and how the shipment will be sent.
- *Body:* Explain the details of the shipment, discuss any irregularities in the order, include resale information, and promote other products and services if appropriate.
- *Closing:* Build goodwill and use a friendly, personalized closing.

GIVING DELIVERY INFORMATION IN THE OPENING

Customers want to know when and how their orders will be sent. Since that news is most important, put it in the first sentence. An inefficient opener such as *We have received your order dated June 20* wastes words and the reader's time by providing information that could be inferred from more effective openers. Instead of stating that you have received an order, imply it in a first sentence that also provides delivery details (*We will ship the books requested in your Order No. 2980 . . .*).

> **✓ Quick Check**
> The first sentence should tell when and how an order will be sent.

PUTTING DETAILS IN THE BODY

You should include details relating to an order in the body of a letter that acknowledges the order. You will also want to discuss any irregularities about the order. If, for example, part of the order will be sent from a different location or prices have changed or items must be back-ordered, present this information.

The body of an order response is also the appropriate place to include resale information. *Resale* refers to the process of reassuring customers that their choices were good ones. You can use resale in an order letter by describing the product favorably (*The books you ordered are among our best-selling editions*). You might mention product features or attributes, popularity among customers, and successful use in certain applications. Perhaps your competitive price recommends the product.

Resale information confirms the discrimination and good judgment of your customers and encourages repeat business. After an opening statement describ-

> **✓ Quick Check**
> When a sales clerk tells you how good you look in the new suit you just purchased, the clerk is practicing "resale."

ing delivery information, resale information such as the following is appropriate: *The multipurpose checks you have ordered allow you to produce several different check formats, including accounts payable and payroll. Customers tell us that these computerized checks are the answer to their check-writing problems.*

Quick Check

Resale emphasizes a product already sold; *promotion* emphasizes additional products to be sold.

Order acknowledgment letters are also suitable channels for sales promotion material. An organization often has other products or services that it wishes to highlight and promote. For example, a computer supply house might include the following sales feature: *Another good buy from Quill is our popular 3 1/2-inch double-sided, high-density diskettes in a rainbow pack of 50 disks for only $21.95. And we will send you a diskette holder at no extra charge.* Use sales promotion material, however, in moderation. Too much can be a burden to read and therefore irritating.

SHOWING APPRECIATION IN THE CLOSING

Quick Check

The best closings are personalized; they relate to one particular letter.

The closing should be pleasant, forward-looking, and appreciative. Above all, it should be personalized. That is, it should relate to the particular customer whose order you are acknowledging. Don't use all-purpose form-letter closings such as *We appreciate your interest in our company* or *Thank you for your order.*

CUSTOMER CLAIM RESPONSE

Quick Check

The writer responding to customer claims seeks to rectify the wrong, regain customer confidence, and promote future business.

As you learned earlier, when an organization receives a claim, it usually means that something has gone wrong. In responding to a claim, you have three goals:

- To rectify the wrong, if one exists
- To regain the confidence of the customer
- To promote future business and goodwill

© Ted Goff (www.tedgoff.com)

If you decide to grant the claim, your response letter will represent good news to the reader. Use the direct strategy described in the following writing plan.

WRITING PLAN FOR GRANTING A CLAIM

- *Subject line:* (optional) Identify the previous correspondence and make a general reference to the main topic.
- *Opening:* Grant the request or announce the adjustment immediately. Include sales promotion if appropriate.
- *Body:* Provide details about how you are complying with the request. Try to regain the customer's confidence; include sales promotion if appropriate.
- *Closing:* End positively with a forward-looking thought; express confidence in future business relations. Avoid referring to unpleasantness.

REVEALING GOOD NEWS IN THE OPENING

Instead of beginning with a review of what went wrong, present the good news immediately. When Amy Hopkins responded to the claim of customer Sound Systems, Inc., about a missing shipment, her first draft, shown at the top of Figure 6.4,

FIGURE 6.4 **Customer Claim Response BEFORE and AFTER Revision**

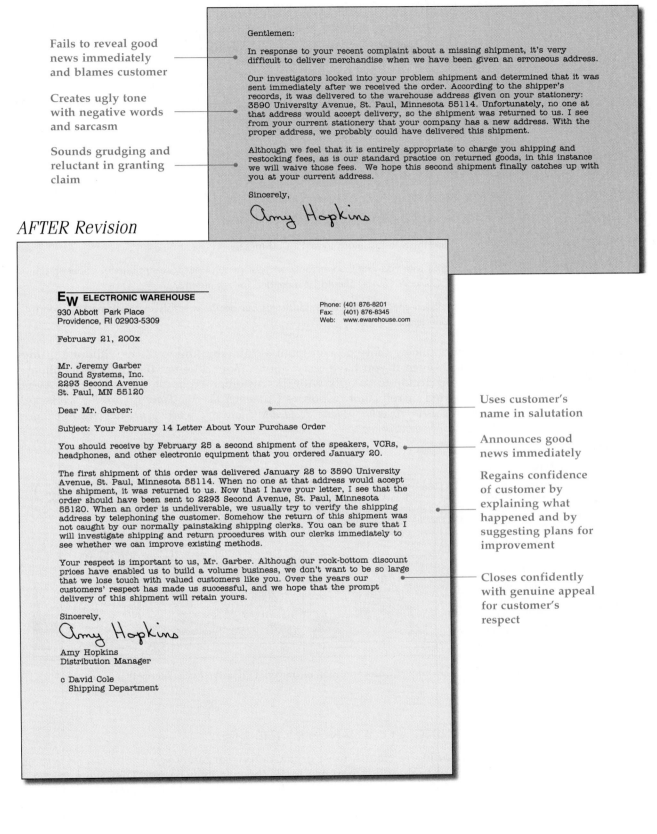

BEFORE Revision

Fails to reveal good news immediately and blames customer

Creates ugly tone with negative words and sarcasm

Sounds grudging and reluctant in granting claim

Gentlemen:

In response to your recent complaint about a missing shipment, it's very difficult to deliver merchandise when we have been given an erroneous address.

Our investigators looked into your problem shipment and determined that it was sent immediately after we received the order. According to the shipper's records, it was delivered to the warehouse address given on your stationery: 3590 University Avenue, St. Paul, Minnesota 55114. Unfortunately, no one at that address would accept delivery, so the shipment was returned to us. I see from your current stationery that your company has a new address. With the proper address, we probably could have delivered this shipment.

Although we feel that it is entirely appropriate to charge you shipping and restocking fees, as is our standard practice on returned goods, in this instance we will waive those fees. We hope this second shipment finally catches up with you at your current address.

Sincerely,

Amy Hopkins

AFTER Revision

E_W **ELECTRONIC WAREHOUSE**

930 Abbott Park Place
Providence, RI 02903-5309

Phone: (401 876-8201
Fax: (401) 876-8345
Web: www.ewarehouse.com

February 21, 200x

Mr. Jeremy Garber
Sound Systems, Inc.
2293 Second Avenue
St. Paul, MN 55120

Dear Mr. Garber:

Subject: Your February 14 Letter About Your Purchase Order

You should receive by February 25 a second shipment of the speakers, VCRs, headphones, and other electronic equipment that you ordered January 20.

The first shipment of this order was delivered January 28 to 3590 University Avenue, St. Paul, Minnesota 55114. When no one at that address would accept the shipment, it was returned to us. Now that I have your letter, I see that the order should have been sent to 2293 Second Avenue, St. Paul, Minnesota 55120. When an order is undeliverable, we usually try to verify the shipping address by telephoning the customer. Somehow the return of this shipment was not caught by our normally painstaking shipping clerks. You can be sure that I will investigate shipping and return procedures with our clerks immediately to see whether we can improve existing methods.

Your respect is important to us, Mr. Garber. Although our rock-bottom discount prices have enabled us to build a volume business, we don't want to be so large that we lose touch with valued customers like you. Over the years our customers' respect has made us successful, and we hope that the prompt delivery of this shipment will retain yours.

Sincerely,

Amy Hopkins

Amy Hopkins
Distribution Manager

c David Cole
  Shipping Department

Uses customer's name in salutation

Announces good news immediately

Regains confidence of customer by explaining what happened and by suggesting plans for improvement

Closes confidently with genuine appeal for customer's respect

was angry. No wonder. Sound Systems had apparently provided the wrong shipping address, and the goods were returned. But once Amy and her company decided to send a second shipment and comply with the customer's claim, she had to give up the anger and strive to retain the goodwill and the business of this customer. The improved version of her letter announces that a new shipment will arrive shortly.

If you decide to comply with a customer's claim, let the receiver know immediately. Don't begin your letter with a negative statement (*We are very sorry to hear that you are having trouble with your Sno-Flake ice crusher*). This approach reminds the reader of the problem and may rekindle the heated emotions or unhappy feelings experienced when the claim was written. Instead, focus on the good news. The following openings for various letters illustrate how to begin a message with good news.

> You may take your Sno-Flake ice crusher to Ben's Appliances at 310 First Street, Myrtle Beach, where it will be repaired at no cost to you.

> Thanks for your letter about your new Toyota Corolla tires. You are certainly justified in expecting them to last more than 12,000 miles.

> We agree with you that the warranty on your general-purpose straight-cut paper shredder GCC Model 22450 should be extended for six months.

> The enclosed check for $325 demonstrates our desire to satisfy our customers and earn their confidence.

In announcing that you will grant a claim, be sure to do so without a grudging tone—even if you have reservations about whether the claim is legitimate. Once you decide to comply with the customer's request, do so happily. Avoid half-hearted or reluctant responses (*Although the Sno-Flake ice crusher works well when it is used properly, we have decided to allow you to take yours to Ben's Appliances for repair at our expense.*)

CATHY

CATHY © Cathy Guisewite. Reprinted with permission of Universal Press Syndicate. All rights reserved.

EXPLAINING COMPLIANCE IN THE BODY

In responding to claims, most organizations sincerely want to correct a wrong. They want to do more than just make the customer happy. They want to stand behind their products and services; they want to do what's right.

In the body of the letter, explain how you are complying with the claim. In all but the most routine claims, you should also seek to regain the confidence of the customer. You might reasonably expect that a customer who has experienced difficulty with a product, with delivery, with billing, or with service has lost faith in your organization. Rebuilding that faith is important for future business.

How to rebuild lost confidence depends on the situation and the claim. If procedures need to be revised, explain what changes will be made. If a product has defective parts, tell how the product is being improved. If service is faulty, describe genuine efforts to improve it. Notice in Figure 6.4 that the writer promises to investigate shipping procedures to see whether improvements might prevent future mishaps.

Sometimes the problem is not with the product but with the way it's being used. In other instances customers misunderstand warranties or inadvertently cause delivery and billing mix-ups by supplying incorrect information. Remember that rational and sincere explanations will do much to regain the confidence of unhappy customers.

In your explanation avoid emphasizing negative words such as *trouble, regret, misunderstanding, fault, defective, error, inconvenience,* and *unfortunately.* Keep your message positive and upbeat.

Deciding Whether to Apologize

Whether to apologize is a debatable issue. Some writing experts argue that apologies remind customers of their complaints and are therefore negative. These writers avoid apologies; instead they concentrate on how they are satisfying the customer. Real letters that respond to customers' claims, however, often include apologies.[2] If you feel that your company is at fault and that an apology is an appropriate goodwill gesture, by all means include it. Be careful, though, not to admit negligence. You'll learn more about responding to negative letters in Chapter 8.

Showing Confidence in the Closing

End positively by expressing confidence that the problem has been resolved and that continued business relations will result. You might mention the product in a favorable light, suggest a new product, express your appreciation for the customer's business, or anticipate future business. It's often appropriate to refer to the desire to be of service and to satisfy customers. Notice how the following closings illustrate a positive, confident tone.

> Your Sno-Flake ice crusher will help you remain cool and refreshed this summer. For your additional summer enjoyment, consider our Smoky Joe tabletop gas grill shown in the enclosed summer catalog. We genuinely value your business and look forward to your future orders.

> We hope that this refund check convinces you of our sincere desire to satisfy our customers. Our goal is to earn your confidence and continue to justify that confidence with quality products and matchless service.

> You were most helpful in telling us about this situation and giving us an opportunity to correct it. We sincerely appreciate your cooperation.

> In all your future dealings with us, you will find us striving our hardest to merit your confidence by serving you with efficiency and sincere concern.

LETTER OF RECOMMENDATION

Letters of recommendation may be written to nominate people for awards and for membership in organizations. More frequently, though, they are written to evaluate present or former employees. The central concern in these messages is honesty. Thus, you should avoid exaggerating or distorting a candidate's qualifications to cover up weaknesses or to destroy the person's chances. Ethically and legally, you have a duty to the candidate as well as to other employers to describe that person truthfully and objectively. You don't, however, have to endorse everyone who asks. Since recommendations are generally voluntary, you can—and should—resist writing letters for individuals you can't truthfully support. Ask these people to find other recommenders who know them better.

Some businesspeople today refuse to write recommendations for former employees because they fear lawsuits. Other businesspeople argue that recommendations are useless because they're always positive. Despite the general avoidance of negatives, well-written recommendations do help match candidates with jobs. Hiring companies learn more about a candidate's skills and potential. As a result, they are able to place a candidate properly. Therefore, you should learn to write such letters because you will surely be expected to do so in your future career.

For letters of recommendation, use the direct strategy as described in the following writing plan.

🌐 WRITING PLAN FOR A LETTER OF RECOMMENDATION

- *Opening:* Identify the applicant, the position, and the reason for writing. State that the message is confidential. Establish your relationship with the applicant. Describe the length of employment or relationship.
- *Body:* Describe job duties. Provide specific examples of the applicant's professional and personal skills and attributes. Compare the applicant with others in his or her field.
- *Closing:* Summarize the significant attributes of the applicant. Offer an overall rating. Draw a conclusion regarding the recommendation.

IDENTIFYING THE PURPOSE IN THE OPENING

Begin an employment recommendation by identifying the candidate and the position sought, if it is known. State that your remarks are confidential, and suggest that you are writing at the request of the applicant. Describe your relationship with the candidate, as shown here:

> Ms. Cindy Rosales, whom your organization is considering for the position of media trainer, requested that I submit confidential information on her behalf. Ms. Rosales worked under my supervision for the past two years in our Video Training Center.

Letters that recommend individuals for awards may open with more supportive statements, such as *I'm very pleased to nominate Robert Walsh for the Employee-of-the-Month award. For the past sixteen months, Mr. Walsh served as staff accountant in my division. During that time he distinguished himself by . . . .*

DESCRIBING PERFORMANCE IN THE BODY

The body of an employment recommendation should describe the applicant's job performance and potential. Employers are particularly interested in such traits as communication skills, organizational skills, people skills, ability to work with a team, ability to work independently, honesty, dependability, ambition, loyalty, and initiative. In describing these traits, be sure to back them up with evidence. One of the biggest weaknesses in letters of recommendation is that writers tend to make global, nonspecific statements (*He was careful and accurate* versus *He completed eight financial statements monthly with about 99 percent accuracy*). Employers prefer definite, task-related descriptions:

> As a training development specialist, Ms. Rosales demonstrated superior organizational and interpersonal skills. She started as a Specialist I, writing scripts for interactive video modules. After six months she was promoted to team leader. In that role she supervised five employees who wrote, produced, evaluated, revised, and installed 14 computer/videodisc training courses over a period of eighteen months.

Be especially careful to support any negative comments with verification (not *He was slower than other customer service reps* but *He answered 25 calls an hour, while most service reps average 40 calls an hour*). In reporting deficiencies, be sure to describe behavior (*Her last two reports were late and had to be rewritten by her supervisor*) rather than evaluate it (*She is unreliable and her reports are careless*).

EVALUATING IN THE CONCLUSION

In the final paragraph of a recommendation, you should offer an overall evaluation. Indicate how you would rank this person in relation to others in similar positions. Many managers add a statement indicating whether they would rehire the applicant, given the chance. If you are strongly supportive, summarize the candidate's best qualities. In the closing you might also offer to answer questions by telephone. Such a statement, though, could suggest that the candidate has weak skills and that you will make damaging statements orally but not in print. Here's how our sample letter might close:

> Ms. Rosales is one of the most productive employees I have supervised. I would rank her in the top 10 percent of all the media specialists with whom I have worked. Were she to return to Bridgeport, we would be pleased to rehire her. If you need additional information, call me at (517) 440-3019.

General letters of recommendation, written when the candidate has no specific position in mind, often begin with the salutation TO PROSPECTIVE EMPLOYERS. More specific recommendations, to support applications to known positions, address an individual. When the addressee's name is unknown, consider using the simplified letter format, shown in Figure 6.5, which avoids a salutation.

Figure 6.5 illustrates a complete employment letter of recommendation and provides a summary of writing tips. After naming the applicant and the position sought, the letter describes the applicant's present duties. Instead of merely naming positive qualities (*He is personable, possesses superior people skills, works well with a team, is creative, and shows initiative*), these attributes are demonstrated with specific examples and details.

WRITING WINNING GOODWILL MESSAGES

Goodwill messages, which include thanks, recognition, and sympathy, seem to intimidate many communicators. Finding the right words to express feelings is sometimes more difficult than writing ordinary business documents. Writers tend

FIGURE 6.5 Employment Recommendation Letter

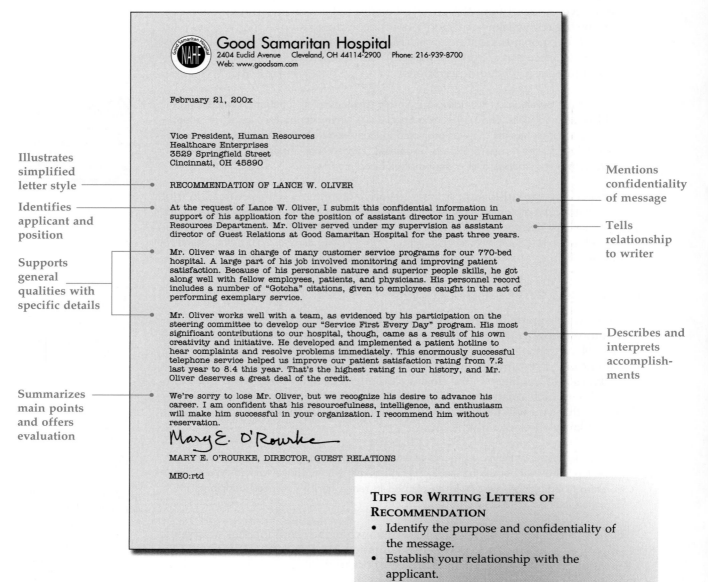

Illustrates simplified letter style

Identifies applicant and position

Supports general qualities with specific details

Summarizes main points and offers evaluation

Good Samaritan Hospital
2404 Euclid Avenue   Cleveland, OH 44114-2900   Phone: 216-939-8700
Web: www.goodsam.com

February 21, 200x

Vice President, Human Resources
Healthcare Enterprises
3529 Springfield Street
Cincinnati, OH 45890

RECOMMENDATION OF LANCE W. OLIVER

At the request of Lance W. Oliver, I submit this confidential information in support of his application for the position of assistant director in your Human Resources Department. Mr. Oliver served under my supervision as assistant director of Guest Relations at Good Samaritan Hospital for the past three years.

Mr. Oliver was in charge of many customer service programs for our 770-bed hospital. A large part of his job involved monitoring and improving patient satisfaction. Because of his personable nature and superior people skills, he got along well with fellow employees, patients, and physicians. His personnel record includes a number of "Gotcha" citations, given to employees caught in the act of performing exemplary service.

Mr. Oliver works well with a team, as evidenced by his participation on the steering committee to develop our "Service First Every Day" program. His most significant contributions to our hospital, though, came as a result of his own creativity and initiative. He developed and implemented a patient hotline to hear complaints and resolve problems immediately. This enormously successful telephone service helped us improve our patient satisfaction rating from 7.2 last year to 8.4 this year. That's the highest rating in our history, and Mr. Oliver deserves a great deal of the credit.

We're sorry to lose Mr. Oliver, but we recognize his desire to advance his career. I am confident that his resourcefulness, intelligence, and enthusiasm will make him successful in your organization. I recommend him without reservation.

Mary E. O'Rourke

MARY E. O'ROURKE, DIRECTOR, GUEST RELATIONS

MEO:rtd

Mentions confidentiality of message

Tells relationship to writer

Describes and interprets accomplishments

TIPS FOR WRITING LETTERS OF RECOMMENDATION
- Identify the purpose and confidentiality of the message.
- Establish your relationship with the applicant.
- Describe the length of employment and job duties, if relevant.
- Provide specific examples of the applicant's professional and personal skills.
- Compare the applicant with others in his or her field.
- Offer an overall rating of the applicant.
- Summarize the significant attributes of the applicant.
- Draw a conclusion regarding the recommendation.

to procrastinate when it comes to goodwill messages, or else they send a ready-made card or pick up the telephone. Remember, though, that the personal sentiments of the sender are always more expressive and more meaningful to readers than are printed cards or oral messages. Taking the time to write gives more importance to our well-wishing. Personal notes also provide a record that can be reread, savored, and treasured.

In expressing thanks, recognition, or sympathy, you should always do so promptly. These messages are easier to write when the situation is fresh in your mind. They also mean more to the recipient. And don't forget that a prompt thank-you note carries the hidden message that you care and that you consider the event to be important. You will learn to write four kinds of goodwill messages—thanks, congratulations, praise, and sympathy. Instead of writing plans for each of them, we recommend that you concentrate on the five Ss. Goodwill messages should be:

✓ Quick Check

Messages that express thanks, recognition, and sympathy should be written promptly.

- **Selfless.** Be sure to focus the message solely on the receiver not the sender. Don't talk about yourself; avoid such comments as *I remember when I . . . .*
- **Specific.** Personalize the message by mentioning specific incidents or characteristics of the receiver. Telling a colleague *Great speech* is much less effective than *Great story about McDonald's marketing in Moscow*. Take care to verify names and other facts.
- **Sincere.** Let your words show genuine feelings. Rehearse in your mind how you would express the message to the receiver orally. Then transform that conversational language to your written message. Avoid pretentious, formal, or flowery language (*It gives me great pleasure to extend felicitations on the occasion of your firm's 20th anniversary*).
- **Spontaneous.** Keep the message fresh and enthusiastic. Avoid canned phrases (*Congratulations on your promotion, Good luck in the future*). Strive for directness and naturalness, not creative brilliance.
- **Short.** Although goodwill messages can be as long as needed, try to accomplish your purpose in only a few sentences. What is most important is remembering an individual. Such caring does not require documentation or wordiness. Individuals and business organizations often use special note cards or stationery for brief messages.

✓ Quick Check

Goodwill messages are most effective when they are selfless, specific, sincere, spontaneous, and short.

THANKS

When someone has done you a favor or when an action merits praise, you need to extend thanks or show appreciation. Letters of appreciation may be written to customers for their orders, to hosts and hostesses for their hospitality, to individuals for kindnesses performed, and especially to customers who complain. After all, complainers are actually providing you with "free consulting reports from the field." Complainers who feel that they were listened to often become the greatest promoters of an organization.[3]

Send letters of thanks to customers, hosts, and individuals who have performed kind acts.

Because the receiver will be pleased to hear from you, you can open directly with the purpose of your message. The letter in Figure 6.6 thanks a speaker who addressed a group of marketing professionals. Although such thank-you notes can be quite short, this one is a little longer because the writer wants to lend importance to the receiver's efforts. Notice that every sentence relates to the receiver and offers enthusiastic praise. And, by using the receiver's name along with contractions and positive words, the writer makes the letter sound warm and conversational.

Written notes that show appreciation and express thanks are significant to their receivers. In expressing thanks, you generally write a short note on special notepaper or heavy card stock. The following messages provide models for expressing thanks for a gift, for a favor, and for hospitality.

FIGURE 6.6 Thank-You for a Favor

Tells purpose and
delivers praise

Personalizes the
message by using
specifics rather
than generalities

Spotlights the
reader's talents

Concludes with
compliments and
thanks

American Marketing Association

Dallas-Fort Worth Chapter
P.O. Box 3598, Dallas, TX 74209   www.dallasama.com   (817) 469-8274

March 20, 200x

Mr. Bryant Huffman
Marketing Manager, Western Division
Toys "R" Us, Inc.
Dallas, TX 75232

Dear Bryant:

You have our sincere gratitude for providing the Dallas–Fort Worth chapter
of the AMA with one of the best presentations our group has ever heard.

Your description of the battle Toys "R" Us waged to begin marketing
products in Japan was a genuine eye-opener for many of us. Nine years of
preparation establishing connections and securing permissions seems an
eternity, but obviously such persistence and patience pay off. We now
understand better the need to learn local customs and nurture relationships
when dealing in Japan.

In addition to your good advice, we particularly enjoyed your sense of
humor and jokes—as you must have recognized from the uproarious
laughter. What a great routine you do on faulty translations!

We're grateful, Bryant, for the entertaining and instructive evening you
provided our marketing professionals. Thanks!

Cordially,

Judy Wagner

Judy Wagner
Program Chair, AMA

JRW:grw

Quick Check

Identify the gift, tell why you appreciate it, and explain how you will use it.

To Express Thanks for a Gift

Thanks, Laura, to you and the other members of the department for honoring me with
the elegant Waterford crystal vase at the party celebrating my twentieth anniversary with
the company.

The height and shape of the vase are perfect to hold roses and other bouquets from
my garden. Each time I fill it, I'll remember your thoughtfulness in choosing this lovely
gift for me.

Quick Check

Tell what the favor means using sincere, simple statements.

To Send Thanks for a Favor

I sincerely appreciate your filling in for me last week when I was too ill to attend the
planning committee meeting for the spring exhibition.

Without your participation much of my preparatory work would have been lost. It's
comforting to know that competent and generous individuals like you are part of our team,
Mark. Moreover, it's my very good fortune to be able to count you as a friend. I'm grateful to you.

To Extend Thanks for Hospitality

Jeffrey and I want you to know how much we enjoyed the dinner party for our department that you hosted Saturday evening. Your charming home and warm hospitality, along with the lovely dinner and sinfully delicious chocolate dessert, combined to create a truly memorable evening.

Most of all, though, we appreciate your kindness in cultivating togetherness in our department. Thanks, Jennifer, for being such a special person.

Compliment the fine food, charming surroundings, warm hospitality, excellent host and hostess, and good company.

RESPONSE

Should you respond when you receive a congratulatory note or a written pat on the back? By all means! These messages are attempts to connect personally; they are efforts to reach out, to form professional and/or personal bonds. Failing to respond to notes of congratulations and most other goodwill messages is like failing to say "You're welcome" when someone says "Thank you." Responding to such messages is simply the right thing to do. Do avoid, though, minimizing your achievements with comments that suggest you don't really deserve the praise or that the sender is exaggerating your good qualities.

Take the time to respond to any goodwill message you may receive.

To Answer a Congratulatory Note

Thanks for your kind words regarding my award, and thanks, too, for sending me the newspaper clipping. I truly appreciate your thoughtfulness and warm wishes.

To Respond to a Pat on the Back

Your note about my work made me feel good. I'm grateful for your thoughtfulness.

SYMPATHY

Most of us can bear misfortune and grief more easily when we know that others care. Notes expressing sympathy, though, are probably more difficult to write than any other kind of message. Commercial "In sympathy" cards make the task easier—but they are far less meaningful. Grieving friends want to know what you think—not what Hallmark's card writers think. To help you get started, you can always glance through cards expressing sympathy. They will supply ideas about the kinds of thoughts you might wish to convey in your own words. In writing a sympathy note, (1) refer to the death or misfortune sensitively, using words that show you understand what a crushing blow it is; (2) in the case of a death, praise the deceased in a personal way; (3) offer assistance without going into excessive detail; and (4) end on a reassuring, forward-looking note. Sympathy messages may be typed, although handwriting seems more personal. In either case, use notepaper or personal stationery.

Sympathy notes should refer to the misfortune sensitively and offer assistance.

To Express Condolences

We are deeply saddened, Gayle, to learn of the death of your husband. Warren's kind nature and friendly spirit endeared him to all who knew him. He will be missed.

Although words seem empty in expressing our grief, we want you to know that your friends at QuadCom extend their profound sympathy to you. If we may help you or lighten your load in any way, you have but to call.

We know that the treasured memories of your many happy years together, along with the support of your family and many friends, will provide strength and comfort in the months ahead.

In condolence notes mention the loss tactfully and recognize the good qualities of the deceased. Assure the receiver of your concern. Offer assistance. Conclude on positive, reassuring note.

SUMMING UP AND LOOKING FORWARD

In this chapter you learned to write letters that respond favorably to information requests, orders, and customer claims. You also learned to write effective responses, letters of recommendation, and a variety of goodwill messages. All of these routine letters use the direct strategy. They open immediately with the main idea followed by details and explanations. But not all letters will carry good news. Occasionally, you must deny requests and deliver bad news. In the next chapter you will learn to use the indirect strategy in conveying negative news.

Interactive Learning @ http://www.westwords.com/guffey/students.html
Prepare for tests and reinforce your chapter knowledge with interactive quizzes and crossword puzzles.

CRITICAL THINKING

1. What's wrong with using the indirect pattern for writing routine requests and replies? If in the end the reader understands the message, why make a big fuss over the organization?
2. Since brevity is valued in business writing, is it ever wise to respond with more information than requested? Why or why not?
3. Which is more effective in claim letters—anger or objectivity? Why?
4. Why is it important to regain the confidence of a customer when you respond to a claim letter?
5. Is it appropriate for businesspeople to write goodwill messages expressing thanks, recognition, and sympathy to business acquaintances? Why or why not?

CHAPTER REVIEW

6. Why do businesspeople still write letters when e-mail is so much faster?

7. What determines whether you write a letter directly or indirectly?

8. What are the two most important positions in a letter?

9. List two ways that you could begin an inquiry letter that asks many questions.

10. What three elements are appropriate in the closing of a request for information?

11. What is a claim letter? Give an original example.

12. What are the three goals of a writer responding to a customer claim letter?

13. Why do some companies comply with nearly all claims?

14. What information should the opening in a letter of recommendation include?

15. The best goodwill messages include what five characteristics?

WRITING IMPROVEMENT EXERCISES

LETTER OPENERS

Your Task. Indicate which of the following entries represents an effective direct opening.

16.a. Please allow me to introduce myself. I am Courtney Wilson, and I am assistant to the director of Human Resources at MicroSynergy. Our company has an intranet, which we would like to use more efficiently to elicit feedback on employee issues and concerns. I understand that you have a software product called "Opinion-ware" that might do this, and I need to ask you some questions about it.

b. Please answer the following questions about your software product "Opinion-ware," which we are considering for our intranet. _____

17.a. Thank you for your e-mail of June 13 in which you inquired about the availability of sprinkler part H640B. _____

b. We have on hand an ample supply of H640B sprinkler parts.

18.a. Yes, the Princess Cruise Club is planning a 15-day Mediterranean cruise beginning October 20. _____

b. This will acknowledge receipt of your letter of December 2 in which you ask about our Mediterranean cruise schedule.

19.a. Your letter of April 15 requesting a refund has been referred to me because Ms. Rivera is away from the office. _____

b. Your refund check for $175 is enclosed.

20.a. We sincerely appreciate your recent order for plywood wallboard panels.

b. The plywood wallboard panels that you requested were shipped today by Coastal Express and should reach you by August 12. _____

DIRECT OPENINGS

Your Task. Revise the following openings so that they are more direct. Add information if necessary.

21. Hello! My name is Todd Thompson, and I am the assistant manager of Body Trends, a fitness equipment center in Miami Shores. My manager has asked me to inquire about the upright and semirecumbent cycling machines that we saw advertised in the June issue of *Your Health* magazine. I have a number of questions.

22. Because I've lost your order blank, I have to write this letter. I hope that it's all right to place an order this way. I am interested in ordering a number of things from your summer catalog, which I still have although the order blank is missing.

23. Pursuant to your letter of January 15, I am writing in regard to your inquiry about whether we offer our European-style patio umbrella in colors. This unique umbrella is a very popular item and receives a number of inquiries. Its 10-foot canopy protects you when the sun is directly overhead, but it also swivels and tilts to virtually any angle for continuous sun protection all day long. It comes in two colors: off white and forest green.

24. I am pleased to receive your inquiry regarding the possibility of my acting as a speaker at the final semester meeting of your business management club on April 30. The topic of online résumés interests me and is one on which I think I could impart helpful information to your members. Therefore, I am responding in the affirmative to your kind invitation.

25. We have just received your letter of March 12 regarding the unfortunate troubles you are having with your Magnum videocassette recorder. In your letter you ask whether you may send the flawed VCR to us for inspection. Although we normally handle all service requests through our local dealers, in your circumstance we are willing to take a look at your unit here at our Richmond plant. Therefore, please send it to us so that we may determine what's wrong.

CLOSING PARAGRAPH

Your Task. The following concluding paragraph to a claim letter response suffers from faults in strategy, tone, and emphasis. Revise and improve.

26. As a result of your complaint of June 2, we are sending a replacement shipment of laser printers by Atlantic Express. Unfortunately, this shipment will not reach you until June 5. We hope that you will not allow this troubling incident and the resulting inconvenience and lost sales you suffered to jeopardize our future business relations. In the past we have been able to provide you with quality products and prompt service.

WRITING IMPROVEMENT CASES

6.1 INFORMATION REQUEST: RÉSUMÉ-SCANNING AT PATAGONIA. You're now in the job market, and you'd really like to apply for a job at Patagonia, the sports clothing and equipment retailer. Patagonia is ranked by *Fortune* magazine as one of the best U.S. employers. You are particularly impressed by its commitment to the environment and staffing diversity. But before you send your résumé, you want to know whether Patagonia scans incoming résumés. If it does, you'll have to make some changes in yours. But what changes? You decide to check the Patagonia Web site; however, you don't see anything about résumés. You telephoned but didn't get a clear answer. You're still wondering whether the company uses software to scan incoming résumés. If so, what should you do to make your résumé scannable? And how about faxing your résumé? Or would it be better to send it by e-mail? Perhaps you should send two résumés—one that is impressive looking and one that is plain but scannable. What about key words? You really don't have a clue about how to prepare a scannable résumé. You decide to write to Patagonia requesting information.

1. What should you include in the opening of an information request?

2. What should the body of your letter contain?

3. How can questions be handled most effectively?

4. How should you close the letter?

Writing Improvement Cases

Your Task. Using your own return address, write a personal business letter to Ms. Kendra Woods, Recruiting, Patagonia, P. O. Box 32060, Reno, NV 89533-2060. Inquire whether Patagonia scans incoming résumés. Ask specific questions about how to prepare and submit yours. Don't ask about jobs just yet!

6.2 INFORMATION RESPONSE: McDONALD'S GOES GREEN.

Fast-food giant McDonald's is often accused of generating excessive litter and abusing the environment with its packaging and products. It receives letters from consumers asking what it is doing to reduce waste and improve the environment.

Your Task. As part of a group of interns at McDonald's, you are to revise the following rough draft of an information response letter to be sent to people inquiring about the company's environmental policies and practices. Analyze the letter; list at least five weaknesses. What writing plan should this letter follow? If your instructor agrees, revise it. Add an appropriate subject line.

Current date

Ms. Julie Kahn
176 Prospect Avenue
Elmhurst, IL 60126

Dear Ms. Kahn:

This is in response to your inquiry about McDonald's environmental policies. As a leader in the fast-food industry, reducing waste and conserving the environment are extremely important to those of us here at McDonald's. Since it began working with the Environmental Defense Fund 80 percent of its restaurant waste stream has been eliminated by McDonald's. McDonald's is reducing it's impact on landfills and world resources. McDonald's have introduced a number of practices that are environmentally-friendly.

For one thing, we are developing new packaging. In fact, we have reduced our polystyrene use by 90 percent. Another thing we are doing is increasing recycling. Our suppliers are using corrugated boxes with at least 35 percent recycled content. Reusable salad lids and shipping pallets, bulk condiment dispensers, and refillable coffee mugs are being tested. Another thing we are doing has to do with composting. More of our restaurants are experimenting with compositing egg shells, coffee grounds, and food scraps. Another thing we are doing has to do with reduced waste. All of our suppliers must meet new waste-reduction goals. And restaurant crews have been retrained to give waste reduction equal priority with quality quickness and cleanliness.

As you can see, MdDonald's cares about preserving the earths resources for today. And for the future. We think we are doing a great job in our commitment to conservation. But you can see for yourself by visiting your local McDonald's We hope you will use the enclosed sandwich coupons and experience first hand the changes we're making at McDonald's.

Sincerely,

1. List at least five weaknesses in the preceding letter.

2. Outline a writing plan for an information response.

   Subject line:

   Opening:

   Body:

   Closing:

6.3 ORDER REQUEST: CAMERA JUMBLE

Your Task. Analyze the following ineffective request for merchandise, and list its weaknesses. Outline a writing plan for an order request. Then revise using block style and your return address above the date. Add any necessary information. Consider a different salutation, such as "Greetings" or "Dear Cameratone."

Current date

Cameratone, Inc.
140 Northern Boulevard
Flushing, NY 11354-1400

Dear Sir:

I saw a number of items in your summer/fall catalog that would fit my Lentax ME camera. I am particularly interested in your Super Zoom 55-200mm lens. Its number is SF39971, and it costs $139.95. To go with this lens I will need a polarizing filter. Its number is SF29032 and costs $22.95 and should fit a 52mm lens. Also include a 05CC magenta filter for a 52mm lens. That number is SF29036 and it costs $9.95. Please send also a Hikemaster camera case for $24.95. Its number is SF28355.

I am interested in having these items charged to my credit card. I'd sure like to get them quickly because my vacation starts soon.

Sincerely,

1. List at least five weaknesses in this letter.

2. Outline a writing plan for an order request.

   Opening:

   Body:

   Closing:

6.4 CLAIM REQUEST: GAS TANK DILEMMA

Your Task. Analyze the following poorly written letter. List its weaknesses, and outline a writing plan. If your instructor directs, revise the letter.

Current date

Mr. Kent Fowler, Manager
Customer Service
Avon Car Rentals
6501 King Lawrence Road
Raleigh, NC 27607

Dear Customer Service Manager Kent Fowler:

This is to inform you that you can't have it both ways. Either you provide customers with cars with full gas tanks or you don't. And if you don't, you shouldn't charge them when they return with empty tanks!

In view of the fact that I picked up a car in Raleigh August 22 with an empty tank, I had to fill it immediately. Then I drove it until August 25. When I returned to Charlotte, I naturally let the tank go nearly empty, since that is the way I received the car in Raleigh.

But your attendant in Charlotte charged me to fill the tank—$26.50 (premium gasoline at premium prices)! Although I explained to him that I had received it with an empty tank, he kept telling me that company policy required that he charge for a fill-up. My total bill came to $266.50, which, you must agree, is a lot of money for a rental period of only three days. I have the signed rental agreement and a receipt showing that I paid the full amount and that it included $26.50 for a gas fill-up when I returned the car.

Inasmuch as my company is a new customer and inasmuch as we had hoped to use your agency for our future car rentals because of your competitive rates, I trust that you will give this matter your prompt attention.

Disappointedly yours,

1. List at least five weaknesses.

2. Outline a writing plan for a claim request.

   Opening:

   Body:

   Closing:

6.5 INFORMATION REQUEST: BREWING "COFFEE SHOP" BEVERAGES IN THE OFFICE.
Workers in your office are big coffee drinkers. Some leave work to go to a nearby Starbucks, and others use instant coffee to brew their own. As manager, you realize that productivity and morale could be improved if your office supplied "coffee shop quality" in freshly brewed coffee. You saw a Flavia beverage system in another office, and you decide to look into purchasing such a system for your office. You have a number of questions about such a system.

The biggest problem is plumbing. If it requires plumbing, you can't use it. You do have cold water available, but not plumbing. You wonder if a Flavia Brewing System offers drinks other than coffee, such as hot chocolate and tea. Since you are a cappuccino fan, you want to know whether it makes authentic cappuccino drinks. You're concerned about cleaning, maintenance, supplies, and repairs. You also worry about how employees will pay for each cup of coffee or other beverage. Perhaps coin operation is available. A number one concern, of course, is how much the system would cost and what kind of warranty is offered.

Your Task. Write a well-organized information request to Mr. Jeffrey Stone, Sales Manager, Flavia Brewing Systems, 1358 Dickens Avenue, Manhattan, KS 66503. Inquire about a Flavia Brewing System for your 25-person office staff. You need the information within two weeks for the next management council meeting.

6.6 INFORMATION REQUEST: REDUCING JUNK MAIL.
As editor of your company newsletter, you have a bright idea. On the radio you heard the tail end of an announcement about reducing the amount of direct mail advertising (junk mail) that people receive. You think you heard that people can write to the Direct Marketing Association and request that their names be removed from direct mail lists. This would make a good article for your newsletter. Nearly everyone hates junk mail. Because you believe that a written request will receive a better response than a phone call or an e-mail, you decide to write a letter to the Direct Marketing Association. You have many questions. You are curious about who sponsors this program. You wonder why the association would support a program to reduce direct mail advertising. How could this program possibly serve its members? You need to know what to tell your readers about how the program works. It occurs to you that your employees might also be interested in how to reduce calls from telephone marketers.

Your Task. Write to the Mail Preference Service, Direct Marketing Association, P.O. Box 9008, Farmingdale, NY 11735-9008. Use your imagination to develop a list of good questions so that you can write an interesting and helpful article for "The Inside Scoop," your company newsletter. You'd like a reply within three weeks to meet your next newsletter deadline. How should the Direct Marketing Association respond to your letter? Call you? Send an e-mail? Write a letter? Since you don't have the name of an individual to address, you can either use "Greetings" or "Dear Direct Marketing Association" as your salutation.

6.7 INFORMATION REQUEST: CHECKING THE BACKGROUND OF JOB CANDIDATES AT WHOLE FOODS MARKET.
After a steady diet of TV dinners in his childhood, John Mackey was intrigued by vegetarian, ethnic, and natural foods. "I was fascinated, and I thought other people would be interested, too," said Mackey. He went on to found Whole Foods Market, the world's largest retailer of natural and organic foods. His chain of 129 markets sells products that are mostly free of additives, artificial preservatives, and pesticides.

Resplendent with overflowing baskets of luscious lettuces, shiny stacks of fruit, and sweet-smelling bakeries, Whole Foods markets delight the senses. Consumers love the aromas, colors, and vast selection, such as 83 varieties of peaches and fresh fish from its own fleet of 18 boats. Although pricey, the merchandise appeals to upscale shoppers who are willing to pay for healthy and attractive foods.

To meet the demand for its products, Whole Foods needs a staff of good workers. "The most important thing for us is to hire good people who will be productive and offer our customers a wonderful shopping experience, and at the same time ensure that we have a safe work environment," says Robin Graf, Whole Foods regional human resources coordinator. "We want to be able to do thorough and quick background checks to investigate possible criminal backgrounds and make sure we get quality people."

But when Whole Foods wants to hire an employee, it is forced to rely on faxes, e-mail transmissions, and other conventional methods of assembling data. Whole Foods worries that the information it receives is not totally accurate or legally compliant with government regulations. And using conventional methods is agonizingly slow. When you find terrific potential employees, "you want them on board as soon as possible," says Graf.

Robin Graf says to you, his assistant, "You know, I heard about a software program from PeopleWise that sounds like just what we need. Would you please find out how it works? Can we check criminal and civil records of potential employees? Can we verify common things such as name, current address, previous address, social security number, and telephone? And what about driving records? We need to know these for some of our truckers. I'd also like to check credit records, but I don't know whether this is really legal. And, of course, we must verify education and previous employment. Most of all, though, I want to know about speed. How fast can they get us the information we need? Oh, yes, I almost forgot. Will they train our employees to use their software program?"

Your Task. Write an information request letter to Ms. Sheryl Marks, Product Manager, PeopleWise, 4301 Sycamore Road, Hollister, CA 94301, to learn more about its software. Decide on a deadline for a response and give a reason.[4]

6.8 INFORMATION REQUEST: MEETING AT CAESARS PALACE, LAS VEGAS.

Your company, Software.com, has just had an enormously successful two-year sales period. The CEO has asked you, as marketing manager, to arrange a fabulous conference/retreat as a thank-you gift for all 75 engineers, product managers, and salespeople. He wants the company to host a four-day combination sales conference/vacation/retreat at some spectacular location. He suggests that you start by inquiring at the fabulous Caesars Palace Las Vegas. You check its Web site and get some good information. However, you decide to write a letter so that you can have a permanent, formal record of all the resorts you investigate.

You estimate that your company will require about 75 rooms. You'll also need about three conference rooms for one and a half days. You want to know room rates, conference facilities, and entertainment possibilities for families. You have two times that would be possible: July 18–22 or August 4–8. You know that these are off-peak times, and you wonder whether you can get a good room rate. What entertainment will be showing at Caesars during these times? One evening you will want to host a banquet for about 140 people. The CEO wants a report from you by April 1.

Your Task. Write a well-organized information request to Mr. Enrique Robles, Manager, Convention Services, Caesars Palace, 257 Palace Drive, Las Vegas, NV 87551. You might take a look at the Caesars Web site at http://www.caesars.com/Caesars/LasVegas/.

6.9 ORDER REQUEST: OLD CATALOG BUT NEW ORDER.

As the office manager of Hart Enterprises, Inc., you must order some items from an office supply catalog. But your catalog is one year old and you have lost the order form. Because you're in a hurry, you decide to place a fax order. Rather than write for a new catalog, you decide to take a chance and order items from the old catalog, realizing that prices may be somewhat different.

You want five boxes of Avery white ink jet address labels, #8460 at $45. The catalog number is MW 473-76. You also want one Panasonic electric pencil sharpener at $18.99. Its catalog number is MW 286-32. You need 250 payroll card envelopes (catalog number MX 454-98) at $25.95. Finally, you want a 25-pack of box-bottom hanging folders (catalog number MW 987-31) at $16.99. Figure tax at 7 percent and shipping at $12.50. Calculate the total and enclose a check. If the amount is not right, MidWest may invoice your company for the additional cost. You would like the items delivered before February 12 (or a date of your choice).

Your Task. Place this order by writing to MidWest Office Supply, 320 Avenue M, Fort Dodge, IA 50501. Between the date and the inside address, type TRANSMITTED BY FAX.

6.10 CLAIM REQUEST: NO-SURPRISE POLICY.

As marketing manager of Rochester Preferred Travel, you are upset with Premier Promos. Premier is a catalog company that provides imprinted promotional products for companies. Your travel company was looking for something special to offer in promoting its cruise ship travel packages. Premier offered free samples of its promotional merchandise under its "No Surprise" policy.

You figured, what could you lose? So on January 11 you placed a telephone order for a number of samples. These included three kinds of jumbo tote bags and a square-ended barrel bag with fanny pack, as well as a deluxe canvas attaché case and two colors of garment-dyed sweatshirts. All items were supposed to be free. You did think it odd that you were asked for your company's Master Card credit number, but Premier promised to bill you only if you kept the samples.

When the items arrived, you weren't pleased, and you returned them all on January 21 (you have a postal receipt showing the return). But your February credit statement showed a charge of $239.58 for the sample items. You called Premier in February and spoke to Diane, who assured you that a credit would be made on your next statement. However, your March statement showed no credit. You called again and received a similar promise. It's now April and no credit has been made. You decide to write and demand action.

Your Task. Write a claim letter that documents the problem and states the action you want taken. Add any information you feel is necessary. Address your letter to Mr. Kevin Chitwood, Customer Services, Premier Promos, 2445 Bermiss Road, Valdosta, GA 31602.

6.11 CLAIM REQUEST: UNHAPPY INTERIOR DESIGNER.

As the owner of Design-Spectrum, you recently completed a kitchen remodel that required double-glazed, made-to-order teak French doors. You ordered them by telephone on June 5 from Pacific Timber Products. When they arrived on June 20, your carpenter gave you the bad news: the doors were cut too small. Instead of measuring a total of 11 feet 8 inches, the doors measured 11 feet 4 inches. In your carpenter's words, "No way can I stretch those doors to fit these openings!" You waited three weeks for these doors, and your clients wanted them installed immediately. Your carpenter said, "I can rebuild this opening for you, but I'm going to have to charge you for my time." His extra charge came to $655.50.

You feel that the people at Pacific Timber should reimburse you for this amount since it was their error. In fact, you actually saved them a bundle of money by not returning the doors. You decide to write to Pacific Timber and enclose a copy of your carpenter's bill. You wonder whether you should also include a copy of Pacific Timber's invoice, even though it does not show the exact door measurements. You are a good customer of Pacific Timber, having used its quality doors and windows on many other jobs. You're confident that it will grant this claim.

Your Task. Write a claim letter to Kevin Rupe, Operations Manager, Pacific Timber Products, 6302 Bronson Boulevard, Seattle, WA 98015.

6.12 CLAIM REQUEST: THE REAL THING.

Have you ever bought a product that didn't work as promised? Have you been disappointed in service at a bank, video store, restaurant, department store, or discount house? Have you had ideas about how a company or organization could improve its image, service, or product? Remember that smart companies want to know what their customers think, especially if a product could be improved.

Your Task. Select a product or service that has disappointed you. Write a claim letter requesting a refund, replacement, explanation, or whatever seems reasonable. For claims about food products, be sure to include bar-code identification from the package, if possible. Your instructor may ask you to actually mail this letter. When you receive a response, share it with your class.

6.13 CLAIM REQUEST: THIS DESK IS GOING BACK.

As the president of Financial Advisors, Inc., 203 Elm Street, Youngwood, PA 15697, you have been doing very well. Your financial planning services firm has been doing so well that you decided to splurge and purchase a fine executive desk for your own office. You ordered an expensive desk described as "North American white oak embellished with hand-inlaid walnut cross-banding." Although you would not ordinarily purchase large, expensive items by mail, you were impressed by the description of this desk and by the money-back guarantee promised in the catalog. You were also reassured because the desk was coming from Hickory, North Carolina, a premier furniture-building area.

When the desk arrived, you knew that you had made a mistake. The wood finish was rough, the grain looked splotchy, and many of the drawers would not pull out easily. The advertisement had promised "full suspension, silent ball-bearing drawer slides." You are disappointed with the desk and decide to send it back, taking advantage of the money-back guarantee. The total cost of the desk, including shipping charges, was $1,524.99.

Your Task. Write a letter to Shane Watkins, Marketing Manager, Carolina Furniture Galleries, P.O. Box 649, Hickory, NC 28603. You want your money refunded. You're not sure whether the freight charges can be refunded, but it's worth a try. Supply any details needed.

INFOTRAC

6.14 INFORMATION RESPONSE: RESTRICTING INTERNET USE ON THE JOB.

As an intern at a large accounting firm, you are surprised at the broad range of expertise expected of the CPAs. In fact, you think they may go too far in trying to please their clients. One client recently asked Greg Moltiere, your boss, to help her out with an Internet use policy for her small company. Although Mr. Moltiere is not an expert in this area, he wants to assist this client, who is not at all computer savvy. She has a growing company, and many of her employees are using the Internet. She called Mr. Moltiere and asked him to help her out with general information about Internet use policies. The client asked these questions: Why does a company need an Internet use policy? What does an Internet policy generally cover? Where can I see a sample Internet policy? Do I really need such a policy for my company?

Your Task. Mr. Moltiere asks you to use the Web to learn more about Internet use policies. For Greg Moltiere's signature, draft an information response letter answering the client's questions. His goal is to provide common information that encourages the client to develop an Internet policy for her company. Offer any additional material that you think will be useful. An InfoTrac search using the keywords "Internet Use Policy" will produce current information. Address the letter to Ms. Sherry Stratton, Stratton Convalescent Services, 2389 Three Rivers Boulevard, Poplar Bluff, MO 63901.

WEB

6.15 INFORMATION RESPONSE: GOING RIVER RAFTING.

As the program chair for the campus Ski Club, you have been asked by president Brian Krauss to investigate river rafting. The Ski Club is an active organization, and its members want to schedule a summer activity. A majority favor rafting. Use a browser such as Google (www.google.com) to search the Web for relevant information. Select five of the most promising Web sites offering rafting. If possible, print a copy of your findings.

Your Task. Summarize your findings in a response letter to the Ski Club president. The next meeting is May 8, but you think it would be a good idea if you could discuss your findings with Brian before the meeting. Address your letter to Brian Krauss, President, SIU Ski Club, 303 Founders Hall, Carbondale, IL 62901.

6.16 INFORMATION RESPONSE: MAKING A RÉSUMÉ SCANNABLE. As part of a team of interns at the catalog store Patagonia, you have been asked to write a form letter to send to job applicants who inquire about your résumé-scanning techniques. The following poorly written response to an inquiry was pulled from the file.

TEAM
CRITICAL THINKING

Dear Mr. Lopez:

Your letter of April 11 has been referred to me for a response. We are pleased to learn that you are considering employment here at Patagonia, and we look forward to receiving your résumé, should you decide to send same to us.

You ask if we scan incoming résumés. Yes, we certainly do. Actually, we use SmartTrack, an automated résumé-tracking system. SmartTrack is wonderful! You know, we sometimes receive as many as 300 résumés a day, and SmartTrack helps us sort, screen, filter, and separate the résumés. It also processes them, helps us organize them, and keeps a record of all of these résumés. Some of the résumés, however, cannot be scanned, so we have to return those—if we have time.

The reasons that résumés won't scan may surprise you. Some applicants send photocopies or faxed copies, and these can cause misreading, so don't do it. The best plan is to send an original copy. Some people use colored paper. Big mistake! White paper (8 1/2 x 11-inch) printed on one side is the best bet. Another big problem is unusual type fonts, such as script or fancy gothic or antique fonts. They don't seem to realize that scanners do best with plain, readable fonts such as Helvetica or Arial in a 10- to 14-point size.

Other problems occur when applicants use graphics, shading, italics, underlining, horizontal and vertical lines, parentheses, and brackets. Scanners like plain "vanilla" résumés! Oh yes, staples can cause misreading. And folding of a résumé can also cause the scanners to foul up. To be safe, don't staple or fold, and be sure to use wide margins and a quality printer (no dot matrixes!!).

When a hiring manager within Patagonia decides to look for an appropriate candidate, he is told to submit key words to describe the candidate he has in mind for his opening. We tell him (or sometimes her) to zero in on nouns and phrases that best describe what they want. Thus, my advice to you is to try to include those words that highlight your technical and professional areas of expertise.

If you do decide to submit your résumé to us, be sure you don't make any of the mistakes described herein that would cause the scanner to misread it.

Sincerely,

Your Task. As a team, discuss how this letter could be improved. Decide what information is necessary to send to potential job applicants. Search for additional information that might be helpful. Then, submit an improved version to your instructor. Although the form letter should be written so that it can be sent to anyone who inquires, address this one to Daryl Black, 629 Massachusetts Avenue, Cambridge, MA 02139.

6.17 INFORMATION RESPONSE: DESCRIBING YOUR MAJOR. A friend in a distant city is considering moving to your area for more education and training in your field. This individual wants to know about your program of study.

Your Task. Write a letter describing a program in your field (or any field you wish to describe). What courses must be taken? Toward what degree, certificate, or employment position does this program lead? Why did you choose it? Would you recommend this program to your friend? How long does it take? Add any information you feel would be helpful.

INFOTRAC

6.18 INFORMATION RESPONSE: AVOIDING EMPLOYEE GIFTS THAT BECOME DOORSTOPS.

A friend of yours, Megan Stowe, is an executive with a large insurance company. One day you see her at a software conference, and afterward you decide to have cappuccino together at a nearby cafe. After the usual small talk, she says, "You know, I'm beginning to hate the holidays. Every year it gets harder and harder to choose presents for our staff. Once we gave fruitcakes, which I thought were excellent, but it turns out that some people used them for doorstops." As an executive training coach, you say, "Well, what is your gift goal? Do you want to encourage your employees? Are you just saying thanks? Or do you want your gifts to act as a retention tool to keep good people on your team?" Megan responds, "I never thought of it that way. Our company doesn't really have a strategy for the gifts. It's just something we do every year. Do you have any ideas?"

As it turns out, you have many ideas. You've developed a gift list based on the reasons talented people stay in organizations. Megan asks you to send her a letter explaining some of the gift ideas. She thinks that she will be able to retain your services for this advice.

Your Task. Using InfoTrac, find the article by Beverly L. Kaye and Sharon Jordan-Evans titled "The ABCs of Management Gift-Giving," *Training & Development*, December 2000, Article No. A68217191. As a consultant, prepare a letter with a sampling of gift-giving ideas addressed to Megan Stowe, Vice President, Alliance Insurance Company, 1004 State Street, Springfield, MA 01109. Because you don't want to give away all of your best advice in this letter, limit your suggestions to ten or twelve. How would you like to present additional ideas?

CRITICAL THINKING

6.19 CLAIM RESPONSE: UNHAPPY INTERIOR DESIGNER.

As Kevin Rupe, manager of Pacific Timber Products, you have a problem. Your firm manufactures quality precut and custom-built doors and frames. You have received a letter dated July 6 from Jessica Loh (described in Activity 6.11). Ms. Loh is an interior designer, and she complains that the teak French doors she recently ordered for a client were made to the wrong dimensions.

Although they were the wrong size, she kept the doors and had them installed because her clients were without outside doors. However, her carpenter charged an extra $655.50 to install them. She claims that you should reimburse her for this amount, since your company was responsible for the error. You check her June 5 order and find that the order was filled correctly. In a telephone order, Ms. Loh requested doors that measured 11 feet 4 inches and that's what you sent. Now she says that the doors should have been 11 feet 8 inches.

Your policy forbids refunds or returns on custom orders. Yet, you remember that around June 5 you had two new people working the phones taking orders. It's possible that they did not hear or record the measurements correctly. You don't know whether to grant this claim or refuse it. But you do know that you must look into the training of telephone order takers and be sure that they verify all custom order measurements. It might also be a good idea to have your craftsmen call a second time to confirm custom measurements.

Ms. Loh is a successful interior designer and has provided Pacific Timber with a number of orders. You value her business but aren't sure how to respond. You'd like to remind her that Pacific Timber has earned a reputation as a premier manufacturer of wood doors and frames. Your doors feature prime woods, meticulous craftsmanship, and award-winning designs. And the engineering is ingenious.

Your Task. Decide how to treat this claim and then respond to Jessica Loh, DesignSpectrum, 2235 Ocean Drive, Pebble Beach, CA 94321. You might mention that you have a new line of greenhouse windows that are available in three sizes. Include a brochure describing these windows.

6.20 CLAIM RESPONSE: THIS DESK IS GOING BACK.

As Shane Watkins, marketing manager, Carolina Furniture Galleries, it is your job to reply to customer claims, and today you must respond to Valerie Vickers (described in Activity 6.13). You are disturbed that she is returning the executive desk (Invoice No. 3499), but your policy is to comply with customer wishes. If she doesn't want to keep the desk, you will certainly return the purchase price plus shipping charges. Desks are occasionally damaged in shipping, and this may explain the marred finish and the sticking drawers.

You want Ms. Vickers to give Carolina Furniture Galleries another chance. After all, your office furniture and other wood products are made from the finest hand-selected woods by master artisans. Since she is apparently furnishing her office, send her another catalog and invite her to look at the traditional conference desk on page 10-E. This is available with a matching credenza, file cabinets, and accessories. She might be interested in your furniture-leasing plan, which can produce substantial savings.

Your Task. Write to Valerie Vickers, President, Financial Advisors, Inc., 203 Elm Street, Youngwood, PA 15697. In granting her claim, promise that you will personally examine any furniture she may order in the future.

6.21 CLAIM RESPONSE: PIGEON POISONING MUST STOP.

You didn't want to do it. But guests were complaining about the pigeons that roost on the Scottsdale Hilton's upper floors and tower. Pigeon droppings splattered sidewalks, furniture, and people. As manager, you had to take action. You called an exterminator who recommended Avitrol. This drug, he promised, would disorient the birds, preventing them from finding their way back to the Hilton. The drugging, however, produced a result you didn't expect: pigeons began dying.

After a story hit the local newspapers, you began to receive complaints. The most vocal came from the Avian Affairs Coalition, a local bird-advocacy group. It said that the pigeons are really Mediterranean rock doves, the original "Dove of Peace" in European history and the same species the Bible said Noah originally released from his ark during the great flood. Activists claimed that Avitrol is a lethal drug causing birds, animals, and even people who ingest as little as 1/600 of a teaspoon to convulse and die lingering deaths of up to two hours.

Repulsed at the pigeon deaths and the bad publicity, you stopped the use of Avitrol immediately. You are now considering installing wires that offer a mild, nonlethal electrical shock. These wires, installed at the Maricopa County Jail in downtown Phoenix for $50,000, keep thousands of pigeons from alighting and could save $1 million in extermination and cleanup costs over the life of the building. You are also considering installing netting that forms a transparent barrier, sealing areas against entry by birds.

Your Task. Respond to Mrs. Meredith Van Huss, 17168 Blackhawk Boulevard, Friendswood, TX 77546, a recent Scottsdale Hilton guest. She sent a letter condemning the pigeon poisoning and threatening to never return to the hotel unless it changed its policy. Try to regain the confidence of Mrs. Van Huss and promote further business.[5]

6.22 EMPLOYMENT RECOMMENDATION: RECOMMENDING YOURSELF.

You are about to leave your present job. When you ask your boss for a letter of recommendation, to your surprise he tells you to write it yourself and then have him sign it. Actually, this is not an unusual practice today. Many businesspeople find that employees are very perceptive and accurate when they evaluate themselves.

Activities and Cases

Your Task. Use specifics from a current or previous job. Describe your duties and skills. Be sure to support general characteristics with specific examples. In writing, speak of yourself in the third person (*Lisa worked under my supervision during the summer of . . . . Lisa was in charge of . . . . I consider her to be reliable . . .*).

6.23 THANKS FOR A FAVOR: GOT THE JOB! Congratulations! You completed your degree and got a terrific job in your field. One of your instructors was especially helpful to you when you were a student. This instructor also wrote an effective letter of recommendation that was instrumental in helping you obtain your job.

Your Task. Write a letter thanking your instructor.

TEAM

6.24 THANKS FOR A FAVOR: THE CENTURY'S BIGGEST CHANGE IN JOB FINDING. Your business communication class was fortunate to have author Joyce Lain Kennedy speak to you. She has written many books including *Electronic Job Search Revolution; Hook Up, Get Hired;* and *Electronic Résumé Revolution.* Ms. Kennedy talked about writing a scannable résumé, using keywords to help employers hire you, keeping yourself visible in databases on the Internet, and finding online classified ads. The class especially liked hearing the many examples of real people who had found jobs on the Internet. Ms. Kennedy shared many suggestions from human resources people, and she described how large and small employers are using computers to read résumés and track employees. You know that she did not come to plug her books, but when she left, most class members wanted to head straight for a bookstore to get some of them. Her talk was a big hit.

Your Task. Individually or in groups, draft a thank-you letter to Joyce Lain Kennedy, P.O. Box 3502, Carlsbad, CA 92009.

6.25 THANKS FOR THE HOSPITALITY: HOLIDAY ENTERTAINING. You and other members of your staff or organization were entertained at an elegant dinner during the winter holiday season.

Your Task. Write a thank-you letter to your boss (supervisor, manager, vice president, president, or chief executive officer) or to the head of an organization to which you belong. Include specific details that will make your letter personal and sincere.

WEB
TEAM

6.26 SENDING GOOD WISHES: PERSONALIZING GROUP GREETING CARDS. When a work colleague has a birthday, gets promoted, or retires, someone generally circulates a group greeting card. In the past it wasn't a big deal. Office colleagues just signed their names and passed the store-bought card along to others. But the current trend is toward personalization with witty, oh-so-clever quips. And that presents a problem. What should you say—or not say?

You know that people value special handwritten quips, but you realize that you're not particularly original and you don't have a store of "bon mots" (clever sayings, witticisms). You're tired of the old standbys, such as "This place won't be the same without you" and "You're only as old as you feel."

Your Task. To be prepared for the next greeting card that lands on your desk at work, you decide to work with some friends to make a list of remarks appropriate for business occasions. Use the Web to research witty sayings appropriate for promotions, birthdays, births, weddings, illnesses, or personal losses. Use a search term such as "birthday sayings," "retirement quotes," or "cool sayings." You may decide to assign each category (birthday, retirement, promotion, and so forth) to a separate team. Submit the best sayings in a memo to your instructor.

6.27 Responding to Good Wishes: Saying Thank You

Your Task. Write a short note thanking a friend who sent you good wishes when you recently completed your degree.

6.28 Extending Sympathy: To a Spouse

Your Task. Imagine that a coworker was killed in an automobile accident. Write a letter of sympathy to his or her spouse.

VIDEO CASE

Responsibilities and Rewards at Ben & Jerry's

View the Ben & Jerry's video either in the classroom or at the Guffey Web site (http://www.meguffey.com). As you learn in the video, Ben & Jerry's changed its ice cream containers to use unbleached paper. The new packaging paper was chosen because chlorine is not used in its manufacture. What's wrong with chlorine? Although it makes paper white, chlorine contains dioxin, which is known to cause cancer, genetic and reproductive defects, and learning disabilities. In producing paper, pulp mills using chlorine are also adding to dioxin contamination of waterways. Finding a chlorine-free, unbleached paperboard for its packages delighted Ben & Jerry's. But the new process resulted in packages whose inner surfaces are brown, rather than white.

You've been hired at Ben & Jerry's to help answer incoming letters. Although you're fairly new, your boss gives you a letter from an unhappy customer. This customer opened a pint container of Ben & Jerry's "World's Best Vanilla" and then threw its contents out. He saw the brown inner lid and inner sides of the package, and he decided that his pint container must have been used for chocolate before it was used for vanilla. Or, he said, "The entire pint has gone bad and somehow turned the insides brown." Whatever the reason, he wasn't taking any chances. Although he's a long-time customer, he now wants his money back. The last comment in his letter was, "I like your stand on environmental and social issues, but I don't like getting my ice cream in used containers."

Your Task. Write a letter that explains the brown interior of the carton, justifies the use of the new packaging material, and retains the customer's business. How could you promote future business with this customer? Address your letter to Mr. Adam W. Johnson, 4030 West Griswold Road, Phoenix, AZ 85051. Use the site index at the Ben & Jerry's Web site (http://www.benjerry.com) to locate more information about dioxin.

VIDEO CASE

MeetingsAmerica

Ask your instructor to show the VHS video about MeetingsAmerica, a company that makes arrangements for meetings and conventions. Businesses planning big conferences often outsource—that is, they hire an outside company—to arrange registration, ground transportation, and special events for the people attending the conference.

Located in Salt Lake City, MeetingsAmerica is a small company owned by Kathleen Barnes and Judy Cannon. In the video Kathleen says, "We can take a meeting from its inception and do everything connected with that meeting, from booking the hotel, the airlines, all of the audiovisual, the packets, the meeting materials, the registration, everything to the tours and the activities and the evening events and all of the extra things that go with a convention and meeting."

As an intern at MeetingsAmerica, you answer the telephone, respond to the mail, and generally assist the owners. They want to give you experience in answering inquiries from potential customers. Sometimes they respond by telephone, but when they receive a letter or e-mail inquiry, they prefer to send a personal letter on their company stationery.

A letter recently arrived from a potential customer. The Association for Dental Health Practitioners is planning a convention for April 15–18 and may select Salt Lake. It wants to know whether MeetingsAmerica could help with registration, ground transportation, and especially with sightseeing trips. What does Salt Lake have to offer?

Kathleen asks you to compose a personalized response to this inquiry. She says, "You know, April 15–18 is one of our busy periods. But if they book us fairly soon, say, before November 1, we could probably work them in." She turns to you and says, "To give you practice in writing personalized letters, I want you to draft a response to these people. Be sure to tell them about our unique services and our terrific tour guides!" Kathleen is in a hurry to leave for an appointment, so she tells you to check out the Salt Lake City Visitors Center Web site for a quick review of the advantages and sightseeing possibilities in Salt Lake. Describe a few of them in your letter, and enclose a copy of "Salt Lake Meeting Planner Guide," which includes detailed information on accommodations, dining, shopping, attractions, culture, and recreation.

Your Task. Draft a letter for Kathleen Barnes to sign when she returns to the office. Address it to Ms. Sally E. Williams, Association for Dental Health Practitioners, 108 Morningside Drive, New York, NY 10025. As you think about this task, you realize that Kathleen didn't tell you how to close this letter. Decide what would be appropriate in encouraging this customer's business. Make up any additional information you need.

GRAMMAR/MECHANICS CHECKUP—6

COMMAS 1

Review the Grammar Review section of the Grammar/Mechanics Handbook Sections 2.01–2.04. Then study each of the following statements and insert necessary commas. In the space provided write the number of commas that you add; write *0* if no commas are needed. Also record the number of the G/M principle illustrated. When you finish, compare your responses with those shown at the end of the book. If your answers differ, study carefully the principles shown in parentheses.

2 _____ (2.01) **Example**   In this class students learn to write clear and concise business letters, memos, and reports.

_____ 1. We do not as a rule allow employees to take time off for dental appointments.

_____ 2. You may be sure Mrs. Schwartz that your car will be ready by 4 p.m.

_____ 3. Anyone who is reliable conscientious and honest should be very successful.

4. A conference on sales motivation is scheduled for May 5 at the Anaheim Marriott Hotel beginning at 2 p.m. _____

5. As a matter of fact I just called your office this morning. _____

6. We are relocating our distribution center from Memphis Tennessee to Des Moines Iowa. _____

7. In the meantime please continue to send your orders to the regional office. _____

8. The last meeting recorded in the minutes was on February 4 2002 in Chicago. _____

9. Mr. Tran Mrs. Adams and Ms. Horne are our new representatives. _____

10. The package mailed to Ms. Leslie Holmes 3430 Larkspur Lane San Diego CA 92110, arrived three weeks after it was mailed. _____

11. The manager feels needless to say that the support of all employees is critical. _____

12. Eric was assigned three jobs: checking supplies replacing inventories and distributing delivered goods. _____

13. We will work diligently to retain your business Mr. Lopez. _____

14. The vice president feels however that all sales representatives need training. _____

15. The name selected for a product should be right for that product and should emphasize its major attributes.

GRAMMAR/MECHANICS CHALLENGE—6

DOCUMENT FOR REVISION

The following letter has faults in grammar, punctuation, spelling, number form, and wordiness. Use standard proofreading marks (see Appendix B) to correct the errors. When you finish, your instructor can show you the revised version of this letter.

January 20, 200x

FAX TRANSMISSION

Mr. Benjamin Spring

322 East Chapman

Fullerton, CA 92634

Dear Mr. Spring:

SUBJECT: Your January 11 Letter Requesting Information About New All Natural Products

We have received your letter of January 11 in which you inquire about our all-natural products. Needless to say, we are pleased to be able to answer in the affirmative. Yes, our new line of freeze dried back packing foods meet the needs of older adults and young people as well. You asked a number of questions, and here are answers to you're questions about our products.

• Our all natural foods contains no perservatives, sugars or additives. The inclosed list of dinner items tell what foods are cholesterol-, fat-, and salt-free.

- Large orders recieve a five percent discount when they're placed direct with Outfitters, Inc. You can also purchase our products at Malibu Sports Center, 19605 Pacific Coast Highway Malibu CA, 90265.

- Outfitters, Inc., food products are made in our sanitary kitchens which I personally supervise. The foods are flash froze in a patented vacum process that retain freshness, texture and taste.

- Outfitters, Inc. food products are made from choice ingredients that combines good taste and healful quality.

- Our foods stay fresh and tasty for up to 18 months.

Mr. Spring I started Outfitters, Inc., two years ago after making custom meals for discerning back packers who rejected typical camping fare. What a pleasure it is now to share my meals with back packers like you.

I hope you'll enjoy the enclosed sample meal, "Saturday Night on the Trail" is a four-coarse meal complete with fruit candys and elegant appetizers. Please call me personally at (213) 459-3342 to place an order, or to ask other questions about my backpacking food products.

Sincerely,

COMMUNICATION WORKSHOP: CAREER SKILLS

Dr. Guffey's Guide to Business Etiquette and Workplace Manners

Etiquette, civility, and goodwill efforts may seem out of place in today's fast-paced, high-tech offices. Yet, etiquette and courtesy are more important than ever if diverse employees are to be able to work cooperatively and maximize productivity and workflow. Many organizations recognize that good manners are good for business. Some colleges and universities offer management programs that include a short course in manners. Companies are also conducting manners seminars for trainee and veteran managers. Why is politeness regaining legitimacy as a leadership tool? Primarily because courtesy works.

Good manners convey a positive image of an organization. People like to do business with people who show respect and treat others civilly. People also like to work in an environment that is pleasant. Considering how much time is spent at work, doesn't it make sense to prefer an agreeable environment to one that is rude and uncivil?

Etiquette is more about attitude than about formal rules of behavior. That attitude is a desire to show others consideration and respect. It includes a desire to make others feel comfortable. You don't have to become a "sissy" or an etiquette nut, but you might need to polish your social competencies a little to be an effective businessperson today.

You can brush up your workplace etiquette skills online at "Dr. Guffey's Guide to Business Etiquette and Workplace Manners" Web page (http://www.westwords. com/guffey/students.html). Click "Book Support," click your book cover, and look for the guide. Of interest to both workplace newcomers and veterans, this guide covers the following topics:

Professional Image	Business Cards
Introductions and Greetings	Dealing With Angry Customers
Networking Manners	Telephone Manners
General Workplace Manners	Cell Phone Etiquette
Coping With Cubicles	E-Mail Etiquette
Interacting With Superiors	Gender-Free Etiquette
Manager's Manners	Business Dining
Business Meetings	Avoiding Social Blunders When Abroad
Business Gifts	

To gauge your current level of knowledge of business etiquette, take the preview quiz at the student Web site. Then, study all 17 business etiquette topics. These easy-to-read topics are arranged in bulleted lists of "Dos" and "Don'ts." After you complete this etiquette module, your instructor may test your comprehension by giving a series of posttests.

Career Application. You've been a manager at OfficeTemps, a company specializing in employment placement and human resources information, for a long time. But you've never received a letter like this before. A reporter preparing an article for a national news organization writes to you requesting information about how workplace etiquette is changing in today's high-tech environment. Her letter lists the following questions:

- Are etiquette and workplace manners still important in today's fast-paced Information Age work environment? Why or why not?
- Do today's workers need help in developing good business manners? Why or why not?
- Are the rules of office conduct changing? If so, how?
- What advice can you give about gender-free etiquette?
- What special manners do people working in shared workspaces need to observe?

The reporter asks for any other information you can share with her regarding her topic, "Information Age Etiquette."

Your Task. In teams or individually, prepare an information response letter addressed to Ms. Lindsey Ann Evans, National Press Association, 443 Riverside Drive, New York, NY 10024. Use the data you learned in this workshop. Conduct additional Web research if you wish. Remember that you will be quoted in her newspaper article, so make it interesting!

Related Web Site: Visit the Guffey Web site (http://www.westwords.com/guffey/ students.html). Click "Book Support," click your book cover, and look for "Dr. Guffey's Guide to Business Etiquette and Workplace Manners."

Chapter

7

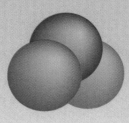

Persuasive Messages

Facts and figures alone will never convince anyone. If you can't connect your facts to the dreams of the client, then all the statistics and charts in the world won't make any impression.[1]

RENÉ NOURSE, Vice President, Investments, Prudential Securities Incorporated

LEARNING OBJECTIVES

1. Request favors and action persuasively.
2. Write persuasive messages within organizations.
3. Make claims and request adjustments successfully.
4. Compose carefully planned sales letters.
5. Implement special techniques in writing online sales messages.

The ability to persuade is a key factor in the success you achieve in your business messages, in your career, and in your interpersonal relations. Persuasive individuals, like René Nourse at Prudential Securities Incorporated, are those who present convincing arguments that influence or win over others.

René Nourse persuades people to invest in stocks and bonds. She knows that facts and figures alone are not convincing; they must be connected to people's desires and needs. Applying this persuasive technique and many others can help you become a persuasive communicator. Because their ideas generally prevail, persuasive individuals become decision makers—managers, executives, and entrepreneurs. This chapter will examine techniques for presenting ideas persuasively.

PERSUASIVE REQUESTS

Persuasion is necessary when resistance is anticipated or when ideas require preparation before they can be presented effectively. For example, let's say you bought a new car and the transmission repeatedly required servicing. When you finally got tired of taking it in for repair, you decided to write to the car manufacturer's district office asking that the company install a new transmission in your car. You knew that your request would be resisted. You had to convince the manufacturer that replacement, not repair, is needed. Routine claim letters, such as those you wrote in Chapter 6, are straightforward and direct. Persuasive requests, on the other hand, are generally more effective when they are indirect. Reasons and explanations should precede the main idea. To overcome possible resistance, the writer lays a logical foundation before the request is delivered. A writing plan for a persuasive request requires deliberate development.

✓ **Quick Check**

Use persuasion when you must change attitudes or produce action.

WRITING PLAN FOR A PERSUASIVE REQUEST

- *Opening:* **Obtain the reader's attention and interest.** Describe a problem, state something unexpected, suggest reader benefits, offer praise or compliments, or ask a stimulating question.
- *Body:* **Build interest.** Explain logically and concisely the purpose of the request. Prove its merit. Use facts, statistics, expert opinion, examples, specific details, and direct and indirect benefits.
- *Body:* **Reduce resistance.** Anticipate objections, offer counterarguments, establish credibility, demonstrate competence, and show the value of your proposal.
- *Closing:* **Motivate action.** Ask for a particular action. Make the action easy to take. Show courtesy and respect.

In this chapter you'll learn to apply the preceding writing plan to messages that (1) request favors and action, (2) persuade within organizations, and (3) make claims and request adjustments.

✓ **Quick Check**

The indirect pattern is appropriate when requesting favors and action, persuading within organizations, and making claims or requesting adjustments.

REQUESTING FAVORS AND ACTIONS

Persuading someone to do something that largely benefits you is not easy. Fortunately, many individuals and companies are willing to grant requests for time, money, information, special privileges, and cooperation. They grant these favors

Getting the president of the United States to speak at Logan High School in LaCrosse, Wisconsin, probably took considerable persuasion. Fortunately, many individuals and companies are willing to grant requests for time, money, information, and special privileges if the request is presented effectively.
© AP/Wide World Photos, Inc.

Quick Check

People are more likely to grant requests if they see direct or indirect benefits to themselves.

for a variety of reasons. They may just happen to be interested in your project, or they may see goodwill potential for themselves. Often, though, they comply because they see that others will benefit from the request. Professionals sometimes feel obligated to contribute their time or expertise to "pay their dues."

You may find that you have few direct benefits to offer in your persuasion. Instead, you'll be focusing on indirect benefits, as the writer does in Figure 7.1. In asking a manager to speak before a marketing meeting, the writer has little to offer as a direct benefit other than a $300 honorarium. But indirectly, the writer offers enticements such as an enthusiastic audience and a chance to help other companies solve overseas marketing problems.

The hurriedly written first version of the request suffers from many faults. It fails to pique the interest of the reader in the opening. It also provides an easy excuse for Mr. Hoffman to refuse (*hate to ask such a busy person*). The body fails to give him any incentive to accept the invitation. The letter also does not anticipate objections and fails to suggest counterarguments. In the closing it doesn't supply a telephone number or e-mail address for an easy response.

In the revised version, the writer gains attention with praise for Mr. Hoffman's company. The letter builds interest with a number of appeals. The primary one is to the reader's desire to serve his profession—although a receptive audience and an opportunity to talk about one's successes have a certain ego appeal as well. Together, these appeals—professional, egoistic, monetary—make a persuasive argument rich and effective. The writer also anticipates objections and counters them by telling Mr. Hoffman that the talk is informal. She provides a list of questions so that he can organize his talk more easily. The closing motivates action and makes acceptance as simple as a telephone call.

PERSUADING WITHIN ORGANIZATIONS

Instructions or directives moving downward from superiors to subordinates usually require little persuasion. Employees expect to be directed in how to perform their jobs. These messages (such as information about procedures, equipment, or customer service) follow the direct pattern, with the purpose immediately stated. However, employees are sometimes asked to perform in a capacity outside their work roles or to accept changes that are not in their best interests (such as pay cuts, job transfers, or reduced benefits). In these instances, a persuasive memo using the indirect pattern may be most effective.

Quick Check

Internal persuasive memos present honest arguments detailing specific reader benefits.

The goal is not to manipulate employees or to seduce them with trickery. Rather, the goal is to present a strong but honest argument, emphasizing points that are important to the receiver. In business, honesty is not just the best policy—it's the *only* policy. People see right through puffery and misrepresentation. For this reason, the indirect pattern is effective only when supported by accurate, honest evidence.

Another form of persuasion within organizations centers on suggestions made by subordinates. Convincing management to adopt a procedure or invest in a product or new equipment generally requires skillful communication. Managers are just as resistant to change as others. Providing evidence is critical when subordinates submit recommendations to their bosses. "The key to making a request of a superior," advises communication consultant Patricia Buhler, "is to know your needs and have documentation [facts, figures, evidence]." Another important factor is moderation. "Going in and asking for the world [right] off the cuff is most likely going to elicit a negative response," she adds.[2] Equally important is focusing on the receiver's needs. What about your suggestion is appealing to the receiver?

The following draft of a request for a second copy machine fails to present convincing evidence of the need. Although the request is reasonable, the argument lacks credibility because of its high-pressure tactics and lack of proof.

FIGURE 7.1 Persuasive Favor Request BEFORE and AFTER Revision

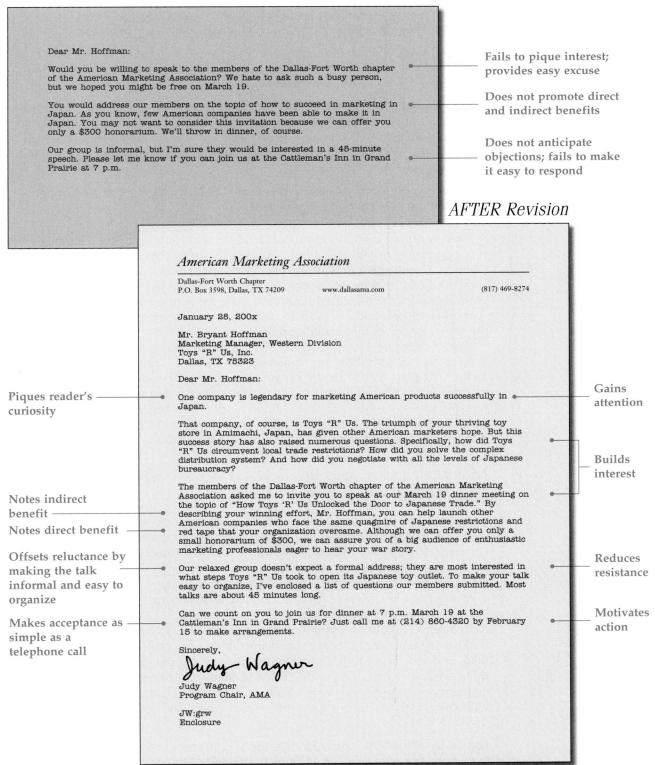

BEFORE Revision

Dear Mr. Hoffman:

Would you be willing to speak to the members of the Dallas-Fort Worth chapter of the American Marketing Association? We hate to ask such a busy person, but we hoped you might be free on March 19.

You would address our members on the topic of how to succeed in marketing in Japan. As you know, few American companies have been able to make it in Japan. You may not want to consider this invitation because we can offer you only a $300 honorarium. We'll throw in dinner, of course.

Our group is informal, but I'm sure they would be interested in a 45-minute speech. Please let me know if you can join us at the Cattleman's Inn in Grand Prairie at 7 p.m.

Fails to pique interest; provides easy excuse

Does not promote direct and indirect benefits

Does not anticipate objections; fails to make it easy to respond

AFTER Revision

American Marketing Association

Dallas-Fort Worth Chapter
P.O. Box 3598, Dallas, TX 74209   www.dallasama.com   (817) 469-8274

January 28, 200x

Mr. Bryant Hoffman
Marketing Manager, Western Division
Toys "R" Us, Inc.
Dallas, TX 75323

Dear Mr. Hoffman:

One company is legendary for marketing American products successfully in Japan.

That company, of course, is Toys "R" Us. The triumph of your thriving toy store in Amimachi, Japan, has given other American marketers hope. But this success story has also raised numerous questions. Specifically, how did Toys "R" Us circumvent local trade restrictions? How did you solve the complex distribution system? And how did you negotiate with all the levels of Japanese bureaucracy?

The members of the Dallas-Fort Worth chapter of the American Marketing Association asked me to invite you to speak at our March 19 dinner meeting on the topic of "How Toys 'R' Us Unlocked the Door to Japanese Trade." By describing your winning effort, Mr. Hoffman, you can help launch other American companies who face the same quagmire of Japanese restrictions and red tape that your organization overcame. Although we can offer you only a small honorarium of $300, we can assure you of a big audience of enthusiastic marketing professionals eager to hear your war story.

Our relaxed group doesn't expect a formal address; they are most interested in what steps Toys "R" Us took to open its Japanese toy outlet. To make your talk easy to organize, I've enclosed a list of questions our members submitted. Most talks are about 45 minutes long.

Can we count on you to join us for dinner at 7 p.m. March 19 at the Cattleman's Inn in Grand Prairie? Just call me at (214) 860-4320 by February 15 to make arrangements.

Sincerely,

Judy Wagner

Judy Wagner
Program Chair, AMA

JW:grw
Enclosure

Piques reader's curiosity

Notes indirect benefit

Notes direct benefit

Offsets reluctance by making the talk informal and easy to organize

Makes acceptance as simple as a telephone call

Gains attention

Builds interest

Reduces resistance

Motivates action

TO: Peggy Brunyansky, Vice President
FROM: Mike Montgomery, Marketing
SUBJECT: COPIERS

Begins by reminding —•
reader of past negative
feelings

Sounds high-pressured —•
and poorly conceived

Presents persuasive —•
arguments illogically
and fails to tell exactly
how much money
could be saved

Doesn't suggest —•
specific action to be
taken

Although you've opposed the purchase of additional copiers in the past, I think I've found a great deal on a copier that's just too good to pass up but we must act before May 1!

Copy City has reconditioned copiers that are practically being given away. If we move fast, they will provide many free incentives—like a free copier stand, free starter supplies, free delivery, and free installation.

We must find a way to reduce copier costs in my department. Our current copier can't keep up with our demand. Thus, we're sending secretaries or sales reps to Copy Quick for an average of 10,000 copies a month. These copies cost 5 cents a page and waste a lot of time. We're making at least eight trips a week, adding up to a considerable expense in travel time and copy costs.

Please give this matter your immediate attention and get back to me as soon as possible. We don't want to miss this great deal!

The preceding memo will probably fail to achieve its purpose. Although the revised version in Figure 7.2 is longer, it's far more effective. Remember that a persuasive message will typically take more space than a direct message because proving a case requires evidence. Notice that the subject line in Figure 7.2 tells the purpose of the memo without disclosing the actual request. By delaying the request until he's had a chance to describe the problem and discuss a solution, the writer prevents the reader's premature rejection.

The strength of this revision, though, is in the clear presentation of comparison figures showing how much money can be saved by purchasing a remanufactured copier. Although the organization pattern is not obvious, the revised memo begins with an attention-getter (frank description of problem), builds interest (with easy-to-read facts and figures), provides benefits, and reduces resistance. Notice that the conclusion tells what action is to be taken, makes it easy to respond, and repeats the main benefit to motivate action.

MAKING CLAIMS AND REQUESTING ADJUSTMENTS (COMPLAINT LETTERS)

Persuasive claim and adjustment letters generally focus on damaged products, mistaken billing, inaccurate shipments, warranty problems, return policies, insurance snafus, faulty merchandise, and so on. The direct pattern is usually best for requesting straightforward adjustments (see Chapter 6). When you feel your request is justified and will be granted, the direct strategy is most efficient. But if a past request has been refused or ignored or if you anticipate reluctance, then the indirect pattern is appropriate.

In a sense, a claim is a complaint letter. Someone is complaining about something that went wrong. Some complaint letters just vent anger; the writers are mad, and they want to tell someone about it. But if the goal is to change something (and why bother to write except to motivate change?), then persuasion is necessary. Effective claim letters make a reasonable claim, present a logical case with clear facts, and adopt a moderate tone. Anger and emotion are not effective persuaders.

Logical Development.   Strive for logical development in a claim letter. You might open with sincere praise, an objective statement of the problem, a point of agreement, or a quick review of what you have done to resolve the problem. Then you can explain precisely what happened or why your claim is legitimate. Don't pro-

FIGURE 7.2   Persuasive Memo

Summarizes problem

Uses columns and headings for easy comparison

Provides more benefits

Repeats main benefit with motivation to act quickly

DATE: April 12, 200x

TO: Peggy Brunyansky, Vice President

FROM: Mike Montgomery, Marketing   MM

SUBJECT: Saving Time and Money on Copying

We're losing money on our current copy sevices and wasting the time of employees as well. Because our Canon copier is in use constantly, we are finding it increasingly necessary to send major jobs out to Copy Quick. Just take a look at how much we are spending each month for outside copy service:

Copy Costs: Outside Service
10,000 copies/month made at Copy Quick	$500.00
Salary costs for secretaries to make 32 trips to drop off originals and pick up copies	240.00
Total	$740.00

When sales reps make the trips, the costs are even greater. Because this expense must be reduced, I've been considering alternatives. New copiers with collating capability and automatic multidrawer paper feeding are very expensive. But reconditioned copiers with all the features we need are available—and at attractive prices and terms. From Copy City we can get a fully remanufactured copier that is guaranteed to work like new. After we make an initial payment of $219, our monthly costs would look like this:

Copy Costs: Remanufactured Copier
Paper supplies for 10,000 copies	$100.00
Toner and copy supplies	75.00
Labor of secretaries to make copies	120.00
Monthly financing charge for copier (purchase price of $1,106 financed at 10% with 29 payments)	41.31
Total	$336.31

As you can see, **a remanufactured copier saves us at least $403.69 per month.**

What's more, for a limited time Copy City is offering a free 15-day trial offer, a free copier stand (worth $165), free starter supplies, and free delivery and installation. We have office space available, and my staff is eager to add a second machine.

Call me at Ext. 630 if you have questions. This copier is such a good opportunity that I've attached a purchase requisition authorizing the agreement with Copy City. With your approval before May 1, we can have our machine by May 10 and start saving time and $403.69 every month. Fast action will also take advantage of Copy City's free start-up incentives.

Enclosure

Describes topic without revealing request

Proves credibility of request with facts and figures

Highlights most important benefit

Counters possible resistance

---

vide a blow-by-blow chronology of details; just hit the highlights. Be sure to enclose copies of relevant invoices, shipping orders, warranties, and payments. And close with a clear statement of what you want done: refund, replacement, credit to your account, or other action. Be sure to think through the possibilities and make your request reasonable.

Moderate Tone.   The tone of the letter is important. Don't suggest that the receiver intentionally deceived you or intentionally created the problem. Rather, appeal to the receiver's sense of responsibility and pride in its good name. Calmly express your disappointment in view of your high expectations of the product and of the company. Communicating your feelings, without rancor, is often your strongest appeal.

Merilee Knapp's letter, shown in Figure 7.3, follows the persuasive pattern. She wants to return three answering machines. Notice her positive opening; her calm, well-documented claims; and her request for specific action.

✓ **Quick Check**

Claim letters should adopt a moderate tone, appeal to the receiver's sense of responsibility, and specify needed actions.

FIGURE 7.3 Claim Request (Complaint Letter)

CHAMPION AUTOMOTIVES
309 Porterville Plaza, Lansing, Michigan 48914 (517) 690-3500
www.chaimpionauto.com

November 29, 200x

Customer Service
Raytronic Electronics
594 Stanton Street
Mobile, AL 36617

Dear Customer Service Representative:

Subject: Code-A-Phone Model 100S

Begins with compliment →

Your Code-A-Phone Model 100S answering unit came well recommended. We liked our neighbor's unit so well that we purchased three for different departments in our business.

Describes problem calmly →

After the three units were unpacked and installed, we discovered a problem. Apparently our office fluorescent lighting interferes with the electronics in these units. When the lights are on, heavy static interrupts every telephone call. When the lights are off, the static disappears.

We can't replace the fluorescent lights; thus we tried to return the Code-A-Phones to the place of purchase (Office Mart, 2560 Haslett Avenue, Lansing, MI 48901). A salesperson inspected the units and said they could not be returned since they were not defective and they had been used.

Suggests responsibility →
Stresses disappointment →

Because the descriptive literature and instructions for the Code-A-Phones say nothing about avoiding use in rooms with fluorescent lighting, we expected no trouble. We were quite disappointed that this well-engineered unit—with its time/date stamp, room monitor, and auto-dial features—failed to perform as we hoped it would.

Appeals to company's desire to preserve good reputation →

Tells what action to take →

If you have a model with similar features that would work in our offices, give me a call. Otherwise, please authorize the return of these units and refund the purchase price of $519.45 (see enclosed invoice). We're confident that a manufacturer with your reputation for excellent products and service will want to resolve this matter quickly.

Sincerely,

Merilee Knapp

Merilee Knapp, President

MK:ett
Enclosure

TIPS FOR MAKING CLAIMS AND COMPLAINTS
- Begin with a compliment, point of agreement, statement of the problem, or brief review of action you have taken to resolve the problem.
- Provide identifying data.
- Prove that your claim is valid; explain why the receiver is responsible.
- Enclose document copies supporting your claim.
- Appeal to the receiver's fairness, ethical and legal responsibilities, and desire for customer satisfaction.
- Describe your feelings and your disappointment.
- Avoid sounding angry, emotional, or irrational.
- Close by telling exactly what you want done.

SALES LETTERS

Traditional direct mail marketing involves the sale of goods and services through letters, catalogs, brochures, and other messages delivered by land mail. Electronic marketing, on the other hand, involves sales messages delivered by e-mail, Web sites, and, less frequently, by fax. Electronic marketing is an increasingly important sales medium. It may one day even eclipse traditional direct-mail campaigns. You'll learn more about online messages later in this chapter.

First, though, we'll focus on traditional direct-mail campaigns featuring letters. Sellers feel that "even with all the new media we have available today, a letter remains one of the most powerful ways to make sales, generate leads, boost retail traffic, and solicit donations."[3] Hard-copy sales letters are still recognized as the most "personal, one-to-one form of advertising there is."[4] Sales letters are generally part of a package that may contain a brochure, price list, illustrations, testimonials, and other persuasive appeals. Professionals who specialize in traditional direct mail services have made a science of analyzing a market, developing an effective mailing list, studying the product, preparing a sophisticated campaign aimed at a target audience, and motivating the reader to act. You've probably received many direct mail packages, often called "junk" mail.

We're most concerned here with the sales letter: its strategy, organization, and evidence. Because sales letters are usually written by specialists, you may never write one on the job. Why, then, learn how to write a sales letter? In many ways, every letter we create is a form of sales letter. We sell our ideas, our organizations, and ourselves. Learning the techniques of sales writing will help you be more successful in any communication that requires persuasion and promotion. Furthermore, you'll recognize sales strategies, thus enabling you to become a more perceptive consumer of ideas, products, and services.

Quick Check

Traditional direct mail marketing uses land mail; electronic marketing uses e-mail, Web sites, and fax.

Quick Check

Learning to write sales letters helps you sell yourself as well as become a smarter consumer.

CRAFTING A WINNING SALES MESSAGE

Your primary goal in writing a sales message is to get someone to devote a few moments of attention to it.[5] You may be promoting a product, a service, an idea, or yourself. In each case the most effective messages will follow a writing plan. This is the same recipe we studied earlier, but the ingredients are different.

When UPS inaugurated its first deliveries to China, it made a big splash by naming a plane "China Express" and unveiling its spectacular dragon logo at a well-attended news ceremony. The first step in developing a sales message is gaining attention and shaping the message to the receiver's interests and benefit.
© AP/Wide World Photos, Inc.

WRITING PLAN FOR A SALES LETTER

- *Opening:* **Gain attention.** Offer something valuable; promise a benefit to the reader; ask a question; or provide a quotation, fact, product feature, testimonial, startling statement, or personalized action setting.
- *Body:* **Build interest.** Describe central selling points and make rational and emotional appeals. **Reduce resistance.** Use testimonials, money-back guarantees, free samples, performance tests, or other techniques.
- *Closing:* **Motivate action.** Offer a gift, promise an incentive, limit the offer, set a deadline, or guarantee satisfaction.

Quick Check

Openers for sales messages should be brief, honest, relevant, and provocative.

Gaining Attention.   One of the most critical elements of a sales letter is its opening paragraph. This opener should be short (one to five lines), honest, relevant, and stimulating. Marketing pros have found that eye-catching typographical arrangements or provocative messages, such as the following, can hook a reader's attention:

© Ted Goff (www.tedgoff.com)

"And these are the benefits to my company if you buy our product."

- **Offer:** *A free trip to Hawaii is just the beginning!*
- **Promise:** *Now you can raise your sales income by 50 percent or even more with the proven techniques found in . . . .*
- **Question:** *Do you yearn for an honest, fulfilling relationship?*
- **Quotation or proverb:** *Necessity is the mother of invention.*
- **Fact:** *The Greenland Eskimos ate more fat than anyone in the world. And yet . . . they had virtually no heart disease.*
- **Product feature:** *Volvo's snazzy new convertible ensures your safety with a roll bar that pops out when the car tips 40 degrees to the side.*
- **Testimonial:** *"The Journal surprises, amuses, investigates, and most of all educates."* (*The New Republic* commenting on *The Wall Street Journal*)
- **Startling statement:** *Let the poor and hungry feed themselves! For just $100 they can.*
- **Personalized action setting:** *It's 4:30 p.m. and you've got to make a decision. You need everybody's opinion, no matter where they are. Before you pick up your phone to call them one at a time, pick up this card: AT&T Teleconference Services.*

Other openings calculated to capture attention might include a solution to a problem, an anecdote, a personalized statement using the receiver's name, or a relevant current event.

Quick Check

Build interest by describing the product or service and making rational or emotional appeals.

Building Interest.   In this phase of your sales message, you should describe clearly the product or service. In simple language emphasize the central selling points that you identified during your prewriting analysis. Those selling points can be developed using rational or emotional appeals.

Rational appeals are associated with reason and intellect. They translate selling points into references to making or saving money, increasing efficiency, or making the best use of resources. In general, rational appeals are appropriate when a product is expensive, long-lasting, or important to health, security, and financial success. Emotional appeals relate to status, ego, and sensual feelings. Appealing to the emotions is sometimes effective when a product is inexpensive, short-lived, or nonessential. Many clever sales messages, however, combine emotional and rational strategies for a dual appeal. Consider these examples:

She had no trouble using her credit card to get this surfboard in Laguna Niguel, California. Credit card companies rely on rational appeals, such as convenience and financial reliability, as well as emotional appeals, such as ego and sensual feelings, to entice new customers to apply for their cards.
© Spencer Grant/ PhotoEdit, Inc.

Rational Appeal
You can buy the things you need and want, pay household bills, pay off higher-cost loans and credit cards—as soon as you're approved and your Credit-Line account is opened.

Emotional Appeal
Leave the urban bustle behind and escape to sun-soaked Bermuda! To recharge your batteries with an injection of sun and surf, all you need is your bathing suit, a little suntan lotion, and your Credit-Line card.

Dual Appeal
New Credit-Line cardholders are immediately eligible for a $100 travel certificate and additional discounts at fun-filled resorts. Save up to 40 percent while lying on a beach in picturesque, sun-soaked Bermuda, the year-round resort island.

A physical description of your product is not enough, however. Zig Ziglar, thought by some to be America's greatest salesperson, points out that no matter how well you know your product, no one is persuaded by cold, hard facts alone. In the end, he contends, "People buy because of the product benefits."[6] Your job is to translate those cold facts into warm feelings and reader benefits. Let's say a

✓ **Quick Check**

Rational appeals focus on making or saving money, increasing efficiency, or making good use of resources.

✓ **Quick Check**

Emotional appeals focus on status, ego, and sensual feelings.

sales letter promotes a hand cream made with aloe and cocoa butter extracts, along with Vitamin A. Those facts become, "Nature's hand helpers—including soothing aloe and cocoa extracts, along with firming Vitamin A—form invisible gloves that protect your sensitive skin against the hardships of work, harsh detergents, and constant environmental assaults."

Reducing Resistance.   Marketing pros use a number of techniques to overcome resistance and build desire.

Quick Check

Techniques for reducing resistance include testimonials, guarantees, warranties, samples, and performance polls.

- **Testimonials:** *"I learned so much in your language courses that I began to dream in French."*—Holly Franker, Beaumont, Texas
- **Names of satisfied users** (with permission, of course): *Enclosed is a partial list of private pilots who enthusiastically subscribe to our service.*
- **Money-back guarantee or warranty:** *We offer the longest warranties in the business—all parts and service on-site for two years!*
- **Free trial or sample:** *We're so confident that you'll like our new accounting program that we want you to try it absolutely free.*
- **Performance tests, polls, or awards:** *Our TP-3000 was named Best Web Phone, and Etown.com voted it Cell Phone of the Year.*

© by Randy Glasbergen.
www..glasbergen.com

"Resistance to our men's fragrance? Nothing that a testimonial from Shaq wouldn't overcome!"

In addition, you need to anticipate objections and questions the receiver may have. When possible, translate these objections into selling points (*If you've never ordered software by mail, let us send you our demonstration disks at no charge*).

When price is an obstacle, consider these suggestions:

- Delay mentioning price until after you've created a desire for the product.
- Show the price in small units, such as the price per issue of a magazine.
- Demonstrate how the reader saves money by, for instance, subscribing for two or three years.
- Compare your prices with those of a competitor.

✓ *Quick Check*

Techniques for motivating action include offering a gift or incentive, limiting an offer, and guaranteeing satisfaction.

Motivating Action.   All the effort put into a sales message is wasted if the reader fails to act. To make it easy for readers to act, you can provide a postage-paid reply card, a stamped and preaddressed envelope, a toll-free telephone number, an easy Web site, or a promise of a follow-up call. Because readers often need an extra push, consider including additional motivators, such as the following:

"I find it hard to believe that we've actually won 20 million dollars when they send the letter bulk mail."

From *The Wall Street Journal*—permission, Cartoon Features Syndicate.

- **Offer a gift:** *You'll receive a free cell phone with the purchase of any new car.*
- **Promise an incentive:** *With every new, paid subscription, we'll plant a tree in one of America's Heritage Forests.*
- **Limit the offer:** *Only the first 100 customers receive free checks.*
- **Set a deadline:** *You must act before June 1 to get these low prices.*
- **Guarantee satisfaction:** *We'll return your full payment if you're not entirely satisfied—no questions asked.*

The final paragraph of the sales letter carries the punch line. This is where you tell readers what you want done and give them reasons for doing it. Most sales letters also include postscripts because they make irresistible reading. Even readers who might skim over or by-pass paragraphs are drawn to a P.S. Therefore, use a postscript to reveal your strongest motivator, to add a special inducement for a quick response, or to reemphasize a central selling point.

Putting It All Together.   Sales letters are a preferred marketing medium because they can be personalized, directed to target audiences, and filled with a more complete message than other advertising media. But direct mail is expensive. That's why the total sales message is crafted so painstakingly.

Let's examine a sales letter, shown in Figure 7.4, addressed to a target group of small-business owners. To sell the new magazine *Small Business Monthly*, the letter incorporates all four components of an effective persuasive message. Notice that the personalized action-setting opener places the reader in a familiar situation (getting into an elevator) and draws an analogy between failing to reach the top floor and failing to achieve a business goal.

The writer develops a rational central selling point (a magazine that provides valuable information for a growing small business) and repeats this selling point in all the components of the letter. Notice, too, how a testimonial from a small-business executive lends support to the sales message, and how the closing pushes for action. Since the price of the magazine is not a selling feature, it's mentioned only on the reply card. This sales letter saves its strongest motivator—a free booklet—for the high-impact P.S. line.

Quick Check

Because direct mail is an expensive way to advertise, messages should present complete information in a personalized tone for specific audiences.

WRITING ONLINE SALES LETTERS

To some marketers, e-mail sounds like "the promised land," guaranteeing instant delivery and costing only pennies per message. However, unsolicited commercial e-mail, called "spam," generates an incredible backlash from recipients. They want their e-mail addresses to remain private and unviolated. One of the leading direct-mail marketers correctly sensed the pulse of the times when he remarked, "Nothing is more powerful than goodwill—except ill will."[7] Unsolicited e-mail seems to create enormous ill will today. However, if your organization requires online sales messages, you can make it more acceptable by following these techniques:

FIGURE 7.4 Sales Letter

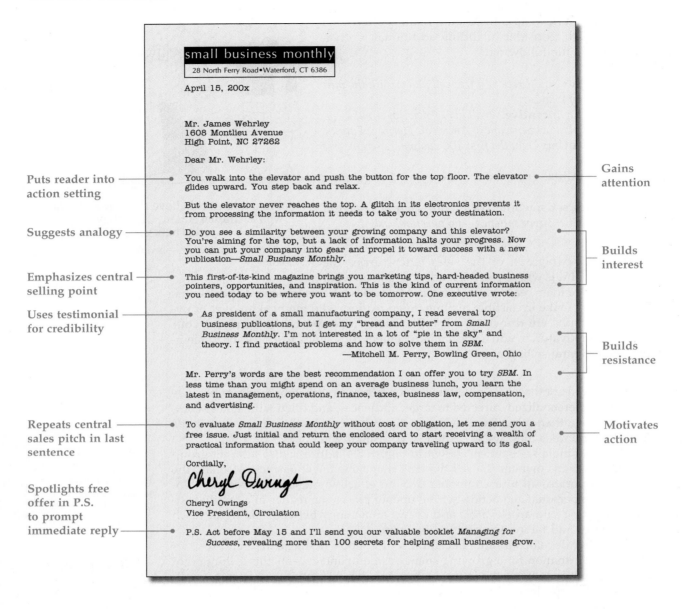

Puts reader into action setting

Suggests analogy

Emphasizes central selling point

Uses testimonial for credibility

Repeats central sales pitch in last sentence

Spotlights free offer in P.S. to prompt immediate reply

Gains attention

Builds interest

Builds resistance

Motivates action

small business monthly
28 North Ferry Road•Waterford, CT 6386

April 15, 200x

Mr. James Wehrley
1608 Montlieu Avenue
High Point, NC 27262

Dear Mr. Wehrley:

You walk into the elevator and push the button for the top floor. The elevator glides upward. You step back and relax.

But the elevator never reaches the top. A glitch in its electronics prevents it from processing the information it needs to take you to your destination.

Do you see a similarity between your growing company and this elevator? You're aiming for the top, but a lack of information halts your progress. Now you can put your company into gear and propel it toward success with a new publication—*Small Business Monthly*.

This first-of-its-kind magazine brings you marketing tips, hard-headed business pointers, opportunities, and inspiration. This is the kind of current information you need today to be where you want to be tomorrow. One executive wrote:

As president of a small manufacturing company, I read several top business publications, but I get my "bread and butter" from *Small Business Monthly*. I'm not interested in a lot of "pie in the sky" and theory. I find practical problems and how to solve them in *SBM*.
—Mitchell M. Perry, Bowling Green, Ohio

Mr. Perry's words are the best recommendation I can offer you to try *SBM*. In less time than you might spend on an average business lunch, you learn the latest in management, operations, finance, taxes, business law, compensation, and advertising.

To evaluate *Small Business Monthly* without cost or obligation, let me send you a free issue. Just initial and return the enclosed card to start receiving a wealth of practical information that could keep your company traveling upward to its goal.

Cordially,

Cheryl Owings

Cheryl Owings
Vice President, Circulation

P.S. Act before May 15 and I'll send you our valuable booklet *Managing for Success*, revealing more than 100 secrets for helping small businesses grow.

✓ Quick Check

Send only targeted, not "blanket," mailings. Include something special for a select group.

- **Be selective.** Send messages only to customers or prospects who have given you permission to send e-mail marketing messages.[8] This is called "opt-in" marketing. Although e-mail users detest "spam" (unsolicited sales and other messages), they are surprisingly receptive to offers from marketers they know and have approved. Remember that today's customer is *somebody*—not *anybody*.
- **Use the receiver's name.** Tests show that receivers are more likely to open messages that have their first names in the subject line or in the first sentence of the body.

- **Keep the message short, conversational, and focused.** Because on-screen text is taxing to read, be brief. Focus on one or two central selling points only.[9] Try to keep your message to 500 or fewer characters. Focus on "you" instead of "we" or "I."
- **Make a strong offer.** Be sure you know your audience so that you can tailor the offer to the buying behavior, needs, and concerns of your readers. Highlight the offer in the subject line or first sentence. Focus on benefits, not features.
- **Motivate a response.** Make it easy to respond. For example, if you want readers to visit a Web site, use a hot link and provide a reward for clicking. Give a discount or gift for an immediate response.
- **Provide a means for being removed from the mailing list.** It's polite and good business tactics to include a statement that tells receivers how to be removed from the sender's mailing database.

SUMMING UP AND LOOKING FORWARD

The ability to persuade is a powerful and versatile communication tool. In this chapter you learned to apply the indirect strategy in making favor and action requests, writing persuasive messages within organizations, making claims and requesting adjustments, and writing sales letters. You also learned techniques for developing successful online sales messages. The techniques suggested here will be useful in many other contexts beyond the writing of these business documents. You will find that logical organization of arguments is also extremely effective in expressing ideas orally or any time you must overcome resistance to change.

In coming chapters you will learn how to modify and generalize the techniques of direct and indirect strategies in preparing and writing informal and formal reports and proposals. Nearly all businesspeople today find that they must write an occasional report.

Interactive Learning @ http://www.westwords.com/guffey/students.html
Prepare for tests and reinforce your chapter knowledge with interactive quizzes and crossword puzzles.

CRITICAL THINKING

1. Why is the ability to persuade a significant trait in both business and personal relations?
2. Why does the organization of a successful persuasive claim center on the reasons and the closing?
3. Should favor requests be written directly or indirectly? Discuss.
4. Why do individuals resist change?
5. Some individuals will never write an actual sales letter. Why is it nevertheless important for them to learn the techniques for doing so?

6. List at least four examples of favor requests.

7. What are the four parts of a writing plan for a persuasive request? Be prepared to explain each part.

8. What kinds of messages within organizations require persuasive techniques?

9. Generally, the direct pattern is best for requesting straightforward claims. When is the indirect pattern appropriate?

10. Name eight tips for making claims and complaints.

11. List at least ten ways to gain a reader's attention in the opening of a sales letter.

12. In selling a product, when are rational appeals most effective? When are emotional appeals most effective?

13. Name six writing techniques that reduce resistance in a sales message.

14. Name five techniques for motivating action in the closing of a sales message.

15. How are online sales letters different from and similar to hard-copy sales letters?

WRITING IMPROVEMENT EXERCISES

7.1 STRATEGIES

Your Task. For each of the following situations, check the appropriate writing strategy.

Direct Strategy	Indirect Strategy	
_____	_____	16. An appeal for a contribution to Children's World, a charity
_____	_____	17. An announcement that henceforth all dental, health, and life insurance benefits for employees will be reduced
_____	_____	18. A request to another company for verification of employment regarding a job applicant
_____	_____	19. A letter to a painting contractor demanding payment for replacing office floor tiles damaged by sloppy painters
_____	_____	20. A request for information about an oak desk and computer workstation
_____	_____	21. A letter to a grocery store asking for permission to display posters advertising a school fund-raising car wash
_____	_____	22. A request for a refund of the cost of a computer program that does not perform the functions it was expected to do

Direct Strategy	Indirect Strategy	
_____	_____	23. A request for a refund of the cost of a hair dryer that stopped working after a month's use (the hair dryer carries a one-year warranty)
_____	_____	24. An invitation to a prominent author to speak before a student rally
_____	_____	25. A memo to employees describing the schedule and selections of a new mobile catering service

WRITING IMPROVEMENT CASES

7.2 FAVOR REQUEST: INVITING A SPEAKER

Your Task. Analyze the following poorly written invitation. List its weaknesses and outline a writing strategy. If your instructor directs, revise it. Add appropriate information, if needed.

Current date

Ms. Joyce Lain Kennedy
P. O. Box 3029
Carlsbad, CA 92009

Dear Ms. Kennedy:

Because you are a local author, we thought it would not be too much trouble for you to be the keynote speaker at our SCU Management Society banquet May 5.

Some of us business students here at South California University have read and admired your many newspaper columns and books on careers. One of our professors said that you were the "dean of career columnists." We were surprised, though, to see that you have written a number of "Dummies" books, including *Resumes for Dummies, Cover Letters for Dummies, College Financial Aid for Dummies,* and *Job Interviews for Dummies.* Perhaps you could tell us why you think that "dummies" is an effective way to address your readers. We are especially interested in learning what a "competency-based" interview is.

Because we have no funds for honoraria, we have to rely on local speakers. We also know that your home in Carlsbad is not too far from our campus in San Diego, so we hoped you could work us into your schedule. Our banquets usually begin at 6:30 with a social hour, followed by dinner at 7:30 and the speaker from 8:30 until 9 or 9:15. We can arrange transportation for you and your husband, if you need it.

We realize that you have a busy schedule, but we hope you'll carve out a space for us. Please let our advisor, Professor Rachel Pierce, have the favor of an early reply.

Cordially,

1. List at least five weaknesses.

2. Outline a writing plan for a persuasive request.

7.3 PERSUASIVE MEMO: OUR TRADE BOOTH

Your Task. Analyze the following memo. List its weaknesses. If your instructor directs, revise it.

DATE: Current
TO: Jennifer Ritter, VP, Media Relations
FROM: Phillip Pitino, Product Manager
SUBJECT: OUR TRADE BOOTH

We have all enjoyed attending the many trade shows where we exhibit our products. I particularly look forward to the Las Vegas Comdex show, which, as you know, is the biggest software and hardware trade show in the country.

My fellow product managers and I try to get visitors to come to our booth, but it's not easy. In the past we've tried promotions with T-shirts, coffee mugs, and pens—all sporting our company logo. We also tried "freemiums," but we lost a bundle on these $50 coupons. You will recall that they were supposed to be used toward future software purchases, but we learned too late that they could be easily photocopied and multiple copies printed out. What a bummer!

But here's a promotion idea that is not going to lose us a lot of money. Digital Equipment Corporation, at its exhibit at Networld a couple of months ago in Las Vegas, had a way of making personalized Web pages for visitors. They used a template, took a picture of the visitor with a digital camera, and made a Web page for each visitor. They then gave a disk to the visitor with the page in HTML format, ready to upload to their personal Web sites. It was a huge hit! The great part about this is that visitors have to leave their names, addresses, and contact information to insert into their Web pages. We get all this great information—they get a free disk. Doesn't this sound like a winner? About all we have to do in the way of preparation is have our Web design team make a Web page template. This shouldn't be too difficult.

Let me know what you think. Our next big trade show is June 10 in Atlanta.

1. List at least five weaknesses.

7.4 CLAIM REQUEST: MOULDY GROUT IS MISSING

Your Task. Analyze the following poorly written claim (complaint) letter. List its weaknesses. If your instructor directs, revise it.

Current date

Ms. Cindy Taylor
Guest Relations
Five Flags Lake Point Park
P.O. Box 4300
Sandusky, OH 45320

Dear Ms. Taylor:

I am really upset with you and your park! I bought two $55 tickets to a concert featuring King Fisher and his Mouldy Grout band at Five Flags. But when my friend and I arrived for the concert May 25, neither King nor the Grout appeared.

Instead, three decidedly not-ready-for-prime-time groups filled in. I had been looking forward to this concert for seven weeks. After the concert started, I stayed through two acts to see whether the talent might improve. It didn't. I know that I saw newspaper advertisements publicizing the Mouldy Grout performance as recently as the day of the concert. Only when we left the Five Flags parking lot did I see a small poster describing a "change in the talent" for the evening's concert.

When I called to demand a refund, I was told that a change had been announced prior to the concert. If you think that a tiny poster is sufficient to announce a major change in talent, you are wrong. I was also told that you would not refund my ticket price because I had stayed for the concert.

This is an obvious rip-off when you advertise a big-name group and then fill in with three no-name talentless groups. And then you refuse to refund the ticket price.

Five Flags used to be one of my favorite local attractions and concert venues, but I have totally lost faith in you.

With disappointment,

1. List at least five weaknesses.

7.5 SALES LETTERS: ANALYZING THE PITCH

Your Task. Select a one- or two-page sales letter received by you or a friend. (If you are unable to find one, your instructor may have a collection.) Study the letter and then answer these questions:

1. What techniques capture the reader's attention?
2. Is the opening effective? Explain.
3. What are the central selling points?
4. Does the letter use rational, emotional, or a combination of appeals? Explain.
5. What reader benefits are suggested?
6. How does the letter build interest in the product or service?
7. How is price handled?
8. How does the letter anticipate reader resistance and offer counterarguments?
9. What action is the reader to take? How is the action made easy?
10. What motivators spur the reader to act quickly?

ACTIVITIES AND CASES

7.6 PERSUASIVE FAVOR/ACTION REQUEST: CELEBRITY AUCTION. Your professional or school organization (such as the Associated Students Organization) must find ways to raise money. The president of your group appoints a team and asks it to brainstorm for ways to meet your group's pledge to aid the United Way's battle against adult illiteracy in your community. The campaign against adult illiteracy has targeted an estimated 10,000 people in your community who cannot read or write. After considering and discarding a number of silly ideas, your team comes up with the brilliant idea of a celebrity auction. At a spring function, items or services from local and other celebrities would be auctioned. Your organization approves your idea and asks your team to persuade an important person in your professional organization (or your college president) to donate one hour of tutoring in a subject he or she chooses. If you have higher aspirations, write to a movie star or athlete of your choice—perhaps one who is part of your organization or who attended your school.

Your Task. As a team, discuss the situation and decide what action to take. Then write a persuasive letter to secure an item for the auction. You might wish to ask a star to donate a prop from a recent movie.

7.7 PERSUASIVE FAVOR REQUEST: INVITING THE DIVA OF RETAIL. As program chair of the National Association of Retail Merchandisers, you must find a speaker for your annual meeting in April. In *Inc.* magazine you saw an impressive article about J'Amy Owens, president of the Retail Group Inc., a Seattle-based strategic retail consulting firm. Owens has become the guru of retail makeovers with a client list of over 400 companies. She believes that the retail economy will increasingly be driven by *experience* as opposed to transactions. "Retail has to feel relevant or it's dead," she says.

Driving the shift in retail focus is Generation Y (those born between 1977 and 1994). They will represent 41 percent of the U.S. population in 10 years. And only 15 percent of this group frequent department stores. Besides being the place where parents shop, department stores specialize in *products* as opposed to *customers*, Owens believes. The store of the future will provide in-store Web access; give environmental controls to customers; furnish lots of sunlight, water, and vegetation; and offer "safe dangers," such as climbing walls and skateboard ramps.

Owens is very much in demand. She has been credited with helping many well-known brands regain lost luster, including McDonald's, Blockbuster Video, Sears, and Starbucks. When Nike lost the devotion of Generation Y, it commissioned her to figure out how to win them back. After her startling redesign of Mega Mart, a consumer electronics firm, it became one of the highest-grossing sellers of consumer electronics in North America.[10]

Your Task. Write a persuasive request inviting J'Amy Owens, President, Retail Group Inc., 240 Pacific Avenue, Seattle, WA 98303. You know that she generally earns $5,000 a pop for industry presentations, but your budget allows only $3,000. You hope, however, that she'll be receptive since you expect about 1,500 of the top retailers to attend the conference April 6 in New Orleans.

7.8 PERSUASIVE FAVOR/ACTION REQUEST: MANDATORY RESTAURANT TIPPING. As a server at the Miami's Bayside Inn, you have occasionally been "stiffed" by a customer who left no tip. You know your service is excellent, but some customers just don't get it. They seem to think that tips are optional, a sign of appreciation. For servers, however, tips are 80 percent of their income. In a recent *New York Times* article, you learned that some restaurants—like the new 16-32 Coach House in New York—automatically add a 15 percent tip to the bill. In Santa Monica the Lula restaurant prints "gratuity guidelines" on checks, showing customers what a 15 or 20 percent tip would be. You also know that American Express recently developed a gratuity calculation feature on its terminals. This means that diners don't even have to do the math!

Your Task. Since they know you are studying business communication, your fellow servers have asked you to write a serious letter to David Rodriguez, general manager of Bayside Inn, 3504 Rickenbacher Causeway, Miami, FL 34607, persuading him to adopt mandatory tipping guidelines. Talk with fellow servers (classmates) to develop logical persuasive arguments.

7.9 PERSONAL PERSUASIVE MEMO: DEAR BOSS. In your own work or organization experience, identify a problem for which you have a solution. Should a procedure be altered to improve performance? Would a new or different piece of equipment help you perform your work better? Could some tasks be scheduled more efficiently? Are employees being used most effectively? Could customers be better served by changing something? Do you want to work other hours or perform other tasks?

Your Task. Once you have identified a situation requiring persuasion, write a memo to your boss or organization head. Use actual names and facts. Employ the concepts and techniques in this chapter to help you convince your boss that your idea should prevail. Include concrete examples, anticipate objections, emphasize reader benefits, and end with a specific action to be taken.

7.10 PERSUASIVE INTERNAL MEMO OR E-MAIL: DALLAS COWBOYS NEED BETTER GRASS. On every NFL staff, one person has the job of worrying about the football field. In Dallas that person is Kevin O'Reilly. He worries so much that even his dreams are in green. What could be the problem when the field is covered with AstroTurf, the famous synthetic grass that never has to be watered? Back in the 1960s, AstroTurf seemed to be the perfect answer to the problem of supplying a playing field inside the "world's eighth wonder," the Houston Astrodome. Natural grass, of course, would not grow without sunshine and rain. That's why AstroTurf, made from the miracle substance nylon, seemed to be faultless. It was tough as nails and provided a no-muss, no-fuss playing service.

But over the years AstroTurf did not prove to be the best surface for sports. In a 1995 survey of 965 NFL players, 93 percent believed that more injuries resulted from playing on AstroTurf than from playing on grass. That year Ki-Jana Carter, a highly touted, first-draft pick Cincinnati Bengals running back, went down on AstroTurf with a knee injury. Asked what he would do with all the domed stadiums in America, he replied, "Bomb 'em." More recently Cowboys wide receiver Michael Irvin had his head slammed into the synthetic turf at Veterans Stadium, reputedly the hardest "rug" in the league. The blow nearly paralyzed Irvin. He was one of at least six significant turf-related injuries the Cowboys suffered in one year.

At the New York Giants Stadium, after numerous player injuries, management decided to cover its AstroTurf field with real grass, at a cost of $4 million—plus $500,000 a year in upkeep. Because real grass is not an option for the Dallas Cowboys, Kevin O'Reilly has been looking for a solution. He was favorably impressed with a new synthetic grass called "FieldTurf." It is a blend of synthetic fibers woven into a carpet filled with layers of sand for stability and ground-up rubber for resilience.

Installed at a heavily used Amarillo, Texas, high school athletic field, FieldTurf proved to be amazingly successful. Amarillo Athletic Director Tex Nolan says that FieldTurf looks and feels like real grass, is resilient, and, according to the team doctor, is safer than grass. In 133 soccer and football games, only two surgery-related injuries were reported. But did it cost a bundle? Not really. AstroTurf bid $1.2 million on the Amarillo job. FieldTurf installed the field for $548,000.

Is it slick in wet weather? Nolan described one Friday night when seven inches of rain fell in the Texas Panhandle, washing out four high school football games. They were rescheduled for the next day on the Amarillo FieldTurf field. It was the only field that remained playable despite the deluge. Well, maybe FieldTurf wears out too fast. Not so, says Nolan. After 74 football games, 59 soccer games, and two all-day band competitions with 40 bands, "it's better than the day it was put down." The fibers have spread out and become even more luxuriant. How about maintenance? A typical grass field costs $60,000 a year to keep up, including $25,000 for water alone. What's the tab for FieldTurf? "Five hundred dollars a year," says Nolan. "We brush the field every six to eight weeks."

But what about warranties? AstroTurf has been around a long time and promises an eight-year warranty. FieldTurf matched this warranty and backed it with insurance from Lloyd's of London.[11]

Your Task. As Kevin O'Reilly, playing field manager, you and your staff are sold on Field-Turf. Now you must convince the Cowboys management that it should give FieldTurf a try. The Cowboys have three practice fields. You decide to ask that one become a pilot test for FieldTurf. Use InfoTrac to read more about artificial turf. Although your memo need not be filled with technical details, you might want to take a look at the FieldTurf Web site. You can find it with any search engine. Discuss with your team how best to persuade the Dallas Cowboys owner and general manager, Mr. Jerry Jones. In a convincing persuasive memo, provide an overview of the problem and a concise solution. Should you ask to have the pilot field installed immediately? Should you ask to arrange a visit by the Field-Turf representative? Should you send Jerry Jones to a Web site for more data?

7.11 PERSUASIVE MEMO: TRAINING TELECOMMUTERS. You see the handwriting on the wall. More and more employees are asking to telecommute. They want to work at home, where they feel they can be more productive and avoid the hassle of driving to work. Some need to telecommute only temporarily, while they take care of family obligations, births, illnesses, or personal problems. Others are highly skilled individuals who can do their work at home as easily as in the office. As human resources director at a large corporation, you know that at least 157 of your current employees have permission to telecommute.

Activities and Cases

But the results have not been totally satisfactory. Teleworkers don't always have the best work habits, and lack of communication is a major problem. Unless the telecommuter is expert at coordinating projects and leaving instructions, productivity can fizzle. Another problem for managers is measuring productivity. Then there's the issue of resentment among other workers in the office.

All the trends seem to indicate that telecommuting will increase in the future. You conclude that if your company is to continue to grant permission for employees to work at remote locations, then workers and their managers must receive training on how to do it effectively. You would like to hire a consultant to train your prospective telecommuters and their managers. Another possibility is to develop an in-house training program. As human resources director, you must convince Robert Richardson, vice president, that your company needs a training program for all individuals who are currently telecommuting or who plan to do so. Their managers should also receive training.

You decide to ask your staff of four to help you gather information. Using InfoTrac, you and your team read several articles on what such training should include. Now you must decide what action you want the vice president to take. Should he meet with you to discuss a training program? Commit to a budget item for future training? Hire a consultant or agency to come in and conduct training programs?

Your Task. Individually or as a team, write a convincing memo that describes the problem, suggests what the training should include, and asks for action by a specific date. Add any reasonable details necessary to build your case. Address your memo or e-mail to Robert Richardson, vice president. Your position is director of Human Resources.[12]

7.12 Persuasive Memo: Scheduling Meetings More Strategically. The following memo, with names changed, was actually sent.

Your Task. Based on what you have learned in this chapter, improve this memo. Expect the staff to be somewhat resistant because they've never before had meeting restrictions.

DATE: Current
TO: All Managers and Employees
FROM: Lynn Wasson, CEO
SUBJECT: SCHEDULING MEETINGS

Please be reminded that travel in the greater Los Angeles area is time consuming. In the future we're asking that you set up meetings that

1. Are of critical importance
2. Consider travel time for the participants
3. Consider phone conferences (or video or e-mail) in lieu of face-to-face meetings
4. Meetings should be at the location where most of the participants work and at the most opportune travel times
5. Traveling together is another way to save time and resources.

We all have our traffic stories. A recent one is that a certain manager was asked to attend a one-hour meeting in Burbank. This required one hour of travel in advance of the meeting, one hour for the meeting, and two and a half hours of travel through Los Angeles afterward. This meeting was scheduled for 4 p.m. Total time consumed by the manager for the one-hour meeting was four and a half hours.

Thank you for your consideration.

7.13 Persuasive Claim: Outrageous Charge for Pancake Breakfast. As regional manager for an electronics parts manufacturer, you and two other employees at-

tended a conference in Washington, DC. You stayed at the Marriott Hotel because your company recommends that employees use this hotel chain. Generally, your employees have liked their accommodations, and the rates have been within your company's budget. The hotel's service has been excellent.

Now, however, you're unhappy with the charges you see on your company's credit statement from the Marriott. When your department's administrative assistant made the reservations, she was assured that you would receive the weekend rates and that a hot breakfast—in the hotel restaurant, the Atrium—would be included in the rate. You hate those cold sweet rolls and instant coffee served in "continental" breakfasts, especially when you have to leave early and won't get another meal until afternoon. So you and the other two employees went to the restaurant and ordered a hot meal from the menu.

When you received the credit statement, though, you see a charge for $79 for three champagne buffet breakfasts in the Atrium. You hit the ceiling! For one thing, you didn't have a buffet breakfast and certainly no champagne. The three of you got there so early that no buffet had been set up. You ordered pancakes and sausage, and for this you were billed $25 each. You're outraged! What's worse, your company may charge you personally for exceeding the expected rates.

In looking back at this event, you remembered that other guests on your floor were having a "continental" breakfast in a lounge on your floor. Perhaps that's where the hotel expected all guests on the weekend rate to eat. However, your administrative assistant had specifically asked about this matter when she made the reservations, and she was told that you could order breakfast from the menu at the hotel's restaurant.

Your Task. You want to straighten out this matter, and you can't do it by telephone because you suspect that you will need a written record of this entire mess. Write a claim request to the Customer Service, Washington Marriott, 1221 22nd Street, N.W., Washington, DC 20037. Should you include a copy of the credit statement showing the charge?

7.14 CLAIM REQUEST: SUPER SUPREME ITALIAN ICE CREAM AND SORBET.

As business manager for Florentino's Super Supreme Italian Ice Cream and Sorbets, you are happy with the growing reputation of your business. Recently your firm was approached by an independent ice cream vendor who wanted to use Florentino's name and recipes for ice cream to be distributed through grocery stores and drugstores. As business manager you worked with a law firm of Jarvis, Simon, and Associates to draw up contracts regarding the use of Florentino's name and quality standards for the product. However, when you received the bill from Gerald Jarvis, you couldn't believe it. The bill itemized 38 hours of attorney preparation, at $300 per hour, and 55 hours of paralegal assistance, at $75 per hour. The bill also showed $415 for telephone calls, which might be accurate because Mr. Jarvis had to converse with Florentino's owners, who were living in Italy at the time. However, you doubt that an experienced attorney would require 38 hours to draw up the contracts in question.

Perhaps some error was made in calculating the total hours. Moreover, you have checked with other businesses and found that excellent legal advice can be obtained for $150 per hour. Florentino's would like to continue using the services of Jarvis, Simon, and Associates for future legal business. Such future business is unlikely if an adjustment is not made on this bill.

Your Task. Write a persuasive request to Gerald Jarvis, Attorney at Law, Jarvis, Simon, and Associates, 5238 Ocean View Place, Panama City, FL 32401.

7.15 SALES LETTER: BECOMING A BRIDAL CONSULTANT.

As a communication consultant, you receive all kinds of requests. Your most recent job is writing a sales letter promoting the Professional Bridal Consultant program. Now, you are the first to admit that you don't know a lot about bridal consulting and weddings, but you do know what it takes to write a good direct-mail letter. You didn't hesitate for a minute in accepting the

WEB

job assignment from Harcourt Learning Direct, an educational institution. It wants you to prepare a letter that sells its online bridal consulting course.

Unfortunately, Harcourt did not provide you with much to go on. You visit its Web site and quickly see that the Web site focuses primarily on instructional information, such as books, learning aids, and access to Web services. But it doesn't provide many details about how important a professional consultant is in achieving a perfect wedding day. To sell this online training program, you feel that you need to make both rational and emotional appeals. You decide to look at other wedding consultant Web sites for more information. Many of them have information about what a consultant does, including establishing a realistic budget; recommending venues, caterers, florists, musicians, and photographers; scheduling appointments; and coordinating everybody on the wedding day. Harcourt's Professional Bridal Consultant program provides training in all of these aspects of wedding planning.

Your Task. Visit the Harcourt site by using a Web search engine (such as http://www. google.com). Search for "Harcourt Professional Bridal Consultant Program." Look at other bridal consultant Web sites also. Then write a letter promoting the Harcourt program. It will be sent to a targeted database of people who sell wedding dresses or gifts, maintain wedding registries, subscribe to selected bridal magazines, or work as caterers. Harcourt figures that within this group some people will be interested in becoming professional bridal consultants. Students can earn a career diploma in as little as nine months. Because your letter will be reviewed thoroughly by Harcourt, you feel free to "pull out all the stops" in your first draft. Your goal is to have receivers return an enclosed postal card requesting more information (free, of course) about the program. If they act by a certain date, they will receive *Basics of a Bridal Business*, a fact-filled book with valuable tips on successful bridal consulting. Address your letter to "Dear Friend."

7.16 SALES LETTER: PROMOTING YOUR PRODUCT OR SERVICE. Identify a situation in your current job or a previous one in which a sales letter is (was) needed. Using suggestions from this chapter, write an appropriate sales letter that promotes a product or service. Use actual names, information, and examples. If you have no work experience, imagine a business you'd like to start: Web site design, word processing, student typing, pet grooming, car detailing, tutoring, specialty knitting, balloon decorating, delivery service, child care, gardening, lawn care, or something else.

Your Task. Write a letter selling your product or service to be distributed to your prospective customers. Be sure to tell them how to respond.

VIDEO CASE

World Gym Persuasive Request

Ask your instructor to show the VHS video about World Gym. You may also see the video and learn more about the case at http://www.westwords.com/guffey/role.html. Many San Franciscans think that World Gym is the best gym in the city for the money. The physical plant is huge, containing over 35,000 square feet of space stocked with free weights, treadmills, lifecycles, Stairmasters, recumbent bikes, rowing machines, and other equipment. But World Gym finds that most of its members come at the same time, from 4 p.m. to 8 p.m. The owners think they could increase profitability and improve service by installing additional security cameras so that members will feel safe using the gym at later hours.

Your Task. Draft a letter to World Gym members that will persuade them to fill out a simple questionnaire regarding proposed additional security cameras. Although you're new to the gym world, the owners value your recent training in business communication.

Related Web site: http://www.westwords.com/guffey/role.html

GRAMMAR/MECHANICS CHECKUP—7

COMMAS 2

Review the Grammar/Mechanics Handbook Sections 2.05–2.09. Then study each of the following statements and insert necessary commas. In the space provided write the number of commas that you add; write *0* if no commas are needed. Also record the number of the G/M principle(s) illustrated. When you finish, compare your responses with those provided at the end of the book. If your answers differ, study carefully the principles shown in parentheses.

Example	When businesses encounter financial problems, they often reduce their administrative staffs.	1 _____ (2.06a)

1. As stated in the warranty this printer is guaranteed for one year. _____
2. Today's profits come from products currently on the market and tomorrow's profits come from products currently on the drawing boards. _____
3. Companies introduce new products in one part of the country and then watch how the product sells in that area. _____
4. One large automobile manufacturer which must remain nameless recognizes that buyer perception is behind the success of any new product. _____
5. The imaginative promising agency opened its offices April 22 in Cambridge. _____
6. The sales associate who earns the highest number of recognition points this year will be honored with a bonus vacation trip. _____
7. Darren Wilson our sales manager in the Panama City area will present the new sales campaign at the June meeting. _____
8. Our new product has many attributes that should make it appealing to buyers but it also has one significant drawback. _____
9. Although they have different technical characteristics and vary considerably in price and quality two or more of a firm's products may be perceived by shoppers as almost the same. _____
10. To motivate prospective buyers we are offering a cash rebate of $2. _____

REVIEW OF COMMAS 1 AND 2

11. When you receive the application please fill it out and return it before Monday January 3. _____
12. On the other hand we are very interested in hiring hard-working conscientious individuals. _____
13. In March we expect to open a new branch in Concord which is an area of considerable growth. _____
14. As we discussed on the telephone the ceremony is scheduled for Thursday June 9 at 3 p.m. _____
15. Dr. Adams teaches the morning classes and Mrs. Wildey is responsible for evening sections. _____

DOCUMENT FOR REVISION

The following letter has faults in grammar, punctuation, spelling, and number form. Look for some commas to remove. Use standard proofreading marks (see Appendix B) to correct the errors. When you finish, your instructor can show you the revised version of this letter.

Current date

Mr. Charles Smith

Eastman Kodak Company

258 West Main Street

Rochester NY 14605

Dear Ms. Smith:

Pictures from a once in a lifetime trip are irreplaceable. Thats why I put my trust in Kodaks Advantix Camera which I bought for a round the world trip I made last fall. Since I am not a camera professional I thought it's easy load feature was exactly what I needed. Your advertisements sold me and I happily purchased the Advantix for my trip.

On my 27 day trip I shot fifteen rolls of film. When I returned I learned that twelve of those roll could not be developed, because the camera malfunctioned. With this letter, I am enclosing the rolls of film, and my purchase slip for the camera.

Needless to say Mr. Smith the value of these photographs is far greater then the cost of the film, or the purchase price of the camera. The real loss is the complete record of a beautiful inspirational trip. If I do not have my pictures I will not remember how I felt, and looked standing in front of the Great Pyramids of Giza exploring the Blue Mosque in Istanbul and dancing with children around a fire in a Thai village.

Replacing the film or camera is not enough. Since I have no pictures I feel as if I never took the trip. I have suffered a tremendous emotional loss and I am requesting that Kodak pay me 20,000 dollars so that I may repeat my trip, and replace the pictures lost because of this faulty camera. I know that Kodak enjoys a excelent reputation among consumers; therefore, I trust that you will do the right thing in helping me replace my lost memorys.

Sincerely,

John W. Streeter

John W. Streeter

Seven Steps to Resolving Workplace Conflicts

"People who never experience conflict on the job are either living in a dream world, blind to their surroundings, or in solitary confinement," says communication expert Diana Booher.[13] Although all workplaces experience conflict from time to time, some people think that workplace conflict is escalating.

Several factors may be tied to increasing problems at work. One factor is our increasingly diverse workforce. Sharing ideas that stem from a variety of backgrounds, experiences, and personalities may lead to better problem solving, but it can also lead to conflict. Another factor related to increased conflict is the trend toward participatory management. In the past only bosses had to resolve problems, but now more employees are making decisions and facing conflict. This is particularly true of teams. Working together harmoniously involves a great deal of give and take, and conflict may result if some people feel that they are being taken advantage of.

Not all conflict is negative or dysfunctional. In fact, conflict can serve a number of healthy functions. In groups, conflict can increase involvement and cohesiveness. When people clash over differing views, they can become more committed to their purpose and to each other. Handled properly, conflict can provide an outlet for hostility and can increase group productivity.[14]

When problems arise in the workplace, it's important for everyone to recognize that conflict is a normal occurrence[15] and that it should be confronted and resolved. Effective conflict resolution requires good listening skills, flexibility, and a willingness to change. Individuals must be willing to truly listen and seek to understand rather than immediately challenge the adversary. In many workplace conflicts, involving a third party to act as a mediator is necessary. Although problems vary greatly, the following seven steps offer a good basic process for resolving conflicts.[16]

1. Make a date. Arrange a time when both parties are willing to have a conversation in a nonthreatening environment.
2. Listen to each side. Encourage each individual to describe the situation from his or her perspective.
3. Paraphrase before responding. To promote empathic communication, follow this rule. No one may respond without first accurately summarizing the other person's previous remarks.
4. Begin problem solving. Brainstorm together to develop multiple options for resolving the conflict. Individuals should try to see each other as allies, rather than opponents, in solving the problem.
5. Negotiate a solution. Ensure that both parties are agreeable to the chosen solution.
6. Record the solution. It is important to formalize the agreement in some way.
7. Implement the solution and follow up. Meet again on an agreed-upon date to ensure satisfactory resolution of the conflict. The deadline makes it more likely that both parties will follow through on their part of the deal.

Career Application. As leader of your work team, you were recently confronted by an angry fellow team member. Laura, a story editor on your film production team, is upset because, for the third time in as many weeks, she was forced to give up part of her weekend for work. This time it was for a black-tie affair that everyone in the office tried to duck. Laura is particularly angry with Bob, who should have represented the team at this awards dinner. But he uttered the magic word: *family*. "Bob says he has plans with his family, and it's like a get-out-of-jail-free card," Laura complains to you. "I don't resent him or his devotion to his family. But I do resent it when my team constantly expects me to give up my personal time because I don't have kids. That's my choice, and I don't think I should be punished for it."[17]

Your Task. Using the principles outlined here, work out a conflict resolution plan for Laura and Bob. Your instructor may wish to divide your class into three-person teams to role-play Laura, Bob, and the team leader. Add any details to make a realistic scenario.

- What are the first steps in resolving this conflict?
- What arguments might each side present?
- What alternatives might be offered?
- What do you think is the best solution?
- How could the solution be implemented with the least friction?

Chapter 8

Negative Messages

More thought goes into bad news messages. That's because we need to explain the whys and try to offer alternatives.[1]

CATHY DIAL, Manager, Consumer Affairs, Frito-Lay, a division of PepsiCo

LEARNING OBJECTIVES

1. Describe a plan for resolving business problems.
2. List the four components of a bad-news message.
3. Distinguish between the direct and indirect patterns for business messages.
4. Discuss methods for applying the indirect pattern to bad-news messages, including buffering the opening, presenting the reasons, cushioning the bad news, and closing pleasantly.
5. Apply the indirect pattern in refusing requests, refusing claims, and announcing bad news to customers and employees.
6. Identify situations in which the direct pattern is appropriate for breaking bad news.
7. Explain when the indirect strategy may be unethical.

STRATEGIES FOR BREAKING BAD NEWS

B reaking bad news is a fact of business life for Cathy Dial at Frito-Lay and for nearly every business communicator. Because bad news disappoints, irritates, and sometimes angers the receiver, such messages must be written carefully.

The direct strategy, which you learned to apply in earlier chapters, frontloads the main idea, even when it's bad news. The direct strategy appeals to efficiency-oriented writers who don't want to waste time with efforts to soften the effects of bad news.[2] Many business writers, however, prefer to use the indirect pattern in delivering negative messages. The indirect strategy is especially appealing to relationship-oriented writers. They care about how a message will affect its receiver.

Although the major focus of this chapter will be on developing the indirect strategy, you'll first learn the procedure that many business professionals follow in resolving business problems. It may surprise you. Then you'll study models of

✓ *Quick Check*

If your message delivers bad news, consider using the indirect strategy.

messages that use the indirect pattern to refuse requests, refuse claims, and announce bad news to customers and employees. Finally, you'll learn to identify instances in which the direct pattern may be preferable in announcing bad news.

RESOLVING BUSINESS PROBLEMS

In all businesses, things occasionally go wrong. Goods are not delivered, a product fails to perform as expected, service is poor, billing gets fouled up, or customers are misunderstood. All businesses offering products or services must sometimes deal with troublesome situations that cause unhappiness to customers and to employees. Whenever possible, these problems should be dealt with immediately and personally. One study found that a majority of business professionals resolve problems in the following manner:[3]

1. Call the individual involved.
2. Describe the problem and apologize.
3. Explain why the problem occurred, what you are doing to resolve it, and how you will prevent it from happening again.
4. Follow up with a letter that documents the phone call and promotes goodwill.

Dealing with problems immediately is important in resolving conflict and retaining goodwill. Written correspondence is generally too slow for problems that demand immediate attention. But written messages are important (1) when personal contact is impossible, (2) to establish a record of the incident, (3) to formally confirm follow-up procedures, and (4) to promote good relations.

A bad-news follow-up letter is shown in Figure 8.1. Consultant Maris Richfield found herself in the embarrassing position of explaining why she had given out the name of her client to a salesperson. The client, Data.com, Inc., had hired her firm, Richfield Consulting Services, to help find an appropriate service for outsourcing its payroll functions. Without realizing it, Maris had mentioned to a po-

When something goes wrong in customer transactions and damage control is necessary, the first thing most businesspeople do is call the individual involved, explain what happened, and apologize. Written messages follow up. © PhotoDisc, Inc./Getty Images

FIGURE 8.1   Bad-News Follow-Up Message

Richfield Consulting Services

4023 Rodeo Drive Plaza, Suite 404
Beverly Hills, CA 90640

Voice: 213.499.8224
Web: www.richfieldconsulting.com

October 23, 200x

Ms. Angela Ranier
Vice President, Human Resources
Data.com, Inc.
21067 Pacific Coast Highway
Malibu, CA 90265

Dear Angela:

You have every right to expect complete confidentiality in your transactions with an independent consultant. As I explained in yesterday's telephone call, I am very distressed that you were called by a salesperson from Payroll Services, Inc. This should not have happened, and I apologize to you again for inadvertently mentioning your company's name in a conversation with a potential vendor, Payroll Services, Inc.

All clients of Richfield Consulting may be sure that we handle all their dealings in the strictest confidence. Because your company's payroll needs are so individual and because you have so many contract workers, I had to explain how your employees differed from those of other companies. The name of your company, however, should never have been mentioned. I can assure you that it will not happen again. I have informed Payroll Services that it had no authorization to call you directly and its actions have forced me to reconsider using its services for my future clients.

A number of other payroll services offer excellent programs. I'm sure we can find the perfect partner to enable you to outsource your payroll responsibilities, thus allowing your company to focus its financial and human resources on its core business. I look forward to our next appointment when you may choose from a number of excellent payroll outsourcing firms.

Sincerely yours,

Maris Richfield

Maris Richfield

Opens with agreement and apology

Explains what caused problem and how it was resolved

Promises to prevent recurrence

Closes with forward look

TIPS FOR RESOLVING PROBLEMS AND FOLLOWING UP
- Whenever possible, call or see the individual involved.
- Describe the problem and apologize.
- Explain why the problem occurred.
- Explain what you are doing to resolve it.
- Explain how it will not happen again.
- Follow up with a letter that documents the personal message.
- Look forward to positive future relations.

tential vendor, Payroll Services, Inc., that her client was considering hiring an outside service to handle its payroll. An overeager salesperson from Payroll Services immediately called on Data.com, thus angering the client. The client had hired the consultant to avoid this very kind of intrusion. Data.com did not want to be hounded by vendors selling their payroll services.

When she learned of the problem, the first thing consultant Maris Richfield did was call her client to explain and apologize. But she also followed up with the letter shown in Figure 8.1. The letter not only confirms the telephone conversation but also adds the right touch of formality. It sends the nonverbal message that the matter is being taken seriously and that it is important enough to warrant a written letter.

USING THE INDIRECT PATTERN TO PREPARE THE READER

Quick Check

The indirect pattern softens the impact of bad news.

When sending a bad-news message that will upset or irritate the receiver, many business communicators use the indirect pattern. Revealing bad news indirectly shows sensitivity to your reader. Whereas good news can be announced quickly, bad news generally should be revealed gradually. By preparing the reader, you soften the impact. A blunt announcement of disappointing news might cause the receiver to stop reading and toss the message aside.

The indirect strategy enables you to keep the reader's attention until you have been able to explain the reasons for the bad news. The most important part of a bad-news letter is the explanation, which you'll learn about shortly. The indirect plan consists of four main parts:

- Buffer
- Reasons
- Bad news
- Closing

BUFFERING THE OPENING

Quick Check

A buffer opens a bad-news letter with a neutral, concise, relevant, and upbeat statement.

A buffer is a device to reduce shock or pain. To buffer the pain of bad news, begin with a neutral but meaningful statement that makes the reader continue reading. The buffer should be relevant and concise. Although it should avoid revealing the bad news immediately, it should not convey a false impression that good news follows. It should provide a natural transition to the explanation that follows. The individual situation, of course, will help determine what you should put in the buffer. Here are some possibilities for opening bad-news messages.

Quick Check

A good buffer may include the best news, a compliment, appreciation, facts regarding the problem, a statement indicating understanding, or an apology.

- **Best news.** Start with the part of the message that represents the best news. In a memo that announces an increase in Internet connection fees, you might begin by describing improved service. For example, *To ensure that your incoming e-mail does not contain spam or viruses, we are installing a new filtering program that you may begin using immediately at no extra charge.*
- **Compliment.** Praise the receiver's accomplishments, organization, or efforts, but do so with honesty and sincerity. For instance, in a letter declining an invitation to speak, you could write, *The Thalians have my sincere admiration for their fund-raising projects on behalf of hungry children. I am honored that you asked me to speak Friday, November 5.*
- **Appreciation.** Convey thanks to the reader for doing business, for sending something, for showing confidence in your organization, for expressing feelings, or simply for providing feedback. In a letter responding to a complaint about poor service, you might say, *Thanks for telling us about your experience at our hotel and for giving us a chance to look into the situation.* Avoid thanking the reader, however, for something you are about to refuse.
- **Agreement.** Make a relevant statement with which both reader and receiver can agree. A letter that rejects a loan application might read, *We both realize how much the export business has been affected by the relative strength of the dollar in the past two years.*

- **Facts.** Provide objective information that introduces the bad news. For example, in a memo announcing cutbacks in the hours of the employees' cafeteria, you might say, *During the past five years the number of employees eating breakfast in our cafeteria has dropped from 32 percent to 12 percent.*
- **Understanding.** Show that you care about the reader. In announcing a product defect, the writer can still manage to express concern for the customer: *We know that you expect superior performance from all the products you purchase from OfficeCity. That's why we're writing personally about the Excell printer cartridges you recently ordered.*
- **Apology.** A study of actual letters responding to customer complaints revealed that 67 percent carried an apology of some sort.[4] If you do apologize, do it early, briefly, and sincerely. For example, a manufacturer of super premium ice cream might respond to a customer's complaint with, *We're genuinely sorry that you were disappointed in the price of the ice cream you recently purchased at one of our scoop shops. Your opinion is important to us, and we appreciate your giving us the opportunity to look into the problem you describe.*

© Ted Goff (www.tedgoff.com)

"Dear Valued Customer: We're sorry, but company policy forbids apologies. Sincerely yours..."

PRESENTING THE REASONS

The most important part of a bad-news letter is the section that explains why a negative decision is necessary. Without sound reasons for denying a request or refusing a claim, a letter will fail, no matter how cleverly it is organized or written. As part of your planning before writing, you analyzed the problem and decided to refuse a request for specific reasons. Before disclosing the bad news, try to explain those reasons. Providing an explanation reduces feelings of ill will and improves the chances that the reader will accept the bad news. A number of techniques such as the following are effective in presenting bad news.

Quick Check

Bad-news messages should explain reasons before stating the negative news.

- **Being cautious in explaining.** If the reasons are not confidential and if they will not create legal liability, you can be specific: *Growers supplied us with a limited number of patio roses, and our demand this year was twice that of last year.* In refusing a speaking engagement, tell why the date is impossible: *On January 17 we have a board of directors meeting that I must attend.*
- **Citing reader benefits.** Readers are more open to bad news if in some way, even indirectly, it may help them. In refusing a customer's request for free hemming of skirts and slacks, Lands' End wrote: *We tested our ability to hem skirts a few months ago. This process proved to be very time-consuming. We have decided not to offer this service because the additional cost would have increased the selling price of our skirts substantially, and we did not want to impose that cost on all our customers.*[5] Readers also accept bad news better if they recognize that someone or something else benefits, such as other workers or the environment: *Although we would like to consider your application, we prefer to fill managerial positions from within.* Avoid trying to show reader benefits, though, if they appear insincere: *To improve our service to you, we're increasing our brokerage fees.*
- **Explaining company policy.** Readers resent blanket policy statements prohibiting something: *Company policy prevents us from making cash refunds* or *Contract bids may be accepted from local companies only* or *Company policy requires us to promote from within.* Instead of hiding behind company policy, gently explain why the policy makes sense: *We prefer to promote from within because it rewards*

Quick Check

Readers accept bad news more readily if they see that someone benefits.

the loyalty of our employees. In addition, we've found that people familiar with our organization make the quickest contribution to our team effort. By offering explanations, you demonstrate that you care about readers and are treating them as important individuals.

Avoid negative words (such as *claim, error, never, fault*) because they make the receiver defensive, angry, and unreceptive to reasoning.

- **Choosing positive words.** Because the words you use can affect a reader's response, choose carefully. Remember that the objective of the indirect pattern is to hold the reader's attention until you've had a chance to explain the reasons justifying the bad news. To keep the reader in a receptive mood, avoid expressions that might cause the reader to tune out. Be sensitive to negative words such as *claim, error, failure, fault, impossible, mistaken, misunderstand, never, regret, unwilling, unfortunately,* and *violate.*

- **Showing that the matter was treated seriously and fairly.** In explaining reasons, demonstrate to the reader that you take the matter seriously, have investigated carefully, and are making an unbiased decision. Consumers are more accepting of disappointing news when they feel that their requests have been heard and that they have been treated fairly.[6] Avoid passing the buck or blaming others within your organization. Such unprofessional behavior makes the reader lose faith in you and your company.

CUSHIONING THE BAD NEWS

Although you can't prevent the disappointment that bad news brings, you can reduce the pain somewhat by breaking the news sensitively. Be especially considerate when the reader will suffer personally from the bad news. A number of thoughtful techniques can cushion the blow.

Techniques for cushioning bad news include positioning it strategically, using the passive voice, emphasizing the positive, implying the refusal, and suggesting alternatives or compromises.

- **Positioning the bad news.** Instead of spotlighting it, sandwich the bad news between other sentences, perhaps among your reasons. Try not to let the refusal begin or end a paragraph—the reader's eye will linger on these high-visibility spots. Another technique that reduces shock is putting a painful idea in a subordinate clause: *Although another candidate was hired, we appreciate your interest in our organization and wish you every success in your job search.* Subordinate clauses often begin with words such as *although, as, because, if,* and *since.*

- **Using the passive voice.** Passive-voice verbs enable you to depersonalize an action. Whereas the active voice focuses attention on a person (*We don't give cash refunds*), the passive voice highlights the action (*Cash refunds are not given because . . .*). Use the passive voice for the bad news. In some instances you can combine passive-voice verbs and a subordinate clause: *Although franchise scoop shop owners cannot be required to lower their ice cream prices, we are happy to pass along your comments for their consideration.*

- **Accentuating the positive.** As you learned earlier, messages are far more effective when you describe what you can do instead of what you can't do. Rather than *We will no longer allow credit card purchases,* try a more positive appeal: *We are now selling gasoline at discount cash prices.*

- **Implying the refusal.** It's sometimes possible to avoid a direct statement of refusal. Often, your reasons and explanations leave no doubt that a request has been denied. Explicit refusals may be unnecessary and at times cruel. In this refusal to contribute to a charity, for example, the writer never actually says no: *Because we will soon be moving into new offices in Glendale, all our funds are earmarked for moving and furnishings. We hope that next year we'll be able to support your worthwhile charity.* The danger of an implied refusal, of course, is that it can be so subtle that the reader misses it. Be certain that you make the bad news clear, thus preventing the need for further correspondence.

- **Suggesting a compromise or an alternative.** A refusal is not so depressing—for the sender or the receiver—if a suitable compromise, substitute, or alternative is available. In denying permission to a class to visit a historical private residence, for instance, this writer softens the bad news by proposing an alternative: *Although private tours of the grounds are not given, we do open the house and its gardens for one charitable event in the fall.*

You can further reduce the impact of the bad news by refusing to dwell on it. Present it briefly (or imply it), and move on to your closing.

CLOSING PLEASANTLY

After explaining the bad news sensitively, close the message with a pleasant statement that promotes goodwill. The closing should be personalized and may include a forward look, an alternative, good wishes, freebies, resale information, or an off-the-subject remark.

✔ *Quick Check*

Closings to bad-news messages might include a forward look, an alternative, good wishes, freebies, and resale or sales promotional information.

- **Forward look.** Anticipate future relations or business. A letter that refuses a contract proposal might read: *Thanks for your bid. We look forward to working with your talented staff when future projects demand your special expertise.*
- **Alternative.** If an alternative exists, end your letter with follow-through advice. For example, in a letter rejecting a customer's demand for replacement of landscaping plants, you might say: *I will be happy to give you a free inspection and consultation. Please call 746-8112 to arrange a date for my visit.*
- **Good wishes.** A letter rejecting a job candidate might read: *We appreciate your interest in our company, and we extend to you our best wishes in your search to find the perfect match between your skills and job requirements.*
- **Freebies.** When customers complain—primarily about food products or small consumer items—companies often send coupons, samples, or gifts to restore confidence and to promote future business. In response to a customer's complaint about a frozen dinner, you could write, *Your loyalty and your concern about our frozen entrees is genuinely appreciated. Because we want you to continue enjoying our healthful and convenient dinners, we're enclosing a coupon that you can take to your local market to select your next Green Valley entree.*
- **Resale or sales promotion.** When the bad news is not devastating or personal, references to resale information or promotion may be appropriate: *The computer workstations you ordered are unusually popular because of their stain-, heat-, and scratch-resistant finishes. To help you locate hard-to-find accessories for these workstations, we invite you to visit our Web site where our online catalog provides a huge selection of surge suppressors, multiple outlet strips, security devices, and PC tool kits.*

Avoid endings that sound canned, insincere, inappropriate, or self-serving. Don't invite further correspondence (*If you have any questions, do not hesitate . . .*), and don't rehash the bad news.

REFUSING REQUESTS

Although the direct strategy is sometimes suitable, most of us prefer to be let down gently when we're being refused something we want. That's why the reasons-before-refusal pattern works well when you must turn down requests for favors, money, information, action, and so forth. The following writing plan is appropriate when you must deny a routine request or claim.

✔ *Quick Check*

The indirect strategy is appropriate when refusing requests for favors, money, information, or action.

WRITING PLAN FOR REFUSING REQUESTS OR CLAIMS

- *Buffer:* Start with a neutral statement on which both reader and writer can agree, such as a compliment, appreciation, a quick review of the facts, or an apology. Try to include a key idea or word that acts as a transition to the reasons.
- *Reasons:* Present valid reasons for the refusal, avoiding words that create a negative tone. Include resale or sales promotion material if appropriate.
- *Bad news:* Soften the blow by deemphasizing the bad news, using the passive voice, accentuating the positive, or implying a refusal. Suggest a compromise, alternative, or substitute if possible. The alternative may be part of the bad news or part of the closing.
- *Closing:* Renew good feelings with a positive statement. Avoid referring to the bad news. Look forward to continued business.

Two versions of a request refusal are shown in Figure 8.2. A magazine writer requested salary information for an article, but the company could not release this information. The ineffective version begins with needless information that could be implied. The second paragraph creates a harsh tone with such negative words as *sorry, must refuse, violate,* and *liable.* Since the refusal precedes the explanation, the reader probably will not be in a receptive frame of mind to accept the reasons for refusing. Notice, too, that the bad news is emphasized by its placement in a short sentence at the beginning of a paragraph. It stands out here and adds more weight to the rejection already felt by the reader.

Moreover, the refusal explanation is overly graphic, containing references to possible litigation. The tone at this point is threatening and unduly harsh. Then, suddenly, the author throws in a self-serving comment about the high salary and commissions of his salespeople. Instead of offering constructive alternatives, the ineffective version reveals only tiny bits of the desired data. Finally, the closing sounds syrupy and insincere.

In the more effective version of this refusal, the opening reflects the writer's genuine interest in the request. But it does not indicate compliance. The second sentence acts as a transition by introducing the words *salespeople* and *salaries,* repeated in the following paragraph. Reasons for refusing this request are objectively presented in an explanation that precedes the refusal. Notice that the refusal (*Although specific salaries and commission rates cannot be released*) is a subordinate clause in a long sentence in the middle of a paragraph. To further soften the blow, the letter offers an alternative. The cordial closing refers to the alternative, avoids mention of the refusal, and looks to the future.

It's always easier to write refusals when alternatives can be offered to soften the bad news. But often no alternatives are possible. The refusal shown in Figure 8.3 involves a delicate situation in which a manager has been asked by her superiors to violate a contract. Several of the engineers for whom she works have privately asked her to make copies of a licensed software program for them. They apparently want this program for their personal computers. Making copies is forbidden by the terms of the software licensing agreement, and the manager refuses to do this. Rather than saying no to each engineer who asks her, she sends all staff computer users the e-mail message shown in Figure 8.3.

The opening tactfully avoids suggesting that any engineer has actually asked to copy the software program. These professionals may prefer not to have their private requests made known. A transition takes the reader to the logical reasons against copying. Notice that the tone is objective, neither preaching nor condemning. The refusal is softened by being linked with a positive statement (*Al-*

FIGURE 8.2   Refusing a Request BEFORE and AFTER Revision

BEFORE Revision

States obvious information

Dear Ms. Brown:

I have your letter of October 21 in which you request information about the salaries and commissions of our top young salespeople.

Sounds harsh, blunt, and unnecessarily negative

I am sorry to inform you that we cannot reveal data of this kind. I must, therefore, refuse your request. To release this information would violate our private employee contracts. Such disclosure could make us liable for damages, should any employee seek legal recourse. I might say, however, that our salespeople are probably receiving the highest combined salary and commissions of any salespeople in this field.

Switches tone

If it were possible for us to help you with your fascinating research, we would certainly be happy to do so.

Sincerely yours,

AFTER Revision

CANON ELECTRONICS

115 Fifth Avenue
New york, NY 10011-1010
(212) 593-1098
www.canon.com

January 15, 200x

Ms. Daniela Brown
1305 Elmwood Avenue
Buffalo, NY 14222-2240

Dear Ms. Brown:

The article you are now researching for *Business Management Weekly* sounds fascinating, and we are flattered that you wish to include our organization. We do have many outstanding young salespeople, both male and female, who are commanding top salaries.

Buffer shows interest, and transition sets up explanation

Each of our salespeople operates under an individual salary contract. During salary negotiations several years ago, an agreement was reached in which both sales staff members and management agree to keep the terms of these individual contracts confidential. Although specific salaries and commission rates cannot be released, we can provide you with a ranked list of our top salespeople for the past five years. Three of the current top salespeople are under the age of thirty-five.

Explanation gives good reasons for refusing request

Refusal is softened by substitute

Enclosed is a fact sheet regarding our top salespeople. We wish you every success with your article, and we hope to see our organization represented in it.

Closing is pleasant and forward looking

Cordially,

Lloyd Kenniston

Lloyd Kenniston
Executive Vice President

LK:je
Enclosure: Sales Fact Sheet

FIGURE 8.3   Refusing a Request

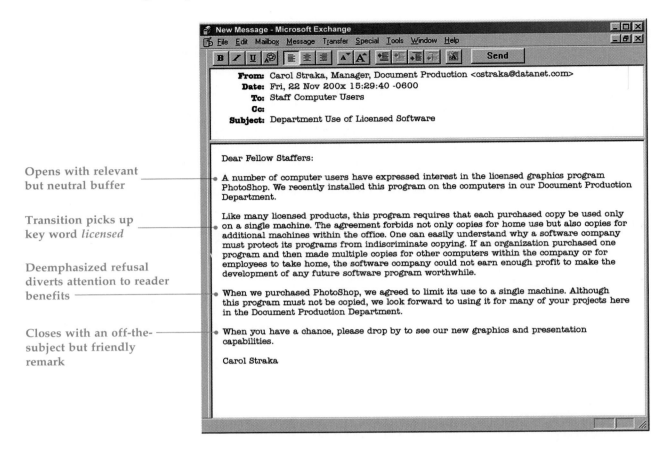

Opens with relevant but neutral buffer

Transition picks up key word *licensed*

Deemphasized refusal diverts attention to reader benefits

Closes with an off-the-subject but friendly remark

New Message - Microsoft Exchange

File Edit Mailbox Message Transfer Special Tools Window Help

From: Carol Straka, Manager, Document Production <cstraka@datanet.com>
Date: Fri, 22 Nov 200x 15:29:40 -0600
To: Staff Computer Users
Cc:
Subject: Department Use of Licensed Software

Dear Fellow Staffers:

A number of computer users have expressed interest in the licensed graphics program PhotoShop. We recently installed this program on the computers in our Document Production Department.

Like many licensed products, this program requires that each purchased copy be used only on a single machine. The agreement forbids not only copies for home use but also copies for additional machines within the office. One can easily understand why a software company must protect its programs from indiscriminate copying. If an organization purchased one program and then made multiple copies for other computers within the company or for employees to take home, the software company could not earn enough profit to make the development of any future software program worthwhile.

When we purchased PhotoShop, we agreed to limit its use to a single machine. Although this program must not be copied, we look forward to using it for many of your projects here in the Document Production Department.

When you have a chance, please drop by to see our new graphics and presentation capabilities.

Carol Straka

though this program must not be copied, we look forward to using it for many of your projects here . . .). To divert attention from the refusal, the memo ends with a friendly, off-the-subject remark.

REFUSING CLAIMS

All businesses offering products or services will receive occasional customer claims for adjustments. Claims may also arise from employees. Most of these claims are valid, and the customer or employee receives a positive response. Even unwarranted claims are sometimes granted because businesses genuinely desire to create a good public image and to maintain friendly relations with employees.

Quick Check

Although most customer claims are granted, occasionally some must be refused.

Some claims, however, cannot be approved because the customer or employee is mistaken, misinformed, unreasonable, or possibly even dishonest. Letters responding to these claims deliver bad news. And the indirect strategy breaks bad news with the least pain. It also allows the writer to explain why the claim must be refused before the reader realizes the bad news and begins resisting.

In the letter shown in Figure 8.4, the writer denies a customer's claim for the difference between the price the customer paid for speakers and the price he saw advertised locally (which would have resulted in a cash refund of $151). While Galaxy does match any advertised lower price, the price-matching policy applies *only* to exact models. This claim must be rejected because the advertisement the customer submitted shows a different, older speaker model.

FIGURE 8.4 Refusing a Claim

Galaxy Sound Sales

3091 Geddes Road
Ann Arbor, Michigan 48104
Telephone: (313) 499-2341

Fax: (313) 499-5904
Web: www.galaxysound.com
E-mail: galaxy2@flash.co

May 24, 200x

Mr. Russell L. Chapman
4205 Evergreen Avenue
Dearborn, MI 48128

Dear Mr. Chapman:

You're absolutely right! We do take pride in selling the finest products at rock-bottom prices. The Boze speakers you purchased last month are premier concert hall speakers. They're the only ones we present in our catalog because they're the best.
> Begins by agreeing with receiver

We have such confidence in our products and prices that we offer the price-matching policy you mention in your letter of May 20. That policy guarantees a refund of the price difference if you see one of your purchases offered at a lower price for 30 days after your purchase. To qualify for that refund, customers are asked to send us an advertisement or verifiable proof of the product price and model. As our catalog states, this price-matching policy applies only to exact models with USA warranties.
> Explains price-matching policy

Our Boze AM-5 II speakers sell for $749. You sent us a local advertisement showing a price of $598 for Boze speakers. This advertisement, however, described an earlier version, the Boze AM-4 model. The AM-5 speakers you received have a wider dynamic range and smoother frequency response than the AM-4 model. Naturally, the improved model you purchased costs a little more than the older AM-4 model that the local advertisement describes. Your speakers have a new three-chamber bass module that virtually eliminates harmonic distortion. Finally, your speakers are 20 percent more compact than the AM-4 model.
> Without actually saying no, shows why claim can't be honored

You bought the finest compact speakers on the market, Mr. Chapman. If you haven't installed them yet, you may be interested in ceiling mounts, shown in the enclosed catalog on page 48. We value your business and invite your continued comparison shopping.
> Renews good feeling by building confidence in wisdom of purchase

Sincerely yours,

Mark L. Johnson

Mark L. Johnson

The letter to Russell Chapman opens with a buffer that agrees with a statement in the customer's letter. It repeats the key idea of product confidence as a transition to the second paragraph. Next comes an explanation of the price-matching policy. The writer does not assume that the customer is trying to pull a fast one. Nor does the writer suggest that the customer is a dummy who didn't read or understand the price-matching policy.

The safest path is a neutral explanation of the policy along with precise distinctions between the customer's speakers and the older ones. The writer also gets a chance to resell the customer's speakers and demonstrate what a quality product they are. By the end of the third paragraph, it's evident to the reader that his claim is unjustified.

Notice how most of the components in an effective claim refusal are woven together in this letter: buffer, reasons, bad news, and closing. The only missing part is an alternative, which was impossible in this situation.

Quick Check

When refusing customer claims, explain objectively and do not assume that the customer is an idiot or a crook.

When Kmart filed for reorganization under Chapter 11 and announced that 284 underperforming stores would close, the company softened the bad news in messages to customers and shareholders by assuring them that reorganization would help Kmart emerge from Chapter 11 the following year and ensure long-term financial growth. Kmart executive Joy Corneliussen supervised an advertising campaign featuring billboards that accentuates the positive despite Kmart's troubles. © AP Topic Gallery

ANNOUNCING BAD NEWS TO CUSTOMERS AND EMPLOYEES

In addition to resolving claims, organizations occasionally must announce bad news to customers or to their own employees. Bad news to customers might involve rate increases, reduced service, changed procedures, new locations, or technical problems. Bad news within organizations might involve declining profits, lost contracts, harmful lawsuits, public relations controversies, and changes in policy.

Whether you use a direct or an indirect pattern in delivering that news depends primarily on the anticipated reaction of the receiver. When the bad news affects customers or employees personally—such as cutbacks in pay, reduction of benefits, or relocation plans—you can generally lessen its impact and promote better relations by explaining reasons before revealing the bad news.

✓ **Quick Check**

The choice of a direct or indirect strategy depends on the expected reaction of the receiver.

WRITING PLAN FOR ANNOUNCING BAD NEWS TO CUSTOMERS AND EMPLOYEES

- *Buffer:* Open with a compliment, appreciation, facts, or some form of good news. Try to include a key idea that leads from the opening to the reasons.
- *Reasons:* Explain the logic behind the bad news; use positive words and try to show reader benefits if possible.
- *Bad News:* Position the bad news so that it does not stand out. Consider implying the bad news. Suggest a compromise or alternative, if possible.
- *Closing:* Look forward positively. Provide information about an alternative, if appropriate.

In many businesses today, employees are being asked to pay more for their health care benefits. Midland Enterprises had to announce a substantial increase to its employees. Figure 8.5 shows two versions of its bad-news message. The first version opens directly with the bad news. The writer does not explain why health

FIGURE 8.5 Memo That Announces Bad News to Employees BEFORE and AFTER Revision

BEFORE Revision

Hits readers with bad news without any preparation

Does not explain why costs are rising

Fails to take credit for absorbing previous increases

Sounds defensive; fails to give reasons

MEMO TO: Staff

Beginning January 1 your monthly payment for health care benefits will be increased to $109 (up from $42 last year).

Every year health care costs go up. Although we considered dropping other benefits, Midland decided that the best plan was to keep the present comprehensive package. Unfortunately, we can't do that unless we pass along some of the extra cost to you. Last year the company was forced to absorb the total increase in health care premiums. However, such a plan this year is inadvisable.

We did everything possible to avoid the sharp increase in costs to you this year. A rate schedule describing the increases in payments for your family and dependents is enclosed.

AFTER Revision

Midland, Inc.
Interoffice Memo

DATE: November 6, 200x

TO: Fellow Employees

FROM: David P. Martinez, President

SUBJECT: MAINTAINING QUALITY HEALTH CARE

Health care programs have always been an important part of our commitment to employees here at Midland, Inc. We're proud that our total benefits package continues to rank among the best in the country.

Such a comprehensive package does not come cheaply. In the last decade health care costs alone have risen over 300 percent. We're told that several factors fuel the cost spiral: inflation, technology improvements, increased cost of outpatient service, and "defensive" medicine practiced by doctors to prevent lawsuits.

Just two years ago our monthly health care cost for each employee was $415. It rose to $469 last year. We were able to absorb that jump without increasing your contribution. But this year's hike to $539 forces us to ask you to share the increase. To maintain your current health care benefits, you will be paying $109 a month. The enclosed rate schedule describes the costs for families and dependents.

Midland continues to pay the major portion of your health care program ($430 each month). We think it's a wise investment.

Enclosure

Begins with positive buffer

Explains why costs are rising

Reveals bad news clearly but embeds it in paragraph

Ends positively by stressing the company's major share of the costs

Announcing Bad News to Customers and Employees

care costs are rising. Although Midland has been absorbing the increasing costs in the past and has not charged employees, it takes no credit for this. Instead, the tone of the memo is defensive and unsatisfying to receivers.

The improved version of this bad-news memo, shown at the bottom of Figure 8.5, uses the indirect pattern. Notice that it opens with a relevant, upbeat buffer regarding health care—but says nothing about increasing costs. For a smooth transition, the second paragraph begins with a key idea from the opening (*comprehensive package*). The reasons section discusses rising costs with explanations and figures. The bad news (*you will be paying $109 a month*) is clearly presented but embedded within the paragraph.

Throughout, the writer strives to show the fairness of the company's position. The ending, which does not refer to the bad news, emphasizes how much the company is paying and what a wise investment it is. Notice that the entire memo demonstrates a kinder, gentler approach than that shown in the first draft. Of prime importance in breaking bad news to employees is providing clear, convincing reasons that explain the decision.

Quick Check

In announcing bad news to employees, consider starting with a neutral statement or something positive.

WHEN TO USE THE DIRECT PATTERN

Many bad-news letters are best organized indirectly, beginning with a buffer and reasons. However, the direct pattern, with the bad news first, may be more effective in situations such as the following:

Quick Check

The direct pattern is appropriate when the bad news is not damaging, when the receiver might overlook the bad news, when the organization expects directness, when the receiver prefers directness, or when firmness is necessary.

- **When the bad news is not damaging.** If the bad news is insignificant (such as a small increase in cost) and doesn't personally affect the receiver, then the direct strategy certainly makes sense.
- **When the receiver may overlook the bad news.** With the crush of mail today, many readers skim messages, looking only at the opening. If they don't find substantive material, they may discard the message. Rate increases, changes in service, new policy requirements—these critical messages may require boldness to ensure attention.
- **When organization policy suggests directness.** Some companies expect all internal messages and announcements—even bad news—to be straightforward and presented without frills.
- **When the receiver prefers directness.** Busy managers may prefer directness. Such shorter messages enable the reader to get in the proper frame of mind immediately. If you suspect that the reader prefers that the facts be presented straightaway, use the direct pattern.
- **When firmness is necessary.** Messages that must demonstrate determination and strength should not use delaying techniques. For example, the last in a series of collection letters that seek payment of overdue accounts may require a direct opener.

ETHICS AND THE INDIRECT STRATEGY

You may worry that the indirect organizational strategy is unethical or manipulative because the writer deliberately delays the main idea. But consider the alternative. Breaking bad news bluntly can cause pain and hard feelings. By delaying bad news, you soften the blow somewhat, as well as ensure that your reasoning will be read while the receiver is still receptive. Your motives are not to deceive the reader or to hide the news. Rather, your goal is to be a compassionate, yet effective communicator.

The key to ethical communication lies in the motives of the sender. Unethical communicators *intend to deceive*. For example, Victoria's Secret, the clothing and lingerie chain, offered free $10 gift certificates. However, when customers tried to cash the certificates, they found that they were required to make a minimum purchase of $50 worth of merchandise.[7] For this misleading, deceptive, and unethical offer, the chain paid a $100,000 fine. Although the indirect strategy provides a setting in which to announce bad news, it should not be used to avoid or misrepresent the truth.

SUMMING UP AND LOOKING FORWARD

When faced with delivering bad news, you have a choice. You can announce it immediately, or you can delay it by presenting a buffer and reasons first. Many business communicators prefer the indirect strategy because it tends to preserve goodwill. In some instances, however, the direct strategy is effective in delivering bad news. In this chapter you learned to write follow-up bad-news messages as well as to apply the indirect strategy in refusing requests, denying claims, and delivering bad news to employees. This same strategy is appropriate when you make persuasive requests or when you try to sell something. Chapter 9 discusses how to apply the indirect strategy to persuasive and sales messages.

Interactive Learning @ http://www.westwords.com/guffey/students.html
Prepare for tests and reinforce your chapter knowledge with interactive quizzes and crossword puzzles.

CRITICAL THINKING

1. A survey of business professionals revealed that nearly every respondent said that every effort should be made to resolve business problems in person.[8] Why is this logical?
2. Does bad news travel faster and farther than good news? Why? What implications would this have for companies responding to unhappy customers?
3. Consider times when you have been aware that others have used the indirect pattern in writing or speaking to you. How did you react?
4. Why is the "reasons" section of a bad-news message so important?
5. Some people feel that all employee news, good or bad, should be announced directly. Do you agree or disagree? Why?

CHAPTER REVIEW

6. List the four steps that many business professionals follow in resolving business problems.

7. List the four main parts of the indirect pattern for revealing bad news.

8. What is a buffer?

9. List seven possibilities for opening bad-news messages.

10. Name at least five words that might affect readers negatively.

11. How can the passive voice be used effectively in bad news messages? Provide an original example.

12. What is the danger in implying a refusal?

13. List five techniques for closing a bad-news message.

14. What determines whether you announce bad news to customers or employees directly or indirectly?

15. List five instances when bad news should be announced directly.

WRITING IMPROVEMENT EXERCISES

8.1 SUBORDINATE CLAUSES. You can soften the effect of bad news by placing it in a subordinate clause that begins with *although, since,* or *because.* The emphasis in a sentence is on the independent clause. Instead of saying *We cannot serve you on a credit basis,* try *Since we cannot serve you on a credit basis, we invite you to take advantage of our cash discounts and sale prices.*

Revise the following so that the bad news appears in a subordinate clause.

16. Unfortunately, our DSL FastAccess Internet service is unavailable in your area. However, we suggest that you use our dial-up modem for Internet access and Web services.

17. We no longer print a complete catalog. However, we now offer all of our catalog choices at our Web site, which is always current.

18. We hope to have our plant remodeling completed by June. We cannot schedule tours of the bottling plant until after we finish remodeling.

19. Island Airways cannot accept responsibility for expenses incurred indirectly from flight delays. However, we do recognize that this delay inconvenienced you.

8.2 PASSIVE-VOICE VERBS. Passive-voice verbs may be preferable in breaking bad news because they enable you to emphasize actions rather than personalities. Compare these two refusals:

Example   Active voice: I cannot authorize you to take three weeks of vacation in July.
Example   Passive voice: Three weeks of vacation in July cannot be authorized.

Revise the following refusals so that they use passive-voice instead of active-voice verbs.

20. Company policy forbids us to give performance reviews until an employee has been on the job for 12 months.

21. We cannot refund cash for the items you purchased on credit.

22. I have already filled my schedule on the date you wish me to speak.

23. We do not examine patients until we have verified their insurance coverage.

8.3 IMPLIED REFUSALS. Bad news can be deemphasized by implying a refusal instead of stating it directly. Compare these refusals:

Example   Direct refusal: We cannot send you a price list, nor can we sell our lawn mowers directly to customers. We sell only through dealers, and your dealer is HomeCo, Inc.
Example   Implied refusal: Our lawn mowers are sold only through dealers, and your dealer is HomeCo, Inc.

Writing Improvement Exercises

Revise the following refusals so that the bad news is implied.

24. We cannot give cash refunds for returned merchandise. Our policy enables us to give only store credit and only for merchandise that is returned in its original packaging and that is resalable.

25. I find it impossible to contribute to the fund-raising campaign this year. At present all the funds of my organization are needed to lease new equipment and offices for our new branch in Richmond. I hope to be able to support this fund in the future.

26. We cannot ship our fresh fruit baskets c.o.d. Your order was not accompanied by payment, so we are not shipping it. We have it ready, though, and will rush it to its destination as soon as you call us with your credit card number.

WRITING IMPROVEMENT CASES

8.4 FOLLOW-UP APOLOGY: MILLION DOLLAR UPGRADE FALLS SHORT. As an Internet service provider, your company, WeConnect, is growing rapidly. To keep up with increased customer demand, you decided to install a million-dollar network upgrade. From USRobotics you bought what you thought were the finest modems on the market. They passed your rigorous lab tests with flying colors, but apparently some bugs in the operating system slipped through the cracks. The modems clearly were not "field ready" when they were installed. Now you are hearing from customers complaining of slower speeds in connecting to the Internet and even disconnections.

Derek Jones, manager, Information Systems, Big Dog Catalog Company, your most profitable local customer, is very upset. Jones says, "You promised a million-dollar upgrade, and now service is worse than ever!" You replied, "Look, we're very sorry. These bugs didn't show up in our lab tests. But USRobotics is providing excellent support for their hardware and we've cleared up most of the initial problems. Although we've fixed all the major technical problems, some other little things remain, and we're fully committed to a complete resolution." You ask for Big Dog's patience. Things will get better, you promise! Discuss the following options in resolving this business problem.

1. Following a telephone call to this unhappy customer, what should you do next?
   a. Cool it. A telephone call is enough. You did what you could to explain the problem, and words will not solve the problem anyway.
   b. Wait to see whether this customer calls again. After all, the next move is up to him. Respond only after repeated complaints.
   c. Send a short e-mail message repeating your apology and explanation.
   d. Immediately send a letter that apologizes, explains, and shows how seriously you have taken the problem and the customer's complaint.

2. You decide to write a follow-up letter. To open this letter, you should begin with a(n)
   a. Neutral statement such as, *This letter is in response to your telephone complaint.*
   b. Defensive statement that protects you from legal liability (*As I mentioned on the telephone, you are the only customer who has complained about connection problems*).
   c. Apologetic statement that shows you understand and take responsibility for the problem.
   d. Off-the-subject remark such as *We're happy to hear that your company is increasing its catalog sales this quarter.*
3. In the body of the follow-up letter, you should
   a. Explain why the problem occurred.
   b. Describe what you are doing to resolve the problem.
   c. Promise that you will do everything possible to prevent the problem from happening again.
   d. All of the above.
4. In the closing of this letter, you should
   a. Avoid apologizing because it may increase your legal liabilities.
   b. Show appreciation for the customer's patience and patronage.
   c. Explain that company policy prohibits you from revealing the exact nature of the software and hardware problems.
   d. Provide an action deadline.

Your Task. After circling your choices and discussing them, write a follow-up letter to Mr. Derek Jones, Manager, Information Systems, Big Dog Catalog Company, 1308 East Tenth Street, Bloomington, IN 47405. You have set up a special Web site where customers can report any connection problems (http://home.weconnect.net/disconnect.html). However, you also want to assure customers that they can contact you personally with questions or comments. You promise that all their issues will be resolved as soon as possible. You might wish to write this letter so that you can use it to respond to other inquiries.

8.5 REQUEST REFUSAL: LEASE PAYMENTS CANNOT BE APPLIED TO PURCHASE.
Analyze the following letter. List its weaknesses and outline a writing plan. Revise the letter if your instructor directs.

Current date

Ms. Kathy Metzinger
Copiers Plus
320 Royal Poinciana Drive
Palm Bay, FL 32909

Dear Ms. Metzinger:

Unfortunately, we cannot permit you to apply the lease payments you've been making for the past ten months toward the purchase of your Sako 600 copier.

Company policy does not allow such conversion. Have you ever wondered why we can offer such low leasing and purchase prices? Converting lease payments to purchases would mean overall higher prices for our customers. Obviously, we couldn't stay in business long if we agreed to proposals such as yours.

You've had the Sako 600 copier for ten months now, Ms. Metzinger, and you say that you like its versatility and reliability. You might be able to afford a cheaper Sako model, such as the Sako 400 series, which has nearly the same features. It may be closer to your price range. Do give us a call.

Sincerely,

1. List at least five weaknesses in this letter.

2. Outline a plan for writing a refusal to a request.

8.6 CLAIM DENIAL: DEPRESSED MATTRESS

Your Task. Analyze the following letter. List its weaknesses and outline a writing plan. Then revise it so that it could be used to answer other, similar letters.

Current date

Mrs. Jason Bridges
2351 Bronson Blvd.
Fennimore, WI 53809

Dear Mrs. Bridges:

We have received your letter of May 23 demanding repair or replacement for your newly purchased BeautyTest mattress. You say that you enjoy sleeping on it, but in the morning when you and your husband get up, you claim that the mattress has body impressions that remain all day.

Unfortunately, Mrs. Bridges, we can neither repair nor replace your mattress because those impressions are perfectly normal. If you will read your warranty carefully, you will find this statement: "Slight body impressions will appear with use and are not indicative of structural failure. The body-conforming coils and comfort-cushioning materials are beginning to work for you and impressions are caused by the natural settling of these materials."

When you purchased your mattress, I'm sure your salesperson told you that the BeautyTest mattress has a unique, scientifically designed system of individually pocketed coils that provide separate support for each person occupying the bed. This unusual construction, with those hundreds of independently operating coils, reacts to every body contour, providing luxurious comfort. At the same time, this system provides firm support. It is this unique design that's causing the body impressions that you see when you get up in the morning.

We never repair or replace a mattress when it merely shows slight impressions. We can, however, send our representative out to inspect your mattress, if it would make you feel better. Please call for an appointment at 1-800-433-9831. Remember, on a BeautyTest mattress you get the best night's rest possible.

Cordially,

1. List at least five weaknesses in this letter.

2. Outline a writing plain for refusing a claim and announcing bad news to customers.

ACTIVITIES AND CASES

8.7 REQUEST REFUSAL: DALLAS COWBOYS OWNER TURNS DOWN NEW ARTIFICIAL TURF.

As owner and general manager of the Dallas Cowboys, Jerry Jones faces a difficult task. He must refuse the request of his playing field manager, Kevin O'Reilly, to install new artificial turf on one of the Cowboys' practice fields (see Activity 7.10 in Chapter 7 for more details). FieldTurf may be the hottest new product for playing fields in years, but Jerry Jones is unconvinced of its effectiveness. He sees no reason to try it out even on one of the three practice fields. But he does value Kevin O'Reilly and doesn't want to damage the good relations he enjoys with his playing field manager. He asks you and your communications staff to draft a memo that refuses the request tactfully. It is possible, though, that he would consider installing FieldTurf in two years when the warranty on the current AstroTurf runs out. He tells you to come up with some plausible reasons for the refusal.

Your Task. As director of communications, you and your staff look over the FieldTurf Web site (use a search engine to find it). You also use InfoTrac to search for information about artificial turf. Then you get together to discuss how to respond. Individually or in teams, draft a memo from Jerry Jones, Dallas Cowboys general manager, to Kevin O'Reilly, playing field manager, refusing his FieldTurf request.

8.8 REQUEST REFUSAL: SAYING NO TO UNDER 21 CROWD ON CARNIVAL CRUISES.

The world's largest cruise line finds itself in a difficult position. Carnival climbed to the number one spot by promoting fun at sea and pitching its appeal to younger customers who were drawn to on-board discos, swim-up bars, and hassle-free partying. But apparently the partying of high school and college students went too far. Roving bands of teens had virtually taken over some cruises in recent years. Travel agents complained of "drunken, loud behavior," as reported by Mike Driscall, editor of *Cruise Week*.[9]

To crack down, Carnival raised the drinking age from 18 to 21 and required more chaperoning of school groups. But young individual travelers were still unruly and disruptive. Thus, Carnival instituted a new policy, effective immediately. No one under 21 may

INFOTRAC
CRITICAL
THINKING
TEAM

travel unless accompanied by an adult over 25. Says Vicki Freed, Carnival's vice president for marketing, "We will turn them back at the docks, and they will not get refunds." As Eric Rivera, a Carnival marketing manager, you must respond to the inquiry of April Corcoran of Counselor Travel, a New York travel agency that features special spring- and summer-break packages for college and high school students.

Counselor Travel has been one of Carnival's best customers. However, Carnival no longer wants to encourage unaccompanied young people. You must refuse the request of Ms. Corcoran to help set up student tour packages. Carnival discourages even chaperoned tours. Its real market is now family packages. You must write to Counselor and break the bad news. Try to promote fun-filled, carefree cruises destined for sunny, exotic ports of call that remove guests from the stresses of everyday life. By the way, Carnival attracts more passengers than any other cruise line—over a million people a year from all over the world. And over 98 percent of Carnival's guests say that they were well satisfied. For more information about Carnival, visit its Web site (http://www.carnival.com). There's no need to register; simply click "About Carnival."

Your Task. Write your letter to April Corcoran, Counselor Travel Agency, 520 West Third Street, New York, NY 10013. Send her a schedule for spring and summer Caribbean cruises. Tell her you will call during the week of January 5 to help her plan special family tour packages.

8.9 REQUEST REFUSAL: GETTING RID OF NOISY TENANT.
As the owner of the Keystone Building, you must respond to the request of Matthew Albano, one of the tenants in your three-story office building. Mr. Albano, a CPA, demands that you immediately evict a neighboring tenant who plays loud music throughout the day, interfering with Mr. Albano's conversations with clients and with his concentration. The noisy tenant, Todd Adler, seems to operate an entertainment booking agency and spends long hours in his office. You know you can't evict Mr. Adler immediately because of his lease. Moreover, you hesitate to do anything drastic because tenants are hard to find. However, Mr. Adler has not been terribly reliable in his rent payments. Occasionally, he's been late.

Your Task. Before responding to Mr. Albano, you decide to use the Internet to find out more about the eviction process. Use InfoTrac to search the keywords "commercial eviction." Then develop a course of action. In writing to Mr. Albano, deny his request but retain his goodwill. Tell him how you plan to resolve the problem. Write to Mr. Matthew Albano, CPA, Suite 203, Keystone Building, 8532 Keystone Crossing Blvd., Indianapolis, IN 46240.

8.10 CLAIM REFUSAL: PLEASE REPLACE MY MP3 PLAYER.
As part of the customer service team at Rio, Inc., you must respond to a customer who wants a replacement for his portable CD player, your best-selling RioVolt. His letter said that he hears "popping" and "skipping" in some MP3 tracks. They are always in the same place, and he thinks his player is defective. He also complains that when he leaves the player in a "stop" or "pause" state, it turns itself off. Although he has heard that this is the best portable CD MP3 player, he thinks that he has a lemon and wants it replaced. The dealer from whom he bought it referred him to the manufacturer.

You know that the "popping" sounds and "skipping" on some MP3 tracks could be the result of a file that had a sound defect that was transferred when the CD was created. When other customers mentioned this problem, you generally told them to reencode the same audio track and therefore verify that the troublesome file was created correctly originally. In regard to the player turning itself off, this is intentional. When the player is left unattended, even if set for "stop" or "pause," it will shut itself off. This preserves battery life.

Your Task. Refuse the request of Jason Jordan, 3404 West 20 Street, Greeley, CO 80615. Although you think it's unreasonable for a customer to expect a replacement for the reasons given, you try to be polite in your response. You wonder why Jason didn't go to your Web site (http://www.riovolt.com) and look at the Frequently Asked Questions. He could have found answers to his questions in the "Troubleshooting" section. You decide to mention this resource for any future problems.

8.11 CLAIM REFUSAL: "POWER ROBOTS" INFECTED WITH VIRUS.

"How could you sell me a program with a virus! I hold your company personally responsible for contaminating my hard drive," wrote Russell R. Wilson in a letter to software game manufacturer ReNex. Mr. Wilson has ample reason to be angry with ReNex. Its Power Robots program carried a computer virus, unknown to ReNex at the time of distribution. Now Mr. Wilson wants ReNex to repair his computer.

Computer viruses are programs written to perform malicious tasks. They attach themselves secretly to other program files and are then spread by disks or by computer networks. Some viruses are carried as attachments to e-mail. The particular virus contaminating ReNex's program is called "Nimbo." First reported in Asia, it represents a class of "stealth" viruses. They mask their location and are therefore especially difficult to detect. Both manufacturers and consumers can get stung by viruses. ReNex already had an extensive virus-detection procedure, but this new virus slipped by. ReNex has just recently licensed special digital-signature software that will make it difficult for future viruses to be spread by the company's products. But this new technology won't do much for current angry customers like Mr. Wilson.

In the past, courts have generally found that if a company has been reasonably prudent in its production process, that company is not liable for damage caused by a third person (in this case, the individual who planted the virus). Nevertheless, ReNex feels an obligation to do whatever it can—within reason—to rectify the situation. Some customers would like to have software companies like ReNex give them new computers, or at the very least, install new hard drives. Mr. Wilson is making what he thinks is a reasonable request. Since he is no computer techie, he wants ReNex to pay for a computer specialist to clean up his hard drive and restore it to its previous uncontaminated state. Such a solution, according to ReNex managers, is out of the question. It's much too expensive. Moreover, ReNex can't be sure that his computer doesn't have problems that have nothing to do with the Power Robot virus. When faced with viruses, other software manufacturers have simply offered a clean program disk and advice.

Because of its vigilance and concern for product quality, ReNex has never previously had a virus contaminate any of its 350 products—until Nimbo. When the virus was discovered, ReNex immediately stopped production and recalled all unsold disks. Like other companies facing virus problems, ReNex has assigned a specialist to answer specific questions from affected customers. He is Kevin Keel at (415) 354-8745. ReNex has also tested and found effective a relevant antivirus program, AntiVirus Max by Integrity Software. AntiVirus Max has special routines that detect, remove, and prevent more than 400 viruses, including Nimbo. AntiVirus Max costs $39.95 and can be purchased by calling Integrity's toll-free number (1-800-690-3220). This program removes the virus and restores the infected computer's hard drive. ReNex fears that as many as 300 of its customers may be affected by the virus. As a small company with a very slim profit margin, ReNex cannot afford to provide AntiVirus Max to that many customers free of charge.

Your Task. You are part of the customer service team at ReNex that must decide how to handle this request and others. Remember that ReNex cannot afford to have technicians make personal visits to sites with infected computers. Discuss possible options, make a group decision, and then individually or as a group write a letter to Mr. Russell R. Wilson, 3562 Market Street, Greensboro, NC 27410.

8.12 BAD NEWS TO CUSTOMERS: J. CREW GOOFS ON CASHMERE TURTLENECK.

Who wouldn't want a cashmere zip turtleneck sweater for $18? At the J. Crew Web site (http://www.jcrew.com), many delighted shoppers scrambled to order the bargain cashmere. Unfortunately, the price should have been $218! Before J. Crew officials could correct the mistake, several hundred e-shoppers had bagged the bargain sweater for their digital shopping carts.

When the mistake was discovered, J. Crew immediately sent an e-mail message to the soon-to-be disappointed shoppers. The subject line shouted "Big Mistake!" Emily Woods, chairwoman of J. Crew, began her message with this statement: "I wish we could sell such an amazing sweater for only $18. Our price mistake on your new cashmere zip turtleneck probably went right by you, but rather than charge you such a large difference, I'm writing to alert you that this item has been removed from your recent order."

As an assistant in the communication department at J. Crew, you saw the e-mail message that was sent to customers and you tactfully suggested that the bad news might have been broken differently. Your boss says, "Okay, hot stuff. Give it your best shot."

Your Task. Although you have only a portion of the message, analyze the customer bad news message sent by J. Crew. Using the principles suggested in this chapter, write an improved e-mail message. In the end, J. Crew decided to allow customers who ordered the sweater at $18 to reorder it for $118.80 to $130.80, depending on the size. Customers were given a special Web site to reorder (make up an address). Remember that J. Crew customers are youthful and hip. Keep your message upbeat.[10]

8.13 BAD NEWS TO CUSTOMERS: NO CREDIT IN PARIS.

Travel writer Arlene Getz was mystified when the sales clerk at the Paris department store refused her credit card. "Sorry," the clerk said, "your credit card is not being accepted. I don't know why." Getz found out soon enough. Her bank had frozen her account because of an "unusual" spending pattern. The problem? "We've never had a charge from you in France before," a bank official told her. The bank didn't seem to remember that Getz had repeatedly used that card in cities ranging from Boston to Tokyo to Cape Town over the past six years, each time without incident.

Getz was a victim of neural-network technology, a tool that is intended to protect credit cardholders from thieves who steal cards and immediately run up huge purchases. This technology tracks spending patterns. If it detects anything unusual—such as a sudden splurge on easy-to-fence items like jewelry—it sets off an alarm. Robert Boxberger, senior vice president of fraud management at Fleet Credit Card Services, says that the system is "geared toward not declining any travel and entertainment expenses, like hotels, restaurants, or car rentals." But somehow it goofed and did not recognize that Arlene Getz was traveling, although she had used her card earlier to rent a car in Paris, a sure sign that she was traveling.

Getz was what the credit card industry calls a false positive—a legitimate cardholder inconvenienced by the hunt for fraudsters. What particularly riled her was finding out that 75 percent of the transactions caught in the neural network turn out to be legitimate. Yet the technology has been immensely successful for credit card companies. Since Visa started using the program, its fraud rate dropped from 15 cents to 6 cents per $100. To avoid inconveniencing cardholders, the company doesn't automatically suspend a card when it suspects fraud. Instead, it telephones the cardholder to verify purchases. Of course, if the cardholder is traveling, the call doesn't reach her.

Angry at the inconvenience and embarrassment she experienced, Getz sent a letter to Visa demanding an explanation in writing.

Your Task. As an assistant to the vice president in charge of fraud detection at Visa, you have been asked to draft a letter that can be used to respond to Arlene Getz as well as to other unhappy customers whose cards were wrongly refused by your software. You know that the program has been an overwhelming success, but it can inconvenience people, especially when they are traveling. You've heard your boss tell travelers that it's a good idea to touch base with your bank before leaving and take along the card's customer service number (1-800-553-0321). Write a letter that explains what happened, retains the goodwill of the customer, and suggests reader benefits. Address your letter to Ms. Arlene Getz, 68 Riverside Drive, Apt. 35, New York, NY 10025.

8.14 BAD NEWS FOR CUSTOMERS: STARBUCKS CHARGES WORLD TRADE CENTER RESCUE WORKERS.

Immediately after the September 11 attack in New York, rescue workers rushed to a Starbucks coffee shop near the World Trade Center to get water to treat shock victims. Starbucks employees demanded $130 for three cases of bottled water. Ambulance workers shelled out the cash from their own pockets. But they weren't happy about it.

When Starbucks president Orin Smith learned about the incident, he made a personal call apologizing to the ambulance service president. Smith also hand delivered a reimbursement check. In expressing his concern, Smith said, "It's totally inconsistent with the kind of behavior we would have expected from our people, so it has been very upsetting to learn of this." In addition to a reimbursement check, Starbucks provided free coffee and other gifts to the Midwood Ambulance Service. Starbucks closed stores nationwide for a day after the attacks. But several Starbucks outlets near the World Trade Center and New York City hospitals served thousands of pounds of coffee, tea, pastries, and water to the Red Cross to aid the relief efforts.

In many ways Starbucks did everything right after the incident. It acknowledged the mistake, took responsibility, apologized directly to those concerned, and followed up with donations in a continuing effort to ease the wrong. Yet it suffered considerable bad publicity. Its own organization seemed to forget that one of the guiding principles in its mission statement involves "contributing positively to our communities and our environment." To show its continuing commitment, Starbucks made a $1 million donation to the September 11th Fund to help victims.

Despite its efforts, Starbucks still receives plenty of angry e-mail messages from people who are upset over the news that Starbucks partners (employees) charged rescue workers for water in a time of dire emergency. The e-mail messages included harsh words calling Starbucks a greedy, uncaring, money-grubbing, and unpatriotic company.

Your Task. As a specialist in the Communications Department of Starbucks, prepare an e-mail form response that apologizes, takes responsibility, explains remedial actions, restores confidence, and offers some form of graceful and upbeat concluding statement. The message will go out under the signature of Orin Smith, president and CEO, Starbucks Coffee Company.[11]

8.15 BAD NEWS FOR CUSTOMERS: STOP TRASHING AMERICA, COKE AND PEPSI!

WEB
TEAM

In the United States this year Coke® and Pepsi® will sell an incredible 70 billion beverages in aluminum cans, plastic containers, and glass bottles. An advertisement in *The New York Times* (24 April 2002) encourages stockholders, voters, and taxpayers to write to The Coca-Cola Company and PepsiCo asking them to stop trashing America by taking responsibility for their bottle and can litter and waste. These companies, according to activists in the GrassRoots Recycling Network and the Container Recycling Institute, actively oppose bottle deposit legislation. Recycling activists say that Coke and Pepsi have spent millions lobbying the National Soft Drink Association to block proposed bills requiring deposits on containers. Yet, container deposits produce the most effective litter reduction tools available—and at almost no cost to taxpayers, according to activists.

Because of current publicity, Coke's public relations offices are receiving many messages from shareholders and consumers accusing the company of "trashing America." Some of the more informed writers want Coke to use at least 25 percent recycled plastic in its container manufacturing process. Actually, Coke claims that one in four PET (polyethylene terephthalate plastic) containers it uses in North American already contains recycled plastic. But when it comes to charging a deposit on soft drink containers, Coke

Activities and Cases

agrees with the rest of the soft drink industry. It argues that narrowly focused programs and mandatory container deposit programs are not "reasonable alternatives given their minimal impact on the waste stream, their high cost, and their counterproductive impact on more comprehensive programs."

Your Task. Assume that you are part of an intern team in a public relations office at The Coca-Cola Company in Atlanta. As a learning experience, your group has been asked to draft a message that can be used in response to the negative incoming mail about container waste and litter. Your intern supervisor tells you to go to the company Web site (http://www.cocacola.com) and read its statement about waste management (use the site map to locate this topic). She also tells you to check out the soft drink industry's policy on packaging at http://www.nsda.org/Recycling/pkgplcy.html. You might find other useful information by visiting http://www.saveabottle.org or by looking for relevant periodical articles. Use the information at these sources as well as your own training in writing bad-news messages to draft a message that could be used as a letter or an e-mail responding to inquiries requesting Coke to stop trashing America. You should produce a polite but responsive message, not a long, data-filled defense. Address your draft to Mrs. Dorothy King, 3956 Roosevelt Boulevard, Jacksonville, FL 32205.

8.16 BAD NEWS FOR EMPLOYEES: SPORTS TEAMS FOR EMPLOYEES ONLY.

Assume you are Linda Rubenstein, vice president of Human Resources at Falls River Paper Company, 1176 Alder Road, Edmonton, Alberta T5B 227, Canada. Recently several of your employees requested that their spouses or friends be allowed to participate in Falls River's intramural sports teams. Although the teams play only once a week during the season, these employees claim that they can't afford more time away from friends and family. More than 100 employees currently participate in the eight coed volleyball, softball, and tennis teams, which are open to company employees only. The teams were designed to improve employee friendships and to give employees a regular occasion to have fun together.

If nonemployees were to participate, you're afraid that employee interaction would be limited. And while some team members might have fun if spouses or friends were included, you're not so sure all employees would enjoy it. You're not interested in turning intramural sports into "date night." Furthermore, the company would have to create additional teams if many nonemployees joined, and you don't want the administrative or equipment costs of more teams. Adding teams also would require changes to team rosters and game schedules, which could be a problem for some employees. You do understand the need for social time with friends and families, but guests are welcome as spectators at all intramural games. Besides, the company already sponsors a family holiday party and an annual company picnic.

Your Task. Write an e-mail or hard-copy memo to the staff denying the request of several employees to include nonemployees on Falls River's intramural sports teams.

WEB
CRITICAL
THINKING

8.17 BAD NEWS FOLLOW-UP: WORMS IN HER POWERBARS!

In a recent trip to her local grocery store, Kelly Keeler decided for the first time to stock up on PowerBars. These are low-fat, high-carbohydrate energy bars that are touted as a highly nutritious snack food specially formulated to deliver long-lasting energy. Since 1986, PowerBar (http://www.powerbar.com) has been dedicated to helping athletes and active people achieve peak performance. It claims to be "the fuel of choice" for top athletes around the world. Kelly is a serious runner and participates in many track meets every year.

On her way to a recent meet, Kelly grabbed a PowerBar and unwrapped it while driving. As she started to take her first bite, she noticed something white and shiny in the corner of the wrapping. An unexpected protein source wriggled out of her energy bar—a worm! Kelly's first inclination was to never buy another PowerBar. On second thought, though, she decided to call the toll-free number on the wrapper. Sophie, who answered the phone, was incredibly nice, extremely apologetic, and very informative about what happened. "I'm very sorry you experienced an infested product," said Sophie.

The infamous Indian meal moth is a pantry pest that causes millions of dollars in damage worldwide. It feeds on grains or grain-based products, such as cereal, flour, dry pasta, crackers, dried fruits, nuts, spices, and pet food. The tiny moth eggs lie dormant for some time or hatch quickly into tiny larvae (worms) that penetrate food wrappers and enter products.

At its manufacturing facilities, PowerBar takes stringent measures to protect against infestation. It inspects incoming grains, supplies proper ventilation, and shields all grain-storage areas with screens to prevent insects from entering. It also uses light traps and electrocuters; these devices eradicate moths with the least environmental impact.

PowerBar President Brian Maxwell makes sure every complaint is followed up immediately with a personal letter. His letters generally tell customers that it is rare for infestations like this to occur. Entomologists say that the worms are not toxic and will not harm humans. Nevertheless, as President Maxwell says, "it is extremely disgusting to find these worms in food."

Your Task. For the signature of Brian Maxwell, PowerBar president, write a bad-news follow-up letter to Kelly Keeler, 932 Opperman Drive, Eagan, MN 55123. Keep the letter informal and personal. Explain how pests get into grain-based products and what you are doing to prevent infestation. You can learn more about the Indian meal moth by searching the Web using http://www.google.com. In your letter include a brochure titled "Notes About the Indian Meal Moth," along with a kit for Kelly to mail the culprit PowerBar to the company for analysis in Boise, Idaho. Also send a check reimbursing Kelly $26.85 for her purchase.[12]

VIDEO CASE

DawnSign Press

View the video describing Joe Dannis and his company, DawnSign Press. Named Small Business Owner of the Year, Joe is a unique entrepreneur. He and many of his employees are deaf. As you watch the video, pay attention to the nature of Joe's business and listen to his reasons for hiring both deaf and hearing employees.

As a staff employee at DawnSign Press, you were surprised but honored when Joe handed you a letter and asked you to answer it for him. The letter was from Melissa Thomas, a customer who had used one of DawnSign Press's books in a class and found it very helpful. However, she said that she was "profoundly disappointed" when she learned that Joe's business was not staffed by deaf people only. As a deaf person, Melissa had experienced great difficulty in finding employment. She felt that DawnSign Press should set an example by hiring an all-deaf staff that provided jobs for many deserving people. She wants DawnSign Press to change its hiring policy.

Joe knows that you have studied business communication. That's why he asks you to prepare a letter that responds to this inquiry but that may be also be used for any future similar inquiries. Because you have heard Joe talk about his employment philosophy, you realize that, in a perfect world, he would hire only deaf employees. But Joe is forced to hire hearing employees as well. Therefore, he cannot agree with Ms. Thomas's suggestion that he hire only deaf employees.

Your Task. For Joe's signature, draft a response to Ms. Melissa Thomas, 4752 Monroe Street, Toledo, OH 43623. You might wish to visit the DawnSign Press Web site (http://www.dawnsign.com) for more information about the business.

COMMAS 3

Review the Grammar/Mechanics Handbook Sections 2.10–2.15. Then study each of the following statements and insert necessary commas. In the space provided write the number of commas that you add; write *0* if no commas are needed. Also record the number of the G/M principle(s) illustrated. When you finish, compare your responses with those provided at the end of the book. If your answers differ, study carefully the principles shown in parentheses.

<u>2</u>   (2.21)   **Example**   The CEO named Glynna Lee, not Melinda Harris, to the supervisory position.

1. "The choice of a good name" said President Zajdel "cannot be overestimated."
2. We hired Donna H. Cox Ph.D. and Catherine Merrikin M.B.A. as consultants.
3. Thomas shipped the August 15 order on Monday didn't he?
4. The Web is useful in providing customer service such as online catalog information and verification of shipping dates.
5. The bigger the investment the greater the profit.

REVIEW COMMAS 1, 2, 3

6. As you requested your order for cartridges file folders and copy paper will be sent immediately.
7. We think however that you should reexamine your Web site and that you should consider redesigning its navigation system.
8. Within the next eight-week period we hope to hire Brenda Woodward who is currently CEO of a small consulting firm.
9. Our convention will attract more participants if it is held in a resort location such as San Diego Monterey or Las Vegas.
10. If everyone who applied for the position were interviewed we would be overwhelmed.
11. In the past ten years we have employed over 30 well-qualified individuals many of whom have selected banking as their career.
12. Sylvia A. Wall who spoke to our class last week is the author of a book entitled *Writing Winning Résumés*.
13. A recent study of productivity that was conducted by authoritative researchers revealed that U.S. workers are more productive than workers in Europe or Japan.
14. The report concluded that America's secret productivity weapons were not bigger companies more robots or even brainier managers.
15. As a matter of fact the report said that America's productivity resulted from the rigors of unprotected hands-off competition.

DOCUMENT FOR REVISION

The following memo has faults in grammar, punctuation, spelling, number form, wordiness, and negative words. Use standard proofreading marks (see Appendix B) to correct the errors. When you finish, your instructor can show you the revised version of this memo.

DATE: August 5, 200x

TO: Arthur W. Rose, Vice President

FROM: Jessica Thomas, Market Research

SUBJECT: ANALYSIS OF GATORADE XL

Here is a summery of the research of James Willis' and myself. Regarding the reduced sugar sports drink being introduced by our No. 1 compititor, Gatorade.

In just under a years time Gatorade developed this new drink, it combines together a mixture of 50 percent sugar and 50 percent artificial sweetener. Apparently Gatorade plans to spend over $8 million to introduce the drink, and to assess consumers reactions to it. It will be tested on the shelfs of convience stores grocerys and other mass merchants in five citys in Florida.

The companys spokesperson said, "The 'X' stands for excelent taste, and the 'L' stands for less sugar." Aimed at young adult's who don't like the taste of sweetener but who want to control calories. The new sports drink is a hybrid sugar and diet drink. Our studys show that simular drinks tryed in this country in the 1980's were unsucessful. On the other hand a 50 calorie low sugar sports drink introduced in Canada two year ago was well received, similarly in Japan a 40 calorie soda is now marketed sucessfully by Coca-Cola.

However our research in regard to trends and our analysis of Gatorade XL fails to indicate that this countrys consumers will be interested in a midcalorie sports drink. Yet Wall Streets response to Gatorades announcement of it's new drink was not unfavorable.

In view of the foregoing the writer and her colleague are of the opinion that we should take a wait and see attitude. Toward the introduction of our own low sugar sports drink.

Presenting Bad News in Other Cultures

To minimize disappointment, Americans generally prefer to present negative messages indirectly. Other cultures may treat bad news differently.

- In Germany business communicators occasionally use buffers but tend to present bad news directly.
- British writers also tend to be straightforward with bad news, seeing no reason to soften its announcement.
- In Latin countries the question is not how to organize negative messages but whether to present them at all. It's considered disrespectful and impolite to report bad news to superiors. Thus, reluctant employees may fail to report accurately any negative messages to their bosses. `
- In Thailand the negativism represented by a refusal is completely alien; the word *no* does not exist. In many cultures negative news is offered with such subtleness or in such a positive light that it may be overlooked or misunderstood by literal-minded Americans.
- In many Asian and some Latin cultures, one must look beyond an individual's actual words to understand what's really being communicated. One must consider the communication style, the culture, and especially the context.
  "I agree" might mean "I agree with 15 percent of what you say."
  "We might be able to" could mean "Not a chance."
  "We will consider" could mean "WE will, but the real decision maker will not."
  "That is a little too much" might equate to "That is outrageous."[14]

Career Application. Interview fellow students or work colleagues who are from other cultures. Collect information regarding the following.

- How is negative news handled in their cultures?
- How would typical business communicators refuse a request for a business favor (such as a contribution to a charity)?
- How would typical business communicators refuse a customer's claim?
- How would an individual be turned down for a job?

Your Task. Report the findings of your interviews in class discussion or in a memo report. In addition, collect samples of foreign business letters. You might ask foreign students, your campus admissions office, or local export/import companies whether they would be willing to share business letters from other countries. Compare letter styles, formats, tone, and writing strategies. How do these elements differ from those in typical North American business letters?

Reporting Workplace Data

Informal Reports

Great leaders are always great simplifiers who can cut through argument, debate, and doubt to offer a solution everybody can understand.[1]

GENERAL COLIN POWELL, Secretary of State and
former Chairman of the Joint Chiefs of Staff

LEARNING OBJECTIVES

1. Describe business report basics, including functions, organizational patterns, and formats.
2. Follow guidelines for developing informal reports, including defining the project, gathering data, using an appropriate writing style, composing effective headings, and being objective.
3. Describe six kinds of informal reports.
4. Write information and progress reports.
5. Write justification/recommendation reports.
6. Write feasibility reports.
7. Write minutes of meetings and summaries.

G ood report writers, like the great leaders Gen. Colin Powell describes, can simplify facts so that anyone can understand them in reports. Why do you need to learn how to write reports? As a business and professional communicator, you'll probably have your share of reports to write. Reports are a fact of life in American business. With increasing emphasis on performance and profits, businesspeople analyze the pros and cons of problems, studying alternatives and assessing facts, figures, and details. This analysis results in reports.

Management decisions in many organizations are based on information submitted in the form of reports. In this chapter we'll concentrate on informal reports. These reports tend to be short (usually ten or fewer pages), use memo or letter format, and are personal in tone. You'll learn about the functions, patterns, formats, and writing styles of typical business reports. You'll learn to write good reports by examining basic techniques and by analyzing appropriate models.

✓ *Quick Check*

Informal reports are relatively short (ten or fewer pages) and usually are written in memo or letter format.

UNDERSTANDING REPORT BASICS

Because of their abundance and diversity, business reports are difficult to define. They may range from informal half-page trip reports to formal 200-page financial forecasts. Reports may be presented orally in front of a group or electronically on a computer screen. Some reports appear as words on paper in the form of memos and letters. Others are primarily numerical data, such as tax reports or profit-and-loss statements. Some seek to provide information only; others aim to analyze and make recommendations. Although reports vary greatly in length, content, form, and formality level, they all have one common purpose: *Business reports are systematic attempts to answer questions and solve problems.*

Business reports are systematic attempts to answer questions and solve problems.

FUNCTIONS OF REPORTS

In terms of what they do, most reports can be placed in two broad categories: information reports and analytical reports.

Information Reports.   Reports that present data without analysis or recommendations are primarily informational. Although writers collect and organize facts, they are not expected to analyze the facts for readers. A trip report describing an employee's visit to a trade show, for example, simply presents information. Other reports that present information without analysis involve routine operations, compliance with regulations, and company policies and procedures.

Information reports present data without analysis or recommendations.

Analytical Reports.   Reports that provide data, analyses, and conclusions are analytical. If requested, writers also supply recommendations. Analytical reports may intend to persuade readers to act or to change their beliefs. Assume you're writing a feasibility report that compares several potential locations for a workout/fitness club. After analyzing and discussing alternatives, you might recommend one site, thus attempting to persuade readers to accept this choice.

Analytical reports provide data, analyses, conclusions, and, if requested, recommendations.

ORGANIZATIONAL PATTERNS

Like letters and memos, reports may be organized directly or indirectly. The reader's expectations and the content of a report determine its pattern of development, as illustrated in Figure 9.1.

Direct Pattern.   When the purpose for writing is presented close to the beginning, the organizational pattern is direct. Information reports, such as the letter report shown in Figure 9.2, are usually arranged directly. They open with an introduction, followed by the facts and a summary. In Figure 9.2 the writer explains a legal services plan. The letter report begins with an introduction. Then it presents the facts, which are divided into three subtopics identified by descriptive headings. The letter ends with a summary and a complimentary close.

The direct pattern places conclusions and recommendations near the beginning of a report.

Analytical reports may also be organized directly, especially when readers are supportive or are familiar with the topic. Many busy executives prefer this pattern because it gives them the results of the report immediately. They don't have to spend time wading through the facts, findings, discussion, and analyses to get to the two items they are most interested in—conclusions and recommendations. You should be aware, though, that unless readers are familiar with the topic, they may find the direct pattern confusing. Some readers prefer the indirect pattern because it seems logical and mirrors the way we solve problems.

FIGURE 9.1 Audience Analysis and Report Organization

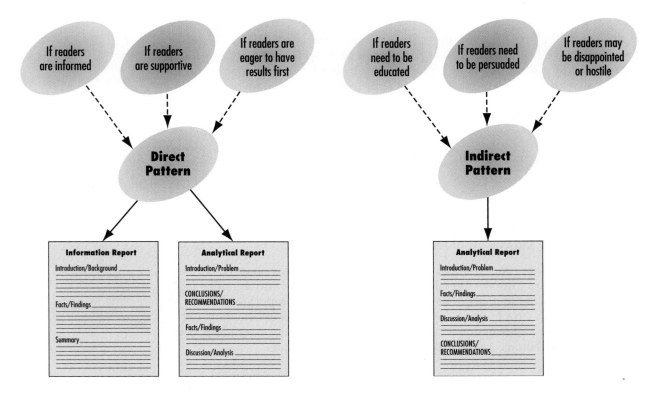

The indirect pattern is appropriate for analytical reports that seek to persuade or that convey bad news.

Indirect Pattern. When the conclusions and recommendations, if requested, appear at the end of the report, the organizational pattern is indirect. Such reports usually begin with an introduction or description of the problem, followed by facts and interpretation from the writer. They end with conclusions and recommendations. This pattern is helpful when readers are unfamiliar with the problem. It's also useful when readers must be persuaded or when they may be disappointed in or hostile toward the report's findings. The writer is more likely to retain the reader's interest by first explaining, justifying, and analyzing the facts and then making recommendations. This pattern also seems most rational to readers because it follows the normal thought process: problem, alternatives (facts), solution.

FORMATS

A report's format depends on its length, topic, audience, and purpose.

The format of a report is governed by its length, topic, audience, and purpose. After considering these elements, you'll probably choose from among the following four formats:

Letter Format. Use letter format for short (say, ten or fewer pages) informal reports addressed outside an organization. Prepared on office stationery, a letter report contains a date, inside address, salutation, and complimentary close, as shown in Figure 9.2. Although they may carry information similar to that found in correspondence, letter reports usually are longer and show more careful organization than most letters. They also include headings.

Memo Format. For short informal reports that stay within organizations, memo format is appropriate. Memo reports begin with DATE, TO, FROM, and SUBJECT.

FIGURE 9.2 Information Report—Letter Format

Center for Consumers of Legal Services ●———— Uses letterhead
P.O. Box 260   stationery for an
Richmond, VA 23219   informal report
                                                                     addressed to an
September 7, 200x   outsider

Ms. Lisa Burgess, Secretary
Lake Austin Homeowners
3902 Oak Hill Drive
Austin, TX 78134

Dear Ms. Burgess:

As executive director of the Center for Consumers of Legal Services, I'm pleased
to send you this information describing how your homeowners' association can
sponsor a legal services plan for its members. After an introduction with
background data, this report will discuss three steps necessary for your group to
start its plan.

Introduction

A legal services plan promotes preventive law by letting members talk to
attorneys whenever problems arise. Prompt legal advice often avoids or prevents
expensive litigation. Because groups can supply a flow of business to the plan's
attorneys, groups can negotiate free consultation, follow-up, and discounts.

Two kinds of plans are commonly available. The first, a free plan, offers free
legal consultation along with discounts for services when the participating groups
are sufficiently large to generate business for the plan's attorneys. These plans
actually act as a substitute for advertising for the attorneys. The second common
type is the prepaid plan. Prepaid plans provide more benefits, but members must
pay annual fees, usually of $200 or more a year. More than 30 million people
are covered by legal services plans today, and a majority belong to free plans.

Since you inquired about a free plan for your homeowners' association, the
following information describes how to set up such a program.

Determine the Benefits Your Group Needs

The first step in establishing a free legal services plan is to meet with the
members of your group to decide what benefits they want. Typical benefits include
the following:

Free consultation. Members may consult a participating attorney—by phone or in
the attorney's office—to discuss any matter. The number of consultations is
unlimited, provided each is about a separate matter. Consultations are generally
limited to 30 minutes, but they include substantive analysis and advice.

Free document review. Important papers—such as leases, insurance policies, and
installment sales contracts—may be reviewed with legal counsel. Members may
ask questions and receive an explanation of terms.

Presents intro-duction and facts without analysis or rec-ommendations

Arranges facts of report into sections with descriptive headings

Emphasizes benefits in paragraph headings with boldface type

TIPS FOR LETTER REPORTS
- Use letter format for short informal reports sent to outsiders.
- Organize the facts section into logical divisions identified by consistent headings.
- Single-space the body.
- Double-space between paragraphs.
- Leave two blank lines above each side heading.
- Create side margins of 1 to 1¼ inches.
- Add a second-page heading, if necessary, consisting of the addressee's name, the page number, and the date.

FIGURE 9.2   **Continued**

Identifies second
and succeeding
pages with
headings

Uses parallel
side headings
for consistency
and readability

Includes
complimentary
close and signature

Ms. Lisa Burgess   Page 2   September 7, 200x

Discount on additional services. For more complex matters, participating attorneys will charge members 75 percent of the attorney's normal fee. However, some organizations choose to charge a flat fee for commonly needed services.

Select the Attorneys for Your Plan

Groups with geographically concentrated memberships have an advantage in forming legal plans. These groups can limit the number of participating attorneys and yet provide adequate service. Generally, smaller panels of attorneys are advantageous.

Assemble a list of candidates, inviting them to apply. The best way to compare prices is to have candidates submit their fees. Your group can then compare fee schedules and select the lowest bidder, if price is important. Arrange to interview attorneys in their offices.

After selecting an attorney or a panel, sign a contract. The contract should include the reason for the plan, what the attorney agrees to do, what the group agrees to do, how each side can end the contract, and the signature of both parties. You may also wish to include references to malpractice insurance, assurance that the group will not interfere with the attorney-client relationship, an evaluation form, a grievance procedure, and responsibility for government filings.

Publicize the Plan to Your Members

Members won't use a plan if they don't know about it, and a plan will not be successful if it is unused. Publicity must be vocal and ongoing. Announce it in newsletters, meetings, bulletin boards, and flyers.

Persistence is the key. All too frequently, leaders of an organization assume that a single announcement is all that's needed. They expect members to see the value of the plan and remember that it's available. Most organization members, though, are not as involved as the leadership. Therefore, it takes more publicity than the leadership usually expects in order to reach and maintain the desired level of awareness.

Summary

A successful free legal services plan involves designing a program, choosing the attorneys, and publicizing the plan. To learn more about these steps or to order a $25 how-to manual, call me at (804) 355-9901.

Sincerely,

Richard M. Ramos

Richard M. Ramos, Esq.
Executive Director

pas

Like letter reports, memo reports differ from regular memos in length, use of headings, and deliberate organization.

Manuscript Format.   For longer, more formal reports, use manuscript format. These reports are usually printed on plain paper instead of letterhead stationery or memo forms. They begin with a title followed by systematically displayed headings and subheadings. You will see examples of proposals and formal reports using manuscript formats in Chapter 10.

Printed Forms.   Prepared forms are often used for repetitive data, such as monthly sales reports, performance appraisals, merchandise inventories, and personnel and financial reports. Standardized headings on these forms save time for the writer. Preprinted forms also make similar information easy to locate and ensure that all necessary information is provided.

GUIDELINES FOR DEVELOPING INFORMAL REPORTS

Your natural tendency in preparing a report is to sit down and begin writing immediately. If you follow this urge, however, you will very likely have to backtrack and start again. Reports take planning, beginning with defining the project and gathering data. The following guidelines will help you plan your project.

Before gaining approval and implementing plans for any big project such as a new park, teams like this one gather facts, inspect locations, and seek consensus. Business reports, which are systematic attempts to answer questions and solve problems, always begin with the collection of solid facts.
© Mark Richards/PhotoEdit, Inc.

DEFINING THE PROJECT

Begin the process of report writing by defining your project. This definition should include a statement of purpose. Ask yourself: Am I writing this report to inform, to analyze, to solve a problem, or to persuade? The answer to this question should be a clear, accurate statement identifying your purpose. In informal reports the statement of purpose may be only one sentence; that sentence usually becomes part of the introduction. Notice how the following introductory statement describes the purpose of the report:

> This report presents data regarding in-service training activities coordinated and supervised by the Human Resources Department between the first of the year and the present.

After writing a statement of purpose, analyze who will read your report. If your report is intended for your immediate supervisors and they are supportive of your project, you need not include extensive details, historical development, definition of terms, or persuasion. Other readers, however, may require background data and persuasive strategies.

The expected audience for your report influences your writing style, research method, vocabulary, areas of emphasis, and communication strategy. Remember, too, that your audience may consist of more than one set of readers. Reports are often distributed to secondary readers who may need more details than the primary reader.

✓ *Quick Check*

Begin a report by formulating a statement of purpose that explains why you are writing the report.

GATHERING DATA

A good report is based on solid, accurate, verifiable facts. Typical sources of factual information for informal reports include (1) company records; (2) observation; (3) surveys, questionnaires, and inventories; (4) interviews; and (5) research.

Company Records.   Many business-related reports begin with an analysis of company records and files. From these records you can observe past performance and methods used to solve previous problems. You can collect pertinent facts that will help determine a course of action.

Observation.   Another logical source of data for many problems lies in personal observation and experience. For example, if you were writing a report on the need for additional computer equipment, you might observe how much the current equipment is being used and for what purpose.

Surveys, Questionnaires, and Inventories.   Data from groups of people can be collected most efficiently and economically by using surveys, questionnaires, and inventories. For example, if you were part of a committee investigating the success of a campus recycling program, you might begin by using a questionnaire to survey use of the program by students and faculty.

Interviews.   Talking with individuals directly concerned with the problem produces excellent first-hand information. Interviews also allow for one-on-one communication, thus giving you an opportunity to explain your questions and ideas in eliciting the most accurate information.

Electronic and Other Research.   An extensive source of current and historical information is available electronically by using a computer to connect to the Web, databases, and other online resources. From a personal or office computer you can access storehouses of information provided by the government, newspapers, magazines, and companies. For short, informal reports the most usable data will probably be found in periodicals and online resources. Chapter 10 gives you more detailed suggestions about online research.

DEVELOPING AN APPROPRIATE WRITING STYLE

Like other business messages, reports can range from informal to formal, depending on their purpose, audience, and setting. Research reports from consultants to their clients tend to be rather formal. Such reports must project an impression of objectivity, authority, and impartiality. But a report to your boss describing a trip to a conference would probably be informal. You can see the differences between formal and informal styles in Figure 9.3.

In this chapter we are most concerned with an informal writing style. Your short reports will probably be written for familiar audiences and involve noncontroversial topics. You may use first-person pronouns (*I, we, me, my, us, our*) and contractions (*I'm, we'll*). You'll emphasize active-voice verbs and strive for shorter sentences using familiar words.

USING EFFECTIVE HEADINGS

Good headings are helpful to both the report reader and the writer. For the reader they serve as an outline of the text, highlighting major ideas and categories. They also act as guides for locating facts and pointing the way through the text. Moreover, headings provide resting points for the mind and for the eye, breaking up large chunks of text into manageable and inviting segments. For the writer, headings force organization of the data into meaningful blocks. To learn more about

FIGURE 9.3 Report-Writing Styles

	INFORMAL WRITING STYLE	FORMAL WRITING STYLE
Use	Short, routine reports Reports for familiar audiences Noncontroversial reports Most reports for company insiders	Theses Research studies Controversial or complex reports (especially to outsiders)
Effect	Feeling of warmth, personal involvement, closeness	Impression of objectivity, accuracy, professionalism, fairness Distance created between writer and reader
Characteristics	Use of first-person pronouns (*I, we, me, my, us, our*)	Absence of first-person pronouns; use of third-person (*the researcher, the writer*)
	Use of contractions (*can't, don't*)	Absence of contractions (*cannot, do not*)
	Emphasis on active-voice verbs (*I conducted the study*)	Use of passive-voice verbs (*the study was conducted*)
	Shorter sentences; familiar words	Complex sentences; long words
	Occasional use of humor, metaphors	Absence of humor and figures of speech
	Occasional use of colorful speech	Reduced use of colorful adjectives and adverbs
	Acceptance of author's opinions and ideas	Elimination of "editorializing" (author's opinions, perceptions)

designing readable headlines, as well as to pick up other tips on designing documents, see Figure 9.4

You may choose functional headings, talking headings, or a combination. Functional headings (such as *Introduction, Discussion of Findings,* and *Summary*) help the writer outline a report. Functional headings are used in the information report shown in Figure 9.2. But talking headings (such as *Students Perplexed by Shortage of Parking* or *Short-Term Parking Solutions*) describe content and provide more information to the reader. Many of the examples in this chapter use functional headings for the purpose of instruction. To provide even greater clarity, you can make headings both functional and descriptive, such as *Recommendations: Shuttle and New Structures.* Whether your headings are talking or functional, keep them brief and clear. Here are general tips on displaying headings effectively:

Quick Check

Functional heads show the outline of a report; talking heads describe the content.

- **Use appropriate heading levels.** The position and format of a heading indicate its level of importance and relationship to other points.
- **Strive for parallel construction.** Use balanced expressions such as *Visible Costs* and *Invisible Costs* rather than *Visible Costs* and *Costs That Don't Show.*
- **For short reports use first- and second-level headings.** Many business reports contain only one or two levels of headings. For such reports use first-level headings (centered, bolded) and/or second-level headings (flush left, bolded).
- **Capitalize and underline carefully.** Most writers use all capital letters (without underlines) for main titles, such as the report, chapter, and unit titles. For first- and second-level headings, they capitalize only the first letter of main words. For additional emphasis, they use a bold font. Don't enclose headings in quotation marks.
- **Keep headings short but clear.** Try to make your headings brief (no more than eight words) but understandable. Experiment with headings that concisely tell who, what, when, where, and why.

Guidelines for Developing Informal Reports

FIGURE 9.4 Ten Tips for Designing Better Documents

Desktop publishing packages, high-level word processing programs, and laser printers now make it possible for you to turn out professional-looking documents. The temptation, though, is to overdo it by incorporating too many features in one document. Here are ten tips for applying good sense and good design principles in "publishing" your documents:

- **Analyze your audience.** Avoid overly flashy type, colors, and borders for conservative business documents. Also consider whether your readers will be reading painstakingly or merely browsing. Lists and headings help readers who are in a hurry.

- **Choose an appropriate type size.** For most business memos, letters, and reports, the body text should be 10 to 12 points tall (a point is 1/72 of an inch). Larger type looks amateurish, and smaller type is hard to read.

- **Use a consistent type font.** Although your software may provide a variety of fonts, stay with a single family of type within one document. The most popular fonts are Times Roman and Helvetica. For emphasis and contrast, you may vary the font size and weight with **bold,** *italic,* ***bold italic,*** and other selections.

- **Generally, don't justify right margins.** Textbooks, novels, newspapers, magazines, and other long works are usually set with justified (even) right margins. However, for shorter works ragged-right margins are recommended because such margins add white space and help readers locate the beginnings of new lines. Slower readers find ragged-right copy more legible.

- **Separate paragraphs and sentences appropriately.** Paragraphs are easier to read if they are indented or preceded by a blank line. To separate sentences, typists have traditionally left two spaces. This spacing is still acceptable for most business documents, but the trend is toward one space after ending punctuation.

Copyright 2002 by Randy Glasbergen.
www.glasbergen.com

"It says our reports stink. We all have to go to writing class to learn to be more objective and sensitive."

- **Don't use headings as antecedents for pronouns** such as *this, that, these,* and *those.* For example, when the heading reads *Laser Printers,* don't begin the next sentence with *These are often used with desktop publishing software.*

BEING OBJECTIVE

Reports are convincing only when the facts are believable and the writer is credible. You can build credibility in a number of ways:

- **Present both sides of an issue.** Even if you favor one possibility, discuss both sides and show through logical reasoning why your position is superior. Remain impartial, letting the facts prove your point.

Reports are more believable if the author is impartial, separates fact from opinion, uses moderate language, and cites sources.

- **Separate fact from opinion.** Suppose a supervisor wrote, *Our department works harder and gets less credit than any other department in the company.* This opinion is difficult to prove, and it damages the credibility of the writer. A more convincing statement might be, *Our productivity has increased 6 percent over the past year, and I'm proud of the extra effort my employees are making.* After you've made a claim or presented an important statement in a report, ask yourself, Is this a verifiable fact? If the answer is *no,* rephrase your statement to make it sound more reasonable.

FIGURE 9.4 **Continued**

- **Design readable headlines.** Use upper- and lowercase letters for the most readable headlines. All caps is generally discouraged because solid blocks of capital letters interfere with recognition of word patterns. To further improve headline readability, many designers select a sans serif typeface (one without cross strokes or embellishment), such as Helvetica or Arial.

- **Strive for an attractive page layout.** In designing title pages or visual aids, provide for a balance between print and white space. Also consider placing the focal point (something that draws the reader's eye) at the optical center of a page—about three lines above the actual center. Moreover, remember that the average reader scans a page from left to right and top to bottom in a Z pattern. Plan your visuals accordingly.

- **Use graphics and clip art with restraint.** Images created with spreadsheet or graphics programs can be imported into documents. Original draw-

ings, photographs, and clip art can also be scanned into documents. Use such images, however, only when they are well drawn, relevant, purposeful, and appropriately sized.

- **Avoid amateurish results.** Many beginning writers, eager to display every graphic device a program offers, produce busy, cluttered documents. Too many typefaces, ruled lines, images, and oversized headlines will overwhelm readers. Strive for simple, clean, and forceful effects.

- **Develop expertise.** Learn to use the desktop publishing features of your current word processing software, or investigate one of the special programs, such as Ventura, Quark XPress, PageMaker, PowerPoint, or CorelDraw. Although the learning curve for many of these programs is steep, such effort is well spent if you will be producing newsletters, brochures, announcements, visual aids, and promotional literature.

- **Be sensitive and moderate in your choice of language.** Don't exaggerate. Instead of saying *Most people think . . .*, it might be more accurate to say *Some people think . . . .* Obviously, avoid using labels and slanted expressions. Calling someone a *turkey,* an *egghead,* or an *elitist* demonstrates bias. If readers suspect that a writer is prejudiced, they may discount the entire argument.

- **Cite sources.** Tell your readers where the information came from. For example, *In a telephone interview with Blake Spence, director of transportation, October 15, he said . . .* OR: *The Wall Street Journal (August 10, p. 40) reports that . . . .* By referring to respected sources, you lend authority and credibility to your statements. Your words become more believable and your argument more convincing.

Six Kinds of Informal Reports

You are about to examine six categories of informal reports frequently written in business. In many instances the boundaries of the categories overlap; distinctions are not always clear-cut. Individual situations, goals, and needs may make one report take on some characteristics of a report in another category. Still, these general categories, presented here in a brief overview, are helpful to beginning writers. Later you'll learn how to fully develop each of these reports.

- **Information reports.** Reports that collect and organize information are informative or investigative. They may record routine activities such as daily, weekly, and monthly reports of sales or profits. They may investigate options, performance, or equipment. Although they provide information, they do not analyze that information.

 Quick Check

Information and progress reports generally present data without analysis.

- **Progress reports.** Progress reports monitor the headway of unusual or non-routine activities. For example, progress reports would keep management informed about a committee's preparations for a trade show 14 months from now. Such reports usually answer three questions: (1) Is the project on schedule? (2) Are corrective measures needed? (3) What activities are next?

- **Justification/Recommendation reports.** Justification and recommendation reports are similar to information reports in that they present information. However, they offer analysis in addition to data. They attempt to solve problems by evaluating options and offering recommendations. These reports are solicited; that is, the writer has been asked to investigate and report.

- **Feasibility reports.** When a company must decide whether to proceed with a plan of action, it may require a feasibility report. For example, should a company invest thousands of dollars to expand its Web site? A feasibility report would examine the practicality of implementing the proposal.

- **Minutes of meetings.** A record of the proceedings of a meeting is called "the minutes." This record is generally kept by a secretary. Minutes may be kept for groups that convene regularly, such as the meetings of clubs, committees, and boards of directors.

- **Summaries.** A summary condenses the primary ideas, conclusions, and recommendations of a longer report or publication. Employees may be asked to write summaries of technical reports. Students may be asked to write summaries of periodical articles or books to sharpen their writing skills. Executive summaries condense long reports such as business plans and proposals.

INFORMATION REPORTS

After the preceding brief overview, we'll now look more closely at each of the categories, beginning with information reports. Writers of information reports provide information without drawing conclusions or making recommendations. Some information reports are highly standardized, such as police reports, hospital admittance reports, monthly sales reports, or government regulatory reports. Other information reports are more personalized, as illustrated in the letter report shown in Figure 9.2. Information reports generally contain three parts: introduction, body (findings), and conclusion. The body may have many subsections. Consider these suggestions for writing information reports:

- In the introduction explain why you are writing. For some reports, describe what methods and sources were used to gather information and why they are credible. Provide any special background information that may be necessary. Preview what is to follow.

- In the findings section organize the facts in a logical sequence. You might group information in one of these patterns: (1) chronological, (2) alphabetical, (3) topical, (4) geographical, (5) journalism style (*who, what, when, where, why,* and *how*), (6) simple-to-complex, or (7) most to least important.

- Decide whether to use functional headings, talking headings, or a combination. Be sure that words used as headings are parallel in structure.

- Conclude by summarizing your findings or highlighting your main points.

In the two-page information report shown in Figure 9.2, Richard Ramos responds to an inquiry about prepaid legal services. In the introduction he explains the purpose of the report and previews the organization of the report. In the findings/facts section, he arranges the information topically. He uses the summary to emphasize the three main topics previously discussed.

PROGRESS REPORTS

Continuing projects often require progress reports to describe their status. These reports may be external (advising customers regarding the headway of their projects) or internal (informing management of the status of activities). Progress reports typically follow this pattern of development:

* Specify in the opening the purpose and nature of the project.
* Provide background information if the audience requires filling in.
* Describe the work completed.
* Explain the work currently in progress, including personnel, activities, methods, and locations.
* Anticipate problems and possible remedies.
* Discuss future activities and provide the expected completion date.

As a location manager in the film industry, Sheila Ryan frequently writes progress reports, such as the one shown in Figure 9.5. Producers want to be informed of what she's doing, and a phone call doesn't provide a permanent record. Notice that her progress report identifies the project and provides brief background information. She then explains what has been completed, what is yet to be completed, and what problems she expects.

This greenhouse at the famous Keukenhof Gardens in Holland became a key point in the justification report of a tour organizer. In supporting his inclusion of the Keukenhof in a proposed itinerary for an American travel company, the writer argued that tourists can never be rained out. In addition to the 70 acres of outdoor gardens, thousands of flowers bloom under glass. Justification and recommendation reports are most persuasive when their recommendations are supported by solid facts. © Dr. Mary Ellen Guffey

JUSTIFICATION/RECOMMENDATION REPORTS

Both managers and employees must occasionally write reports that justify or recommend something, such as buying equipment, changing a procedure, hiring an employee, consolidating departments, or investing funds. Large organizations sometimes prescribe how these reports should be organized; they use forms with conventional headings. When you are free to select an organizational plan your-

FIGURE 9.5 Progress Report

QuaStar Productions
Interoffice Memo

DATE: January 7, 200x

TO: Rick Willens, Executive Producer

FROM: Sheila Ryan, Location Manager   *SR*

SUBJECT: Sites for "Bodega Bay" Telefilm

Identifies project and previews report → This memo describes the progress of my search for an appropriate rustic home, villa, or ranch to be used for the wine country sequences in the telefilm "Bodega Bay." Three sites will be available for you to inspect on January 21, as you requested.

Background: In preparation for this assignment, I consulted Director Dave Durslag, who gave me his preferences for the site. He suggested a picturesque ranch home situated near vineyards, preferably with redwoods in the background. I also consulted Producer Teresa Silva, who told me that the site must accommodate 55 to 70 production crew members for approximately three weeks of filming. Ben Waters, telefilm accountant, requested that the cost of the site not exceed $24,000 for a three-week lease.

Saves space by integrating headings into paragraphs → **Work Completed:** For the past eight days I have searched the Russian River area in the Northern California wine country. Possible sites include turn-of-the-century estates, Victorian mansions, and rustic farmhouses in the towns of Duncans Mills, Monte Rio, and Guerneville. One exceptional site is the Country Meadow Inn, a 97-year-old farmhouse nestled among vineyards with a breathtaking view of valleys, redwoods, and distant mountains.

Work To Be Completed. In the next five days, I'll search the Sonoma County countryside, including wineries at Korbel, Field Stone, and Napa. Many old wineries contain charming structures that may present exactly the degree of atmosphere and mystery we need. These wineries have the added advantage of easy access. I will also inspect possible structures at the Armstrong Redwoods State Reserve and the Kruse Rhododendron Reserve, both within 100 miles of Guerneville. I've made an appointment with the director of state parks to discuss our project, use of state lands, restrictions, and costs.

Tells the bad news as well as the good → **Anticipated Problems:** You should be aware of two complications for filming in this area.

1. Property owners seem unfamiliar with the making of films and are suspicious of short-term leases.

2. Many trees won't have leaves again until May. You may wish to change the filming schedule somewhat.

Concludes by giving completion date and describing what follows → By January 14 you'll have my final report describing the three most promising locations. Arrangements will be made for you to visit these sites January 21.

TIPS FOR WRITING PROGRESS REPORTS

- Identify the purpose and the nature of the project immediately.
- Supply background information only if the reader must be educated.
- Describe the work completed.
- Discuss the work in progress, including personnel, activities, methods, and locations.
- Identify problems and possible remedies.
- Consider future activities.
- Close by telling the expected date of completion.

self, however, let your audience and topic determine your choice of direct or indirect structure.

For nonsensitive topics and recommendations that will be agreeable to readers, you can organize directly according to the following sequence:

- In the introduction identify the problem or need briefly.
- Announce the recommendation, solution, or action concisely and with action verbs.
- Discuss pros, cons, and costs. Explain more fully the benefits of the recommendation or steps to be taken to solve the problem.
- Conclude with a summary specifying the recommendation and action to be taken.

Justin Brown applied the preceding process in writing the recommendation report shown in Figure 9.6. Justin is operations manager in charge of a fleet of trucks for a large parcel delivery company in Atlanta. When he heard about a new Goodyear smart tire with an electronic chip, Justin thought his company should give the new tire a try. His recommendation report begins with a short introduction to the problem followed by his two recommendations. Then he explains the product and how it would benefit his company. He concludes by highlighting his recommendation and specifying the action to be taken.

FEASIBILITY REPORTS

Feasibility reports examine the practicality and advisability of following a course of action. They answer this question: Will this plan or proposal work? Feasibility reports typically are internal reports written to advise on matters such as consolidating departments, offering a wellness program to employees, or hiring an outside firm to handle a company's accounting or computing operations. These reports may also be written by consultants called in to investigate a problem. The focus in these reports is on the decision: stopping or proceeding with the proposal. Since your role is not to persuade the reader to accept the decision, you'll want to present the decision immediately. In writing feasibility reports, consider these suggestions:

✓ **Quick Check**
Feasibility reports analyze whether a proposal or plan will work.

- Announce your decision immediately.
- Describe the background and problem necessitating the proposal.
- Discuss the benefits of the proposal.
- Describe any problems that may result.
- Calculate the costs associated with the proposal, if appropriate.
- Show the time frame necessary for implementation of the proposal.

Elizabeth Webb, customer service manager for a large insurance company in Omaha, Nebraska, wrote the feasibility report shown in Figure 9.7. Because her company had been losing customer service reps (CSRs) after they were trained, she talked with the vice president about the problem. He didn't want her to take time away from her job to investigate what other companies were doing to retain their CSRs. Instead, he suggested that they hire a consultant to investigate what other companies were doing to keep their CSRs. The vice president then wanted to know whether the consultant's plan was feasible. Although Elizabeth's report is only one page long, it provides all the necessary information: background, benefits, problems, costs, and time frame.

FIGURE 9.6 Justification/Recommendation Report—Memo Format

Applies memo format for short informal internal report

Interoffice Memo   **Atlantic Trucking, Inc.**

DATE: July 19, 200x
TO: Bill Montgomery, Vice President
FROM: Justin Brown, Operations Manager *JB*
SUBJECT: Pilot Testing Smart Tires

Next to fuel, truck tires are our biggest operating cost. Last year we spent $211,000 replacing and retreading tires for 495 trucks. This year the costs will be greater because prices have jumped at least 12 percent and because we've increased our fleet to 550 trucks. Truck tires are an additional burden since they require labor-intensive paperwork to track their warranties, wear, and retread histories. To reduce our long-term costs and to improve our tire tracking system, I recommend that we do the following:

Introduces problem briefly

Presents recommendations immediately

- Purchase 24 Goodyear smart tires.
- Begin a one-year pilot test on four trucks.

How Smart Tires Work

Smart tires have an embedded computer chip that monitors wear, performance, and durability. The chip also creates an electronic fingerprint for positive identification of a tire. By passing a hand-held sensor next to the tire, we can learn where and when a tire was made (for warranty and other information), how much tread it had originally, and its serial number.

Justifies recommendation by explaining product and benefits

How Smart Tires Could Benefit Us

Although smart tires are initially more expensive than other tires, they could help us improve our operations and save us money in four ways:

1. **Retreads.** Goodyear believes that the wear data is so accurate that we should be able to retread every tire three times, instead of our current two times. If that's true, in one year we could save at least $27,000 in new tire costs.
2. **Safety.** Accurate and accessible wear data should reduce the danger of blowouts and flat tires. Last year, drivers reported six blowouts.
3. **Record keeping and maintenance.** Smart tires could reduce our maintenance costs considerably. Currently, we use an electric branding iron to mark serial numbers on new tires. Our biggest headache is manually reading those serial numbers, decoding them, and maintaining records to meet safety regulations. Reading such data electronically could save us thousands of dollars in labor.
4. **Theft protection.** The chip can be used to monitor each tire as it leaves or enters the warehouse or yard, thus discouraging theft.

Enumerates items for maximum impact and readability

Explains recommendation in more detail

Summary and Action

Specifically, I recommend that you do the following:
- Authorize the special purchase of 24 Goodyear smart tires at $450 each, plus one electronic sensor at $1,200.
- Approve a one-year pilot test in our Atlanta territory that equips four trucks with smart tires and tracks their performance.

Specifies action to be taken

TIPS FOR MEMO REPORTS
- Use memo format for most short (ten or fewer pages) informal reports within an organization.
- Leave side margins of 1 to 1¼ inches.
- Sign your initials on the FROM line.
- Use an informal, conversational style.
- For a receptive audience, put recommendations first.
- For an unreceptive audience, put recommendations last.

FIGURE 9.7 Feasibility Report

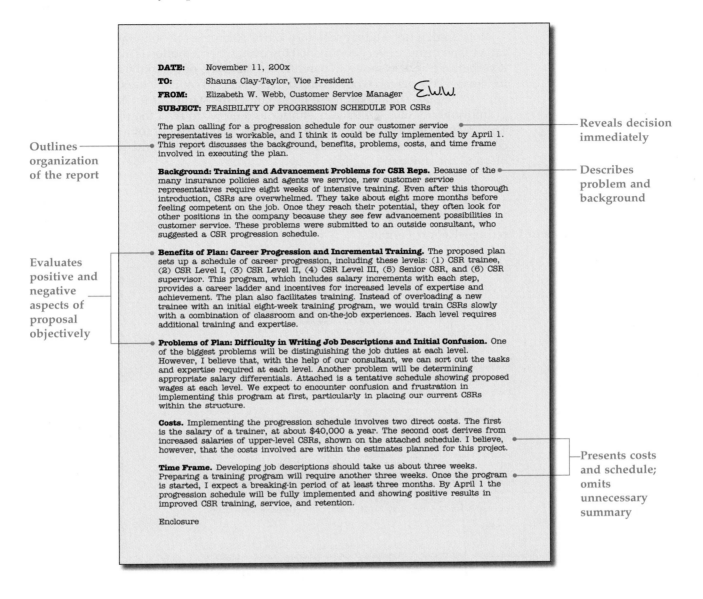

Outlines organization of the report

Evaluates positive and negative aspects of proposal objectively

Reveals decision immediately

Describes problem and background

Presents costs and schedule; omits unnecessary summary

DATE: November 11, 200x
TO: Shauna Clay-Taylor, Vice President
FROM: Elizabeth W. Webb, Customer Service Manager   EWW
SUBJECT: FEASIBILITY OF PROGRESSION SCHEDULE FOR CSRs

The plan calling for a progression schedule for our customer service representatives is workable, and I think it could be fully implemented by April 1. This report discusses the background, benefits, problems, costs, and time frame involved in executing the plan.

Background: Training and Advancement Problems for CSR Reps. Because of the many insurance policies and agents we service, new customer service representatives require eight weeks of intensive training. Even after this thorough introduction, CSRs are overwhelmed. They take about eight more months before feeling competent on the job. Once they reach their potential, they often look for other positions in the company because they see few advancement possibilities in customer service. These problems were submitted to an outside consultant, who suggested a CSR progression schedule.

Benefits of Plan: Career Progression and Incremental Training. The proposed plan sets up a schedule of career progression, including these levels: (1) CSR trainee, (2) CSR Level I, (3) CSR Level II, (4) CSR Level III, (5) Senior CSR, and (6) CSR supervisor. This program, which includes salary increments with each step, provides a career ladder and incentives for increased levels of expertise and achievement. The plan also facilitates training. Instead of overloading a new trainee with an initial eight-week training program, we would train CSRs slowly with a combination of classroom and on-the-job experiences. Each level requires additional training and expertise.

Problems of Plan: Difficulty in Writing Job Descriptions and Initial Confusion. One of the biggest problems will be distinguishing the job duties at each level. However, I believe that, with the help of our consultant, we can sort out the tasks and expertise required at each level. Another problem will be determining appropriate salary differentials. Attached is a tentative schedule showing proposed wages at each level. We expect to encounter confusion and frustration in implementing this program at first, particularly in placing our current CSRs within the structure.

Costs. Implementing the progression schedule involves two direct costs. The first is the salary of a trainer, at about $40,000 a year. The second cost derives from increased salaries of upper-level CSRs, shown on the attached schedule. I believe, however, that the costs involved are within the estimates planned for this project.

Time Frame. Developing job descriptions should take us about three weeks. Preparing a training program will require another three weeks. Once the program is started, I expect a breaking-in period of at least three months. By April 1 the progression schedule will be fully implemented and showing positive results in improved CSR training, service, and retention.

Enclosure

MINUTES OF MEETINGS

Minutes provide a summary of the proceedings of meetings. Formal, traditional minutes, illustrated in Figure 9.8, are written for large groups and legislative bodies. If you are the secretary of a meeting, you'll want to write minutes that do the following:

- Provide the name of the group, as well as the date, time, and place of the meeting.
- Identify the names of attendees and absentees, if appropriate.
- Describe the disposition of previous minutes.
- Record old business, new business, announcements, and reports.

✓ *Quick Check*

Meeting minutes record summaries of old business, new business, announcements, and reports as well as the precise wording of motions.

- Include the precise wording of motions; record the vote and action taken.
- Conclude with the name and signature of the person recording the minutes.

Notice in Figure 9.8 that secretary Carol Allen tries to summarize discussions rather than capture every comment. However, when a motion is made, she records it verbatim. She also shows in parentheses the name of the individual making the motion and the person who seconded it. By using all capital letters for "MOTION" and "PASSED," she makes these important items stand out for easy reference.

Informal minutes are usually shorter and easier to read than formal minutes. They may be formatted with three categories: summaries of topics discussed, decisions reached, and action items (showing the action item, the person responsible, and the due date).

FIGURE 9.8   Minutes of Meeting—Report Format

Shows attendees and absentees

Summarizes discussion; does not record every word

Summarizes new business and announcements

International Association of Administrative Professionals
Planning Committee Meeting
Conference Room B, Marriott Century Hotel
November 4, 200x, 10 a.m.

Present: Carol Allen, Kim Jobe, LeeAnn Johnson, Barbara Leonard, Lee Schultz, Doris Williamson, Margaret Zappa

Absent: Ellen Williams

The meeting was called to order by Chair Kim Jobe at 10:05 a.m. Minutes from the July 11 meeting were read and approved.

Old Business

LeeAnn Johnson and Barbara Leonard reviewed the information distributed at the last meeting about hotels being considered for the Houston conference. LeeAnn said that the Hilton Regency has ample conference rooms and remodeled interiors. Barbara reported that the Embassy Suites Houston also has excellent banquet facilities, adequate meeting facilities, and rooms at $112 per night.
MOTION: To recommend that IAAP hold its International Convention at the Embassy Suites Houston, July 21-24, 2005. (Allen/Leonard). PASSED 6-1.

Reports

Lee Schultz reported on convention exhibits and her desire to involve more companies and products. Discussion followed regarding how this might be accomplished.
MOTION: That IAAP office staff develop a list of possible convention exhibitors. The list should be submitted at the next meeting. (Leonard/Schultz). PASSED 7-0.

New Business

The chair announced three possible themes for the convention, all of which focused on technology and the changing role of administrative assistants. Doris Williamson suggested the following possible title: "Vision Without Boundaries." Carol Allen suggested a communication theme. Several other possibilities were discussed. The chair appointed a subcommittee of Doris and Margaret to bring to the next committee meeting two or three concrete theme ideas.

Margaret Zappa thought that IAAP should be doing more to help members stay ahead in the changing workplace. She suggested workshops to polish skills in word processing, spreadsheet, database, presentations, and scheduling software.
MOTION: To recommend to IAAP that it investigate offering fee-based technology workshops at the national and regional conventions. (Zappa/Schultz). PASSED 5-2.

The meeting was adjourned at 11:50 by Kim Jobe.

Respectfully submitted,

Carol Allen

Carol Allen, Secretary

Describes disposition of previous minutes

Highlights motions, showing name of person making motion and person seconding it

Shows name and signature of person recording minutes

SUMMARIES

A summary compresses the main points from a book, report, article, Web site, meeting, or convention. A summary saves time because it can reduce a report or article 85 to 95 percent. Employees are sometimes asked to write summaries that condense technical reports, periodical articles, or books so that their staffs or superiors may grasp the main ideas quickly. Students may be asked to write summaries of articles, chapters, or books to sharpen their writing skills and to confirm their knowledge of reading assignments. In writing a summary, you'll follow these general guidelines:

- Present the goal or purpose of the document being summarized. Why was it written?
- Highlight the research methods (if appropriate), findings, conclusions, and recommendations.
- Omit illustrations, examples, and references.
- Organize for readability by including headings and bulleted or enumerated lists.
- Include your reactions or an overall evaluation of the document if asked to do so.

An *executive summary* condenses a long report, proposal, or business plan. It concentrates on what management needs to know from a longer report. The executive summary shown in Figure 9.9 summarizes main points from a business plan prepared by Bluewater Koi fish farm. This company wants to expand, and it needs $72,000 to acquire additional land for three fish ponds. To secure financial backing, Bluewater wrote a business plan explaining its operation, service, product, marketing, and finances. Part of that business plan is an executive summary, which you see in Figure 9.9.

Quick Check

A summary condenses the primary ideas, conclusions, and recommendations of a longer publication.

Quick Check

An executive summary presents an overview of a longer report and focuses on key points.

Breeding beautifully colored koi for collectors is a profitable but hazardous and costly business. Commercial growers need acreage to build breeding and growing ponds, expensive equipment to monitor water quality and prevent diseases, and caring personnel to oversee the intricate breeding program. To secure financial backing, businesses, such as Bluewater Koi, submit proposals that often include executive summaries, such as that shown in Figure 9.9.
© Vince Stearno/CORBIS

FIGURE 9.9   Executive Summary (excerpt from business plan)

Summarizes purpose of longer report

Uses headings to improve readability

Follows sequence of longer report

Provides overview of main points

Focuses on most important parts of business plan, including marketing, finances, and payback

EXECUTIVE SUMMARY

Bluewater Koi Expansion Plan

The purpose of this business plan is to acquaint venture capitalists with Bluewater Koi fish farm and to solicit support for an expansion plan to be undertaken over the next two years. This report will do the following:
- Profile the current Bluewater Koi operation
- Explain the need for expansion to meet market demands
- Summarize expansion costs and expected payback

Business Profile

Bluewater Creek is a 45-acre ornamental fish farm located in South Alabama. Bluewater specializes in breeding and selling koi, which are exotic and beautifully colored carp developed in Japan. Koi are collected by hobbyists and usually live in lushly landscaped fish ponds indoors or outside. Although a grand champion koi in Asia has sold for over a million dollars, the koi sold at Bluewater Creek range in price from $2.20 to $90 each. Bluewater had total sales of $347,000 last year in its retail and wholesale operations. The fish at Bluewater are grown in five surface ponds, and the operation ranges from breeding to shipping.

Expansion to Meet Market Demands

Bluewater has enjoyed increasing sales and profits since its inception as a fish hatchery in 1981. It has developed a large clientele, selling to retailers and wholesalers through its print catalog and its Web site. Fish quality and health are of utmost importance at Bluewater. Because koi are susceptible to viruses, Bluewater has adopted a policy of not buying or reselling fish from other U.S. growers. As a result, all Bluewater koi are bred and grown on site. This policy, coupled with constantly increasing sales, makes it necessary to acquire a 9-acre farm to accommodate three additional growing ponds.

Financial Needs and Payback

Acquiring the 9-acre farm is expected to cost $38,000. An additional $12,000 is needed to move 60,000 cubic yards of earth to enable the ponds to reach the natural water table necessary for maintaining water levels in the ponds. Other expenses include $22,000 to expand the breeding operation, which involves matching high-quality male and female brood fish imported from Japan. Artificial spawning yields high hatching rates. But this practice is labor intensive. Equally laborious is the following culling process in which only the best colored, patterned, and conformed fish are kept. A total investment of $72,000 will enable Bluewater to complete its needed expansion. Projected annual sales and costs indicate that Bluewater should be able to repay the loan in five years.

Summing Up and Looking Forward

This chapter presented six types of informal business reports: information reports, progress reports, justification/recommendation reports, feasibility reports, minutes of meetings, and summaries. Information reports generally provide data only. Justification/recommendation and feasibility reports are more analytical in that they also evaluate the information, draw conclusions, and make recommendations. This chapter also discussed four formats for reports. Letter format is used for reports sent outside an organization; memo format is used for internal reports. More formal reports are formatted on plain paper with a manuscript design, while routine reports may be formatted on prepared forms. The chapter presented numerous model documents illustrating the many kinds of reports and their formats.

All of the examples in this chapter are considered relatively informal. Longer, more formal reports are necessary for major investigations and research. These reports and proposals, along with suggestions for research methods, are presented in Chapter 10.

CRITICAL THINKING

1. Why are reports necessary to businesses, and why do today's businesspeople write so many?
2. How do business reports differ from business letters?
3. How are information reports different from analytical reports? Give an original example of each.
4. Of the reports presented in this chapter, discuss those that require indirect development versus those that require direct development.
5. How are the reports that you write for your courses similar to those presented here? How are they different?

CHAPTER REVIEW

6. List six kinds of informal reports. Be prepared to describe each.

7. List four formats suitable for reports. Be prepared to discuss each.

8. From the lists you made in Questions 6 and 7, select a report category and appropriate format for each of the following situations.

   a. Your supervisor asks you to read a long technical report and write a report that condenses the important points.

   b. You want to tell management about an idea you have for improving a procedure that you think will increase productivity.

   c. You are in charge of planning your company's booth for next year's big trade show. Your boss wants to know what you have done thus far.

   d. You are asked to record the proceedings of a meeting of your school's student association.

   e. As Engineering Department office manager, you have been asked to describe your highly regarded computer system for another department.

   f. As a police officer, you are writing a report of an arrest.

g. At a mail-order catalog company, your boss asks you to investigate ways to reduce the time that customers are kept waiting for service representatives to take their telephone orders. He wants your report to examine the problem and offer solutions.

9. If you were about to write the following reports, where would you gather information? Be prepared to discuss the specifics of each choice.

   a. You are a student representative on a curriculum committee. You are asked to study the course requirements in your major and make recommendations.

   b. As department manager, you must write job descriptions for several new positions you wish to establish in your department.

   c. You are proposing to management the replacement of a copier in your department.

   d. You must document the progress of a 12-month campaign to alter the image of Levi-Strauss jeans.

10. What three questions do progress reports typically address?

11. What one factor distinguishes reports developed directly from those developed indirectly?

12. What is the difference between a functional heading and a talking heading? Give an example of each for a report about consumer reactions to a new shampoo product.

13. Information reports generally contain what three parts?

14. What should the minutes of a meeting include?

15. What should a summary of a long article or report contain?

WRITING IMPROVEMENT EXERCISES

9.1 EVALUATING HEADINGS AND TITLES. Identify the following report headings and titles as "talking" or "functional/descriptive." Discuss the usefulness and effectiveness of each.

TEAM

a. Problem

b. Need for Tightening Computer ID System

c. Annual Budget

d. How Direct Mail Can Deliver Profits for Your Business

e. Case History: Improving Service at Royal Palace Hotel

f. Solving Our Networking Problems With an Extranet

g. Comparing Copier Volume, Ease of Use, and Speed

h. Alternatives

ACTIVITIES AND CASES

9.2 INFORMATION REPORT: DESCRIBING YOUR JOB. Your instructor wants to learn about your employment. Select a position you now hold or one that you have held in the past. If you have not been employed, choose an organization to which you belong.

Your Task. Write an information report describing your employment. As an introduction describe the company and its products or services, its ownership, and its location. As the main part of the report, describe your position, including its tasks and the skills required to perform these tasks. Summarize by describing the experience you gained. Your memo report should be single-spaced and 1½ to 2 pages long and should be addressed to your instructor.

9.3 INFORMATION REPORT: LEARNING ABOUT AN OCCUPATION. Gather information about a career or position in which you might be interested. Learn about the nature of the job. Discover whether certification, a license, or experience is required. One of the best places to search is the latest *Occupational Outlook Handbook*. Use a search engine such as Google (http://www.google.com) to locate the handbook, sponsored by the U.S. Bureau of Labor Statistics. Click on an occupation, listed along the left side of the Web page.

WEB

Your Task. Write an information report that characterizes the working conditions in your target career area. Describe typical entry-level salaries and the potential for advancement. If your instructor wishes to make this an extended report, collect information about two companies where you might apply. Investigate each company's history, products and/or services, size, earnings, reputation, and number of employees. Describe the functions of an employee working in the position you have investigated. To do this, interview one or more individuals who are working in that position. Devote several sections of your report to the specific tasks, functions, duties, and opinions of these individuals. You can make this into a recommendation report by drawing conclusions and making recommendations. One conclusion that you could draw relates to success in this career area. Who might be successful in this field?

CRITICAL THINKING

9.4 RECOMMENDATION REPORT: RETAINING EMPLOYEES. An employer for whom you worked last year regarded you highly. Although you are no longer employed there, this individual called to ask your candid opinion on how to retain employees. He is concerned about the high rate of turnover. What advice can you offer? How do similar businesses recruit and retain their employees?

Your Task. Using actual experiences, write a recommendation report with your suggestions for retaining employees. Use letter format and organize your remarks under a number of descriptive headings, such as "Problem," "Possible Causes," and "Suggestions for Retaining Staff."

CRITICAL THINKING

9.5 RECOMMENDATION REPORT: EXPANDING THE COMPANY LIBRARY. Despite the interest in online publications, managers and employees at your company still like to browse through magazines in the company library. Bonnie Finley, the company librarian, wants to add business periodicals to the library subscription list and has requested help from various company divisions.

Your Task. You've been asked to recommend four periodicals in your particular specialty (accounting, marketing, etc.). Visit your library and use appropriate indexes and guides to select four periodicals to recommend. Write a memo report to Ms. Finley describing the particular readership, usual contents, and scope of each periodical. To judge each adequately, you should examine several issues. Explain why you think each periodical should be ordered and who would read it. Convince the librarian that your choices would be beneficial to your department.

TEAM

9.6 JUSTIFICATION/RECOMMENDATION REPORT: EVALUATING YOUR CURRICULUM. You have been serving as a student member of a college curriculum advisement committee. The committee is expected to examine the course requirements for a degree or certificate in your major.

Your Task. In teams of three to five people, decide whether the requirements are realistic and practical. What improvements can your team suggest? Interview other students and faculty members for their suggestions. Prepare a justification report in letter or memo format to send to the dean of your college proposing your suggestions. You anticipate that the dean may need to be persuaded to make any changes. Consider delaying your recommendations until after you have developed a foundation of explanation and reasons.

9.7 JUSTIFICATION/RECOMMENDATION REPORT: PURCHASING NEW EQUIPMENT. In your work or your training, identify equipment that needs to be purchased or replaced (computer, printer, modem, VCR, copier, digital camera, etc.). Gather information about two different models or brands.

Your Task. Write a justification report comparing the two items. Establish a context by describing the need for the equipment. Discuss the present situation, emphasizing the current deficiencies. Describe the advantages of acquiring the new equipment.

9.8 PROGRESS REPORT: MAKING HEADWAY TOWARD YOUR DEGREE. You made an agreement with your parents (or spouse, relative, or significant friend) that you would submit a progress report at this time describing headway toward your educational goal (employment, certificate, or degree).

Your Task. In memo format write a progress report that fulfills your promise to describe your progress toward your educational goal. Address your progress report to your parents, spouse, relative, or significant friend. In your memo (1) describe your goal; (2) summarize the work you have completed thus far; (3) discuss thoroughly the work currently in progress, including your successes and anticipated obstacles; and (4) forecast your future activities in relation to your scheduled completion date.

9.9 MINUTES: RECORDING THE PROCEEDINGS OF A MEETING. Attend an open meeting of an organization at your school or elsewhere. Assume that you are asked to record the proceedings.

Your Task. Record the meeting proceedings in formal or informal minutes. Review the chapter to be sure you include all the data necessary for minutes. Focus on motions, votes, decisions reached, and action taken.

9.10 SUMMARY: CONDUCTING AN E-MAIL SURVEY. Your boss at a large catalog retailer wants to conduct a customer e-mail survey that will help him decide how to expand the print and online catalog business. He doesn't know how to prepare his e-mail survey. Should the list of questions be sent as an attachment or embedded in the message? He also wants to know whether other ways exist for conducting an online survey. He asks you to conduct Internet research to see what has been written on the subject.

INFOTRAC

Your Task. Using InfoTrac, find an article by Curt J. Dommeyer and Eleanor Moriarty titled "Comparing Two Forms of an E-Mail Survey: Embedded Vs. Attached," appearing in *International Journal of Market Research*, Winter 1999, Article A61298911. In a memo report addressed to your boss, Jason Owens, cover the following points:

a. Discuss the goal of the article.
b. Summarize the four methods suggested for conducting online surveys.
c. Summarize past research on this subject.
d. Discuss the research methods used for this study.
e. Present the results (findings) and conclusions drawn by the authors.
f. Include your recommendation to your boss based on this article.

9.11 EXECUTIVE SUMMARY: KEEPING THE BOSS INFORMED. Like many executives, your boss is too rushed to read long journal articles. But she is eager to keep up with developments in her field. Assume she has asked you to help her stay abreast of research in her field. She asks you to submit to her one executive summary every month on an article of interest.

INFOTRAC

Your Task. In your field of study, select a professional journal, such as the *Journal of Management*. Using an InfoTrac Power search, look for articles in your target journal. Select an article that is at least five pages long and is interesting to you. Write an executive summary in a memo format. Include an introduction that might begin with *As you requested, I am submitting this executive summary of* . . . . Identify the author, article name, journal, and date of publication. Explain what the author intended to do in the study or article. Summarize three or four of the most important findings of the study or article. Use descriptive rather than functional headings. Summarize any recommendations made. Your boss would also like a concluding statement indicating your reaction to the article. Address your memo to Kendra Halle.

9.12 LONGER REPORT: SOLVING A PROBLEM. Choose a business or organization with which you are familiar and identify a problem such as sloppy workmanship, indifferent service, poor attendance at organization meetings, uninspired cafeteria food, antique office equipment, arrogant management, lack of communication, underappreciated employees, or wasteful procedures.

Your Task. Describe the problem in detail. Assume you are to report to management (or to the leadership of an organization) about the nature and scope of the problem. Decide which kind of report to prepare (information, recommendation/justification), and choose the format. Naturally, you will gather data from reputable sources to lend authority to your conclusions and recommendations. Determine the exact topic and report length after consultation with your instructor.

9.13 CONNECTING WITH E-MAIL: PROGRESS REPORT. If you are working on a long report for either this chapter or Chapter 10, keep your instructor informed of your progress.

Your Task. Send your instructor a report detailing the progress you are making on your long report assignment. Discuss (1) the purpose of the report, (2) the work already completed, (3) the work currently in progress, and (4) your schedule for completing the report.

WEB
CRITICAL
THINKING

9.14 REPORT TOPICS. A list of over 70 report topics is available at the Guffey Web site (http://www.westwords.com/guffey/students.html). The topics are divided into the following categories: accounting, finance, personnel/human resources, marketing, information systems, management, and general business/education/campus issues. You can collect information for many of these reports by using InfoTrac and the Web. Your instructor may assign them as individual or team projects. All involve critical thinking in collecting and organizing information into logical reports.

GRAMMAR/MECHANICS CHECKUP—9

SEMICOLONS AND COLONS

Review Sections 2.16–2.19 in the Grammar/Mechanics Handbook. Then study each of the following statements. Insert any necessary punctuation. Use the delete sign to omit unnecessary punctuation. In the space provided indicate the number of changes you made and record the number of the G/M principle(s) illustrated. (When you replace one punctuation mark with another, count it as one change.) If you make no changes, write *0*. This exercise concentrates on semicolon and colon use, but you will also be responsible for correct comma use. When you finish, compare your responses with those shown at the end of the book. If your responses differ, study carefully the specific principles shown in parentheses.

2 _____ (2.16a) **Example** The job of Mr. Wellworth is to make sure that his company has enough cash to meet its obligations; moreover, he is responsible for locating credit when needed.

_____ 1. Short-term financing refers to a period of under one year long-term financing on the other hand refers to a period of ten years or more.

_____ 2. Cash resulting from product sales does not arrive until December therefore our cash flow becomes critical in October and November.

_____ 3. We must negotiate short-term financing during the following months September October and November.

_____ 4. Large American corporations that offer huge amounts of trade credit are, Ford Motor Company and General Electric Company.

5. Although some firms rarely need to borrow short-term money many businesses find that they require significant credit to pay for current production and sales costs. _____

6. A supermarket probably requires no short-term credit a greeting card manufacturer however typically would need considerable short-term credit. _____

7. We offer three basic types of credit open-book accounts promissory notes and trade acceptances. _____

8. Speakers at the conference on credit include the following businesspeople Mary Ann Mahan financial manager Holmes Industries Terry L. Buchanan comptroller Metropolitan Bank and Mark Kendall legal counsel Security Federal Banking. _____

9. The prime interest rate is set by one or more of the nation's largest banks and this rate goes up or down as the cost of money to the bank itself fluctuates. _____

10. Most banks are in business to lend money to commercial customers for example retailers service companies manufacturers and construction firms. _____

11. Avionics Enterprises, Inc., which is a small electronics firm with a solid credit rating recently applied for a loan but First Federal refused the loan application because the bank was short on cash. _____

12. When Avionics, Inc., was refused by First Federal its financial managers submitted applications to: Fidelity Trust, Farmers Mutual, and Mountain Federal. _____

13. The cost of financing capital investments at the present time is very high therefore Avionics' managers elected to postpone certain expansion projects. _____

14. If interest rates reach as high as 18 percent the cost of borrowing becomes prohibitive and many businesses are forced to reconsider or abandon projects that require financing. _____

15. Several investors decided to pool their resources then they could find attractive investments for large-scale projects. _____

GRAMMAR/MECHANICS CHALLENGE—9

DOCUMENT FOR REVISION

The following progress report has faults in grammar, punctuation, spelling, number form, wordiness, and word use. Use standard proofreading marks (see Appendix B) to correct the errors. When you finish, your instructor can show you the revised version of this report.

DATE: April 20, 200x

TO: Dorothy Prevatt, President

FROM: Jay Thorson, Development Officer

SUBJECT: Progress Report on Construction of Miami Branch Office

Construction of Prevatt Realtys Miami Branch Office has entered Phase three. Although we are 1 week behind the contractors original schedule the building should be already for occupancie on August 15.

Past Progress

Phaze one involved development of the architects plans, this process was completed onFebruary 5. Phaze two involved submission of the plan's for county building department approval. Each of the plans were then given to the following 2 contractors for the purpose of eliciting estimates, Holst Brothers Contractors, and Ocean Beach Builders. The lowest bidder was Holst Brothers, consequently this firm began construction on March 25.

Present Status

Phase three includes initial construction processes. We have completed the following steps as of April 20:

- Demolition of existing building at 11485 NW 27 Avenue
- Excavation of foundation footings for the building and for the surrounding wall
- Steel reinforcing rods installed in building pad and wall
- Pouring of concrete foundation

Holst Brothers Contractors indicated that he was 1 week behind schedule for these reasons. The building inspectors required more steel reinforcement then was showed on the architects blueprints. In addition excavation of the footings required more time then the contractor anticipated because the 18 inch footings were all below grade.

Future Schedule

In spite of the fact that we lost time in Phase 3 we are substantially on target for the completion of this office building by August 1. Phase 4 include the following activities, framing drywalling and installation of plumbing.

COMMUNICATION WORKSHOP: COLLABORATION

Laying the Groundwork for Team Writing Projects

The chances are that you can look forward to some kind of team writing in your future career. You may collaborate voluntarily (seeking advice and differing perspectives) or involuntarily (through necessity or by assignment). Working with other people can be frustrating, particularly when some team members don't carry their weight or when conflict breaks out. Team projects, though, can be harmonious and productive when members establish ground rules at the outset and adhere to guidelines such as the following.

Preparing to Work Together

Before you discuss the project, talk about how your group will function.

- Limit the size of your team, if possible, to three or four members. Larger groups have more difficulties. An odd number is usually preferable to avoid ties in voting.
- Name a meeting leader (to plan and conduct meetings), a recorder (to keep a record of group decisions), and an evaluator (to determine whether the group is on target and meeting its goals).
- Decide whether your team will be governed by consensus (everyone must agree) or by majority rule.
- Compare schedules of team members, and set up the best meeting times. Plan to meet often. Avoid other responsibilities during meetings.
- Discuss the value of conflict. By bringing conflict into the open and encouraging confrontation, your team can prevent personal resentment and group dysfunction. Confrontation can actually create better final documents by promoting new ideas and avoiding "groupthink."
- Discuss how you will deal with members who are not pulling their share of the load.

Planning the Document

Once you've established ground rules, you're ready to discuss the project and resulting document. Be sure to keep a record of the decisions your team makes.

- Establish the document's specific purpose and identify the main issues involved.
- Decide on the final form of the document. What parts will it have?
- Discuss the audience(s) for the document and what appeal would help it achieve its purpose.
- Develop a work plan. Assign jobs. Set deadlines.
- Decide how the final document will be written: individuals working separately on assigned portions, one person writing the first draft, the entire group writing the complete document together, or some other method.

Collecting Information

The following suggestions help teams gather accurate information.

- Brainstorm for ideas as a group.
- Decide who will be responsible for gathering what information.
- Establish deadlines for collecting information.
- Discuss ways to ensure the accuracy of the information collected.

Organizing, Writing, and Revising

As the project progresses, your team may wish to modify some of its earlier decisions.

- Review the proposed organization of your final document, and adjust it if necessary.
- Write the first draft. If separate team members are writing segments, they should use the same word processing program to facilitate combining files.
- Meet to discuss and revise the draft(s).
- If individuals are working on separate parts, appoint one person (probably the best writer) to coordinate all the parts, striving for consistent style and format.

Editing and Evaluating

Before the document is submitted, complete these steps.

- Give one person responsibility for finding and correcting grammatical and mechanical errors.
- Meet as a group to evaluate the final document. Does it fulfill its purpose and meet the needs of the audience?

Career Application. Select a report topic from this chapter or Chapter 10. Assume that you must prepare the report as a team project. If you are working on a long report, your instructor may ask you to prepare individual progress reports as you develop your topic.

Your Task

- Form teams of three to five members.
- Prepare to work together by using the suggestions provided here.
- Plan your report by establishing its purpose, identifying the main issues, developing a work plan, and assigning tasks.
- Collect information, organize the data, and write the first draft.
- Decide how the document will be revised, edited, and evaluated.

Your instructor may assign grades not only on the final report but also on your team effectiveness and your individual contribution, as determined by fellow team members.

Chapter 10

Proposals and Formal Reports

Today, more than ever, success in business requires knowing how to write powerful, persuasive proposals and reports. From large corporations to the smallest entrepreneurial operations, businesspeople are demanding proposals so that they can compare apples to apples.[1]

THOMAS SANT, consultant and author of over $11 billion worth of business reports and proposals

LEARNING OBJECTIVES

1. Identify and explain the parts of informal and formal proposals.
2. Describe the preparatory steps for writing a formal report.
3. Collect data from secondary sources including print and electronic sources.
4. Understand how to use Web browsers and search engines to locate reliable data.
5. Discuss how to generate primary data from surveys, interviews, observation, and experimentation.
6. Understand the need for accurate documentation of data.
7. Describe how to organize report data, create an outline, and make effective titles.
8. Illustrate data using tables, charts, and graphs.
9. Describe and sequence the parts of a formal report.

P roposals are written offers to solve problems, provide services, or sell equipment. Let's say that sports shoe manufacturer Nike wants to upgrade the computers and software in its human resources department. If it knows exactly what it wants, it would prepare a request for proposals (RFP) specifying its requirements. It then publicizes this RFP, and companies interested in bidding on the job submit proposals. Both large and small companies, as proposal consultant Tom Sant says, are increasingly likely to use RFPs to solicit competitive bids on their projects. This enables them to compare "apples to apples." That is, they can compare prices from different companies on their projects. They also want the legal protection offered by proposals, which are legal contracts.

Many companies earn a sizable portion of their income from sales resulting from proposals. That's why creating effective proposals is especially important today. In writing proposals, the most important thing to remember is that pro-

✓ *Quick Check*

Proposals are persuasive offers to solve problems, provide services, or sell equipment.

posals are sales presentations. They must be persuasive, not merely mechanical descriptions of what you can do. You may recall from Chapter 7 that effective persuasive sales messages (1) emphasize benefits for the reader, (2) "toot your horn" by detailing your expertise and accomplishments, and (3) make it easy for the reader to understand and respond.

Quick Check

Both large and small companies today often use requests for proposals (RFPs) to solicit competitive bids on projects.

INFORMAL PROPOSALS

Quick Check

Informal proposals may contain an introduction, background information, the proposal, staffing requirements, a budget, and an authorization request.

Proposals may be informal or formal; they differ primarily in length and format. Informal proposals are often presented in two- to four-page letters. Sometimes called *letter proposals*, they contain six principal parts: introduction, background, proposal, staffing, budget, and authorization. The informal letter proposal shown in Figure 10.1 illustrates all six parts of a letter proposal. This proposal is addressed to a Pittsburgh dentist who wants to improve patient satisfaction.

INTRODUCTION

Quick Check

Effective proposal openers "hook" readers by promising extraordinary results or resources or by identifying key benefits, issues, or outcomes.

Most proposals begin by explaining briefly the reasons for the proposal and by highlighting the writer's qualifications. To make your introduction more persuasive, you need to provide a "hook" to capture the reader's interest. One proposal expert suggests these possibilities:[2]

- Hint at extraordinary results, with details to be revealed shortly.
- Promise low costs or speedy results.
- Mention a remarkable resource (well-known authority, new computer program, well-trained staff) available exclusively to you.
- Identify a serious problem (worry item) and promise a solution, to be explained later.
- Specify a key issue or benefit that you feel is the heart of the proposal.

For example, Joseph Geckle, in the introduction of the proposal shown in Figure 10.1, focused on a key benefit. In this proposal to conduct a patient satisfaction survey, Joe Geckle thought that his client, Dr. Hricik, would be most interested in specific recommendations for improving service to his patients. But Geckle didn't hit on this hook until after the first draft had been written. Indeed, it's often a good idea to put off writing the introduction to a proposal until after you have completed other parts. For longer proposals the introduction also describes the scope and limitations of the project, as well as outlining the organization of the material to come.

BACKGROUND, PROBLEM, PURPOSE

The background section identifies the problem and discusses the goals or purposes of the project. Your aim is to convince the reader that you understand the problem completely. Thus, if you are responding to an RFP, this means repeating its language. For example, if the RFP asks for the *design of a maintenance program for high-speed mail-sorting equipment*, you would use the same language in explaining the purpose of your proposal. This section might include segments titled *Basic Requirements, Most Critical Tasks,* and *Most Important Secondary Problems.*

Trade show business consumes more than $1.5 billion today. Every day hundreds of shows go on in every major city around the globe. Designing exhibit booths for these shows has become a huge business. To compete for business, companies that design and sell trade booths submit proposals that describe the problem (how to attract visitors to their booth), plan (strategy for designing and constructing the exhibit booth), staffing, and budget.
© Davis Barber/PhotoEdit, Inc.

Proposal, Plan, Schedule

In the proposal section itself, you should discuss your plan for solving the problem. In some proposals this is tricky because you want to disclose enough of your plan to secure the contract without giving away so much information that your services aren't needed. Without specifics, though, your proposal has little chance, so you must decide how much to reveal. Tell what you propose to do and how it will benefit the reader. Remember, too, that a proposal is a sales presentation. Sell your methods, product, and "deliverables"—items that will be left with the client. In this section some writers specify how the project will be managed and how its progress will be audited. Most writers also include a schedule of activities or timetable showing when events will take place.

Quick Check
The proposal section must give enough information to secure the contract but not so much detail that the services are not needed.

Staffing

The staffing section of a proposal describes the credentials and expertise of the project leaders. It may also identify the size and qualifications of the support staff, along with other resources such as computer facilities and special programs for analyzing statistics. In longer proposals, résumés of key people may be provided. The staffing or personnel section is a good place to endorse and promote your staff.

Budget

A central item in most proposals is the budget, a list of project costs. You need to prepare this section carefully because it represents a contract; you can't raise the price later—even if your costs increase. You can—and should—protect yourself with a deadline for acceptance. In the budget section some writers itemize hours and costs; others present a total sum only. A proposal to install a complex computer system might, for example, contain a detailed line-by-line budget. In the proposal shown in Figure 10.1, Joseph Geckle felt that he needed to justify the

Quick Check
Because a proposal is a legal contract, the budget must be researched carefully.

FIGURE 10.1 Informal Proposal

Grabs attention with "hook" that focuses on key benefit

Identifies four goals of survey

Announces heart of proposal

Divides total plan into logical segments for easy reading

GECKLE RESEARCH ASSOCIATES

One Patriot Plaza
Youngwood, PA 15697
(614) 435-8933
www.geckleresearch.com

May 15, 200x

Michael Hricik, D.D.S.
4032 Wilkinsburg Place
Pittsburgh, PA 15673

Dear Dr. Hricik:

Helping you improve your practice is of the highest priority to us at Geckle Research Associates. That's why we are pleased to submit the following proposal outlining our plan to help you more effectively meet your patients' needs by analyzing their views about your practice.

Background and Goals

We understand that you have been incorporating a total quality management system in your practice. Although you have every reason to believe your patients are pleased with the service you provide, you would like to give them an opportunity to discuss what they like and possibly don't like about your service. Based on our conversations, we understand that you would like the patient surveys to allow you to do the following:

- Determine the level of satisfaction with you and your staff
- Elicit suggestions for improvement
- Learn more about how your patients discovered you
- Compare your "preferred" and "standard" patients

Proposed Plan

To help you achieve the goals listed above, Geckle Research proposes the following plan:

Survey. A short but thorough questionnaire will probe the data you desire. This questionnaire will measure your patients' reactions to such elements as courtesy, professionalism, accuracy of billing, friendliness, and waiting time. After you approve it, the questionnaire will be sent to a carefully selected sample of 300 patients whom you have separated into groupings of "preferred" and "standard."

Analysis. Survey data will be analyzed by demographic segments, such as patient type, age, and gender. Our experienced team of experts, using state-of-the-art computer systems and advanced statistical measures, will study the (1) degree of patient satisfaction, (2) reasons for satisfaction or dissatisfaction, and (3) relationship between your "preferred" and "standard" patients. Moreover, our team will give you specific suggestions for making patient visits more pleasant.

Report. You will receive a final report with the key findings outlined here. The report will include tables summarizing all responses categorized by "preferred" and "standard" clients. Our staff will also draw conclusions based on these findings.

---

budget for his firm's patient satisfaction survey, so he itemized the costs. But the budget included for a proposal to conduct a one-day seminar to improve employee communication skills might be a lump sum only. Your analysis of the project will help you decide what kind of budget to prepare.

AUTHORIZATION

Informal proposals often close with a request for approval or authorization. In addition, the closing should remind the reader of key benefits and motivate action. It might also include a deadline date beyond which the offer is invalid. At some companies, such as Hewlett-Packard, authorization to proceed is not part of the proposal. Instead, it is usually discussed after the customer has received the proposal. In this way the customer and the sales account manager are able to negotiate terms before a formal agreement is drawn.

FIGURE 10.1 (Continued)

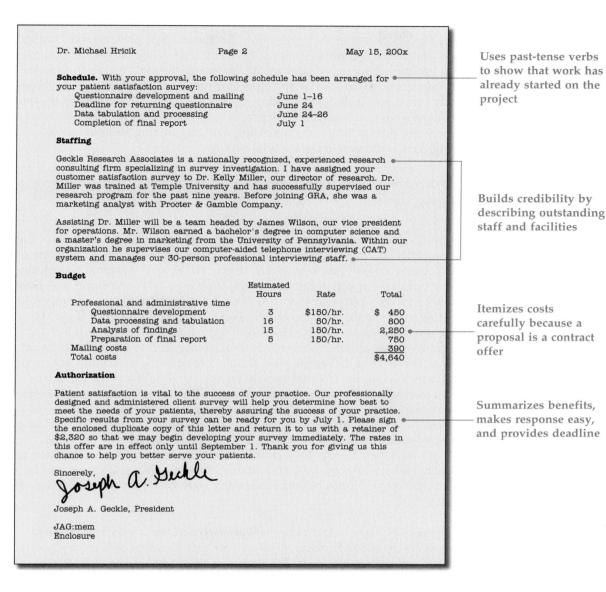

Dr. Michael Hricik   Page 2   May 15, 200x

Schedule. With your approval, the following schedule has been arranged for your patient satisfaction survey:

Questionnaire development and mailing	June 1–16
Deadline for returning questionnaire	June 24
Data tabulation and processing	June 24–26
Completion of final report	July 1

Uses past-tense verbs to show that work has already started on the project

Staffing

Geckle Research Associates is a nationally recognized, experienced research consulting firm specializing in survey investigation. I have assigned your customer satisfaction survey to Dr. Kelly Miller, our director of research. Dr. Miller was trained at Temple University and has successfully supervised our research program for the past nine years. Before joining GRA, she was a marketing analyst with Procter & Gamble Company.

Assisting Dr. Miller will be a team headed by James Wilson, our vice president for operations. Mr. Wilson earned a bachelor's degree in computer science and a master's degree in marketing from the University of Pennsylvania. Within our organization he supervises our computer-aided telephone interviewing (CAT) system and manages our 30-person professional interviewing staff.

Builds credibility by describing outstanding staff and facilities

Budget

	Estimated Hours	Rate	Total
Professional and administrative time			
Questionnaire development	3	$150/hr.	$ 450
Data processing and tabulation	16	50/hr.	800
Analysis of findings	15	150/hr.	2,250
Preparation of final report	5	150/hr.	750
Mailing costs			390
Total costs			$4,640

Itemizes costs carefully because a proposal is a contract offer

Authorization

Patient satisfaction is vital to the success of your practice. Our professionally designed and administered client survey will help you determine how best to meet the needs of your patients, thereby assuring the success of your practice. Specific results from your survey can be ready for you by July 1. Please sign the enclosed duplicate copy of this letter and return it to us with a retainer of $2,320 so that we may begin developing your survey immediately. The rates in this offer are in effect only until September 1. Thank you for giving us this chance to help you better serve your patients.

Summarizes benefits, makes response easy, and provides deadline

Sincerely,

Joseph A. Geckle

Joseph A. Geckle, President

JAG:mem
Enclosure

FORMAL PROPOSALS

Formal proposals differ from informal proposals not in style but in size and format. Formal proposals respond to big projects and may range from 5 to 200 or more pages. To facilitate comprehension and reference, they are organized into many parts. In addition to the six basic parts just described, formal proposals contain some or all of the following additional parts: copy of the RFP, letter of transmittal, abstract and/or executive summary, title page, table of contents, figures, and appendix.

Well-written proposals win contracts and business for companies and individuals. In fact, many companies depend entirely on proposals to generate their income. Companies such as Microsoft, Hewlett-Packard, and IBM employ staffs

Quick Check

Formal proposals respond to big projects and may contain 200 or more pages.

of people who do nothing but prepare proposals to compete for new business. For more information about industry standards and resources, visit the Web site of the Association of Proposal Management Professionals (http://www.apmp.org).

Quick Check

The primary differences between formal and informal reports are tone, structure, and length.

Formal reports, whether they offer only information or also analyze that information and make recommendations, typically have three characteristics: formal tone, traditional structure, and length. Although formal reports in business are seen infrequently, they serve an important function. They provide management with vital data for decision making. In this section we will consider the entire process of writing a formal report: preparing to write, researching secondary data, generating primary data, documenting data, organizing and outlining data, illustrating data, and presenting the final report.

PREPARING TO WRITE FORMAL REPORTS

Like proposals and informal reports, formal reports begin with a definition of the project. Probably the most difficult part of this definition is limiting the scope of the report. Every project has limitations. If you are writing a formal report, decide at the outset what constraints influence the range of your project and how you will achieve your purpose. How much time do you have for completing your report? How much space will you be allowed for reporting on your topic? How accessible are the data you need? How thorough should your research be?

If you are writing about low morale among swing-shift employees, for example, how many of your 475 employees should you interview? Should you limit your research to company-related morale factors, or should you consider external factors over which the company has no control? In investigating variable-rate mortgages, should you focus on a particular group, such as first-time homeowners in a specific area, or should you consider all mortgage holders? The first step in writing a report, then, is determining the precise boundaries of the topic.

Quick Check

The planning of every report begins with a statement of purpose explaining the goal, significance, and limitations of the report.

Once you have defined the project and limited its scope, write a statement of purpose. The statement of purpose should describe the goal, significance, and limitations of the report. Notice how the following statement pinpoints the research and report:

> The purpose of this report is to explore employment possibilities for entry-level paralegal workers in the city of San Francisco. It will consider typical salaries, skills required, opportunities, and working conditions. This research is significant because of the increasing number of job openings in the paralegal field. This report will not consider legal secretarial employment, which represents a different employment focus.

RESEARCHING SECONDARY DATA

One of the most important steps in the process of writing a report is research. Because a report is only as good as its data, you'll want to spend considerable time collecting data before you begin writing.

Quick Check

Primary data come from firsthand experience and observation; secondary data, from reading.

Data fall into two broad categories, primary and secondary. Primary data result from firsthand experience and observation. Secondary data come from reading what others have experienced and observed. Coca-Cola and Pepsi-Cola, for example, produce primary data when they stage taste tests and record the reactions of consumers. These same sets of data become secondary after they have been published and, let's say, a newspaper reporter uses them in an article about soft drinks. Secondary data are easier and cheaper to develop than primary data, which might involve interviewing large groups or sending out questionnaires.

You're going to learn first about secondary data because that's where nearly every research project should begin. Often, something has already been written about your topic. Reviewing secondary sources can save time and effort and prevent you from "reinventing the wheel." Most secondary material is available either in print or electronically.

PRINT RESOURCES

Although we're seeing a steady movement away from print to electronic data, much information is available only in print.

Although researchers are increasingly turning to electronic data, much data is available only in print.

If you are an infrequent library user, begin your research by talking with a reference librarian about your project. These librarians won't do your research for you, but they will steer you in the right direction. And they are very accommodating. Several years ago a *Wall Street Journal* poll revealed that librarians are among the friendliest, most approachable people in the working world. Many libraries help you understand their computer, cataloging, and retrieval systems by providing brochures, handouts, and workshops.

Books. Although quickly outdated, books provide excellent historical, in-depth data on a large variety of subjects. Books can be located through print catalogs or online catalogs. Most automated systems today enable you to learn not only whether a book is in the library but whether it is currently available.

Books provide historical, in-depth data; periodicals provide limited but current coverage.

Periodicals. Magazines, pamphlets, and journals are called *periodicals* because of their recurrent or periodic publication. Journals, by the way, are compilations of scholarly articles. Articles in journals and other periodicals will be extremely useful to you because they are concise, limited in scope, current, and can supplement information in books.

Print, CD-ROM, and Web-Based Bibliographic Indexes. *The Readers' Guide to Periodical Literature* is a valuable index of general-interest magazine article titles. It includes such magazines as *Time, Newsweek, The New Yorker,* and *U.S. News & World Report*. More useful to business writers, though, will be the titles of articles appearing in business and industrial magazines (such as *Forbes, Fortune,* and *Business Week*). For an index of these publications, consult the *Business Periodicals Index*. Most indexes today are available in print, CD-ROM, and Web versions for easy searching. When using CD-ROM and Web-based online indexes, follow the on-screen instructions or ask for assistance from a librarian. It's a good idea to begin with a subject search because it generally turns up more relevant citations than keyword searches (especially when searching for names or people or companies). Once you locate usable references, print a copy of your findings and then check the shelf listings to see whether the publications are available.

ELECTRONIC DATABASES

As a writer of business reports today, you will probably begin your secondary research with electronic resources. Most writers turn to them first because they are fast, cheap, and easy to use. Some are even accessible from remote locations. This means that you can conduct detailed searches without ever leaving your office, home, or dorm room. Although some databases are still offered on CD-ROM, information is increasingly available in online databases. They have become the staple of secondary research.

Most researchers today begin by looking in electronic databases.

A database is a collection of information stored electronically so that it is accessible by computer and digitally searchable. Databases, such as InfoTrac, provide both bibliographic (titles of documents and brief abstracts) and full-text documents. Most researchers prefer full-text documents. Various databases contain a rich array of magazine, newspaper, and journal articles, as well as newsletters, business reports, company profiles, government data, reviews, and directories.

THE INTERNET

The best-known area of the Internet is the World Wide Web. Growing at a dizzying pace, the Web includes an enormous collection of specially formatted documents called *Web pages* located at Web sites around the world. Web offerings include online databases, magazines, newspapers, library resources, job and résumé banks, sound and video files, and many other information resources. Creators of Web pages use a special system of codes (HTML, i.e., Hypertext Markup Language) to format their offerings. The crucial feature of these hypertext pages is their use of links to other Web pages. Links are identified by underlined words and phrases or, occasionally, images. When clicked, the links open up related Web pages. These pages immediately download to your computer screen, thus creating a vast web of resources at your fingertips.

Web Opportunities and Frustrations.   To a business researcher, the Web offers a wide range of organizational and commercial information. You can expect to find such items as product and marketing information, public relations material, mission statements, staff directories, press releases, current company news, government information, selected article reprints, collaborative scientific project reports, and employment information. The Web is unquestionably one of the greatest sources of information now available to anyone needing facts quickly and inexpensively. But finding that information can be frustrating and time-consuming. The constantly changing contents of the Web and its lack of organization frustrate researchers. And content is not always reliable. Check out the Communication Workshop at the end of this chapter to learn more about what questions to ask in assessing the quality of a Web document.

Web Browsers and URLs.   Searching the Web requires a Web browser, such as Netscape Navigator or Microsoft Internet Explorer. Browsers are software programs that enable you to view the graphics and text of, as well as access links to, Web pages. To locate the Web page of a specific organization, you need its URL (Uniform Resource Locator). URLs are case and space sensitive, so be sure to type the address exactly as it is printed. For most companies, the URL is http://www.xyzcompany.com.   Your goal is to locate the top-level Web page of an organization's site. On this page you'll generally find an overview of the site contents or a link to a site map. If you

Copyright 2002 by Randy Glasbergen.   www.glasbergen.com

"I'm looking up some important stuff: Does tail wagging count as aerobic exercise? How long should you know someone before you lick their face? What do the etiquette rules say about drinking from the toilet?"

can't guess a company's URL, you can usually find it quickly at Hoover's (http://www.hoovers.com).

Search Tools.   The Web is packed with amazing information. Instead of visiting libraries or searching reference books when you need to find something, you can now turn to the Web for all kinds of facts. However, you'll need a good search tool, such as Google, AltaVista, or Yahoo!. A search tool is a service that indexes, organizes, and often rates and reviews Web pages. Some search tools rely on people to maintain a catalog of Web sites or pages. Others use software to identify key information. They all begin a search based on the keywords that you type in. The most-used search tool at this writing is Google. It has developed a cult-like following with its "uncanny ability to sort through millions of Web pages and put the sites you really want at the top of its results pages."[3]

Like everything else about the Web, search tools are constantly evolving as developers change their features to attract more users. Check the Guffey Web site (http://www.westwords.com/guffey/students.html) to find links to up-to-date reviews of search engines. And always read the help sections of any search engine when you first use it.

Dumb as Rocks? Internet Search Tips and Techniques.   "Search engines are dumber than a box of rocks," claims one Web veteran. For example, he says, "If you ask one to look up *bathing suits*, it will find sites on *bathing* and on *suits*,"[4] but not necessarily on the combined concept of *bathing suits*. A researcher must enclose the phrase in quotation marks so that the search engine will look for the words together. Knowing how to use search engines can transform that dumb box of rocks into a jewel case bulging with gems of useful information. Here are a few tips to make you a savvy Internet researcher:[5]

- **Use quotation marks.** When searching for a phrase, such as *cost benefit analysis*, most search tools will retrieve documents having all or some of the terms. This AND/OR strategy is the default of most search tools. To locate occurrences of a specific phrase, enclose it in quotation marks.
- **Prefer uncommon words.** Commonly used words make poor search keywords. For example, instead of *keeping employees*, use *employee retention*.
- **Omit articles and prepositions.** These are known as "stop words," and they do not add value to a search. Instead of *request for proposal*, use *proposal request*.
- **Know your search tool.** When connecting to a search service for the first time, always read the description of its service, including its FAQs (Frequently Asked Questions), Help, and How to Search sections.
- **Bookmark the best.** To keep better track of your favorite Internet sites, save them on your browser as bookmarks.
- **Use two or three search tools.** Different Internet search engines turn up different results. However, at this writing, Google consistently turns up more reliable "hits" than other search tools.
- **Understand case sensitivity.** Generally use lowercase for your searches, unless you are searching for a term that is typically written in upper- and lowercase, such as a person's name.
- **Be persistent.** If a search produces no results, check your spelling. Try synonyms and variations on words. Try to be less specific in your search term. If your search produces too many hits, try to be more specific. Think of words that uniquely identify what you're looking for. And use as many relevant keywords as possible. Repeat your search a few days later.

GENERATING PRIMARY DATA

Quick Check

Primary data come from firsthand experience.

Although you'll begin a business report by probing for secondary data, you'll probably need primary data to give a complete picture. Business reports that solve specific current problems typically rely on primary, firsthand data. If, for example, management wants to discover the cause of increased employee turnover in its Seattle office, it must investigate conditions in Seattle by collecting recent information. Providing answers to business problems often means generating primary data through surveys, interviews, observation, or experimentation.

SURVEYS

Quick Check

Surveys yield efficient and economical primary data for reports.

Surveys collect data from groups of people. When companies develop new products, for example, they often survey consumers to learn their needs. The advantages of surveys are that they gather data economically and efficiently. Mailed surveys reach big groups nearby or at great distances. Moreover, people responding to mailed surveys have time to consider their answers, thus improving the accuracy of the data.

Mailed surveys, of course, have disadvantages. Most of us rank them with junk mail, so response rates may be no higher than 2 percent. Furthermore, those who do respond may not represent an accurate sample of the overall population, thus invalidating generalizations from the group. Let's say, for example, that an insurance company sends out a survey questionnaire asking about provisions in a new policy. If only older people respond, the survey data cannot be used to generalize what people in other age groups might think. A final problem with surveys has to do with truthfulness. Some respondents exaggerate their incomes or distort other facts, thus causing the results to be unreliable. Nevertheless, surveys may be the best way to generate data for business and student reports.

INTERVIEWS

Quick Check

Interviews with experts produce useful report data, especially when little has been written about a topic.

Some of the best report information, particularly on topics about which little has been written, comes from individuals. These individuals are usually experts or veterans in their fields. Consider both in-house and outside experts for business reports. Tapping these sources will call for in-person or telephone interviews. To elicit the most useful data, try these techniques:

- **Locate an expert.** Ask managers and individuals working in an area whom they consider to be most knowledgeable. Check membership lists of professional organizations, and consult articles about the topic or related topics. Most people enjoy being experts or at least recommending them. You could also post an inquiry to an Internet *newsgroup*. An easy way to search newsgroups in a topic area is through the browse groups now indexed by the popular search tool Google.
- **Prepare for the interview.** Learn about the individual you're interviewing as well as the background and terminology of the topic. Let's say you're interviewing a corporate communication expert about producing an in-house newsletter. You ought to be familiar with terms such as *font* and software such as QuarkXpress, Adobe Pagemaker, and Ventura Publisher. In addition, be prepared by making a list of questions that pinpoint your focus on the topic. Ask the interviewee if you may record the talk.
- **Make your questions objective and friendly.** Don't get into a debating match with the interviewee. And remember that you're there to listen, not to talk! Use open-ended, rather than yes-or-no, questions to draw experts out.

Firsthand observation inspired today's best-selling toothbrush, SpinBrush. John Osher, who invented the SpinBrush with three colleagues, walked the aisles of Wal-Mart to learn more about the pricing, packaging, and styles of competitors. The information he collected, considered primary data, led to the development of the first low-priced electric brush that uses Spin Pop technology.
© Susan Van Etten

- **Watch the time.** Tell interviewees in advance how much time you expect to need for the interview. Don't overstay your appointment.
- **End graciously.** Conclude the interview with a general question, such as *Is there anything you'd like to add?* Express your appreciation, and ask permission to telephone later if you need to verify points.

OBSERVATION AND EXPERIMENTATION

Some kinds of primary data can be obtained only through firsthand observation and investigation. How long does a typical caller wait before a customer service rep answers the call? How is a new piece of equipment operated? Are complaints of sexual harassment being taken seriously? Observation produces rich data, but that information is especially prone to charges of subjectivity. One can interpret an observation in many ways. Thus, to make observations more objective, try to quantify them. For example, record customer telephone wait-time for 60-minute periods at different times throughout a week. Or compare the number of sexual harassment complaints made with the number of investigations undertaken and resulting actions.

Experimentation produces data suggesting causes and effects. Informal experimentation might be as simple as a pretest and posttest in a college course. Did students expand their knowledge as a result of the course? More formal experimentation is undertaken by scientists and professional researchers who control variables to test their effects. Assume, for example, that the Hershey Company wants to test the hypothesis (which is a tentative assumption) that chocolate lifts people out of the doldrums. An experiment testing the hypothesis would separate depressed individuals into two groups: those who ate chocolate (the experimental group) and those who did not (the control group). What effect did chocolate have? Such experiments are not done haphazardly, however. Valid experiments require sophisticated research designs and careful attention to matching the experimental and control groups.

✓ *Quick Check*

Some of the best report data come from firsthand observation and investigation.

DOCUMENTING DATA

Whether you collect data from primary or secondary sources, the data must be documented; that is, you must indicate where the data originated. Careful documentation in a report serves three purposes:

- **Strengthens your argument.** Including good data from reputable sources will convince readers of your credibility and the logic of your reasoning.
- **Protects you.** Acknowledging your sources keeps you honest. It's unethical and illegal to use others' ideas without proper documentation.
- **Instructs the reader.** Citing references enables readers to pursue a topic further and make use of the information themselves.

Using the ideas of someone else without giving credit is called *plagiarism* and is unethical. Even if you paraphrase (put the information in your own words), the ideas must be documented. You can learn more about documenting sources by studying the formal report in Figure 10.16 and by consulting Appendix C.

Citing Electronic Sources.   Standards for researchers using electronic sources are still evolving. When citing electronic media, you should hold the same goals as for print sources. That is, you want to give credit to the authors and allow others to locate the same or updated information easily. However, traditional formats for identifying authors, publication dates, and page numbers become confusing when applied to sources on the Internet. Strive to give correct credit for electronic sources by including the author's name (when available), document title, Web page title, access date, and Web address (in angle brackets). Here's an example of an Internet bibliographic citation:

> Jacobson, Trudi and Laura Cohen. "Evaluating Internet Resources." *University of Albany Libraries.* Retrieved 13 January 2003 <http://www.albany.edu/library/internet/evaluate.html>.

Formats for some electronic sources are shown in Appendix C. For more comprehensive electronic citation formats, visit the Guffey Web site.

ORGANIZING AND OUTLINING DATA

Once you've collected the data for a report and recorded that information on notes or printouts, you're ready to organize it into a coherent plan of presentation. First, you should decide on an organizational strategy, and then, following your plan, you'll want to outline the report.

ORGANIZATIONAL STRATEGIES

The readability and effectiveness of a report are greatly enhanced by skillful organization of the information presented. As you begin the process of organization, you ask yourself two important questions. (1) Where should I place the conclusions/recommendations? (2) How should I organize the findings?

Where To Place the Conclusions/Recommendations.   As you recall from earlier instruction, the direct strategy presents main ideas first. In formal reports that would mean beginning with your conclusions and recommendations. For example, if you were studying five possible locations for a proposed shopping center, you would begin with the recommendation of the best site. Use this strategy when the reader is supportive and knowledgeable. However, if the reader is not supportive or needs to be informed, the indirect strategy may be better. This involves presenting facts and discussion first, followed by conclusions and recommendations. Since formal reports often seek to educate the reader, this order of presentation is often most effective. Following this sequence, a study of possible locations for a shopping center would begin with data regarding all proposed sites followed by analysis of the information and conclusions drawn from that analysis.

"Ten crates of data and one little envelope of information. Sign here."

How To Organize the Findings.   After collecting your facts, you need a coherent plan for presenting them. We describe here three principal organizational patterns: chronological, geographical, and topical. You will find these and other patterns summarized in Figure 10.2. The pattern you choose depends on the material collected and the purpose of your report.

FIGURE 10.2 Organizational Patterns for Report Findings

PATTERN	DEVELOPMENT	USE
Chronology	Arrange information in a time sequence to show history or development of topic.	Useful in showing time relationships, such as 5-year profit figures or series or events leading to a problem
Geography/Space	Organize information by regions or areas.	Appropriate for topics that are easily divided into locations, such as East Coast, West Coast, etc.
Topic/Function	Arrange by topics or functions.	Works well for topics with established categories, such as a report about categories of company expenses
Compare/Contrast	Present problem and show alternative solutions. Use consistent criteria. Show how the solutions are similar and different.	Best used for "before and after" scenarios or for problems with clear alternatives
Journalism Pattern	Arrange information in paragraphs devoted to *who, what, when, where, why,* and *how.* May conclude with recommendations.	Useful with audiences that need to be educated or persuaded
Value/Size	Start with the most valuable, biggest, or most important item. Discuss other items in descending order.	Useful for classifying information in, for example, a realtor's report on home values
Importance	Arrange from most important to least importance or build from least to most important.	Appropriate when persuading the audience to take a specific action or change a belief
Simple/Complex	Begin with simple concept; proceed to more complex idea.	Useful for technical or abstract topics
Best Case/Worst Case	Describe the best and possibly the worst possible outcomes.	Useful when dramatic effect is needed to achieve results; helpful when audience is uninterested or uninformed

Organizing and Outlining Data

Organize report findings chronologically, geographically, spatially,
functionally, or by one of the
methods shown in Figure 10.2.

- **Chronological sequence.** Information sequenced along a time frame is arranged chronologically. This plan is effective for presenting historical data or for describing a procedure. A description of the development of a multinational company, for example, would be chronological. A report explaining how to obtain federal funding for a project might be organized chronologically. Often topics are arranged in a past-to-present or present-to-past sequence.
- **Geographical or spatial arrangement.** Information arranged geographically or spatially is organized by physical location. For instance, a report analyzing a company's national sales might be divided into sections representing different geographical areas such as the East, South, Midwest, West, and Northwest.
- **Topical or functional arrangement.** Some subjects lend themselves to arrangement by topic or function. A report analyzing changes in the management hierarchy of an organization might be arranged in this manner. First, the report would consider the duties of the CEO followed by the functions of the general manager, business manager, marketing manager, and so forth.

OUTLINES AND HEADINGS

✓ Quick Check

Huge amounts of data collected
for a report must be analyzed
into meaningful information and
organized into coherent sections.

Most writers agree that the clearest way to show the organization of a report topic is by recording its divisions in an outline. Although the outline is not part of the final report, it is a valuable tool of the writer. It reveals at a glance the overall organization of the report. As you learned in Chapter 3, outlining involves dividing a topic into major sections and supporting those with details. Figure 10.3 shows an abbreviated outline of a report about forms of business ownership. Rarely is a real outline so perfectly balanced; some sections are usually longer than others. Remember, though, not to put a single topic under a major component. If you have only one subpoint, integrate it with the main item above it or reorganize. Use details, illustrations, and evidence to support subpoints.

The main points used to outline a report often become the main headings of the written report. In Chapter 9 you studied tips for writing talking and functional headings. Formatting those headings depends on what level they represent. Major headings, as you can see in Figure 10.4, are centered and typed in bold font. Second-level headings start at the left margin, and third-level headings are indented and become part of a paragraph.

FIGURE 10.3 Outline Format

FORMS OF BUSINESS OWNERSHIP

I. Sole of proprietorship (*first main topic*)
   A. Advantages of sole proprietorship (*first subdivision of Topic I*)
      1. Minimal capital requirements (*first subdivision of Topic A*)
      2. Control by owner (*second subdivision of Topic A*)
   B. Disadvantages of sole proprietorship (*second subdivision of Topic I*)
      1. Unlimited liability (*first subdivision of Topic B*)
      2. Limited management talent (*second subdivision of Topic B*)
II. Partnership (*second main topic*)
   A. Advantages of partnership (*first subdivision of Topic II*)
      1. Access to capital (*first subdivision of Topic A*)
      2. Management talent (*second subdivision of Topic A*)
      3. Ease of formation (*third subdivision of Topic A*)
   B. Disadvantages of partnership (*second subdivision of Topic II*)
      1. Unlimited liability (*first subdivision of Topic B*)
      2. Personality conflicts (*second subdivision of Topic B*)

FIGURE 10.4 Levels of Headings in Reports

↓ 2-inch top margin

REPORT, CHAPTER, AND PART TITLES

↓ 2 blank lines

The title of a report, chapter heading, or major part (such as CONTENTS or NOTES) should be centered in all caps. If the title requires more than one line, arrange it in an inverted triangle with the longest lines at the top. Begin the text a triple space (two blank lines) below the title, as shown here.

↓ 2 blank lines

First-Level Subheading

↓ 1 blank line

Headings indicating the first level of division are centered and bolded. Capitalize the first letter of each main word. Whether a report is single-spaced or double-spaced, most typists triple-space (leaving two blank lines) before and double-space (leaving one blank line) after a first-level subheading.

↓ 1 blank line

Every level of heading should be followed by some text. For example, we could not jump from "First-Level Subheading," shown above, to "Second-Level Subheading," shown below, without some discussion between.

Good writers strive to develop coherency and fluency by ending most sections with a lead-in that introduces the next section. The lead-in consists of a sentence or two announcing the next topic.

↓ 2 blank lines

Second-Level Subheading

Headings that divide topics introduced by first-level subheadings are bolded and begin at the left margin. Use a triple space above and a double space after a second-level subheading. If a report has only one level of heading, use either first- or second-level subheading style.

Always be sure to divide topics into two or more subheadings. If you have only one subheading eliminate it and absorb the discussion under the previous major heading. Try to make all headings within a level grammatically equal. For example, all second-level headings might use verb forms (*Preparing*, *Organizing*, and *Composing*) or noun forms (*Preparation*, *Organization*, and *Composition*).

↓ 1 blank line

Third-level subheading. Because it is part of the paragraph that follows, a third-level subheading is also called a "paragraph subheading." Capitalize only the first word and proper nouns in the subheading. Bold the subheading and end it with a period. Begin typing the paragraph text immediately following the period, as shown here. Double-space before a paragraph subheading.

Left side annotations:
- Capitalizes initial letters of main words
- Starts at left margin
- Makes heading part of paragraph

Right side annotations:
- Places major headings in the center
- Does not indent paragraphs because report is single-spaced

ILLUSTRATING DATA

After collecting information and interpreting it, you need to consider how best to present it to your audience. Whether you are delivering your report orally or in writing to company insiders or to outsiders, it will be easier to understand and remember if you include suitable graphics. Appropriate graphics make numerical data meaningful, simplify complex ideas, and provide visual interest. In contrast, readers tend to be bored and confused by text paragraphs packed with complex data and numbers. The same information summarized in a table or chart becomes clear.

Because data can be shown in many different forms (for example, in a chart, table, or graph), you need to recognize how to match the appropriate graphic with

Quick Check
Effective graphics clarify numerical data and simplify complex ideas.

FIGURE 10.5 Matching Graphics to Objectives

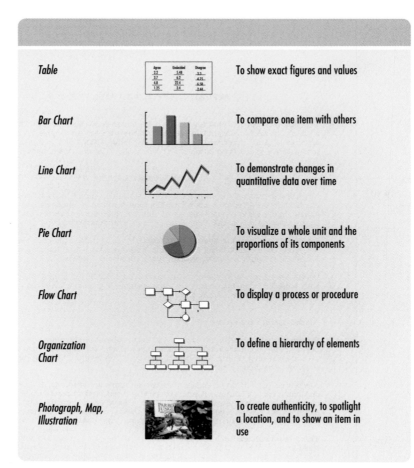

your objective. In addition, you need to know how to incorporate graphics into your reports.

MATCHING GRAPHICS AND OBJECTIVES

In developing the best graphics, you should first decide what data you want to highlight. Chances are you will have many points you would like to show in a table or chart. But which graphics are most appropriate to your objectives? Figure 10.5 summarizes appropriate uses for each type of graphics. Let's look at each kind of graphic in greater detail so that you can use it effectively.

TABLES

Tables permit systematic presentation of large amounts of data, while charts enhance visual comparisons.

Probably the most frequently used visual aid in reports is the table. A table presents quantitative information in a systematic order of columns and rows. Here are tips for making good tables, one of which is illustrated in Figure 10.6.

- Provide clear heads for the rows and columns.
- Identify the units in which figures are given (percentages, dollars, units per worker hour, and so forth) in the table title, in the column or row head, with the first item in a column, or in a note at the bottom.

FIGURE 10.6 Table Summarizing Precise Data

FIGURE 1
MPM ENTERTAINMENT COMPANY
Income by Division (in millions of dollars)

	THEME PARKS	MOTION PICTURES	VIDEO	TOTAL
2000	$15.8	$39.3	$11.2	$66.3
2001	18.1	17.5	15.3	50.9
2002	23.8	21.1	22.7	67.6
2003	32.2	22.0	24.3	78.5
2004 (projected)	35.1	21.0	26.1	82.2

Source: *Industry Profiles* (New York: DataPro, 2003), 225.

- Place titles and labels at the top of the table.
- Arrange items in a logical order (alphabetical, chronological, geographical, highest to lowest) depending on what you need to emphasize.
- Use *N/A* (not available) for missing data.
- Make long tables easier to read by shading alternate lines or by leaving a blank line after groups of five.
- Place tables as close as possible to the place where they are mentioned in the text.

BAR CHARTS

Although they lack the precision of tables, bar charts enable you to make emphatic visual comparisons. Bar charts can be used to compare related items, illustrate changes in data over time, and show segments as part of a whole. Figures 10.7 through 10.10 show vertical, horizontal, grouped, and segmented bar charts that highlight some of the data shown in the MPM Entertainment Company table (Figure 10.6). Note how the varied bar charts present information in different ways.

FIGURE 10.7 Vertical Bar Chart

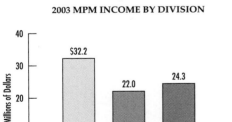

Source: *Industry Profiles* (New York: DataPro, 2003), 225.

FIGURE 10.8 Horizontal Bar Chart

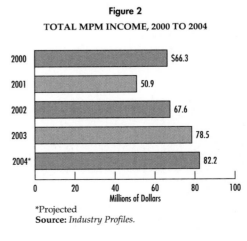

*Projected
Source: *Industry Profiles.*

Illustrating Data

FIGURE 10.9 Grouped Bar Chart FIGURE 10.10 Segmented 100% Bar Chart

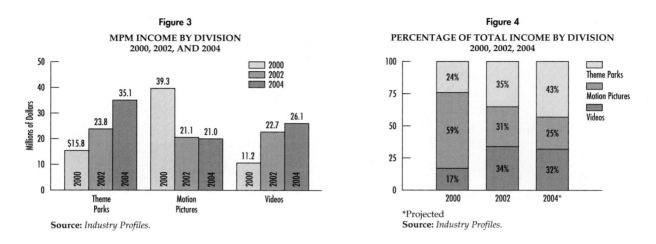

Many suggestions for tables also hold true for bar charts. Here are a few additional tips:

- Keep the length of each bar and segment proportional.
- Include a total figure in the middle of a bar or at its end if the figure helps the reader and does not clutter the chart.
- Start dollar or percentage amounts at zero.
- Avoid showing too much information, which produces clutter and confusion.

LINE CHARTS

✓ *Quick Check*

Line charts illustrate trends and changes in data over time.

The major advantage of line charts is that they show changes over time, thus indicating trends. Figures 10.11 through 10.13 show line charts that reflect income trends for the three divisions of MPM. Notice that line charts do not provide precise data, such as the 2003 MPM Videos income. Instead, they give an overview or impression of the data. Experienced report writers use tables to list exact data; they use line charts or bar charts to spotlight important points or trends.

FIGURE 10.11 Simple Line Chart   **FIGURE 10.12 Multiple Line Chart**

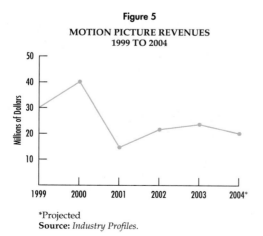

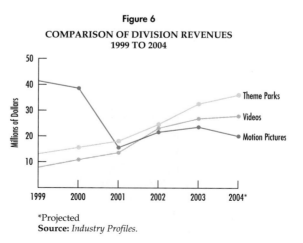

Chapter 10   Proposals and Formal Reports

FIGURE 10.13 Segmented Line (Surface) Chart　　　　**FIGURE 10.14 Pie Chart**

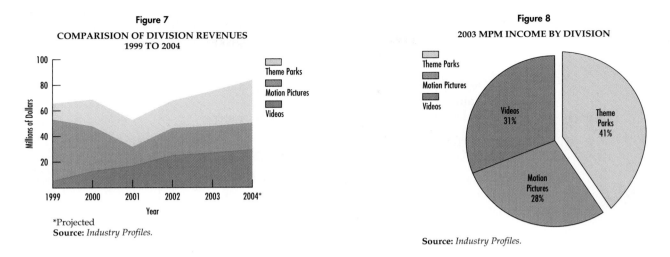

Figure 7
COMPARISION OF DIVISION REVENUES
1999 TO 2004

*Projected
Source: *Industry Profiles.*

Figure 8
2003 MPM INCOME BY DIVISION

Source: *Industry Profiles.*

Simple line charts (Figure 10.11) show just one variable. Multiple line charts combine several variables (Figure 10.12). Segmented line charts (Figure 10.13), also called *surface charts*, illustrate how the components of a whole change over time. Notice that Figure 10.13 helps you visualize the shift in total MPM income from motion pictures to videos and theme parks. By contrast, tables don't permit such visualization.

Here are tips for preparing line charts:

- Begin with a grid divided into squares.
- Arrange the time component (usually years) horizontally across the bottom; arrange values for the other variable vertically.
- Draw small dots at the intersections to indicate each value at a given year.
- Connect the dots and add color if desired.
- To prepare a segmented (surface) chart, plot the first value (say, video income) across the bottom; add the next item (say, motion picture income) to the first figures for every increment; for the third item (say, theme park income) add its value to the total of the first two items. The top line indicates the total of the three values.

PIE CHARTS

Pie, or circle, charts enable readers to see a whole and the proportion of its components, or wedges. Although less flexible than bar or line charts, pie charts are useful in showing percentages, as Figure 10.14 illustrates. Notice that a wedge can be "exploded" or popped out for special emphasis, as seen in Figure 10.14. For the most effective pie charts, follow these suggestions:

- Begin at the 12 o'clock position, drawing the largest wedge first. (Computer software programs don't always observe this advice, but if you're drawing your own charts, you can.)
- Include, if possible, the actual percentage or absolute value for each wedge.
- Use four to eight segments for best results; if necessary, group small portions into one wedge called "Other."
- Distinguish wedges with color, shading, or cross-hatching.
- Keep all labels horizontal.

✓ *Quick Check*

Pie charts are most useful in showing the proportion of parts to a whole.

FLOW CHARTS

Quick Check

Flow charts use standard symbols to illustrate a process or procedure.

Procedures are simplified and clarified by diagramming them in a flow chart, as shown in Figure 10.15. Whether you need to describe the procedure for handling a customer's purchase order or outline steps in solving a problem, flow charts help the reader visualize the process. Traditional flow charts use the following symbols:

- Ovals to designate the beginning and end of a process
- Diamonds to denote decision points
- Rectangles to represent major activities or steps

USING YOUR COMPUTER TO PRODUCE CHARTS

Quick Check

Computer software programs enable you to produce top-quality graphics quickly and cheaply.

Designing effective bar charts, pie charts, figures, and other graphics is easy with today's software. Spreadsheet programs such as Excel, Lotus 1-2-3, and Corel QuattroPro, as well as presentation graphics programs such as Microsoft PowerPoint, allow even nontechnical people to design high-quality graphics. These graphics can be printed directly on paper for written reports or used for transparency masters and slides for oral presentations. The benefits of preparing visual aids on a computer are near-professional quality, shorter preparation time, and substantial cost savings. To prepare computer graphics, follow these steps:

- Assemble your data, usually in table form (such as that in Figure 10.6).
- Choose a chart type, such as pie chart, grouped bar chart, vertical bar chart, horizontal bar chart, organization chart, or some other graphic.
- To make a pie chart, key in the data or select the data from an existing file.
- Add a title for the chart as well as any necessary labels.
- To make a bar or line chart, indicate the horizontal and vertical axes (reference lines or beginning points).
- Verify the legend, which your program may generate automatically.
- Print the final chart on paper or import into another program.

FIGURE 10.15 Flow Chart

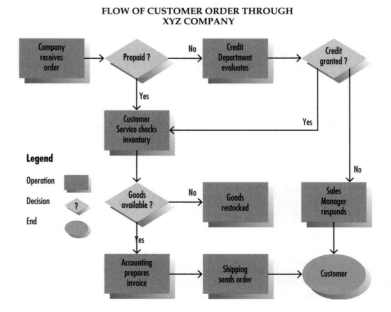

Presenting the Final Report

Long reports are generally organized into three major divisions: (1) prefatory parts, (2) body, and (3) supplementary parts. Following is a description of the order and content of each part. Refer to the model formal report in Figure 10.16 for illustrations of most of these parts.

Prefatory Parts (Preceding the Body of Report)

Title Page.   A report title page, as illustrated in Figure 10.16, begins with the name of the report typed in uppercase letters (no underscore and no quotation marks). Next comes *Prepared for* (or *Submitted to*) and the name, title, and organization of the individual receiving the report. Lower on the page is *Prepared by* (or *Submitted by*) and the author's name plus any necessary identification. The last item on the title page is the date of submission. All items after the title appear in a combination of upper- and lowercase letters.

Letter of Transmittal.   Generally written on organization stationery, a letter or memorandum of transmittal introduces a formal report. You will recall that letters are sent to outsiders and memos to insiders. A transmittal letter or memo follows the direct pattern and is usually less formal than the report itself. For example, the letter or memo may use contractions and first-person pronouns such as *I* and *we*. The following suggestions will help you structure an effective letter of transmittal:

- Deliver the report ("Here is the report you authorized").
- Present an overview of the report.
- Suggest how to read or interpret it.
- Describe limitations, if they exist.
- Acknowledge those who assisted you.
- Suggest follow-up studies, if appropriate.
- Offer to discuss the report personally.
- Express appreciation for the assignment.

Table of Contents.   The table of contents shows the headings in a report and their page numbers. It gives an overview of the report topics and helps readers locate them. You should wait to prepare the table of contents until after you've completed the report. For short reports include all headings. For longer reports you might want to list only first- and second-level headings. Leaders (spaced or unspaced dots) help guide the eye from the heading to the page number. Items may be indented in outline form or typed flush with the left margin.

Executive Summary, Abstract, Synopsis, or Epitome.   A summary condensing the entire report may carry any of these names. This time-saving device summarizes the purpose, findings, and conclusions. Chapter 9 discussed how to write an executive summary and included an example in Figure 9.9. You can see another executive summary on page iii of Figure 10.16.

> **✓ Quick Check**
>
> A letter or memo of transmittal presents an overview of the report, suggests how to read it, describes limitations, acknowledges assistance, and expresses appreciation.

FIGURE 10.16 Model Format Report

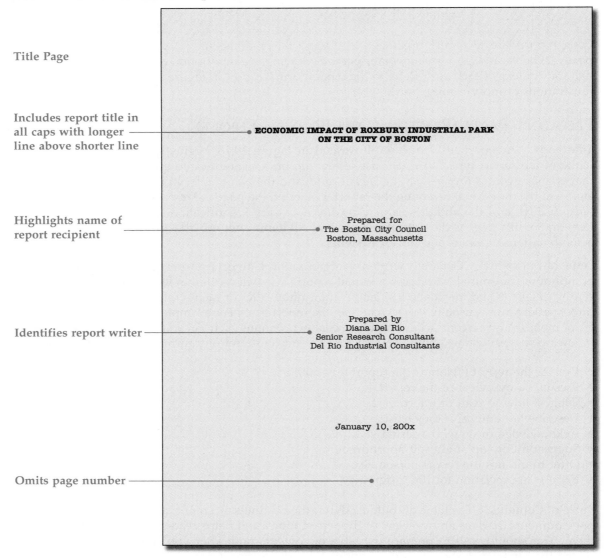

Title Page

Includes report title in all caps with longer line above shorter line

> **ECONOMIC IMPACT OF ROXBURY INDUSTRIAL PARK**
> **ON THE CITY OF BOSTON**

Highlights name of report recipient

> Prepared for
> The Boston City Council
> Boston, Massachusetts

Identifies report writer

> Prepared by
> Diana Del Rio
> Senior Research Consultant
> Del Rio Industrial Consultants

> January 10, 200x

Omits page number

The title page is usually arranged in four evenly balanced areas. If the report is to be bound on the left, move the left margin and center point ¼ inch to the right. Notice that no page number appears on the title page, although it is counted as page i. In designing the title page, be careful to avoid anything unprofessional—such as too many type fonts, italics, oversized print, and inappropriate graphics. Keep the title page simple and professional.

FIGURE 10.16 (Continued) Letter of Transmittal

DEL RIO INDUSTRIAL CONSULTANTS

588 Park Avenue
Boston, Massachusetts 02116

www.delrio.com
(617) 549-1101

January 12, 200x

City Council
City of Boston
Boston, MA 02290

Dear Council Members:

The attached report, requested by the Boston City Council in a letter to Goldman-Lyon & Associates dated May 20, describes the economic impact of Roxbury Industrial Park on the city of Boston. We believe you will find the results of this study useful in evaluating future development of industrial parks within the city limits. — Announces report and identifies authorization

This study was designed to examine economic impact in three areas:

- Current and projected tax and other revenues accruing to the city from Roxbury Industrial Park — Gives broad overview of report purposes

- Current and projected employment generated by the park

- Indirect effects on local employment, income, and economic growth

Primary research consisted of interviews with 15 Roxbury Industrial Park tenants and managers, in addition to a 2001 survey of over 5,000 RIP employees. Secondary research sources included the Annual Budget of the City of Boston, county and state tax records, government publications, periodicals, books, and online resources. Results of this research, discussed more fully in this report, indicate that Roxbury Industrial Park exerts a significant beneficial influence on the Boston metropolitan economy. — Describes primary and secondary research

We would be pleased to discuss this report and its conclusions with you at your request. My firm and I thank you for your confidence in selecting our company to prepare this comprehensive report. — Offers to discuss report; expresses appreciation

Sincerely,

Diana Del Rio

Diana Del Rio
Senior Research Consultant

DDR:mef
Attachment

A letter or memo of transmittal announces the report topic and explains who authorized it. It briefly describes the project and previews the conclusions, if the reader is supportive. Such messages generally close by expressing appreciation for the assignment, suggesting follow-up actions, acknowledging the help of others, or offering to answer questions. The margins for the transmittal should be the same as for the report, about 1 to 1¼ inches on all sides.

FIGURE 10.16 **(Continued) Table of Contents and List of Figures**

Uses leaders to guide eye from heading to page number

Indents secondary headings to show levels of outline

Includes tables and figures in one list for simplified numbering

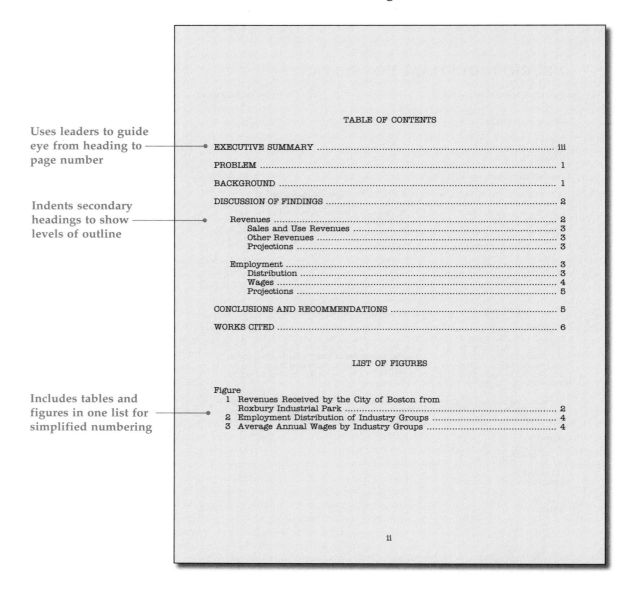

TABLE OF CONTENTS

LIST OF FIGURES

Figure

ii

Because the table of contents and the list of figures for this report are small, they are combined on one page. Notice that the titles of major report parts are in all caps, while other headings are a combination of upper- and lowercase letters. The style duplicates those within the report. Advanced word processing capabilities enable you to generate a contents page automatically—including leaders and accurate page numbering—no matter how many times you revise.

FIGURE 10.16 (Continued) Executive Summary

EXECUTIVE SUMMARY

The city of Boston can benefit from the development of industrial parks like the Roxbury Industrial Park. Both direct and indirect economic benefits result, as shown by this in-depth study conducted by Del Rio Industrial Consultants. The study was authorized by the Boston City Council when Goldman-Lyon & Associates sought the City Council's approval for the proposed construction of a G-L industrial park. The City Council requested evidence demonstrating that an existing development could actually benefit the city.

Our conclusion that the city of Boston benefits from industrial parks is based on data supplied by a survey of 5,000 Roxbury Industrial Park employees, personal interviews with managers and tenants of RIP, city and state documents, and professional literature.

Analysis of the data revealed benefits in three areas:

• Revenues. The city of Boston earned nearly $1 million in tax and other revenues from the Roxbury Industrial Park in 1997. By 2004 this income is expected to reach $1.7 million (in constant 1997 dollars).

• Employment. In 1997, RIP businesses employed a total of 7,035 workers, who earned an average wage of $24,920. By 2004, RIP businesses are expected to employ directly nearly 15,000 employees who will earn salaries totaling over $450 million.

• Indirect benefits. Because of the multiplier effect, by 2004 Roxbury Industrial Park will directly and indirectly generate a total of 38,362 jobs in the Boston metropolitan area.

On the basis of these findings, it is recommended that development of additional industrial parks be encouraged to stimulate local economic growth.

iii

Opens directly with major research findings

Identifies data sources

Summarizes organization of report

Condenses recommendations

An executive summary or abstract highlights report findings, conclusions, and recommendations. Its length depends on the report it summarizes. A 100-page report might require a 10-page summary. Shorter reports may contain 1-page summaries, as shown here. Unlike letters of transmittal (which may contain personal pronouns and references to the writer), the executive summary of a long report is formal and impersonal. It uses the same margins as the body of the report. See Chapter 9 for additional discussion of executive summaries and for an example of a business plan summary.

FIGURE 10.16 (Continued) Page 1

ECONOMIC IMPACT OF ROXBURY INDUSTRIAL PARK

PROBLEM

This study was designed to analyze the direct and indirect economic impact of Roxbury Industrial Park on the city of Boston. Specifically, the study seeks answers to these questions:

Lists three problem questions

- What current tax and other revenues result directly from this park? What tax and other revenues may be expected in the future?

- How many and what kind of jobs are directly attributable to the park? What is the employment picture for the future?

- What indirect effects has Roxbury Industrial Park had on local employment, incomes, and economic growth?

BACKGROUND

Describes authorization for report and background of study

The development firm of Goldman-Lyon & Associates commissioned this study of Roxbury Industrial Park at the request of the Boston City Council. Before authorizing the development of a proposed Goldman-Lyon industrial park, the City Council requested a study examining the economic effects of an existing park. Members of the City Council wanted to determine to what extent industrial parks benefit the local community, and they chose Roxbury Industrial Park as an example.

For those who are unfamiliar with it, Roxbury Industrial Park is a 400-acre industrial park located in the city of Boston about 4 miles from the center of the city. Most of the area lies within a specially designated area known as Redevelopment Project No. 2, which is under the jurisdiction of the Boston Redevelopment Agency. Planning for the park began in 1989; construction started in 1991.

1

The first page of a formal report contains the title printed 2 inches from the top edge. Titles for major parts of a report are centered in all caps. In this model document we show functional headings such as *PROBLEM, BACKGROUND, FINDINGS,* and *CONCLUSIONS.* However, most business reports would use descriptive headings or a combination such as *FINDINGS REVEAL REVENUE AND EMPLOYMENT BENEFITS.* First-level headings (such as *Employment* on page 3) are printed with bold upper- and lowercase letters. Second-level headings (such as *Distribution* on page 3) begin at the side. See Figure 10.4 for an illustration of heading formats.

FIGURE 10.16 (Continued) Page 2

The park now contains 14 building complexes with over 1.25 million square feet of completed building space. The majority of the buildings are used for office, research and development, marketing and distribution, or manufacturing uses. Approximately 50 acres of the original area are yet to be developed.

Data for this report came from a 2001 survey of over 5,000 Roxbury Industrial Park employees, interviews with 15 RIP tenants and managers, the Annual Budget of the City of Boston, county and state tax records, current books, articles, journals, and online resources. Projections for future revenues resulted from analysis of past trends and "Estimates of Revenues for Debt Service Coverage, Redevelopment Project Area 2" (Miller 79).

Provides specifics for data sources

DISCUSSION OF FINDINGS

Uses functional heading

The results of this research indicate that major direct and indirect benefits have accrued to the city of Boston and surrounding metropolitan areas as a result of the development of Roxbury Industrial Park. The research findings presented here fall into three categories: (a) revenues, (b) employment, and (c) indirect effects.

Previews organization of report

Revenues

Roxbury Industrial Park contributes a variety of tax and other revenues to the city of Boston, as summarized in Figure 1. Current revenues are shown, along with projections to the year 2006. At a time when the economy is unstable, revenues from an industrial park such as Roxbury can become a reliable income stream for the city of Boston.

Figure 1

Places figure close to textual reference

REVENUES RECEIVED BY THE CITY OF BOSTON
FROM ROXBURY INDUSTRIAL PARK

Current Revenues and Projections to 2006

	2001	2006
Sales and use taxes	$604,140	$1,035,390
Revenues from licenses	126,265	216,396
Franchise taxes	75,518	129,424
State gas tax receipts	53,768	92,134
Licenses and permits	48,331	82,831
Other revenues	64,039	111,987
Total	$972,061	$1,668,162

Source: Massachusetts State Board of Equalization *Bulletin*. Boston: State Printing Office, 2003, 103.

2

Notice that this formal report is single-spaced. Many businesses prefer this space-saving format. However, some organizations prefer double-spacing, especially for preliminary drafts. If you single-space, do not indent paragraphs. If you double-space, do indent the paragraphs. Page numbers may be centered 1 inch from the bottom of the page or placed 1 inch from the upper right corner at the margin. Strive to leave a minimum of 1 inch for top, bottom, and side margins. References follow the parenthetical citation style of the Modern Language Association (MLA). Notice that the author's name and a page reference appear in parentheses. This model document uses functional headings to clarify sections for student readers. Business readers might prefer "talking" or descriptive headings such as *RESEARCH REVEALS REVENUE AND EMPLOYMENT BENEFITS*.

FIGURE 10.16 (Continued) Page 3

Continues interpreting figures in table

Sales and Use Revenues

As shown in Figure 1, the city's largest source of revenues from RIP is the sales and use tax. Revenues from this source totaled $604,140 in 2001, according to figures provided by the Massachusetts State Board of Equalization (26). Sales and use taxes accounted for more than half of the park's total contribution to the city of $972,061.

Other Revenues

Other major sources of city revenues from RIP in 2001 include alcohol licenses, motor vehicle in lieu fees, trailer coach licenses ($126,265), franchise taxes ($75,518), and state gas tax receipts ($53,768). Although not shown in Figure 1, other revenues may be expected from the development of recently acquired property. The U.S. Economic Development Administration has approved a grant worth $775,000 to assist in expanding the current park eastward on an undeveloped parcel purchased last year. Revenues from leasing this property may be sizeable.

Projections

Includes ample description of electronic reference

Total city revenues from RIP will nearly double by 2006, producing an income of $1.7 million. This estimate is based on an annual growth rate of 1.4 percent, as projected by the Bureau of Labor Statistics and reported at the Web site of Infoplease.com ("Economic Outlook Through 2008").

Employment

One of the most important factors to consider in the overall effect of an industrial park is employment. In Roxbury Industrial Park the distribution, number, and wages of people employed will change considerably in the next five years.

Sets stage for next topics to be discussed

Distribution

A total of 7,035 employees currently work in various industry groups at Roxbury Industrial Park. The distribution of employees is shown in Figure 2. The largest number of workers (58 percent) is employed in manufacturing and assembly operations. In the next largest category, the computer and electronics industry employs 24 percent of the workers. Some overlap probably exists because electronics assembly could be included in either group. Employees also work in publishing (9 percent), warehousing and storage (5 percent), and other industries (4 percent).

Although the distribution of employees at Roxbury Industrial Park shows a wide range of employment categories, it must be noted that other industrial parks would likely generate an entirely different range of job categories.

3

Only the most important research findings are interpreted and discussed for readers. The depth of discussion depends on the intended length of the report, the goal of the writer, and the expectations of the reader. Because the writer wants this report to be formal in tone, she avoids *I* and *we* in all discussions.

FIGURE 10.16 (Continued) Page 4

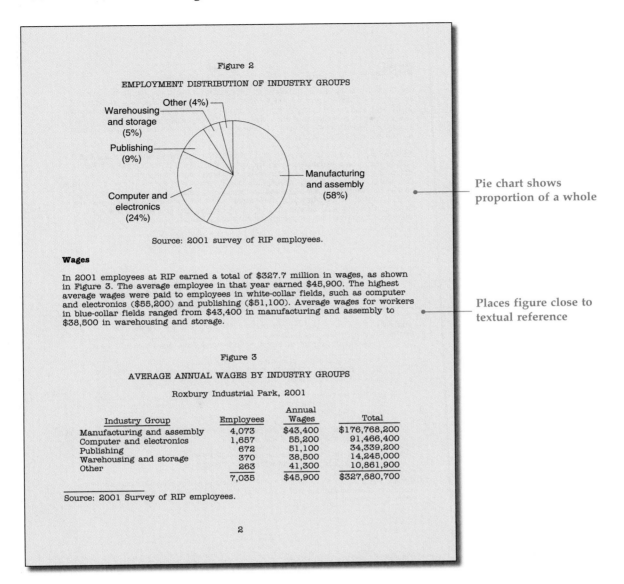

Figure 2

EMPLOYMENT DISTRIBUTION OF INDUSTRY GROUPS

Other (4%)

Warehousing
and storage
(5%)

Publishing
(9%)

Manufacturing
and assembly
(58%)

Computer and
electronics
(24%)

Source: 2001 survey of RIP employees.

Pie chart shows
proportion of a whole

Wages

In 2001 employees at RIP earned a total of $327.7 million in wages, as shown in Figure 3. The average employee in that year earned $45,900. The highest average wages were paid to employees in white-collar fields, such as computer and electronics ($55,200) and publishing ($51,100). Average wages for workers in blue-collar fields ranged from $43,400 in manufacturing and assembly to $38,500 in warehousing and storage.

Places figure close to
textual reference

Figure 3

AVERAGE ANNUAL WAGES BY INDUSTRY GROUPS

Roxbury Industrial Park, 2001

Industry Group	Employees	Annual Wages	Total
Manufacturing and assembly	4,073	$43,400	$176,768,200
Computer and electronics	1,657	55,200	91,466,400
Publishing	672	51,100	34,339,200
Warehousing and storage	370	38,500	14,245,000
Other	263	41,300	10,861,900
	7,035	$45,900	$327,680,700

Source: 2001 Survey of RIP employees.

2

If you use figures or tables, be sure to introduce them in the text (for example, *as shown in Figure 3*). Although it's not alway possible, try to place them close to the spot where they are first mentioned. To save space, you can print the title of a figure at its side. Because this report contains few tables and figures, the writer named them all "Figures" and numbered them consecutively.

FIGURE 10.16 (Continued) Page 5

Projections

By 2006 Roxbury Industrial Park is expected to more than double its number of employees, bringing the total to over 15,000 workers. The total payroll in 2006 will also more than double, producing over $656 million (using constant 2001 dollars) in salaries to RIP employees. These projections are based on an 8 percent growth rate (Miller 78), along with anticipated increased employment as the park reaches its capacity.

Future development in the park will influence employment and payrolls. One RIP project manager stated in an interview that much of the remaining 50 acres is planned for medium-rise office buildings, garden offices, and other structures for commercial, professional, and personal services (Novak). Average wages for employees are expected to increase because of an anticipated shift to higher-paying white-collar jobs. Industrial parks often follow a similar pattern of evolution (Badri 41). Like many industrial parks, RIP evolved from a warehousing center into a manufacturing complex.

CONCLUSIONS AND RECOMMENDATIONS

Analysis of tax revenues, employment data, personal interviews, and professional literature leads to the following conclusions and recommendations about the economic impact of Roxbury Industrial Park on the city of Boston:

1. Sales tax and other revenues produced nearly $1 million in income to the city of Boston in 2001. By 2006 sales tax and other revenues are expected to produce $1.7 million in city income.

2. RIP currently employs 7,035 employees, the majority of whom are working in manufacturing and assembly. The average employee in 2001 earned $45,900.

3. By 2006 RIP is expected to employ more than 15,000 workers producing a total payroll of over $656 million.

4. Employment trends indicate that by 2006 more RIP employees will be engaged in higher-paying white-collar positions.

On the basis of these findings, we recommend that the City Council of Boston authorize the development of additional industrial parks to stimulate local economic growth.

5

Clarifies information and tells what it means in relation to original research questions

Summarizes conclusions and recommendations

After discussing and interpreting the research findings, the writer articulates what she considers the most important conclusions and recommendations. Longer, more complex reports may have separate sections for conclusions and resulting recommendations. In this report they are combined. Notice that it is unnecessary to start a new page for the conclusions.

FIGURE 10.16 (Continued) Bibliography

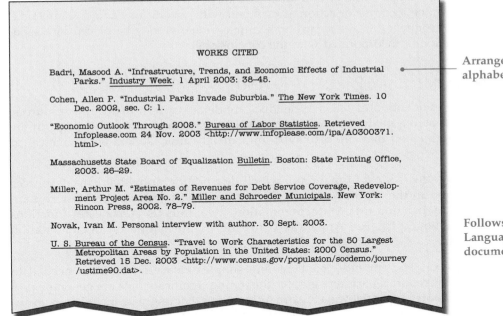

WORKS CITED

Badri, Masood A. "Infrastructure, Trends, and Economic Effects of Industrial Parks." Industry Week. 1 April 2003: 38–45.

Cohen, Allen P. "Industrial Parks Invade Suburbia." The New York Times. 10 Dec. 2002, sec. C: 1.

"Economic Outlook Through 2008." Bureau of Labor Statistics. Retrieved Infoplease.com 24 Nov. 2003 <http://www.infoplease.com/ipa/A0300371.html>.

Massachusetts State Board of Equalization Bulletin. Boston: State Printing Office, 2003. 26–29.

Miller, Arthur M. "Estimates of Revenues for Debt Service Coverage, Redevelopment Project Area No. 2." Miller and Schroeder Municipals. New York: Rincon Press, 2002. 78–79.

Novak, Ivan M. Personal interview with author. 30 Sept. 2003.

U. S. Bureau of the Census. "Travel to Work Characteristics for the 50 Largest Metropolitan Areas by Population in the United States: 2000 Census." Retrieved 15 Dec. 2003 <http://www.census.gov/population/socdemo/journey/ustime90.dat>.

Arranges references in alphabetical order

Follows Modern Language Association documentation style

BODY OF REPORT

Introduction or Background. After the prefatory parts, begin the body of the report with an introduction that includes any or all of the following items:

- Explanation of how the report originated and why it was authorized
- Description of the problem that prompted the report and the specific research questions to be answered
- Purpose of the report
- Scope (boundaries) and limitations or restrictions of the research
- Sources and methods of collecting data
- Summary of findings, if the report is written deductively
- Preview of the major sections of the report to follow, thus providing coherence and transition for the reader

Discussion of Findings. This is the main section of the report and contains numerous headings and subheadings. It is unnecessary to use the title *Discussion of Findings*; many business report writers prefer to begin immediately with the major headings into which the body of the report is divided. As summarized in Figure 10.2, you may organize the findings chronologically, geographically, topically, or by some other method. Regardless of the organizational pattern, present your findings logically and objectively. Avoid the use of first-person pronouns (*I, we*). Include tables, charts, and graphs if necessary to illustrate findings. Analytic and scientific reports may include another section titled *Implications of Findings*, in which the findings are analyzed and related to the problem. Less formal reports contain the author's analysis of the research findings within the *Discussion* section.

Summary, Conclusions, Recommendations. If the report has been largely informational, it ends with a summary of the data presented. If the report analyzes re-

> **✓ Quick Check**
>
> The body of a report includes an introduction; discussion of findings; and summary, conclusions, or recommendations.

search findings, then it ends with conclusions drawn from the analyses. An analytic report frequently poses research questions. The conclusion to such a report reviews the major findings and answers the research questions. If a report seeks to determine a course of action, it may end with conclusions and recommendations. Recommendations regarding a course of action may be placed in a separate section or incorporated with the conclusions.

SUPPLEMENTARY PARTS OF REPORT

Footnotes or Endnotes.   See Appendix C for details on how to document sources. In the footnote method the source notes appear at the foot of each page. In the endnote method they are displayed immediately after the text on a page called *Notes*.

Quick Check

Endnotes, a bibliography, and appendixes may appear after the body of the report.

Bibliography.   Most formal reports include a bibliography that lists all sources consulted in the report research. Our model report follows the Modern Language Association (MLA) documentation style; thus its *Works Cited* functions as a bibliography. See Appendix C for more information on documentation formats.

Appendix.   The appendix contains any supplementary information needed to clarify the report. Charts and graphs illustrating significant data are generally part of the report proper. However, extra information that might be included in an appendix are such items as a sample survey, a survey cover letter, correspondence relating to the report, maps, other reports, and optional tables.

SUMMING UP AND LOOKING FORWARD

Proposals are offers to solve problems, provide services, or sell equipment. Both small and large businesses today write proposals to generate income. Informal proposals may be as short as 2 pages; formal proposals may be 200 pages or more. Regardless of the size, proposals contain standard parts that must be developed persuasively.

Formal reports present well-organized information systematically. The information may be collected from primary or secondary sources. All ideas borrowed from others must be documented. Good reports contain appropriate headings and illustrations.

Written reports are vital to decision makers. But oral reports can be equally important. In the next chapter you will learn how to organize and make oral presentations, as well as how to conduct meetings and communicate effectively on the telephone.

CRITICAL THINKING

1. Why is proposal writing an important function in many businesses?
2. Discuss this statement, made by three well-known professional business writers: "Nothing you write will be completely new."[6]
3. Is information obtained on the Web as reliable as information obtained from journals, newspapers, and magazines? Explain.
4. Should all reports be written so that they follow the sequence of investigation—that is, description of the initial problem, analysis of issues, data collection, data analysis, and conclusions? Why or why not?
5. Distinguish between primary and secondary data. Which data are more likely to be useful in a business report?

CHAPTER REVIEW

6. What are the six principal parts of an informal proposal? Be prepared to explain each.

7. How are formal proposals different from informal proposals?

8. What is the first step in writing a formal report?

9. Do formal business reports generally rely more heavily on primary or secondary data?

10. List four sources of secondary information, and be prepared to discuss how valuable each might be in writing a formal report about updating your company's accounting procedures.

11. Define these terms: browser, URL, search tool

Chapter Review

295

12. List four levels of headings, and explain how they are different.

13. Pie charts are most helpful in showing what?

    Line graphs are most effective in showing what?

14. List three reasons for documenting data in a business report.

15. List the parts of a formal report. Be prepared to discuss each.

ACTIVITIES AND CASES

TEAM

10.1 RESEARCHING SECONDARY AND PRIMARY DATA. In teams, discuss how you would collect information for each of the following report topics. Would your research be primary, secondary, or a combination of methods? What resources would be most useful—books, articles, the Web, interviewing?

a. The history of unions

b. Which public relations firm will best improve the image of a company so that its stock price increases

c. The cause of the high absenteeism in one department of a company

d. The latest Occupational Safety and Health Administration (OSHA) rulings that might affect your small business

e. The traffic count at a possible location for a fast-food restaurant

f. What the heads of three departments think about changing the official routine for developing each year's budget in your company

g. The costs and features of a new telephone/voice mail system for your company

h. How users are reacting to a new accounting software program recently released

i. How to meet international quality standards (ISO certification) so that you can sell your products in Europe

10.2 OUTLINING.   You work for a recruiting firm that helps businesses find candidates for jobs. Over the years, many clients have asked for suggestions on the best way to interview job candidates. Your boss asks you to write a short report on how to become a great interviewer. Here are some ideas you gathered from your own experience and that of other recruiters:

One of the most important qualities of a successful interview is efficient use of the interview time. Most businesspeople hate the hiring process because it interrupts their daily routine and throws off their schedules. But you have found that if you block out an afternoon or a whole day, you don't feel so frustrated. Shutting out all interruptions and setting aside 45 minutes for each interview can also be helpful.

Interviewing is an inexact art because judging the talents and abilities of people is subjective. To select the best candidate, you must begin with a list of all the job duties. Then you select the three duties with the highest priorities. Naturally, you would then ask questions to discover what candidate can perform those duties best.

Every interview should have objectives. What do you want to achieve? One of the most important goals is uncovering the experience that qualifies the candidate to do the job. Another important element is the correlation you see between the candidate and your company's values. A major final objective is selling the candidate on the opportunity with your company.

Your Task. Select the most important information and organize it into an outline such as that shown in Figure 10.3. You should have three main topics with three subdivisions under each. Assume that you would gather more information later. Add a title.

10.3 SELECTING VISUAL AIDS.   In teams identify the best visual aid (table, bar chart, line chart, pie chart, flow chart, organization chart) to illustrate the following data:

TEAM

a. Instructions for workers telling them how to distinguish between worker accidents that must be reported to state and federal agencies and those that need not be reported

b. Figures showing what proportion of every state tax dollar is spent on education, social services, transportation, debt, and other expenses

Activities and Cases

c. Data showing the academic, administrative, and operation divisions of a college, from the president to department chairs and division managers

d. Figures showing the operating profit of a company for the past five years

e. Figures comparing the sales of VCRs, color TVs, and personal computers for the past five years

f. Percentages showing the causes of Rocky Mountains forest fires (lightning, 73 percent; arson, 5 percent; campfires, 9 percent; and so on).

g. Figures comparing the cost of basic TV cable service in ten areas of the United States for the past ten years (the boss wants to see exact figures)

10.4 EVALUATING VISUAL AIDS. From *U.S. News & World Report, USA Today, Business Week,* a textbook, or some other publication, locate one example each of a table, a pie chart, a line chart, a bar chart, and an organization chart. Bring copies of these visual aids to class. How effectively could the data have been expressed in words, without the graphics? Is the appropriate graphic form used? How is the graphic introduced in the text? Your instructor may ask you to submit a memo discussing visual aids.

10.5 STUDYING VISUAL AIDS IN ANNUAL REPORTS. In a memo to your instructor, evaluate the effectiveness of visual aids in three to five corporation annual reports. Critique their readability, clarity, and success in visualizing data. How were they introduced in the text? What suggestions would you make to improve them?

10.6 LIBRARY RECOMMENDATION. You have been asked to recommend a library to fellow students who have little library experience. Visit your school or public library. Observe its resources, method of operation, shelf lists, electronic capabilities, and personnel. Write a one-page memo report describing your findings.

10.7 BIBLIOGRAPHY. Select a business topic that interests you. Prepare a bibliography of at least five current magazine articles, three books, and five other references that contain relevant information regarding the topic. Your instructor may ask you to divide your bibliography into sections: *Books, Periodicals, Other Resources.* You may also be asked to annotate your bibliography, that is, to compose a brief description of each reference, such as this:

> Rash, Wayne, Jr. "Dawn of the Dead Disk." *Byte,* July 2003, 137–140. This article discusses the need for timely, complete backups of data stored on hard disks so that when a hard disk crashes, a business may continue with the least interruption.

10.8 PROPOSAL: LOOKING FOR CLIENTS FOR YOUR BUSINESS. A new medical clinic, ProMed Institute, is opening its doors in your hometown; and a mutual friend has recommended your small business to the administrator of the clinic. You have received a letter asking you to provide information about your service. The new medical clinic specializes in sports medicine, physical therapy, and cardiac rehabilitation services. It is interested in retaining your company, rather than hiring its own employees to perform the service your company offers.

Your Task. Working in teams, first decide what service you will offer. It could be landscaping, uniform supply, laundry of uniforms, general cleaning, computerized no-paper filing systems online medical supplies, patient transportation, supplemental hospice care, temporary office support, or food service. As a team, develop a letter proposal outlining your plan, staffing, and budget. Use persuasion to show why contracting your services is better than hiring in-house employees. In the proposal letter, request a meeting with the administrative board. In addition to a written proposal, you may be expected to make an oral presentation that includes visual aids and/or handouts. Send your proposal to Mr. Jack Dawson, Director, ProMed Institute. Supply a local address.

10.9 PROPOSAL: STARTING YOUR OWN BUSINESS. You and your buddies have a terrific idea for a new business in your town. For example, you might want to propose to Starbucks the concept of converting some of its coffee shops into Internet cafes. Or you might propose to the city or another organization a better Web site, which you and your team would design and maintain. You might want to start a word processing business that offers production, editing, and printing services. Often businesses, medical centers, attorneys, and other professionals have overload transcribing or word processing to farm out to a service.

TEAM
CRITICAL
THINKING

Your Task. Working in teams, explore entrepreneurial ventures based on your experience and expertise. Write a proposal to secure approval and funding. Your report should include a transmittal letter, as well as a description of your proposed company, its product or service, market analysis, operations and management plan, and financial plan.

10.10 FORMAL REPORT: INTERCULTURAL COMMUNICATION. American businesses are expanding into foreign markets with manufacturing plants, sales offices, and branch offices abroad. Unfortunately, most Americans have little knowledge of or experience with people from other cultures. To prepare for participation in the global marketplace, you are to collect information for a report focused on a Pacific Rim, Latin American, or European country where English is not regularly spoken. Before selecting the country, though, consult your campus international student program for volunteers who are willing to be interviewed. Your instructor may make advance arrangements seeking international student volunteers.

TEAM

Your Task. In teams of three to five, collect information about your target country from the library and other sources. Then invite an international student representing your target country to be interviewed by your group. As you conduct primary and secondary research, investigate the topics listed in Figure 10.17.[7] Confirm what you learn in your secondary research by talking with your interviewee. When you complete your research, write a report for the CEO of your company (make up a name and company). Assume that your company plans to expand its operations abroad. Your report should advise the company's executives of social customs, family life, attitudes, religions, education, and values in the target country. Remember that your company's interests are business-oriented; don't dwell on tourist information. Write your report individually or in teams.

10.11 PROPOSAL AND GRANT WRITING: LEARNING FROM THE NONPROFITS. You'd like to learn more about writing business proposals and especially about writing grants. The latter involve funding supplied by an institution, foundation, or the government. You might one day even decide to become a professional grant/proposal writer. But first you need experience.

INFOTRAC

FIGURE 10.17   Intercultural Interview Topics and Questions

SOCIAL CUSTOMS

1. How do people react to strangers? Friendly? Hostile? Reserved?
2. How do people greet each other?
3. What are the appropriate manners when you enter a room? Bow? Nod? Shake hands with everyone?
4. How are names used for introductions? Is it appropriate to inquire about one's occupation or family?
5. What are the attitudes toward touching?
6. How does one express appreciation for an invitation to another's home? Bring a gift? Send flowers? Write a thank-you note? Are any gifts taboo?
7. Are there any customs related to how or where one sits?
8. Are any facial expressions or gestures considered rude?
9. How close do people stand when talking?
10. What is the attitude toward punctuality in social situations? In business situations?
11. What are acceptable eye contact patterns?
12. What gestures indicate agreement? Disagreement?

FAMILY LIFE

1. What is the basic unit of social organization? Basic family? Extended family?
2. Do women work outside of the home? In what occupations?

HOUSING, CLOTHING, AND FOOD

1. Are there differences in the kind of housing used by different social groups? Differences in location? Differences in furnishings?
2. What occasions require special clothing?
3. Are some types of clothing considered taboo?
4. What is appropriate business attire for men? For women?
5. How many times a day do people eat?
6. What types of places, food, and drink are appropriate for business entertainment? Where is the seat of honor at a table?

CLASS STRUCTURE

1. Into what classes is society organized?
2. Do racial, religious, or economic factors determine social status?
3. Are there any minority groups? What is their social standing?

POLITICAL PATTERNS

1. Are there any immediate threats to the political survival of the country?
2. How is political power manifested?
3. What channels are used for expression of popular opinion?
4. What information media are important?
5. Is it appropriate to talk politics in social situations?

RELIGION AND FOLK BELIEFS

1. To which religious groups do people belong? Is one predominant?
2. Do religious beliefs influence daily activities?
3. Which places have sacred value? Which objects? Which events?
4. How do religious holidays affect business activities?

ECONOMIC INSTITUTIONS

1. What are the country's principal products?
2. Are workers organized in unions?
3. How are businesses owned? By family units? By large public corporations? By the government?
4. What is the standard work schedule?
5. Is it appropriate to do business by telephone?
6. How has technology affected business procedures?
7. Is participatory management used?
8. Are there any customs related to exchanging business cards?
9. How is status shown in an organization? Private office? Secretary? Furniture?
10. Are businesspeople expected to socialize before conducting business?

VALUE SYSTEMS

1. Is competitiveness or cooperation more prized?
2. Is thrift or enjoyment of the moment more valued?
3. Is politeness more important than factual honesty?
4. What are the attitudes toward education?
5. Do women own or manage businesses? If so, how are they treated?
6. What are your people's perceptions of Americans? Do Americans offend you? What has been hardest for you to adjust to in America? How could Americans make this adjustment easier for you?

Your Task. Volunteer your services for a local nonprofit organization, such as a United Way (http://www.unitedway.org) member agency, an educational institution, or your local church. To learn more about writing grants, complete an InfoTrac subject guide search for "proposal." Click on articles under the categories of "business proposal writing" and "grant proposal writing." Your instructor may ask you to submit a preliminary memo report outlining ten or more pointers you learn about writing proposals and grants for nonprofit organizations.

10.12 FORMAL REPORT: READABILITY OF INSURANCE POLICIES. The 21st Century Insurance Company is concerned about the readability of its policies. State legislators are beginning to investigate complaints of policyholders who say they can't understand their insurance policies. One judge lambasted insurers, saying, "The language in these policies is bureaucratic gobbledygook, jargon, double-talk, a form of officialese, federalese, and insurancese that does not qualify as English. The burden upon organizations is to write policies in a manner designed to communicate rather than to obfuscate." Taking the initiative in improving its policies, 21st Century hires you as a consultant to study its standard policy and make recommendations.

CRITICAL THINKING

Examine a life, fire, or health insurance policy that you or a friend or relative holds. Select one that is fairly complex. Study the policy for jargon, confusing language, long sentences, and unclear antecedents. Evaluate its format, print size, paper and print quality, amount of white space, and use of headings. Does it have an index or glossary? Are difficult terms defined? How easy is it to find specifics, should a policyholder want to check something?

In addition to the data you collect from your own examination of the policy, 21st Century gives you the following data from a recent policyholder survey:

Response to statement: "I am able to read and understand the language and provisions of my policy."

Age Group	Strongly Agree	Agree	Undecided	Disagree	Strongly Disagree
18–34	2%	9%	34%	41%	14%
35–49	2	17	38	33	10
50–64	1	11	22	35	31
65+	1	2	17	47	33

Your Task. Prepare a report for Heather Garcia, vice president, 21st Century Insurance Company, discussing your analysis, conclusions, and recommendations for improving its basic policy.

10.13 FORMAL REPORT: FAST-FOOD CHECKUP. The national franchising headquarters for a fast-food chain has received complaints about the service, quality, and cleanliness of one of its restaurants in your area. You have been sent to inspect and to report on what you see.

Your Task. Select a nearby fast-food restaurant. Visit on two or more occasions. Make notes about how many customers were served, how quickly they received their food, and how courteously they were treated. Observe the number of employees and supervisors working. Note the cleanliness of observable parts of the restaurant. Inspect the restroom as well as the exterior and surrounding grounds. Sample the food. Your boss is a stickler for details; he has no use for general statements such as *The restroom was not clean.* Be specific. Draw conclusions. Are the complaints justified? If improvements are necessary, make recommendations. Address your report to Lawrence C. Kelsey, President.

10.14 FORMAL REPORT: CONSUMER PRODUCT INVESTIGATION. Study a consumer product that you might consider buying. Are you, your family, or your business interested

INFOTRAC

in purchasing a VCR, computer, digital camera, microwave, car, SUV, camcorder, or some other product?

Your Task. Use at least five primary and five secondary sources in researching your topic. Your primary research will be in the form of interviews with individuals (owners, users, salespeople, technicians) in a position to comment on attributes of your product. Secondary research will be in the form of print or electronic sources, such as magazine articles, owner manuals, and Web sites. Be sure to use InfoTrac to find appropriate articles. Your report should analyze and discuss at least three comparable models or versions of the target product. Decide what criteria you will use to compare the models, such as price, features, warranty, service, and so forth. The report should include these components: letter of transmittal, table of contents, executive summary, introduction (including background, purpose, scope of the study, and research methods), findings (organized by comparison criteria), summary of findings, conclusions, recommendations, and bibliography. Address the report to your instructor. You may work individually, in pairs, or in teams.

10.15 FORMAL REPORT: COMMUNICATION SKILLS ON THE JOB. Collect information regarding communication skills used by individuals in a particular career field (accounting, management, marketing, office administration, paralegal, and so forth). Interview three or more individuals in a specific occupation in that field. Determine how much and what kind of writing they do. Do they make oral presentations? How much time do they spend in telephone communication? Do they use e-mail? If so, how much and for what? What recommendations do they have for training for this position?

Your Task. Write a report that discusses the findings from your interviews. What conclusions can you draw regarding communication skills in this field? What recommendations would you make for individuals entering this field? Your instructor may ask you to research the perception of businesspeople over the past ten years regarding the communication skills of employees. To gather such data, conduct library or online research.

10.16 MORE PROPOSAL AND REPORT TOPICS. A list with over 70 report topics is available at the Guffey Student Web site (http://www.meguffey.com). Click "Book Support" and "Report Topics." The topics are divided into the following categories: accounting, finance, personnel/human resources, marketing, information systems, management, and general business/education/campus issues. You can collect information for many of these reports by using InfoTrac and the Web. Your instructor may assign them as individual or team projects. All involve critical thinking in organizing information, drawing conclusions, and making recommendations. The topics include assignments appropriate for proposals, business plans, and formal reports.

VIDEO CASE

Technology in Communication at Burke Marketing Research

Burke Marketing Research is one of the premier international marketing research and consulting firms in the industry. It's the world's seventh largest research company with offices in 40 countries around the world. For it to remain successful, effective internal and external communication is vital.

Your Task. After viewing the Burke video, discuss these questions:

- What technological tools does Burke use for written communication?
- What are the advantages and disadvantages of e-mail for Burke?
- Why is Burke moving from paper to paperless reports?
- What technological tools does Burke use for oral communication?
- Why has videoconferencing been less successful than teleconferencing? (Video-conferencing involves the transmission of images; teleconferencing generally means the transmission of voice only.)
- How does Burke use the Internet to collect and deliver information?

GRAMMAR/MECHANICS CHECKUP—10

POSSESSIVES

Review Sections 2.20–2.22 in the Grammar/Mechanics Handbook. Then study each of the following statements. Underscore any inappropriate form. Write a correction in the space provided and record the number of the G/M principle(s) illustrated. If a sentence is correct, write C. When you finish, compare your responses with those at the back of the book. If your answers differ, study carefully the principles shown in parentheses.

Example   In just two <u>years</u> time, the accountants and managers devised an entirely new system.   <u>years'</u>   (2.20b)

1. Two supervisors said that <u>Mr. Wilsons</u> work was excellent.   _____
2. In less than a <u>years</u> time, the offices of both attorneys were moved.   _____
3. None of the employees in our Electronics Department had taken more than two <u>weeks</u> vacation.   _____
4. All the secretaries agreed that <u>Ms. Lanhams</u> suggestions were practicable.   _____
5. After you obtain your <u>boss</u> approval, send the application to Human Resources.   _____
6. We tried to sit at our favorite <u>waitress</u> station, but all her tables were filled.   _____
7. Despite <u>Kevin</u> grumbling, his wife selected two bonds and three stocks for her investments.   _____
8. The apartment owner requires two <u>months</u> rent in advance from all applicants.   _____
9. Four <u>companies</u> buildings were damaged in the fire.   _____
10. In one <u>months</u> time we hope to be able to complete all the address files.   _____
11. Only one <u>ladies</u> car had its engine running.   _____
12. One <u>secretaries</u> desk will have to be moved to make way for the computer.   _____
13. Several <u>sellers</u> permits were issued for two years.   _____

14. <u>Marks</u> salary was somewhat higher than <u>David</u>.   _____
15. <u>Lisas</u> job in accounts receivable ends in two months.   _____

GRAMMAR/MECHANICS CHALLENGE—10

DOCUMENT FOR REVISION

The following executive summary has faults in grammar, punctuation, spelling, number form, wordiness, and word use. Use standard proofreading marks (see Appendix B) to correct the errors. When you finish, your instructor can show you the revised version of this summary.

EXECUTIVE SUMMARY

Problem

The U.S. tuna industry must expand it's markets abroad particularly in regard to Japan. Although consumption of tuna is decreasing in the United States they are increasing in Japan. The problem that is for the american tuna industry is developing apropriate marketing strategies to boost its current sale in Japanese markets.

Summary of Findings

This report analyzes the Japanese market which currently consumes six hundred thousand tons of tuna per year, and is growing rapidly. Much of this tuna is supplied by imports which at this point in time total about 35% of sales. Our findings indicate that not only will this expand, but the share of imports will continue to grow. The trend is alarming to Japanese tuna industry leaders, because this important market, close to a $billion a year, is increasingly subject to the influence of foreign imports. Declining catches by Japans own Tuna fleet as well as a sharp upward turn in food preference by affluent Japanese consumers, has contributed to this trend.

Recommendations

Based on our analisys we reccommend the following 5 marketing strategys for the U.S. Tuna industry.

1. Farm greater supplys of bluefin tuna to export.
2. We should market our own value added products.
3. Sell fresh tuna direct to the Tokyo Central Wholesale market.
4. Sell to other Japanese markets also.
5. Direct sales should be made to Japanese Supermarket chains.

Trash or Treasure: Assessing the Quality of Web Documents

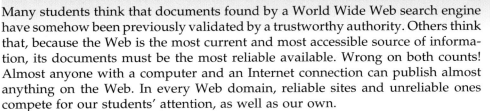

Many students think that documents found by a World Wide Web search engine have somehow been previously validated by a trustworthy authority. Others think that, because the Web is the most current and most accessible source of information, its documents must be the most reliable available. Wrong on both counts! Almost anyone with a computer and an Internet connection can publish almost anything on the Web. In every Web domain, reliable sites and unreliable ones compete for our students' attention, as well as our own.

Unlike the contents of the journals, magazines, and newspapers found in research-oriented libraries, the contents of most Web sites have not been carefully scrutinized by experienced editors and peer writers. To put it another way, print journals, magazines, and newspapers have traditionally featured reasonably unbiased, trustworthy articles; all too many Web sites, however, have another goal in mind. They are above all else interested in promoting a cause or in selling a product.

To use the Web meaningfully, students must learn to scrutinize carefully what they find in the documents it offers. A number of instructors and librarians have given a lot of thought to this issue, and some of them have created Web pages that offer relevant guidelines for student researchers. To access up-to-date links to many of these highly useful pages, first go to the home page (http://www.meguffey.com) of the Guffey Web site for students. Then click "Internet" and "Assessing the Quality of Web Documents."

Many of the writers who have dealt with the problem of teaching students how to evaluate Web pages have emphasized the utility of a quality-assessment checklist. With their experiences, insights, and recommendations in mind, we have developed the following checklist. Used properly, it will help you distinguish Web trash from Web treasure.

Checklist for Assessing the Quality of a Web Page

Authority

☑ Who publishes or sponsors this Web page?
☑ What makes the presenter of the page an authority?
☑ Is a contact, such as an e-mail address, available for the presenter?
☑ To what domain (.com, .org, .edu, .gov) does the site containing it belong?
☑ Is the site "personal" (often indicated by "~" or "%" in the site's URL)?

Currency

☑ What is the date of the Web page?
☑ Is some of the information obviously out of date?

Content

☑ Is the purpose of the page to entertain, inform, convince, or sell?
☑ Who is the intended audience of the page, based on its content, tone, and style?
☑ Can you judge the overall value of content as compared with other resources on this topic?

Accuracy

- ☑ Do the page's assertions ("facts") seem reliable to you?
- ☑ Do you find spelling, grammar, or usage errors? Broken links?
- ☑ Do you see any evidence of bias?
- ☑ Are footnotes necessary? If so, have they been provided?

Career Application. As interns at a news-gathering service, you have been asked to assess the quality of the following Web sites. Which of these could you recommend as sources of valid information?

- Beef Nutrition (http://www.beefnutrition.org)
- Edmunds—Where Smart Car Buyers Start (http://www.edmunds.com)
- Clones-R-US (http://www.d-b.net/dti)
- EarthSave International (http://www.earthsave.org)
- The Vegetarian Resource Group (http://www.vrg.org/nutshell/nutshell.htm)
- National Anti-Vivisection Society (http://www.navs.org)
- Home Depot Sucks (http://www.homedepotsucks.com)
- Smithsonian Institution (http://www.si.edu)

Task. If you are working with a team, divide the preceding list among team members. If you are working individually, select four of the sites. Answer the questions in the preceding checklist as you evaluate each site. Summarize your evaluation of each site in a memo report to your instructor or in team or class discussion.

Developing
Speaking Skills

Communicating in Person, by Telephone, and in Meetings

Communication is the most important element of doing business today. So, think before you speak—because you can never take it back.[1]

Kris Pomianek, public relations specialist and communication seminar leader

LEARNING OBJECTIVES

1. Discuss improving face-to-face workplace communication including using your voice as a communication tool.
2. Specify procedures for promoting positive workplace relations through conversation.
3. Review techniques for offering constructive criticism on the job, responding professionally to workplace criticism, and resolving workplace conflicts.
4. Identify ways to polish your professional telephone skills, including traditional phones and cell phones.
5. List techniques for making the best use of voice mail.
6. Discuss procedures for planning and participating in productive business and professional meetings.

> **✓ Quick Check**
> Strong oral communication skills can help you be hired and succeed on the job.

*O*ral communication skills consistently rank near the top of competencies valued by employers. Companies are looking for employees who can interact successfully with customers, work smoothly with coworkers, and provide meaningful feedback to managers. Expressing yourself well and communicating effectively with others are skills that are critical to job placement, workplace performance, career advancement, and organizational success.

Earlier in this book you studied the communication process, effective listening techniques, and nonverbal communication skills. Many intervening chapters helped you develop good writing skills. The next two chapters will round out your communication expertise by focusing on oral communication skills. In your business or professional career, you will be judged not only by what you say but also by the way you say it. In this chapter we'll help you become a more successful speaker when you communicate in person, by telephone, and in meetings.

IMPROVING FACE-TO-FACE WORKPLACE COMMUNICATION

Because today's technologies provide many alternate communication channels, you may think that face-to-face communication is no longer essential or even important in business and professional transactions. You've already learned that e-mail is now the preferred communication channel because it is faster, cheaper, and easier than telephone, mail, or fax. Yet, despite their popularity and acceptance, alternate communication technologies can't replace the richness or effectiveness of face-to-face communication.[2] Imagine that you want to tell your boss how you solved a problem. Would you settle for a one-dimensional phone call, a fax, or an e-mail when you could step into her office and explain in person?

Face-to-face conversation has many advantages. It allows you to be persuasive and expressive because you can use your voice and body language to make a point. You are less likely to be misunderstood because you can read feedback and make needed adjustments. In conflict resolution, you can reach a solution more efficiently and cooperate to create greater levels of mutual benefit when communicating face to face.[3] Moreover, people want to see each other to satisfy a deep human need for social interaction. For numerous reasons communicating in person remains the most effective of all communication channels. In this chapter you'll explore helpful business and professional interpersonal speaking techniques, starting with viewing your voice as a communication tool.

✓ Quick Check
One-dimensional communication technologies cannot replace the richness or effectiveness of face-to-face communication.

USING YOUR VOICE AS A COMMUNICATION TOOL

It's been said that language provides the words, but your voice is the music that makes words meaningful.[4] You may believe that a beautiful or powerful voice is unattainable. After all, this is the voice you were born with, and it can't be changed. Actually, the voice is a flexible instrument. Actors hire coaches to help them eliminate or acquire accents or proper inflection for challenging roles. Julia Roberts worked with a voice coach to shed her Georgia accent; and Robert DeNiro, Leonardo DeCaprio, and Tony Danza all studied to lose their native accents. Celebrities, business executives, and everyday people consult voice and speech therapists to help them shake bad habits or just help them speak so that they can be understood and not sound less intelligent than they are. Rather than consult a high-paid specialist, you can pick up useful tips for using your voice most

✓ Quick Check
Like an actor, you can change your voice to make it a more powerful communication tool.

One of the most important figures in popular culture, Oprah Winfrey has cultivated a distinctive speaking style. To use your voice as a communication tool, pay attention to how you sound. Practice techniques that improve your pronunciation, voice quality, pitch, volume, and emphasis.
© AP/Wide World Photos, Inc.

effectively by learning how to control such elements as pronunciation, voice quality, pitch, volume, rate, and emphasis.

Pronunciation.   *Pronunciation* involves saying words correctly and clearly with the accepted sounds and accented syllables. You'll be at a distinct advantage in your job if, through training and practice, you learn to pronounce words correctly. Some of the most common errors, shown in Figure 11.1, include adding or omitting vowels, omitting consonants, reversing sounds, and slurring sounds. In casual conversation with your friends, correct pronunciation is not a big deal. But on the job you want to sound intelligent, educated, and competent. If you mispronounce words or slur phrases together, you risk being misunderstood as well as giving a poor impression of yourself. How can you improve your pronunciation skills? The best way is to listen carefully to educated people, look words up in the dictionary, and avoid errors such as those in Figure 11.1.

Voice Quality.   The quality of your voice sends a nonverbal message to listeners. It identifies your personality and your mood. Some voices sound enthusiastic and friendly, conveying the impression of an upbeat person who is happy to be with the listener. But voices can also sound controlling, patronizing, slow-witted, angry, or childish. This doesn't mean that the speaker necessarily has that attribute. It may mean that the speaker is merely carrying on a family tradition or pattern learned in childhood. To check your voice quality, record your voice and listen to it critically. Is it projecting a positive quality about you?

Pitch.   Effective speakers use a relaxed, controlled, well-pitched voice to attract listeners to their message. *Pitch* refers to sound vibration frequency; that is, it indicates the highness or lowness of a sound. In North America, speakers and listeners prefer a variety of pitch patterns. Voices are most attractive when they rise and fall in conversational tones. Flat, monotone voices are considered boring and ineffectual. In business, communicators strive for a moderately low voice, which is thought to be pleasing and professional.

FIGURE 11.1 Pronunciation Errors to Avoid

Adding vowel sounds	*athlete* (NOT *ath-a-lete*)
	disastrous (NOT *disas-ter-ous*)
Omitting vowel sounds	*federal* (NOT *fed-ral*)
	ridiculous (NOT *ri-dic-lous*)
	generally (NOT *gen-rally*)
Substituting vowel sounds	*get* (NOT *git*)
	creek (NOT *crick*)
	separate (NOT *sep-e-rate*)
Adding consonant sounds	*butter* (NOT *budder*)
	statistics (NOT *sta-stis-tics*)
Omitting consonant sounds	*library* (NOT *libery*)
	perhaps (NOT *praps*)
Confusing or distorting sounds	*ask* (NOT *aks*)
	hundred (NOT *hunderd*)
	accessory (NOT *assessory*)
Slurring sounds	*didn't you* (NOT *dint ya*)
	going to (NOT *gonna*)

Volume and Rate. *Volume* indicates the degree of loudness or the intensity of sound. Just as you adjust the volume on your radio or television set, you should adjust the volume of your speaking to the occasion and your listeners. When speaking face to face, you generally know whether you are speaking too loudly or softly by looking at your listeners. Are they straining to hear you? To judge what volume to use, listen carefully to the other person's voice. Use it as a guide for adjusting your voice. *Rate* refers to the pace of your speech. If you speak too slowly, listeners are bored and their attention wanders. If you speak too quickly, listeners can't understand you. Most people normally talk at about 125 words a minute. Again, monitor the nonverbal signs of your listeners and adjust your rate as needed.

Emphasis. By emphasizing or stressing certain words, you can change the meaning you are expressing. For example, read these sentences aloud, emphasizing the italicized words:

Matt said the hard drive failed again. (Matt knows what happened.)
Matt *said* the hard drive failed again. (But he may be wrong.)
Matt said the hard drive failed *again*? (Did he really say that?)

As you can see, emphasis affects the meaning of the words and the thought expressed. To make your message interesting and natural, use emphasis appropriately. You can raise your volume to sound authoritative and raise your pitch to sound disbelieving. Lowering your volume and pitch makes you sound professional or reasonable.

Some speakers today are prone to *uptalk*. This is a habit of using a rising inflection at the end of a sentence resulting in a singsong pattern that makes statements sound like questions. Once used exclusively by teenagers, uptalk is increasingly found in the workplace with negative results. When statements sound like questions, speakers seem weak and tentative. Their messages lack conviction and authority. On the job, managers afflicted by uptalk may have difficulty convincing staff members to follow directions because their voice inflection implies that other valid options are available. If you want to sound confident and competent, avoid uptalk.

PROMOTING POSITIVE WORKPLACE RELATIONS THROUGH CONVERSATION

In the workplace, conversations may involve giving and taking instructions, providing feedback, exchanging ideas on products and services, participating in performance appraisals, or engaging in small talk about such things as families and sports. Face-to-face conversation helps people work together harmoniously and feel that they are part of the larger organization. Our goal here is to provide you with several guidelines, starting with using correct names and titles, that promote positive workplace conversations.

Use correct names and titles. Although the world seems increasingly informal, it's still wise to use titles and last names when addressing professional adults (*Mrs. Smith, Mr. Rivera*). In some organizations senior staff members will speak to junior employees on a first-name basis, but the reverse may not be encouraged. Probably the safest plan is to ask your superiors how they want to be addressed. Customers and others outside the organization should always be addressed by title and last name.

When you meet strangers, do you have trouble remembering their names? You can improve your memory considerably if you associate the person with an object, place, color, animal, job, adjective, or some other memory hook. For example, *computer pro Kevin, Miami Kim, silver-haired Mr. Lee, bull-dog Chris, bookkeeper Lynn, traveler Ms. Janis.* The person's name will also be more deeply imbedded in your memory if you use it immediately after being introduced, in subsequent conversation, and when you part.

Choose appropriate topics. In some workplace activities, such as social gatherings or interviews, you will be expected to engage in small talk. Be sure to stay away from controversial topics with someone you don't know very well. Avoid politics, religion, or current event items that can start heated arguments. To initiate appropriate conversations, read newspapers and listen to radio and TV shows discussing current events. Make a mental note of items that you can use in conversation, taking care to remember where you saw or heard the news items so that you can report accurately and authoritatively. Try not to be defensive or annoyed if others present information that upsets you.

© Ted Goff (www.tedgoff.com)

"I had to spend the money I budgeted for your raise on a therapist after listening to your endless complaining."

Avoid negative remarks. Workplace conversations are not the place to complain about your colleagues, your friends, the organization, or your job. No one enjoys listening to whiners. And your criticism of others may come back to haunt you. A snipe at your boss or a complaint about a fellow worker may reach him or her, sometimes embellished or distorted with meanings you did not intend. Be circumspect in all negative judgments. Remember, some people love to repeat statements that will stir up trouble or set off internal workplace wars. Don't give them the ammunition!

Listen to learn. In conversations with colleagues, subordinates, and customers, train yourself to expect to learn something from what you are hearing. Being attentive is not only instructive but also courteous. Beyond displaying good manners, you'll probably find that your conversation partner has information that you don't have. Being receptive and listening with an open mind means not interrupting or prejudging. Let's say you want very much to be able to work at home for part of your workweek. You try to explain your ideas to your boss, but he cuts you off shortly after you start. He says, "It's out of the question; we need you here every day." Suppose instead he says, "I have strong reservations about your telecommuting, but maybe you'll change my mind"; and he settles in to listen to your presentation. Even if your boss decides against your request, you will feel that your ideas were heard and respected.

Give sincere and specific praise. A wise person once said, "Man does not live by bread alone. He needs to be buttered up once in a while." Probably nothing promotes positive workplace relationships better than sincere and specific praise. Whether the compliments and appreciation are traveling upward to management, downward to workers, or horizontally to colleagues, everyone responds well to recognition. Organizations run more smoothly and morale is higher when people feel appreciated. In your workplace conversations, look for ways to recognize good work and good people. And try to be specific. Instead of "You did a good job in leading that meeting," try something more specific, such as "Your excellent leadership skills certainly kept that meeting short, focused, and productive."

OFFERING CONSTRUCTIVE CRITICISM ON THE JOB

No one likes to receive criticism, and most of us don't like to give it either. But in the workplace cooperative endeavors demand feedback and evaluation. How are we doing on a project? What went well? What failed? How can we improve our efforts? Today's workplace often involves team projects. As a team member, you will be called on to judge the work of others. In addition to working on teams, you can also expect to become a supervisor or manager one day. As such, you will need to evaluate subordinates. Good employees seek good feedback from their supervisors. They want and need timely, detailed observations about their work to reinforce what they do well and help them overcome weak spots. But making that feedback palatable and constructive is not always easy. Depending on your situation, you may find some or all of the following suggestions helpful when you must deliver constructive criticism:

© Ted Goff (www.tedgoff.com)

"Would you like a little more constructive criticism?"

- **Mentally outline your conversation.** Think carefully about what you want to accomplish and what you will say. Find the right words at the right time and in the right setting.
- **Generally, use face-to-face communication.** Most constructive criticism is better delivered in person rather than in e-mail messages or memos. Personal feedback offers an opportunity for the listener to ask questions and give explanations. Occasionally, however, complex situations may require a different strategy. You might prefer to write out your opinions and deliver them by telephone or in writing. A written document enables you to organize your thoughts, include all the details, and be sure of keeping your cool. Remember, though, that written documents create permanent records—for better or worse.
- **Focus on improvement.** Instead of attacking, use language that offers alternative behavior. Use phrases such as "Next time, you could . . . ."
- **Offer to help.** Criticism is accepted more readily if you volunteer to help in eliminating or solving the problem.
- **Be specific.** Instead of a vague assertion such as "Your work is often late," be more specific: "The specs on the Riverside job were due Thursday at 5 p.m., and you didn't hand them in until Friday." Explain how the person's performance jeopardized the entire project.
- **Avoid broad generalizations.** Don't use words such as *should, never, always,* and other encompassing expressions as they may cause the listener to shut down and become defensive.
- **Discuss the behavior, not the person.** Instead of "You seem to think you can come to work any time you want," focus on the behavior: "Coming to work late means that we have to fill in with someone else until you arrive."
- **Use the word *we* rather than *you.*** "We need to meet project deadlines," is better than saying "You need to meet project deadlines." Emphasize organizational expectations rather than personal ones. Avoid sounding accusatory.
- **Encourage two-way communication.** Even if well-planned, criticism is still hard to deliver. It may surprise or hurt the feelings of the employee. Considering ending your message with, "It can be hard to hear this type of feedback. If you would like to share your thoughts, I'm listening."

> ✓ **Quick Check**
>
> Offering constructive criticism is easier if you plan what you will say, focus on improvement, offer to help, be specific, discuss the behavior and not the person, speak privately face to face, and avoid anger.

- **Avoid anger, sarcasm, and a raised voice.** Criticism is rarely constructive when tempers flare. Plan in advance what you will say and deliver it in low, controlled, and sincere tones.
- **Keep it private.** Offer praise in public; offer criticism in private. "Setting an example" through public criticism is never a wise management policy.

RESPONDING PROFESSIONALLY TO WORKPLACE CRITICISM

As much as we hate giving criticism, we dislike receiving it even more. Yet, the workplace requires not only dishing it out but also being able to take it. When being criticized, you probably will feel that you are being attacked. You can't just sit back and relax. Your heart beats faster, your temperature shoots up, your face reddens, and you respond with classic "fight or flight" syndrome. You feel that you want to instantly retaliate or escape from the attacker. But focusing on your feelings distracts you from hearing the content of what is being said, and it prevents you from responding professionally. Some or all of the following suggestions will guide you in reacting positively to criticism so that you can benefit from it:

- **Listen without interrupting.** Even though you might want to protest, make yourself hear the speaker out.
- **Determine the speaker's intent.** Unskilled communicators may throw "verbal bricks" with unintended negative-sounding expressions. If you think the intent is positive, focus on what is being said rather than reacting to poorly chosen words.
- **Acknowledge what you are hearing.** Respond with a pause, a nod, or a neutral statement such as "I understand you have a concern." This buys you time. Do not disagree, counterattack, or blame, which may escalate the situation and harden the speaker's position.
- **Paraphrase what was said.** In your own words restate objectively what you are hearing.
- **Ask for more information if necessary.** Clarify what is being said. Stay focused on the main idea rather than interjecting side issues.
- **Agree—if the comments are accurate.** If an apology is in order, give it. Explain what you plan to do differently. If the criticism is on target, the sooner you agree, the more likely you will engender respect from the other person.
- **Disagree respectfully and constructively—if you feel the comments are unfair.** After hearing the criticism, you might say, "May I tell you my perspective?" Or you could try to solve the problem by saying, "How can we improve this situation in a way you believe we can both accept?" If the other person continues to criticize, say "I want to find a way to resolve your concern. When do you want to talk about it next?"
- **Look for a middle position.** Search for a middle position or a compromise. Be genial even if you don't like the person or the situation.

RESOLVING WORKPLACE CONFLICTS

Conflict is a normal part of every workplace. Although the word alone is enough to make your heart go into overdrive, conflict is not always negative. When managed properly, conflict can improve decision-making, clarify values, increase group cohesiveness, stimulate creativity, decrease tensions, and reduce dissatisfaction. Unresolved conflict, however, can destroy productivity and seriously reduce morale. You will be better prepared to resolve workplace conflict if you know the five most common response patterns as well as a six-step procedure for dealing with conflict.

Workplace conflict is not always negative. If workplace conflict is resolved, it can lead to better decision-making, improved group cohesiveness, enhanced creativity, and improved morale. Collaboration and cooperation can help resolve conflict effectively.
© David Young Wolff/PhotoEdit, Inc.

Common Conflict Response Patterns.   Imagine a time when you were very upset with a workplace colleague, boss, or a teammate. How did you respond? Experts who have studied conflict say that most of us deal with it in one of the following predictable patterns:[5]

- **Avoidance/withdrawal.** Instead of trying to resolve the conflict, one person or the other simply withdraws. Avoidance of conflict generally results in a "lose–lose" situation because the problem festers and no attempt is made to understand the issues causing the conflict. On the other hand, avoidance may be the best response when the issue is trivial, when potential losses from an open conflict outweigh potential gains, or when insufficient time is available to work through the issue adequately.
- **Accommodation/smoothing.** When one person gives in quickly, the conflict is smoothed over and surface harmony results. This may be the best method when the issue is minor, when damage to the relationship would harm both parties, and when tempers are too hot for productive discussion.
- **Compromise.** In this pattern both people give up something of lesser importance to gain something more important. Compromise may be the best approach when both parties stand to gain, when a predetermined "ideal" solution is not required, and when time is short.
- **Competition/forcing.** This approach results in a contest in which one person comes out on top, leaving the other with a sense of failure. This method ends the conflict, but it may result in hurt feelings and potential future problems from the loser. This strategy is appropriate when a decision or action must be immediate and when the parties recognize the power relationship between themselves.
- **Collaboration/problem-solving.** In this pattern both parties lay all the cards on the table and attempt to reach consensus. This approach works when the involved people have common goals but they disagree over how to reach them. Conflict may arise from misunderstanding or a communication breakdown. Collaboration works best when all parties are trained in problem-solving techniques.

Quick Check

Although avoidance does not solve conflicts, it may be the best response for some situations, such as when the issue is trivial.

Quick Check

Resolving conflict through the collaboration/problem-solving method is best, but this technique requires training and commitment.

Six-Step Procedure for Dealing With Conflict. Probably the best pattern for resolving conflicts entails collaboration and problem-solving procedures. But this method requires a certain amount of training. Fortunately, experts in the field of negotiation have developed a six-step pattern that you can try the next time you need to resolve a conflict.[6]

1. **Listen.** To be sure you understand the problem, listen carefully. If the other person doesn't seem to be listening to you, you need to set the example and be the first to listen.
2. **Understand the other point of view.** Once you listen, it's much easier to understand the other's position. Show your understanding by asking questions and paraphrasing. This will also verify what you think the other person means.
3. **Show a concern for the relationship.** By focusing on the problem, not the person, you can build, maintain, and even improve relationships. Show an understanding of the other person's situation and needs. Show an overall willingness to come to an agreement.
4. **Look for common ground.** Identify your interests and help the other side to identify its interests. Learn what you have in common, and look for a solution to which both sides can agree.
5. **Invent new problem-solving options.** Spend time identifying the interests of both sides. Then brainstorm to invent new ways to solve the problem. Be open to new options.
6. **Reach an agreement based on what's fair.** Seek to determine a standard of fairness that is acceptable to both sides. Then weigh the possible solutions, and choose the best option.

✔ *Quick Check*

Following an effective six-step procedure can help you resolve conflicts through collaboration and cooperation.

POLISHING YOUR PROFESSIONAL TELEPHONE AND VOICE MAIL SKILLS

✔ *Quick Check*

For most businesses, telephones—both traditional and wireless—are a primary contact with the outside world.

The telephone is the most universal—and, some would say, the most important—piece of equipment in offices today.[7] For many businesspeople, it is a primary contact with the outside world. Some observers predicted that e-mail and faxes would "kill off phone calls."[8] The amazing expansion of wireless communication, however, has given the telephone a new and vigorous lease on life. Telephones are definitely here to stay. But many of us do not use them efficiently or effectively. In this chapter we'll focus on traditional telephone techniques as well as voice mail efficiency.

MAKING PRODUCTIVE TELEPHONE CALLS

Before making a telephone call, decide whether the intended call is really necessary. Could you find the information yourself? If you wait a while, would the problem resolve itself? Perhaps your message could be delivered more efficiently by some other means. One West Coast company found that telephone interruptions consumed about 18 percent of staff members' workdays. Another study found that two thirds of all calls were less important than the work they interrupted.[9] Alternatives to telephone calls include e-mail, memos, or calls to voice mail systems. If a telephone call must be made, consider using the following suggestions to make it fully productive.

- **Plan a mini-agenda.** Have you ever been embarrassed when you had to make a second telephone call because you forgot an important item the first time? Before placing a call, jot down notes regarding all the topics you need to discuss. Following an agenda guarantees not only a complete call but also a quick one. You'll be less likely to wander from the business at hand while rummaging through your mind trying to remember everything.

- **Use a three-point introduction.** When placing a call, immediately (1) name the person you are calling, (2) identify yourself and your affiliation, and (3) give a brief explanation of your reason for calling. For example: "May I speak to Larry Lopez? This is Hillary Dahl of Sebastian Enterprises, and I'm seeking information about a software program called Power Presentations." This kind of introduction enables the receiving individual to respond immediately without asking further questions.

- **Be brisk if you are rushed.** For business calls when your time is limited, avoid questions such as "How are you?" Instead, say, "Lisa, I knew you'd be the only one who could answer these two questions for me." Another efficient strategy is to set a "contract" with the caller: "Look, Lisa, I have only ten minutes, but I really wanted to get back to you."

- **Be cheerful and accurate.** Let your voice show the same kind of animation that you radiate when you greet people in person. In your mind try to envision the individual answering the telephone. A smile can certainly affect the tone of your voice, so smile at that person. Moreover, be accurate about what you say. "Hang on a second; I'll be right back" rarely is true. Better to say, "It may take me two or three minutes to get that information. Would you prefer to hold or have me call you back?"

- **Bring it to a close.** The responsibility for ending a call lies with the caller. This is sometimes difficult to do if the other person rambles on. You may need to use suggestive closing language, such as "I've certainly enjoyed talking with you," "I've learned what I needed to know, and now I can proceed with my work," "Thanks for your help," or "I must go now, but may I call you again in the future if I need . . . ?"

- **Avoid telephone tag.** If you call someone who's not in, ask when it would be best for you to call again. State that you will call at a specific time—and do it. If you ask a person to call you, give a time when you can be reached—and then be sure you are in at that time.

- **Leave complete voice mail messages.** Remember that there's no rush when you leave a voice mail message. Always enunciate clearly. And be sure to provide a complete message, including your name, telephone number, and the time and date of your call. Explain your purpose so that the receiver can be ready with the required information when returning your call.

> **✓ Quick Check**
>
> You can make productive telephone calls by planning an agenda, identifying the purpose, being courteous and cheerful, and avoiding rambling.

RECEIVING PRODUCTIVE TELEPHONE CALLS

With a little forethought you can make your telephone a productive, efficient work tool. Developing good telephone manners also reflects well on you and on your organization.

- **Identify yourself immediately.** In answering your telephone or someone else's, provide your name, title or affiliation, and, possibly, a greeting. For example, "Larry Lopez, Proteus Software. How may I help you?" Force yourself to speak clearly and slowly. Remember that the caller may be unfamiliar with what you are saying and fail to recognize slurred syllables.

- **Be responsive and helpful.** If you are in a support role, be sympathetic to callers' needs. Instead of "I don't know," try "That's a good question; let me investigate." Instead of "We can't do that," try "That's

© Ted Goff (www.tedgoff.com)

"Who is this, what do you want, and why are you angry with me already?"

a tough one; let's see what we can do." Avoid "No" at the beginning of a sentence. It sounds especially abrasive and displeasing because it suggests total rejection.

- **Be cautious when answering calls for others.** Be courteous and helpful, but don't give out confidential information. Better to say, "She's away from her desk" or "He's out of the office" than to report a colleague's exact whereabouts.
- **Take messages carefully.** Few things are as frustrating as receiving a potentially important phone message that is illegible. Repeat the spelling of names and verify telephone numbers. Write messages legibly and record their time and date. Promise to give the messages to intended recipients, but don't guarantee return calls.
- **Explain what you're doing when transferring calls.** Give a reason for transferring, and identify the extension to which you are directing the call in case the caller is disconnected.

✓ *Quick Check*

You can improve your telephone reception skills by identifying yourself, acting responsive, being helpful, and taking accurate messages.

USING CELL PHONES FOR BUSINESS

✓ *Quick Check*

Cell phones are essential workplace communication tools, but they must be used without offending others.

Cell phones enable you to conduct business from virtually anywhere at any time. More than a plaything or a mere convenience, the cell phone has become an essential part of communication in today's workplace. As with many new technologies, a set of rules or protocol on usage is still evolving for cell phones. How are they best used? When is it acceptable to take calls? Where should calls be made? Most of us have experienced thoughtless and rude cell phone behavior. To avoid offending, smart business communicators practice cell phone etiquette, as outlined in Figure 11.2. In projecting a professional image, they are careful about location, time, and volume in relation to their cell phone calls.

Location.　Use good judgment in placing or accepting cell phone calls. Some places are dangerous or inappropriate for cell phone use. Turn off your cell phone when entering a conference room, interview, theater, place of worship, or any other place where it could be distracting or disruptive to others. Taking a call in

FIGURE 11.2 Practicing Courteous and Responsible Cell Phone Use

Business communicators find cell phones to be enormously convenient and real time-savers. But rude users have generated a backlash against inconsiderate callers. Here are specific suggestions for using cell phones safely and responsibly:

- **Be courteous to those around you.** Don't force those near you to hear your business. Apologize and make amends gracefully for occasional cell phone blunders.
- **Observe wireless-free quiet areas.** Don't allow your cell phone to ring in theaters, restaurants, museums, classrooms, important meetings, and similar places. Use the cell phone's silent/vibrating ring option. A majority of travelers prefer that cell phone conversations *not* be held on most forms of public transportation.
- **Speak in low, conversational tones.** Microphones on cell phones are quite sensitive, thus making it unnecessary to talk loudly. Avoid "cell yell."
- **Take only urgent calls.** Make full use of your cell phone's caller ID feature to screen incoming calls. Let voice mail take those calls that are not pressing.
- **Drive now, talk later.** Pull over if you must make a call. Talking while driving increases the chance of accidents fourfold, about the same as driving while intoxicated.

a crowded room or bar makes it difficult to hear and reflects poorly on you as a professional. A bad connection also makes a bad impression. Static or dropped signals create frustration and miscommunication. Don't sacrifice professionalism for the sake of a garbled phone call. It's smarter to turn off your phone in an area where the signal is weak and when you are likely to have interference. Use voice mail and return the call when conditions are better.

Time. Often what you are doing is more important than whatever may come over the air waves to you on your phone. For example, when you have having an important discussion with a business partner, customer, or superior, it is rude to allow yourself to be interrupted by an incoming call. It's also poor manners to practice multitasking while on the phone. What's more, it's dangerous. Although you might be able to read and print out e-mail messages, deal with a customer at the counter, and talk on your cell phone simultaneously, it's impolite and risky. Lack of attention results in errors. If a phone call is important enough to accept, then it's important enough to stop what you are doing and attend to the conversation.

Volume. Many people raise their voices when using their cell phones. "Cell yell" results, much to the annoyance of anyone nearby. Raising your voice is unnecessary since most phones have excellent microphones that can pick up even a whisper. If the connection is bad, louder volume will not improve the sound quality. As in face-to-face conversations, a low, modulated voice sounds professional and projects the proper image.

MAKING THE BEST USE OF VOICE MAIL

Voice mail links a telephone system to a computer that digitizes and stores incoming messages. Some systems also provide functions such as automated attendant menus, allowing callers to reach any associated extension by pushing specific buttons on a touch-tone telephone. For example, a ski resort in Colorado uses voice mail to answer routine questions that once were routed through an operator: *Welcome to Snow Paradise. For information on accommodations, touch 1; for snow conditions, touch 2; for ski equipment rental, touch 3,* and so forth.

Within some companies, voice mail accounts for 90 percent of all telephone messages.[10] Its popularity results from serving many functions, the most important of which is message storage. Because as many as half of all business calls require no discussion or feedback, the messaging capabilities of voice mail can mean huge savings for businesses. Incoming information is delivered without interrupting potential receivers and without all the niceties that most two-way conversations require. Stripped of superfluous chitchat, voice mail messages allow communicators to focus on essentials. Voice mail also eliminates telephone tag, inaccurate message-taking, and time-zone barriers. Critics complain, nevertheless, that automated systems seem cold and impersonal and are sometimes confusing and irritating. In any event, here are some ways that you can make voice mail work more effectively for you.

- **Announce your voice mail.** If you rely principally on a voice mail message system, identify it on your business stationery and cards. Then, when people call, they will be ready to leave a message.
- **Prepare a warm and informative greeting.** Make your mechanical greeting sound warm and inviting, both in tone and content. Identify yourself and your organization so that callers know they have reached the right number. Thank the caller and briefly explain that you are unavailable. Invite the caller to leave a message or, if appropriate, call back. Here's a typical voice mail greeting: "Hi! This is Larry Lopez of Proteus Software, and I appreciate your call. You've

reached my voice mailbox because I'm either working with customers or talking on another line at the moment. Please leave your name, number, and reason for calling so that I can be prepared when I return your call." Give callers an idea of when you will be available, such as "I'll be back at 2:30" or "I'll be out of my office until Wednesday, May 20." If you screen your calls as a time-management technique, try this message: "I'm not near my phone right now, but I should be able to return calls after 3:30."

- **Test your message.** Call your number and assess your message. Does it sound inviting? Sincere? Understandable? Are you pleased with your tone? If not, says one consultant, have someone else, perhaps a professional, record a message for you.

PLANNING AND PARTICIPATING IN PRODUCTIVE BUSINESS AND PROFESSIONAL MEETINGS

Quick Check

Because you can expect to attend many workplace meetings, learn to make them efficient, satisfying, and productive.

As businesses become more team-oriented and management becomes more participatory, people are attending more meetings than ever. One survey of managers found that they were devoting as many as two days a week to various gatherings.[11] Yet, meetings are almost universally disliked. Typical comments include "We have too many of them," "They don't accomplish anything," and "What a waste of time!" In spite of employee reluctance and despite terrific advances in communication and team technology, face-to-face meetings are not going to disappear. In discussing the future of meetings, Akio Morita, former chairman of the Sony Corporation, said that he expects "face-to-face meetings will still be the number one form of communication in the twenty-first century."[12] So, get used to them. Meetings are here to stay. Our task, then, as business communicators, is to learn how to make them efficient, satisfying, and productive.

Meetings, by the way, consist of three or more individuals who gather to pool information, solicit feedback, clarify policy, seek consensus, and solve problems. But meetings have another important purpose for you. They represent opportunities. Because they are a prime tool for developing staff, they are career-critical. "If you can't orchestrate a meeting, you're of little use to the corporation," says Morris Schechtman, head of a leadership training firm.[13] At meetings judgments are formed and careers are made. Therefore, instead of treating them as thieves of your valuable time, try to see them as golden opportunities to demonstrate your leadership, communication, and problem-solving skills. So that you can make the most of these opportunities, here are techniques for planning and conducting successful meetings.

DECIDING WHETHER A MEETING IS NECESSARY

Quick Check

Call meetings only when necessary, and invite only key people.

No meeting should be called unless the topic is important, can't wait, and requires an exchange of ideas. If the flow of information is strictly one way and no immediate feedback will result, then don't schedule a meeting. For example, if people are merely being advised or informed, send an e-mail, memo, or letter. Leave a telephone or voice mail message, but don't call a costly meeting. Remember, the real expense of a meeting is the lost productivity of all the people attending. To decide whether the purpose of the meeting is valid, it's a good idea to consult the key people who will be attending. Ask them what outcomes are desired and how to achieve those goals. This consultation also sets a collaborative tone and encourages full participation.

FIGURE 11.3 Meeting Purpose and Number of Participants

PURPOSE	IDEAL SIZE
Intensive problem-solving	5 or fewer
Problem identification	10 or fewer
Information reviews and presentations	30 or fewer
Motivational	Unlimited

SELECTING PARTICIPANTS

The number of meeting participants is determined by the purpose of the meeting, as shown in Figure 11.3. If the meeting purpose is motivational, such as an awards ceremony for sales reps of Mary Kay Cosmetics, then the number of participants is unlimited. But to make decisions, according to studies at 3-M Corporation, the best number is five or fewer participants.[14] Ideally, those attending should be people who will make the decision and people with information necessary to make the decision. Also attending should be people who will be responsible for implementing the decision and representatives of groups who will benefit from the decision.

Quick Check
Problem-solving meetings should involve five or fewer people.

DISTRIBUTING AN AGENDA

At least two days in advance of a meeting, distribute an agenda of topics to be discussed. Also include any reports or materials that participants should read in advance. For continuing groups, you might also include a copy of the minutes of the previous meeting. To keep meetings productive, limit the number of agenda items. Remember, the narrower the focus, the greater the chances for success. A good agenda, as illustrated in Figure 11.4, covers the following information:

Quick Check
Before a meeting, pass out a meeting agenda showing topics to be discussed and other information.

- Date and place of meeting
- Start time and end time
- Brief description of each topic, in order of priority, including the names of individuals who are responsible for performing some action
- Proposed allotment of time for each topic
- Any premeeting preparation expected of participants

GETTING THE MEETING STARTED

To avoid wasting time and irritating attendees, always start meetings on time—even if some participants are missing. Waiting for latecomers causes resentment and sets a bad precedent. For the same reasons, don't give a quick recap to anyone who arrives late. At the appointed time, open the meeting with a 3- to 5-minute introduction that includes the following:

Quick Check
Start meetings on time and open with a brief introduction.

- Goal and length of the meeting
- Background of topics or problems
- Possible solutions and constraints
- Tentative agenda
- Ground rules to be followed

A typical set of ground rules might include arriving on time, communicating openly, being supportive, listening carefully, participating fully, confronting conflict frankly, and following the agenda. More formal groups follow parliamentary

FIGURE 11.4 **Typical Meeting Agenda**

AGENDA
Quantum Travel International
Staff Meeting
September 4, 200x
10 to 11 a.m.
Conference Room

		Person	Proposed Time
I. Call to order; roll call			
II. Approval of agenda			
III. Approval of minutes from previous meeting			
IV. Committee reports			
A. Web site update		Kevin	5 minutes
B. Tour packages		Lisa	10 minutes
V. Old business			
A. Equipment maintenance		John	5 minutes
B. Client escrow accounts		Alicia	5 minutes
C. Internal newsletter		Adrienne	5 minutes
VI. New business			
A. New accounts		Sarah	5 minutes
B. Pricing policy for trips		Marcus	15 minutes
VII. Announcements			
VIII. Chair's summary, adjournment			

procedures based on Robert's Rules. After establishing basic ground rules, the leader should ask whether participants agree thus far. The next step is to assign one attendee to take minutes and one to act as a recorder. The recorder stands at a flipchart or whiteboard and lists the main ideas being discussed and agreements reached.

© Ted Goff (www.tedgoff.com)

"Wow. That was a great ghost story. But I still want to know why our data center keeps crashing."

✓ *Quick Check*

Keep the meeting moving by avoiding issues that sidetrack the group.

MOVING THE MEETING ALONG

After the preliminaries, the leader should say as little as possible. Like a talk show host, an effective leader makes "sure that each panel member gets some air time while no one member steals the show."[15] Remember that the purpose of a meeting is to exchange views, not to hear one person, even the leader, do all the talking. If the group has one member who monopolizes, the leader might say, "Thanks, Kurt, for that perspective, but please hold your next point while we hear how Ann would respond to that." This technique also encourages quieter participants to speak up.

To avoid allowing digressions to sidetrack the group, try generating a "Parking Lot" list. This is a list of important but divergent issues that should be discussed at a later time. Another way to handle digressions is to say, "Folks, we are getting off track here. Forgive me for pressing on, but I need to bring us back to the central issue of . . . ."[16] It's important to adhere to the agenda and the time schedule. Equally important, when the group seems to have reached a consensus, is to summarize the group's position and check to see whether everyone agrees.

DEALING WITH CONFLICT

Conflict is natural and even desirable in workplaces, but it can cause awkwardness and uneasiness. In meetings, conflict typically develops when people feel unheard or misunderstood. If two people are in conflict, the best approach is to encourage each to make a complete case while group members give their full attention. Let each one question the other. Then, the leader should summarize what was said, and the group should offer comments. The group may modify a recommendation or suggest alternatives before reaching consensus on a direction to follow.

Quick Check

When a conflict develops between two members, allow each to make a complete case before the group.

HANDLING DYSFUNCTIONAL GROUP MEMBERS

When individuals are performing in a dysfunctional role (such as blocking discussion, attacking other speakers, joking excessively, or withdrawing), they should be handled with care and tact. The following specific techniques can help a meeting leader control some group members and draw others out.[17]

- **Lay down the rules in an opening statement.** Give a specific overall summary of topics, time allotment, and expected behavior. Warn that speakers who digress will be interrupted.
- **Seat potentially dysfunctional members strategically.** Experts suggest seating a difficult group member immediately next to the leader. It's easier to bypass a person in this position. Make sure the person with dysfunctional behavior is not seated in a power point, such as at the end of table or across from the leader.
- **Avoid direct eye contact.** In American society direct eye contact is a nonverbal signal that encourages talking. Thus, when asking a question of the group, look only at those whom you wish to answer.
- **Assign dysfunctional members specific tasks.** Ask a potentially disruptive person, for example, to be the group recorder.
- **Ask members to speak in a specific order.** Ordering comments creates an artificial, rigid climate and should be done only when absolutely necessary. But such a regimen ensures that everyone gets a chance to participate.
- **Interrupt monopolizers.** If a difficult member dominates a discussion, wait for a pause and then break in. Summarize briefly the previous comments or ask someone else for an opinion.
- **Encourage nontalkers.** Give only positive feedback to the comments of reticent members. Ask them direct questions about which you know they have information or opinions.
- **Give praise and encouragement** to those who seem to need it, including the distracters, the blockers, and the withdrawn.

Quick Check

To control dysfunctional behavior, team leaders should establish rules and seat problem people strategically.

ENDING WITH A PLAN

End the meeting at the agreed time. The leader should summarize what has been decided, who is going to do what, and by what time. It may be necessary to ask people to volunteer to take responsibility for completing action items agreed to in the meeting. No one should leave the meeting without a full understanding of what was accomplished. One effective technique that encourages full participation is "once around the table." Everyone is asked to summarize briefly his or her interpretation of what was decided and what happens next. Of course, this closure technique works best with smaller groups. The leader should conclude by asking the group to set a time for the next meeting. He or she should also assure the group that a report will follow and thank participants for attending.

Quick Check

End the meeting with a summary of accomplishments and a review of action items; follow up by reminding participants of their assigned tasks.

FOLLOWING UP ACTIVELY

If minutes were taken, they should be distributed within a couple of days after the meeting. It is up to the leader to see that what was decided at the meeting is accomplished. The leader may need to call people to remind them of their assignments and also to volunteer to help them if necessary.

SUMMING UP AND LOOKING FORWARD

In this chapter you studied how to improve face-to-face communication in the workplace. You can use your voice as a communication tool by focusing on pronunciation, voice quality, pitch, volume, rate, and emphasis. In workplace conversations, you should use correct names and titles, choose appropriate topics, avoid negative remarks, listen to learn, and be willing to offer sincere and specific praise. You studied how to give and take constructive criticism on the job. In regard to workplace conflicts, you learned about five common response patterns as well as a six-step plan for resolving interpersonal conflicts. The chapter also presented techniques for polishing your professional telephone and voice mail skills, including making and receiving productive telephone calls. Finally, you learned how to plan and participate in productive business and professional meetings.

This chapter focused on developing speaking skills in face-to-face workplace communication. The next chapter covers an additional facet of oral communication, that of making presentations. Learning to speak before groups is important to your career success because you will probably be expected to do so occasionally. You'll learn helpful techniques and get practice applying them so that you can control stage fright in making polished presentations.

CRITICAL THINKING

1. Is face-to-face communication always preferable to one-dimensional channels of communication such as e-mail and fax? Why or why not?
2. In what ways can conflict be a positive force in the workplace?
3. Commentators are constantly predicting that new communications media will destroy old ones. Do you think e-mail and fax will kill off phone calls? Why or why not?
4. Why do so many people hate voice mail when it is an efficient system for recording messages?
5. How can business meetings help you advance your career?

6. Name five elements that you control in using your voice as a communication tool.

7. What topics should be avoided in workplace conversations?

8. List six techniques that you consider most important when delivering constructive criticism.

9. If you are criticized at work, what are eight ways that you can respond professionally?

10. What are five common responses to workplace conflicts? Which response do you think is most constructive?

11. What is a three-point introduction for a telephone call?

12. Name five ways in which callers can practice courteous and responsible cell phone use.

13. When should a business meeting be held?

14. What is an agenda and what should it include?

15. List eight tactics that a meeting leader can use in dealing with dysfunctional participants.

ACTIVITIES

TEAM

11.1 PRONUNCIATION. You can improve your effectiveness and credibility as a speaker if you pronounce words correctly.

Your Task. In teams or in class discussion, study the following list of words. What vowel do you think is frequently omitted or mispronounced? How can you be sure of the correct pronunciation? How can you improve your own pronunciation of these words?

accurate	manufacturer
burglar	original
company	popular
disastrous	positive
eleven	responsible
entrance	separately
excellent	singular
family	terrible
federal	usually
history	variable
liability	veteran

11.2 VOICE QUALITY. Recording your voice gives you a chance to learn how your voice sounds to others and provides an opportunity for you to improve its effectiveness. Don't be surprised if you fail to recognize your own voice.

Your Task. Record yourself reading a newspaper or magazine article.

a. If you think your voice sounds a bit high, practice speaking slightly lower.
b. If your voice is low or expressionless, practice speaking slightly louder and with more inflection.
c. Ask a colleague, teacher, or friend to provide feedback on your pronunciation, pitch, volume, rate, and professional tone.

11.3 DELIVERING AND RESPONDING TO CRITICISM. Develop your skills in handling criticism by joining with a partner to role play critical messages you might deliver and receive on the job.

Your Task. Designate one person "A" and the other "B." A describes the kinds of critical messages she or he is likely to receive on the job and identifies who might deliver them. In Scenario 1, B takes the role of the critic and delivers the criticism in an unskilled manner. A responds using techniques described in this chapter. In Scenario 2, B again is the critic but delivers the criticism using techniques described in this chapter. A responds again. Then A and B reverse roles and repeat Scenarios 1 and 2.

11.4 DISCUSSING WORKPLACE CRITICISM. In the workplace, criticism is often delivered thoughtlessly.

TEAM

Your Task. In teams of two or three, describe a time when you were criticized by an untrained superior or colleague. What made the criticism painful? What goal do you think the critic had in mind? How did you feel? How did you respond? Considering techniques discussed in this chapter, how could the critic have improved his or her delivery? How does the delivery technique affect the way a receiver responds to criticism? Your instructor may ask you to submit a memo analyzing an experience in which you were criticized.

11.5 RESPONDING TO WORKPLACE CONFLICTS. Experts say that we generally respond to conflict in one of the following patterns: avoidance/withdrawal, accommodation/smoothing, compromise, competition/forcing, or collaboration/problem-solving.

Your Task. For each of the following conflict situations, name an appropriate response pattern(s) and be prepared to explain your choice.

a. A company policy manual is posted and updated at an internal Web page. Employees must sign that they have read and understand the manual. A conflict arises when one manager insists that employees should sign electronically. Another manager thinks that a paper form should be signed by employees so that better records may be kept. What conflict response pattern is most appropriate?

b. Jeff and Mark work together but frequently disagree. Today they disagree on what computer disks to purchase for an order that must be submitted immediately. Jeff insists on buying Brand X computer disks. Mark knows that Brand X is made by a company that markets an identical disk at a slightly lower price. However, Mark doesn't have stock numbers for the cheaper disks at his fingertips. How should Mark respond?

c. A manager and his assistant plan to attend a conference together at a resort location. Six weeks before the conference, the company announces a cutback and limits conference support to only one person. The assistant, who has developed a presentation specifically for the conference, feels that he should be the one to attend. Travel arrangements must be made immediately. What conflict response pattern will most likely result?

d. Two vice presidents disagree on a company e-mail policy. One wants to ban personal e-mail totally. The other thinks that an outright ban is impossible to implement. He is more concerned with limiting Internet misuse, including visits to online game, porn, and shopping sites. The vice presidents agree that they need an e-mail policy, but they disagree on what to allow and what to prohibit. What conflict response pattern is appropriate?

e. Customer service rep Jackie comes to work one morning and finds Alexa sitting at Workstation 2. Although the customer service reps have no special workstation assigned to them, Jackie has the longest seniority and has always assumed that Workstation 2 was hers. Other workstations were available, but the supervisor told Alexa to use Workstation 2 that morning because she didn't know that Jackie would be coming in. When Jackie arrives and sees her workstation occupied, she becomes angry and demands that Alexa vacate "her" station. What conflict response pattern might be most appropriate for Alexa and the supervisor?

TEAM
INFOTRAC

11.6 RULES FOR WIRELESS PHONE USE IN SALES. As one of the managers of LaReve, a hair care and skin products company, you are alarmed at a newspaper article you just saw. A stockbroker for Smith Barney was making cold calls on his personal phone while driving. His car hit and killed a motorcyclist. The brokerage firm was sued and accused of contributing to an accident by encouraging employees to use cellular telephones while driving. To avoid the risk of paying huge damages awarded by an emotional jury, the brokerage firm offered the victim's family a $500,000 settlement. Read the rest of this case in Chapter 5, Activity 5.6.

Your Task. Individually or in teams write a memo to LaReve sales reps outlining company suggestions (or should they be rules?) for safe wireless phone use in cars. Check InfoTrac for articles that discuss cell phone use in cars. Look for additional safety ideas. In your message to sales reps, try to suggest receiver benefits. How is safe cell phone use beneficial to the sales rep?

11.7 IMPROVING TELEPHONE SKILLS BY ROLE PLAYING. Acting out the roles of telephone caller and receiver is an effective technique for improving skills. To give you such practice, your instructor will divide the class into pairs.

Your Task. For each scenario take a moment to read and rehearse your role silently. Then play the role with your partner. If time permits, repeat the scenarios, changing roles.

PARTNER 1	**PARTNER 2**
A. You are the personnel manager of Datatronics, Inc. Call Elizabeth Franklin, office manager at Computers Plus. Inquire about a job applicant, Chelsea Chavez, who listed Ms. Franklin as a reference.	You are the receptionist for Computers Plus. The caller asks for Elizabeth Franklin, who is home sick today. You don't know when she will be able to return. Answer the call appropriately.

PARTNER 1	**PARTNER 2**
B. Call Ms. Franklin again the following day to inquire about the same job applicant, Chelsea Chavez. Ms. Franklin answers today, but she talks on and on, describing the applicant in great detail. Tactfully close the conversation.	You are now Ms. Franklin, office manager. Describe Chelsea Chavez, an imaginary employee. Think of someone with whom you've worked. Include many details, such as her ability to work with others, her appearance, her skills at computing, her schooling, her ambition, and so forth.
C. You are now the receptionist for Tom Wing, of Wing Imports. Answer a call for Mr. Wing, who is working in another office, at ext. 134, where he will accept calls.	You are now an administrative assistant for attorney Michael Murphy. Call Tom Wing to verify a meeting date Mr. Murphy has with Mr. Wing. Use your own name in identifying yourself.
D. You are now Tom Wing, owner of Wing Imports. Call your attorney, Michael Murphy, about a legal problem. Leave a brief, incomplete message.	You are now the receptionist for attorney Michael Murphy. Mr. Murphy is skiing in Aspen and will return in two days, but he doesn't want his clients to know where he is. Take a message.
E. Call Mr. Murphy again. Leave a message that will prevent telephone tag.	Take a message again.

11.8 ANALYZING A MEETING. You've learned a number of techniques in this chapter for planning and participating in meetings. Here's your chance to put your knowledge to work.

Your Task. Attend a structured meeting of a college, social, business, or other organization. Compare the manner in which the meeting is conducted with the suggestions presented in this chapter. Why did the meeting succeed or fail? Prepare a memo for your instructor or be ready to discuss your findings in class.

11.9 PLANNING A MEETING. Assume that the next meeting of your associated students organization will discuss preparations for a careers day in the spring. The group will hear reports from committees working on speakers, business recruiters, publicity, reservations of campus space, setup of booths, and any other matters you can think of.

Your Task. As president of your ASO, prepare an agenda for the meeting. Compose your introductory remarks to open the meeting. Your instructor may ask you to submit these two documents or use them in staging an actual meeting in class.

11.10 LEADING A MEETING. Your boss is unhappy at the way some employees lead meetings. Because he knows that you have studied this topic, he asks you to send him a memo listing specific points that he can use in an in-house training session in which he plans to present ideas on how to conduct business meetings.

INFOTRAC

Your Task. Using InfoTrac, locate articles providing tips on leading meetings. One particularly good article is Cathrine L. Carlozzi's "Make Your Meetings Count" (*Journal of Accountancy*, February 1999, Article A53878198). Prepare a memo to your boss, Douglas Hawkins, outlining eight or more points on how to lead a meeting.

OTHER PUNCTUATION

Although this checkup concentrates on Sections 2.23–2.29 in the Grammar/Mechanics Handbook, you may also refer to other punctuation principles. Insert any necessary punctuation. In the space provided, indicate the number of changes you make and record the number of the G/M principle(s) illustrated. Count each mark separately; for example, a set of parentheses counts as 2. If you make no changes, write *0*. When you finish, compare your responses with those provided at the end of the book. If your responses differ, study carefully the specific principles shown in parentheses.

2	(2.27)	**Example**	(De-emphasize.) The consumption of Mexican food products is highest in certain states (California, Arizona, New Mexico, and Texas), but this food trend is spreading to other parts of the country.

1. (Emphasize.) The convention planning committee has invited three managers Jim Lowey, Frank Beyer, and Carolyn Wong to make presentations.
2. Would you please Miss Sanchez use your computer to recalculate these totals
3. (Deemphasize.) A second set of demographic variables see Figure 13 on page 432 includes nationality, religion, and race.
4. Because the word recommendation is frequently misspelled we are adding it to our company style book.
5. Recruiting, hiring, and training these are three important functions of a personnel officer.
6. The office manager said, Who placed an order for two dozen printer cartridges
7. Have any of the research assistants been able to locate the article entitled How Tax Reform Will Affect You
8. (Emphasize.) The biggest oil-producing states Texas, California, and Alaska are experiencing severe budget deficits.
9. Have you sent invitations to Mr Ronald E Harris, Miss Michelle Hale, and Ms Sylvia Mason
10. Dr. Y. W. Yellin wrote the chapter entitled Trading on the Options Market that appeared in a book called Securities Markets.
11. James said, "I'll be right over" however he has not appeared yet.
12. In business the word liability may be defined as any legal obligation requiring payment in the future.
13. Because the work was scheduled to be completed June 10,; we found it necessary to hire temporary workers to work June 8 and 9.
14. Did any cod shipments arrive today
15. Hooray I have finished this checkup haven't I

GRAMMAR/MECHANICS CHALLENGE—11

DOCUMENT FOR REVISION

The following report showing meeting minutes has faults in grammar, punctuation, spelling, number form, wordiness, and word use. Use standard proofreading marks (see Appendix B) to correct the errors. When you finish, your instructor can show you the revised version of this summary.

Honolulu-Pacific Federal Interagency Board
Policy Board Committee
Room 25, 310 Ala Moana Boulevard, Honolulu
February 4, 200x

Present: Debra Chinnapongse, Tweet Jackson, Irene Kishita, Barry Knaggs, Kevin Poepoe, and Ralph Mason

Absent: Alex Watanabe

The meeting was call to order by Chair Kevin Poepo at 9:02 a.m. in the morning. Minutes from the January 6th meeting was read and approve.

Old Business

Debra Chinnapongse discussed the cost of the annual awards luncheon. That honors outstanding employees. The ticket price ticket does not cover all the expenses incured. Major expenses include: awards, leis, and complementary lunches for the judges, VIP guests and volunteers. Honolulu-Pacific Federal Interagency Board can not continue to make up the difference between income from tickets and costs for the luncheon. Ms. Chinnapongse reported that it had come to her attention that other interagency boards relied on members contributions for their awards' programs.

MOTION: To send a Letter to board members asking for there contributions to support the annual awards luncheon. (Chinapongse/Kishita). PASSED 6-0.

Reports

Barry Knaggs reported that the homeland defense committee sponsored a get acquainted meeting in November. More than eighty people from various agencys attended.

The Outreach Committee reports that they have been asked to assist the Partnership for Public Service, a non profit main land organization in establishing a speakers bureau of Hawaiian Federal employees. It would be available to speak at schools and colleges about Federal jobs and employment.

New Business

The chair announced a Planning Meeting to be held in March regarding revising the emergency dismissal plan. In other New Business Ralph Mason reported that the staff had purchased fifty tickets for members, and our committees to attend the Zig Ziglar seminar in the month of March.

Next Meeting

The next meeting of the Policy Boare Committee will be held in early Aprl at the Fleet and Industrial Supply Center, Pearl harbor. At that time the meeting will include a tour of the Red Hill under ground fuel storage facility.

The meeting adjourned at 10:25 am by Keven Poepoe.

Respectfully submitted,

Communication Workshop: Career Skills   **331**

How to Deal With Difficult People at Work

Difficult people in the workplace challenge your patience and your communication skills. In your work life and in your personal life, you are often confronted by people who are negative, manipulative, uncooperative, or just plain difficult. Although everyone is irritable or indecisive at times, some people are so difficult that they require us to react with special coping skills. In his famous book *Coping With Difficult People*, psychologist and management consultant Robert M. Bramson provides helpful advice in dealing with a number of personality types.

Sherman tanks try to bully and overwhelm with intimidation, arrogance, righteous indignation, and outright anger. To cope, try the following:

- Give them time to run down; maintain eye contact.
- Don't worry about being polite; state your opinions forcefully.
- Don't argue or be sarcastic; be ready to be friendly.

Snipers hide behind cover. They attack by teasing and making not-too-subtle digs. To cope, try the following:

- "Smoke" them out; refuse to be attacked indirectly. Ask questions such as, "What did you mean by your remark?" "Sounds as if you are ridiculing me. Are you?"
- Ask the group to confirm or deny the sniper's criticism. "Anyone else see it that way?" Get other points of view.
- Acknowledge the underlying problem and try to find a feasible solution.

Exploders blow up in frustrated rage; they have an adult tantrum. To cope, try the following:

- Give them time to run down and regain control on their own.
- If they don't stop, break into the tirade by saying, "Stop!"
- Show that you take them seriously.
- Find a way to take a breather and get some privacy with them.

Complainers find fault with everything. Some complaints are made directly; others are made indirectly to third parties. To cope,

- Listen attentively, even if you feel guilty or impatient.
- Acknowledge what they are saying and paraphrase to see whether you understand.
- Don't agree or apologize, even if you feel you should.
- Avoid the accusation–defense–reaccusation pattern.
- Try to solve the problem by (a) asking specific informational questions, (b) assigning fact-finding tasks, or (c) asking for the complaint in writing.
- If all else fails, ask the complainer, "How do you want this discussion to end?"

Indecisive stallers are unable to make decisions. Their stalling makes them difficult to work with. To cope,

- Encourage stallers to tell you about conflicts or reservations that prevent the decision. Listen for clues.

- Help stallers solve their problems by (a) acknowledging past problems non-defensively, (b) examining the facts, and (c) proposing alternative solutions in priority order.
- Give support after a decision has been made.

Career Application. In most workplaces you can expect to meet one or more truly difficult people. To provide practice in dealing with such people, develop a coping plan.

Your Task. In a memo to yourself, write responses to the following:

1. Describe in detail the behavior of a person whom you find to be difficult.
2. Analyze and describe your understanding of that behavior.
3. Review your past interactions with this person. Did you get along better with this person before?
4. Decide what coping behavior would be appropriate.
5. Acknowledge what might need to change in yourself to best carry out the most promising coping behavior.
6. Prepare an action plan explaining what you will do and by what date.

Chapter 12

Making Oral Presentations

Public speaking skills have risen to the top of nearly every company's wish list of executive attributes.[1]

HAL LANCASTER, *Wall Street Journal* columnist

LEARNING OBJECTIVES

1. Discuss two important first steps in preparing effective oral presentations.
2. Explain the major elements in organizing the content of a presentation, including the introduction, body, and conclusion.
3. Identify techniques for gaining audience rapport, including using effective imagery, providing verbal signposts, and sending appropriate nonverbal messages.
4. Discuss designing and using effective visual aids, handouts, and electronic presentation materials.
5. Specify delivery techniques for use before, during, and after a presentation.
6. Explain effective techniques for adapting oral presentations to cross-cultural audiences.

*O*rganizations today are increasingly interested in hiring people with good presentation skills. Why? The business world is changing. Technical skills aren't enough to guarantee success. You also need to be able to communicate ideas effectively in presentations to customers, vendors, members of your team, and management. Your presentations will probably be made to inform, influence, or motivate action. And the opportunities to make these presentations are increasing, even for nonmanagement employees.[2] Powerful speaking skills draw attention to you and advance your career. But reading a textbook is not enough to help you develop solid speaking skills. You also need coaching and chances to practice your skills. In this book you will learn the fundamentals, and in your course you will be able to try out your skills and develop confidence.

Today's work environments require employees to fully develop their presentation skills so that they are prepared to share information in informal settings as well as in more formal presentations. Preparing for a team presentation involves deciding what you want to accomplish, understanding your audience, gathering information, and working together to develop a polished performance.
© Mark Richards/ PhotoEdit, Inc.

GETTING READY FOR AN ORAL PRESENTATION

In getting ready for an oral presentation, you probably feel a great deal of anxiety. For many people fear of speaking before a group is almost as great as the fear of dying. We get butterflies in our tummies just thinking about it. When you feel those butterflies, though, speech coach Dianne Booher advises getting them in formation and visualizing the swarm as a powerful push propelling you to a peak performance.[3] For any presentation, you can reduce your fears and lay the foundation for a professional performance by focusing on five areas: preparation, organization, audience rapport, visual aids, and delivery.

DECIDING WHAT YOU WANT TO ACCOMPLISH

The most important part of your preparation is deciding your purpose. Do you want to sell a health care program to a prospective client? Do you want to persuade management to increase the marketing budget? Do you want to inform customer service reps of three important ways to prevent miscommunication? Whether your goal is to persuade or to inform, you must have a clear idea of where you are going. At the end of your presentation, what do you want your listeners to remember or do?

Eric Evans, a loan officer at First Fidelity Trust, faced such questions as he planned a talk for a class in small business management. (You can see the outline for his talk in Figure 12.3.) Eric's former business professor had asked him to return to campus and give the class advice about borrowing money from banks in order to start new businesses. Because Eric knew so much about this topic, he found it difficult to extract a specific purpose statement for his presentation. After much thought he narrowed his purpose to this: *To inform potential entrepreneurs about three important factors that loan officers consider before granting start-up loans to launch small businesses.* His entire presentation focused on ensuring that the class members understood and remembered three principal ideas.

UNDERSTANDING YOUR AUDIENCE

A second key element in preparation is analyzing your audience, anticipating its reactions, and making appropriate adaptations. Understanding four different audience types, summarized in Figure 12.1, helps you decide how to organize your presentation. A friendly audience, for example, will respond to humor and personal experiences. A neutral audience requires an even, controlled delivery style. The talk would probably be filled with facts, statistics, and expert opinions. An uninterested audience that is forced to attend requires a brief presentation. Such an audience might respond best to humor, cartoons, colorful visuals, and startling statistics. A hostile audience demands a calm, controlled delivery style with objective data and expert opinion.

Other elements, such as age, gender, education, experience, and size of audience will affect your style and message content. Analyze the following questions to help you determine your organizational pattern, delivery style, and supporting material.

- How will this topic appeal to this audience?
- How can I relate this information to their needs?
- How can I earn respect so that they accept my message?

FIGURE 12.1 Succeeding With Four Audience Types

AUDIENCE MEMBERS	ORGANIZATIONAL PATTERN	DELIVERY STYLE	SUPPORTING MATERIAL
Friendly They like you and your topic	Use any pattern; try something new; involve the audience	Be warm, pleasant, open; use lots of eye contact, smiles	Include humor, personal examples and experiences
Neutral They are calm, rational; their minds are made up but they think they are objective	Present both sides of issue; use pro–con or problem–solution patterns; save time for audience questions	Be controlled; do nothing showy; use confident, small gestures	Use facts, statistics, expert opinion, comparison and contrast; avoid humor, personal stories, and flashy visuals
Uninterested They have short attention spans; they may be there against their will	Be brief, no more than three points; avoid topical and pro–con patterns that seem lengthy to audience	Be dynamic and entertaining; move around, use large gestures	Use humor, cartoons, colorful visuals, powerful quotations, startling statistics
	Avoid darkening the room, standing motionless, passing out handouts, using boring visuals, or expecting audience to participate		
Hostile They want to take charge or to ridicule speaker; defensive, emotional	Use noncontroversial pattern such as topical, chronological, or geographical	Be calm, controlled; speak evenly and slowly	Include objective data and expert opinion; avoid anecdotes and humor
	Avoid question-and-answer period, if possible; otherwise, use a moderator or accept only written questions		

- What would be most effective in making my point? Facts? Statistics? Personal experiences? Expert opinion? Humor? Cartoons? Graphic illustrations? Demonstrations? Case histories? Analogies?
- What measures must I take to ensure that this audience remembers my main points?

ORGANIZING CONTENT FOR A POWERFUL IMPACT

Once you have determined your purpose and analyzed the audience, you're ready to collect information and organize it logically. Good organization and conscious repetition are the two most powerful keys to audience comprehension and retention. In fact, many speech experts recommend the following admittedly repetitious, but effective, plan:

Step 1: Tell them what you're going to say.
Step 2: Say it.
Step 3: Tell them what you've just said.

In other words, repeat your main points in the introduction, body, and conclusion of your presentation. Although it sounds deadly, this strategy works surprisingly well. Let's examine how to construct the three parts of an effective presentation.

CAPTURING ATTENTION IN THE INTRODUCTION

How many times have you heard a speaker begin with, *It's a pleasure to be here.* Or, *I'm honored to be asked to speak.* Boring openings such as these get speakers off to a dull start. Avoid such banalities by striving to accomplish three goals in the introduction to your presentation:

- Capture listeners' attention and get them involved.
- Identify yourself and establish your credibility.
- Preview your main points.

If you're able to appeal to listeners and involve them in your presentation right from the start, you're more likely to hold their attention until the finish. Consider some of the same techniques that you used to open sales letters: a question, a startling fact, a joke, a story, or a quotation. Some speakers achieve involvement by opening with a question or command that requires audience members to raise their hands or stand up. You'll find additional techniques for gaining and keeping audience attention in Figure 12.2.

To establish your credibility, you need to describe your position, knowledge, or experience—whatever qualifies you to speak. Try also to connect with your audience. Listeners are particularly drawn to speakers who reveal something of themselves and identify with them. A consultant addressing office workers might reminisce about how he started as a temporary worker; a CEO might tell a funny story in which the joke is on herself.

After capturing attention and establishing yourself, you'll want to preview the main points of your topic, perhaps with a visual aid. You may wish to put off

© Ted Goff (www.tedgoff.com)

"Please don't make me use another water balloon to keep your attention."

FIGURE 12.2 Nine Winning Techniques for Gaining and Keeping Audience Attention

Experienced speakers know how to capture the attention of an audience and how to maintain that attention during a presentation. You can give your presentations a boost by trying these nine proven techniques.

- **A promise.** Begin with a promise that keeps the audience expectant. For example, *By the end of this presentation I will have shown you how you can increase your sales by 50 percent!*
- **Drama.** Open by telling an emotionally moving story or by describing a serious problem that involves the audience. Throughout your talk include other dramatic elements, such as a long pause after a key statement. Change your vocal tone or pitch. Professionals use high-intensity emotions such as anger, joy, sadness, and excitement.
- **Eye contact.** As you begin, command attention by surveying the entire audience to take in all listeners. Take two to five seconds to make eye contact with as many people as possible.
- **Movement.** Leave the lectern area whenever possible. Walk around the conference table or between the aisles of your audience. Try to move toward your audience, especially at the beginning and end of your talk.
- **Questions.** Keep listeners active and involved with rhetorical questions. Ask for a show of hands to get each listener thinking. The response will also give you a quick gauge of audience attention.
- **Demonstrations.** Include a member of the audience in a demonstration. For example, *I'm going to show you exactly how to implement our four-step customer courtesy process, but I need a volunteer from the audience to help me.*
- **Samples/gimmicks.** If you're promoting a product, consider using items to toss out to the audience or to award as prizes to volunteer participants. You can also pass around product samples or promotional literature. Be careful, though, to maintain control.
- **Visuals.** Give your audience something to look at besides yourself. Use a variety of visual aids in a single session. Also consider writing the concerns expressed by your audience on a flipchart or on the board as you go along.
- **Self-interest.** Review your entire presentation to ensure that it meets the critical *What's-in-it-for-me* audience test. Remember that people are most interested in things that benefit them.

---

actually writing your introduction, however, until after you have organized the rest of the presentation and crystallized your principal ideas.

Take a look at Eric Evans's introduction, shown in Figure 12.3, to see how he integrated all the elements necessary for a good opening.

ORGANIZING THE BODY

The best oral presentations focus on a few key ideas.

The biggest problem with most oral presentations is a failure to focus on a few principal ideas. Thus, the body of your short presentation (20 or fewer minutes) should include a limited number of main points, say, two to four. Develop each main point with adequate, but not excessive, explanation and details. Too many details can obscure the main message, so keep your presentation simple and logical. Remember, listeners have no pages to leaf back through should they become confused.

FIGURE 12.3 Oral Presentation Outline

What Makes a Loan Officer Say "Yes"?

I. INTRODUCTION

A. How many of you expect one day to start your own businesses? How many of you have all the cash available to capitalize that business when you start?

B. Like you, nearly every entrepreneur needs cash to open a business, and I promise you that by the end of this talk you will have inside information on how to make a loan application that will be successful.

C. As a loan officer at First Fidelity Trust, which specializes in small business loans, I make decisions on requests from entrepreneurs like you applying for start-up money.

Transition: Your professor invited me here today to tell you how you can improve your chances of getting a loan from us or from any other lender. I have suggestions in three areas: experience, preparation, and projection.

II. BODY

A. First, let's consider experience. You must show that you can hit the ground running.
1. Demonstrate what experience you have in your proposed business.
2. Include your résumé when you submit your business plan.
3. If you have little experience, tell us whom you would hire to supply the skills that you lack.

Transition: In addition to experience, loan officers will want to see that you have researched your venture thoroughly.

B. My second suggestion, then, involves preparation. Have you done your homework?
1. Talk to local businesspeople, especially those in related fields.
2. Conduct traffic counts or other studies to estimate potential sales.
3. Analyze the strengths and weaknesses of the competition.

Transition: Now that we've discussed preparation, we're ready for my final suggestion.

C. My last tip is the most important one. It involves making a realistic projection of your potential sales, cash flow, and equity.
1. Present detailed monthly cash-flow projections for the first year.
2. Describe "what-if" scenarios indicating both good and bad possibilities.
3. Indicate that you intend to supply at least 25 percent of the initial capital yourself.

Transition: The three major points I've just outlined cover critical points in obtaining start-up loans. Let me review them for you.

III. CONCLUSION

A. Loan officers are most likely to say "yes" to your loan application if you do three things: (1) prove that you can hit the ground running when your business opens; (2) demonstrate that you've researched your proposed business seriously; and (3) project a realistic picture of your sales, cash flow, and equity.

B. Experience, preparation, and projection, then, are the three keys to launching your business with the necessary start-up capital so that you can concentrate on where your customers, not your funds, are coming from.

Left margin annotations:
Captures attention
Involves audience
Identifies speaker
Establishes main points
Summarizes main points

Right margin annotations:
Previews three main points
Develops coherence with planned transitions
Provides final focus

When Eric Evans began planning his presentation, he realized immediately that he could talk for hours on his topic. He also knew that listeners are not good at separating major and minor points. Thus, instead of submerging his listeners in a sea of information, he sorted out a few principal ideas. In the mortgage business, loan officers generally ask the following three questions of each applicant for a small business loan: (1) Are you ready to "hit the ground running" in starting your business? (2) Have you done your homework? and (3) Have you made realistic projections of potential sales, cash flow, and equity investment? These questions would become his main points, but Eric wanted to streamline them further so that his audience would be sure to remember them. He capsulized the questions in three words: *experience, preparation,* and *projection.* As you can see in Figure 12.3, Eric prepared a sentence outline showing these three main ideas. Each is supported by examples and explanations.

How to organize and sequence main ideas may not be immediately obvious when you begin working on a presentation. In Chapter 10 (Figure 10.2) you studied a number of patterns for organizing written reports. Those patterns—reviewed, amplified, and illustrated here—are equally appropriate for oral presentations.

- **Chronology.** Example: A presentation describing the history of a problem, organized from the first sign of trouble to the present.
- **Geography/space.** Example: A presentation about the changing diversity of the workforce, organized by regions in the country (East Coast, West Coast, and so forth).
- **Topic/function/conventional grouping.** Example: A report discussing mishandled airline baggage, organized by names of airlines.
- **Comparison/contrast (pro/con).** Example: A report comparing organic farming methods with those of modern industrial farming.
- **Journalism pattern.** Example: A report describing how identity thieves can ruin your good name. Organized by *who, what, when, where, why,* and *how.*
- **Value/size.** Example: A report describing fluctuations in housing costs, organized by prices of homes.
- **Importance.** Example: A report describing five reasons that a company should move its headquarters to a specific city, organized from the most important reason to the least important.
- **Problem/solution.** Example: A company faces a problem such as declining sales. A solution such as reducing the staff is offered.
- **Simple/complex.** Example: A report explaining genetic modification of plants, organized from simple seed production to complex gene introduction.
- **Best case/worst case.** Example: A report analyzing whether two companies should merge, organized by the best case result (improved market share, profitability, employee morale) opposed to the worse case result (devalued stock, lost market share, employee malaise).

In the presentation shown in Figure 12.3, Eric arranged the main points by importance, placing the most important point last where it had maximum effect. When organizing any presentation, prepare a little more material than you think you will actually need. Savvy speakers always have something useful in reserve (such as an extra handout, transparency, or idea)—just in case they finish early.

Summarizing in the Conclusion

Nervous speakers often rush to wrap up their presentations because they can't wait to flee the stage. But listeners will remember the conclusion more than any part of a speech. That's why you should spend some time to make it most effective. Strive to achieve two goals:

- Summarize the main themes of the presentation.
- Include a statement that allows you to leave the podium gracefully.

Some speakers end limply with comments such as "I guess that's about all I have to say." This leaves bewildered audience members wondering whether they should continue listening. Skilled speakers alert the audience that they are finishing. They use phrases such as, *In conclusion, As I end this presentation,* or *It's time for me to stop.* Then they proceed immediately to the conclusion. Audiences become justly irritated with a speaker who announces the conclusion but then digresses with one more story or talks on for ten more minutes.

A straightforward summary should review major points and focus on what you want the listeners to do, think, or remember. You might say, "In bringing my

Organize your report by time, geography, function, importance, or some other method that is logical to the receiver.

Effective conclusions summarize main points and allow the speaker to exit gracefully.

presentation to a close, I will restate my major purpose. . . ." Or, "In summary, my major purpose has been to . . ."; "in support of my purpose, I have presented three major points. They are (a) . . . , (b) . . . , and (c). . . ." Notice how Eric Evans, in the conclusion shown in Figure 12.3, summarized his three main points and provided a final focus to listeners.

If you are promoting a recommendation, you might end as follows: "In conclusion, I recommend that we retain Matrixx Marketing to conduct a telemarketing campaign beginning September 1 at a cost of X dollars. To complete this recommendation, I suggest that we (a) finance this campaign from our operations budget, (b) develop a persuasive message describing our new product, and (c) name Lisa Beck to oversee the project."

In your conclusion you might want to use an anecdote, an inspiring quotation, or a statement that ties in the opener and offers a new insight. Whatever you choose, be sure to include a closing thought that indicates you are finished. For example, "This concludes my presentation. After investigating many marketing firms, we are convinced that Matrixx is the best for our purposes. Your authorization of my recommendations will mark the beginning of a very successful campaign for our new product. Thank you."

HOW THE BEST SPEAKERS BUILD AUDIENCE RAPPORT

Good speakers are adept at building audience rapport. They form a bond with the audience; they entertain as well as inform. How do they do it? Based on observations of successful and unsuccessful speakers, we learn that the good ones use a number of verbal and nonverbal techniques to connect with the audience. Some of their helpful techniques include providing effective imagery, supplying verbal signposts, and using body language strategically.

EFFECTIVE IMAGERY

You'll lose your audience quickly if your talk is filled with abstractions, generalities, and dry facts. To enliven your presentation and enhance comprehension, try using some of these techniques:

- **Analogies.** A comparison of similar traits between dissimilar things can be effective in explaining and drawing connections. For example, *Product development is similar to the process of conceiving, carrying, and delivering a baby.* Or, *Downsizing and restructuring is similar to an overweight person undergoing a regimen of dieting, habit changing, and exercise.*
- **Metaphors.** A comparison between otherwise dissimilar things without using the words *like* or *as* results in a metaphor. For example, *Our competitor's CEO is a snake when it comes to negotiating* or *My desk is a garbage dump.*
- **Similes.** A comparison that includes the words *like* or *as* is a simile. For example, *Our critics used our background report as a drunk uses a lamppost—for support rather than for illumination.* Or, *She's as happy as someone who just won the lottery.*
- **Personal anecdotes.** Nothing connects you faster or better with your audience than a good personal story. In a talk about e-mail techniques, you could reveal your own blunders that became painful learning experiences. In a talk to potential investors, the founder of a new ethnic magazine might tell a story about growing up without positive ethnic role models.
- **Personalized statistics.** Although often misused, statistics stay with people—particularly when they relate directly to the audience. A speaker discussing job searching might say, *Look around the room. Only three out of five graduates will*

✓ *Quick Check*

Use analogies, metaphors, similes, personal anecdotes, personalized statistics, and worst- and best-case scenarios instead of dry facts.

Patricia F. Russo, CEO of Lucent Technologies, the largest maker of equipment for telephone companies, used an excellent metaphor to suggest her company's troubles. Describing her effort to reduce Lucent's work force and return to profitability during an economic downturn, she said: "We're trying to fly a 747 in the middle of a storm and change the engines while we're at it." In comparing two dissimilar things, this apt metaphor helps us visualize the difficulty of Lucent's tasks.

find a job immediately after graduation. If possible, simplify and personalize facts. For example, *The sales of Coca-Cola totaled 2 billion cases last year. That means that six full cases of Coke were consumed by every man, woman, and child in the U.S.*

- **Worst- and best-case scenarios.** Hearing the worst that could happen can be effective in driving home a point. For example, *If we do nothing about our computer backup system now, it's just a matter of time before the entire system crashes and we lose all of our customer contact information. Can you imagine starting from scratch in building all of your customer files again? However, if we fix the system now, we can expand our customer files and actually increase sales at the same time.*

VERBAL SIGNPOSTS

Speakers must remember that listeners, unlike readers of a report, cannot control the rate of presentation or flip back through pages to review main points. As a result, listeners get lost easily. Knowledgeable speakers help the audience recognize the organization and main points in an oral message with verbal signposts. They keep listeners on track by including helpful previews, summaries, and transitions, such as these:

- **Previewing**
  The next segment of my talk presents three reasons for . . . .
  Let's now consider the causes of . . . .

- **Summarizing**
  Let me review with you the major problems I've just discussed . . . .
  You see, then, that the most significant factors are . . . .

- **Switching directions**
  Thus far we've talked solely about . . . ; now let's move to . . . .
  I've argued that . . . and . . . , but an alternate view holds that . . . .

You can further improve any oral presentation by including appropriate transitional expressions such as *first, second, next, then, therefore, moreover, on the other hand, on the contrary,* and *in conclusion.* These expressions lend emphasis and tell listeners where you are headed. Notice in Eric Evans' outline, in Figure 12.3, the specific transitional elements designed to help listeners recognize each new principal point.

NONVERBAL MESSAGES

Although what you say is most important, the nonverbal messages you send can also have a potent effect on how well your message is received. How you look, how you move, and how you speak can make or break your presentation. The following suggestions focus on nonverbal tips to ensure that your verbal message is well-received.

- **Look terrific.** Like it or not, you will be judged by your appearance. For everything but small in-house presentations, be sure you dress professionally. The rule of thumb is that you should dress at least as well as the best-dressed person in the audience.
- **Animate your body.** Be enthusiastic and let your body show it. Emphasize ideas to enhance points about size, number, and direction. Use a variety of gestures, but don't consciously plan them in advance.
- **Punctuate your words.** You can keep your audience interested by varying your tone, volume, pitch, and pace. Use pauses before and after important points. Allow the audience to take in your ideas.
- **Get out from behind the podium.** Avoid being planted to the podium. Movement makes you look natural and comfortable. You might pick a few places in the room to walk to. Even if you must stay close to your visual aids, make a point of leaving them occasionally so that the audience can see your whole body.
- **Vary your facial expression.** Begin with a smile, but change your expressions to correspond with the thoughts you are voicing. You can shake your head to show disagreement, roll your eyes to show disdain, look heavenward for guidance, or wrinkle your brow to show concern or dismay. To see how speakers convey meaning without words, mute the sound on your TV and watch the facial expressions of a talk show personality.

PLANNING VISUAL AIDS, HANDOUTS, AND ELECTRONIC PRESENTATIONS

Before you make a business presentation, consider this wise Chinese proverb: "Tell me, I forget. Show me, I remember. Involve me, I understand." Your goals as a speaker are to make listeners understand, remember, and act on your ideas. To get them interested and involved, include effective visual aids. Some experts say that we acquire 85 percent of all our knowledge visually. Therefore, an oral presentation that incorporates visual aids is far more likely to be understood and retained than one lacking visual enhancement.

Good visual aids have many purposes. They emphasize and clarify main points, thus improving comprehension and retention. They increase audience interest, and they make the presenter appear more professional, better prepared, and more persuasive. Furthermore, research shows that the use of visual aids actually shortens meetings.[4] Visual aids are particularly helpful for inexperienced speakers because the audience concentrates on the aid rather than on the speaker. Good visuals also serve to jog the memory of a speaker, thus improving self-confidence, poise, and delivery.

TYPES OF VISUAL AIDS

Fortunately for today's speakers, many forms of visual media are available to enhance a presentation. Figure 12.4 describes a number of visual aids and compares their cost, degree of formality, and other considerations. Three of the most popular visuals are overhead transparencies, handouts, and computer visuals.

Overhead Transparencies.   Student and professional speakers alike rely on the overhead projector for many reasons. Most meeting areas are equipped with pro-

FIGURE 12.4 Presentation Enhancers

MEDIUM	COST	AUDIENCE SIZE	FORMALITY LEVEL	ADVANTAGES AND DISADVANTAGES
Computer slides	Low	2–200	Formal or informal	Presentation software programs are easy to use and cheap and produce professional results. They should not, however, replace or distract from the speaker's message. Darkened room can put audience to sleep.
Overhead projector	Low	2–200	Formal or informal	Transparencies produce neat, legible visuals that are cheap and easy to make. Speaker keeps contact with audience. Transparencies may, however, look low tech.
Flipchart	Low	2–200	Informal	Easels and charts are readily available and portable. Useful for working discussions and informational presentations. Speaker can prepare display in advance or on the spot.
Write-and-wipe board	Medium	2–200	Informal	Porcelain-on-steel surface replaces messy chalkboard. Speaker can wipe clean with cloth. Useful for working discussions.
Video monitor	Medium	2–100	Formal or informal	A VCR display features motion and sound. Videos, however, require skill, time, and equipment to prepare.
Props	Varies	2–200	Formal or informal	Product samples, prototypes, symbols, or gimmicks can produce vivid images that audiences remember.
Handouts	Varies	Unlimited	Formal or informal	Audience appreciates take-home items such as outlines, tables, charts, reports, brochures, or summaries. Handouts, however, can divert attention from speaker.

Chapter 12   Making Oral Presentations

jectors and screens. Moreover, acetate transparencies for the overhead are cheap, easily prepared on a computer or copier, and simple to use. And, because rooms need not be darkened, a speaker using transparencies can maintain eye contact with the audience. A word of caution, though: stand to the side of the projector so that you don't obstruct the audience's view.

Handouts. You can enhance and complement your presentations by distributing pictures, outlines, brochures, articles, charts, summaries, or other supplements. Speakers who use computer presentation programs often prepare a set of their slides along with notes to hand out to viewers. Timing the distribution of any handout, though, is tricky. If given out during a presentation, your handouts tend to distract the audience, causing you to lose control. Thus, it's probably best to discuss most handouts during the presentation but delay distributing them until after you finish.

Computer Visuals. With today's excellent software programs—such as Power-Point, Harvard Graphics Advanced Presentation, Freelance Graphics, and Corel Presentations—you can create dynamic, colorful presentations with your PC. The output from these programs is generally shown on a PC monitor, a TV monitor, an LCD (liquid crystal display) panel, or a screen. With a little expertise and advanced equipment, you can create a multimedia presentation that includes stereo sound, video clips, and hyperlinks, as described in the following discussion of electronic presentations.

DESIGNING AN IMPRESSIVE ELECTRONIC PRESENTATION

The content of most presentations today hasn't changed, but the medium certainly has. At meetings and conferences smart speakers now use computer programs, such as PowerPoint, to present, defend, and sell their ideas most effectively. PowerPoint is a software program that facilitates design of text and graphics on slides that can be displayed on a laptop computer or projected to a screen. Power-Point slides can also be sent out as an e-mail attachment, distributed via Web download, or printed as a booklet. The latest gadgets even enable you to plan your PowerPoint presentation on a PDA (personal digital assistant computer).[5] Many business speakers use PowerPoint because it helps them organize their thoughts, is inexpensive, and produces flashy high-tech visuals. Used skillfully, PowerPoint can make an impressive, professional presentation.

Yet, PowerPoint has its critics. They charge that the program dictates the way in which information is structured and presented. PowerPoint stifles "the storyteller, the poet, the person whose thoughts cannot be arranged in the shape of an AutoContent slide."[6] PowerPoint, say its detractors, is turning the nation's businesspeople into a "mindless gaggle of bullet-pointed morons."[7] Although storytellers and poets may find that PowerPoint smothers their creativity, business speakers know that it increases audience enjoyment, enhances comprehension, and promotes retention. PowerPoint speakers, however, are effective only when they are skillful. To stay clear of the "bullet-pointed moron" category, you must learn about using templates, working with color, building bullet points, and adding multimedia effects.

USING TEMPLATES TO YOUR ADVANTAGE

To begin your training in using an electronic presentation program, you'll want to examine its templates. These professionally designed formats combine harmonious colors, borders, and fonts for pleasing visual effects. One of the biggest prob-

✓ **Quick Check**

Computer-aided presentations are economical, flexible, professional, and easy to prepare.

✓ **Quick Check**

Critics say that PowerPoint is too regimented and produces "bullet-pointed morons."

lems in corporate presentations is inconsistency. Presentations include a hodge-podge collection of informal slides with different fonts and clashing colors. Templates avoid this problem by showing what fonts should be used for different level headings.

Templates also provide guidance in laying out each slide, as shown in Figure 12.5. You can select a layout for a title page, a bulleted list, a bar chart, a double-column list, an organization chart, and so on. To present a unified and distinctive image, some companies develop a customized template with their logo and a pre-defined color scheme. As one expert says, "This prevents salespeople from creating horrid color combinations on their own."[8] But templates are helpful only if you use them when you first begin preparing your presentation. Applying a template when you are nearly finished would involve a lot of rekeying and rewriting.

WORKING WITH COLOR

✓ **Quick Check**

Background and text colors depend on the lightness of the room.

You don't need training in color theory to create presentation images that impress your audience rather than confuse them. You can use the color schemes from the design templates that come with your presentation program, as shown in Figure 12.6, or you can alter them. Generally, you're smart to use a color palette of five or fewer colors for an entire presentation. Use warm colors—reds, oranges, and yellows—to highlight important elements. Use the same color for like elements. For example, all slide titles should be the same color. The color for backgrounds and text depends on where the presentation will be given. Use light text on a dark background for presentations in darkened rooms. Use dark text on a light background for computer presentations in lighted rooms and for projecting transparencies.

When many people are working together to prepare a slide presentation, be sure that they all choose colors that are in PowerPoint's color scheme menu. When

FIGURE 12.5 Selecting a Slide Layout

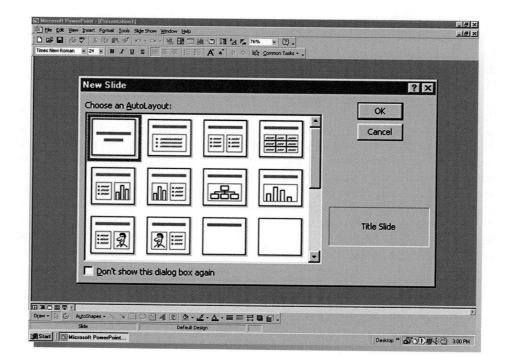

Chapter 12   Making Oral Presentations

FIGURE 12.6 Choosing a Color Scheme

TIPS FOR CHOOSING THE BEST COLORS IN VISUALS
- Develop a color palette of five or fewer colors.
- Use the same color for similar elements.
- Use dark text on a light background for presentations in bright rooms.
- Use light text on a dark background for presentations in darkened rooms.
- Use dark text on a light background for transparencies.
- Beware of light text on light backgrounds and dark text on dark backgrounds.

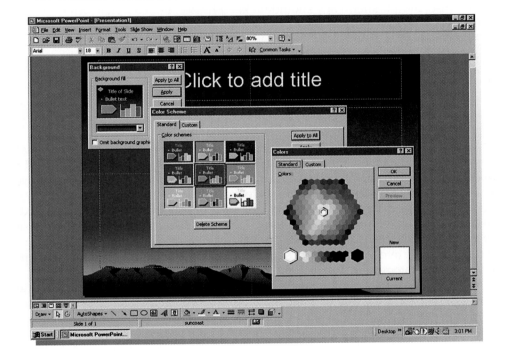

PowerPoint software provides a selection of designed templates, but you can also develop your own color scheme.

other colors are used, making changes becomes a tedious exercise in individual slide-editing.[9]

BUILDING BULLET POINTS

When you prepare your slides, translate the major headings in your presentation outline into titles for slides. Then build bullet points using short phrases. In Chapter 5 you learned to improve readability by using graphic highlighting techniques, including bullets, numbers, and headings. In preparing a PowerPoint presentation, you will use those same techniques.

Let's say, for example, that Matt wants to persuade management to install a voice mail system. Management is resisting because it says that voice mail will cost too much. Matt wants to emphasize benefits that result in increased productivity. Here is a portion of the text he wrote.

✓ *Quick Check*

Bullet points should be short phrases that are parallel.

Text of Presentation

Because voice mail allows callers to deliver detailed information to office personnel with just one telephone call, telephone tag can be eliminated. In addition, some research has found that up to 75 percent of all business calls do not reach the desired party. Whatever the actual number, people do tend to make far fewer callbacks when they have a voice mailbox in which their callers can leave messages. Although voice mail can't match the timeliness of a live telephone call, it's the next best thing for getting the word out when time is of the essence. Finally, voice mail frees callers from the prospect of being placed on hold indefinitely when the person they want is temporarily unavailable. Callers can immediately leave a voice message, bypassing the hold interval altogether.

Quick Check

Text can be converted to bullet points by experimenting with key phrases that are concise and balanced grammatically.

To convert the preceding text into bullet points, Matt started with a title and then listed the main ideas that related to that title. He worked with the list until all the items were parallel. That meant considerable experimenting with different wording. Matt went through many revisions before creating the following bulleted list. Notice that the heading promotes reader benefits. Notice also that the bullet points are concise and parallel. They should be key phrases, not complete sentences.

Text Converted to Bullet Points
Voice Mail Can Make Your Calls More Efficient
- Eliminates telephone tag
- Reduces callbacks
- Improves timely communication
- Shortens "hold" times

Quick Check

Incremental bullet points enable a speaker to animate the presentation and control the flow of ideas.

One of the best features of electronic presentation programs is the "build" capability. You can focus the viewer's attention on each specific item as you add bullet points line by line. The bulleted items may "fly" in from the left, right, top, or bottom. They can also build or dissolve from the center. As you add each new bullet point, leave the previous ones on the slide but show them in lightened text. In building bulleted points or in moving from one slide to the next, you can use *slide transition* elements, such as "wipe-outs," glitter, ripple, liquid, and vortex effects. But don't overdo it. Experts suggest choosing one transition effect and applying it consistently.[10]

For the most readable slides, apply the *Rule of Seven*. Each slide should include no more than seven words in a line, no more than seven total lines, and no more than 7×7 or 49 total words. And remember that presentation slides summarize; they don't tell the whole story. That's the job of the presenter.

ADDING MULTIMEDIA AND OTHER EFFECTS

Quick Check

Multimedia elements include sound, animation, and video features.

Many presentation programs also provide libraries of *multimedia* features to enhance your content. These include sound, animation, and video elements. For example, you could use sound effects to "reward" correct answers from your audience. But using the sound of screeching tires in a Department of Motor Vehicles presentation is probably unwise. Similarly, video clips—when used judiciously—can add excitement and depth to a presentation. You might use video to capture attention in a stimulating introduction, to show the benefits of a product in use, or to bring the personality of a distant expert or satisfied customer right into the meeting room.

Another way to enliven a presentation is with real-life photographic images, which are now easy to obtain thanks to the prevalence of low-cost scanners and digital cameras. Some programs are also capable of generating hyperlinks ("hot" spots on the screen) that allow you to jump instantly to relevant data or multimedia content.

FIGURE 12.7 Preparing a PowerPoint Presentation

TIPS FOR PREPARING AND USING SLIDES
- Keep all visuals simple; spotlight major points only.
- Use the same font size and style for similar headings.
- Apply the Rule of Seven: No more than seven words on a line, seven total lines, and 7 × 7 or 49 total words.
- Be sure that everyone in the audience can see the slides.
- Show a slide, allow the audience to read it, then paraphrase it. Do NOT read from a slide.
- Rehearse by practicing talking to the audience, not to the slides.
- Bring backup transparencies in case of equipment failure.

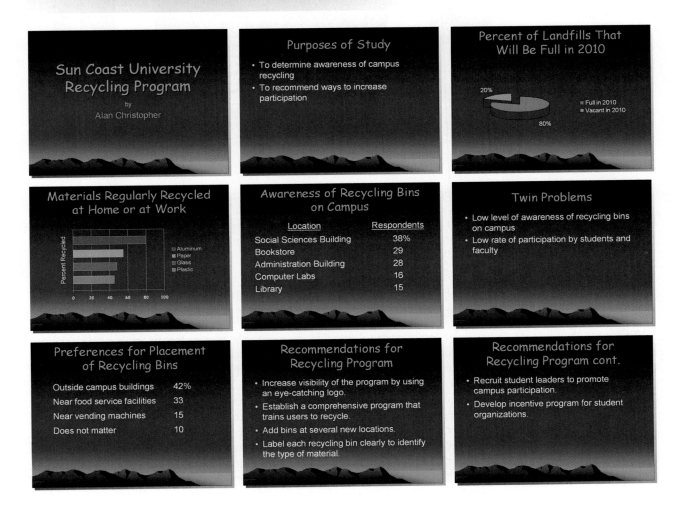

PRODUCING SPEAKER'S NOTES AND HANDOUTS

Most electronic presentation programs offer a variety of presentation options. In addition to printouts of your slides, you can make speaker's notes, as shown in Figure 12.8. These are wonderful aids for practicing your talk; they remind you

Designing an Impressive Electronic Presentation

FIGURE 12.8 Making Speaker's Notes for an Electronic Presentation

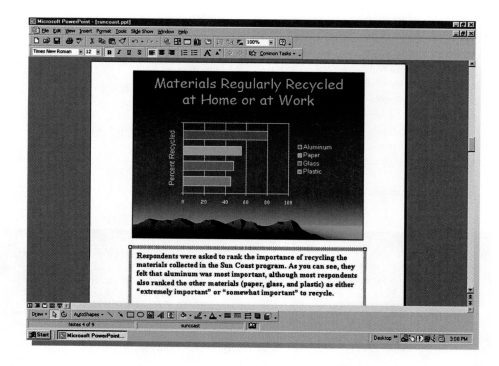

Speaker's notes enable you to print discussion items beneath each slide, thus providing handy review material for practice.

of the supporting comments for the abbreviated material in your slides. Many programs allow you to print miniature versions of your slides with numerous slides to a page, if you wish. These miniatures are handy if you want to preview your talk to a sponsoring organization or if you wish to supply the audience with a summary of your presentation.

DEVELOPING WEB-BASED PRESENTATIONS AND ELECTRONIC HANDOUTS

Web presentations are more convenient and less expensive than videoconferencing.

Because of many technological improvements, you can now give a talk without even traveling off-site. In other words, you can put your slides "on the road." Web presentations with slides, narration, and speaker control are emerging as a less costly alternative to videoconferencing, which can be expensive. For example, you could initiate a meeting via a conference call, narrate using a telephone, and have participants see your slides from the browsers on their computers. If you prefer, you could skip the narration and provide a prerecorded presentation. Web-based presentations have many applications, including providing access to updated training or sales data whenever needed.[11] Larry Magid, computer expert and noted speaker, suggests still another way that speakers can use the Web. He recommends posting your slides on the Web even if you are giving a face-to-face presentation. Attendees appreciate these *electronic handouts* because they don't have to lug them home.[12]

AVOIDING BEING UPSTAGED BY YOUR SLIDES

Although electronic presentations supply terrific sizzle, they cannot replace the steak. In developing a presentation, don't expect your slides to carry the show.

Your goal is to avoid letting PowerPoint "steal your thunder." Here are suggestions for keeping control in your slide presentation:[13]

- Use your slides primarily to summarize important points. For each slide have one or more paragraphs of narration to present to your audience.
- Remember that your responsibility is to *add value* to the information you present. Explain the analyses leading up to the major points and what each point means.
- Look at the audience, not the screen.
- Leave the lights as bright as you can. Make sure the audience can see your face and eyes.
- Darken the screen while you discuss points, tell a story, give an example, or involve the audience.
- Maintain a connection with the audience by using a laser pointer to highlight slide items to discuss.
- Don't rely totally on PowerPoint. Help the audience visualize your points by using other techniques. Drawing a diagram on a white board or flip chart can be more engaging than showing slide after slide of static drawings. Showing real objects is a welcome relief from slides.
- Remember that your slides merely supply a framework for your presentation. Your audience came to see and hear you!

✔ Quick Check

Don't allow PowerPoint to replace you as the main event; look at the audience, not the screen; leave the lights on; and use other visualization techniques.

POLISHING YOUR DELIVERY AND FOLLOWING UP

Once you've organized your presentation and prepared visuals, you're ready to practice delivering it. Here are suggestions for selecting a delivery method, along with specific techniques to use before, during, and after your presentation.

DELIVERY METHOD

Inexperienced speakers often feel that they must memorize an entire presentation to be effective. Unless you're a professional performer, however, you will sound wooden and unnatural. Moreover, forgetting your place can be disastrous! Therefore, memorizing an entire oral presentation is not recommended. However, memorizing significant parts—the introduction, the conclusion, and perhaps a meaningful quotation—can be dramatic and impressive.

If memorizing won't work, is reading your presentation the best plan? Definitely not! Reading to an audience is boring and ineffective. Because reading suggests that you don't know your topic well, the audience loses confidence in your expertise. Reading also prevents you from maintaining eye contact. You can't see audience reactions; consequently, you can't benefit from feedback.

Neither the memorizing nor the reading method creates convincing presentations. The best plan, by far, is a "notes" method. Plan your presentation carefully and talk from note cards or an outline containing key sentences and major ideas. By preparing and then practicing with your notes, you can talk to your audience in a conversational manner. Your notes should be neither entire paragraphs nor single words. Instead, they should contain a complete sentence or two to introduce each major idea. Below the topic sentence(s), outline subpoints and illustrations. Note cards will keep you on track and prompt your memory, but only if you have rehearsed the presentation thoroughly.

✔ Quick Check

The best method for delivering your presentation is speaking from carefully prepared note cards.

"In this seminar we'll discuss a simple technique for overcoming your fear of speaking in public."

✔ **Quick Check**

Stage fright is both natural and controllable.

DELIVERY TECHNIQUES

Nearly everyone experiences some degree of stage fright when speaking before a group. "If you hear someone say he or she isn't nervous before a speech, you're talking either to a liar or a very boring speaker," says corporate speech consultant Dianna Booher.[14] In other words, you can capitalize on the adrenaline that is coursing through your body by converting it to excitement and enthusiasm for your performance. But you can't just walk in and "wing it." People who don't prepare suffer the most anxiety and give the worst performances. You can learn to make effective oral presentations by focusing on four areas: preparation, organization, visual aids, and delivery.

Being afraid is quite natural and results from actual physiological changes occurring in your body. Faced with a frightening situation, your body responds with the fight-or-flight response, discussed more fully in Figure 12.9. You can learn to control and reduce stage fright, as well as to incorporate techniques for effective speaking, by using the following strategies and techniques before, during, and after your presentation.

BEFORE YOUR PRESENTATION

- **Prepare thoroughly.** One of the most effective strategies for reducing stage fright is knowing your subject thoroughly. Research your topic diligently and

FIGURE 12.9 Conquer Stage Fright With These Techniques

Ever get nervous before giving a speech? Everyone does! And it's not all in your head, either. When you face something threatening or challenging, your body reacts in what psychologists call the *fight-or-flight* response. This response provides your body with increased energy to deal with threatening situations. It also creates those sensations—dry mouth, sweaty hands, increased heartbeat, and stomach butterflies—that we associate with stage fright. The fight-or-flight response arouses your body for action—in this case, giving a speech.

Since everyone feels some form of apprehension before speaking, it's impossible to eliminate the physiological symptoms altogether. But you can help reduce their effects with the following techniques:

- **Breathe deeply.** Use deep breathing to ease your fight-or-flight symptoms. Inhale to a count of ten, hold this breath to a count of ten, and exhale to a count of ten. Concentrate on your counting and your breathing; both activities reduce your stress.

- **Convert your fear.** Don't view your sweaty palms and dry mouth as evidence of fear. Interpret them as symptoms of exuberance, excitement, and enthusiasm to share your ideas.
- **Know your topic.** Feel confident about your topic. Select a topic that you know well and that is relevant to your audience.
- **Use positive self-talk.** Remind yourself that you know your topic and are prepared. Tell yourself that the audience is on your side—because it is!
- **Shift the spotlight to your visuals.** At least some of the time the audience will be focusing on your slides, transparencies, handouts, or whatever you have prepared—and not on you.
- **Ignore any stumbles.** Don't apologize or confess your nervousness. If you keep going, the audience will forget any mistakes quickly.
- **Feel proud when you finish.** You'll be surprised at how good you feel when you finish. Take pride in what you've accomplished, and your audience will reward you with applause and congratulations. And, of course, your body will call off the fight-or-flight response and return to normal!

prepare a careful sentence outline. Those who try to "wing it" usually suffer the worst butterflies—and make the worst presentations.

- **Rehearse repeatedly.** When you rehearse, practice your entire presentation, not just the first half. Place your outline sentences on separate cards. You may also wish to include transitional sentences to help you move to the next topic. Use these cards as you practice, and include your visual aids in rehearsal. Rehearse alone or before friends and family. Also try rehearsing on audio- or videotape so that you can evaluate your effectiveness.
- **Time yourself.** Most audiences tend to get restless during longer talks. Thus, try to complete your presentation in no more than 20 minutes. Set a timer during your rehearsal to measure your speaking time.
- **Request a lectern.** Every beginning speaker needs the security of a high desk or lectern from which to deliver a presentation. It serves as a note holder and a convenient place to rest wandering hands and arms.
- **Check the room.** Before you talk, make sure that a lectern has been provided. If you are using sound equipment or a projector, be certain they are operational. Check electrical outlets and the position of the viewing screen. Ensure that the seating arrangement is appropriate to your needs.
- **Greet members of the audience.** Try to make contact with a few members of the audience when you enter the room, while you are waiting to be introduced, or when you walk to the podium. Your body language should convey friendliness, confidence, and enjoyment.
- **Practice stress reduction.** If you feel tension and fear while you are waiting your turn to speak, use stress-reduction techniques, such as deep breathing. Additional techniques to help you conquer stage fright are presented in Figure 12.9.

DURING YOUR PRESENTATION

- **Begin with a pause.** When you first approach the audience, take a moment to adjust your notes and make yourself comfortable. Establish your control of the situation.
- **Present your first sentence from memory.** By memorizing your opening, you can immediately establish rapport with the audience through eye contact. You'll also sound confident and knowledgeable.
- **Maintain eye contact.** If the size of the audience overwhelms you, pick out two individuals on the right and two on the left. Talk directly to these people.
- **Control your voice and vocabulary.** This means speaking in moderated tones but loudly enough to be heard. Eliminate verbal static, such as *ah, er, you know,* and *um.* Silence is preferable to meaningless fillers when you are thinking of your next idea.
- **Put the brakes on.** Many novice speakers talk too rapidly, displaying their nervousness and making it difficult for audience members to understand their ideas. Slow down and listen to what you are saying.
- **Move naturally.** You can use the lectern to hold your notes so that you are free to move about casually and naturally. Avoid fidgeting with your notes, your clothing, or items in your pockets. Learn to use your body to express a point.
- **Use visual aids effectively.** Discuss and interpret each visual aid for the audience. Move aside as you describe it so that it can be seen fully. Use a pointer if necessary.
- **Avoid digressions.** Stick to your outline and notes. Don't suddenly include clever little anecdotes or digressions that occur to you on the spot. If it's not part of your rehearsed material, leave it out so that you can finish on time. Remember, too, that your audience may not be as enthralled with your topic as you are.

- **Summarize your main points.** Conclude your presentation by reiterating your main points or by emphasizing what you want the audience to think or do. Once you have announced your conclusion, proceed to it directly.

AFTER YOUR PRESENTATION

- **Distribute handouts.** If you prepared handouts with data the audience will need, pass them out when you finish.
- **Encourage questions.** If the situation permits a question-and-answer period, announce it at the beginning of your presentation. Then, when you finish, ask for questions. Set a time limit for questions and answers.
- **Repeat questions.** Although the speaker may hear the question, audience members often do not. Begin each answer with a repetition of the question. This also gives you thinking time. Then, direct your answer to the entire audience.
- **Reinforce your main points.** You can use your answers to restate your primary ideas ("I'm glad you brought that up because it gives me a chance to elaborate on . . ."). In answering questions, avoid becoming defensive or debating the questioner.
- **Keep control.** Don't allow one individual to take over. Keep the entire audience involved.
- **Avoid *Yes, but* answers.** The word *but* immediately cancels any preceding message. Try replacing it with *and*. For example, *Yes, X has been tried. And Y works even better because . . . .*
- **End with a summary and appreciation.** To signal the end of the session before you take the last question, say something like *We have time for just one more question.* As you answer the last question, try to work it into a summary of your main points. Then, express appreciation to the audience for the opportunity to talk with them.

ADAPTING TO INTERNATIONAL AND CROSS-CULTURAL AUDIENCES

Every good speaker adapts to the audience, and cross-cultural presentations call for special adjustments and sensitivity. When working with an interpreter or speaking before individuals whose English is limited, you'll need to be very careful about your language.

Beyond these basic language adaptations, however, more fundamental sensitivity is often necessary. In organizing a presentation for a cross-cultural audience, think twice about delivering your main idea up front. Many people (notably those in Japanese, Latin American, and Arabic cultures) consider such directness to be brash and inappropriate. Remember that others may not share our cultural emphasis on straightforwardness.[15]

Also consider breaking your presentation into short, discrete segments. Such organization enables participants to ask questions and digest what has been presented. This technique is especially effective in cultures where people communicate in "loops." In the Middle East, for example, Arab speakers "mix circuitous, irrelevant (by American standards) conversations with short dashes of information that go directly to the point." Presenters who are patient, tolerant, and "mature" (in the eyes of the audience) will make the sale or win the contract.[16]

Match your presentation to the expectations of your audience. In Germany, for instance, successful presentations tend to be dense with facts and precise statistics. Americans might say "around 30 percent" while a German presenter might say "30.4271958 percent."

Remember, too, that some cultures prefer greater formality than Americans exercise. Writing on a flipchart or transparency seems natural and spontaneous in this country. Abroad, though, such informal techniques may suggest that the speaker does not value the audience enough to prepare proper visual aids in advance.[17]

This caution aside, you'll still want to use visual aids to communicate your message. These visuals should be written in both languages, so that you and your audience understand them. Never use numbers without writing them out for all to see. If possible, say numbers in both languages. Distribute translated handouts, summarizing your important information, when you finish. Finally, be careful of your body language. Looking people in the eye suggests intimacy and self-confidence in this country, but in other cultures such eye contact may be considered disrespectful.

SUMMING UP AND LOOKING FORWARD

This chapter presented techniques for making effective oral presentations. Good presentations begin with analysis of your purpose and your audience. Organizing the content involves preparing an effective introduction, body, and closing. The introduction should capture the listener's attention, identify the speaker, establish credibility, and preview the main points. The body should discuss two to four main points, with appropriate explanations, details, and verbal signposts to guide listeners. The conclusion should review the main points, provide a final focus, and allow the speaker to leave the podium gracefully. You can improve audience rapport by using effective imagery including analogies, metaphors, similes, personal anecdotes, statistics, and worst/best-case scenarios. In illustrating a presentation, use simple, easily understood visual aids to emphasize and clarify main points. If you employ PowerPoint, you can enhance the presentation by using templates, layout designs, and bullet points.

In delivering your presentation, outline the main points on note cards and rehearse repeatedly. During the presentation consider beginning with a pause and presenting your first sentence from memory. Make eye contact, control your voice, speak and move naturally, and avoid digressions. After your talk distribute handouts and answer questions. End gracefully and express appreciation.

The final two chapters of this book focus on your ultimate goal—getting a job or advancing in your career. You'll learn how to write a persuasive résumé and how to ace an employment interview.

Interactive Learning @ http://www.westwords.com/guffey/students.html
Prepare for tests and reinforce your chapter knowledge with interactive quizzes and crossword puzzles.

CRITICAL THINKING

1. Why is it necessary to repeat key points in an oral presentation?
2. How can a speaker make the most effective use of visual aids?
3. If PowerPoint is so effective, why are people speaking out against using it in presentations?

4. How can speakers prevent electronic presentation software from stealing their thunder?

5. What techniques are most effective for reducing stage fright?

CHAPTER REVIEW

6. The planning of an oral presentation should begin with serious thinking about what two factors?

7. Name three goals to be achieved in the introduction of an oral presentation.

8. What should the conclusion to an oral presentation include?

9. Name three ways for a speaker to use verbal signposts in a presentation. Illustrate each.

10. List six techniques for creating effective imagery in a presentation. Be prepared to discuss each.

11. List ten ways that an oral presentation may be organized.

12. Name specific advantages and disadvantages of electronic presentation software.

13. How is the Rule of Seven applied in preparing bulleted points?

14. What delivery method is most effective for speakers?

15. How might presentations before international or cross-cultural audiences be altered to be most effective?

ACTIVITIES

12.1 CRITIQUING A SPEECH

Your Task. Visit your library and select a speech from *Vital Speeches of Our Day*. Write a memo report to your instructor critiquing the speech in terms of the following:

a. Effectiveness of the introduction, body, and conclusion
b. Evidence of effective overall organization
c. Use of verbal signposts to create coherence
d. Emphasis of two to four main points
e. Effectiveness of supporting facts (use of examples, statistics, quotations, and so forth)

12.2 PREPARING AN ORAL PRESENTATION FROM AN ARTICLE

Your Task. Select a newspaper or magazine article and prepare an oral report based on it. Submit your outline, introduction, and conclusion to your instructor, or present the report to your class.

12.3 OVERCOMING STAGE FRIGHT.   What makes you most nervous when making a presentation before class? Being tongue-tied? Fearing all eyes on you? Messing up? Forgetting your ideas and looking silly?

Your Task. Discuss the previous questions as a class. Then, in groups of three or four talk about ways to overcome these fears. Your instructor may ask you to write a memo (individual or collective) summarizing your suggestions, or you may break out of your small groups and report your best ideas to the entire class.

12.4 INVESTIGATING ORAL COMMUNICATION IN YOUR FIELD.   One of the best sources of career information is someone in your field.

Your Task. Interview one or two individuals in your professional field. How is oral communication important in this profession? Does the need for oral skills change as one advances? What suggestions can these people make to newcomers to the field for developing proficient oral communication skills? Discuss your findings with your class.

12.5 OUTLINING AN ORAL PRESENTATION. For many people the hardest part of preparing an oral presentation is developing the outline.

Your Task. Select an oral presentation topic from the list in Activity 12.8 or suggest an original topic. Prepare an outline for your presentation using the following format.

Title   _____

Purpose   _____

	I. INTRODUCTION
Gain attention of audience	A.
Involve audience	B.
Establish credibility	C.
Preview main points	D.
Transition	
	II. BODY
Main point	A.
Illustrate, clarify, contrast	1.
	2.
	3.
Transition	
Main point	B.
Illustrate, clarify, contrast	1.
	2.
	3.
Transition	
Main point	C.
Illustrate, clarify, contrast	1.
	2.
	3.
Transition	
	III. CONCLUSION
Summarize main points	A.
Provide final focus	B.
Encourage questions	C.

INFOTRAC

12.6 DISCOVERING NEW PRESENTATION TIPS

Your Task. Using InfoTrac, perform a subject guide search for *business presentations*. Read at least three articles that provide suggestions for giving business presentations. If possible, print the most relevant findings. Select at least eight good tips or techniques that you did *not* learn from this chapter. Your instructor may ask you to bring them to class for discussion or submit a short memo report outlining your tips.

INFOTRAC

12.7 RESEARCHING JOB-APPLICATION INFORMATION

Your Task. Using InfoTrac, perform a subject search for one of the following topics. Find as many articles as you can. Then organize and present a five- to ten-minute informative talk to your class.

a. Do recruiters prefer one- or two-page résumés?
b. How do applicant tracking systems work?
c. How are inflated résumés detected and what are the consequences?

Interactive Learning @ http://www.westwords.com/guffey/students.html

d. What's new in writing cover letters in job applications?
e. What is online résumé fraud?
f. What are some new rules for résumés?

12.8 CHOOSING A TOPIC FOR AN ORAL PRESENTATION

Your Task. Select a topic from the list below or from the report topics at the end of Chapter 10. For an expanded list of report topics, go to the Guffey Web site. Prepare a five- to ten-minute oral presentation. Consider yourself an expert who has been called in to explain some aspect of the topic before a group of interested people. Since your time is limited, prepare a concise yet forceful presentation with effective visual aids.

a. What is the career outlook in a field of your choice?
b. How has the Internet changed job searching?
c. How can attendance be improved in a minor sports field (your choice) at your school?
d. How do employees use online services?
e. What is telecommuting, and for what kind of workers is it an appropriate work alternative?
f. How much choice should parents have in selecting schools for their young children (parochial, private, and public)?
g. What travel location would you recommend for college students at Christmas (or another holiday or in summer)?
h. What is the economic outlook for a given product (such as domestic cars, laptop computers, digital cameras, fitness equipment, or a product of your choice)?
i. How can your organization or institution improve its image?
j. Why should people invest in a company or scheme of your choice?
k. What brand and model of computer and printer represent the best buy for college students today?
l. What franchise would offer the best investment opportunity for an entrepreneur in your area?
m. How should a job candidate dress for an interview?
n. What should a guide to proper cell phone use include?
o. Are internships worth the effort?
p. How is an administrative assistant different from a secretary?
q. Where should your organization hold its next convention?
r. What is your opinion of the statement "Advertising steals our time, defaces the landscape, and degrades the dignity of public institutions"?[18]
s. How can businesspeople reduce the amount of e-mail spam they receive?
t. What is the outlook for real estate (commercial or residential) investment in your area?
u. What are the pros and cons of videoconferencing for [name an organization]?
v. What do the personal assistants for celebrities do, and how does one become a personal assistant? (Investigate the Association of Celebrity Personal Assistants.)
w. What kinds of gifts are appropriate for businesses to give clients and customers during the holiday season?
x. What scams are on the Federal Trade Commission's List of Top 10 Consumer Scams, and how can consumers avoid falling for them?
y. How are businesses and conservationists working together to protect the world's dwindling tropical forests?
z. Should employees be able to use computers in a work environment for anything other than work-related business?

Designing and Delivering Oral Presentations at Burke Marketing

Burke Marketing Research is one of the premier international marketing research and consulting firms in the industry. It is the world's seventh largest research company, and a large part of its business revolves around presenting research findings to clients. In the video a Burke vice president says that to be most meaningful, research results should be explained in person. This is usually done in an oral presentation accompanied by a written report. In this video Burke consultants discuss how to plan, organize, and deliver an effective presentation. They also present tips regarding dress, honesty, repetition, animation, and brevity.

Your Task. After watching the video, be prepared to answer these questions:

- What are the four main steps that Burke consultants follow in creating an effective oral presentation?
- What tips do Burke consultants mention for improving the delivery of a presentation?
- How can unfavorable results be successfully presented?
- What is the worst error a presenter can make?

GRAMMAR/MECHANICS CHECKUP—12

CAPITALIZATION

Review Sections 3.01–3.16 in the Grammar/Mechanics Handbook. Then study each of the following statements. Circle any lowercase letter that should be capitalized. Draw a slash (/) through any capital letter that you wish to change to lowercase. Indicate in the space provided the number of changes you made in each sentence and record the number of the G/M principle(s) illustrated. If you made no changes, write *0*. When you finish, compare your responses with those provided at the back of the book. If your responses differ, study carefully the principles in parentheses.

4   (3.01, 3.06a)   **Example**   After consulting our ~~A~~ttorneys for ~~l~~egal advice, Vice ~~p~~resident Mills signed the ~~c~~ontract.

_____ 1. All american passengers from Flight 402 must pass through Customs Inspection at Gate 17 upon arrival at Baltimore international airport.

_____ 2. Personal tax rates for japanese citizens are low by International standards; rates for japanese corporations are high, according to Iwao Nakatani, an Economics Professor at Osaka university.

_____ 3. In the end, Business passes on most of the burden to the Consumer: What looks like a tax on Business is really a tax on Consumption.

_____ 4. Lisa enrolled in courses in History, Sociology, Spanish, and Computer Science.

_____ 5. Did you see the *Forbes* article entitled "Careers in horticulture are nothing to sneeze at"?

_____ 6. Although I recommend the Minex Diskettes sold under the brandname Maxidisk, you may purchase any Diskettes you choose.

_____ 7. According to a Federal Government report, any regulation of State and County banking must receive local approval.

8. The vice president of the united states said, "this country continues to encourage Foreign investments." _____

9. The Comptroller of Ramjet International reported to the President and the Board of Directors that the internal revenue service was beginning an investigation of their Company. _____

10. My Mother, who lives near St. Petersburg, reports that protection from the Sun's rays is particularly important in the South.

11. Our Managing Editor met with Leslie Hawkins, Manager of the Advertising Sales Department, to plan an Ad Campaign for our special issue. _____

12. In the fall, Editor in Chief Porter plans an article detailing the astounding performance of the austrian, german, and italian currencies. _____ _____

13. To reach Belle Isle park, which is located on an Island in the Detroit river, tourists pass over the Douglas MacArthur bridge. _____

14. On page 6 of the catalog, you will see that the computer science department is offering a number of courses in programming. _____

15. Please consult figure 3.2 in chapter 5 for U.S. census bureau figures regarding non-english-speaking residents. _____

GRAMMAR/MECHANICS CHALLENGE—12

DOCUMENT FOR REVISION

The following executive summary of a report has faults in grammar, punctuation, spelling, number form, wordiness, and word use. Use standard proofreading marks (see Appendix B) to correct the errors. When you finish, your instructor can show you the revised version of this abstract.

EXECUTIVE SUMMARY

Purpose of Report

The purposes of this report is (1) To determine the Sun coast university campus communitys awareness of the campus recycling program and (2) To recommend ways to increase participation. Sun Coasts recycling program was intended to respond to the increasing problem of waste disposal, to fulfil it's social responsibility as an educational institution, and to meet the demands of legislation that made it a requirement for individuals and organizations to recycle.

A Survey was conducted in an effort to learn about the campus communities recycling habits and to make an assessment of the participation in the recycling program that is current. 220 individuals responded to the Survey but twenty-seven Surveys could not be used. Since Sun coast universitys recycling program include only aluminum, glass, paper and plastic at this point in time these were the only materials considered in this Study.

Recycling at Sun coast

Most Survey respondants recognized the importance of recycling, they stated that they do recycle aluminum, glass, paper and plastic on a regular basis either at home or at work.

However most respondants displayed a low-level of awareness, and use of the on campus program. Many of the respondants was unfamilar with the location of the bins around campus; and therefore had not participated in the Recycling Program. Other responses indicated that the bins were not located in convenent locations.

Reccommendations for increasing recycling participation

Recommendations for increasing participation in the Program include the following;

1. relocating the recycling bins for greater visability

2. development of incentive programs to gain the participation of on campus groups

3. training student volunteers to give on campus presentations that give an explanation of the need for recycling, and the benefits of using the Recycling Program

4. we should increase Advertising in regard to the Program

COMMUNICATION WORKSHOP: ETHICS

The Worst Deadly Sin in a Presentation

Audiences appreciate speakers with polished delivery techniques, but they are usually relatively forgiving when mistakes occur. One thing they don't suffer gladly, though, is unethical behavior. Executives in a comprehensive research survey agreed that the "worst deadly sin" a speaker can commit in a presentation is demonstrating a lack of integrity.

What kinds of unethical behavior do audiences reject? They distrust speakers who misrepresent, exaggerate, and lie. They also dislike cover-ups and evasiveness. The following situations clearly signal trouble for speakers because of the unethical actions involved:

- A sales rep, instead of promoting his company's products, suggests that his competitor's business is mismanaged, is losing customers, or offers seriously flawed products.
- A manager distorts a new employee insurance plan, underemphasizing its deficiencies and overemphasizing its strengths.
- A sales rep fabricates an answer to a tough question instead of admitting ignorance.
- A financial planner tries to prove her point by highlighting an irrelevant statistic.

Career Application. America's largest brokerage firm, Merrill Lynch, recently suffered a major blow to its credibility and paid a $100 million settlement. Why? Its analysts privately called particular Internet stocks "crap" or "dogs," while publicly recommending them in presentations to customers.

Your Task. In small groups or with the entire class, discuss what might motivate a speaker to commit "the worst deadly sin." When have you heard presentations in which you doubted the integrity of the speaker? What unethical presentation techniques have you seen on television? What happens when a speaker loses credibility?

Communicating for Employment

The Job Search, Résumés, and Job Application Letters

If your résumé isn't a winner, it's a killer.

JOYCE LAIN KENNEDY, renowned careers author and nationally syndicated columnist

LEARNING OBJECTIVES

1. Prepare for employment by identifying your interests, evaluating your assets, recognizing the changing nature of jobs, choosing a career path, and studying traditional and electronic job search techniques.
2. Compare and contrast chronological, functional, and combination résumés.
3. Organize and format the parts of a résumé to produce a persuasive product.
4. Identify techniques that prepare a résumé for computer scanning, posting at a Web site, faxing, and e-mailing.
5. Write a persuasive job application letter to accompany your résumé.

W hether you are applying for your first permanent position, competing for promotion, or changing careers, you'll be more successful if you understand employment strategies and how to promote yourself with a winning résumé. This chapter provides expert current advice in preparing for employment, searching the job market, writing a persuasive résumé, and developing an effective job application letter.

PREPARING FOR EMPLOYMENT

Quick Check

Finding a satisfying career means learning about oneself, the job market, and the employment process.

You may think that the first step in finding a job is writing a résumé. Wrong! The job search process actually begins long before you are ready to prepare your résumé. Regardless of the kind of employment you seek, you must invest time and effort getting ready. You can't hope to find the position of your dreams without (1) knowing yourself, (2) knowing the job market, and (3) knowing the employment process.

In addition to searching for career information and choosing a specific job objective, you should be studying the job market and becoming aware of the substantial changes in the nature of work. You'll also want to understand how to use the latest Internet resources in your job search. When you have finished all this preparation, you're ready to design a persuasive résumé and job application letter. These documents should be appropriate for small businesses as well as for larger organizations that may be using résumé-scanning programs. Following these steps, summarized in Figure 13.1 and described in this chapter, gives you a master plan for landing a job you really want.

IDENTIFYING YOUR INTERESTS

The employment process begins with introspection. This means looking inside yourself to analyze what you like and dislike so that you can make good employment choices. Career counselors charge large sums for helping individuals learn about themselves. You can do the same kind of self-examination—without spending a dime. For guidance in choosing a field that eventually proves to be satisfying, answer the following questions. If you have already chosen a field, think carefully about how your answers relate to that choice.

- *Do I enjoy working with people, data, or things?*
- *How important is it to be my own boss?*
- *How important are salary, benefits, technology support, and job stability?*
- *How important are working environment, colleagues, and job stimulation?*

✓ **Quick Check**

Analyzing your likes and dislikes helps you make wise employment decisions.

✓ **Quick Check**

Answering specific questions can help you choose a career.

FIGURE 13.1 The Employment Search

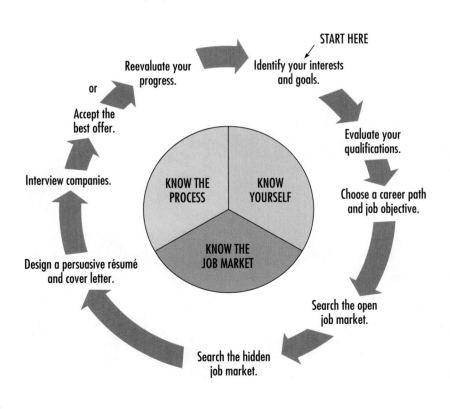

- *Would I rather work for a large or a small company?*
- *Must I work in a specific city, geographical area, or climate?*
- *Am I looking for security, travel opportunities, money, power, or prestige?*
- *How would I describe the perfect job, boss, and coworkers?*

EVALUATING YOUR QUALIFICATIONS

Assessing your skills and experience prepares you to write a persuasive résumé.

In addition to your interests, assess your qualifications. Employers today want to know what assets you have to offer them. Your responses to the following questions will target your thinking as well as prepare a foundation for your résumé. Remember, though, that employers seek more than empty assurances; they will want proof of your qualifications.

- *What computer skills can I offer?* Employers are often interested in specific software programs.
- *What other skills have I acquired in school, on the job, or through activities?* How can I demonstrate these skills?
- *Do I work well with people?* What proof can I offer? Consider extracurricular activities, clubs, and jobs.
- *Am I a leader, self-starter, or manager?* What evidence can I offer?
- *Do I speak, write, or understand another language?*
- *Do I learn quickly? Am I creative?* How can I demonstrate these characteristics?
- *Do I communicate well in speech and in writing?* How can I verify these talents?

RECOGNIZING THE CHANGING NATURE OF JOBS

✓ *Quick Check*

Downsizing and flatter organizations have resulted in less job security.

As you learned in Chapter 1, the nature of the workplace is changing. One of the most significant changes involves the concept of the "job." Following the downsizing in recent years and the movement toward flattened organizations, fewer people are employed in permanent positions. Many employees are feeling less job security, although they are doing more work.

In his best-selling book *JobShift*, William Bridges describes the disappearance of the traditional job. The notion of a full-time permanent job with a specific job de-

Employees who are most valuable to their employers are willing to broaden their skills through training, show flexibility in adapting to a changing work environment, and work successfully with fellow employees or on a team. These employees have the best chance of job security and career advancement.
© Julie Dennis/Index Stock Imagery, Inc.

scription, he claims, is giving way to more flexible work arrangements. Work is completed by teams assigned to projects, or work is outsourced to a group that's not even part of an organization.[1] He sees the migration of work away from fixed "boxes" that we've always called jobs.

At the same time that work is becoming more flexible, big companies are no longer the main employers. Only 20 percent of new jobs are created by big companies.[2] Only one third of people currently employed work for companies with 500 or more employees.[3] People seem to be working for smaller companies, or they are becoming consultants or specialists who work on tasks or projects under arrangements too fluid to be called "jobs." And because new technologies can spring up overnight, making today's skills obsolete, employers are less willing to hire people into jobs with narrow descriptions.

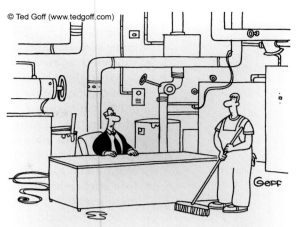

© Ted Goff (www.tedgoff.com)

"I don't need computer skills, I said. I can do all my work with a pad and paper, I told them."

What do these changes mean for you? For one thing, you should probably no longer think in terms of a lifelong career with a single company. In fact, you can't even expect reasonably permanent employment for work well done. This social contract between employer and employee is no longer a given. And predictable career paths within companies have largely disappeared. The result is that career advancement is in your own hands.[4] In the new workplace you can expect to work for multiple employers on flexible job assignments associated with teams and projects. You'll strive for career durability rather than job security.[5] For maximum durability, you should be prepared for constant retraining to update your skills. People who learn quickly and adapt to change are "high-value-added" individuals who will always be in demand even in a climate of surging change.

✓ **Quick Check**

Employees should expect to continually update their skills as new technologies change their jobs.

CHOOSING A CAREER PATH

There's no escaping the fact that the employment picture today is much different from that of a decade or two ago. By the time you are 30, you can expect to have had five to seven jobs. The average employee will have worked at 12 to 15 jobs over the course of a career, staying an average of 3.6 years at each job.[6] Some of you probably have not yet settled on your first career choice; others are returning to college to retrain for a new career. Although you may be changing jobs in the future, you still need to train for a specific career area now. In choosing an area, you'll make the best decisions when you can match your interests and qualifications with the requirements and rewards in specific careers. But where can you find career data? Here are some suggestions:

✓ **Quick Check**

The average employee will have worked at 12 to 15 jobs over the course of a career.

- **Visit your campus career center.** Most have literature, inventories, software programs, and Internet connections that allow you to investigate such fields as accounting, finance, office technology, information systems, hotel management, and so forth.
- **Search the Web.** Many job search sites on the Web offer career-planning information and resources. Updated descriptions of and links to the best career counseling and job search Web sites may be found at the Guffey Web site. Click "Jobs."
- **Use your library.** Many print and online resources are especially helpful. Consult the latest edition of the *Dictionary of Occupational Titles, Occupational Outlook Handbook,* and *The Jobs Rated Almanac* for information about career duties, qualifications, salaries, and employment trends.
- **Take a summer job, internship, or part-time position in your field.** Nothing is better than trying out a career by actually working in it or an allied area.

✓ **Quick Check**

Career information can be obtained at campus career centers and libraries, from the Internet, in classified ads, and from professional organizations.

Quick Check

Summer and part-time jobs and internships are good opportunities to learn about different careers.

Many companies offer internships and temporary jobs to begin training college students and to develop relationships with them. These relationships sometimes blossom into permanent positions.

- **Interview someone in your chosen field.** People are usually flattered when asked to describe their careers. Inquire about needed skills, required courses, financial and other rewards, benefits, working conditions, future trends, and entry requirements.
- **Monitor the classified ads.** Early in your college career, begin monitoring want ads and Web sites of companies in your career area. Check job availability, qualifications sought, duties, and salary range. Don't wait until you're about to graduate to see how the job market looks.
- **Join professional organizations in your field.** Frequently, they offer student membership status and reduced rates. You'll get inside information on issues, career news, and possibly jobs.

USING TRADITIONAL JOB SEARCH TECHNIQUES

Quick Check

Finding a great job often means beginning to think about it in the first or second year of college.

Finding the perfect job requires an early start and a determined effort. Whether you use traditional or online job search techniques, you should be prepared to launch an aggressive campaign. And you can't start too early. Some universities now require first- and second-year students to take an employment seminar called "Reality 101." Students are told early on that a college degree alone doesn't guarantee a job. They are cautioned that grade-point averages make a difference to employers. And they are advised of the importance of experience. Here are some traditional steps that job candidates take:

- **Check classified ads in local and national newspapers.** Be aware, though, that classified ads are only one small source of jobs.
- **Examine announcements in publications of professional organizations.** If you do not have a student membership, ask your professors to share current copies of professional journals, newsletters, and so on. Your college library is another good source.

Traditional job search techniques include checking classified ads, examining announcements in professional publications, and especially developing your own personal network of people who may help you find the right position. Maintaining communication with the people in your network is made easier by the rich array of communication options available today including cell phones, e-mail, instant messaging, voice mail, and fax.
© Charlie Borland/Index Stock Imagery, Inc.

- **Contact companies in which you're interested, even if you know of no current opening.** Write an unsolicited letter and include your résumé. Follow up with a telephone call. Check the company's Web site for employment possibilities and procedures.
- **Sign up for campus interviews with visiting company representatives.** Campus recruiters may open your eyes to exciting jobs and locations.
- **Ask for advice from your professors.** They often have contacts and ideas for expanding your job search.
- **Develop your own network of contacts.** Networking still accounts for most of the jobs found by candidates. Therefore, plan to spend a considerable portion of your job search time developing a personal network. The Communication Workshop at the end of this chapter gives you step-by-step instructions for traditional networking as well as some ideas for online networking.

✓ *Quick Check*

A traditional job search campaign might include checking classified ads, studying announcements in professional publications, contacting companies, and developing a network of contacts.

USING ELECTRONIC JOB SEARCH TECHNIQUES

Just as the Internet has changed the way the world works, it's also changing the nature of the job search. One software maker observed, "Employers are more proactive now, and there's less 'pounding the pavement' for job seekers."[7] Increasing numbers of employers are listing their job openings at special Web sites that are similar to newspaper classified ads. Companies are also listing job openings at their own Web sites, providing a more direct connection to employment opportunities. Although we will describe six of the best Internet job sites here, you can find a more extensive and continuously updated list with clickable hot links at the Guffey Student Web site. Our site includes many job lists for recent college graduates and entry-level positions.

✓ *Quick Check*

An electronic job search campaign includes searching career and company Web sites for job listings.

- **America's Job Bank** is a partnership between the U.S. Department of Labor and the state-operated Public Employment Service. Its free service claims to be the "biggest and busiest job market in cyberspace."
- **CareerBuilder** joined forces with media giants to offer "industry's most targeted online network of career centers." Users have access to the classified ads of major newspapers.
- **CareerCity** claims to "search millions of jobs at all leading career sites with one click."
- **College Grad Job Hunter** offers job postings and helpful hints for novices to the job market, such as how to write a résumé, interview, and negotiate.
- **Monster Board** offers access to information on more than 500,000 jobs worldwide. You may search for jobs by category, city, or nation, as shown in Figure 13.2. Many consider it to be the Web's premier job site.
- **WetFeet** provides expert advice on everything from résumés to getting dressed.

Perhaps even better are the job openings listed at company Web sites. Check out a promising company to see what positions are open. What's the fastest way to find a company's Web address? We recommend Hoover's (http://www.hoovers.com) for quick company information and Web site links. If that fails, use your favorite search engine to learn whether a company has its own Web site. Some companies even provide online résumé forms that encourage job candidates to submit their qualifications immediately.

Hundreds of job sites now flood the Internet and increasing numbers of companies offer online recruiting. However, the harsh reality is that landing a job still depends largely on personal contacts. One employment expert said, "Online recruiting is a little like computer dating. People may find dates that way, but they don't get married that way."[8] Another professional placement expert said, "If you think just [posting] your résumé will get you a job, you're crazy. [Electronic services are] just a supplement to a core strategy of networking your buns off."[9]

✓ *Quick Check*

Many jobs are posted on the Internet, but most hiring is still done through personal contact.

FIGURE 13.2 Using the Web to Search for a Job

To begin a job search at Monster.com, click "Search Jobs." You'll next see a form enabling you to search by location, job category, or keyword.

Searching for "Administrative and Support Services" reveals a long list of open positions, a few or which are shown here.

THE PERSUASIVE RÉSUMÉ

After using both traditional and online resources to learn about the employment market and to develop job leads, you'll focus on writing a persuasive résumé. Such a résumé does more than merely list your qualifications. It packages your assets into a convincing advertisement that sells you for a specific job. The goal of a persuasive résumé is winning an interview. Even if you are not in the job market at this moment, preparing a résumé now has advantages. Having a current résumé makes you look well organized and professional should an unexpected employment opportunity arise. Moreover, preparing a résumé early can help you recognize weak areas and give you time to bolster them.

CHOOSING A RÉSUMÉ STYLE

Your qualifications and career goal will help you choose from among three résumé styles: chronological, functional, and combination.

Chronological. Most popular with recruiters is the chronological résumé, shown in Figure 13.3. It lists work history job by job, starting with the most recent position. Recruiters favor the chronological format because such résumés quickly reveal a candidate's education and experience record. One corporate recruiter said, "I'm looking for applicable experience; chronological résumés are the easiest to assess."[10] The chronological style works well for candidates who have experience in their field of employment and for those who show steady career growth. But for many college students and others who lack extensive experience, the functional résumé format may be preferable.

Functional. The functional résumé, shown in Figure 13.4, focuses attention on a candidate's skills rather than on past employment. Like a chronological résumé, the functional résumé begins with the candidate's name, address, telephone

Quick Check

Chronological résumés focus on past employment; functional résumés focus on skills.

FIGURE 13.3 Chronological Résumé

ROBERTA M. SANCHEZ
1148 Lambert Road
Naperville, IL 60144

Phone: (708) 814-9322   E-mail: rsanchez@sprint.com

OBJECTIVE   Position with financial services organization installing accounting
software and providing user support, where computer experience and
proven communication and interpersonal skills can be used to
improve operations

Includes detailed objective in response to advertisement

EXPERIENCE   **Accounting software consultant,** Financial Specialists, Elmhurst,
Illinois
June 2002 to present
• Design and install accounting systems for businesses such as 21st
Century Real Estate, Illini Insurance, Aurora Lumber Company,
and others
• Provide ongoing technical support and consultation for regular clients
• Help write proposals, such as recent one that won $250,000 contract

Uses present-tense verbs for current job

Office manager (part-time), Post Premiums, Naperville, Illinois
June 1998 to May 2002
• Conceived and implemented improved order processing and filing
system
• Managed computerized accounting system; trained new employees
to use it
• Helped install local area network

Shows job title in bold for readability

Chronological format arranges jobs and education by dates

Bookkeeper (part-time), Sunset Avionics, Downers Grove, Illinois
August 1996 to May 1998
• Kept books for small airplane rental and repair service.
• Performed all bookkeeping functions including quarterly internal
audit

EDUCATION   **College of DuPage,** Glen Ellyn, Illinois
Associate of Arts degree in business administration, June 2002
GPA in major 3.6/4.0

Computer Associates training seminars, summer and fall 2002
Certificates of completion
Seminars in consulting ethics, marketing, and ACCPAC accounting
software

White space around headings creates open look

SPECIAL SKILLS   • Proficient in Word, PageMaker, Lotus, and Excel
• Skilled in ACCPAC Plus, MAS90, and Solomon IV accounting soft-
ware
• Trained in technical writing, including proposals and documentation
• Experienced in office administration and management
• Competent at speaking and writing Spanish

Highlights technical, management, and communication skills

**HONORS AND
ACTIVITIES**   Dean's list, 3 semesters
Member, Beta Alpha Gamma (business student honorary)
Member, Academic Affairs Advisory Committee, College of DuPage,
1999–01

Roberta Sanchez uses a chronological résumé to highlight her work
experience, most of which is related directly to the position she seeks.
Although she is a recent graduate, she has accumulated experience in two
part-time jobs and one full-time job. If she had wished to emphasize her
special skills (which is not a bad idea considering her heavy computer
expertise), she could have placed the special skills section just after her
objective.

The Persuasive Résumé

FIGURE 13.4 Functional Résumé

Uses general objective for all-purpose résumé

Avoids dense look by starring items on separate lines (could have used bullets, dashes, periods, or boxes)

Emphasizes relevant skills for sales/marketing position

Employs action verbs to describe skills

Deemphasizes employment by listing it near end

DONALD W. VINTON
2250 Turtle Creek Drive
Monroeville, Pennsylvania 15146

PHONE: (412) 724-4981   E-mail: dwvinton@aol.com

OBJECTIVE   Position in sales or marketing with opportunity for advancement and travel

SALES/   *Demonstrated lawn-care equipment in central and western Penn-
MARKETING   sylvania
SKILLS   *Achieved product sales amounting to 120 percent of forecast in competitive field
                   *Personally generated over $25,000 in telephone subscriptions as part of President's Task Force for the Penn Foundation
                   *Conducted telephone survey of selected businesses in two counties to determine potential users of farm equipment and to promote company services
                   *Successfully served 40 or more retail customers daily as clerk in electrical appliance department of national home hardware store

COMMUNICATION *Conducted survey, analyzed results, and wrote a 20-page report
SKILLS   regarding the need for developing a recycling program at Penn State
                   *Presented talks before selected campus classes and organizations encouraging students to participate in recycling program
                   *Spoke for award-winning delegation defending U.S. policies before mock U.N. meeting
                   *Announced sports news for WGNF, college radio station

ORGANIZA-   *Helped conceptualize, organize, and conduct highly successful
TIONAL/   campus campaign to register student voters
MANAGEMENT   *Scheduled events and arranged weekend student retreat for
SKILLS   Newman Club
                   *Trained and supervised two counter employees at Pizza Bob's
                   *Organized courses, extracurricular activities, and part-time employment to graduate in seven semesters; earned 3.4 grade-point average (A = 4.0)

EDUCATION   Pennsylvania State University, State College, PA. B.S., 2002
                   Major: Business Administration with sales and marketing emphasis GPA in major: 3.6 (A = 4.0)

                   Community College of Allegheny County, Monroeville, PA
                   Courses in General Studies and Business Administration

EMPLOYMENT   2000–2002, Pizza Bob's, State College, Pennsylvania
                   Summer 1999, Bellefonte Manufacturers Representatives,
                   Pittsburgh
                   Summer 1996, Home Depot, Inc., Pittsburgh

INTERESTS   Basketball, soccer, mountain biking, skiing

Donald Vinton, a recent graduate, chose this functional format to de-emphasize his meager work experience and emphasize his potential in sales and marketing. Within each of the three major categories, he lists specific achievements, all of which are introduced by action verbs. He has also included a number of keywords that could be helpful if his résumé is scanned. He included an employment section to satisfy recruiters.

number, job objective, and education. Instead of listing jobs, though, the functional résumé groups skills and accomplishments in special categories, such as *Supervisory and Management Skills* or *Retailing and Marketing Experience*. This résumé style highlights accomplishments and can deemphasize a negative employment history. People who have changed jobs frequently or who have gaps in their employment records may prefer the functional résumé. Recent graduates with little employment experience often find the functional résumé useful.

Functional résumés are also called *skill* résumés. Although the functional résumé of Donald Vinton shown in Figure 13.4 concentrates on skills, it does include a short employment section because recruiters expect it. Notice that Donald breaks his skills into three categories. An alternative—and easier—method is to make one large list, perhaps with a title such as *Areas of Accomplishment, Summary of Qualifications,* or *Areas of Expertise and Ability.*

Combination.   The combination résumé style, shown in Figure 13.5, draws on the best features of the chronological and functional résumés. It emphasizes a candidate's capabilities while also including a complete job history. The combination résumé is a good choice for recent graduates because it enables them to profile what they can do for a prospective employer. If the writer has a specific job in mind, the items should be targeted to that job description.

DECIDING ON ITS LENGTH

Experts simply do not agree on how long a résumé should be. Conventional wisdom has always held that recruiters prefer one-page résumés. A recent carefully controlled study of 570 recruiters revealed that they *claimed* they preferred one-page résumés. However, the recruiters actually *chose* to interview the applicants with two-page résumés.[11] Apparently, recruiters who are serious about candidates often prefer a full picture with the kind of details that can be provided in a two-page résumé.

The entire question may become moot as recruiters increasingly encourage online résumés, which are not restricted by page lengths. Perhaps the best advice is to make your résumé as long as needed to sell your skills.

Quick Check

Recruiters may say they prefer one-page résumés, but many choose to interview those with longer résumés.

ARRANGING THE PARTS

Although résumés have standard parts, their arrangement and content should be strategically planned. The most persuasive résumés emphasize skills and achievements aimed at a particular job or company. They show a candidate's most important qualifications first, and they deemphasize any weaknesses. In arranging the parts, try to create as few headings as possible; more than six generally looks cluttered. No two résumés are ever exactly alike, but most writers consider the following parts.

Quick Check

The parts of résumés should be arranged with the most important qualifications first.

Main Heading.   Your résumé should always begin with your name, address, cell and land phone numbers, and e-mail address, if available. If possible, include a telephone number where messages may be left for you. Don't give a number that is always busy because you're using a modem on that line. Prospective employers tend to call the next applicant when no one answers. Avoid showing both permanent and temporary addresses; some specialists say that dual addresses immediately identify about-to-graduate college students. Choose one address to use. Keep the main heading as uncluttered and simple as possible. And don't include the word *résumé*; it's like putting the word *letter* above correspondence.

Career Objective.   Opinion is divided on the effect of including a career objective on a résumé. Recruiters think such statements indicate that a candidate has

FIGURE 13.5 Combination Résumé

Omits objective to keep all options open

Focuses on skills and aptitudes that employers seek

Arranges employment by job titles for easy reading

Combines activities and awards to fill out section

Includes references because local employers expect them (most résumés today omit references)

SUSAN R. SNOW
Route 2, Box 180
Dodgeville, Wisconsin 53533
Residence: (608) 935-3196   Messages: (608) 935-4399

SKILLS AND CAPABILITIES
- Keyboard 70 wpm with accuracy
- Take symbol shorthand at 90 wpm with accurate transcription
- Skilled in the production of legal documents and correspondence
- Competent in producing mailable copy from machine transcription
- Experienced in personal computer use, including the following software: Word, Lotus, and Excel.
- Ability to perform office tasks and interact effectively using excellent written and oral communication skills

EXPERIENCE
Word Processing Operator 1, Limited-term employee
University of Wisconsin-Madison, May 2002 to August 2002
- Transcribed confidential letters, memos, reports, and other documents from machine dictation using Word Me
- Proofread documents for other operators, marking grammar and content errors

Student Assistant
Southwest Wisconsin Technical College, Fennimore, WI 53809, June 2001 to August 2001
- Typed memos and input financial aid data on terminal to mainframe; printed and verified monthly report totals for $70,000 budget
- Helped financial aid applicants understand and complete five-page form
- Screened incoming telephone calls for supervisor and three counselors

Part-Time Cook and Cashier
Souprrr Subs, Fennimore, WI 53809, May 2000 to May 2001
- Prepared menu items, accepted customer payments, and balanced cash drawer

EDUCATION
Southwest Wisconsin Technical College, Fennimore, WI 53809
Major: Office assistant and word processing specialist programs
A.A. degree expected May 2003. GPA in major: 3.6 (4.0 = A)

ACTIVITIES AND AWARDS
- Received the Fennimore Times award from Southwest Wisconsin Technical College Foundation for academic excellence and contribution to campus life
- Elected secretary of Business Professionals of America Club; represented SWTC chapter at state and national competitions

REFERENCES

Ms. Shirley A. Yost	Professor Lois Wagner	Mr. James W. Loy
College of Letters & Science	SW Wisconsin Technical College	SW Wisconsin Technical College
University of Wisconsin	Highway 18 East	Highway 18 East
Madison, WI 53489	Fennimore, WI 53809	Fennimore, WI 53809
(413) 390-4491	(608) 822-8931	(608) 822-8749

Because Susan Snow wanted to highlight her skills and capabilities along with her experience, she combined the best features of functional and traditional résumés. This résumé style is becoming increasingly popular. Although it's not standard practice, Susan included references because employers in her area expect them.

Note: For more résumé models, see Figures 13.10–13.13.

made a commitment to a career. Moreover, career objectives make recruiters' lives easier by allowing them to classify the résumé quickly. But such declarations can also disqualify a candidate if the stated objective doesn't match a company's job description.[12] One expert warned that putting a job objective on a résumé has "killed more opportunities for candidates . . . than typos."[13]

You have four choices regarding career objectives.

✓ **Quick Check**

Career objectives are most appropriate for specific, targeted positions, but they may limit a broader job search.

1. Include a career objective only when applying for a specific, targeted position. For example, the following responds to an advertised position: *Objective: To work in the health care industry as a human resources trainee with exposure to recruiting, training, and benefits administration.*
2. Omit a career objective, especially if you are preparing an all-purpose résumé.
3. Include a general statement, such as *Objective: Challenging position in urban planning* or *Job Goal: Position in sales/marketing.*
4. Omit an objective on the résumé but include it in the application letter, where it can be tailored to a specific position.[14]

Some consultants warn against using the words *entry-level* in your objective, as these words emphasize lack of experience. Many aggressive job applicants today prepare individual résumés that are targeted for each company or position sought. Thanks to word processing, the task is easy.

Education. The next component on your résumé is your education—if it is more noteworthy than your work experience. In this section you should include the name and location of schools, dates of attendance, major fields of study, and degrees received. Your grade-point average and/or class ranking are important to prospective employers. One way to enhance your GPA is to calculate it in your major courses only (for example, *3.6/4.0 in major*). By the way, it is not unethical to showcase your GPA in your major—as long as you clearly indicate what you are doing.

✓ **Quick Check**

Recent graduates with little job experience should place their education section ahead of the experience section.

Under *Education* you might be tempted to list all the courses you took, but such a list makes for very dull reading. Refer to courses only if you can relate them to the position sought. When relevant, include certificates earned, seminars attended, and workshops completed. Because employers are interested in your degree of self-sufficiency, you might want to indicate the percentage of your education for which you paid. If your education is incomplete, include such statements as *B.S. degree expected 6/02* or *80 units completed in 120-unit program.* Entitle this section *Education, Academic Preparation,* or *Professional Training.*

Work Experience or Employment History. If your work experience is significant and relevant to the position sought, this information should appear before education. List your most recent employment first and work backward, including only those jobs that you think will help you win the targeted position. A job application form may demand a full employment history, but your résumé may be selective. (Be aware, though, that time gaps in your employment history will probably be questioned in the interview.) For each position show the following:

- Employer's name, city, and state
- Dates of employment
- Most important job title
- Significant duties, activities, accomplishments, and promotions

© Ted Goff (www.tedgoff.com)

"You should hire me because I'm unhindered by any outdated work experience."

FIGURE 13.6 Action Verbs to Highlight Your Skills and Accomplishments

MANAGEMENT SKILLS	COMMUNICATION SKILLS	RESEARCH SKILLS	TECHNICAL SKILLS	TEACHING SKILLS
administered	addressed	clarified	assembled	adapted
analyzed	arbitrated	collected	built	advised
consolidated	arranged	critiqued	calculated	clarified
coordinated	collaborated	diagnosed	computed	coached
delegated	convinced	evaluated	designed	communicated
developed	developed	examined	devised	coordinated
directed	drafted	extracted	engineered	developed
evaluated	edited	identified	executed	enabled
improved	explained	inspected	fabricated	encouraged
increased	formulated	interpreted	maintained	evaluated
organized	interpreted	interviewed	operated	explained
oversaw	negotiated	investigated	overhauled	facilitated
planned	persuaded	organized	programmed	guided
prioritized	promoted	summarized	remodeled	informed
recommended	publicized	surveyed	repaired	instructed
scheduled	recruited	systematized	solved	persuaded
strengthened	translated		upgraded	set goals
supervised	wrote			trained

*The underlined words are especially good for pointing out accomplishments.

Quick Check

The work experience section of a résumé should list specifics and quantify achievements.

Describe your employment achievements concisely but concretely. Avoid generalities such as *Worked with customers.* Be more specific, with statements such as *Served 40 or more retail customers a day; Successfully resolved problems about custom stationery orders;* or *Acted as intermediary among customers, printers, and suppliers.* If possible, quantify your accomplishments, such as *Conducted study of equipment needs of 100 small businesses in Phoenix; Personally generated orders for sales of $90,000 annually; Keyed all the production models for a 250-page employee procedures manual;* or *Assisted editor in layout, design, and news writing for 12 issues of division newsletter.* One professional recruiter said, "I spend a half hour every day screening 50 résumés or more, and if I don't spot some [quantifiable] results in the first 10 seconds, the résumé is history."[15]

In addition to technical skills, employers seek individuals with communication, management, and interpersonal capabilities. This means you'll want to select work experiences and achievements that illustrate your initiative, dependability, responsibility, resourcefulness, and leadership. Employers also want people who can work together in teams. Thus, include statements such as *Collaborated with interdepartmental task force in developing 10-page handbook for temporary workers* and *Headed student government team that conducted most successful voter registration in campus history.*

Statements describing your work experience can be made forceful and persuasive by using action verbs, such as those listed in Figure 13.6 and illustrated in Figure 13.7

Quick Check

Emphasize the skills and aptitudes that recommend you for a specific position.

Capabilities and Skills. Recruiters want to know specifically what you can do for their companies. Therefore, list your special skills, such as *Proficient in preparing correspondence and reports using Word.* Include your ability to use computer programs, office equipment, foreign languages, or sign language. Describe proficiencies you have acquired through training and experience, such as *Trained in computer accounting, including general ledger, accounts receivable, accounts payable, and*

FIGURE 13.6 **Continued**

FINANCIAL SKILLS	CREATIVE SKILLS	HELPING SKILLS	CLERICAL OR DETAIL SKILLS	MORE VERBS FOR ACCOMLISHMENTS
administered	acted	assessed	approved	achieved
allocated	conceptualized	assisted	catalogued	expanded
analyzed	created	clarified	classified	improved
appraised	customized	coached	collected	pioneered
audited	designed	counseled	compiled	reduced (losses)
balanced	developed	demonstrated	generated	resolved (problems)
budgeted	directed	diagnosed	inspected	restored
calculated	established	educated	monitored	spearheaded
computed	founded	expedited	operated	transformed
developed	illustrated	facilitated	organized	
forecasted	initiated	familiarized	prepared	
managed	instituted	guided	processed	
marketed	introduced	motivated	purchased	
planned	invented	referred	recorded	
projected	originated	represented	screened	
researched	performed		specified	
	planned		systematized	
	revitalized		tabulated	

Source: Adapted from Yana Parker, *The Damn Good Résumé Guide* (Berkeley, CA: Ten Speed Press). Reprinted with permission.

payroll. Use expressions such as *competent in, skilled in, proficient with, experienced in,* and *ability to;* for example, *Competent in typing, editing, and/or proofreading reports, tables, letters, memos, manuscripts, and business forms.*

You'll also want to highlight exceptional aptitudes, such as working well under stress and learning computer programs quickly. If possible, provide details and evidence that back up your assertions; for example, *Mastered PhotoShop in 25 hours with little instruction.* Search for examples of your writing, speaking, management, organizational, and interpersonal skills—particularly those talents that are relevant to your targeted job.

FIGURE 13.7 **Using Action Verbs to Strengthen Your Résumé**

Identified weaknesses in internships and **researched** five alternate programs
Reduced delivery delays by an average of three days per order
Streamlined filing system, thus reducing 400-item backlog to 0
Organized holiday awards program for 1200 attendees and 140 awardees
Created a 12-point checklist for use when requesting temporary workers
Designed five posters announcing new employee suggestion program
Calculated shipping charges for overseas deliveries and **recommended** most economical rates
Managed 24-station computer network linking data in three departments
Distributed and **explained** voter registration forms to over 500 prospective student voters
Praised by top management for enthusiastic teamwork and achievement
Secured national recognition from National Arbor Foundation for tree project

Source: Cathy, © Universal Press Syndicate. Reprinted with permission.

For recent graduates, this section can be used to give recruiters evidence of your potential. Instead of *Capabilities*, the section might be called *Skills and Abilities*.

Awards, Honors, and Activities. If you have three or more awards or honors, highlight them by listing them under a separate heading. If not, put them with activities. Include awards, scholarships (financial and other), fellowships, honors, recognition, commendations, and certificates. Be sure to identify items clearly. Your reader may be unfamiliar, for example, with Greek organizations, honoraries, and awards; tell what they mean. Instead of saying *Recipient of Star award*, give more details: *Recipient of Star award given by Pepperdine University to outstanding graduates who combine academic excellence and extracurricular activities.*

It's also appropriate to include school, community, and professional activities. Employers are interested in evidence that you are a well-rounded person. This section provides an opportunity to demonstrate leadership and interpersonal skills. Strive to use action statements. For example, instead of saying *Treasurer of business club*, explain more fully: *Collected dues, kept financial records, and paid bills while serving as treasurer of 35-member business management club.*

Personal Data. Today's résumés omit personal data, such as birth date, marital status, height, weight, and religious affiliation. Such information doesn't relate to genuine occupational qualifications, and recruiters are legally barred from asking for such information. Some job seekers do, however, include hobbies or interests (such as skiing or photography) that might grab the recruiter's attention or serve as conversation starters. Naturally, you wouldn't mention dangerous pastimes (such as bungee jumping or sports car racing) or time-consuming interests. But you should indicate your willingness to travel or to relocate, since many companies will be interested.

References. Listing references on a résumé is favored by some recruiters and opposed by others.[16] Such a list takes up valuable space. Moreover, it is not normally instrumental in securing an interview—few companies check references before the interview. Instead, they prefer that a candidate bring to the interview a list of individuals willing to discuss her or his qualifications. If you do list them, use parallel form. For example, if you show a title for one person (*Professor, Dr., Mrs.*), show titles for all. Include addresses and telephone numbers.

Whether or not you include references on your résumé, you should have their names available when you begin your job search. Ask three to five instructors or previous employers whether they will be willing to answer inquiries regarding your qualifications for employment. Be sure, however, to provide them with an opportunity to refuse. No reference is better than a negative one. Do not include personal or character references, such as friends or neighbors, because recruiters

Quick Check

Awards, honors, and activities are appropriate for the résumé.

Quick Check

Omit personal data not related to job qualifications.

Quick Check

References are unnecessary for the résumé, but they should be available for the interview.

rarely consult them. Companies are more interested in the opinions of objective individuals.

One final note: human resources officers see little reason for including the statement *References furnished upon request*. "It's like saying the sun comes up every morning," remarked one human resources professional.[17]

MAKING YOUR RÉSUMÉ COMPUTER FRIENDLY

So far, our résumé advice aimed at human readers. However, the first reader of your résumé may well be a computer. Hiring companies now use computer programs to reduce hiring costs and make résumé information more accessible. The process of a résumé-scanning program is shown in Figure 13.8

Before you send your résumé, you should learn whether the recipient uses scanning software. One simple way to find out is to call any company where you plan to apply and ask whether it scans résumés electronically. If you can't get a clear answer and you have even the slightest suspicion that your résumé might be read electronically, you'll be smart to prepare a plain, scannable version.

A scannable résumé must sacrifice many of the graphics possibilities that savvy writers employ. Computers aren't impressed by graphics; they prefer "vanilla" résumés—free of graphics and fancy fonts. To make a computer-friendly "vanilla" résumé, you'll want to apply the following suggestions about its physical appearance.

- **Avoid unusual typefaces, underlining, and italics.** Moreover, don't use boxing, shading, or other graphics to highlight text. These features don't scan well. Most applicant-tracking programs, however, can accurately read bold print, solid bullets, and asterisks.
- **Use 10- to 14-point type.** Because touching letters or unusual fonts are likely to be misread, it's safest to use a large, well-known font, such as 12-point Times Roman or Helvetica. This may mean that your résumé will require two pages. After printing, inspect your résumé to see whether any letters touch—especially in your name.
- **Use smooth white paper, black ink, and quality printing.** Avoid colored and textured papers as well as dot-matrix printing.
- **Be sure that your name is the first line on the page.** Don't use fancy layouts that may confuse a scanner.
- **Provide white space.** To ensure separation of words and categories, leave plenty of white space. For example, instead of using parentheses to enclose a telephone area code, insert blank spaces, such as 212 799-2415. Leave blank lines around headings.

✓ Quick Check
Increasing use of scanners requires job candidates to prepare computer-friendly résumés.

✓ Quick Check
Computer-friendly résumés are free of graphics and fancy fonts.

✓ Quick Check
Today's employees must contribute to improving productivity and profitability.

FIGURE 13.8 **What a Résumé-Scanning Program Does**

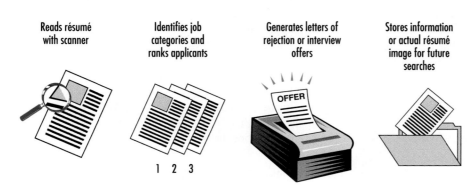

Reads résumé with scanner

Identifies job categories and ranks applicants
1 2 3

Generates letters of rejection or interview offers
OFFER

Stores information or actual résumé image for future searches

- **Avoid double columns.** When listing job duties, skills, computer programs, and so forth, don't tabulate items into two- or three-column lists. Scanners read across and may convert tables into gobbledygook.
- **Don't fold or staple your résumé.** Send it in a large envelope so that you can avoid folds. Words that appear on folds may not be scanned correctly. Avoid staples because the indentions left after they are removed may cause pages to stick.
- **Use abbreviations carefully.** Minimize unfamiliar abbreviations, but maximize easily recognized abbreviations—especially those within your field, such as CAD, COBRA, or JIT. When in doubt, though, spell out! Computers are less confused by whole words.
- **Include all your addresses and telephone numbers.** Be sure your résumé contains your e-mail address, as well as your land address, telephone numbers, and fax number, if available.
- **Be prepared to send your résumé in ASCII.** Pronounced "AS kee," this format offers text only and is immediately readable by all computer programs. It eliminates italics, bold, underlining, and unusual keyboard characters.

EMPHASIZING KEYWORDS

Keywords are usually nouns that describe specific candidate traits or job requirements.

In addition to paying attention to the physical appearance of your résumé, you must also be concerned with keywords. These are usually nouns that describe what an employer wants. Suppose a supervisor at Nike wants to hire an administrative assistant with special proficiencies. That supervisor might submit the following keywords to the Nike applicant-tracking system: *Administrative Assistant, Computer Skills, Word Me, Self-Starter, Report Writing, Proofreading, Communication Skills.* The system would then search through all the résumés on file to see which ones best match the requirements.

A computer-friendly résumé may contain a keyboard summary filled with words (usually nouns) that describe the job or candidate.

Joyce Lain Kennedy, nationally syndicated career columnist and author of *Electronic Résumé Revolution*,[18] suggests using a keyword summary. This list of keyword descriptors immediately follows your name and address on your résumé. A keyword summary, as illustrated in Figure 13.9, should contain your targeted job title and alternative labels, as well as previous job titles, skills, software programs, and selected jargon known in your field. It concentrates on nouns rather than on verbs or adjectives.

FIGURE 13.9 Interpersonal Keywords Most Requested by Employers Using Résumé-Scanning Software*

Ability to delegate	Creative	Leadership	Self-accountable
Ability to implement	Customer oriented	Multitasking	Self-managing
Ability to plan	Detail minded	Open communication	Setting priorities
Ability to train	Ethical	Open minded	Supportive
Accurate	Flexible	Oral communication	Takes initiative
Adaptable	Follow instructions	Organizational skills	Team building
Aggressive work	Follow through	Persuasive	Team player
Analytical ability	Follow up	Problem solving	Tenacious
Assertive	High energy	Public speaking	Willing to travel
Communication skills	Industrious	Results oriented	
Competitive	Innovative	Safety conscious	

*Reported by Resumix, a leading producer of résumé-scanning software.
Source: Joyce Lain Kennedy and Thomas J. Morrow, *Electronic Résumé Revolution* (New York: John Wiley & Sons), 70. Reprinted by permission of John Wiley & Sons, Inc.

To construct your summary, go through your core résumé and mark all relevant nouns. Also try to imagine what eight to ten words an employer might use to describe the job you want. Then select the 25 best words for your summary. Because interpersonal traits are often requested by employers, consult Figure 13.9. It shows the most frequently requested interpersonal traits, as reported by Resumix, one of the leaders in résumé-scanning software.

You may entitle your list *Keyword Summary, Keyword Profile,* or *Keyword Index.* Here's an example of a possible keyword summary for a junior accountant:

Keyword Summary
Accountant: Public, Junior, Staff. A.A., Delgado Community College—Business Administration. BA, Nicholls State University—Accounting. Payables. Receivables. Payroll Experience. Quarterly Reports. Unemployment Reports. Communication Skills. Computer Skills. Excel. Word Me. PCs. Mainframes. Internet. Web. Networks. J. D. Edwards Software. Ability to learn software. Accurate. Dean's List. Award of Merit. Team player. Willing to travel. Relocate.

After an introductory keyword summary, your résumé should contain the standard parts discussed in this chapter. Remember that the keyword section merely helps ensure that your résumé will be selected for inspection. Then human eyes take over. Therefore, you'll want to observe the other writing tips you've learned to make your résumé attractive and forceful. Figures 13.10 through 13.12 show additional examples of chronological and combination résumés. Notice that the scannable résumé in Figure 13.13 is not drastically different from the others. It does, however, include a keyword summary.

PREPARING AN ONLINE, HYPERTEXT RÉSUMÉ

To give your résumé life and make it stand out from others, you might wish to prepare an online résumé. This is actually an HTML (Hypertext Markup Language) document located at a Web site. Posting an online résumé has some distinct advantages—and a few disadvantages.

On the plus side, merely preparing an online résumé suggests that you have exceptional technical savvy. (You would, of course, give credit for any borrowed graphics or code.) An online résumé can be viewed whenever it is convenient for an employer, and it can be seen by many individuals in an organization without circulating a paper copy. But the real reason for preparing an online résumé is that it can become an electronic portfolio with links to examples of your work.

You could include clickable links to reports you have written, summaries of projects completed, a complete list of your coursework, letters of recommendation (with permissions from your recommenders), and extra information about your work experience. An advanced portfolio might include links to electronic copies of your artwork, film projects, blueprints, and photographs of classwork that might otherwise be difficult to share with potential employers. Moreover, you can include razzle-dazzle effects such as color, animation, sound, and graphics. An online résumé provides ample opportunity to show off your creative talents, but only if the position calls for creativity.

On the minus side, online résumés must be more generic than print résumés. They cannot be altered easily if you apply for different positions. Moreover, they present a security problem unless password protected. You may want to include only an e-mail address instead of offering your address and telephone number. Perhaps the best approach is to submit a traditional résumé and letter of application and treat your online résumé only as a portfolio of your work.

Quick Check
An online résumé contains hypertext links to work samples or a portfolio of additional information.

FIGURE 13.10 Enhanced Résumé

Places honors first for emphasis

Quantifies many experiences

Organizes computer skills into three categories

Shows leadership qualities and well-rounded personality

2590 Roxbury Drive
Montpelier, Vermont 05602
(802) 672-5590
joneill@aol.com

Jeffrey V. O'Neill

Objective
To obtain a challenging position using my financial education and experience

Education
- Millikin School of Commerce, University of Virginia
  Bachelor of Science in Commerce, May 2002. GPA: 3.8
  Concentrations in Finance and Management Information Systems
- University of Vermont, Burlington, VT, 1998–2002

Honors
Golden Key National Honor Society	Dean's List 1998–2002
Phi Eta Sigma Freshman Honor Society	Vermont State Scholarship

Experience
Kraft General Foods International, Ryebrook, New York (Summer 2001) Systems Engineer
- Independently analyzed and documented purchasing system and reengineered procedures to improve efficiency
- Evaluated use of 25 PCs and made recommendations to CIO that would save over $30,000
- Conducted cost-benefit study to update PCs and improve network integration for 150 users

Millikin Computer Lab, Charlottesville, Virginia (Fall 2000 to present) Lab Consultant
- Solve problems and maintain LAN of the Commerce School
- Provide technical assistance to over 300 students and 25 faculty members in the use of lab hardware and software

Shearson-Lehman Brothers, Stamford, Connecticut (March 2000) Extern
- Gained valuable insights into U.S. capital markets while assisting financial consultants
- Analyzed equity-options trades to determine how financial securities are evaluated

Computer Experience
Languages: TruBasic, COBOL
Environments: Microsoft Windows, DOS, UNIX
Applications: Lotus, Excel, Word, WordPerfect, PowerPoint

Activities
- Student Council Representative to Admissions Committee, Fall 2001
- Commerce School Representative to Student Council, Spring 2001 to present
- Finance Society Executive Board, Chairman for Investments Game, Spring 2001
- Intramural soccer and basketball, tennis, guitar

Although Jeffrey O'Neill had little paid work experience off campus, his résumé looks impressive because of his relevant summer, campus, and extern experiences. He describes specific achievements related to finance, his career goal. This version of his résumé is enhanced with desktop publishing features because he knows it will not be scanned.

FIGURE 13.11 Combination Résumé

RICK M. JAMESON

4938 Mountain View Avenue
Sunnyvale, CA 94255
(415) 479-1982
Messages: (415) 412-5540

Objective: Position as Staff Accountant with progressive Bay Area firm, where my technical, computer, and communication skills will be useful in managing accounts and acquiring new clientele — Responds to specific job advertisement

SKILLS AND CAPABILITIES

Accounting
- Ability to journalize entries accurately in general and specialized journals
- Proficient in posting to general ledger, preparing trial balance, and detecting discrepancies
- Trained in preparing and analyzing balance sheet and other financial statements — Highlights skills named in advertisement

Computer
- Experienced in using Lotus, dBASE, and WordPerfect for Windows
- Comfortable in personal computer (MS-DOS), mainframe, or network environments
- Ability to learn new computer programs and applications quickly, with little instruction

Communication and Interpersonal
- Enjoy working with details and completing assignments accurately and on time
- Demonstrate sound writing and speaking skills acquired and polished in business letter writing, report writing, and speech classes
- interact well with people as evidenced in my successful sales, volunteer, and internship work

EXPERIENCE

Tax Preparer, Volunteer Income Tax Assistance program (VITA)
Sponsored by the Internal Revenue Service and California State University, San Jose. Prepared state and federal tax returns for individuals with incomes under $25,000. Conducted interviews with over 50 individuals to elicit data regarding taxes. Determined legitimate tax deductions and recorded them accurately. (Tax seasons, 2000 to present) — Combines skills and experience for most forceful appeal

Accounting Intern, Software, Inc., Accounting Department, Santa Clara, CA
Assisted in analyzing data for weekly accounts payable aging report. Prepared daily cash activity report for sums up to $10,000. Calculated depreciation on 12 capital asset accounts with a total valuation of over $900,000. Researched and wrote report analyzing one division's budget of $150,000.(Spring 2000) — Quantifies descriptions of experience

Salesperson, Kmart, Santa Clara, CA
Helped customers select gardening and landscaping supplies. Assisted in ordering merchandise, stocking the department, and resolving customer problems. (Summers 2000, 2001)

EDUCATION

California State University, San Jose. B.S. degree expected 6/02
Major: Business Administration
Specialization: Accounting Theory and Practice. GPA: 3.2 (A = 4.0)
Participated as member of Accounting Club for two years. — Includes activities and awards with education because of limited space

San Jose Community College. A.A. degree 6/99
Major: Business Administration and Accounting. GPA: 3.4 (A = 4.0)
Received Award of Merit for volunteer work as orientation guide and peer tutor

Rick Jameson's résumé responds to an advertisement specifying skills for a staff accountant. He uses the combination format to allow him to highlight the skills his education and limited experience have provided. To make the résumé look professional, he uses the italics, bold, and scalable font features of his word processing program.

FIGURE 13.12 Chronological Résumé

Explains nature of employer's business because it is not immediately recognizable

Emphasizes steady employment history by listing dates FIRST

Describes and quantifies specific achievements

Uses action verbs but includes many good nouns for possible computer scanning

Deemphasizes education because work history is more important for mature candidates

---

RACHEL M. CHOWDHRY

P.O. Box 3310   E-mail: rchowdhry@west.net
Thousand Oaks, CA 91359   (805) 490-3310

OBJECTIVE: SENIOR FINANCIAL MANAGEMENT

PROFESSIONAL HISTORY AND ACHIEVEMENTS

11/98 to 5/02   CONTROLLER
United Plastics, Inc., Newbury Park, CA (extruder of polyethylene film for plastic aprons and gloves)
- Directed all facets of accounting and cash management for 160-employee, $3 billion business
- Supervised inventory and production data processing operations and tax compliance
- Talked owner into reducing sales prices, resulting in doubling first quarter 1997 sales
- Created cost accounting by product and pricing based on gross margin
- Increased line of credit with 12 major suppliers

11/96 to 10/98   CONTROLLER
Burgess, Inc., Freeport, IL (major manufacturer of flashlight and lantern batteries)
- Managed all accounting, cash, payroll, credit, and collection operations for 175-employee business
- Implemented a new system for cost accounting, inventory control, and accounts payable, resulting in a $100,000 annual savings in computer operations
- Reduced staff from 10 persons to 5 with no loss in productivity
- Successfully reduced inventory levels from $1.1 million to $600,000
- Helped develop new cash management system that significantly increased cash flow

8/94 to 8/96   TREASURER/CONTROLLER
The Builders of Winter, Winter, WI (manufacturer of modular housing)
- Supervised accounts receivable/payable, cash management, payroll, and insurance
- Directed monthly and year-end closings, banking relations, and product costing
- Refinanced company with long-term loan, ensuring continued operational stability
- Successfully lowered company's insurance premiums by 7 percent

4/90 to 6/94   SUPERVISOR OF GENERAL ACCOUNTING
Levin National Batteries, St. Paul, MN (local manufacturer of flashlight batteries)
- Completed monthly and year-end closing of ledgers for $2 million business
- Audited freight bills, acted as interdepartmental liaison, prepared financial reports

ADDITIONAL INFORMATION

Education: B.S.B.A. degree, University of Minnesota, major in Accounting, 1987
Certification: CPA Review, Academy of Accountancy, Minneapolis, Minnesota
Personal: Will travel and/or relocate

Because Rachel Chowdhry has many years of experience and seeks high-level employment, she focuses on her experience. Notice how she includes specific achievements and quantifies them whenever possible.

FIGURE 13.13 Computer-Friendly Résumé

CASANDRA L. JOHNSON
3340 Bay Drive
Clearwater, FL 33704
813 742-4490

KEYWORDS
Operations Officer. Operations Department. Bank Teller. Head Teller. Customer Service. Accountant. Bookkeeper. Payables. Receivables. Management. Communication Skills. Organizational Skills. Computer Proficiency. A.A. Hillsborough Community College. B.S. in progress, University of South Florida.

OBJECTIVE
Customer-oriented, fast-learning individual seeks to work in financial institution in career leading to management

EXPERIENCE
First Federal Bank, Pinellas Park, FL 33705
July 2000 to present
Teller

    Cheerfully greet customers, make deposits and withdrawals, accurately enter on computer. Balance up to $10,000 in cash with computer journal tape daily within 15-minute time period. Solve customer problems and answer questions patiently. Issue cashier's checks, savings bonds, and traveler's checks.

Ames Aviation Maintenance Company, St. Petersburg, FL 33706
June 1998 to June 2000
Bookkeeper

    Managed all bookkeeping functions, including accounts payable, accounts receivable, payroll, and tax reports for a small business

EDUCATION
Hillsborough Community College, Tampa, FL
Associate of Arts Degree, 2000
Major: Business Administration and Accounting

University of South Florida, Tampa, FL
*Bachelor of Science in Business Management

STRENGTHS

Computer: Accounting software, banking CRT experience, Excel spreadsheet, Word Perfect. Learn new programs quickly.

Interpersonal: Persuasive, communicative, open-minded. Selected to represent our branch on company diversity committee. Able to set priorities and follow through. Maintain 3.2 GPA while working nearly full time to pay for college.

Professional: Certificate of Merit, presented by First Federal to outstanding new employees

*Will complete in 2003

Annotations (right margin):

Places name alone at top of résumé where scanner expects to find it

Includes job title desired, alternative titles, skills, and other words that might match job description

Surrounds headings with white space for accurate scanning

Prevents inaccurate scanning by using type font in which letters do not touch

Uses synonyms for some data (B.S. in keyword section and Bachelor of Science here) to protect against possible scanning confusion

Mentions some interpersonal traits known to be most requested by employers

Casandra Johnson prepared this "vanilla" résumé (free of graphics and fancy formatting) so that it would scan well if read by a computer. Notice that she begins with a keyword summary that contains job titles, skills, traits, and other descriptive words. She hopes that some of these keywords will match those submitted by an employer. To improve accurate scanning, she avoids italics, vertical and horizontal lines, and double columns.

The Persuasive Résumé

Newly appointed Notre Dame football coach George O'Leary resigned in disgrace after admitting that he had lied about his academic and athletic credentials on his résumé. His revelation touched off a wave of investigations into résumés and biographical sketches. Several coaches, athletic directors, and even the president of the U.S. Olympic Committee lost their jobs over long-forgotten lies or half-truths in their résumés. Once a lie becomes part of your résumé, it's difficult to correct it later. © AP Topic Gallery

RISKING YOUR FUTURE WITH AN INFLATED RÉSUMÉ

✓ Quick Check

Even if discovered much later, deception on a résumé can result in firing.

A résumé is expected to showcase a candidate's strengths and minimize weaknesses. For this reason, recruiters expect a certain degree of self-promotion. But some résumé writers step over the line that separates honest self-marketing from deceptive half-truths and flat-out lies. Distorting facts on a résumé is unethical; lying is illegal. And either practice can destroy a career.

Although recruiters can't check everything, most will verify previous employment and education before hiring candidates. More than half will require official transcripts. And after hiring, the checking process may continue. At one of the nation's top accounting firms, the human resources director described the posthiring routine: "If we find a discrepancy in GPA or prior experience due to an honest mistake, we meet with the new hire to hear an explanation. But if it wasn't a mistake, we terminate the person immediately. Unfortunately, we've had to do that too often."[19]

No job seeker wants to be in the unhappy position of explaining résumé errors or defending misrepresentation. Avoiding the following common problems can keep you off the hot seat:

✓ Quick Check

Beware of inflating education, grades, honors, job titles, or accomplishments.

- **Inflated education, grades, or honors.** Some job candidates claim degrees from colleges or universities when in fact they merely attended classes. Others increase their grade-point averages or claim fictitious honors. Any such dishonest reporting is grounds for dismissal when discovered.
- **Enhanced job titles.** Wanting to elevate their status, some applicants misrepresent their titles. For example, one technician called himself a "programmer" when he had actually programmed only one project for his boss. A mail clerk who assumed added responsibilities conferred upon herself the title of "supervisor." Even when the description seems accurate, it's unethical to list any title not officially granted.
- **Puffed-up accomplishments.** Some job seekers inflate their employment experience or achievements. One clerk, eager to make her photocopying duties sound more important, said that she assisted the *vice president in communicat-*

ing and distributing employee directives. An Ivy League graduate who spent the better part of six months watching rented videos on his VCR described the activity as *Independent Film Study.* That statement may have helped win an interview, but it lost him the job.[20] In addition to avoiding puffery, guard against taking sole credit for achievements that required the efforts of many people. When recruiters suspect dubious claims on résumés, they nail applicants with specific—and often embarrassing—questions during their interviews.[21]

- **Altered employment dates.** Some candidates extend the dates of employment to hide unimpressive jobs or to cover up periods of unemployment and illness. Let's say that several years ago Cindy was unemployed for fourteen months between working for Company A and being hired by Company B. To make her employment history look better, she adds seven months to her tenure with Company A and seven months to Company B. Now her employment history has no gaps, but her résumé is dishonest and represents a potential booby trap for her.

© Ted Goff (www.tedgoff.com)

"How long were you the Decision Enhancement Coordinator for the Acme Company Janitorial Department?"

Applying the Final Touches

Because your résumé is probably the most important document you will ever write, you should expect to revise it many times. With so much information in concentrated form and with so much riding on its outcome, your résumé demands careful polishing, proofreading, and critiquing.

As you revise, be certain to verify all the facts, particularly those involving your previous employment and education. Don't be caught in a mistake, or worse, distortion of previous jobs and dates of employment.

As you continue revising, look for other ways to improve your résumé. For example, consider consolidating headings. By condensing your information into as few headings as possible, you'll produce a clean, professional-looking document. Study other résumés for valuable formatting ideas. Ask yourself what graphics highlighting techniques you can use to improve readability: capitalization, underlining, indenting, and bulleting. Experiment with headings and styles to achieve a pleasing, easy-to-read message. Moreover, look for ways to eliminate wordiness. For example, instead of *Supervised two employees who worked at the counter,* try *Supervised two counter employees.* Review Chapter 4 for more tips on writing concisely.

Above all, make your résumé look professional. Avoid anything humorous or "cute," such as a help-wanted poster with your name or picture inside. Eliminate the personal pronoun *I.* The abbreviated, objective style of a résumé precludes the use of personal pronouns. Use white, off-white, or buff-colored heavy bond paper (24-pound) and a first-rate printer.

After revising, proofread, proofread, and proofread again: for spelling and mechanics, for content, and for format. Then, have a knowledgeable friend or relative proofread it again. This is one document that must be perfect.

By now you may be thinking that you'd like to hire someone to write your résumé. Don't. First, you know yourself better than anyone else could know you. Second, you'll end up with either a generic or a one-time résumé. A generic résumé in today's highly competitive job market will lose out to a targeted résumé nine times out of ten. Equally useless is a one-time résumé aimed at a single job. What if you don't get that job? Because you will need to revise your résumé

✓ *Quick Check*

In addition to being well written, a résumé must be carefully formatted and meticulously proofread.

✓ *Quick Check*

Because résumés must be perfect, they should be proofread many times.

many times as you seek a variety of jobs, be prepared to write (and rewrite) it yourself.

A final word about résumé-writing services. Some tend to produce eye-catching, elaborate documents with lofty language, fancy borders, and fuzzy thinking. Here's an example of empty writing: "Seeking a position which will utilize academic achievements and hands-on experience while providing for career-development opportunities."[22] Save your money and buy a good interview suit instead.

FAXING OR E-MAILING YOUR RÉSUMÉ

In this hurry-up world, employers increasingly want information immediately. If you must fax or e-mail your résumé, take a second look at it. The key to success is SPACE. Without it, characters blur. Underlines blend with the words above, and bold print may look like an ink blot.[23] How can you improve your chances of making a good impression when you must fax or e-mail your résumé?

If you are faxing your printed résumé, select a font with adequate space between characters. Thinner fonts—such as Times, Palatino, New Century Schoolbook, Courier, and Bookman—are clearer than thicker ones. Use a 12-point or larger font, and avoid underlines, which may look broken or choppy when faxed. To be safe, get a transmission report to ensure that all pages were transmitted satisfactorily. Finally, follow up with your polished, printed résumé.

If you are e-mailing your résumé, you may wish to prepare an ASCII version (text only). It will eliminate bold, italics, underlining, tabulated indentions, and unusual characters. To prevent lines from wrapping at awkward spots, keep your line length to 65 characters or less. You can, of course, transmit a fully formatted, attractive résumé if you send it as an attachment and your receiver is using a compatible e-mail program

Nearly everyone writes a résumé by adapting a model, such as those in Figures 13.3 through 13.5 and 13.10 through 13.13. The chronological résumé for Rachel Chowdhry shown in Figure 13.12 is typical of candidates with considerable working experience. Although she describes four positions that span a 14-year period, she manages to fit her résumé on one page. However, two-page résumés are justified for people with long work histories.

THE PERSUASIVE JOB APPLICATION LETTER

To accompany your résumé, you'll need a persuasive job application letter (also called a cover letter). The job application letter has three purposes: (1) introducing the résumé, (2) highlighting your strengths in terms of benefits to the reader, and (3) gaining an interview. In many ways your application letter is a sales letter; it sells your talents and tries to beat the competition. It will, accordingly, include many of the techniques you learned for sales presentations in Chapter 7.

Human resources professionals disagree on how long to make job application letters. Many prefer short letters with no more than four paragraphs. Instead of concentrating on the letter, these readers focus on the résumé. Others desire longer letters that supply more information, thus giving them a better opportunity to evaluate a candidate's qualifications. The latter human resources professionals argue that hiring and training new employees is expensive and time-consuming; therefore, they welcome extra data to guide them in making the best choice the first time. Follow your judgment in writing a brief or a lengthier letter. If you feel, for example, that you need space to explain in more detail what you can do for a prospective employer, do so.

Regardless of its length, an application letter should have three primary parts: (1) an opening that gains attention, (2) a body that builds interest and reduces resistance, and (3) a closing that motivates action.

GAINING ATTENTION IN THE OPENING

The first step in gaining the interest of your reader is addressing that individual by name. Rather than sending your letter to the "Personnel Manager" or "Human Resources Department," try to identify the name of the appropriate individual. Make it a rule to call the organization for the correct spelling and the complete address. This personal touch distinguishes your letter and demonstrates your serious interest.

How you open your letter of application depends largely on whether the application is solicited or unsolicited. If an employment position has been announced and applicants are being solicited, you can use a direct approach. If you do not know whether a position is open and you are prospecting for a job, use an indirect approach. Whether direct or indirect, the opening should attract the attention of the reader. Strive for openings that are more imaginative than *Please consider this letter an application for the position of* . . . or *I would like to apply for.* . . .

Openings for Solicited Jobs.   Here are some of the best techniques to open a letter of application for a job that has been announced:

- **Refer to the name of an employee in the company.** Remember that employers always hope to hire known quantities rather than complete strangers:

  Mitchell Sims, a member of your Customer Service Department, told me that IntriPlex is seeking an experienced customer service representative. The attached summary of my qualifications demonstrates my preparation for this position.

  At the suggestion of Ms. Jennifer Larson of your Human Resources Department, I submit my qualifications for the position of staffing coordinator.

- **Refer to the source of your information precisely.** If you are answering an advertisement, include the exact position advertised and the name and date of the publication. For large organizations it's also wise to mention the section of the newspaper where the ad appeared:

  Your advertisement in Section C-3 of the June 1 *Daily News* for an accounting administrator greatly appeals to me. With my accounting training and computer experience, I believe I could serve Quad Graphics well.

  The September 10 issue of *The Washington Post* reports that you are seeking a mature, organized, and reliable administrative assistant with excellent communication skills.

  Susan Butler, placement director at Sierra University, told me that DataTech has an opening for a technical writer with knowledge of Web design and graphics.

- **Refer to the job title and describe how your qualifications fit the requirements.** Human resources directors are looking for a match between an applicant's credentials and the job needs:

  Will an honors graduate with a degree in recreation and two years of part-time experience organizing social activities for a convalescent hospital qualify for your position of activity director?

  Because of my specialized training in computerized accounting at Boise State University, I feel confident that I have the qualifications you described in your advertisement for a cost accountant trainee.

The Persuasive Job Application Letter

Openings for Unsolicited Jobs.   If you are unsure whether a position actually exists, you may wish to use a more persuasive opening. Since your goal is to convince this person to read on, try one of the following techniques:

Openers for unsolicited jobs show interest in and knowledge of the company, as well as spotlight reader benefits.

- **Demonstrate interest in and knowledge of the reader's business.** Show the personnel director that you have done your research and that this organization is more than a mere name to you:

    Since Signa HealthNet, Inc., is organizing a new information management team for its recently established group insurance division, could you use the services of a well-trained information systems graduate who seeks to become a professional systems analyst?

- **Show how your special talents and background will benefit the company.** Personnel directors need to be convinced that you can do something for them:

    Could your rapidly expanding publications division use the services of an editorial assistant who offers exceptional language skills, an honors degree from the University of Maine, and two years' experience in producing a campus literary publication?

In applying for an advertised job, Kendra A. Hawkins wrote the solicited letter of application shown in Figure 13.14. Notice that her opening identifies the position and the newspaper completely so that the reader knows exactly what advertisement Kendra means. Using features on her word processing program, Kendra designed her own letterhead that uses her name and looks like professionally printed letterhead paper.

More challenging are unsolicited letters of application, such as Donald Vinton's shown in Figure 13.15. Because he hopes to discover or create a job, his opening must grab the reader's attention immediately. To do that, he capitalizes on company information appearing in the newspaper. Donald purposely kept his application letter short and to the point because he anticipated that a busy executive would be unwilling to read a long, detailed letter. Donald's unsolicited letter "prospects" for a job. Some job candidates feel that such letters may be even more productive than efforts to secure advertised jobs, since "prospecting" candidates face less competition. Notice that Donald's letter uses a standard return address consisting of his street, city, and the date.

BUILDING INTEREST IN THE BODY

✓ Quick Check

The body of a letter of application should build interest, reduce resistance, and discuss relevant personal traits.

Once you have captured the attention of the reader, you can use the body of the letter to build interest and reduce resistance. Keep in mind that your résumé emphasizes what you have *done;* your application letter stresses what you *can do* for the employer.

Your first goal is to relate your remarks to a specific position. If you are responding to an advertisement, you'll want to explain how your preparation and experience fill the stated requirements. If you are prospecting for a job, you may not know the exact requirements. Your employment research and knowledge of your field, however, should give you a reasonably good idea of what is expected for this position.

It's also important to emphasize reader benefits. In other words, you should describe your strong points in relation to the needs of the employer. In one employment survey many personnel professionals expressed the same view: "I want you to tell me what you can do for my organization. This is much more important to me than telling me what courses you took in college or what 'duties' you performed on your previous jobs."[24] Instead of *I have completed courses in business communication, report writing, and technical writing*, try this:

FIGURE 13.14 Solicited Application Letter

Kendra A. Hawkins
1770 Hawthorne Place, Boulder, CO 80304

May 23, 2003

Ms. Courtney L. Donahue
Director, Human Resources
Del Rio Enterprises
305 Westminster Avenue
Denver, CO 82511

Dear Ms. Donahue:

Your advertisement for an assistant product manager, appearing May 22 in Section C of the *Denver Post*, immediately caught my attention because my education and training closely parallel your needs.

According to your advertisement, the job includes "assisting in the coordination of a wide range of marketing programs as well as analyzing sales results and tracking marketing budgets." A recent internship at Ventana Corporation introduced me to similar tasks. Assisting the marketing manager enabled me to analyze the promotion, budget, and overall sales success of two products Ventana was evaluating. My ten-page report examined the nature of the current market, the products' life cycles, and their sales/profit return. In addition to this research, I helped formulate a product merchandising plan and answered consumers' questions at a local trade show.

Intensive course work in marketing and management, as well as proficiency in computer spreadsheets and databases, has given me the kind of marketing and computer training that Del Rio probably demands in a product manager. Moreover, my recent retail sales experience and participation in campus organizations have helped me develop the kind of customer service and interpersonal skills necessary for an effective product manager.

After you have examined the enclosed résumé for details of my qualifications, I would be happy to answer questions. Please call me to arrange an interview at your convenience so that we may discuss how my marketing experience, computer training, and interpersonal skills could contribute to Del Rio Enterprises.

Sincerely,

Kendra A. Hawkins

Kendra A. Hawkins

Enclosure

Annotations (right margin):
- Uses personally designed letterhead
- Addresses proper person by name and title
- Identifies job and exact page where ad appeared
- Relates writer's experiences to job requirements
- Discusses schooling
- Discusses experience
- Refers reader to résumé
- Asks for interview and repeats main qualifications

Courses in business communication, report writing, and technical writing have helped me develop the research and writing skills required of your technical writers.

Choose your strongest qualifications and show how they fit the targeted job. And remember, students with little experience are better off spotlighting their education and its practical applications, as these candidates did:

Because you seek an architect's apprentice with proven ability, I submit a drawing of mine that won second place in the Sinclair College drafting contest last year.

Successfully transcribing over 100 letters and memos in my college transcription class gave me experience in converting the spoken word into the written word, an exacting communication skill demanded of your administrative assistants.

In the body of your letter, you'll also want to discuss relevant personal traits. Employers are looking for candidates who, among other things, are team players,

✓ Quick Check
Spotlighting reader benefits means matching one's personal strengths to an employer's needs.

The Persuasive Job Application Letter

FIGURE 13.15 Unsolicited Letter of Application

Uses standard return address format, but could have designed his own letterhead

Shows knowledge of company and resourcefulness

Keeps letter brief to retain reader's attention

Refers to résumé

Takes initiative for follow-up

> 2250 Turtle Creek Drive
> Monroeville, PA 15146
> May 29, 2003
>
> Mr. Richard M. Jannis
> Vice President, Operations
> Sports World, Inc.
> 4907 Allegheny Boulevard
> Pittsburgh, PA 16103
>
> Dear Mr. Jannis:
>
> Today's Pittsburgh *Examiner* reports that your organization plans to expand its operations to include national distribution of sporting goods, and it occurs to me that you will be needing highly motivated, self-starting sales representatives and marketing managers. Here are three significant qualifications I have to offer:
>
> - Four years of formal training in business administration, including specialized courses in sales management, retailing, marketing promotion, and consumer behavior
>
> - Practical experience in demonstrating and selling consumer products, as well as successful experience in telemarketing
>
> - Good communication skills and a strong interest in most areas of sports (which helped me become a sportscaster at Penn State radio station WGNF)
>
> May we talk about how I can put these qualifications, and others summarized in the enclosed résumé, to work for Sports World as it develops its national sales force? I'll call during the week of June 5 to discuss your company's expansion plans and the opportunity for an interview.
>
> Sincerely yours,
>
> *Donald W. Vinton*
>
> Donald W. Vinton
>
> Enclosure

take responsibility, show initiative, and learn easily. Finally, in this section or the next, you should refer the reader to your résumé. Do so directly or as part of another statement, as shown here:

> Please refer to the attached résumé for additional information regarding my education, experience, and references.
>
> As you will notice from my résumé, I will graduate in June with a bachelor's degree in business administration.

MOTIVATING ACTION IN THE CLOSING

After presenting your case, you should conclude with a spur to action. This is where you ask for an interview. If you live in a distant city, you may request an employment application or an opportunity to be interviewed by the organization's nearest representative. However, never ask for the job. To do so would be presumptuous and naive. In requesting an interview, suggest reader benefits or review your strongest points. Sound sincere and appreciative. Remember to make it easy for the reader to agree by supplying your telephone number and the best times to call you. And keep in mind that some personnel directors prefer that you take the initiative to call them. Here are possible endings:

> I hope this brief description of my qualifications and the additional information on my résumé indicate to you my genuine desire to put my skills in accounting to work for you. Please call me at (405) 488-2291 before 10 a.m. or after 3 p.m. to arrange an interview.

> To add to your staff an industrious, well-trained administrative assistant with proven word processing and communication skills, call me at (350) 492-1433 to arrange an interview. I can meet with you at any time convenient to your schedule.

> Next week, after you have examined the attached résumé, I will call you to discuss the possibility of arranging an interview.

AVOIDING "I" DOMINANCE

As you revise your application letter, notice how many sentences begin with *I*. Although it's impossible to talk about yourself without using *I*, you can reduce the number of sentences beginning with this pronoun by using two techniques. First, place *I* in the middle of sentences instead of dominating the opening. Instead of *I was the top salesperson in my department*, try *While working in X department, I did Y and Z* and *Among 15 coworkers, I received top ratings from my managers.* Incorporating *I* into the middle of sentences considerably reduces its domination.

Another technique for avoiding "I" dominance involves making activities and outcomes, and not yourself, the subjects of sentences. For example, rather than *I took classes in business communication and computer applications*, say *Classes in business communication and computer applications prepared me to. . . .* Instead of *I enjoyed helping customers*, say *Helping customers was a real pleasure.*

FINAL TIPS

Like the résumé, your application letter must look professional and suggest quality. This means using a traditional letter style, such as block or modified block. Also, be sure to print it on the same bond paper as your résumé. More and more writers today are designing their own letterhead paper, or they adapt one of the "wizards" available with their word processing programs. Be sure to use restraint, though, so that your letterhead looks truly professional, such as that shown in Figure 13.14. Finally, proofread your application letter several times; then, have a friend read it for content and mechanics.

✓ *Quick Check*

A letter of application should look professional and suggest quality.

SUMMING UP AND LOOKING FORWARD

In today's competitive job market, an employment search begins with identifying your interests, evaluating your qualifications, and choosing a career path. Finding the perfect job will mean a concentrated effort devoted to checking classified advertisements, networking, and studying online job possibilities. In applying for jobs, you'll want to submit a persuasive résumé that sells your skills and experience. Whether you choose a chronological, functional, or combination résumé style, you should tailor your assets to fit the position sought. If you think your résumé might be scanned, emphasize keywords and keep the format simple. A persuasive application letter should introduce your résumé and describe how your skills and experiences match those required.

Now, if your résumé and application letter have been successful, you'll proceed to the employment interview, one of life's most nerve-wracking experiences. The last chapter in this book provides helpful suggestions for successful interviewing and follow-up communication.

Interactive Learning @ http://www.westwords.com/guffey/students.html
Prepare for tests and reinforce your chapter knowledge with interactive quizzes and crossword puzzles.

CRITICAL THINKING

1. How has the concept of the job changed, and how will it affect your employment search?
2. How is a résumé different from a company employment application?
3. Some job candidates think that applying for unsolicited jobs can be more fruitful than applying for advertised openings. Discuss the advantages and disadvantages of letters that "prospect" for jobs.
4. What are the advantages and disadvantages of developing a hypertext résumé?
5. Ethical Issue: At work fellow employee Kevin lets it slip that he did not complete the degree he claims on his résumé. You have never liked Kevin, but he does satisfactory work. You are both competing for the same promotion. You are considering writing an anonymous note to the boss telling him to verify Kevin's degree. Use the tools on page 78 to decide whether this is an ethical action.

CHAPTER REVIEW

6. List five questions that you should ask yourself to identify your employment interests.

7. List five or more sources of career information.

8. How are most jobs likely to be found? Through the classified ads? Employment agencies? Networking? Explain.

9. What is the goal of your résumé?

10. Describe a chronological résumé and discuss its advantages.

11. Describe a functional résumé and discuss its advantages.

12. What are the disadvantages of a functional résumé?

13. When does it make sense to include a career objective on your résumé?

14. On a chronological résumé what information should you include for the jobs you list?

15. In addition to technical skills, what traits and characteristics do employers seek?

16. List some suggestions for making a résumé easily scannable by a computer.

17. What are keywords, and why are they important in résumé scanning? Give examples.

18. If you are e-mailing your résumé, why is it wise to send a text-only version?

19. What are the three purposes of a job application letter?

20. How can you make it easy for a recruiter to reach you?

ACTIVITIES AND CASES

13.1 IDENTIFYING YOUR EMPLOYMENT INTERESTS

Your Task. In a memo addressed to your instructor, answer the questions in the section "Identifying Your Interests" at the beginning of the chapter. Draw a conclusion from your answers. What kinds of career, company, position, and location seem to fit your self-analysis?

13.2 EVALUATING YOUR QUALIFICATIONS

Your Task. Prepare four worksheets that inventory your qualifications in the areas of employment, education, capabilities and skills, and honors and activities. Use active verbs when appropriate.

a. **Employment.** Begin with your most recent job or internship. For each position list the following information: employer; job title; dates of employment; and three to five duties, activities, or accomplishments. Emphasize activities related to your job goal. Strive to quantify your achievements.

b. **Education.** List degrees, certificates, and training accomplishments. Include courses, seminars, or skills that are relevant to your job goal. Calculate your grade-point average in your major.

c. **Capabilities and skills.** List all capabilities and skills that recommend you for the job you seek. Use words such as *skilled, competent, trained, experienced,* and *ability to.* Also list five or more qualities or interpersonal skills necessary for a successful individual in your chosen field. Write action statements demonstrating that you possess some of these qualities. Empty assurances aren't good enough; try to show evidence (*Developed teamwork skills by working with a committee of eight to produce a . . .*).

d. **Awards, honors, and activities.** Explain any awards so that the reader will understand them. List campus, community, and professional activities that suggest you are a well-rounded individual or possess traits relevant to your target job.

WEB

13.3 CHOOSING A CAREER PATH. Many people know surprisingly little about the work done in various occupations and the training requirements.

Your Task. Use the online *Occupational Outlook Handbook* (http://www.bls.gov/oco), prepared by the Bureau of Labor Statistics, to learn more about an occupation of your choice. Find the description of a position for which you could apply in two to five years.

Learn about what workers do on the job, working conditions, training and education needed, earnings, and expected job prospects. Print the pages from the *Occupational Outlook Handbook* that describe employment in the area in which you are interested. If your instructor directs, attach these copies to the letter of application you will write in Activity 13.8.

13.4 SEARCHING THE JOB MARKET

Your Task. Clip a job advertisement from the classified section of a newspaper or print one from a career site on the Web. Select an ad describing the kind of employment you are seeking now or plan to seek when you graduate. Save this advertisement to attach to the résumé you will write in Activity 13.8.

13.5 POSTING A RÉSUMÉ ON THE WEB

Your Task. Prepare a list of at least three online employment sites where you could post your résumé. Describe the procedure involved and the advantages for each site.

WEB

13.6 DRAFT DOCUMENT: RÉSUMÉ

Your Task. Analyze the following résumé. Discuss its strengths and weaknesses. Your instructor may ask you to revise sections of this résumé before showing you an improved version.

Wendy Lee Cox
5349 East Zion Place
Tulsa, OK 74115-3394
Phone: (d) (918) 834-4583 (n) (918) 594-2985

Seeking to be hired at Mead Products as an intern in Accounting

SKILLS: Accounting, Internet, Windows XP, Excel, PowerPoint, Freelance Graphics

EDUCATION
Now working on B.S. in Business Administration. Major, Management and Accounting; GPA is 3.5. Expect to graduate in June, 2004.

EXPERIENCE:
Assistant Accountant, 1999 to present. March and McLennan, Inc., Bookkeeping/Tax Service, Tulsa. I keep accounting records for several small businesses accurately. I prepare 150 to 200 individual income tax returns each year. For Hill and Hill Truck Line I maintain accurate and up-to-date A/R records. And I prepare payroll records for 16 employees at three firms.

Peterson Controls Inc., Tulsa. Data Processing Internship, 2003 to present. I design and maintain spreadsheets and also process weekly and monthly information for production uptime and downtime. I prepare graphs to illustrate uptime and downtime data.

Tulsa Country Club. Accounts Payable Internship, 2002 to 2003. Took care of accounts payable including filing system for the club. Responsible for processing monthly adjusting entries for general ledger. Worked closely with treasurer to give the Board budget/disbursement figures regularly.

Langston University, Tulsa. I marketed the VITA program to Langston students and organized volunteers and supplies. Official title: Coordinator of Volunteer Income Tax Assistance Project.

COMMUNITY SERVICE: March of Dimes Drive, Central Park High School; All Souls Unitarian Church, coordinator for Children's Choir

13.7 DRAFT DOCUMENT: LETTER OF APPLICATION

Your Task. Analyze each section of the following letter of application written by an accounting major about to graduate.

Dear Human Resources Director:

Please consider this letter as an application for the position of staff accountant that I saw advertised in the *Houston Post*. Although I have had no paid work experience in this field, accounting has been my major in college and I'm sure I could be an asset to your company.

For four years I have studied accounting, and I am fully trained for full-charge bookkeeping as well as electronic accounting. I have taken 36 units of college accounting and courses in business law, economics, statistics, finance, management, and marketing. In addition to my course work, during the tax season I have been a student volunteer for VITA. This is a project to help individuals in the community prepare their income tax returns, and I learned a lot from this experience. I have also received some experience in office work and working with figures when I was employed as an office assistant for Copy Quick, Inc.

I am a competent and responsible person who gets along pretty well with others. I have been a member of some college and social organizations and have even held elective office.

I feel that I have a strong foundation in accounting as a result of my course work and my experience. Along with my personal qualities and my desire to succeed, I hope that you will agree that I qualify for the position of staff accountant with your company.
Sincerely,

13.8 RÉSUMÉ

Your Task. Using the data you developed in Activity 13.2, write your résumé. Aim it at a full-time job, part-time position, or internship. Attach a job listing for a specific position (from Activity 13.4). Use a computer. Revise your résumé until it is perfect.

13.9 JOB APPLICATION LETTER

Your Task. Write an application letter introducing your résumé. Again, use a computer. Revise your application letter until it is perfect.

INFOTRAC 13.10 SPECIAL TIPS FOR TODAY'S RÉSUMÉ WRITERS

Your Task. Using InfoTrac, research the topic of employment résumés. Read at least three recent articles. In a memo to your instructor list eight or more good tips that are not covered in this chapter. Pay special attention to advice concerning the preparation of online résumés. The subject line of your memo should be "Special Tips for Today's Résumé Writers."

GRAMMAR/MECHANICS CHECKUP—13

NUMBER STYLE

Review Sections 4.01–4.13 in the Grammar/Mechanics Handbook. Then study each of the following pairs. Assume that these expressions appear in the context of letters, reports, or memos. Write *a* or *b* in the space provided to indicate the preferred number style and record the number of the G/M principle illustrated. When you finish, compare your response with those at the end of the book. If your responses differ, study carefully the principles in parentheses.

Example   (a) six investments (b) 6 investments   a _____ (4.01a)

1. (a) sixteen credit cards   (b) 16 credit cards   _____
2. (a) Fifth Avenue   (b) 5th Avenue   _____
3. (a) 34 newspapers   (b) thirty-four newspapers   _____
4. (a) July eighth   (b) July 8   _____
5. (a) twenty dollars   (b) $20   _____
6. (a) on the 15th of June   (b) on the fifteenth of June   _____
7. (a) at 4:00 p.m.   (b) at 4 p.m.   _____
8. (a) 3 200-page reports   (b) three 200-page reports   _____
9. (a) over 18 years ago   (b) over eighteen years ago   _____
10. (a) 2,000,000 people   (b) 2 million people   _____
11. (a) fifteen cents   (b) 15 cents   _____
12. (a) a thirty-day warranty   (b) a 30-day warranty   _____
13. (a) 2/3 of the e-mails   (b) two thirds of the e-mails _____
14. (a) two telephones for   (b) 2 telephones for
        fifteen employees   15 employees   _____
15. (a) 6 of the 130 letters   (b) six of the 130 letters   _____

GRAMMAR/MECHANICS CHALLENGE—13

DOCUMENT FOR REVISION

The following résumé (shortened for this exercise) has faults in grammar, punctuation, spelling, number form, verb form, wordiness, and word use. Use standard proofreading marks (see Appendix B) to correct the errors. When you finish, your instructor can show you the revised version of this résumé.

MEGAN A. RYAN

2450 1st Street

Miami, Flor., 33133

EDUCATION

Coastal Community College, Miami, Florida

Degree expected approximately in June of 2004

Major Office Technology

EXPERIENCE:

• **Office Assistant.** Host Systems, Miami. 2002 too pressent. Responsible for entering data on Macintosh computer. I had to insure accuracy and completness of data that was to be entered. Another duty was maintaining a clean and well-organized office. I also served as Office Courier.

- **Lechter's Housewares.** Miami Shores. 2nd Asst. Mgr I managed store in absence of mgr. and asst. mgr. I open and close registers. Ballanced daily reciepts. Ordered some mds. I also had to supervise 2 employes, earning rabid promotion.

- **Clerk typist.** Caribean Cruises Miami. 1999-00. (part time) Entered guest data on IBM PC. Did personalized followup letters to customer inquirys. Was responsible for phones. I also handled all errands as courier.

STRENGTHS

IBM PC, transcription, poofreading.

Can type 50 words/per/minute.

I am a fast learner, and very accurate.

Word, Excell, InterNet

COMMUNICATION WORKSHOP: CAREER SKILLS

How to Use Traditional and Online Networking to Explore the Hidden Job Market

Not all jobs are advertised in classified ads or listed in job databases. The "hidden" job market, according to some estimates, accounts for as much as two thirds of all positions available. Companies don't always announce openings publicly because it's time-consuming to interview all the applicants, many of whom are not qualified. But the real reason that companies resist announcing a job is that they dislike hiring "strangers." One recruiter says that when she needs to hire, she first looks around among her friends and acquaintances. If she can't find anyone suitable, she then turns to advertising.[25] It's clear that many employers are more comfortable hiring a person they know.

The key to finding a good job, then, is converting yourself from a "stranger" into a known quantity. One way to become a known quantity is by networking. You can use either traditional methods or online resources.

Traditional Networking

- *Step 1: Develop a list.* Make a list of anyone who would be willing to talk with you about finding a job. List your friends, relatives, former employers, former coworkers, classmates from grade school and high school, college friends, members of your church, people in social and athletic clubs, present and former teachers, neighbors, and friends of your parents.
- *Step 2: Make contacts.* Call the people on your list or, even better, try to meet with them in person. To set up a meeting, say "Hi, Aunt Martha! I'm looking for a job and I wonder if you could help me out. When could I come over to talk about it?" During your visit be friendly, well-organized, polite, and inter-

ested in what your contact has to say. Provide a copy of your résumé, and try to keep the conversation centered on your job search area. Your goal is to get two or more referrals. In pinpointing your request, ask two questions. "Do you know of anyone who might have an opening for a person with my skills?" If not, "Do you know of anyone else who might know of someone who would?"

- *Step 3: Follow up on your referrals.* Call the people whose names are on your referral list. You might say something like, "Hello. I'm Carlos Ramos, a friend of Connie Cole. She suggested that I call and ask you for help. I'm looking for a position as a marketing trainee, and she thought you might be willing to see me and give me a few ideas." Don't ask for a job. During your referral interview ask how the individual got started in this line of work, what he or she likes best (or least) about the work, what career paths exist in the field, and what problems must be overcome by a newcomer. Most important, ask how a person with your background and skills might get started in the field. Send an informal thank-you note to anyone who helps you in your job search, and stay in touch with the most promising contacts. Ask whether you may call every three weeks or so during your job search.

Online Networking

As with traditional networking, the goal is to make connections with people who are advanced in their fields. Ask for their advice about finding a job. Most people like talking about themselves, and asking them about their experiences is an excellent way to begin an online correspondence that might lead to "electronic mentoring" or a letter of recommendation from an expert in the field. "Hanging out" at an online forum, discussion group, or newsgroup where industry professionals can be found is also a great way to keep tabs on the latest business trends and potential job leads.

- *Web-Based Discussion Groups, Forums, and Boards.* An especially good discussion group resource for beginners is Yahoo! Groups (http://groups.yahoo .com). You may choose from groups ranging from Business/Finance to Romance/Relationship and on to Science. If you click the "Business/Finance" listing, you will see listings for more specialized groups. Click "Employment and Work," and you will find career groups including construction, customer service, secretaries, court reporting, interior design, and so on.
- *Mailing Lists and Newsgroups.* The most relevant Internet discussions can be found on mailing lists. You can subscribe to an e-mail newsletter or discussion group at Topica (http://www.topica.com). To post and read newsgroup (Usenet) messages, try the Google Web site (http://www.google.com) and click "Groups."

Career Application. Everyone who goes out on the job market needs to develop his or her own network. Assume you are ready to change jobs or look for a permanent position. Begin developing your personal network.

Your Task

- Conduct at least one referral interview and report on it to your class.
- Join one professional mailing list. Ask your instructor to recommend an appropriate mailing list for your field.
- Take notes on discussions at your mailing list and report your reactions and findings to your class.

Chapter

14

Employment Interviewing and Follow-Up Messages

Very often the difference between the person hired and the person rejected is not who is the better candidate but who is better prepared for the interview. Careers can be made and lost at that point alone.[1]

JOHN D. SHINGLETON, former placement director, Michigan State University

LEARNING OBJECTIVES

1. Distinguish between screening interviews and hiring/placement interviews.
2. Identify information resources in investigating target employers.
3. Explain how to prepare for employment interviews.
4. Recognize how to control nonverbal messages and how to fight interview fears.
5. Be prepared to answer favorite interview questions and know how to close an interview.
6. Itemize topics and behaviors to avoid in interviews.
7. Write follow-up letters and other employment messages.

Job interviews, for most of us, are intimidating; no one enjoys being judged and, possibly, rejected. Should you expect to be nervous about an upcoming job interview? Of course! Everyone is uneasy about being scrutinized and questioned. But think of how much *more* nervous you would be if you had no idea what to expect in the interview and if you were unprepared.

This chapter presents different kinds of interviews and shows you how to prepare for them. You'll learn how to gather information about an employer, as well as how to reduce nervousness, control body language, and fight fear during an interview. You'll pick up tips for responding to recruiters' favorite questions and learn how to cope with illegal questions and salary matters. Moreover, you'll receive pointers on significant questions you can ask during an interview. Finally, you'll learn what you should do as a successful follow-up to an interview.

Yes, you can expect to be nervous. But you can also expect to ace an interview when you know what's coming and when you prepare thoroughly. Remember, it's often the degree of preparation that determines who gets the job.

The primary goal of an interviewer is to learn whether you have the skills, training, experience, and interest necessary to fulfill the requirements of the position. Because most employers want to establish a lasting relationship, they will ask a series of questions to determine whether you, the job, and the company are compatible.
© Omni Photo Communications, Inc./ Index Stock Imagery, Inc.

SUCCEEDING IN VARIOUS KINDS OF EMPLOYMENT INTERVIEWS

Job applicants generally face two kinds of interviews: screening interviews and hiring/placement interviews. You must succeed in the first to proceed to the second.

SCREENING INTERVIEWS

Screening interviews do just that—they screen candidates to eliminate those who fail to meet minimum requirements. Initial screening may be done by telephone or by computer.[2]

A telephone screening interview may be as short as five minutes. But don't treat it casually. It's not just another telephone call. If you don't perform well during the telephone interview, it may be your last interview with that organization. Here's how you can be prepared:

 Quick Check

Screening interviews are intended to eliminate those who fail to meet minimum requirements.

- Keep a list near the telephone of positions for which you have applied.
- Have your résumé, references, a calendar, and a notepad handy.
- If caught off guard, ask whether you can call back in a few minutes from the telephone in your office. Organize your materials and yourself.
- Sell your qualifications, and, above all, sound enthusiastic!

One recruiter said that the mistakes most often made in telephone screening interviews were bringing up money too soon and exhibiting disinterest by typing on a keyboard. Another mistake, made by individuals using company telephones for their job search, was whispering so that coworkers would not hear them.[3]

A new trend in screening interviews involves computers. Many well-known retailers—such as Target, Macy's, Hollywood Video, and Longs Drug Stores—are replacing paper applications and in-person interviews with computer kiosks for the initial screening of applicants.[4] Athletic shoe manufacturer Nike used computer interviews to select 2,500 candidates from the 6,000 who responded to ads for workers at its Las Vegas Niketown.[5]

 Quick Check

Computer interviews are used by companies to screen candidates and identify qualifications quickly.

HIRING/PLACEMENT INTERVIEWS

The most promising candidates selected from screening interviews will be invited to hiring/placement interviews. Although these interviews are the real thing, in some ways they are like a game. Trained interviewers try to uncover any negative information that will eliminate a candidate. The candidate, of course, tries to minimize faults and emphasize strengths to avoid being eliminated. More common, however, are interviewers who genuinely want to learn how the candidate would fit into their organization. Conducted in depth, hiring/placement interviews may take many forms.

© Ted Goff (www.tedgoff.com)

"I can't tell you how much getting this interview means to me, Ms. Whatsyourname."

- **One-on-one interviews** are most common. You can expect to sit down with a company representative and talk about the job and your qualifications. If the representative is the hiring manager, questions will be specific and job-related. If the representative is from human resources, the questions will probably be more general.

- **Sequential and group interviews** are common with companies that rule by consensus. You may face many interviewers in sequence, all of whom you must listen to carefully and respond to positively. Many group interviews are conducted by teams. With team interviews, begin to think in terms of "we" instead of "I." Explain how you contributed to a team effort instead of emphasizing individual achievements.[6] Strive to stay focused, summarize important points, and ask good questions.

- **Stress interviews** are meant to test your reactions. If asked rapid-fire questions from many directions, take the time to slow things down. For example, *I would be happy to answer your question Ms. X, but first I must finish responding to Mr. Z.* If greeted with silence, another stress technique, you might say, *Would you like me to begin the interview? Let me tell you about myself.* Or ask a question such as *Can you give me more information about the position?* A stress interviewer might confront a job candidate with, *It's obvious your background makes you totally unqualified for this position. Why should we even waste our time talking?* The best way to handle stress questions is to remain calm and give carefully considered answers.

INVESTIGATING THE TARGET

One of the most important steps in effective interviewing is gathering information about a prospective employer. In learning about a company, you may uncover information that convinces you that this is not the company for you. It's always better to learn about negatives early in the process. More likely, though, the information you collect will help you tailor your application and interview responses to the organization's needs.

DIGGING FOR COMPANY INFORMATION

Recruiters are impressed by candidates who have done their homework. You can find information from annual reports, books, employment Web sites, and company Web sites. Some of the best research data about companies comes from *Gale's Job Seeker's Guide to Private and Public Companies, Hoover's Handbook of American*

Companies, *The Million Dollar Directory, Moody's Complete Corporate Index, Standard and Poor's Registry of Corporations,* and *The 100 Best Companies to Work for in America.* In addition to these books, you might try three Web sites that provide good company information: (1) http://www.wetfeet.com, (2) http://www.flipdog.com, and (3) http://www.hoovers.com.

If you want specific information on both big and small companies, go to their own Web sites. They are often bursting with juicy information. Another way to learn about an organization is to call the receptionist or the interviewer directly. Ask what you can read to prepare you for the interview. Here are some specifics to research:

- Find out all you can about company leaders. Their goals, ambitions, and values often are adopted by the entire organization—including your interviewer.
- Investigate the business philosophy of the leaders, such as their priorities, strategies, and managerial approaches. Are you a good match with your target employer? If so, be sure to let the employer know that there is a correlation between the company's needs and your qualifications.
- Learn about the company's accomplishments and setbacks. This information should help you determine where you might make your best contribution.
- Study the company's finances. Are they so shaky that a takeover is imminent? If so, look elsewhere. Try to get your hands on an annual report. Many larger companies now post them at their Web sites.
- Examine its products and customers. What excites you about this company?
- Check out the competition. What are its products, strengths, and weaknesses?
- Analyze the company's advertising, including sales and marketing brochures. One candidate, a marketing major, spent a great deal of time poring over brochures from an aerospace contractor. During his initial interview, he shocked and impressed the recruiter with his knowledge of the company's guidance systems. The candidate had, in fact, relieved the interviewer of his least-favorite task—explaining the company's complicated technology.[7]

Study company leaders, organizational strategies, finances, products, customers, competition, and advertising.

LEARNING ABOUT SMALLER COMPANIES

For smaller companies and those that are not publicly owned, you'll probably have to do a little more footwork. You might start with the local library. Ask the reference librarian to help you locate information. Newspapers might contain stories or press releases with news of an organization. Visit the Better Business Bureau to discover whether the company has had any difficulties with other companies or consumers. Investigate the Chamber of Commerce to see what you can learn about the target company.

Talking with company employees is always a good idea, if you can manage it. They are probably the best source of inside information. Try to be introduced to someone who is currently employed—but not working in the immediate area where you wish to be hired. Be sure to seek out someone who is discreet.

The best source of inside information is company employees.

You know how flattered you feel when an employer knows about you and your background. That feeling works both ways. Employers are pleased when job candidates take an interest in them. Be ready to put in plenty of effort in investigating a target employer because this effort really pays off at interview time.

PREPARING AND PRACTICING

After you have learned about the target organization, study the job description. It not only helps you write a focused résumé but also enables you to match your education, experience, and interests with the employer's position. Finding out the duties and responsibilities of the position will help you practice your best response strategies.

One of the best ways to prepare for an interview involves itemizing your (1) most strategic skills, (2) greatest areas of knowledge, (3) strongest personality traits, and (4) key accomplishments. Write this information down and practice relating these strengths to the kinds of questions frequently asked in interviews. Here are some specific tips for preparation:

Quick Check

Practice success stories that emphasize your most strategic skills, areas of knowledge, strongest personality traits, and key accomplishments.

- Practice, practice, practice. Recite answers to typical interview questions in a mirror, with a friend, while driving in your car, or in spare moments. Keep practicing until you have the best responses down pat.
- Consider videotaping or tape recording a practice session to see and hear how you really come across. Do you look and sound enthusiastic?
- Be ready to answer questions about alcohol and drug use. It is legal to ask whether a candidate drinks alcohol, but it is not legal to ask how much. If you take a job with a large company, you can count on being asked to take a drug test.
- Expect to explain problem areas on your résumé. For example, if you have little or no experience, you might emphasize your recent training and up-to-date skills. If you have gaps in your résumé, be prepared to answer questions about them positively and truthfully.
- Try to build interviewing experience with less important jobs first. You will become more confident and better able to sell your strengths with repeated interviewing exposure. Think of it as a game that requires practice.

SENDING POSITIVE NONVERBAL MESSAGES

What comes out of your mouth and what's written on your résumé are not the only messages an interviewer receives from you. Nonverbal messages also create powerful impressions on people. Here are suggestions that will help you send the right nonverbal messages during interviews:

- Arrive on time or a little early. If necessary, find the location on a trial run a few days before the interview so that you know where to park, how much time the drive takes, and what office to find.
- Be courteous and congenial to everyone. Remember that you are being judged not only by the interviewer but by the receptionist and anyone else who sees you before and after the interview. They will notice how you sit, what you read, and how you look.
- Introduce yourself to the receptionist, and wait to be invited to sit.

✓ **Quick Check**

Send positive nonverbal messages by arriving on time, being courteous, dressing professionally, greeting the interviewer confidently, controlling your body movements, making eye contact, and smiling.

- Dress professionally. Even if some employees in the organization dress casually, you should look qualified, competent, and successful. One young applicant complained to his girlfriend about having to wear a suit for an interview when everyone at the company dressed casually. She replied, "You don't get to wear the uniform, though, until you make the team!"
- Greet the interviewer confidently. Extend your hand, look him or her directly in the eye, and say, "I'm pleased to meet you, Mr. X. I am Z." In this culture a firm, not crushing, handshake sends a nonverbal message of poise and assurance.
- Wait for the interviewer to offer you a chair. Make small talk with upbeat comments, such as "This is a beautiful headquarters. How many employees work here?" Don't immediately begin rummaging in your briefcase for your résumé. Being at ease and unrushed suggest that you are self-confident.

- Control your body movements. Keep your hands, arms, and elbows to yourself. Don't lean on a desk. Sit erect, leaning forward slightly. Keep your feet on the floor.
- Make eye contact frequently, but don't get into a staring contest. A direct eye gaze, at least in North America, suggests interest and trustworthiness.
- Smile enough to convey a positive attitude. Have a friend give you honest feedback on whether you generally smile too much or not enough.
- Sound enthusiastic and interested—but sincere.

FIGHTING FEAR

Expect to be nervous. It's natural! Other than public speaking, employment interviews are the most dreaded events in people's lives. One of the best ways to overcome fear is to know what happens in a typical interview. Figure 14.1 describes how a recruiter usually structures an interview. You can further reduce your fears by following these suggestions.

- Practice interviewing as much as you can—especially with real companies. The more times you experience the interview situation, the less nervous you will be.
- Prepare 110 percent! Know how you will answer the most frequently asked questions. Be ready with success stories. Rehearse your closing statement. One of the best ways to reduce butterflies is to know that you have done all you can to be ready for the interview.

> ✓ **Quick Check**
>
> Fight fear by practicing, preparing 110 percent, breathing deeply, and knowing that you are in charge for part of the interview.

FIGURE 14.1 Steps in an Employment Interview From a Recruiter's Perspective

Step 1
Before interview, review candidate's résumé.

Step 2
Check career objective. Look for skills; note items to pursue.

Step 3
Greet candidate. Introduce self. Make candidate feel comfortable.

Step 4
Describe open position. Confirm candidate's interest in position.

Step 5
Give brief overview of organization.

Step 6
Using résumé, probe for evidence of relevant skills and traits.

Step 7
Solicit questions from candidate.

Step 8
Close interview by promoting organization and explaining next step.

Step 9
Fill out evaluation form.

- Take deep breaths, particularly if you feel anxious while waiting for the interviewer. Deep breathing makes you concentrate on something other than the interview and also provides much-needed oxygen.
- Remember that the interviewer isn't the only one who is gleaning information. You have come to learn about the job and the company. In fact, during some parts of the interview, you will be in charge. This should give you courage.

ANSWERING QUESTIONS

✓ Quick Check

How you answer questions can be as important as the answers themselves.

The way you answer questions can be almost as important as what you say. Use the interviewer's name and title from time to time when you answer. *Ms. Lyon, I would be pleased to tell you about. . . .* People like to hear their own names. But be sure you are pronouncing the name correctly!

Occasionally it may be necessary to refocus and clarify vague questions. Some interviewers are inexperienced and ill at ease in the role. You may even have to ask your own question to understand what was asked, *By _____ do you mean _____?*

Consider closing out some of your responses with *Does that answer your question?* or *Would you like me to elaborate on any particular experience?*

✓ Quick Check

Stay focused on the skills and traits that employers seek; don't reveal weaknesses.

Always aim your answers at the key characteristics interviewers seek: expertise and competence, motivation, interpersonal skills, decision-making skills, enthusiasm for the job, and a pleasing personality. And remember to stay focused on your strengths. Don't reveal weaknesses, even if you think they make you look human. You won't be hired for your weaknesses, only for your strengths.

Use good English, and enunciate clearly. Remember, you will definitely be judged by how well you communicate. Avoid slurred words such as *gonna* and *din't*, as well as slangy expressions such as *yeah, like,* and *you know*. Also eliminate verbal static (*ah, and, uhm*). As you practice answering expected interview questions, it's always a good idea to make a tape recording. Is your speech filled with verbal static?

You can't expect to be perfect in an employment interview. No one is. But you can avert sure disaster by avoiding certain topics and behaviors such as those described in Figure 14.2.

ALL-TIME FAVORITE QUESTIONS WITH SELECTED ANSWERS

✓ Quick Check

You can anticipate 90 to 95 percent of all questions you will be asked in an interview.

Employment interviews are all about questions. And most of the questions are not new. You can actually anticipate 90 to 95 percent of all questions that will be asked before you ever walk into an interview room.[8]

The following questions represent all-time favorites asked of recent graduates and other job seekers. You'll find get-acquainted questions, experience and accomplishment questions, crystal-ball questions, squirm questions, and money questions. To get you thinking about how to respond, we've provided an answer or discussion for the first question in each group. As you read the remaining questions in each group, think about how you could respond most effectively.

QUESTIONS TO GET ACQUAINTED

After opening introductions, recruiters generally try to start the interview with personal questions that put the candidate at ease. They are also striving to gain a picture of the candidate to see whether he or she will fit into the organization's culture.

FIGURE 14.2 Ten Interview Actions to Avoid

1. Don't ask for the job. It's naive, undignified, and unprofessional. Wait to see how the interview develops.
2. Don't trash your previous employer, supervisors, or colleagues. The tendency is for interviewers to wonder whether you would speak about their companies similarly.
3. Don't be a threat to the interviewer. Avoid suggesting directly or indirectly that your goal is to become head honcho, a path that might include the interviewer's job.
4. Don't be late or too early for your appointment. Arrive five minutes before you are scheduled.
5. Don't discuss controversial subjects, and don't use profanity.
6. Don't smoke unless the interviewer smokes.
7. Don't emphasize salary or benefits. If the interview goes well and these subjects have not been addressed, you may mention them toward the end of the interview.
8. Don't be negative about yourself or others. Never dwell on your liabilities.
9. Don't interrupt. It is not only impolite but also prevents you from hearing a complete question or remark.
10. Don't accept an offer until you have completed all your interviews.

---

1. Tell me about yourself.

   Experts agree that you must keep this answer short (1 to 2 minutes tops) but on target. Try practicing this formula: "My name is _____. I have completed _____ degree with a major in _____. Recently I worked for _____ as a _____. Before that I worked for _____ as a _____. My strengths are _____ (interpersonal) and _____ (technical)." Try rehearsing your response in 30-second segments devoted to your education, your work experience, and your qualities/skills. Some candidates end with, "Now that I've told you about myself, can you tell me a little more about the position?"

   ✓ *Quick Check*

   Prepare for get-acquainted questions by practicing a short formula response.

2. What was your major in college, and why did you choose it?
3. If you had it to do over again, would you choose the same major? Why?
4. Tell me about your college (or your major) and why you chose it.
5. Do you prefer to work by yourself or with others? Why?
6. What are your key strengths?
7. What are some things you do in your spare time? Hobbies? Sports?
8. How did you happen to apply for this job?
9. What particular qualifications do you have for this job?
10. Do you consider yourself a team player? Describe your style as a team player.

QUESTIONS ABOUT YOUR EXPERIENCE AND ACCOMPLISHMENTS

After questions about your background and education, the interview generally becomes more specific with questions about your experience and accomplishments.

1. Why should we hire you when we have applicants with more experience or better credentials?

   In answering this question, remember that employers often hire people who present themselves well instead of others with better credentials. Emphasize your personal strengths

Quick Check

Employers will hire a candidate with less experience and fewer accomplishments if he or she can demonstrate the skills required.

that could be an advantage with this employer. Are you a hard worker? How can you demonstrate it? Have you had recent training? Some people have had more years of experience but actually have less knowledge because they have done the same thing over and over. Stress your experience using the latest methods and equipment. Be sure to mention your computer training and use of the Internet and Web. Emphasize that you are open to new ideas and learn quickly.

2. Tell me about your part-time jobs, internships, or other experience.
3. What were your major accomplishments in each of your past jobs?
4. Why did you change jobs?
5. What was a typical work day like?
6. What job functions did you enjoy most? Least? Why?
7. Who was the toughest boss you ever worked for and why?
8. What were your major achievements in college?

CRYSTAL BALL GAZING AND QUESTIONS ABOUT THE FUTURE

Questions that look into the future tend to stump some candidates, especially those who have not prepared adequately. Some of these questions give you a chance to discuss your personal future goals, while others require you to think on your feet and tell how you would respond in hypothetical situations.

1. Where do you expect to be five years from now?

Quick Check

When asked about the future, show ambition and interest in succeeding with this company.

It's a sure kiss of death to respond that you'd like to have the interviewer's job! Instead, show an interest in the current job and in making a contribution to the organization. Talk about the levels of responsibility you'd like to achieve. One employment counselor suggests showing ambition but not committing to a specific job title. Suggest that you will have learned enough to have progressed to a position where you will continue to grow.

2. If you got this position, what would you do to be sure you fit in?
3. If your supervisor gave you an assignment and then left town for two weeks, what would you do?
4. This is a large (or small) organization. Do you think you'd like that environment?
5. If you were aware that a coworker was falsifying data, what would you do?
6. If your supervisor was dissatisfied with your work and you thought it was acceptable, how would you resolve the conflict?
7. Do you plan to continue your education?

QUESTIONS TO MAKE YOU SQUIRM

The following questions may make you squirm, but the important thing to remember is to answer truthfully without dwelling on your weaknesses. As quickly as possible, convert any negative response into a discussion of your strengths.

Quick Check

Strive to convert discussion of your weaknesses to topics that show your strengths.

1. What are your key weaknesses?

It's amazing how many candidates knock themselves out of the competition by answering this question poorly. Actually, you have many choices. You can present a strength as a weakness (*Some people complain that I'm a workaholic or too attentive to details*). You can mention a corrected weakness (*I found that I really needed to learn about the Internet, so I took a course.*) You could cite an unrelated skill (*I really need to brush up on my Spanish*). You can cite a learning objective (*One of my long-term goals is to learn more about international management. Does your company have any plans to expand overseas?*) Another possibility is to reaffirm your qualifications (*I have no weaknesses that affect my ability to do this job*).

2. If you could change one thing about your personality, what would it be and why?
3. What would your former boss say about you?
4. What do you want the most from your job? Money? Security? Power?
5. How did you prepare for this interview?
6. Do you feel you achieved the best grade-point average of which you were capable in college?
7. Have you ever used drugs?
8. Relate an incident in which you faced an ethical dilemma. How did you react? How did you feel?
9. If your supervisor told you to do something a certain way, and you knew that way was dead wrong, what would you do?

QUESTIONS ABOUT MONEY

Although money is a very important consideration, don't let it enter the interview process too soon. Some interviewers forget to mention money at all, while others ask what you think you are worth. Here are some typical money questions.

1. How much money are you looking for?

    One way to handle salary questions is to ask politely to defer the discussion until it's clear that a job will be offered to you. (*I'm sure when the time comes, we'll be able to work out a fair compensation package. Right now, I'd rather focus on whether we have a match*). Another possible response is to reply candidly that you can't know what to ask until you know more about the position and the company. If you continue to be pressed for a dollar figure, give a salary range. Be sure to do research before the interview so that you know what similar jobs are paying. For example, check weekly salary surveys published in the *National Business Employment Weekly*.

2. How much are you presently earning?
3. How did you finance your education?
4. How much money do you expect to earn at age _____?
5. Are you willing to take a pay cut from your current (or previous) job?

For more tips on how to negotiate a salary, see the Communication Workshop for this chapter.

QUESTIONS FOR YOU TO ASK

At some point in the interview, you will be asked whether you have any questions. Your questions should not only help you gain information, but they should also impress the interviewer with your thoughtfulness and interest in the position. Remember, though, that this interview is a two-way street. You must be happy with the prospect of working for this organization. You want a position for which your skills and personality are matched. Use this opportunity to find out whether this job is right for you.

1. What will my duties be (if not already discussed)?
2. Tell me what it's like working here in terms of the people, management practices, workloads, expected performance, and rewards.
3. Why is this position open? Did the person who held it previously leave?
4. What training programs are available from this organization? What specific training will be given for this position?
5. What are the possibilities for promotion from this position?
6. Who would be my immediate supervisor?

Quick Check
Defer a discussion of salary until later in the interview when you know more about the job and whether it will be offered.

Quick Check
Your questions should impress the interviewer but also provide valuable information about the job.

7. What is the organizational structure, and where does this position fit in?
8. Is travel required in this position?
9. How is job performance evaluated?
10. Assuming my work is excellent, where do you see me in five years?
11. How long do employees generally stay with this organization?
12. What are the major challenges for a person in this position?
13. What can I do to make myself more employable to you?
14. What is the salary for this position?
15. When will I hear from you regarding further action on my application?

FIELDING ILLEGAL QUESTIONS

✓ **Quick Check**

You may respond to an illegal question by asking tactfully how it relates to the responsibilities of the position.

Because federal laws prohibit discrimination, interviewers may not ask questions such as those in the following list. Nevertheless, you may face an inexperienced or unscrupulous interviewer who does ask some of these questions. How should you react? If you find the question harmless and if you want the job, go ahead and answer it. If you think that answering it would damage your chance to be hired, try to deflect the question tactfully with a response such as *Could you tell me how my marital status relates to the responsibilities of this position?* Another option, of course, is to respond to any illegal question by confronting the interviewer and threatening a lawsuit. However, you could not expect to be hired under these circumstances. In any case, you might wish to reconsider working for an organization that sanctions such procedures.

Here are some illegal questions that you may or may not want to answer:

✓ **Quick Check**

Learn to recognize the difference between legal and illegal questions.

1. Are you married, divorced, separated, or single?
2. Do you have any disabilities that would prevent you from doing this job? (But it is legal to ask *Can you carry a 50-pound sack up a 10-foot ladder five times daily?*)
3. What is your corrected vision? (But it is legal to ask *Do you have 20/20 corrected vision?*)
4. Does stress ever affect your ability to be productive? (But it is legal to ask *How well can you handle stress?*)
5. How much alcohol do you drink per week? (But it is legal to ask *Do you drink alcohol?*)
6. Have you ever been arrested? (But it is legal to ask *Have you ever been convicted of a crime?*)
7. How old are you? What is your date of birth? (But it is legal to ask *Are you 18 years old or older?*)
8. Of what country are you a citizen? (But it is legal to ask *Are you a citizen of the United States?*)
9. What is your maiden name? (But it is legal to ask *What is your full name?*)
10. What is your religious preference?
11. Do you have children?
12. Are you practicing birth control?
13. Are you living with anyone?
14. Do you own or rent your home?
15. How much do you weigh? How tall are you?

CLOSING THE INTERVIEW

After the recruiter tells you about the organization and after you have asked your questions, the interviewer will signal the end of the interview, usually by standing up or by expressing appreciation that you came. If not addressed earlier, you

End the interview by thanking the interviewer, reviewing your strengths for this position, and inquiring about what action will follow. Ask whether you may leave another copy of your résumé and a list of your references. You might also ask when you could expect to hear from the company. Finally, say, "If I don't hear from you by then, may I call you?"
© Getty Images Digital Vision

should at this time find out what action will follow. Too many candidates leave the interview without knowing their status or when they will hear from the recruiter.

You may learn that your résumé will be distributed to several departments for review. If this is the case, be sure to ask when you will be contacted. When you are ready to leave, briefly review your strengths for the position and thank the interviewer for telling you about the organization and for considering you for the position. Ask whether you may leave an additional copy of your résumé or your list of references. If the recruiter says nothing about notifying you, ask ,"When can I expect to hear from you?" You can follow this by saying, "If I don't hear from you by then, may I call you?"

✓ Quick Check

End the interview by thanking the interviewer, reviewing your strengths for this position, and asking what action will follow.

After leaving the interview, make notes of what was said in case you are called back for a second interview. Also note your strengths and weaknesses so that you can work to improve in future interviews. Be sure to alert your references (whom you prepared in advance with a copy of your résumé, highlighted with sales points). Finally, write a thank-you letter, which will be discussed shortly.

If you don't hear from the recruiter within five days (or at the specified time), call him or her. Practice saying something like, "I'm wondering what else I can do to convince you that I'm the right person for this job."

FOLLOW-UP LETTERS AND OTHER EMPLOYMENT DOCUMENTS

Although the résumé and letter of application are your major tasks, other important letters and documents are often required during the employment process. You may need to make requests, write follow-up letters, or fill out employment applications. Because each of these tasks reveals something about you and your communication skills, you'll want to put your best foot forward. These documents often subtly influence company officials to extend an interview or offer a job.

© Ted Goff (www.tedgoff.com)

"Why do all your references scream and slam down the phone when I mention your name?"

REFERENCE REQUEST

Most employers expect job candidates at some point to submit names of individuals who are willing to discuss the candidates' qualifications. Before you list anyone as a reference, however, be sure to ask permission. Try to do this in person. Ask an instructor, for example, whether he or she would be willing and has the time to act as your recommender. If you detect any sign of reluctance, don't force the issue. Your goal is to find willing individuals who think well of you.

What your recommenders need most is information about you. What should they stress to prospective employers? Let's say you're applying for a specific job that requires a letter of recommendation. Professor Smith has already agreed to be a reference for you. To get the best letter of recommendation from Professor Smith, help her out. Write a letter telling her about the position, its requirements, and the recommendation deadline. Include a copy of your résumé. You might remind her of a positive experience with you (*You said my report was well-organized*) that she could use in the recommendation. Remember that recommenders need evidence to support generalizations. Give them appropriate ammunition, as the student has done in the following request:

Quick Check

Identify the target position and company. Tell immediately why you are writing.

Quick Check

Specify the job requirements so that the recommender knows what to stress in the letter. Provide a stamped, addressed envelope.

Dear Professor Smith:

Recently I applied for the position of administrative assistant in the Human Resources Department of Host International. Because you kindly agreed to help me, I am now asking you to write a letter of recommendation to Host.

The position calls for good organizational, interpersonal, and writing skills, as well as computer experience. To help you review my skills and training, I enclose my résumé. As you may recall, I earned an A in your business communication class; and you commended my long report for its clarity and organization.

Please send your letter before July 1 in the enclosed stamped, addressed envelope. I'm grateful for your support, and I promise to let you know the results of my job search.

APPLICATION REQUEST LETTER

Some organizations consider candidates only when they submit a completed application form. To secure a form, write a routine letter of request. But provide enough information about yourself, as shown in the following example, to assure the reader that you are a serious applicant:

Quick Check

In an application request letter, announce your request immediately. Close with an end date, if appropriate.

Dear Mr. Adams:

Please send me an application form for work in your Human Resources Department. In June I will be completing my studies in psychology and communications at Northwestern University in Evanston, Illinois. My program included courses in public relations, psychology, and communications.

I would appreciate receiving this application by May 15 so that I may complete it before making a visit to your city in June. I'm looking forward to beginning a career in personnel management.

APPLICATION OR RÉSUMÉ FOLLOW-UP LETTER

If your letter or application generates no response within a reasonable time, you may decide to send a short follow-up letter such as the following. Doing so (1) jogs the memory of the personnel officer, (2) demonstrates your serious interest, and (3) allows you to emphasize your qualifications or to add new information.

Dear Ms. Lopez:

Please know I am still interested in becoming an administrative support specialist with Quad, Inc.

Since I submitted an application in May, I have completed my schooling and have been employed as a summer replacement for office workers in several downtown offices. This experience has honed my word processing and communication skills. It has also introduced me to a wide range of office procedures.

Please keep my application in your active file and let me know when I may put my formal training, technical skills, and practical experience to work for you.

Quick Check
Use an application or résumé follow-up letter to emphasize your serious interest and to review your strengths.

INTERVIEW FOLLOW-UP LETTER

After a job interview you should always send a brief letter of thanks. This courtesy sets you apart from other applicants (most of whom will not bother). Your letter also reminds the interviewer of your visit as well as suggesting your good manners and genuine enthusiasm for the job.

Follow-up letters are most effective if sent immediately after the interview. In your letter refer to the date of the interview, the exact job title for which you were interviewed, and specific topics discussed. Avoid worn-out phrases, such as *Thank you for taking the time to interview me.* Be careful, too, about overusing *I,* especially to begin sentences. Most important, show that you really want the job and that you are qualified for it. Notice how the following letter conveys enthusiasm and confidence:

Dear Ms. Cogan:

Talking with you Thursday, May 23, about the graphic designer position was both informative and interesting.

Thanks for describing the position in such detail and for introducing me to Ms. Thomas, the senior designer. Her current project designing the annual report in four colors on a Macintosh sounds fascinating as well as quite challenging.

Now that I've learned in greater detail the specific tasks of your graphic designers, I'm more than ever convinced that my computer and creative skills can make a genuine contribution to your graphic productions. My training in Macintosh design and layout ensures that I could be immediately productive on your staff.

You will find me an enthusiastic and hard-working member of any team effort. I'm eager to join the graphics staff at your Santa Barbara headquarters, and I look forward to hearing from you soon.

Quick Check
Mention the interview date and specific position.

Quick Check
Personalize your letter by mentioning topics discussed in the interview. Highlight a specific skill you have for the job.

REJECTION FOLLOW-UP LETTER

If you didn't get the job and you think it was perfect for you, don't give up. Employment consultant Patricia Windelspecht advises, "You should always respond to a rejection letter. . . . I've had four clients get jobs that way." In a rejection follow-up letter, it's okay to admit you're disappointed. Be sure to add, however, that you're still interested and will contact them again in a month in case a job opens up. Then follow through for a couple of months—but don't overdo it. "There's a fine line between being professional and persistent and being a pest," adds consultant Windelspecht.[9] Here's an example of an effective rejection follow-up letter:

Dear Mr. Crenshaw:

Although I'm disappointed that someone else was selected for your accounting position, I appreciate your promptness and courtesy in notifying me.

Because I firmly believe that I have the technical and interpersonal skills needed to work in your fast-paced environment, I hope you will keep my résumé in your active file. My desire to become a productive member of your Transamerica staff remains strong.

I enjoyed our interview, and I especially appreciate the time you and Mr. Samson spent describing your company's expansion into international markets. To enhance my qualifications, I've enrolled in a course in International Accounting at CSU.

Should you have an opening for which I am qualified, you may reach me at (818) 719-3901. In the meantime, I will call you in a month to discuss employment possibilities.

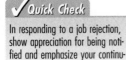
Quick Check

In responding to a job rejection, show appreciation for being notified and emphasize your continuing interest.

APPLICATION FORM

Some organizations require job candidates to fill out job application forms instead of submitting résumés. This practice permits them to gather and store standardized data about each applicant. Here are some tips for filling out such forms:

Quick Check

When applying for jobs, keep with you a card summarizing your important data.

- Carry a card summarizing vital statistics not included on your résumé. If you are asked to fill out an application form in an employer's office, you will need a handy reference to the following data: social security number, graduation dates, beginning and ending dates of all employment; salary history; full names, titles, and present work addresses of former supervisors; and full names, occupational titles, occupational addresses, and telephone numbers of persons who have agreed to serve as references.
- Look over all the questions before starting. Fill out the form neatly, printing if your handwriting is poor.
- Answer all questions. Write *Not applicable* if appropriate.
- Be prepared for a salary question. Unless you know what comparable employees are earning in the company, the best strategy is to suggest a salary range or to write *Negotiable* or *Open*.
- Ask whether you may submit your résumé in addition to the application form.

SUMMING UP AND LOOKING FORWARD

Whether you face a screening interview or a hiring/placement interview, you must be well-prepared. You can increase your chances of success and reduce your sweaty palms considerably by knowing how interviews are typically conducted and by investigating the target company thoroughly. Practice answering typical questions, including legal and illegal ones. Consider tape recording or videotaping a mock interview so that you can check your body language and improve your answering techniques.

Close the interview by thanking the interviewer, reviewing your main strengths for this position, and asking what the next step is. Follow up with a thank-you letter and a call back, if appropriate.

You have now completed 14 chapters of rigorous instruction aimed at developing your skills so that you can be a successful business communicator in today's rapidly changing world of information. Remember that this is but a starting point. Your skills as a business communicator will continue to grow on the job as you apply the principles you have learned and expand your expertise.

Interactive Learning @ http://www.westwords.com/guffey/students.html
Prepare for tests and reinforce your chapter knowledge with interactive quizzes and crossword puzzles.

CRITICAL THINKING

1. Is it normal to be nervous about an employment interview, and what can be done to overcome this fear?
2. What can you do to improve the first impression you make at an interview?
3. In employment interviews, do you think that behavioral questions (such as *Tell me about a business problem you have had and how you solved it*) are more effective than traditional questions (such as *Tell me what you are good at*)? Why?
4. Why is it important to avoid discussing salary early in an interview?
5. Why should a job candidate write a thank-you letter after an interview?

CHAPTER REVIEW

6. If you have sent out your résumé to many companies, what information should you keep near your telephone and why?

7. Your first interview is with a small local company. What kind of information should you seek about this company and where could you expect to find it?

8. Name at least two ways in which you can practice for the interview and receive feedback on your performance.

9. Name at least six interviewing behaviors you can exhibit that send positive nonverbal messages.

10. What is your greatest fear of what you might do or what might happen to you during an employment interview? How can you overcome your fears?

11. Should you be candid with an interviewer when asked about your weaknesses?

12. How can you clarify vague questions from recruiters?

13. How should you respond if you are asked why a company should hire you when it has applicants with more experience or better credentials?

14. How should you respond to questions you feel are illegal?

15. List various kinds of follow-up letters.

ACTIVITIES AND CASES

14.1 RESEARCHING AN ORGANIZATION. An important part of your preparation for an interview is finding out about the target company.

WEB

Your Task. Select an organization where you would like to be employed. Assume you've been selected for an interview. Using resources described in this chapter, locate information about the organization's leaders and their business philosophy. Find out about the organization's accomplishments, setbacks, finances, products, customers, competition, and advertising. Prepare a summary report documenting your findings. Good Web sites to visit include Hoovers (http://www.hoovers.com), WetFeet (http://www.wetfeet.com), and FlipDog (http://www.flipdog.com).

14.2 LEARNING WHAT JOBS ARE REALLY ABOUT THROUGH INFORMATIONAL IN-TERVIEWING. An informational interview is a brief meeting between a person who wants to investigate a career and a person working in that career. These interviews help students learn more about the realities of working in a particular occupation. Sometimes people find out that their dream job is not so dreamy after all.

INFOTRAC

Your Task. Using InfoTrac, locate Olivia Crosby's article, "Informational Interviewing: Get the Inside Scoop on Careers," *Occupational Outlook Quarterly*, Summer 2002, 32–37 (Article A89388395). In reading the article, find the following information:

a. Name six purposes of an informational interview.
b. Whom should you interview?
c. What are three ways you can arrange for an informational interview?
d. Name eight questions that you would find most interesting to ask in an interview.

14.3 BUILDING INTERVIEW SKILLS. Successful interviews require diligent preparation and repeated practice. To be best prepared, you need to know what skills are required for your targeted position. In addition to computer and communication skills, employers generally want to know whether a candidate works well with a team, accepts responsibility, solves problems, is efficient, meets deadlines, shows leadership, saves time and money, and is a hard worker.

Your Task. Consider a position for which you are eligible now or one for which you will be eligible when you complete your education. Identify the skills and traits necessary for this position. If you prepared a résumé in Chapter 13, be sure that it addresses these targeted areas. Now prepare interview worksheets listing at least ten technical and other skills or traits you think a recruiter will want to discuss in an interview for your targeted position.

14.4 PREPARING SUCCESS STORIES. You can best showcase your talents if you are ready with your own success stories that show how you have developed the skills or traits required for your targeted position.

Your Task. Using the worksheets you prepared in Activity 14.3, prepare success stories that highlight the required skills or traits. Select three to five stories to develop into answers to potential interview questions. For example, here's a typical question: "How does your background relate to the position we have open?" A possible response: "As you know, I have just completed an intensive training program in _____. In addition, I have over three years of part-time work experience in a variety of business settings. In one position I was selected to manage a small business in the absence of the owner. I developed responsibility and customer-service skills in filling orders efficiently, resolving shipping problems, and monitoring key accounts. I also inventoried and organized products worth over $200,000. When the owner returned from a vacation to Florida, I was commended for increasing sales and was given a bonus in recognition of his gratitude." People relate to and remember stories. Try to shape your answers into memorable stories.

14.5 POLISHING ANSWERS TO INTERVIEW QUESTIONS. Practice makes perfect in interviewing. The more often you rehearse responses to typical interview questions, the closer you are to getting the job.

Your Task. Select three questions from each of the five question categories discussed in this chapter. Write your answers to each set of questions. Try to incorporate skills and traits required for the targeted position. Polish these answers and your delivery technique by practicing in front of a mirror or into a tape recorder.

14.6 KNOWING WHAT TO ASK. When it is your turn to ask questions during the interview process, be ready.

Your Task. Decide on three to five questions that you would like to ask during an interview. Write these questions out and practice asking them so that you sound confident and sincere.

TEAM

14.7 PRACTICING ANSWERING INTERVIEW QUESTIONS. One of the best ways to understand interview dynamics and to develop confidence is to role-play the parts of interviewer and candidate.

Your Task. Choose a partner from your team. Make a list of five interview questions from those presented in this chapter. In team sessions you and your partner will role-play an actual interview. One acts as interviewer; the other is the candidate. Prior to the interview, the candidate tells the interviewer what job and company he or she is applying to. For the interview, the interviewer and candidate should dress appropriately and sit in chairs facing each other. The interviewer greets the candidate and makes the candidate comfortable. The candidate gives the interviewer a copy of his or her résumé. The interviewer asks three (or more depending on your instructor's time schedule) questions from the candidate's list. The interviewer may also ask follow-up questions if appropriate. When finished, the interviewer ends the meeting graciously. After one interview, reverse roles and repeat.

14.8 VIDEOTAPING AN INTERVIEW. Seeing how you look during an interview can help you improve your body language and presentation style. Your instructor may act as interviewer, or an outside businessperson may be asked to conduct mock interviews in your classroom.

Your Task. Engage a student or campus specialist to videotape each interview. Review your performance, and critique it, looking for ways to improve. Your instructor may ask class members to offer comments and suggestions on individual interviews.

14.9 HANDLING ILLEGAL INTERVIEW QUESTIONS. Although some questions are considered illegal by the government, many interviewers will ask them anyway—whether intentionally or unknowingly. Being prepared is important.

Your Task. How would you respond in the following scenario? Let's assume you are being interviewed at one of the top companies on your list of potential employers. The interviewing committee consists of a human resources manager and the supervising manager of the department where you would work. At various times during the interview the supervising manager has asked questions that made you feel uncomfortable. For example, he asked whether you were married. You know this question is illegal, but you saw no harm in answering it. But then he asked how old you were. Since you started college early and graduated in three and a half years, you are worried that you may not be considered mature enough for this position. But you have most of the other qualifications required and you are convinced you could succeed on the job. How should you answer this question?

14.10 REQUESTING AN APPLICATION FORM. You decide to apply for a position with a company, and you need an application form.

Your Task. Send a letter addressed to Douglas Tyson, Human Resources Manager, KillerAp Software, 2443 Pacific Grove Drive, Cupertino, CA 94510. Request an employment application.

14.11 SAYING THANKS FOR THE INTERVIEW. You've just completed an exciting employment interview, and you want the interviewer to remember you.

Your Task. Write a follow-up thank-you letter to Ronald T. Ranson, Human Resources Development, Electronic Data Sources, 1328 Peachtree Plaza, Atlanta, GA 30314 (or a company of your choice).

14.12 REFUSING TO TAKE NO FOR AN ANSWER. After an excellent interview with Electronic Data Sources (or a company of your choice), you're depressed to learn that it hired someone else. But you really want to work for EDS.

Your Task. Write a follow-up letter to Ronald T. Ranson, Human Resources Development, Electronic Data Sources, 1328 Peachtree Plaza, Atlanta, GA 30314 (or a company of your choice). Indicate that you are disappointed but still interested.

14.13 AVOIDING INTERVIEW PERILS. Nervous, shy, and inexperienced interviewees can make mistakes. Long-time career counselor Denis Claveloux gives advice on what to avoid.

INFOTRAC

Your Task. Using InfoTrac, locate an article titled "Career Counselor Advises Bridgeport, Conn., Audience on Job-Interview Perils," 8 May 2002 (ArticleCJ85587780). In a memo to your instructor, name at least 15 actions that the author considers perilous during a job interview.

14.14 POLISHING YOUR INTERVIEW SKILLS WITH A VIRTUAL INTERVIEW. The Career Services Center at Western State College of Colorado offers a good online interview with questions, multiple-choice answers, and an evaluation of each answer. If this Web site is still available (pages are often removed), by all means try out your skills with this interactive tool that provides insightful and helpful feedback. The questions are particularly appropriate for recent college graduates.

WEB

Your Task. Visit the Career Services site and answer the virtual interview questions (http://www.western.edu/career/Interview_virtual/Virtual_interview.htm). If this URL doesn't work, search Google with this term: "virtual interview."

14.15 SEARCHING FOR ADVICE. You can find wonderful, free, and sometimes entertaining information about job search strategies, career tips, and interview advice on the Web.

WEB
E-MAIL

Your Task. Use a search engine or visit the Guffey Web site (http://www.westwords.com/guffey/students.html) to locate links to job search and résumé sites. From any Web site featuring interview information, make a list of at least five good interview pointers—ones that were not covered in this chapter. Send an e-mail message to your instructor describing your findings.

Activities and Cases

Interviewing in Business

Dayton Hudson Corporation, with headquarters in Minneapolis, is the fourth-largest retailer in the United States. It consists of Target, Dayton's, Hudson's, and Marshall Field's. In our video, members of Hudson's management team discuss hiring requirements as they begin staffing a new suburban store. Management team members discuss their hiring goals, what they look for during an interview, and how to follow up an interview.

Your Task. After viewing the Hudson's video, respond to these questions:

- How should a job candidate prepare for a job interview?
- How can a candidate send positive body language?
- What problems are typically suffered by job candidates during interviewing?
- What are the characteristics of a good résumé?
- What follow-up is expected after an interview?

GRAMMAR/MECHANICS CHECKUP—PUNCTUATION REVIEW

Review Sections 1.17 and 2.01–2.29 in the Grammar/Mechanics Handbook. Study the groups of sentences below. In the space provided, write the letter of the one that is correctly punctuated. When you finish, compare your responses with those at the end of the book. If your responses differ, study carefully the principles in parentheses.

_____
1.a. Our accounting team makes a point of analyzing your business operations, and getting to know what's working for you and what's not.
  b. We are dedicated to understanding your business needs over the long term, and taking an active role when it comes to creating solutions.
  c. We understand that you may be downsizing or moving into new markets, and we want to help you make a seamless transition.

_____
2.a. If you are growing, or connecting to new markets, our team will help you accomplish your goals with minimal interruptions.
  b. When you look at our organization chart, you will find the customer at the top.
  c. Although we offer each customer a dedicated customer account team we also provide professional general services.

_____
3.a. The competition is changing; therefore, we have to deliver our products and services more efficiently.
  b. Although delivery systems are changing; the essence of banking remains the same.
  c. Banks will continue to be available around the corner, and also with the click of a mouse.

_____
4.a. One of the reasons we are decreasing the number of our ATMs, is that two thirds of the bank's customers depend on tellers for transactions.
  b. We are looking for an article entitled, "Online Banking."
  c. Banks are at this time competing with nontraditional rivals who can provide extensive financial services.

_____
5.a. We care deeply about the environment; but we also care about safety and good customer service.

b. The president worked with environmental concerns; the vice president focused on customer support.

c. Our Web site increases our productivity, it also improves customer service.

6.a. Employees who will be receiving salary increases are: Terri, Mark, Rob, and Ellen. _____

b. The following employees are eligible for bonuses: Robin, Jeff, Bill, and Jose.

c. Our consulting firm is proud to offer Web services for: site design, market analysis, e-commerce, and hosting.

7.a. All secretaries' computers were equipped with Excel. _____

b. Both attorneys statements confused the judge.

c. Some members names and addresses must be rekeyed.

8.a. Our committee considered convention sites in Scottsdale, Arizona, Palm Springs, California; and Dallas, Texas. _____

b. Serena was from Columbus, Ohio; Josh was from Denver, Colorado, and Rachel was from Seattle, Washington.

c. The following engineers were approved: J. W. Ellis, civil; Dr. Thomas Lee, structural; and W. R. Verey, mechanical.

9.a. The package from Albany, New York was never delivered. _____

b. We have scheduled an inspection tour on Tuesday, March 5, at 4 p.m.

c. Send the check to M. E. Williams, 320 Summit Ridge, Ogden, Utah 84404 before the last mail pickup.

10.a. The best plan of action in my opinion, is a straightforward approach. _____

b. Under the circumstances we could not have hoped for better results.

c. Our department will, in the meantime, reduce its services.

11.a. If you demand reliable, competent service, you should come to us. _____

b. We could not resist buying cookies from the enthusiastic, young Girl Scout.

c. Our highly trained technicians, with years of experience are always available to evaluate and improve your network environment.

12.a. We guarantee same-day, not next-day, service. _____

b. Our departmental budget requests are considerably reduced yet adequate.

c. The nominating committee selected Todd Shimoyama, not Suzette Chase as its representative.

13.a. Their wealthy uncle left $1 million to be distributed to Bob, Carol, and Sue. _____

b. Their wealthy uncle left $1 million to be distributed to Bob, Carol and Sue.

c. Our agency will maintain and upgrade your computers, printers, copiers and fax machines.

14.a. Beginning June 1, we will service many top vendors, including: Compaq, Hewlett Packard, IBM, Dell and Mita. _____

b. To promote our new business we are offering a 10 percent discount.

c. In a period of only one month, we gained 150 new customers.

15.a. We specialize in network design, however we also offer troubleshooting and consulting. _____

b. We realize that downtime is not an option; therefore, you can count on us for reliable, competent service.

c. Our factory-trained and certified technicians perform repair at your location, or in our own repair depot for products under warranty and out of warranty.

DOCUMENT FOR REVISION

The following interview thank-you letter has faults in grammar, punctuation, spelling, wordiness, and word use. Use standard proofreading marks (see Appendix B) to correct the errors. When you finish, your instructor can show you the revised version of this letter.

4201 North Harrison
Shawnee, OK 74801
June 4, 200x

Mr. Anthony R. Masters
Human Resources Department
Biolage Enterprises
7246 South May Avenue
Oklahoma City, OK 73159

Dear Mr. Master:

I appriciate the opportunity for the interview yesterday for the newly-listed Position of Sales Trainee. It was really a pleasure meeting yourself and learning more about Biolage Enterprises, you have a fine staff and a sophisticated approach to marketing.

You're organization appears to be growing in a directional manner that parralels my interests' and career goals. The interview with yourself and your staff yesterday confirmed my initale positive impressions of Biolage Enterprises and I want to reiterate my strong interest in working with and for you. My prior Retail sales experience as a sales associate with Sears; plus my recent training in Microsoft Word and Excel would enable me to make progress steadily through your programs of training and become a productive member of your sales team in no time at all.

Again, thank-you for your kind and gracius consideration. In the event that you need any additional information from me, all you have to do is give me a call me at (405) 391-7792.

Sincerly yours,

_____

Let's Talk Money: Negotiating a Salary

When to talk about salary causes many job applicants concern. Some advisors recommend bringing the issue up immediately; others suggest avoiding the topic entirely. The best plan is probably to avoid discussing salary during a screening interview but be ready to discuss it later. The important thing to remember is that almost all salaries are negotiable. The following negotiating rules, recommended by career guru Ron Farr, can guide you to a better beginning salary.[10]

Rule No. 1: Never talk money until after the interviewing company decides it wants you.

Your goal is to avoid discussing salary until you know for sure that the interviewing company is making a job offer. If salary comes up and you are not sure whether the job is being offered to you, it's time for you to be blunt. Here are some things you could say:

Are you making me a job offer?
What salary range do you pay for positions with similar requirements?
I'm very interested in the position, and my salary would be negotiable.
Tell me what you have in mind for the salary range.

Rule No. 2: Know in advance the probable salary range for similar jobs in similar organizations.

Some job search Web sites provide salary information. But it's probably better for you to call around in your area to learn what similar jobs are paying. The important thing here is to think in terms of a wide range. Let's say you are hoping to start at between $35,000 and $40,000. To an interviewer, you might say, *I was looking for a salary in the high thirties to the low forties*. This technique is called bracketing.

Rule No. 3: Always bracket your salary range to begin within their probable salary range and end a bit above what you expect to settle for.

Remember to be realistic. You probably have some idea of what the interviewing company is willing to pay for this position. If you guess that the salary for this position might be about $35,000, your bracketed range should begin with that figure and extend beyond what you expect to settle for.

Rule No. 4: Never say no to a job offer before it is offered.

Why would anyone refuse a job offer before it's made? It happens all the time. Let's say you were hoping for a salary of, say, $35,000. The interviewer tells you that the salary scheduled for this job is $30,000. You respond, *Oh, that's out of the question!* Before you were offered the job, you have, in effect, refused it.

Rule No. 5: Be ready to bargain if offered a low starting salary.

Many salaries are negotiable. Companies are often willing to pay more for someone who interviews well and fits their culture. If the company seems right to you and you are pleased with the sound of the open position but you have been offered a low salary, say, *That is somewhat lower than I had hoped but this position does sound exciting. If I were to consider this, what sorts of things could I do to quickly become more valuable to this organization?*

Even if the salary offered is an insult, don't kick the desk, grab your résumé, and stomp out. Hold your temper and say something like, *Thanks for the offer. The position is very much what I wanted in many ways, and I am delighted at your interest. If I start at this salary, may I be reviewed within six months with the goal of raising the salary to _____?*

Another possibility is to ask for more time to think about the low offer. Tell the interviewer that this is an important decision, and you need some time to consider the offer. The next day you can call and say, *I am flattered by your offer, but I cannot accept because the salary is lower than I would like. Perhaps you could reconsider your offer or keep me in mind for future openings.*

Career Application. You've just passed the screening interview and have been asked to come in for a personal interview with the human resources representative and the hiring manager of a company where you are very eager to work. Although you are delighted with the company, you have promised yourself that you will not accept any position that pays less than $35,000 to start.

Your Task

- In teams of two, role-play the position of interviewer and interviewee.
- Interviewer: Set the interview scene. Discuss preliminaries, and then offer a salary of $32,500.
- Interviewee: Respond to preliminary questions and then to the salary offer of $32,500.
- Reverse roles so that the interviewee becomes the interviewer. Repeat the scenario.

Reference Guide to Document Formats

Business documents carry two kinds of messages. Verbal messages are conveyed by the words chosen to express the writer's ideas. Nonverbal messages are conveyed largely by the appearance of a document. If you compare an assortment of letters and memos from various organizations, you will notice immediately that some look more attractive and more professional than others. The nonverbal message of the professional-looking documents suggests that they were sent by people who are careful, informed, intelligent, and successful. Understandably, you're more likely to take seriously documents that use attractive stationery and professional formatting techniques.

Over the years certain practices and conventions have arisen regarding the appearance and formatting of business documents. Although these conventions offer some choices (such as letter and punctuation styles), most business letters follow standardized formats. To ensure that your documents carry favorable nonverbal messages about you and your organization, you'll want to give special attention to the appearance and formatting of your letters, envelopes, memos, e-mail messages, and fax cover sheets.

APPEARANCE

To ensure that a message is read and valued, you need to give it a professional appearance. Two important elements in achieving a professional appearance are stationery and placement of the message on the page.

Stationery. Most organizations use high-quality stationery for business documents. This stationery is printed on select paper that meets two qualifications: weight and cotton-fiber content.

Paper is measured by weight and may range from 9 pounds (thin onionskin paper) to 32 pounds (thick card and cover stock). Most office stationery is in the 16- to 24-pound range. Lighter 16-pound paper is generally sufficient for internal documents including memos. Heavier 20- to 24-pound paper is used for printed letterhead stationery.

Paper is also judged by its cotton-fiber content. Cotton fiber makes paper stronger, softer in texture, and less likely to yellow. Good-quality stationery contains 25 percent or more cotton fiber.

Spacing After Punctuation. For some time typists left two spaces after end punctuation (periods, question marks, and so forth). This practice was necessary, it was thought, because typewriters did not have proportional spacing and sentences were easier to read if two spaces separated them. Professional typesetters, however, never followed this practice because they used proportional spacing, and readability was not a problem. Fortunately, today's word processors now make available the same fonts used by typesetters.

The question of how many spaces to leave after concluding punctuation is one of the most frequently asked questions at the Modern Language Association Web site (http://www.mla.org). MLA experts point out that most publications in this country today have the same spacing after a punctuation mark as between words on the same line. Influenced by the look of typeset publications, many writers now leave only one space after end punctuation. As a practical matter, however, it is not wrong to use two spaces.

Letter Placement. The easiest way to place letters on the page is to use the defaults of your word processing program. These are usually set for side margins of 1 inch. Many companies today find these margins acceptable.

If you want to adjust your margins to better balance shorter letters, use the following chart:

WORDS IN BODY OF LETTER	SIDE MARGINS	BLANK LINES AFTER DATE
Under 200	$1\frac{1}{2}$ inches	4 to 10
Over 200	1 inch	2 to 3

Experts say that a "ragged" right margin is easier to read than a justified (even) margin. You might want to turn off the justification feature of your word processing program if it automatically justifies the right margin.

LETTER PARTS

Professional-looking business letters are arranged in a conventional sequence with standard parts. Following is a discussion of how to use these letter parts properly. Figure A.1 illustrates the parts in a block-style letter. (See Chapter 6 for additional discussion of letters and their parts.)

Letterhead. Most business organizations use $8\frac{1}{2}$- × 11-inch paper printed with a letterhead displaying their official name, street address, Web address, e-mail address, and telephone and fax numbers. The letterhead may also include a logo and an advertising message such as *Frontier Bank: A new brand of banking*.

Dateline. On letterhead paper you should place the date two blank lines below the last line of the letterhead or 2 inches from the top edge of the paper (line 13). On plain paper place the date immediately below your return address. Since the date goes on line 13, start the return address an appropriate number of lines above it. The most common dateline format is as follows: *June 9, 2004*. Don't use *th* (or *rd*) when the date is written this way. For European or military correspondence, use the following dateline format: *9 June 2004*. Notice that no commas are used.

Addressee and Delivery Notations. Delivery notations such as *FAX TRANSMISSION, FEDERAL EXPRESS, MESSENGER DELIVERY, CONFIDENTIAL*, or *CERTIFIED MAIL* are typed in all capital letters two blank lines above the inside address.

Inside Address. Type the inside address—that is, the address of the organization or person receiving the letter—single-spaced, starting at the left margin. The

*island*graphics

893 Dillingham Boulevard Honolulu, HI 96817-8817 — **Letterhead**

↓ line 13 or 1 blank line below letterhead

September 13, 200x — **Dateline**

↓ 1 to 9 blank lines

Mr. T. M. Wilson, President
Visual Concept Enterprises
1901 Kaumualii Highway — **Inside address**
Lihue, HI 96766

↓ 1 blank line

Dear Mr. Wilson: — **Salutation**

↓ 1 blank line

SUBJECT: BLOCK LETTER STYLE — **Subject line**

↓ 1 blank line

This letter illustrates block letter style, about which you asked. All typed lines begin at the left margin. The date is usually placed two inches from the top edge of the paper or two lines below the last line of the letterhead, whichever position is lower.

This letter illustrates mixed punctuation. It includes a colon (not a comma) after the salutation and a comma after the complimentary close. Most of our customers prefer this form of punctuation. — **Body**

If a subject line is included, it appears 1 blank line below the salutation. The word *SUBJECT* is optional. Most readers will recognize a statement in this position as the subject without an identifying label. The subject line may appear in all capital letters or in lowercase letters with the main words capitalized.

↓ 1 blank line

Sincerely,

Mark H. Wong   ↓ 3 blank lines

Mark H. Wong — **Complimentary close and signature block**
Graphics Designer

↓ 1 blank line

MHW:pil

In block-style letters, as shown above, all lines begin at the left margin. In modified block-style letters, as shown at the right, the date is centered or aligned with the complimentary close and signature block, which start at the center. Paragraphs may be blocked or indented. Mixed punctuation includes a colon after the salutation and a comma after the complimentary close. Open punctuation omits the colon following the salutation and omits the comma following the complimentary closing. However, open punctuation is rarely used today.

number of lines between the dateline and the inside address depends on the size of the letter body, the type size (point or pitch size), and the length of the typing lines. Generally, one to nine blank lines are appropriate.

Be careful to duplicate the exact wording and spelling of the recipient's name and address on your documents. Usually, you can copy this information from the letterhead of the correspondence you are answering. If, for example, you are responding to *Jackson & Perkins Company*, don't address your letter to *Jackson and Perkins Corp.*

Always be sure to include a courtesy title such as *Mr., Ms., Mrs., Dr.,* or *Professor* before a person's name in the inside address—for both the letter and the envelope. Although many women in business today favor *Ms.,* you'll want to use whatever title the addressee prefers.

Remember that the inside address is not included for readers (who already know who and where they are). It's there to help writers accurately file a copy of the message.

In general, avoid abbreviations (such as *Ave.* or *Co.*) unless they appear in the printed letterhead of the document being answered.

Attention Line.   An attention line allows you to send your message officially to an organization but to direct it to a specific individual, officer, or department. However, if you know an individual's complete name, it's always better to use it as the first line of the inside address and avoid an attention line. Here are two common formats for attention lines:

MultiMedia Enterprises
931 Calkins Road
Rochester, NY 14301

ATTENTION MARKETING DIRECTOR

MultiMedia Enterprises
Attention: Marketing Director
931 Calkins Road
Rochester, NY 14301

Attention lines may be typed in all caps or with upper- and lowercase letters. The colon following *Attention* is optional. Notice that an attention line may be placed two lines below the address block or printed as the second line of the inside address. You'll want to use the latter format if you're composing on a word processor because the address block may be copied to the envelope and the attention line will not interfere with the last-line placement of the zip code. (Mail can be sorted more easily if the zip code appears in the last line of a typed address.)

Whenever possible, use a person's name as the first line of an address instead of putting that name in an attention line. Some writers use an attention line because they fear that letters addressed to individuals at companies may be considered private. They worry that if the addressee is no longer with the company, the letter may be forwarded or not opened. Actually, unless a letter is marked "Personal" or "Confidential," it will very likely be opened as business mail.

Salutation.   For most letter styles place the letter greeting, or salutation, one blank line below the last line of the inside address or the attention line (if used). If the letter is addressed to an individual, use that person's courtesy title and last name (*Dear Mr. Lanham*). Even if you are on a first-name basis (*Dear Leslie*), be sure to add a colon (not a comma or a semicolon) after the salutation. Do not use an individual's full name in the salutation (not *Dear Mr. Leslie Lanham*) unless you are unsure of gender (*Dear Leslie Lanham*).

For letters with attention lines or those addressed to organizations, the selection of an appropriate salutation has become more difficult. Formerly, *Gentlemen* was used generically for all organizations. With increasing numbers of women in business management today, however, *Gentlemen* is problematic. Because no universally acceptable salutation has emerged as yet, you could use *Ladies and Gentlemen* or *Gentlemen and Ladies*.

One way to avoid the salutation dilemma is to address a document to a specific person. Another alternative is to use the simplified letter style (shown in Figure A.2), which conveniently omits the salutation (and the complimentary close).

Subject and Reference Lines.   Although experts suggest placing the subject line one blank line below the salutation, many businesses actually place it above the salutation. Use whatever style your organization prefers. Reference lines often show policy or file numbers; they generally appear two lines above the salutation. Use initial capital letters for the main words or all capital letters.

Body.   Most business letters and memorandums are single-spaced, with double-spacing between paragraphs. Very short messages may be double-spaced with indented paragraphs.

Complimentary Close.   Typed one blank line below the last line of the letter, the complimentary close may be formal (*Very truly yours*) or informal (*Sincerely yours* or *Cordially*). The simplified letter style omits a complimentary close.

Signature Block.   In most letter styles the writer's typed name and optional identification appear three to four blank lines below the complimentary close. The combination of name, title, and organization information should be arranged to achieve a balanced look. The name and title may appear on the same line or on separate lines, depending on the length of each. Use commas to separate categories within the same line, but not to conclude a line.

Sincerely yours,

Jeremy M. Wood

Jeremy M. Wood, Manager
Technical Sales and Services

Cordially yours,

Casandra Baker-Murillo

Casandra Baker-Murillo
Executive Vice President

Courtesy titles (*Ms., Mrs.,* or *Miss*) should be used before female names that are not readily distinguishable as male or female. They should also be used before names containing only initials and international names. The title is usually placed in parentheses, but it may appear without them.

Yours truly,

Ms. K.C. Tripton

(Ms.) K. C. Tripton
Project Manager

Sincerely,

Mr. Leslie Hill

(Mr.) Leslie Hill
Public Policy Department

Some organizations include their names in the signature block. In such cases the organization name appears in all caps one blank line below the complimentary close, as shown here.

Cordially,

LITTON COMPUTER SERVICES

Ms. Shelina A. Simpson

Ms. Shelina A. Simpson
Executive Assistant

Reference Initials.   If used, the initials of the typist and writer are typed one blank line below the writer's name and title. Generally, the writer's initials are capitalized and the typist's are lowercased, but this format varies.

Enclosure Notation.   When an enclosure or attachment accompanies a document, a notation to that effect appears one blank line below the reference initials. This notation reminds the typist to insert the enclosure in the envelope, and it reminds the recipient to look for the enclosure or attachment. The notation may be spelled out (*Enclosure, Attachment*), or it may be abbreviated (*Enc., Att.*). It may indicate the number of enclosures or attachments, and it may also identify a specific enclosure (*Enclosure: Form 1099*).

Copy Notation.   If you make copies of correspondence for other individuals, you may use *cc* to indicate carbon copy, *pc* to indicate photocopy, or merely *c* for any kind of copy. A colon following the initial(s) is optional.

Second-page Heading.   When a letter extends beyond one page, use plain paper of the same quality and color as the first page. Identify the second and succeeding pages with a heading consisting of the name of the addressee, the page number, and the date. Use either of the following two formats:

Ms. Rachel Ruiz   2   May 3, 2004

Ms. Rachel Ruiz
Page 2
May 3, 2004

Both headings appear on line 7 followed by two blank lines to separate them from the continuing text. Avoid using a second page if you have only one line or the complimentary close and signature block to fill that page.

Plain-Paper Return Address.   If you prepare a personal or business letter on plain paper, place your address immediately above the date. Do not include your name; you will type (and sign) your name at the end of your letter. If your return address contains two lines, begin typing it on line 11 so that the date appears on line 13. Avoid abbreviations except for a two-letter state abbreviation.

580 East Leffels Street
Springfield, OH 45501
December 14, 2004

Ms. Ellen Siemens
Escrow Department
TransOhio First Federal
1220 Wooster Boulevard
Columbus, OH 43218-2900

Dear Ms. Siemens:

For letters prepared in the block style, type the return address at the left margin. For modified block-style letters, start the return address at the center to align with the complimentary close.

LETTER SYLES

Business letters are generally prepared in one of three formats. The most popular is the block style, but the simplified style has much to recommend it.

Block Style.   In the block style, shown in Figure A.1, all lines begin at the left margin. This style is a favorite because it is easy to format.

Modified Block Style.   The modified block style differs from block style in that the date and closing lines appear in the center, as shown at the bottom of Figure A.1. The date may be (1) centered, (2) begun at the center of the page (to align with the closing lines), or (3) backspaced from the right margin. The signature block—including the complimentary close, writer's name and title, or organization identification—begins at the center. The first line of each paragraph may begin at the left margin or may be indented five or ten spaces. All other lines begin at the left margin.

Simplified Style.   Introduced by the Administrative Management Society a number of years ago, the simplified letter style, shown in Figure A.2, requires little formatting. Like the block style, all lines begin at the left margin. A subject line appears in all caps two blank lines below the inside address and two blank lines above the first paragraph. The salutation and complimentary close are omitted. The signer's name and identification appear in all caps four blank lines below the last paragraph. This letter style is efficient and avoids the problem of appropriate salutations and courtesy titles.

PUNCTUATION STYLES

Two punctuation styles are commonly used for letters. *Mixed* punctuation, shown in Figure A.1, requires a colon after the salutation and a comma after the complimentary close. *Open* punctuation contains no punctuation after the salutation or complimentary close. It is seldom used in business today.

With mixed punctuation, be sure to use a colon—not a comma or semicolon—after the salutation. Even when the salutation is a first name, the colon is appropriate.

ENVELOPES

An envelope should be of the same quality and color of stationery as the letter it carries. Because the envelope introduces your message and makes the first impression, you need to be especially careful in addressing it. Moreover, how you fold the letter is important.

Return Address.   The return address is usually printed in the upper left corner of an envelope, as shown in Figure A.3. In large companies some form of identification (the writer's initials, name, or location) may be typed above the company name and return address. This identification helps return the letter to the sender in case of nondelivery.

On an envelope without a printed return address, single-space the return address in the upper left corner. Beginning on line 3 on the fourth space ($\frac{1}{2}$ inch) from the left edge, type the writer's name, title, company, and mailing address.

ABC ★ Automation Business Consultants
One Peachtree Plaza
Atlanta, GA 30312   (404) 369-1109

↓ line 13 or 1 blank line below letterhead

July 19, 200x

↓ 2 to 7 blank lines

Identifies method of
delivery
FAX TRANSMISSION

↓ 1 blank line

Ms. Sara Hendricks, Manager
American Land and Home Realty
P.O. Box 3392A
Atlanta, GA 30308

↓ 2 blank lines

Replaces salutation
with subject line
SIMPLIFIED LETTER STYLE

↓ 2 blank lines

Leaves 2 blank lines
above and below
subject line

You may be interested to learn, Ms. Hendricks, that some years ago the Administrative Management Society recommended the simplified letter format illustrated here. Notice the following efficient features:

1. All lines begin at the left margin.

2. The salutation and complimentary close are omitted.

3. A subject line in all caps appears 2 blank lines below the inside address and 2 blank lines above the first paragraph.

4. The writer's name and identification appear 4 blank lines below the last paragraph.

In addition to its efficiency, this letter style is helpful in dealing with the problem of appropriate salutations. Since it has no salutation, your writers need not worry about which to choose. For many reasons we recommend this style to your staff.

Omits complimentary
close

Holly Higgins

↓ 4 blank lines

Highlights writer's
name and
identification
with all caps
HOLLY HIGGINS, MANAGER, OFFICE DIVISION

↓ 1 blank line

HH:tlb

↓ 1 blank line

Identifies copy
c John Fox

Mailing Address.   On legal-sized No. 10 envelopes ($4\frac{1}{8} \times 9\frac{1}{2}$ inches), begin the address on line 13 about $4\frac{1}{4}$ inches from the left edge, as shown in Figure A.3. For small envelopes ($3\frac{5}{8} \times 6\frac{1}{2}$ inches), begin typing on line 12 about $2\frac{1}{2}$ inches from the left edge.

The U.S. Postal Service recommends that addresses be typed in all caps without any punctuation. This Postal Service style, shown in the small envelope in Figure A.3, was originally developed to facilitate scanning by optical character readers. Today's OCRs, however, are so sophisticated that they scan upper- and lowercase letters easily. Many companies today do not follow the Postal Service format because they prefer to use the same format for the envelope as for the inside address. If the same format is used, writers can take advantage of word processing programs to "copy" the inside address to the envelope, thus saving keystrokes and reducing errors. Having the same format on both the inside address and the envelope also looks more professional and consistent. For these reasons you may choose to use the familiar upper- and lowercase combination format. But you will want to check with your organization to learn its preference.

FIGURE A.3 Envelope Formats

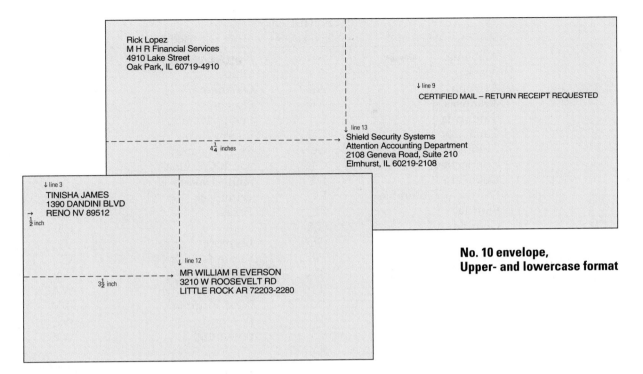

Rick Lopez
M H R Financial Services
4910 Lake Street
Oak Park, IL 60719-4910

↓ line 9

CERTIFIED MAIL – RETURN RECEIPT REQUESTED

↓ line 13

Shield Security Systems
Attention Accounting Department
2108 Geneva Road, Suite 210
Elmhurst, IL 60219-2108

$4\frac{1}{4}$ inches

**No. 10 envelope,
Upper- and lowercase format**

↓ line 3

TINISHA JAMES
1390 DANDINI BLVD
RENO NV 89512

→ $\frac{1}{2}$ inch

↓ line 12

MR WILLIAM R EVERSON
3210 W ROOSEVELT RD
LITTLE ROCK AR 72203-2280

$3\frac{1}{2}$ inch

No. $6\frac{3}{4}$ envelope, Postal Service uppercase format

In addressing your envelopes for delivery in this country or in Canada, use the two-letter state and province abbreviations shown in Figure A.4. Notice that these abbreviations are in capital letters without periods.

Folding.   The way a letter is folded and inserted into an envelope sends additional nonverbal messages about a writer's professionalism and carefulness. Most businesspeople follow the procedures shown here, which produce the least number of creases to distract readers.

For large No. 10 envelopes, begin with the letter face up. Fold slightly less than one third of the sheet toward the top, as shown in the following diagram. Then fold down the top third to within $\frac{1}{3}$ inch of the bottom fold. Insert the letter into the envelope with the last fold toward the bottom of the envelope.

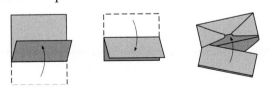

For small No. $6\frac{3}{4}$ envelopes, begin by folding the bottom up to within $\frac{1}{3}$ inch of the top edge. Then fold the right third over to the left. Fold the left third to within $\frac{1}{3}$ inch of the last fold. Insert the last fold into the envelope first.

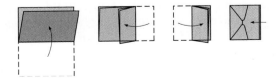

Envelopes

FIGURE A.4 Abbreviations of States, Territories, and Provinces

STATE OR TERRITORY	TWO-LETTER ABBREVIATION	STATE OR TERRITORY	TWO-LETTER ABBREVIATION
Alabama	AL	North Dakota	ND
Alaska	AK	Ohio	OH
Arizona	AZ	Oklahoma	OK
Arkansas	AR	Oregon	OR
California	CA	Pennsylvania	PA
Canal Zone	CZ	Puerto Rico	PR
Colorado	CO	Rhode Island	RI
Connecticut	CT	South Carolina	SC
Delaware	DE	South Dakota	SD
District of Columbia	DC	Tennessee	TN
Florida	FL	Texas	TX
Georgia	GA	Utah	UT
Guam	GU	Vermont	VT
Hawaii	HI	Virgin Islands	VI
Idaho	ID	Virginia	VA
Illinois	IL	Washington	WA
Indiana	IN	West Virginia	WV
Iowa	IA	Wisconsin	WI
Kansas	KS	Wyoming	WY
Kentucky	KY		
Louisiana	LA		**Two-Letter**
Maine	ME	**Canadian Province**	**Abbreviation**
Maryland	MD	Alberta	AB
Massachusetts	MA	British Columbia	BC
Michigan	MI	Labrador	LB
Minnesota	MN	Manitoba	MB
Mississippi	MS	New Brunswick	NB
Missouri	MO	Newfoundland	NF
Montana	MT	Northwest Territories	NT
Nebraska	NE	Nova Scotia	NS
Nevada	NV	Ontario	ON
New Hampshire	NH	Prince Edward Island	PE
New Jersey	NJ	Quebec	PQ
New Mexico	NM	Saskatchewan	SK
New York	NY	Yukon Territory	YT
North Carolina	NC		

MEMORANDUMS

As discussed in Chapter 5, memorandums deliver messages within organizations. Some offices use memo forms imprinted with the organization name and, optionally, the department or division names. Although the design and arrangement of memo forms vary, they usually include the basic elements of *TO, FROM, DATE,* and *SUBJECT.* Large organizations may include other identifying headings, such as *FILE NUMBER, FLOOR, EXTENSION, LOCATION,* and *DISTRIBUTION.*

Because of the difficulty of aligning computer printers with preprinted forms, many business writers use a standardized memo template (sometimes called a

FIGURE A.5 Memo on Plain Paper

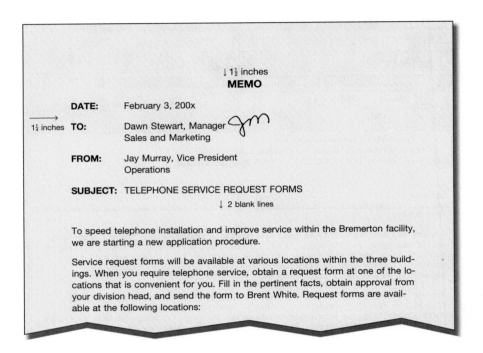

↓ 1½ inches
MEMO

DATE: February 3, 200x

1¼ inches **TO:**   Dawn Stewart, Manager
          Sales and Marketing

FROM: Jay Murray, Vice President
          Operations

SUBJECT: TELEPHONE SERVICE REQUEST FORMS

↓ 2 blank lines

To speed telephone installation and improve service within the Bremerton facility, we are starting a new application procedure.

Service request forms will be available at various locations within the three buildings. When you require telephone service, obtain a request form at one of the locations that is convenient for you. Fill in the pertinent facts, obtain approval from your division head, and send the form to Brent White. Request forms are available at the following locations:

"wizard"). This template automatically provides attractive headings with appropriate spacing and formatting. Other writers store their own preferred memo formats. Either method eliminates alignment problems.

If no printed or stored computer forms are available, memos may be typed on company letterhead or on plain paper, as shown in Figure A.5. On a full sheet of paper, leave a 1½-inch top margin; on a half sheet, leave a 1-inch top margin. Double-space and type in all caps the guide words *TO:, FROM:, DATE:, SUBJECT:*. Align all the fill-in information two spaces after the longest guide word (*SUBJECT:*). Leave 2 blank lines after the last line of the heading and begin typing the body of the memo. Like business letters, memos are single-spaced.

Memos are generally formatted with side margins of 1¼ inches, or they may conform to the printed memo form. (For more information about memos, see Chapter 5.)

E-MAIL MESSAGES

Because e-mail is a developing communication medium, formatting and usage are still fluid. The following suggestions, illustrated in Figure A.6 and also in Figure 5.2 in Chapter 5, may guide you in setting up the parts of an e-mail message. Always check, however, with your organization so that you can follow its practices.

To Line.   Include the receiver's e-mail address after *To*. If the receiver's address is recorded in your address book, you just have to click on it. Be sure to enter all addresses very carefully since one mistyped letter prevents delivery.

From Line.   Most mail programs automatically include your name and e-mail address after *From*.

Includes descriptive subject line

Incorporates recipient's name in first sentence

Uses single spacing within paragraphs and double spacing between

Closes with name and title to ensure identification

Cc and Bcc.   Insert the e-mail address of anyone who is to receive a copy of the message. *Cc* stands for carbon copy or courtesy copy. Don't be tempted, though, to send needless copies just because it's so easy. *Bcc* stands for blind carbon copy. Some writers use *bcc* to send a copy of the message without the addressee's knowledge. Writers are also using the *bcc* line for mailing lists. When a message is being sent to a number of people and their e-mail addresses should not be revealed, the *bcc* line works well to conceal the names and addresses of all receivers.

Subject.   Identify the subject of the e-mail message with a brief but descriptive summary of the topic. Be sure to include enough information to be clear and compelling. Capitalize the initial letters of principal words, or capitalize the entire line if space permits.

Salutation.   Include a brief greeting, if you like. Some writers use a salutation such as *Dear Sondra* followed by a comma or a colon. Others are more informal with *Hi, Sondra!*, or *Good morning* or *Greetings*. Some writers simulate a salutation by including the name of the receiver in an abbreviated first line, as shown in Figure A.6. Other writers treat an e-mail message like a memo and skip the salutation entirely. See Chapter 5 for a more complete discussion of e-mail salutations.

Message.   Cover just one topic in your message, and try to keep your total message under two screens in length. Single-space and be sure to use both upper- and lowercase letters. Double-space between paragraphs.

Closing.   Conclude an external message, if you like, with *Cheers, Best wishes,* or *Warm regards,* followed by your name and e-mail address (because some programs and routers do not transmit your address automatically). If the recipient is unlikely to know you, it's not a bad idea to include your title and organization. Some veteran e-mail users include a *signature file* with identifying information embellished with keyboard art. Use restraint, however, because signature files take up precious space. Writers of e-mail messages sent within organizations may omit a closing and even skip their names at the ends of messages because receivers recognize them from identification in the opening lines.

Attachment.   Use the attachment window or button to select the path and file name of any file you wish to send with your e-mail message. You can also attach a Web page to your message.

FAX COVER SHEET

Documents transmitted by fax are usually introduced by a cover sheet, such as that shown in Figure A.7. As with memos, the format varies considerably. Important items to include are (1) the name and fax number of the receiver, (2) the name and fax number of the sender, (3) the number of pages being sent, and (4) the name and telephone number of the person to notify in case of unsatisfactory transmission.

When the document being transmitted requires little explanation, you may prefer to attach an adhesive note (such as a Post-it™ fax transmittal form) instead of a full cover sheet. These notes carry essentially the same information as shown in our printed fax cover sheet. They are perfectly acceptable in most business organizations and can save considerable paper and transmission costs.

FIGURE A.7   **Fax Cover Sheet**

```
                        FAX TRANSMISSION

        DATE: _____
                                    FAX
                                    NUMBER: _____
        TO:   _____
              _____
              _____
                                    FAX
        FROM: _____  NUMBER _____
              _____
              _____

        NUMBER OF PAGES TRANSMITTED INCLUDING THIS COVER SHEET: ___

        MESSAGE:




        If any part of this fax transmission is missing or not clearly received,
        please call:

        NAME: _____

        PHONE: _____
```

Appendix
B

Correction Symbols and Proofreading Marks

In marking your papers, your instructor may use the following symbols or abbreviations to indicate writing weaknesses. You'll find that studying these symbols and suggestions will help you understand your instructor's remarks. Knowing this information can also help you evaluate and improve your own letters, memos, reports, and other writing.

STRATEGY AND ORGANIZATION

Coh   Develop coherence between ideas. Repeat key idea or add transitional expression.
DS   Use direct strategy. Start with main idea or good news.
IS   Use indirect strategy. Explain before introducing main idea.
Org   Improve organization. Keep similar topics together.
Plan   Apply appropriate plan for message.
Trans   Include transition to join ideas.

CONTENT AND STYLE

Acc   Verify accuracy of names, places, amounts, and other data.
ACE   Avoid copying examples.
ACP   Avoid copying case problems.
Act   Use active voice.
AE   Use action ending that tells reader what to do.
Awk   Rephrase to avoid awkward or unidiomatic expression.
Asn   Check assignment for instructions or facts.
Chop   Use longer sentences to avoid choppiness. Vary sentence patterns.
Cl   Improve clarity of ideas or expression.
Con   Condense into shorter form.
Emp   Emphasize this idea.
Eth   Use language that projects honest, ethical business practices.
Exp   Explain more fully or clearly.
Inc   Expand an incomplete idea.
Jar   Avoid jargon or specialized language that reader may not know.
Log   Remedy faulty logic.
Neg   Revise negative expression with more positive view.
Obv   Avoid saying what is obvious.
Par   Use parallel (balanced) expression.

PV	Express idea from reader's point of view.
RB	Show reader benefits. What's in it for reader?
Rdn	Revise to eliminate redundant idea or expression.
Rep	Avoid unintentional repetition of word, idea, or sound.
Sin	Use language that sounds sincere.
Spec	Develop idea with specific details.
Sub	Subordinate this point to lessen its impact.
SX	Avoid sexist language.
Tone	Use more conversational or positive tone.
You	Emphasize "you"-view.
Var	Vary sentences with different patterns.
Vag	Avoid vague pronoun. Don't use *they, that, this, which, it,* or other pronouns unless their references are clear.
Vb	Use correct verb tense. Avoid verb shift.
W	Condense to avoid wordiness.
WC	Improve word choice. Find a more precise word.

GRAMMAR AND MECHANICS

Abv	Avoid most abbreviations in text. Use correct abbreviation if necessary.
Agr	Make each subject and verb or pronoun and noun agree.
Apos	Use an apostrophe to show possession or contraction.
Art	Choose a correct article (*a, an,* or *the*).
Cap	Capitalize appropriately.
Cm	Use a comma.
CmConj	Use a comma preceding coordinating conjunction (*and, or, nor, but*) that joins independent clauses.
CmIntro	Use a comma following introductory dependent clause or long phrase.
CmSer	Use commas to separate items in a series.
CS	Rectify a comma splice by separating independent clauses with a period or a semicolon.
Div	Improve word division by hyphenating between syllables.
DM	Rectify a dangling modifier by supplying a clear subject for modifying element.
Exp	Avoid expletives such as *there is, there are,* and *it is.*
Frag	Revise fragment to form complete sentence.
Gram	Use correct grammar.
Hyp	Hyphenate a compound adjective.
lc	Use lowercase instead of capital.
MM	Correct misplaced modifier by moving modifier closer to word it describes or limits.
Num	Express numbers in correct word or figure form.
Pn	Use correct punctuation.
Prep	Correct use of preposition.
RO	Rectify run-on sentence with comma or semicolon to separate independent clauses.
Sem	Use semicolon to join related independent clauses.
Sp	Check spelling.
SS	Shorten sentences.
UnCm	Avoid unnecessary comma.

FORMAT

Cen   Center a document appropriately on the page.

DSp	Insert a double space, or double-space throughout.
F	Choose appropriate format for this item or message.
GH	Use graphic highlighting (bullets, lists, indentions, and headings) to improve readability.
Mar	Improve margins to frame a document on the page.
SSp	Insert a single space, or single-space throughout.
TSp	Insert a triple space.

PROOFREADING MARKS

PROOFREADING MARK	DRAFT COPY	FINAL COPY
⌇ Align horizontally	TO: Rick Munoz	TO: Rick Munoz
‖ Align vertically	166.32 132.45	166.32 132.45
☰ Capitalize	Coca-cola runs on ms-dos	Coca-Cola runs on MS-DOS
⊂ Close up space	meeting at 3 p. m.	meeting at 3 p.m.
⊐⊏ Center	Recommendations	Recommendations
⸜ Delete	in my final judgement	in my judgment
⌄ Insert apostrophe	our companys product	our company's product
⋀ Insert comma	you will of course	you will, of course,
⋀̄ Insert hyphen	tax free income	tax-free income
⊙ Insert period	Ms Holly Hines	Ms. Holly Hines
⌄ Insert quotation mark	shareholders receive a bonus.	shareholders receive a "bonus."
# Insert space	wordprocessing program	word processing program
/ Lowercase (remove capitals)	the Vice President	the vice president
	HUMAN RESOURCES	Human Resources
⊏ Move to left	I. Labor costs	I. Labor costs
⊐ Move to right	A. Findings of study	A. Findings of study
○ Spell out	aimed at 2 depts	aimed at two departments
¶ Start new paragraph	Keep the screen height of your computer at eye level.	Keep the screen height of your computer at eye level.
⋯ Stet (don't delete)	officials talked openly	officials talked openly
∿ Transpose	accounts recievable	accounts receivable
bf Use boldface	Conclusions	**Conclusions**
ital Use italics	The Perfect Résumé	*The Perfect Résumé*

Appendix C

Documentation Formats

For many reasons business writers are careful to properly document report data. Citing sources strengthens a writer's argument, as you learned in Chapter 10. Acknowledging sources also shields writers from charges of plagiarism. Moreover, good references help readers pursue further research.

Before we discuss specific documentation formats, you must understand the difference between *source* notes and *content* notes. Source notes identify quotations, paraphrased passages, and author references. They lead readers to the sources of cited information, and they must follow a consistent format. Content notes, on the other hand, enable writers to add comments, explain information not directly related to the text, or refer readers to other sections of a report. Because content notes are generally infrequent, most writers identify them in the text with a raised asterisk (*). At the bottom of the page, the asterisk is repeated with the content note following. If two content notes appear on one page, a double asterisk identifies the second reference.

Your real concern will be with source notes. These identify quotations or paraphrased ideas in the text, and they direct readers to a complete list of references (a bibliography) at the end of your report. Researchers have struggled for years to develop the perfect documentation system, one that is efficient for the writer and crystal clear to the reader. As a result, many systems exist, each with its advantages. The important thing for you is to adopt one system and use it consistently.

Students frequently ask, "But what documentation system is most used in business?" Actually, no one method dominates. Many businesses have developed their own hybrid systems. These companies generally supply guidelines illustrating their in-house style to employees. Before starting any research project on the job, you'll want to inquire about your organization's preferred documentation style. You can also look in the files for examples of previous reports.

References are usually cited in two places: (1) a brief citation appears in the text, and (2) a complete citation appears in a bibliography at the end of the report. The two most common formats for citations and bibliographies are those of the Modern Language Association (MLA) and the American Psychological Association (APA). Each has its own style for textual references and bibliography lists. For more discussion and examples of citations for electronic formats, visit the Guffey Web site at http://www.westwords.com/guffey/students.html and click "Documentation."

Writers in the humanities frequently use the MLA format, as illustrated in Figure C.1. The author's name and page number appear in parentheses close to the textual reference. If no author is known, a shortened version of the source title is used. At the end of the report, the writer lists all references alphabetically in a bibliography called "Works Cited." To see a long report illustrating MLA documentation, turn to Figure 14.4 in Chapter 14. For more information consult Joseph Gibaldi, *MLA Handbook for Writers of Research Papers*, Fifth Edition (New York: The Modern Language Association of America, 1999).

MLA In-Text Format. In-text citations generally appear close to the point where the reference is mentioned or at the end of the sentence inside the closing period. Follow these guidelines:

- Include the last name of the author(s) and the page number. Omit a comma, as (Smith 310).
- If the author's name is mentioned in the text, cite only the page number in parentheses. Do not include either the word *page* or the abbreviations *p.* or *pp.*
- If no author is known, refer to the document title or a shortened version of it, as (Facts at Fingertips 102).

MLA Bibliographic Format. The "Works Cited" bibliography lists all references cited in a report. Some writers include all works consulted. A portion of an MLA

FIGURE C.1 Portions of MLA Text Page and Bibliography

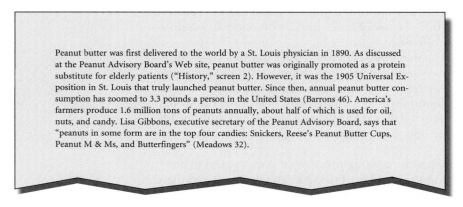

Peanut butter was first delivered to the world by a St. Louis physician in 1890. As discussed at the Peanut Advisory Board's Web site, peanut butter was originally promoted as a protein substitute for elderly patients ("History," screen 2). However, it was the 1905 Universal Exposition in St. Louis that truly launched peanut butter. Since then, annual peanut butter consumption has zoomed to 3.3 pounds a person in the United States (Barrons 46). America's farmers produce 1.6 million tons of peanuts annually, about half of which is used for oil, nuts, and candy. Lisa Gibbons, executive secretary of the Peanut Advisory Board, says that "peanuts in some form are in the top four candies: Snickers, Reese's Peanut Butter Cups, Peanut M & Ms, and Butterfingers" (Meadows 32).

Works Cited

Barrons, Elizabeth Ruth. "A Comparison of Domestic and International Consumption of Legumes." *Journal of Economic Agriculture 23* (1998): 45–49.

"History of Peanut Butter." *Peanut Advisory Board*. Retrieved 19 Jan. 2004 <http://www.peanut butterlovers.com/History/index.html>.

Meadows, Mark Allen. "Peanut Crop Is Anything but Peanuts at Home and Overseas." *Business Monthly*, 30 Sept. 2002, 31–34.

FIGURE C.2 MLA Bibliography Sample References

Works Cited

American Airlines. *2002 Annual Report*. Fort Worth, TX: AMR Corporation. ●——— Annual report

Berss, Marcia. "Protein Man." *Forbes* 24 Oct. 2001: 65–66. ●——— Magazine article

Connors, H. Lee. "Saturn's Orbit Still High With Consumers." *Marketing News Online*. 31 ●——— Magazine article, online
    Aug. 2002. Retrieved 1 Sept. 2003 <http://www.marketingnews.com/08-31-02.htm>.

"Globalization Often Means That the Fast Track Leads Overseas." *The Washington Post* 17 ●——— Newspaper article, no author
    June 2002: A10.

Lancaster, Hal. "When Taking a Tip From a Job Network, Proceed With Caution." *The Wall* ●——— Newspaper article, one author
    Street Journal 7 Feb. 2001: B1.

Markoff, John. "Voluntary Rules Proposed to Help Insure Privacy for Internet Users." *New* ●——— Newspaper article, online
    York Times on the Web 5 June 2002. Retrieved 9 June 2003 <http://www.nytimes.com/
    library/tech/02/05/biztech/articles/05privacy.html>.

Pinkerton Investigation Services. *The Employer's Guide to Investigation Services*, 2nd ed. ●——— Brochure
    Atlanta: Pinkerton Information Center, 2002.

Rivera, Francisco. Personal interview. 16 May 2003. ●——— Interview

Rose, Richard C., and Echo Montgomery Garrett. *How to Make a Buck and Still Be a Decent* ●——— Book, two authors
    Human Being. New York: HarperCollins, 2001.

"Spam: How to Eliminate It From Your Workplace." *SmartPros*. 8 Aug. 1997. Retrieved 12 ●——— Internet document, no author
    Sept. 2003 <http://accounting.smartpros.com/x10434.xml>.

U.S. Dept. of Labor. *Child Care as a Workforce Issue*: An Update. Washington, DC: GPO, ●——— Government publication
    2003.

Wetherbee, James C., Nicholas P. Vitalari, and Andrew Milner. "Key Trends in Systems ●——— Journal article with volume
    Development in Europe and North America." *Journal of Global Information Management*   and issue numbers
    3.2 (2001): 5–20. ["3.2" signifies volume 3, issue 2]

Wilson, Craig M. "E-Mail Bill May Fail to Curtail Spamming." *eWeek*. 9 July 2001: 49. ●——— Article from online database
    Retrieved 26 Aug 2003 from Infotrac College Edition database, Article No. A76563183.

Yeller, Martin. "E-commerce challenges and victories" [Msg. 4]. Online posting 4 Dec 2002
    to Google Group biz—ecommerce. Retrieved 14 Jan. 2003 from <http://groups.google.
    com/groups?h1-en@safe=off&group=biz.eco>. ●——— Message from online forum
    or discussion group

Note: If a printed document is viewed electronically and you have no reason to believe the electronic version is different from the print version, use the same format as for the print citation. More information about electronic documentation formats can be found at http://www.westwords.com/guffey/students.html.

bibliography is shown in Figure C.1. A more complete list of model references appears in Figure C.2. Following are selected guidelines summarizing important points regarding MLA bibliographic format:

- Use italics or underscores for the titles of books, magazines, newspapers, and journals. Check with your organization or instructor for guidance. Capitalize all important words.
- Enclose the titles of magazine, newspaper, and journal articles in quotation marks. Include volume and issue numbers for journals only.
- For Internet citations, include a retrieval date. Although MLA format does not include the words "Retrieved" or "Accessed," such wording helps distinguish the retrieval date from the document date.

AMERICAN PSYCHOLOGICAL ASSOCIATION FORMAT

Popular in the social and physical sciences, the American Psychological Association (APA) documentation style uses parenthetic citations. That is, each author reference is shown in parentheses when cited in the text, as shown in Figure C.3. At the end of the report, all references are listed alphabetically in a bibliography called "References." For more information about APA formats, see the *Publication Manual of the American Psychological Association*, Fifth Edition (Washington, DC: American Psychological Association, 2001).

FIGURE C.3 Portions of APA Text Page and Bibliography

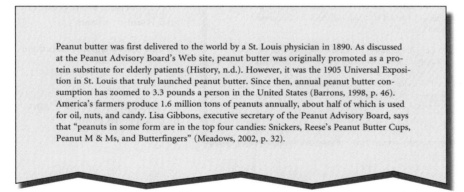

Peanut butter was first delivered to the world by a St. Louis physician in 1890. As discussed at the Peanut Advisory Board's Web site, peanut butter was originally promoted as a protein substitute for elderly patients (History, n.d.). However, it was the 1905 Universal Exposition in St. Louis that truly launched peanut butter. Since then, annual peanut butter consumption has zoomed to 3.3 pounds a person in the United States (Barrons, 1998, p. 46). America's farmers produce 1.6 million tons of peanuts annually, about half of which is used for oil, nuts, and candy. Lisa Gibbons, executive secretary of the Peanut Advisory Board, says that "peanuts in some form are in the top four candies: Snickers, Reese's Peanut Butter Cups, Peanut M & Ms, and Butterfingers" (Meadows, 2002, p. 32).

References

Barrons, E. (1998). A comparison of domestic and international consumption of legumes. *Journal of Economic Agriculture*, 23(3), 45–49.

Meadows, M. (2002). Peanut crop is anything but peanuts at home and overseas. *Business Monthly, 14*, 31–34.

History of peanut butter (n.d.). Peanut Advisory Board. Retrieved January 17, 2004, from http://www.peanutbutterlovers.com/History/index.html

FIGURE C.4 Model APA Bibliography Sample References

References

American Airlines. (2003). *2003 Annual Report*. Fort Worth, TX: AMR Corporation. •——— Annual report

Atamian, R. M., & Ferranto, M. (2000). *Driving market forces*. New York: HarperCollins. •——— Book, two authors

Berss, M. (2001, October 24). Protein man. *Forbes*, 154, 64–66. •——— Magazine article

Cantrell, M. R., & Watson, H. (2002). Violence in today's workplace [Electronic version]. •——— Magazine article, viewed electronically
    Office Review, 26(1), 24–29.

Globalization often means that the fast track leads overseas. (2002, June 16). *The Washington* •——— Newspaper article, no author
    Post, p. A10.

Lancaster, H. (2002, February 7). When taking a tip from a job network, proceed with caution. •——— Newspaper article, one author
    The Wall Street Journal, p. B1.

Lang, R. T. (2001, March 2). Most people fail to identify nonverbal signs. *The New York Times*. •——— Newspaper article, online
    Retrieved November 15, 2001, from http://www.nytimes.com

Moon, J. (1999). Solid waste disposal. *Microsoft Encarta 2000* [CD-ROM]. Redmond, WA: •——— CD-ROM encyclopedia article
    Microsoft.

Pinkerton Investigation Services. (2001). *The employer's guide to investigation services* (3rd ed.) •——— Brochure
    [Brochure]. Atlanta: Pinkerton Information Center.

Wetherbee, J. C., Vitalari, N. P., & Milner, A. (2001). Key trends in systems development in •——— Journal article with volume and issue numbers
    Europe and North America. *Journal of Global Information Management*, 3(2), 5–20.
    ["3(2)" signifies volume 3, series or issue 2]

Wilson, G. & Simmons, P. (2003). *Plagiarism: What it is, and how to avoid it*. Retrieved July •——— World Wide Web document with author and date
    4, 2003, from Biology Program Guide 2001/2002 at the University of British Columbia
    Web site: http://www.zoology.ubc.ca/bpg/plagiarism.htm

WWW user survey reveals consumer trends. (n.d.). Retrieved August 2, 2003, from http://www •——— World Wide Web document, no author, no date
    .cc.gatech.edu/gvu/user_surveys/survey-2002-10/

Yudkin, M. (2003, July 4). The marketing minute: Truth is always in season [Msg. ID:ruf6kt0 •——— Message from online forum or discussion group
    aiu5eui6523qsrofhu70h21evoj@4ax.com]. Message posted to news://biz.ecommerce

APA In-Text Format.   Within the text, document each specific textual source with a short description in parentheses. Following are selected guidelines summarizing important elements of APA style:

- Include the last name of the author(s), date of publication, and page number, as (Jones, 2002, p. 36). Use "n.d." if no date is available.
- If no author is known, refer to the first few words of the reference list entry and the year, as (Computer Privacy, 2004, p. 59).
- Omit page numbers for general references, but always include page numbers for direct quotations.

APA Bibliographic Format.   List all citations alphabetically in a section called "References." A portion of an APA bibliography is shown in Figure C.3. A more complete list of model references appears in Figure C.4. APA style requires specific capitalization and sequencing guidelines, some of which are summarized here:

- Include an author's name with the last name first followed by initials, such as *Smith, M. A.* First and middle names are not used.
- Show the date of publication in parentheses immediately after the author's name, as *Smith M. A. (2002).*
- Italicize the titles of books. Use "sentence-style" capitalization. This means that only the first word of a title, proper nouns, and the first word after an internal colon is capitalized.
- Do not italicize or underscore the titles of magazine and journal articles. Use sentence-style capitalization for article titles.
- Italicize the names of magazines and journals. Capitalize the initial letters of all important words.

CITING ELECTRONIC SOURCES

Standards for researchers using electronic sources are still emerging. When citing electronic media, you should hold the same goals as for print sources. That is, you try to give credit to the authors and to allow others to easily locate the same or updated information. However, traditional formats for identifying authors, publication dates, and page numbers become confusing when applied to sources on the Internet. Strive to give correct credit for electronic sources by including the author's name (when available), document title, Web page title, Web address, and retrieval date. Formats for some electronic sources are shown here. For more comprehensive electronic citation formats, visit the Guffey Web site at http://www.westwords.com/guffey/students.html, which is updated as new formats emerge.

Grammar/Mechanics Handbook

Because many students need a quick review of basic grammar and mechanics, we provide a number of resources in condensed form. The Grammar/Mechanics Handbook, which offers you a rapid systematic review, consists of four parts:

- **Grammar/Mechanics Diagnostic Test.** This 65-point Grammar/Mechanics Diagnostic Test helps you assess your strengths and weaknesses in eight areas of grammar and mechanics.
- **Grammar/Mechanics Profile.** The G/M Profile enables you to pinpoint specific areas in which you need remedial instruction or review.
- **Grammar Review With Reinforcement and Editing Exercises.** A concise set of guidelines reviews basic principles of grammar, punctuation, capitalization, and number style. The review also provides reinforcement and quiz exercises that help you interact with the principles of grammar and test your comprehension. The guidelines not only provide a study guide for review but will also serve as a reference manual throughout the writing course. The grammar review can be used for classroom-centered instruction or for self-guided learning.
- **Confusing Words and Frequently Misspelled Words.** A list of selected confusing words, along with a list of 160 frequently misspelled words, completes the Grammar/Mechanics Handbook.

For additional assistance in helping you strengthen your language skills, we suggest the following resources:

- **On-line interactive skill builders.** At the Guffey Web Site (http://www.westwords.com/guffey/students.html), you will find sentence competency drills that are similar to the grammar/mechanics exercises provided in this book. Click "Book Support," your book cover, and "Skill Builders." You can also work on your spelling and vocabulary skills at this Web site.
- **Reference books.** More comprehensive treatment of grammar and punctuation guidelines can be found in Clark and Clark's *A Handbook for Office Workers* (South-Western, 2001) and Guffey's *Business English* (South-Western, 2002).

The first step in your systematic review of grammar and mechanics involves completing a diagnostic test found on the next page.

Name _____

This diagnostic test is intended to reveal your strengths and weaknesses in using the following:

plural nouns	adjectives	punctuation
possessive nouns	adverbs	capitalization style
pronouns	prepositions	number style
verbs	conjunctions	

The test is organized into sections corresponding to these categories. In sections A–H, each sentence is either correct or has one error related to the category under which it is listed. If a sentence is correct, write C. If it has an error, underline the error and write the correct form in the space provided. Use ink to record your answers. When you finish, check your answers with your instructor and fill out the Grammar/Mechanics Profile at the end of the test.

A. PLURAL NOUNS

branches _____

Example   The newspaper named editors in chief for both <u>branchs</u>.

1. Three of the attornies representing the defendants were from cities in other states.
2. Four freshmans discussed the pros and cons of attending colleges or universities.
3. Since the 1990s, most companys have begun to send bills of lading with shipments.
4. Neither the Johnsons nor the Morris's knew about the changes in beneficiaries.
5. The manager asked all secretaries to work on the next four Saturday's.

B. POSSESSIVE NOUNS

_____

_____

_____

_____

_____

6. We sincerely hope that the jurys judgment reflects the stories of all the witnesses.
7. In a little over two months time, the secretaries had finished three reports for the president.
8. Mr. Franklins staff is responsible for all accounts receivable contracted by customers purchasing electronics parts.
9. At the next stockholders meeting, we will discuss benefits for employees and dividends for shareholders.
10. Three months ago several employees in the sales department complained of Mrs. Smiths smoking.

C. PRONOUNS

me _____

Example   Whom did you ask to replace Tom and <u>I</u>?

11. My manager and myself were willing to send the copies to whoever needed them.
12. Some of the work for Mr. Benson and I had to be reassigned to Mark and him.
13. Although it's motor was damaged, the car started for the mechanic and me.

14. Just between you and me, only you and I know that she will be transferred. _____
15. My friend and I applied for employment at Reynolds, Inc., because of their excellent employee benefits. _____

D. VERB AGREEMENT

Example   The list of arrangements <u>have</u> to be approved by Tim and her.   has _____

16. The keyboard, printer, and monitor costs less than I expected. _____
17. A description of the property, together with several other legal documents, were submitted by my attorney. _____
18. There was only two enclosures and the letter in the envelope. _____
19. Neither the manager nor the employees in the office think the solution is fair. _____
20. Because of the holiday, our committee prefer to delay its action. _____

E. VERB MOOD, VOICE, AND TENSE

21. If I was able to fill your order immediately, I certainly would. _____
22. To operate the machine, first open the disk drive door and then you insert the diskette. _____
23. If I could chose any city, I would select Honolulu. _____
24. Those papers have laid on his desk for more than two weeks. _____
25. The auditors have went over these accounts carefully, and they have found no discrepancies. _____

F. ADJECTIVES AND ADVERBS

26. Until we have a more clearer picture of the entire episode, we shall proceed cautiously. _____
27. For about a week their newly repaired copier worked just beautiful. _____
28. The recently elected official benefited from his coast to coast campaign. _____
29. Mr. Snyder only has two days before he must complete the end-of-the-year report. _____
30. The architects submitted there drawings in a last-minute attempt to beat the deadline. _____

G. PREPOSITIONS AND CONJUNCTIONS

31. Can you tell me where the meeting is scheduled at? _____
32. It seems like we have been taking this test forever. _____
33. Our investigation shows that the distribution department is more efficient then the sales department. _____
34. My courses this semester are totally different than last semester's. _____
35. Do you know where this shipment is going to? _____

H. COMMAS

For each of the following sentences, insert any necessary commas. Count the number of commas that you added. Write that number in the space provided. All punctuation must be correct to receive credit for the sentence. If a sentence requires no punctuation, write C.

Example   However, because of developments in theory and computer applications, management is becoming more of a science.   2 _____

36. For example management determines how orders assignments and responsibilities are delegated to employees.
_____
37. Your order Mrs. Swift will be sent from Memphis Tennessee on July 1.
_____
38. When you need service on any of your pieces of equipment we will be happy to help you Mr. Lopez.
_____
39. Kevin Long who is the project manager at Techdata suggested that I call you.
_____
40. You have purchased from us often and your payments in the past have always been prompt.

I. COMMAS AND SEMICOLONS 1

Add commas and semicolons to the following sentences. In the space provided, write the number of punctuation marks that you added.

_____
41. The salesperson turned in his report however he did not indicate what time period it covered.
_____
42. Interest payments on bonds are tax deductible dividend payments are not.
_____
43. We are opening a branch office in Kettering and hope to be able to serve all your needs from that office by the middle of January.
_____
44. As suggested by the committee we must first secure adequate funding then we may consider expansion.
_____
45. When you begin to conduct research for a report consider the many library sources available namely books, periodicals, government publications, and databases.

J. COMMAS AND SEMICOLONS 2

_____
46. After our office manager had the printer repaired it jammed again within the first week although we treated it carefully.
_____
47. Our experienced courteous staff has been trained to anticipate your every need.
_____
48. In view of the new law that went into effect April 1 our current liability insurance must be increased however we cannot immediately afford it.
_____
49. As stipulated in our contract your agency will supervise our graphic arts and purchase our media time.
_____
50. As you know Mrs. Simpson we aim for long-term business relationships not quick profits.

K. OTHER PUNCTUATION

Each of the following sentences may require dashes, colons, question marks, quotation marks, periods, and underscores, as well as commas and semicolons. Add the appropriate punctuation to each sentence. Then, in the space provided, write the total number of marks that you added.

3 _____
Example   Price,service,and reliability these are our prime considerations.

_____
51. The following members of the department volunteered to help on Saturday Kim Carlos Dan and Sylvia.
_____
52. Mr Danner, Miss Reed, and Mrs Garcia usually arrived at the office by 830 am.
_____
53. Three of our top managers Tim, Marcy, and Thomas received cash bonuses.
_____
54. Did the vice president really say "All employees may take Friday off
_____
55. We are trying to locate an edition of Newsweek that carried an article entitled Who Is Reading Your E-Mail

L. CAPITALIZATION

For each of the following sentences, circle any letter that should be capitalized. In the space provided, write the number of circles that you marked.

Example   (V)ice (P)resident (D)aniels devised a procedure for expediting purchase orders from (A)rea 4 warehouses.   4 _____

56. although english was his native language, he also spoke spanish and could read french.   _____

57. on a trip to the east coast, uncle henry visited the empire state building.   _____

58. karen enrolled in classes in history, german, and sociology.   _____

59. the business manager and the vice president each received a new compaq computer.   _____

60. james lee, the president of kendrick, inc., will speak to our conference in the spring.   _____

M. NUMBER STYLE

Decide whether the numbers in the following sentences should be written as words or as figures. Each sentence either is correct or has one error. If it is correct, write C. If it has an error, underline it and write the correct form in the space provided.

Example   The bank had <u>5</u> branches in three suburbs.   five _____

61. More than 2,000,000 people have visited the White House in the past five years.   _____

62. Of the 35 letters sent out, only three were returned.   _____

63. We set aside forty dollars for petty cash, but by December 1 our fund was depleted.   _____

64. The meeting is scheduled for May 5th at 3 p.m.   _____

65. In the past 20 years, nearly 15 percent of the population changed residences at least once.   _____

GRAMMAR/MECHANICS PROFILE

In the spaces at the right, place a check mark to indicate the number of correct answers you had in each category of the Grammar/Mechanics Diagnostic Test.

		NUMBER CORRECT*				
		5	4	3	2	1
1–5	Plural Nouns	____	____	____	____	____
6–10	Possessive Nouns	____	____	____	____	____
11–15	Pronouns	____	____	____	____	____
16–20	Verb Agreement	____	____	____	____	____
21–25	Verb Mood, Voice, and Tense	____	____	____	____	____
26–30	Adjectives and Adverbs	____	____	____	____	____
31–35	Prepositions and Conjunctions	____	____	____	____	____
36–40	Commas	____	____	____	____	____
41–45	Commas and Semicolons 1	____	____	____	____	____

	NUMBER CORRECT*				
	5	4	3	2	1
46–50 Commas and Semicolons 2	_____	_____	_____	_____	_____
51–55 Other Punctuation	_____	_____	_____	_____	_____
56–60 Capitalization	_____	_____	_____	_____	_____
61–65 Number Style	_____	_____	_____	_____	_____

Note: 5 = have excellent skills; 4 = need light review; 3 = need careful review; 2 = need to study rules; 1 = need serious study and follow-up reinforcement.

GRAMMAR REVIEW

PARTS OF SPEECH (1.01)

1.01 Functions.   English has eight parts of speech. Knowing the functions of the parts of speech helps writers better understand how words are used and how sentences are formed.

    a. ***Nouns:*** name persons, places, things, qualities, concepts, and activities (for example, *Kevin, Phoenix, computer, joy, work, banking*).
    b. ***Pronouns:*** substitute for nouns (for example, *he, she, it, they*).
    c. ***Verbs:*** show the action of a subject or join the subject to words that describe it (for example, *walk, heard, is, was jumping*).
    d. ***Adjectives:*** describe or limit nouns and pronouns and often answer the questions *what kind? how many?* and *which one?* (for example, *red* car, *ten* items, *good* manager).
    e. ***Adverbs:*** describe or limit verbs, adjectives, or other adverbs and frequently answer the questions *when? how? where?* or *to what extent?* (for example, *tomorrow, rapidly, here, very*).
    f. ***Prepositions:*** join nouns or pronouns to other words in sentences (for example, desk *in* the office, ticket *for* me, letter *to* you).
    g. ***Conjunctions:*** connect words or groups of words (for example, you *and* I, Mark *or* Jill).
    h. ***Interjections:*** express strong feelings (for example, *Wow! Oh!*).

NOUNS (1.02–1.06)

Nouns name persons, places, things, qualities, concepts, and activities. Nouns may be classified into a number of categories.

1.02 Concrete and Abstract.   Concrete nouns name specific objects that can be seen, heard, felt, tasted, or smelled. Examples of concrete nouns are *telephone, dollar, IBM,* and *tangerine*. Abstract nouns name generalized ideas such as qualities or concepts that are not easily pictured. *Emotion, power,* and *tension* are typical examples of abstract nouns.

    Business writing is most effective when concrete words predominate. It's clearer to write *We need 16-pound copy paper* than to write *We need office supplies.* Chapter 4 provides practice in developing skill in the use of concrete words.

1.03 Proper and Common.   Proper nouns name specific persons, places, or things and are always capitalized (*General Electric, Baltimore, Jennifer*). All other nouns are common nouns and begin with lowercase letters (*company, city, student*). Rules for capitalization are presented in Sections 3.01–3.16.

1.04 Singular and Plural.   Singular nouns name one item; plural nouns name more than one. From a practical view, writers seldom have difficulty with singular nouns. They may need help, however, with the formation and spelling of plural nouns.

1.05 Guidelines for Forming Noun Plurals

a. Add *s* to most nouns (*chair, chairs; mortgage, mortgages; Monday, Mondays*).
b. Add *es* to nouns ending in *s, x, z, ch,* or *sh* (*bench, benches; boss, bosses; box, boxes; Lopez, Lopezes*).
c. Change the spelling in irregular noun plurals (*man, men; foot, feet; mouse, mice; child, children*).
d. Add *s* to nouns that end in *y* when *y* is preceded by a vowel (*attorney, attorneys; valley, valleys; journey, journeys*).
e. Drop the *y* and add *ies* to nouns ending in *y* when *y* is preceded by a consonant (*company, companies; city, cities; secretary, secretaries*).
f. Add *s* to the principal word in most compound expressions (*editors in chief, fathers-in-law, bills of lading, runners-up*).
g. Add *s* to most numerals, letters of the alphabet, words referred to as words, degrees, and abbreviations (*5s, 1990s, Bs, ands, CPAs, qts.*).
h. Add *'s* only to clarify letters of the alphabet that might be misread, such as *A's, I's, M's,* and *U's* and *i's, p's,* and *q's.* An expression like *c.o.d.s* requires no apostrophe because it would not easily be misread.

1.06 Collective Nouns.   Nouns such as *staff, faculty, committee, group,* and *herd* refer to a collection of people, animals, or objects. Collective nouns may be considered singular or plural depending upon their action. See Section 1.10i for a discussion of collective nouns and their agreement with verbs.

REVIEW EXERCISE A—NOUNS

In the space provided for each item, write *a* or *b* to complete the following statements accurately. When you finish, compare your responses with those provided. Answers are provided for odd-numbered items. Your instructor has the remaining answers. For each item on which you need review, consult the numbered principle shown in parentheses.

1. Nearly all (a) *editor in chiefs,* (b) *editors in chief* demand observance of standard punctuation. _____
2. Several (a) *attorneys,* (b) *attornies* worked on the case together. _____
3. Please write to the (a) *Davis's,* (b) *Davises* about the missing contract. _____
4. The industrial complex has space for nine additional (a) *companys,* (b) *companies.* _____
5. That accounting firm employs two (a) *secretaries,* (b) *secretarys* for five CPAs. _____
6. Four of the wooden (a) *benches,* (b) *benchs* must be repaired. _____
7. The home was constructed with numerous (a) *chimneys,* (b) *chimnies.* _____
8. Tours of the production facility are made only on (a) *Tuesdays,* (b) *Tuesday's.* _____
9. We asked the (a) *Lopez's,* (b) *Lopezes* to contribute to the fund-raising drive. _____
10. Both my (a) *sister-in-laws,* (b) *sisters-in-law* agreed to the settlement. _____
11. The stock market is experiencing abnormal (a) *ups and downs,* (b) *up's and down's.* _____
12. Three (a) *mouses,* (b) *mice* were seen near the trash cans. _____
13. This office is unusually quiet on (a) *Sundays,* (b) *Sunday's.* _____
14. Several news (a) *dispatchs,* (b) *dispatches* were released during the strike. _____
15. Two major (a) *countries,* (b) *countrys* will participate in arms negotiations. _____

16. Some young children have difficulty writing their (a) *bs and ds*, (b) *b's and d's*.
17. The (a) *board of directors*, (b) *boards of directors* of all the major companies participated in the surveys.
18. In their letter the (a) *Metzes*, (b) *Metzs* said they intended to purchase the property.
19. In shipping we are careful to include all (a) *bill of sales*, (b) *bills of sale*.
20. Over the holidays many (a) *turkies*, (b) *turkeys* were consumed.

1. b (1.05f)   3. b (1.05b)   5. a (1.05e)   7. a (1.05d)   9. b (1.05b)   11. a (1.05g)   13. a (1.05a)   15. a (1.05e)   17. b (1.05f)   19. b (1.05f) (Only odd-numbered answers are provided. Consult your instructor for the others.)

PRONOUNS (1.07–1.09)

Pronouns substitute for nouns. They are classified by case.

1.07 Case.   Pronouns function in three cases, as shown in the following chart.

Nominative Case (Used for subjects of verbs and subject complements)	Objective Case (Used for objects of prepositions and objects of verbs)	Possessive Case (Used to show possession)
I	me	my, mine
we	us	our, ours
you	you	your, yours
he	him	his
she	her	her, hers
it	it	its
they	them	their, theirs
who, whoever	whom, whomever	whose

1.08 Guidelines for Selecting Pronoun Case

a. Pronouns that serve as subjects of verbs must be in the nominative case:

   He and *I* (not *Him* and *me*) decided to apply for the jobs.

b. Pronouns that follow linking verbs (such as *am, is, are, was, were, be, being, been*) and rename the words to which they refer must be in the nominative case.

   It must have been *she* (not *her*) who placed the order. (The nominative-case pronoun *she* follows the linking verb *been* and renames *it*.)

   If it was *he* (not *him*) who called, I have his number. (The nominative-case pronoun *he* follows the linking verb *was* and renames *it*.)

c. Pronouns that serve as objects of verbs or objects of prepositions must be in the objective case:

   Mr. Andrews asked *them* to complete the proposal. (The pronoun *them* is the object of the verb *asked*.)

   All computer printouts are sent to *him*. (The pronoun *him* is the object of the preposition *to*.)

   Just between you and *me*, profits are falling. (The pronoun *me* is one of the objects of the preposition *between*.)

d. Pronouns that show ownership must be in the possessive case. Possessive pronouns (such as *hers, yours, ours, theirs,* and *its*) require no apostrophes:

We found my diskette, but *yours* (not *your's*) may be lost.

All parts of the machine, including *its* (not *it's*) motor, were examined.

The house and *its* (not *it's*) contents will be auctioned.

Don't confuse possessive pronouns and contractions. Contractions are shortened forms of subject-verb phrases (such as *it's* for *it is*, *there's* for *there is*, and *they're* for *they are*).

e. When a pronoun appears in combination with a noun or another pronoun, ignore the extra noun or pronoun and its conjunction. In this way pronoun case becomes more obvious:

The manager promoted Jeff and *me* (not *I*). (Ignore *Jeff and*.)

f. In statements of comparison, mentally finish the comparative by adding the implied missing words:

Next year I hope to earn as much as *she*. (The verb *earns* is implied here: . . . *as much as she earns*.)

g. Pronouns must be in the same case as the words they replace or rename. When pronouns are used with appositives, ignore the appositive:

A new contract was signed by *us* (not *we*) employees. (Temporarily ignore the appositive *employees* in selecting the pronoun.)

We (not *us*) citizens have formed our own organization. (Temporarily ignore the appositive *citizens* in selecting the pronoun.)

h. Pronouns ending in *self* should be used only when they refer to previously mentioned nouns or pronouns:

The CEO *himself* answered the telephone.

Robert and *I* (not *myself*) are in charge of the campaign.

i. Use objective-case pronouns as objects of the prepositions *between, but, like,* and *except*:

Everyone but John and *him* (not *he*) qualified for the bonus.

Employees like Miss Gillis and *her* (not *she*) are hard to replace.

j. Use *who* or *whoever* for nominative-case constructions and *whom* or *whomever* for objective-case constructions. In making the correct choice, it's sometimes helpful to substitute *he* for *who* or *whoever* and *him* for *whom* or *whomever*:

For *whom* was this book ordered? (*This book was ordered for him/whom?*)

Who did you say would drop by? (*Who/he . . . would drop by?*)

Deliver the package to *whoever* opens the door. (In this sentence the clause *whoever opens the door* functions as the object of the preposition *to*. Within the clause itself *whoever* is the subject of the verb *opens*. Again, substitution of *he* might be helpful: *He/Whoever opens the door*.)

1.09 Guidelines for Making Pronouns Agree With Their Antecedents.   Pronouns must agree with the words to which they refer (their antecedents) in gender and in number.

a. Use masculine pronouns to refer to masculine antecedents, feminine pronouns to refer to feminine antecedents, and neuter pronouns to refer to antecedents without gender:

The man opened *his* office door. (Masculine gender applies.)

A woman sat at *her* desk. (Feminine gender applies.)

This computer and *its* programs fit our needs. (Neuter gender applies.)

b. Use singular pronouns to refer to singular antecedents:

Common-gender pronouns (such as *him* or *his*) traditionally have been used when the gender of the antecedent is unknown. Sensitive writers today, however, prefer to recast such constructions to avoid the need for common-gender pronouns. Study these examples for alternatives to the use of common-gender pronouns:*

Each student must submit a report on Monday.

All students must submit *their* reports on Monday.

Each student must submit *his* or *her* report on Monday. (This alternative is least acceptable since it is wordy and calls attention to itself.)

c. Use singular pronouns to refer to singular indefinite subjects and plural pronouns for plural indefinite subjects. Words such as *anyone, something,* and *anybody* are considered indefinite because they refer to no specific person or object. Some indefinite pronouns are always singular; others are always plural.

Always Singular			**Always Plural**
anybody	everyone	somebody	both
anyone	everything	someone	few
anything	neither		many
each	nobody		several
either	no one		

Somebody in the group of touring women left *her* (not *their*) purse in the museum.

Either of the companies has the right to exercise *its* (not *their*) option to sell stock.

d. Use singular pronouns to refer to collective nouns and organization names:

The engineering staff is moving *its* (not *their*) facilities on Friday. (The singular pronoun *its* agrees with the collective noun *staff* because the members of *staff* function as a single unit.)

Jones, Cohen, & James, Inc., *has* (not *have*) canceled *its* (not *their*) contract with us. (The singular pronoun *its* agrees with *Jones, Cohen, & James, Inc.,* because the members of the organization are operating as a single unit.)

e. Use a plural pronoun to refer to two antecedents joined by *and*, whether the antecedents are singular or plural:

Our company president and our vice president will be submitting *their* expenses shortly.

f. Ignore intervening phrases—introduced by expressions such as *together with, as well as,* and *in addition to*—that separate a pronoun from its antecedent:

One of our managers, along with several salespeople, is planning *his* retirement. (If you wish to emphasize both subjects equally, join them with *and*: One of our managers *and* several salespeople are planning *their* retirements.)

---

*See Chapter 2, page 38, for additional discussion of common-gender pronouns and inclusive language.

g. When antecedents are joined by *or* or *nor*, make the pronoun agree with the antecedent closest to it.

Neither Jackie nor Kim wanted her (not their) desk moved.

REVIEW EXERCISE B—PRONOUNS

In the space provided for each item, write *a, b,* or *c* to complete the statement accurately. When you finish, compare your responses with those provided. For each item on which you need review, consult the numbered principle shown in parentheses.

1. Mr. Behrens and (a) *I,* (b) *myself* will be visiting sales personnel in the Wilmington district next week. _____
2. James promised that he would call; was it (a) *him,* (b) *he* who left the message? _____
3. Much preparation for the seminar was made by Mrs. Washington and (a) *I,* (b) *me* before the brochures were sent out. _____
4. The Employee Benefits Committee can be justly proud of (a) *its,* (b) *their* achievements. _____
5. A number of inquiries were addressed to Jeff and (a) *I,* (b) *me,* (c) *myself.* _____
6. (a) *Who,* (b) *Whom* did you say the letter was addressed to? _____
7. When you visit Sears Savings Bank, inquire about (a) *its,* (b) *their* certificates. _____
8. Copies of all reports are to be reviewed by Mr. Sanders and (a) *I,* (b) *me,* (c) *myself.* _____
9. Apparently one of the female applicants forgot to sign (a) *her,* (b) *their* application. _____
10. Both the printer and (a) *it's,* (b) *its* cover are missing. _____
11. I've never known any man who could work as fast as (a) *him,* (b) *he.* _____
12. Just between you and (a) *I,* (b) *me,* the stock price will fall by afternoon. _____
13. Give the supplies to (a) *whoever,* (b) *whomever* ordered them. _____
14. (a) *Us,* (b) *We* employees have been given an unusual voice in choosing benefits. _____
15. On her return from Mexico, Mrs. Sanchez, along with many other passengers, had to open (a) *her,* (b) *their* luggage for inspection. _____
16. Either James or Robert will have (a) *his,* (b) *their* work reviewed next week. _____
17. Any woman who becomes a charter member of this organization will be able to have (a) *her,* (b) *their* name inscribed on a commemorative plaque. _____
18. We are certain that (a) *our's,* (b) *ours* is the smallest wristwatch available. _____
19. Everyone has completed the reports except Debbie and (a) *he,* (b) *him.* _____
20. Lack of work disturbs Mr. Thomas as much as (a) *I,* (b) *me.* _____

1. a (1.08h) 3. b (1.08c) 5. b (1.08c, 1.08e) 7. a (1.09d) 9. a (1.09b) 11. b (1.08f) 13. a (1.08j) 15. a (1.09f) 17. a (1.09b) 19. b (1.08i)

CUMULATIVE EDITING QUIZ 1

Use proofreading marks (see Appendix B) to correct errors in the following sentences. All errors must be corrected to receive credit for the sentence. Check with your instructor for the answers.

Example   Nicholas and ~~him~~ *he* made all ~~there~~ *their* money in the 1990~~'~~s.

1. Just between you and I, whom do you think would make the best manager?

2. Either Stacy or me is responsible for correcting all errors in news dispatchs.

3. Several attornies asked that there cases be postponed.

4. One of the secretarys warned Bill and I to get the name of whomever answered the phone.

5. The committee sent there decision to the president and I last week.

6. Who should Susan or me call to verify the three bill of sales received today?

7. Several of we employees complained that it's keyboard made the new computer difficult to use.

8. All the CEO's agreed that the low interest rates of the early 2000s could not continue.

9. Every customer has a right to expect there inquirys to be treated courteously.

10. You may send you're contribution to Eric or myself or to whomever is listed as your representative.

VERBS (1.10–1.15)

Verbs show the action of a subject or join the subject to words that describe it.

1.10 Guidelines for Agreement With Subjects.   One of the most troublesome areas in English is subject-verb agreement. Consider the following guidelines for making verbs agree with subjects.

a. A singular subject requires a singular verb:

The stock market *opens* at 10 a.m. (The singular verb *opens* agrees with the singular subject *market.*)

He *doesn't* (not *don't*) work on Saturday.

b. A plural subject requires a plural verb:

On the packing slip several items *seem* (not *seems*) to be missing.

c. A verb agrees with its subject regardless of prepositional phrases that may intervene:

This list of management objectives *is* extensive. (The singular verb *is* agrees with the singular subject *list.*)

Every one of the letters *shows* (not *show*) proper form.

d. A verb agrees with its subject regardless of intervening phrases introduced by *as well as, in addition to, such as, including, together with,* and similar expressions:

An important memo, together with several letters, *was* misplaced. (The singular verb *was* agrees with the singular subject *memo.*)

The president as well as several other top-level executives *approves* of our proposal. (The singular verb *approves* agrees with the subject *president.*)

e. A verb agrees with its subject regardless of the location of the subject:

Here *is* one of the contracts about which you asked. (The verb *is* agrees with its subject *one,* even though it precedes *one.* The adverb *here* cannot function as a subject.)

There *are* many problems yet to be resolved. (The verb *are* agrees with the subject *problems.* The adverb *there* cannot function as a subject.)

In the next office *are* several printers. (In this inverted sentence the verb *are* must agree with the subject *printers*.)

f. Subjects joined by *and* require a plural verb:

Analyzing the reader and organizing a strategy *are* the first steps in letter writing. (The plural verb *are* agrees with the two subjects, *analyzing* and *organizing*.)

The tone and the wording of the letter *were* persuasive. (The plural verb *were* agrees with the two subjects, *tone* and *wording*.)

g. Subjects joined by *or* or *nor* may require singular or plural verbs. Make the verb agree with the closer subject:

Neither the memo nor the report *is* ready. (The singular verb *is* agrees with *report*, the closer of the two subjects.)

h. The following indefinite pronouns are singular and require singular verbs: *anyone, anybody, anything, each, either, every, everyone, everybody, everything, many a, neither, nobody, nothing, someone, somebody,* and *something*:

Either of the alternatives that you present *is* acceptable. (The verb *is* agrees with the singular subject *either*.)

i. Collective nouns may take singular or plural verbs, depending on whether the members of the group are operating as a unit or individually:

Our management team *is* united in its goal.

The faculty *are* sharply *divided* on the tuition issue. (Although acceptable, this sentence sounds better recast: The faculty *members* are sharply divided on the tuition issue.)

j. Organization names and titles of publications, although they may appear to be plural, are singular and require singular verbs.

Clark, Anderson, and Horne, Inc., *has* (not *have*) hired a marketing consultant.

Thousands of Investment Tips is (not *are*) again on the best-seller list.

1.11 Voice.   Voice is that property of verbs that shows whether the subject of the verb acts or is acted upon. Active-voice verbs direct action from the subject toward the object of the verb. Passive-voice verbs direct action toward the subject.

Active voice: Our employees *send* many e-mail messages.

Passive voice: Many e-mail messages *are sent* by our employees.

Business writing that emphasizes active-voice verbs is generally preferred because it is specific and forceful. However, passive-voice constructions can help a writer be tactful. Strategies for effective use of active- and passive-voice verbs are presented in Chapter 3.

1.12 Mood.   Three verb moods express the attitude or thought of the speaker or writer toward a subject: (1) the indicative mood expresses a fact; (2) the imperative mood expresses a command; and (3) the subjunctive mood expresses a doubt, a conjecture, or a suggestion.

Indicative: I *am looking* for a job.

Imperative: *Begin* your job search with the want ads.

Subjunctive: I wish I *were* working.

Only the subjunctive mood creates problems for most speakers and writers. The most common use of subjunctive mood occurs in clauses including *if* or *wish*. In such clauses substitute the subjunctive verb *were* for the indicative verb *was*:

If he *were* (not *was*) in my position, he would understand.

Mr. Simon acts as if he *were* (not *was*) the boss.

We wish we *were* (not *was*) able to ship your order.

The subjunctive mood may be used to maintain goodwill while conveying negative information. The sentence *We wish we were able to ship your order* sounds more pleasing to a customer than *We cannot ship your order*, although, for all practical purposes, both sentences convey the same negative message.

1.13 Tense. Verbs show the time of an action by their tense. Speakers and writers can use six tenses to show the time of sentence action; for example:

Present tense:	I *work*; he *works*.
Past tense:	I *worked*; she *worked*.
Future tense:	I *will work*; he *will work*.
Present perfect tense:	I *have worked*; he *has worked*.
Past perfect tense:	I *had worked*; she *had worked*.
Future perfect tense:	I *will have worked*; he *will have worked*.

1.14 Guidelines for Verb Tense

a. Use present tense for statements that, although they may be introduced by past-tense verbs, continue to be true:

What did you say his name *is*? (Use the present tense *is* if his name has not changed.)

b. Avoid unnecessary shifts in verb tenses:

The manager *saw* (not *sees*) a great deal of work yet to be completed and *remained* to do it herself.

Although unnecessary shifts in verb tense are to be avoided, not all the verbs within one sentence have to be in the same tense; for example:

She *said* (past tense) that she *likes* (present tense) to work late.

1.15 Irregular Verbs. Irregular verbs cause difficulty for some writers and speakers. Unlike regular verbs, irregular verbs do not form the past tense and past participle by adding *-ed* to the present form. Here is a partial list of selected troublesome irregular verbs. Consult a dictionary if you are in doubt about a verb form.

TROUBLESOME IRREGULAR VERBS

Present	**Past**	**Past Participle** *(always use helping verbs)*
begin	began	begun
break	broke	broken
choose	chose	chosen
come	came	come
drink	drank	drunk
go	went	gone
lay (to place)	laid	laid
lie (to rest)	lay	lain
ring	rang	rung
see	saw	seen
write	wrote	written

a. Use only past-tense verbs to express past tense. Notice that no helping verbs are used to indicate simple past tense:

The auditors *went* (not *have went*) over our books carefully.

He *came* (not *come*) to see us yesterday.

b. Use past participle forms for actions completed before the present time. Notice that past participle forms require helping verbs:

Steve *had gone* (not *went*) before we called. (The past participle *gone* is used with the helping verb *had*.)

c. Avoid inconsistent shifts in subject, voice, and mood. Pay particular attention to this problem area, for undesirable shifts are often characteristic of student writing.

Inconsistent:	When Mrs. Taswell read the report, the error was found. (The first clause is in the active voice; the second, passive.)
Improved:	When Mrs. Taswell read the report, she found the error. (Both clauses are in the active voice.)
Inconsistent:	The clerk should first conduct an inventory. Then supplies should be requisitioned. (The first sentence is in the active voice; the second, passive.)
Improved:	The clerk should first conduct an inventory. Then he or she should requisition supplies. (Both sentences are in the active voice.)
Inconsistent:	All workers must wear security badges, and you must also sign a daily time card. (This sentence contains an inconsistent shift in subject from *all workers* in first clause to *you* in second clause.)
Improved:	All workers must wear security badges, and they must also sign a daily time card.
Inconsistent:	Begin the transaction by opening an account; then you enter the customer's name. (This sentence contains an inconsistent shift from the imperative mood in first clause to the indicative mood in second clause.)
Improved:	Begin the transaction by opening an account; then enter the customer's name. (Both clauses are now in the indicative mood.)

REVIEW EXERCISE C—VERBS

In the space provided for each item, write *a* or *b* to complete the statement accurately. When you finish, compare your responses with those provided. For each item on which you need review, consult the numbered principle shown in parentheses.

1. A list of payroll deductions for our employees (a) *was*, (b) *were* sent to the personnel manager. _____
2. There (a) *is*, (b) *are* a customer service engineer and two salespeople waiting to see you. _____
3. Increased computer use and more complex automated systems (a) *is*, (b) *are* found in business today. _____
4. Crews, Meliotes, and Bove, Inc., (a) *has*, (b) *have* opened an office in Boston. _____
5. Yesterday Mrs. Phillips (a) *choose*, (b) *chose* a new office on the second floor. _____
6. The man who called said that his name (a) *is*, (b) *was* Johnson. _____
7. *Office Computing and Networks* (a) *is*, (b) *are* beginning a campaign to increase readership. _____
8. Either of the flight times (a) *appears*, (b) *appear* to fit my proposed itinerary. _____
9. If you had (a) *saw*, (b) *seen* the rough draft, you would better appreciate the final copy. _____

10. Across from our office (a) *is*, (b) *are* the parking structure and the information office.
11. Although we have (a) *began*, (b) *begun* to replace outmoded equipment, the pace is slow.
12. Specific training as well as ample experience (a) *is*, (b) *are* important for that position.
13. Inflation and increased job opportunities (a) *is*, (b) *are* resulting in increased numbers of working women.
14. Neither the organizing nor the staffing of the program (a) *has been*, (b) *have been* completed.
15. If I (a) *was*, (b) *were* you, I would ask for a raise.
16. If you had (a) *wrote*, (b) *written* last week, we could have sent a brochure.
17. The hydraulic equipment that you ordered (a) *is*, (b) *are* packed and will be shipped Friday.
18. One of the reasons that sales have declined in recent years (a) *is*, (b) *are* lack of effective advertising.
19. Either of the proposed laws (a) *is*, (b) *are* going to affect our business negatively.
20. Merger statutes (a) *requires*, (b) *require* that a failing company accept bids from several companies before merging with one.

1. a (1.10c)   3. b (1.10f)   5. b (1.15a)   7. a (1.10j)   9. b (1.15b)   11. b (1.15b)   13. b (1.10f)
15. b (1.12)   17. a (1.10a)   19. a (1.10h)

REVIEW EXERCISE D—VERBS

In the following sentence pairs, choose the one that illustrates consistency in use of subject, voice, and mood. Write *a* or *b* in the space provided. When you finish, compare your responses with those provided. For each item on which you need review, consult the numbered principle shown in parentheses.

1. (a) You need more than a knowledge of equipment; one also must be able to interact well with people.
   (b) You need more than a knowledge of equipment; you also must be able to interact well with people.
2. (a) Tim and Jon were eager to continue, but Bob wanted to quit.
   (b) Tim and Jon were eager to continue, but Bob wants to quit.
3. (a) The salesperson should consult the price list; then you can give an accurate quote to a customer.
   (b) The salesperson should consult the price list; then he or she can give an accurate quote to a customer.
4. (a) Read all the instructions first; then you install the printer program.
   (b) Read all the instructions first, and then install the printer program.
5. (a) She was an enthusiastic manager who always had a smile for everyone.
   (b) She was an enthusiastic manager who always has a smile for everyone.

1. b (1.15c)   3. b (1.15c)   5. a (1.14b)

CUMULATIVE EDITING QUIZ 2

Use proofreading marks (see Appendix B) to correct errors in the following sentences. All errors must be corrected to receive credit for the sentence. Check with your instructor for the answers.

1. Assets and liabilitys is what my partner and myself must investigate.

2. If I was you, I would ask whomever is in charge for their opinion.

3. The faculty agree that it's first concern is educating students.

4. The book and it's cover was printed in Japan.

5. Waiting to see you is a sales representative and a job applicant who you told to drop by.

6. Every employee could have picked up his ballot if he had went to the cafeteria.

7. Your choice of hospitals and physicians are reduced by this plan and it's restrictions.

8. My uncle and her come to visit my parents and myself last night.

9. According to both editor in chiefs, the tone and wording of all our letters needs revision.

10. The Davis'es, about who the article was written, said they were unconcerned with the up's and down's of the stock market.

ADJECTIVES AND ADVERBS (1.16–1.17)

Adjectives describe or limit nouns and pronouns. They often answer the questions *what kind? how many?* or *which one?* Adverbs describe or limit verbs, adjectives, or other adverbs. They often answer the questions *when? how? where?* or *to what extent?*

1.16 Forms.   Most adjectives and adverbs have three forms, or degrees: positive, comparative, and superlative.

	Positive	Comparative	Superlative
Adjective:	clear	clearer	clearest
Adverb:	clearly	more clearly	most clearly

Some adjectives and adverbs have irregular forms.

	Positive	Comparative	Superlative
Adjective:	good	better	best
	bad	worse	worst
Adverb:	well	better	best

Adjectives and adverbs composed of two or more syllables are usually compared by the use of *more* and *most*; for example:

The Payroll Department is *more efficient* than the Shipping Department.

Payroll is the *most efficient* department in our organization.

1.17 Guidelines for Use

a. Use the comparative degree of the adjective or adverb to compare two persons or things; use the superlative degree to compare three or more:

Of the two plans, which is *better* (not *best*)?

Of all the plans, we like this one *best* (not *better*).

b. Do not create a double comparative or superlative by using *-er* with *more* or *-est* with *most*:

His explanation couldn't have been *clearer* (not *more clearer*).

c. A linking verb (*is, are, look, seem, feel, sound, appear,* and so forth) may introduce a word that describes the verb's subject. In this case be certain to use an adjective, not an adverb:

The characters on the monitor look *bright* (not *brightly*). (Use the adjective *bright* because it follows the linking verb *look* and modifies the noun *characters*. It answers the question *What kind of characters?*)

The company's letter made the customer feel *bad* (not *badly*). (The adjective *bad* follows the linking verb *feel* and describes the noun *customer*.)

d. Use adverbs, not adjectives, to describe or limit the action of verbs:

The business is running *smoothly* (not *smooth*). (Use the adverb *smoothly* to describe the action of the verb *is running*. *Smoothly* tells how the business is running.)

Don't take his remark *personally* (not *personal*). (The adverb *personally* describes the action of the verb *take*.)

e. Two or more adjectives that are joined to create a compound modifier before a noun should be hyphenated:

The *four-year-old* child was tired.

Our agency is planning a *coast-to-coast* campaign.

Hyphenate a compound modifier following a noun only if your dictionary shows the hyphen(s):

Our speaker is very *well-known*. (Include the hyphen because most dictionaries do.)

The tired child was four years old. (Omit the hyphens because the expression follows the word it describes, *child*, and because dictionaries do not indicate hyphens.)

f. Keep adjectives and adverbs close to the words that they modify:

She asked for a cup of *hot* coffee (not a *hot cup of coffee*).

Patty had *only* two days of vacation left (not Patty *only had two days*).

Students may sit in the *first* five rows (not *in the five first rows*).

He has saved *almost* enough money for the trip (not *He has almost saved*).

g. Don't confuse the adverb *there* with the possessive pronoun *their* or the contraction *they're*:

Put the documents *there*. (The adverb *there* means "at that place or at that point.")

There are two reasons for the change. (The adverb *there* is used as filler preceding a linking verb.)

We already have *their* specifications. (The possessive pronoun *their* shows ownership.)

They're coming to inspect today. (The contraction *they're* is a shortened form of *they are*.)

REVIEW EXERCISE E—ADJECTIVES AND ADVERBS

In the space provided for each item, write *a, b,* or *c* to complete the statement accurately. If two sentences are shown, select *a* or *b* to indicate the one expressed more effectively. When you finish, compare your responses with those provided. For each item on which you need review, consult the numbered principle shown in parentheses.

1. After the interview, Tim looked (a) *calm*, (b) *calmly*.
2. If you had been more (a) *careful*, (b) *carefuler*, the box might not have broken.

3. Because a new manager was appointed, the advertising campaign is running very (a) *smooth*, (b) *smoothly*.   _____

4. To avoid a (a) *face to face*, (b) *face-to-face* confrontation, she wrote a letter.   _____

5. Darren completed the employment test (a) *satisfactorily*, (b) *satisfactory*.   _____

6. I felt (a) *bad*, (b) *badly* that he was not promoted.   _____

7. Which is the (a) *more*, (b) *most* dependable of the two models?   _____

8. Can you determine exactly what (a) *there*, (b) *their*, (c) *they're* company wants us to do?   _____

9. Of all the copiers we tested, this one is the (a) *easier*, (b) *easiest* to operate.   _____

10. (a) Mr. Aldron almost was ready to accept the offer.
    (b) Mr. Aldron was almost ready to accept the offer.   _____

11. (a) We only thought that it would take two hours for the test.
    (b) We thought that it would take only two hours for the test.   _____

12. (a) Please bring me a glass of cold water.
    (b) Please bring me a cold glass of water.   _____

13. (a) The committee decided to retain the last ten tickets.
    (b) The committee decided to retain the ten last tickets.   _____

14. New owners will receive a (a) *60-day*, (b) *60 day* trial period.   _____

15. The time passed (a) *quicker*, (b) *more quickly* than we expected.   _____

16. We offer a (a) *money back*, (b) *money-back* guarantee.   _____

17. Today the financial news is (a) *worse*, (b) *worst* than yesterday.   _____

18. Please don't take his comments (a) *personal*, (b) *personally*.   _____

19. You must check the document (a) *page by page*, (b) *page-by-page*.   _____

20. (a) We try to file only necessary paperwork.
    (b) We only try to file necessary paperwork.   _____

---

1. a (1.17c)   3. b (1.17d)   5. a (1.17d)   7. a (1.17a)   9. b (1.17a)   11. b (1.17f)   13. a (1.17f)
15. b (1.17d)   17. a (1.17a)   19. a (1.17e)

PREPOSITIONS (1.18)

Prepositions are connecting words that join nouns or pronouns to other words in a sentence. The words *about, at, from, in,* and *to* are examples of prepositions.

1.18 Guidelines for Use

a. Include necessary prepositions:

> What type *of* software do you need (not *what type software*)?
> I graduated *from* high school two years ago (not *I graduated high school*).

b. Omit unnecessary prepositions:

> Where is the meeting? (Not *Where is the meeting at?*)
> Both printers work well. (Not *Both of the printers.*)
> Where are you going? (Not *Where are you going to?*)

c. Avoid the overuse of prepositional phrases.

> **Weak:**   We have received your application for credit at our branch in the Fresno area.
> **Improved:**   We have received your Fresno credit application.

d. Repeat the preposition before the second of two related elements:

> Applicants use the résumé effectively by summarizing their most important experiences and *by* relating their education to the jobs sought.

e. Include the second preposition when two prepositions modify a single object:

> George's appreciation *of* and aptitude *for* computers led to a promising career.

CONJUNCTIONS (1.19)

Conjunctions connect words, phrases, and clauses. They act as signals, indicating when a thought is being added, contrasted, or altered. Coordinate conjunctions (such as *and, or, but*) and other words that act as connectors (such as *however, therefore, when, as*) tell the reader or listener in what direction a thought is heading. They're like road signs signaling what's ahead.

1.19 Guidelines for Use

a. Use coordinating conjunctions to connect only sentence elements that are parallel or balanced.

Weak: His report was correct and written in a concise manner.
Improved: His report was correct and concise.

Weak: Management has the capacity to increase fraud, or reduction can be achieved through the policies it adopts.
Improved: Management has the capacity to increase or reduce fraud through the policies it adopts.

b. Do not use the word *like* as a conjunction:

It seems *as if* (not *like*) this day will never end.

c. Avoid using *when* or *where* inappropriately. A common writing fault occurs in sentences with clauses introduced by *is when* and *is where*. Written English ordinarily requires a noun (or a group of words functioning as a noun) following the linking verb *is*. Instead of acting as conjunctions in these constructions, the words *where* and *when* function as adverbs, creating faulty grammatical equations (adverbs cannot complete equations set up by linking verbs). To avoid the problem, revise the sentence, eliminating *is when* or *is where*.

Weak: A bullish market is when prices are rising in the stock market.
Improved: A bullish market is created when prices are rising in the stock market.

Weak: A flowchart is when you make a diagram showing the step-by-step progression of a procedure.
Improved: A flowchart is a diagram showing the step-by-step progression of a procedure.

Weak: Word processing is where you use a computer and software to write.
Improved: Word processing involves the use of a computer and software to write.

A similar faulty construction occurs in the expression *I hate when*. English requires nouns, noun clauses, or pronouns to act as objects of verbs, not adverbs.

Weak: I hate when we're asked to work overtime.
Improved: I hate it when we're asked to work overtime.
Improved: I hate being asked to work overtime.

d. Don't confuse the adverb *then* with the conjunction *than*. *Then* means "at that time"; *than* indicates the second element in a comparison:

We would rather remodel *than* (not *then*) move.
First, the equipment is turned on; *then* (not *than*) the program is loaded.

Review Exercise F—Prepositions and Conjunctions

In the space provided for each item, write *a* or *b* to indicate the sentence that is expressed more effectively. When you finish, compare your responses with those provided. For each item on which you need review, consult the numbered principle shown in parentheses.

1. (a) Do you know where this shipment is being sent?   _____
   (b) Do you know where this shipment is being sent to?
2. (a) She was not aware of nor interested in the company insurance plan.   _____
   (b) She was not aware nor interested in the company insurance plan.
3. (a) Mr. Samuels graduated college last June.   _____
   (b) Mr. Samuels graduated from college last June.
4. (a) "Flextime" is when employees arrive and depart at varying times.   _____
   (b) "Flextime" is a method of scheduling worktime in which employees arrive and depart at varying times.
5. (a) Both employees enjoyed setting their own hours.   _____
   (b) Both of the employees enjoyed setting their own hours.
6. (a) I hate when the tape sticks in my VCR.   _____
   (b) I hate it when the tape sticks in my VCR.
7. (a) What style of typeface should we use?   _____
   (b) What style typeface should we use?
8. (a) Business letters should be concise, correct, and written clearly.   _____
   (b) Business letters should be concise, correct, and clear.
9. (a) Mediation in a labor dispute occurs when a neutral person helps union and management reach an agreement.   _____
   (b) Mediation in a labor dispute is where a neutral person helps union and management reach an agreement.
10. (a) It looks as if the plant will open in early January.   _____
    (b) It looks like the plant will open in early January.
11. (a) We expect to finish up the work soon.   _____
    (b) We expect to finish the work soon.
12. (a) At the beginning of the program in the fall of the year at the central office, we experienced staffing difficulties.   _____
    (b) When the program began last fall, the central office experienced staffing difficulties.
13. (a) Your client may respond by e-mail or a telephone call may be made.   _____
    (b) Your client may respond by e-mail or by telephone.
14. (a) A résumé is when you make a written presentation of your education and experience for a prospective employer.   _____
    (b) A résumé is a written presentation of your education and experience for a prospective employer.

15. (a) Stacy exhibited both an awareness of and talent for developing innovations.
   (b) Stacy exhibited both an awareness and talent for developing innovations.

16. (a) This course is harder then I expected.
   (b) This course is harder than I expected.

17. (a) An ombudsman is an individual hired by management to investigate and resolve employee complaints.
   (b) An ombudsman is when management hires an individual to investigate and resolve employee complaints.

18. (a) I'm uncertain where to take this document to.
   (b) I'm uncertain where to take this document.

19. (a) By including accurate data and by writing clearly, you will produce effective memos.
   (b) By including accurate data and writing clearly, you will produce effective memos.

20. (a) We need computer operators who can load software, monitor networks, and files must be duplicated.
   (b) We need computer operators who can load software, monitor networks, and duplicate files.

1. a (1.18b)   3. b (1.18a)   5. a (1.18b)   7. a (1.18a)   9. a (1.19c)   11. b (1.18b)   13. b (1.19a)
15. a (1.18e)   17. a (1.19c)   19. a (1.18d)

CUMULATIVE EDITING QUIZ 3

Use proofreading marks (see Appendix B) to correct errors in the following sentences. All errors must be corrected to receive credit for the sentence. Check with your instructor for the answers.

1. If Cindy works faster then her, shouldn't Cindy be hired?

2. We felt badly that Mark's home was not chose for the tour.

3. Neither the company nor the workers is pleased at how slow the talks seems to be progressing.

4. Just between you and I, it's better not to take his remarks personal.

5. After completing there floor by floor inventory, managers will deliver there reports to Mr. Quinn and I.

6. If my cell phone was working, Jean and myself could have completed our calls.

7. Powerful software and new hardware allows us to send the newsletter to whomever is currently listed in our database.

8. The eighteen year old girl and her mother was given hot cups of tea after there ordeal.

9. We begun the work two years ago, but personnel and equipment has been especially difficult to obtain.

10. Today's weather is worst then yesterday.

COMMAS 1 (2.01–2.04)

2.01 Series.   Commas are used to separate three or more equal elements (words, phrases, or short clauses) in a series. To ensure separation of the last two elements, careful writers always use a comma before the conjunction in a series:

> Business letters usually contain a dateline, address, salutation, body, and closing. (This series contains words.)

> The job of an ombudsman is to examine employee complaints, resolve disagreements between management and employees, and ensure fair treatment. (This series contains phrases.)

> Trainees complete basic keyboarding tasks, technicians revise complex documents, and editors proofread completed projects. (This series contains short clauses.)

2.02 Direct Address.   Commas are used to set off the names of individuals being addressed:

> Your inquiry, *Mrs. Johnson*, has been referred to me.

> We genuinely hope that we may serve you, *Mr. Lee.*

2.03 Parenthetical Expressions.   Skilled writers use parenthetical words, phrases, and clauses to guide the reader from one thought to the next. When these expressions interrupt the flow of a sentence and are unnecessary for its grammatical completeness, they should be set off with commas. Examples of commonly used parenthetical expressions follow:

all things considered	however	needless to say
as a matter of fact	in addition	nevertheless
as a result	incidentally	no doubt
as a rule	in fact	of course
at the same time	in my opinion	on the contrary
consequently	in the first place	on the other hand
for example	in the meantime	therefore
furthermore	moreover	under the circumstances

> *As a matter of fact*, I wrote to you just yesterday. (Phrase used at the beginning of a sentence.)

> We will, *in the meantime*, send you a replacement order. (Phrase used in the middle of a sentence.)

> Your satisfaction is our first concern, *needless to say.* (Phrase used at the end of a sentence.)

Do not use commas if the expression is necessary for the completeness of the sentence:

> Kimberly had *no doubt* that she would finish the report. (Omit commas because the expression is necessary for the completeness of the sentence.)

2.04 Dates, Addresses, and Geographical Items.   When dates, addresses, and geographical items contain more than one element, the second and succeeding elements are normally set off by commas.

a. Dates:

The conference was held February 2 at our home office. (No comma is needed for one element.)

The conference was held February 2, 2003, at our home office. (Two commas set off the second element.)

The conference was held Tuesday, February 2, 2003, at our home office. (Commas set off the second and third elements.)

In February 2003 the conference was held. (This alternate style omitting commas is acceptable if only the month and year are written.)

b. Addresses:

The letter addressed to Mr. Jim W. Ellman, 600 Via Novella, Agoura, CA 91306, should be sent today. (Commas are used between all elements except the state and zip code, which in this special instance are considered a single unit.)

c. Geographical items:

She moved from Toledo, Ohio, to Champaign, Illinois. (Commas set off the state unless it appears at the end of the sentence, in which case only one comma is used.)

In separating cities from states and days from years, many writers remember the initial comma but forget the final one, as in the examples that follow:

The package from Austin, Texas {,} was lost.

We opened June 1, 2001 {,} and have grown steadily since.

REVIEW EXERCISE G—COMMAS 1

Insert necessary commas in the following sentences. In the space provided write the number of commas that you add. Write C if no commas are needed. When you finish, compare your responses with those provided. For each item on which you need review, consult the numbered principle shown in parentheses.

1. As a rule we do not provide complimentary tickets.
2. You may be certain Mr. Martinez that your policy will be issued immediately.
3. I have no doubt that your calculations are correct.
4. The safety hazard on the contrary can be greatly reduced if workers wear rubber gloves.
5. Every accredited TV newscaster radio broadcaster and newspaper reporter had access to the media room.
6. Deltech's main offices are located in Boulder Colorado and Seattle Washington.
7. The employees who are eligible for promotions are Terry Evelyn Vicki Rosanna and Steve.
8. During the warranty period of course you are protected from any parts or service charges.
9. Many of our customers include architects engineers attorneys and others who are interested in database management programs.
10. I wonder Mrs. Stevens if you would send my letter of recommendation as soon as possible.
11. The new book explains how to choose appropriate legal protection for ideas trade secrets copyrights patents and restrictive covenants.
12. The factory is scheduled to be moved to 2250 North Main Street Ann Arbor Michigan 48107 within two years.

13. You may however prefer to correspond directly with the manufacturer in Hong Kong. _____

14. Are there any alternatives in addition to those that we have already considered? _____

15. The rally has been scheduled for Monday January 12 in the football stadium. _____

16. A check for the full amount will be sent directly to your home Mr. Jefferson. _____

17. Goodstone Tire & Rubber for example recalled 400,000 steelbelted radial tires because some tires failed their rigorous tests. _____

18. Kevin agreed to unlock the office open the mail and check all the equipment in my absence. _____

19. In the meantime thank you for whatever assistance you are able to furnish. _____

20. Research facilities were moved from Austin Texas to Santa Cruz California. _____

1. rule, (2.03) 3. C (2.03) 5. newscaster, radio broadcaster, (2.01) 7. Terry, Evelyn, Vicki, Rosanna, (2.01) 9. architects, engineers, attorneys, (2.01) 11. ideas, trade secrets, copyrights, patents, (2.01) 13. may, however, (2.03) 15. Monday, January 12, (2.04a) 17. Rubber, for example, (2.03) 19. meantime, (2.03)

COMMAS 2 (2.05–2.09)

2.05 Independent Clauses.   An independent clause is a group of words that has a subject and a verb and that could stand as a complete sentence. When two such clauses are joined by *and, or, nor,* or *but*, use a comma before the conjunction:

> We can ship your merchandise July 12, but we must have your payment first.

> Net income before taxes is calculated, and this total is then combined with income from operations.

Notice that each independent clause in the preceding two examples could stand alone as a complete sentence. Do not use a comma unless each group of words is a complete thought (that is, has its own subject and verb).

> Net income before taxes is calculated *and* is then combined with income from operations. (No comma is needed because no subject follows *and*.)

2.06 Dependent Clauses.   Dependent clauses do not make sense by themselves; for their meaning they depend on independent clauses.

a. *Introductory clauses.* When a dependent clause precedes an independent clause, it is followed by a comma. Such clauses are often introduced by *when, if,* and *as*:

> *When your request came,* we responded immediately.

> *As I mentioned earlier,* Mrs. James is the manager.

b. *Terminal clauses.* If a dependent clause falls at the end of a sentence, use a comma only if the dependent clause is an afterthought:

> The meeting has been rescheduled for October 23, *if this date meets with your approval.* (Comma used because dependent clause is an afterthought.)

> We responded immediately *when we received your request.* (No comma is needed.)

c. *Essential versus nonessential clauses.* If a dependent clause provides information that is unneeded for the grammatical completeness of a sentence, use commas to set it off. In determining whether such a clause is essential or nonessential, ask yourself whether the reader needs the information contained in the clause to identify the word it explains:

Our district sales manager, *who just returned from a trip to the Southwest District,* prepared this report. (This construction assumes that there is only one district sales manager. Since the sales manager is clearly identified, the dependent clause is not essential and requires commas.)

The salesperson *who just returned from a trip to the Southwest District* prepared this report. (The dependent clause in this sentence is necessary to identify which salesperson prepared the report. Therefore, use no commas.)

The position of assistant sales manager, *which we discussed with you last week,* is still open. (Careful writers use *which* to introduce nonessential clauses. Commas are also necessary.)

The position *that we discussed with you last week* is still open. (Careful writers use *that* to introduce essential clauses. No commas are used.)

2.07 Phrases. A phrase is a group of related words that lacks both a subject and a verb. A phrase that precedes a main clause is followed by a comma only if the phrase contains a verb form or has five or more words:

Beginning November 1, Worldwide Savings will offer two new combination checking/savings plans. (A comma follows this introductory phrase because the phrase contains the verb form *beginning.*)

To promote their plan, we will conduct an extensive direct mail advertising campaign. (A comma follows this introductory phrase because the phrase contains the verb form *to promote.*)

In a period of only one year, we were able to improve our market share by 30 percent. (A comma follows the introductory phrase—actually two prepositional phrases—because its total length exceeds five words.)

In 2002 our organization installed a multiuser system that could transfer programs easily. (No comma needed after the short introductory phrase.)

2.08 Two or More Adjectives. Use a comma to separate two or more adjectives that equally describe a noun. A good way to test the need for a comma is this: mentally insert the word *and* between the adjectives. If the resulting phrase sounds natural, a comma is used to show the omission of *and*:

We're looking for a *versatile, error-free* operating system. (Use a comma to separate *versatile* and *error-free* because they independently describe *operating system. And* has been omitted.)

Our *experienced, courteous* staff is ready to serve you. (Use a comma to separate *experienced* and *courteous* because they independently describe *staff. And* has been omitted.)

It was difficult to refuse the *sincere young* telephone caller. (No commas are needed between *sincere* and *young* because and has not been omitted.)

2.09 Appositives. Words that rename or explain preceding nouns or pronouns are called *appositives.* An appositive that provides information not essential to the identification of the word it describes should be set off by commas:

James Wilson, *the project director for Sperling's,* worked with our architect. (The appositive, *the project director for Sperling's,* adds nonessential information. Commas set it off.)

Review Exercise H—Commas 2

Insert only necessary commas in the following sentences. In the space provided, indicate the number of commas that you add for each sentence. If a sentence requires no commas, write *C.* When you finish, compare your responses with those provided. For each item on which you need review, consult the numbered principle shown in parentheses.

1. A corporation must be registered in the state in which it does business and it must operate within the laws of that state. _____
2. The manager made a point-by-point explanation of the distribution dilemma and then presented his plan to solve the problem. _____
3. If you will study the cost analysis you will see that our company offers the best system at the lowest price. _____
4. Molly Epperson who amassed the greatest number of sales points was awarded the bonus trip to Hawaii. _____
5. The salesperson who amasses the greatest number of sales points will be awarded the bonus trip to Hawaii. _____
6. To promote goodwill and to generate international trade we are opening offices in the Far East and in Europe. _____
7. On the basis of these findings I recommend that we retain Jane Rada as our counsel. _____
8. Mary Bantle is a dedicated hard-working employee for our company. _____
9. The bright young student who worked for us last summer will be able to return this summer. _____
10. When you return the completed form we will be able to process your application. _____
11. We will be able to process your application when you return the completed form. _____
12. The employees who have been with us over ten years automatically receive additional insurance benefits. _____
13. Knowing that you wanted this merchandise immediately I took the liberty of sending it by Express Parcel Services. _____
14. The central processing unit requires no scheduled maintenance and has a self-test function for reliable performance. _____
15. Foreign competition nearly ruined the American shoe industry but the textile industry remains strong. _____
16. Stacy Wilson our newly promoted office manager has made a number of worthwhile suggestions. _____
17. For the benefit of employees recently hired we are offering a two-hour seminar regarding employee benefit programs. _____
18. Please bring your suggestions and those of Mr. Mason when you attend our meeting next month. _____
19. The meeting has been rescheduled for September 30 if this date meets with your approval. _____
20. Some of the problems that you outline in your recent memo could be rectified through more stringent purchasing procedures. _____

---

1. business, (2.05)   3. analysis, (2.06a)   5. C (2.06c)   7. findings, (2.07)   9. C (2.08)   11. C (2.06b)   13. immediately, (2.07)   15. industry, (2.05)   17. hired, (2.07)   19. September 30, (2.06b)

COMMAS 3 (2.10–2.15)

2.10 Degrees and Abbreviations. Degrees following individuals' names are set off by commas. Abbreviations such as *Jr.* and *Sr.* are also set off by commas unless the individual referred to prefers to omit the commas:

Anne G. Turner, M.B.A., joined the firm.

Michael Migliano, Jr., and Michael Migliano, Sr., work as a team.

Anthony A. Gensler Jr. wrote the report. (The individual referred to prefers to omit commas.)

The abbreviations *Inc.* and *Ltd.* are set off by commas only if a company's legal name has a comma just before this kind of abbreviation. To determine a company's practice, consult its stationery or a directory listing:

Firestone and Blythe, *Inc.*, is based in Canada. (Notice that two commas are used.)

Computers *Inc.* is extending its franchise system. (The company's legal name does not include a comma before *Inc.*)

2.11 Omitted Words.   A comma is used to show the omission of words that are understood:

On Monday we received 15 applications; on Friday, only 3. (Comma shows the omission of *we received.*)

2.12 Contrasting Statements.   Commas are used to set off contrasting or opposing expressions. These expressions are often introduced by such words as *not, never, but,* and *yet*:

The consultant recommended dual-tape storage, *not* floppy-disk storage, for our operations.

Our budget for the year is reduced, *yet* adequate.

The greater the effort, the greater the reward.

If increased emphasis is desired, use dashes instead of commas, as in *Only the sum of $100—not $1,000—was paid on this account.*

2.13 Clarity.   Commas are used to separate words repeated for emphasis. Commas are also used to separate words that may be misread if not separated:

The building is a long, long way from completion.

Whatever is, is right.

No matter what, you know we support you.

2.14 Quotations and Appended Questions
a. A comma is used to separate a short quotation from the rest of a sentence. If the quotation is divided into two parts, two commas are used:

The manager asked, "Shouldn't the managers control the specialists?"

"Not if the specialists," replied Tim, "have unique information."

b. A comma is used to separate a question appended (added) to a statement:

You will confirm the shipment, won't you?

2.15 Comma Overuse.   Do not use commas needlessly. For example, commas should not be inserted merely because you might drop your voice if you were speaking the sentence:

One of the reasons for expanding our East Coast operations is {,} that we anticipate increased sales in that area. (Do not insert a needless comma before a clause.)

I am looking for an article entitled {,} "State-of-the-Art Communications." (Do not insert a needless comma after the word *entitled.*)

A number of food and nonfood items are carried in convenience stores *such as* {,} 7-Eleven and Stop-N-Go. (Do not insert a needless comma after *such as.*)

We have {,} at this time {,} an adequate supply of parts. (Do not insert needless commas around prepositional phrases.)

REVIEW EXERCISE I—COMMAS 3

Insert only necessary commas in the following sentences. Remove unnecessary commas with the delete sign ( ). In the space provided, indicate the number of commas inserted or deleted in each sentence. If a sentence requires no changes, write C. When you finish, compare your responses with those provided. For each item on which you need review, consult the numbered principle shown in parentheses.

1. We expected Charles Bedford not Tiffany Richardson to conduct the audit. _____
2. Brian said "We simply must have a bigger budget to start this project." _____
3. "We simply must have" said Brian "a bigger budget to start this project." _____
4. In August customers opened at least 50 new accounts; in September only about 20. _____
5. You returned the merchandise last month didn't you? _____
6. In short employees will now be expected to contribute more to their own retirement funds. _____
7. The better our advertising and recruiting the stronger our personnel pool will be. _____
8. Mrs. Delgado investigated selling her stocks not her real estate to raise the necessary cash. _____
9. "On the contrary" said Mrs. Mercer "we will continue our present marketing strategies." _____
10. Our company will expand into surprising new areas such as, women's apparel and fast foods. _____
11. What we need is more not fewer suggestions for improvement. _____
12. Randall Clark Esq. and Jonathon Georges M.B.A. joined the firm. _____
13. "America is now entering" said President Saunders "the Age of Information." _____
14. One of the reasons that we are inquiring about the publisher of the software is, that we are concerned about whether that publisher will be in the market five years from now. _____
15. The talk by D. A. Spindler Ph.D. was particularly difficult to follow because of his technical and abstract vocabulary. _____
16. The month before a similar disruption occurred in distribution. _____
17. We are very fortunate to have, at our disposal, the services of excellent professionals. _____
18. No matter what you can count on us for support. _____
19. Mrs. Sandoval was named legislative counsel; Mr. Freeman executive adviser. _____
20. The data you are seeking can be found in an article entitled, "The Fastest Growing Game in Computers." _____

1. Bedford, Richardson, (2.12)   3. have," said Brian, (2.14a)   5. month, (2.14b)   7. recruiting, (2.12)   9. contrary," Mercer, (2.14a)   11. more, not fewer, (2.12)   13. entering," Saunders, (2.14a)   15. Spindler, Ph.D., (2.10)   17. have at our disposal (2.15)   19. Freeman, (2.11)

CUMULATIVE EDITING QUIZ 4

Use proofreading marks (see Appendix B) to correct errors and omissions in the following sentences. All errors must be corrected to receive credit for the sentence. Check with your instructor for the answers.

1. Business documents must be written clear, to ensure that readers comprehend the message quick.

2. Needless to say the safety of our employees have always been most important to the president and I.

3. The Small Business Administration which provide disaster loans are setting up an office in Miami Florida.

4. Many entrepreneurs who want to expand there markets, have choosen to advertise heavy.

5. Our arbitration committee have unanimously agreed on a compromise package but management have been slow to respond.

6. Although the business was founded in the 1970's its real expansion took place in the 1990s.

7. According to the printed contract either the dealer or the distributor are responsible for repair of the product.

8. Next June, Lamont and Jones, Inc., are moving their headquarters to Denton Texas.

9. Our company is looking for intelligent, articulate, young, people who has a desire to grow with an expanding organization.

10. As you are aware each member of the jury were asked to avoid talking about the case.

SEMICOLONS (2.16)

2.16 Independent Clauses, Series, Introductory Expressions

a. *Independent clauses with conjunctive adverbs.* Use a semicolon before a conjunctive adverb that separates two independent clauses. Some of the most common conjunctive adverbs are *therefore, consequently, however,* and *moreover*:

Business messages should sound conversational; *therefore,* familiar words and contractions are often used.

The bank closes its doors at 3 p.m.; *however,* the ATM is open 24 hours a day.

Notice that the word following a semicolon is *not* capitalized (unless, of course, that word is a proper noun).

b. *Independent clauses without conjunctive adverbs.* Use a semicolon to separate closely related independent clauses when no conjunctive adverb is used:

Bond interest payments are tax deductible; dividend payments are not.

Ambient lighting fills the room; task lighting illuminates each workstation.

Use a semicolon in *compound* sentences, not in *complex* sentences:

After one week the paper feeder jammed; we tried different kinds of paper. (Use a semicolon in a compound sentence.)

After one week the paper feeder jammed, although we tried different kinds of paper. (Use a comma in a complex sentence. Do not use a semicolon after *jammed.*)

The semicolon is very effective for joining two closely related thoughts. Don't use it, however, unless the ideas are truly related.

c. *Independent clauses with other commas.* Normally, a comma precedes *and, or,* and *but* when those conjunctions join independent clauses. However, if either clause contains commas, change the comma preceding the conjunction to a semicolon to ensure correct reading:

> If you arrive in time, you may be able to purchase a ticket; but ticket sales close promptly at 8 p.m.

> Our primary concern is financing; and we have discovered, as you warned us, that money sources are quite scarce.

d. *Series with internal commas.* Use semicolons to separate items in a series when one or more of the items contains internal commas:

> Delegates from Miami, Florida; Freeport, Mississippi; and Chatsworth, California, attended the conference.

> The speakers were Kevin Lang, manager, Riko Enterprises; Henry Holtz, vice president, Trendex, Inc.; and Margaret Slater, personnel director, West Coast Productions.

e. *Introductory expressions.* Use a semicolon when an introductory expression such as *namely, for instance, that is,* or *for example* introduces a list following an independent clause:

> Switching to computerized billing are several local companies; namely, Ryson Electronics, Miller Vending Services, and Black Advertising.

> The author of a report should consider many sources; for example, books, periodicals, databases, and newspapers.

COLONS (2.17–2.19)

2.17 Listed Items

a. *With colon.* Use a colon after a complete thought that introduces a formal list of items. A formal list is often preceded by such words and phrases as *these, thus, the following,* and *as follows.* A colon is also used when words and phrases like these are implied but not stated:

> Additional costs in selling a house involve *the following*: title examination fee, title insurance costs, and closing fee. (Use a colon when a complete thought introduces formal list.)

> Collective bargaining focuses on several key issues: cost-of-living adjustments, fringe benefits, job security, and hours of work. (The introduction of the list is implied in the preceding clause.)

b. *Without colons.* Do not use a colon when the list immediately follows a *to be* verb or a preposition:

> The employees who should receive the preliminary plan are James Sears, Monica Spears, and Rose Lopez. (No colon is used after the verb *are*.)

> We expect to consider equipment for Accounting, Legal Services, and Payroll. (No colon is used after the preposition *for*.)

2.18 Quotations.
Use a colon to introduce long one-sentence quotations and quotations of two or more sentences:

> Our consultant said: "This system can support up to 32 users. It can be used for decision support, computer-aided design, and software development operations at the same time."

2.19 Salutations.
Use a colon after the salutation of a business letter:

> Gentlemen: Dear Mrs. Seaman: Dear Jamie:

REVIEW EXERCISE J—SEMICOLONS, COLONS

In the following sentences, add semicolons, colons, and necessary commas. For each sentence indicate the number of punctuation marks that you add. If a sentence requires no punctuation, write C. When you finish, compare your responses with those provided. For each item on which you need review, consult the numbered principle shown in parentheses.

_____ 1. A strike in Canada has delayed shipments of parts consequently our production has fallen behind schedule.

_____ 2. Our branch in Sherman Oaks specializes in industrial real estate our branch in Canoga Park concentrates on residential real estate.

_____ 3. The sedan version of the automobile is available in these colors Olympic red metallic silver and Aztec gold.

_____ 4. If I can assist the new manager please call me however I will be gone from June 10 through June 15.

_____ 5. The individuals who should receive copies of this announcement are Jeff Doogan Alicia Green and Kim Wong.

_____ 6. We would hope of course to send personal letters to all prospective buyers but we have not yet decided just how to do this.

_____ 7. Many of our potential customers are in Southern California therefore our promotional effort will be strongest in that area.

_____ 8. Since the first of the year we have received inquiries from one attorney two accountants and one information systems analyst.

_____ 9. Three dates have been reserved for initial interviews January 15 February 1 and February 12.

_____ 10. Several staff members are near the top of their salary ranges and we must reclassify their jobs.

_____ 11. Several staff members are near the top of their salary ranges we must reclassify their jobs.

_____ 12. Several staff members are near the top of their salary ranges therefore we must reclassify their jobs.

_____ 13. If you open an account within two weeks you will receive a free cookbook moreover your first 500 checks will be imprinted at no cost to you.

_____ 14. Monthly reports from the following departments are missing Legal Department Human Resources Department and Engineering Department.

_____ 15. Monthly reports are missing from the Legal Department Human Resources Department and Engineering Department.

_____ 16. Since you became director of that division sales have tripled therefore I am recommending you for a bonus.

_____ 17. The convention committee is considering Portland Oregon New Orleans Louisiana and Phoenix Arizona.

_____ 18. Several large companies allow employees access to their personnel files namely General Electric Eastman Kodak and Infodata.

_____ 19. Sherry first asked about salary next she inquired about benefits.

_____ 20. Sherry first asked about the salary and she next inquired about benefits.

---

1. parts; consequently, (2.16a)   3. colors: Olympic red, metallic silver, (2.01, 2.17a)   5. Doogan, Alicia Green, (2.01, 2.17b)   7. California; therefore, (2.16a)   9. interviews: January 15, February 1, (2.01, 2.17a)   11. ranges; (2.16b)   13. weeks, cookbook; moreover, (206a, 2.16a)   15. Department, Human Resources Department, (2.01, 2.17b)   17. Portland, Oregon; New Orleans, Louisiana; Phoenix, (2.16d)   19. salary; (2.16b)

APOSTROPHES (2.20–2.22)

2.20 Basic Rule.   The apostrophe is used to show ownership, origin, authorship, or measurement.

Ownership:	We are looking for *Brian's keys.*
Origin:	At the *president's* suggestion, we doubled the order.
Authorship:	The *accountant's annual report* was questioned.
Measurement:	In *two years' time* we expect to reach our goal.

a. *Ownership words not ending in* s. To place the apostrophe correctly, you must first determine whether the ownership word ends in an *s* sound. If it does not, add an apostrophe and an *s* to the ownership word. The following examples show ownership words that do not end in an *s* sound:

the employee's file	(the file of a single employee)
a member's address	(the address of a single member)
a year's time	(the time of a single year)
a month's notice	(notice of a single month)
the company's building	(the building of a single company)

b. *Ownership words ending in* s. If the ownership word does end in an *s* sound, usually add only an apostrophe:

several employees' files	(files of several employees)
ten members' addresses	(addresses of ten members)
five years' time	(time of five years)
several months' notice	(notice of several months)
many companies' buildings	(buildings of many companies)

A few singular nouns that end in *s* are pronounced with an extra syllable when they become possessive. To these words, add *'s*.

my boss's desk
the waitress's table
the actress's costume

Use no apostrophe if a noun is merely plural, not possessive:

All the sales representatives, as well as the secretaries and managers, had their names and telephone numbers listed in the directory.

2.21 Names.   The writer may choose either traditional or popular style in making singular names that end in an *s* sound possessive. The traditional style uses the apostrophe plus an *s*, while the popular style uses just the apostrophe. Note that only with singular names ending in an *s* sound does this option exist.

Traditional style	Popular style
Russ's computer	Russ' computer
Mr. Jones's car	Mr. Jones' car
Mrs. Morris's desk	Mrs. Morris' desk
Ms. Horowitz's job	Ms. Horowitz' job

The possessive form of plural names is consistent: the Joneses' car, the Horowitzes' home, the Lopezes' daughter.

2.22 Gerunds.   Use *'s* to make a noun possessive when it precedes a gerund, a verb form used as a noun:

Mr. Smith's smoking prompted a new office policy. (*Mr. Smith* is possessive because it modifies the gerund *smoking*.)

It was Betsy's careful proofreading that revealed the discrepancy.

REVIEW EXERCISE K—APOSTROPHES

Insert necessary apostrophes in the following sentences. In the space provided for each sentence, indicate the number of apostrophes that you added. If none were added, write C. When you finish, compare your responses with those provided. For each item on which you need review, consult the numbered principle shown in parentheses.

1. Your account should have been credited with six months interest.
2. If you go to the third floor, you will find Mr. Londons office.
3. All the employees personnel folders must be updated.
4. In a little over a years time, that firm was able to double its sales.
5. The Harrises daughter lived in Florida for two years.
6. An inventors patent protects his or her invention for seventeen years.
7. Both companies headquarters will be moved within the next six months.
8. That position requires at least two years experience.
9. Some of their assets could be liquidated; therefore, a few of the creditors were satisfied.
10. All secretaries workstations were equipped with Internet access.
11. The package of electronics parts arrived safely despite two weeks delay.
12. Many nurses believe that nurses notes are not admissable evidence.
13. According to Mr. Cortez [or Cortezs] latest proposal, all employees would receive an additional holiday.
14. Many of our members names and addresses must be checked.
15. His supervisor frequently had to correct Jacks financial reports.
16. We believe that this firms service is much better than that firms.
17. Mr. Jackson estimated that he spent a years profits in reorganizing his staff.
18. After paying six months rent, we were given a receipt.
19. The contract is not valid without Mrs. Harris [or Harriss] signature.
20. It was Mr. Smiths signing of the contract that made us happy.

1. months' (2.20b)   3. employees' (2.20b)   5. Harrises' (2.21)   7. companies' (2.20b)   9. C (2.20b)   11. weeks' (2.20b)   13. Cortez' or Cortez's (2.21)   15. Jack's (2.21)   17. year's (2.20a)   19. Harris' or Harris's (2.21)

CUMULATIVE EDITING QUIZ 5

Use proofreading marks (see Appendix B) to correct errors and omissions in the following sentences. All errors must be corrected to receive credit for the sentence. Check with your instructor for the answers.

1. The three C's of credit are the following character capacity and capital.

2. We hope that we will not have to sell the property however that may be our only option.

3. As soon as the supervisor and her can check this weeks sales they will place an order.

4. Any of the auditors are authorized to proceed with an independent action however only the CEO can alter the councils directives.

5. Although reluctant technicians sometimes must demonstrate there computer software skills.

6. On April 6 2004 we opened an innovative fully-equipped fitness center.

7. A list of maintenance procedures and recommendations are in the owners manual.

8. The Morrises son lived in Flint Michigan however there daughter lived in Albany New York.

9. Employment interviews were held in Dallas Texas Miami Florida and Chicago Illinois.

10. Mr. Lees determination courage and sincerity could not be denied however his methods was often questioned.

OTHER PUNCTUATION (2.23–2.29)

2.23 Periods

a. *Ends of sentences.* Use a period at the end of a statement, command, indirect question, or polite request. Although a polite request may have the same structure as a question, it ends with a period:

Corporate legal departments demand precise skills from their workforce. (End a statement with a period.)

Get the latest data by reading current periodicals. (End a command with a period.)

Mr. Rand wondered whether we had sent any follow-up literature. (End an indirect question with a period.)

Would you please reexamine my account and determine the current balance. (A polite request suggests an action rather than a verbal response.)

b. *Abbreviations and initials.* Use periods after initials and after many abbreviations.

R. M. Johnson	c.o.d.	Ms.
M.D.	a.m.	Mr.
Inc.	i.e.	Mrs.

Use just one period when an abbreviation falls at the end of a sentence:

Guests began arriving at 5:30 p.m.

2.24 Question Marks. Direct questions are followed by question marks:

Did you send your proposal to Datatronix, Inc.?

Statements with questions added are punctuated with question marks.

We have completed the proposal, haven't we?

2.25 Exclamation Points. Use an exclamation point after a word, phrase, or clause expressing strong emotion. In business writing, however, exclamation points should be used sparingly:

Incredible! Every terminal is down.

2.26 Dashes. The dash (constructed at a keyboard by striking the hyphen key twice in succession) is a legitimate and effective mark of punctuation when used according to accepted conventions. As an emphatic punctuation mark, however, the dash loses effectiveness when overused.

a. *Parenthetical elements.* Within a sentence a parenthetical element is usually set off by commas. If, however, the parenthetical element itself contains internal commas, use dashes (or parentheses) to set it off:

Three top salespeople—Tom Judkins, Tim Templeton, and Mary Yashimoto—received bonuses.

b. *Sentence interruptions.* Use a dash to show an interruption or abrupt change of thought:

News of the dramatic merger—no one believed it at first—shook the financial world.

Ship the materials Monday—no, we must have them sooner.

Sentences with abrupt changes of thought or with appended afterthoughts can usually be improved through rewriting.

c. *Summarizing statements.* Use a dash (not a colon) to separate an introductory list from a summarizing statement:

Sorting, merging, and computing—these are tasks that our data processing programs must perform.

2.27 Parentheses. One means of setting off nonessential sentence elements involves the use of parentheses. Nonessential sentence elements may be punctuated in one of three ways: (1) with commas, to make the lightest possible break in the normal flow of a sentence; (2) with dashes, to emphasize the enclosed material; and (3) with parentheses, to deemphasize the enclosed material. Parentheses are frequently used to punctuate sentences with interpolated directions, explanations, questions, and references:

The cost analysis (which appears on page 8 of the report) indicates that the copy machine should be leased.

Units are lightweight (approximately 13 oz.) and come with a leather case and operating instructions.

The IBM laser printer (have you heard about it?) will be demonstrated for us next week.

A parenthetical sentence that is not imbedded within another sentence should be capitalized and punctuated with end punctuation:

The Model 20 has stronger construction. (You may order a Model 20 brochure by circling 304 on the reader service card.)

2.28 Quotation Marks

a. *Direct quotations.* Use double quotation marks to enclose the exact words of a speaker or writer:

"Keep in mind," Mrs. Frank said, "that you'll have to justify the cost of networking our office."

The boss said that automation was inevitable. (No quotation marks are needed because the exact words are not quoted.)

b. *Quotations within quotations.* Use single quotation marks (apostrophes on the keyboard) to enclose quoted passages within quoted passages:

In her speech, Mrs. Deckman remarked, "I believe it was the poet Robert Frost who said, 'All the fun's in how you say a thing.' "

c. *Short expressions.* Slang, words used in a special sense, and words following *stamped* or *marked* are often enclosed within quotation marks:

Jeffrey described the damaged shipment as "gross." (Quotation marks enclose slang.)

Students often have trouble spelling the word "separate." (Quotation marks enclose words used in a special sense.)

Grammar/Mechanics Handbook

Jobs were divided into two categories: most stressful and least stressful. The jobs in the "most stressful" list involved high risk or responsibility. (Quotation marks enclose words used in a special sense.)

The envelope marked "Confidential" was put aside. (Quotation marks enclose words following *marked.*)

In the four preceding sentences, the words enclosed within quotation marks can be set in italics, if italics are available.

d. *Definitions.* Double quotation marks are used to enclose definitions. The word or expression being defined should be underscored or set in italics:

The term *penetration pricing* is defined as "the practice of introducing a product to the market at a low price."

e. *Titles.* Use double quotation marks to enclose titles of literary and artistic works, such as magazine and newspaper articles, chapters of books, movies, television shows, poems, lectures, and songs. Names of major publications—such as books, magazines, pamphlets, and newspapers—are set in italics (underscored) or typed in capital letters.

Particularly helpful was the chapter in Smith's EFFECTIVE WRITING TECHNIQUES entitled "Right Brain, Write On!"

In the Los Angeles Times appeared John's article, "E-Mail Blunders"; however, we could not locate it in a local library.

f. *Additional considerations.* In this country periods and commas are always placed inside closing quotation marks. Semicolons and colons, on the other hand, are always placed outside quotation marks:

Mrs. James said, "I could not find the article entitled 'Cell Phone Etiquette.' "

The president asked for "absolute security": all written messages were to be destroyed.

Question marks and exclamation points may go inside or outside closing quotation marks, as determined by the form of the quotation:

Sales Manager Martin said, "Who placed the order?" (The quotation is a question.)

When did the sales manager say, "Who placed the order?" (Both the incorporating sentence and the quotation are questions.)

Did the sales manager say, "Ryan placed the order"? (The incorporating sentence asks question; the quotation does not.)

"In the future," shouted Bob, "ask me first!" (The quotation is an exclamation.)

2.29 Brackets.   Within quotations, brackets are used by the quoting writer to enclose his or her own inserted remarks. Such remarks may be corrective, illustrative, or explanatory:

Mrs. Cardillo said, "OSHA [Occupational Safety and Health Administration] has been one of the most widely criticized agencies of the federal government."

REVIEW EXERCISE L—OTHER PUNCTUATION

Insert necessary punctuation in the following sentences. In the space provided for each item, indicate the number of punctuation marks that you added. Count sets of parentheses and dashes as two marks. Emphasis or deemphasis will be indicated for some parenthetical elements. When you finish, compare your responses with those provided. For each item on which you need review, consult the numbered principle shown in parentheses.

_____ 1. Will you please stop payment on my Check No. 233

_____ 2. (Emphasize.) Your order of October 16 will be on its way you have my word by October 20.

_____ 3. Mr Sirakides Mrs Sylvester, and Miss Sanchez have not yet responded.

_____ 4. Mrs Franklin asked whether the order had been sent cod

_____ 5. Interviews have been scheduled for 3:15 pm, 4 pm, and 4:45 pm

_____ 6. (Deemphasize.) Three knowledgeable individuals the plant manager, the construction engineer, and the construction supervisor all expressed concern about soil settlement.

_____ 7. Fantastic The value of our stock just rose 10 points on the stock market exchange

_____ 8. The word de facto means exercising power as if legally constituted.

_____ 9. (Deemphasize.) Although the appliance now comes in limited colors brown, beige, and ivory, we expect to see new colors available in the next production run.

_____ 10. Was it the manager who said "What can't be altered must be endured

_____ 11. The stock market went bonkers over the news of the takeover.

_____ 12. Because the envelope was marked Personal, we did not open it.

_____ 13. Price, service, and reliability these are our prime considerations in equipment selection.

_____ 14. The lettercarrier said Would you believe that this package was marked Fragile

_____ 15. (Emphasize.) Three branch managers Carmen Lopez, Stan Meyers, and Ivan Sergo will be promoted.

_____ 16. (Deemphasize.) The difference between portable and transportable computers see Figure 4 for weight comparisons may be considerable.

_____ 17. All the folders marked Current Files should be sent to Human Resources.

_____ 18. I am trying to find the edition of *Newsweek* that carried an article entitled The Future Without Shock

_____ 19. Martin Simon MD and Gail Nemire RN were hired by Healthnet, Inc

_____ 20. The computer salesperson said This innovative, state-of-the-art laptop sells for a fraction of the cost of big-name computers.

---

1. 233. (2.23a) 3. Mr. Mrs. responded. (2.23a, 2.23b) 5. p.m. p.m. p.m. (2.23b) 7. Fantastic! exchange! (2.25) 9. (brown ivory) (2.27) 11. "bonkers" (2.28c) 13. reliability— (2.26c) 15. managers— Sergo— (2.26a) 17. "Current Files" (2.28c) 19. Simon, M.D., Nemire, R.N., Inc. (2.23b)

CUMULATIVE EDITING QUIZ 6

Use proofreading marks (see Appendix B) to correct errors and omissions in the following sentences. All errors must be corrected to receive credit for the sentence. Check with your instructor for the answers.

1. Although the envelope was marked Confidential the vice presidents secretary thought it should be opened.

2. Would you please send my order c.o.d?

3. To be eligible for an apartment you must pay two months rent in advance.

4. We wanted to use Russ computer, but forgot to ask for permission.

5. Wasnt it Jeff Song not Eileen Lee who requested a 14 day leave.

6. Miss. Judith L. Beam is the employee who the employees council elected as their representative.

7. The Evening Post Dispatch our local newspaper featured an article entitled The Worlds Most Expensive Memo.

8. As soon as my manager or myself can verify Ricks totals we will call you, in the meantime you must continue to disburse funds.

9. Just inside the entrance, is the receptionists desk and a complete directory of all departments'.

10. Exports from small companys has increased thereby affecting this countrys trade balance positively.

STYLE AND USAGE

CAPITALIZATION (3.01–3.16)

Capitalization is used to distinguish important words. However, writers are not free to capitalize all words they consider important. Rules or guidelines governing capitalization style have been established through custom and use. Mastering these guidelines will make your writing more readable and more comprehensible.

3.01 Proper Nouns. Capitalize proper nouns, including the *specific* names of persons, places, schools, streets, parks, buildings, religions, holidays, months, agreements, programs, services, and so forth. Do not capitalize common nouns that make only *general* references.

Proper nouns	Common nouns
Michael DeNiro	a salesperson in electronics
Germany, Japan	major trading partners of the United States
El Camino College	a community college
Sam Houston Park	a park in the city
Phoenix Room, Statler Inn	a meeting room in the hotel
Catholic, Presbyterian	two religions
Memorial Day, New Year's Day	two holidays
Express Mail	a special package delivery service
George Washington Bridge	a bridge
Consumer Product Safety Act	a law to protect consumers
Greater Orlando Chamber of Commerce	a chamber of commerce
Will Rogers World Airport	a municipal airport

3.02 Proper Adjectives. Capitalize most adjectives that are derived from proper nouns:

Greek symbol	British thermal unit
Roman numeral	Norwegian ship
Xerox copy	Hispanic markets

Do not capitalize the few adjectives that, although originally derived from proper nouns, have become common adjectives through usage. Consult your dictionary when in doubt:

manila folder	diesel engine
india ink	china dishes

3.03 Geographic Locations.

Capitalize the names of *specific* places such as cities, states, mountains, valleys, lakes, rivers, oceans, and geographic regions:

New York City
Allegheny Mountains
San Fernando Valley
the East Coast

Great Salt Lake
Pacific Ocean
Delaware Bay
the Pacific Northwest

3.04 Organization Names.

Capitalize the principal words in the names of all business, civic, educational, governmental, labor, military, philanthropic, political, professional, religious, and social organizations:

Inland Steel Company
*The Wall Street Journal**
New York Stock Exchange
United Way
Commission to Restore the Statue
  of Liberty

Board of Directors, Midwest Bank
San Antonio Museum of Art
Securities and Exchange Commission
National Association of Letter Carriers
Association of Information Systems
  Professionals

3.05 Academic Courses and Degrees.

Capitalize particular academic degrees and course titles. Do not capitalize references to general academic degrees and subject areas:

Professor Bernadette Ordian, *Ph.D.*, will teach *Accounting* 221 next fall.

Mrs. Snyder, who holds *bachelor's* and *master's degrees*, teaches *marketing* classes.

Jim enrolled in classes in *history, business English,* and *management.*

3.06 Personal and Business Titles

a. Capitalize personal and business titles when they precede names:

Vice President Ames
Board Chairman Frazier
Governor G. W. Thurmond
Professor McLean

Uncle Edward
Councilman Herbert
Sales Manager Klein
Dr. Samuel Washington

b. Capitalize titles in addresses, salutations, and closing lines:

Mr. Juan deSanto
Director of Purchasing
Space Systems, Inc.
Boxborough, MA 01719

Very truly yours,

Clara J. Smith
Supervisor, Marketing

c. Generally, do not capitalize titles of high government rank or religious office when they stand alone or follow a person's name in running text.

The president conferred with the joint chiefs of staff and many senators.

Meeting with the chief justice of the Supreme Court were the senator from Ohio and the mayor of Cleveland.

Only the cardinal from Chicago had an audience with the pope.

d. Do not capitalize most common titles following names:

The speech was delivered by Robert Lynch, *president*, South-Western Publishing.

Lois Herndon, *chief executive officer*, signed the order.

Note: Capitalize *the* only when it is part of the official name of an organization, as printed on the organization's stationery.

e. Do not capitalize common titles appearing alone:

Please speak to the *supervisor* or to the *office manager*.

Neither the *president* nor the *vice president* was asked.

However, when the title of an official appears in that organization's minutes, bylaws, or other official document, it may be capitalized.

f. Do not capitalize titles when they are followed by appositives naming specific individuals:

We must consult our *director of research*, Ronald E. West, before responding.

g. Do not capitalize family titles used with possessive pronouns:

my mother   our aunt   your father   his cousin

h. Capitalize titles of close relatives used without pronouns:

Both *Mother* and *Father* must sign the contract.

3.07 Numbered and Lettered Items.   Capitalize nouns followed by numbers or letters (except in page, paragraph, line, and verse references):

Flight 34, Gate 12	Plan No. 2
Volume I, Part 3	Warehouse 33-A
Invoice No. 55489	Figure 8.3
Model A5673	Serial No. C22865404-2
State Highway 10	page 6, line 5

3.08 Points of the Compass.   Capitalize *north, south, east, west,* and their derivatives when they represent *specific* geographical regions. Do not capitalize the points of the compass when they are used in directions or in general references.

Specific regions	**General references**
from the South	heading north on the highway
living in the Midwest	west of the city
Easterners, Southerners	western Nevada, southern Indiana
going to the Middle East	the northern part of the United States
from the East Coast	the east side of the street

3.09 Departments, Divisions, and Committees.   Capitalize the names of departments, divisions, or committees within your own organization. Outside your organization capitalize only *specific* department, division, or committee names:

The inquiry was addressed to the *Legal Department* in our *Consumer Products Division*.

John was appointed to the *Employee Benefits Committee*.

Send your résumé to their *human resources division*.

A *planning committee* will be named shortly.

3.10 Governmental Terms.   Do not capitalize the words *federal, government, nation,* or *state* unless they are part of a specific title:

Unless *federal* support can be secured, the *state* project will be abandoned.

The *Federal Deposit Insurance Corporation* protects depositors from bank failure.

3.11 Product Names.   Capitalize product names only when they refer to trademarked items. Except in advertising, common names following manufacturers' names are not capitalized:

Magic Marker	Dell computer
Kleenex tissues	Swingline stapler
Q-tips	3M diskettes
Levi 501 jeans	Sony dictation machine
DuPont Teflon	Canon camera

3.12 Literary Titles. Capitalize the principal words in the titles of books, magazines, newspapers, articles, movies, plays, songs, poems, and reports. Do *not* capitalize articles (*a, an, the*), short conjunctions (*and, but, or, nor*), and prepositions of fewer than four letters (*in, to, by, for,* etc.) unless they begin or end the title:

Jackson's *What Job Is for You?* (Capitalize book titles.)

Gant's "Software for the Executive Suite" (Capitalize principal words in article titles.)

"Performance Standards to Go By" (Capitalize article titles.)

"The Improvement of Fuel Economy With Alternative Motors" (Capitalize report titles.)

3.13 Beginning Words. In addition to capitalizing the first word of a complete sentence, capitalize the first word in a quoted sentence, independent phrase, item in an enumerated list, and formal rule or principle following a colon:

The business manager said, "*All* purchases must have requisitions." (Capitalize first word in a quoted sentence.)

Yes, if you agree. (Capitalize an independent phrase.)

Some of the duties of the position are as follows:
1. *Editing* and formatting Word files
2. *Receiving* and routing telephone calls
3. *Verifying* records, reports, and applications (Capitalize items in an enumerated list.)

One rule has been established through the company: *No* smoking is allowed in open offices. (Capitalize a rule following a colon.)

3.14 Celestial Bodies. Capitalize the names of celestial bodies such as *Mars, Saturn,* and *Neptune.* Do not capitalize the terms *earth, sun,* or *moon* unless they appear in a context with other celestial bodies:

Where on *earth* did you find that manual typewriter?

Venus and *Mars* are the closest planets to *Earth.*

3.15 Ethnic References. Capitalize terms that refer to a particular culture, language, or race:

Oriental	Hebrew
Caucasian	Indian
Latino	Japanese
Persian	Judeo-Christian

3.16 Seasons. Do not capitalize seasons:

In the *fall* it appeared that *winter* and *spring* sales would increase.

REVIEW EXERCISE M—CAPITALIZATION

In the following sentences correct any errors that you find in capitalization. Circle any lowercase letter that should be changed to a capital letter. Draw a slash

(/) through a capital letter that you wish to change to a lowercase letter. In the space provided, indicate the total number of changes you have made in each sentence. If you make no changes, write *0*. When you finish, compare your responses with those provided. For each item on which you need review, consult the numbered principle shown in parentheses.

Example   Bill McAdams, currently ~~A~~ssistant ~~M~~anager in our Personnel ~~D~~epartment, will be promoted to ~~M~~anager of the Employee Services ~~D~~ivision.   5 _____

1. The social security act, passed in 1935, established the present system of social security.   _____
2. Our company will soon be moving its operations to the west coast.   _____
3. Marilyn Hunter, m.b.a., received her bachelor's degree from Ohio university in athens.   _____
4. The President of Datatronics, Inc., delivered a speech entitled "Taking off into the future."   _____
5. Please ask your Aunt and your Uncle if they will come to the Attorney's office at 5 p.m.   _____
6. Your reservations are for flight 32 on american airlines leaving from gate 14 at 2:35 p.m.   _____
7. Once we establish an organizing committee, arrangements can be made to rent holmby hall.   _____
8. Bob was enrolled in history, spanish, business communications, and physical education courses.   _____
9. Either the President or the Vice President of the company will make the decision about purchasing xerox copiers.   _____
10. Rules for hiring and firing Employees are given on page 7, line 24, of the Contract.   _____
11. Some individuals feel that american companies do not have the sense of loyalty to their employees that japanese companies do.   _____
12. Where on Earth can we find better workers than Robots?   _____
13. The secretary of state said, "we must protect our domestic economy from Foreign competition."   _____
14. After crossing the sunshine skyway bridge, we drove to Southern Florida for our vacation.   _____
15. All marketing representatives of our company will meet in the empire room of the red lion motor inn.   _____
16. Richard Elkins, ph.d., has been named director of research for spaceage strategies, inc.   _____
17. The special keyboard for the IBM Computer must contain greek symbols for Engineering equations.   _____
18. After she received a master's degree in electrical engineering, Joanne Dudley was hired to work in our product development department.   _____
19. In the Fall our organization will move its corporate headquarters to the franklin building in downtown los angeles.   _____
20. Dean Amador has one cardinal rule: always be punctual.   _____

1. Social Security Act (3.01)   3. M.B.A.   University   Athens (3.01, 3.05)   5. aunt   uncle   attorney's (3.06e, 3.06g)   7. Holmby Hall (3.01)   9. president   vice president   Xerox (3.06e, 3.11)   11. American   Japanese (3.02)   13. We   foreign (3.10, 3.13)   15. Empire Room   Red Lion Motor Inn (3.01)   17. computer   Greek   engineering (3.01, 3.02, 3.11)   19. fall   Franklin Building   Los Angeles (3.01, 3.03, 3.16)

Use proofreading marks (see Appendix B) to correct errors and omissions in the following sentences. All errors must be corrected to receive credit for the sentence. Check with your instructor for the answers.

1. The Manager thinks that you attending the three day seminar is a good idea, however we must find a replacement.

2. We heard that professor watson invited edward peters, president of micropro, inc. to speak to our business law class.

3. Carla Jones a new systems programmer in our accounting department will start monday.

4. After year's of downsizing and restructuring the u.s. has now become one of the worlds most competitive producers.

5. When our company specialized in asian imports our main office was on the west coast.

6. Company's such as amway discovered that there unique door to door selling methods was very successful in japan.

7. If you had given your sony camera to she or I before you got on the roller coaster it might have stayed dry.

8. Tracy recently finished a bachelors degree in accounting, consequently she is submitting many résumé's to companys across the country.

9. The Lopezs moved from San Antonio Texas to Urbana Illinois when mr lopez enrolled at the university of illinois.

10. When we open our office in montréal we will need employees whom are fluent in english and french.

NUMBER STYLE (4.01–4.13)

Usage and custom determine whether numbers are expressed in the form of figures (for example, *5, 9*) or in the form of words (for example, *five, nine*). Numbers expressed as figures are shorter and more easily understood, yet numbers expressed as words are necessary in certain instances. The following guidelines are observed in expressing numbers in written sentences. Numbers that appear on business forms—such as invoices, monthly statements, and purchase orders—are always expressed as figures.

4.01 General Rules

a. The numbers *one* through *ten* are generally written as words. Numbers above *ten* are written as figures:

The bank had a total of *nine* branch offices in *three* suburbs.

All 58 employees received benefits in the *three* categories shown.

A shipment of *45,000* light bulbs was sent from *two* warehouses.

b. Numbers that begin sentences are written as words. If a number beginning a sentence involves more than two words, however, the sentence should be written so that the number does not fall at the beginning.

Fifteen different options were available in the annuity programs.

A total of 156 companies participated in the promotion (not *One hundred fifty-six companies participated in the promotion*).

4.02 Money. Sums of money $1 or greater are expressed as figures. If a sum is a whole dollar amount, omit the decimal and zeros (whether or not the amount appears in a sentence with additional fractional dollar amounts):

We budgeted *$30* for diskettes, but the actual cost was *$37.96*.

On the invoice were items for *$6.10, $8, $33.95,* and *$75*.

Sums less than $1 are written as figures that are followed by the word *cents*:

By shopping carefully, we can save *15 cents* per diskette.

4.03 Dates. In dates, numbers that appear after the name of the month are written as cardinal figures (*1, 2, 3,* etc.). Those that stand alone or appear before the name of a month are written as ordinal figures (*1st, 2d, 3d,** etc.):

The Personnel Practices Committee will meet *May 7*.

On the *5th* day of February and again on the *25th*, we placed orders.

In domestic business documents, dates generally take the following form: *January 4, 2004*. An alternative form, used primarily in military and foreign correspondence, begins with the day of the month and omits the comma: *4 January 2004*.

4.04 Clock Time. Figures are used when clock time is expressed with *a.m.* or *p.m.* Omit the colon and zeros in referring to whole hours. When exact clock time is expressed with the contraction *o'clock*, either figures or words may be used:

Mail deliveries are made at *11 a.m.* and *3:30 p.m.*

At *four* (or *4*) *o'clock* employees begin to leave.

4.05 Addresses and Telephone Numbers

a. Except for the number *one*, house numbers are expressed in figures:

540 Elm Street   17802 Washington Avenue
One Colorado Boulevard 2 Highland Street

b. Street names containing numbers *ten* or lower are written entirely as words. For street names involving numbers greater than *ten*, figures are used:

330 Third Street   3440 Seventh Avenue
6945 East 32 Avenue   4903 West 103 Street

If no compass direction (*North, South, East, West*) separates a house number from a street number, the street number is expressed in ordinal form (*-st, -d, -th*).

256 42d Street   1390 11th Avenue

c. Telephone numbers are expressed with figures. When used, the area code is placed in parentheses preceding the telephone number:

Please call us at *(818) 347-0551* to place an order.
Mr. Sims asked you to call *(619) 554-8923*, Ext. 245, after 10 a.m.

Note: Some writers today are using the more efficient *2d* and *3d* instead of *2nd* and *3rd*.

4.06 Related Numbers. Numbers are related when they refer to similar items in a category within the same reference. All related numbers should be expressed as the largest number is expressed. Thus if the largest number is greater than *ten*, all the numbers should be expressed in figures:

Only *5* of the original *25* applicants completed the processing. (Related numbers require figures.)

The *two* plans affected *34* employees working in *three* sites. (Unrelated numbers use figures and words.)

Getty Oil operated *86* rigs, of which *6* were rented. (Related numbers require figures.)

The company hired *three* accountants, *one* customer service representative, and *nine* sales representatives. (Related numbers under ten use words.)

4.07 Consecutive Numbers. When two numbers appear consecutively and both modify a following noun, generally express the first number in words and the second in figures. If, however, the first number cannot be expressed in one or two words, place it in figures also (*120 37-cent* stamps). Do not use commas to separate the figures.

Historians divided the era into *four 25-year* periods. (Use word form for the first number and figure form for the second.)

We ordered *ten 30-page* color brochures. (Use word form for the first number and figure form for the second.)

Did the manager request *150 100-watt* bulbs? (Use figure form for the first number since it would require more than two words.)

4.08 Periods of Time. Periods of time are generally expressed in word form. However, figures may be used to emphasize business concepts such as discount rates, interest rates, warranty periods, credit terms, loan or contract periods, and payment terms:

This business was incorporated over *fifty* years ago. (Use words for a period of time.)

Any purchaser may cancel a contract within *72* hours. (Use figures to explain a business concept.)

The warranty period is *5* years. (Use figures for a business concept.)

Cash discounts are given for payment within *30* days. (Use figures for a business concept.)

4.09 Ages. Ages are generally expressed in word form unless the age appears immediately after a name or is expressed in exact years and months:

At the age of *twenty-one*, Elizabeth inherited the business.

Wanda Tharp, *37*, was named acting president.

At the age of *4 years and 7 months*, the child was adopted.

4.10 Round Numbers. Round numbers are approximations. They may be expressed in word or figure form, although figure form is shorter and easier to comprehend:

About *600* (or *six hundred*) stock options were sold.

It is estimated that *1,000* (or *one thousand*) people will attend.

For ease of reading, round numbers in the millions or billions should be expressed with a combination of figures and words:

At least *1.5 million* readers subscribe to the ten top magazines.

Deposits in money market accounts totaled more than *$115 billion*.

4.11 Weights and Measurements. Weights and measurements are expressed with figures:

The new deposit slip measures *2* by *6 inches*.

Her new suitcase weighed only *2 pounds 4 ounces*.

Toledo is *60 miles* from Detroit.

4.12 Fractions. Simple fractions are expressed as words. Complex fractions may be written either as figures or as a combination of figures and words:

Over *two thirds* of the stockholders voted.

This microcomputer will execute the command in *1 millionth* of a second. (Combination of words and numbers is easier to comprehend.)

She purchased a *one-fifth* share in the business.*

4.13 Percentages and Decimals. Percentages are expressed with figures that are followed by the word *percent*. The percent sign (%) is used only on business forms or in statistical presentations:

We had hoped for a *7 percent* interest rate, but we received a loan at *8 percent*.

Over *50 percent* of the residents supported the plan.

Decimals are expressed with figures. If a decimal expression does not contain a whole number (an integer) and does not begin with a zero, a zero should be placed before the decimal point:

The actuarial charts show that *1.74* out of 1,000 people will die in any given year.

Inspector Norris found the setting to be *.005* inch off. (Decimal begins with a zero and does not require a zero before the decimal point.)

Considerable savings will accrue if the unit production cost is reduced *0.1* percent. (A zero is placed before a decimal that neither contains a whole number nor begins with a zero).

Quick Chart—Expression of Numbers

Use Words	**Use Figures**
Numbers *ten* and under	Numbers *11* and over
Numbers at beginning of sentence	Money
Periods of time	Dates
Ages	Addresses and telephone numbers
Fractions	Weights and measurements
	Percentages and decimals

REVIEW EXERCISE N—NUMBER STYLE

Circle *a* or *b* to indicate the preferred number style. Assume that these numbers appear in business correspondence. When you finish, compare your responses

---

Note: Fractions used as adjectives require hyphens.

with those provided. For each item on which you need review, consult the numbered principle shown in parentheses.

1. (a) 2 alternatives   (b) two alternatives
2. (a) Seventh Avenue   (b) 7th Avenue
3. (a) sixty sales reps   (b) 60 sales reps
4. (a) November ninth   (b) November 9
5. (a) forty dollars   (b) $40
6. (a) on the 23d of May   (b) on the twenty-third of May
7. (a) at 2:00 p.m.   (b) at 2 p.m.
8. (a) 4 two-hundred-page books   (b) four 200-page books
9. (a) at least 15 years ago   (b) at least fifteen years ago
10. (a) 1,000,000 viewers   (b) 1 million viewers
11. (a) twelve cents   (b) 12 cents
12. (a) a sixty-day warranty   (b) a 60-day warranty
13. (a) ten percent interest rate   (b) 10 percent interest rate
14. (a) 4/5 of the voters   (b) four fifths of the voters
15. (a) the rug measures four by six feet   (b) the rug measures 4 by 6 feet
16. (a) about five hundred people attended   (b) about 500 people attended
17. (a) at eight o'clock   (b) at 8 o'clock
18. (a) located at 1 Wilshire Boulevard   (b) located at One Wilshire Boulevard
19. (a) three computers for twelve people   (b) three computers for 12 people
20. (a) 4 out of every 100 licenses   (b) four out of every 100 licenses

1. b (4.01a)   3. b (4.01a)   5. b (4.02)   7. b (4.04)   9. b (4.08)   11. b (4.02)   13. b (4.13)   15. b (4.11)   17. a or b (4.04)   19. b (4.06)

CUMULATIVE EDITING QUIZ 8

Use proofreading marks (see Appendix B) to correct errors and omissions in the following sentences. All errors must be corrected to receive credit for the sentence. Check with your instructor for the answers.

1. The president of the U.S. recommended a 30 day cooling off period in the middle east peace negotiations.

2. Please meet at my attorneys office at four p.m. on May 10th to sign our papers of incorporation.

3. A Retail Store at 405 7th avenue had sales of over one million dollars last year.

4. Every new employee must receive their permit to park in lot 5-A or there car will be cited.

5. Mr thompson left three million dollars to be divided among his 4 children rachel, timothy, rebecca and kevin.

6. Most companys can boost profits almost one hundred percent by retaining only 5% more of there current customers.

7. Although the bill for coffee and doughnuts were only three dollars and forty cents Phillip and myself had trouble paying it.

8. Only six of the 19 employees, who filled out survey forms, would have went to hawaii as their vacation choice.

9. Danielles report is more easier to read then david because her's is better organized and has good headings.

10. At mcdonald's we devoured 4 big macs 3 orders of french fries and 5 coca colas for lunch.

CONFUSING WORDS

accede:	to agree or consent	elicit:	to draw out
exceed:	over a limit	illicit:	unlawful
accept:	to receive	every day:	each single day
except:	to exclude; (prep) but	everyday:	ordinary
advice:	suggestion, opinion	farther:	a greater distance
advise:	to counsel or recommend	further:	additional
		formally:	in a formal manner
affect:	to influence	formerly:	in the past
effect:	(n) outcome, result; (v) to bring about, to create	hole:	an opening
		whole:	complete
all ready:	prepared	imply:	to suggest indirectly
already:	by this time	infer:	to reach a conclusion
all right:	satisfactory	liable:	legally responsible
alright:	unacceptable variant spelling	libel:	damaging written statement
altar:	structure for worship	loose:	not fastened
alter:	to change	lose:	to misplace
appraise:	to estimate	miner:	person working in a mine
apprise:	to inform		
assure:	to promise	minor:	a lesser item; person under age
ensure:	to make certain		
insure:	to protect from loss	patience:	calm perseverance
capital:	(n) city that is seat of government; wealth of an individual; (adj) chief	patients:	people receiving medical treatment
		personal:	private, individual
capitol:	building that houses state or national lawmakers	personnel:	employees
		precede:	to go before
		proceed:	to continue
cereal:	breakfast food	precedence:	priority
serial:	arranged in sequence	precedents:	events used as an example
cite:	to quote; to summon		
site:	location	principal:	(n) capital sum; school official; (adj) chief
sight:	a view; to see		
complement:	that which completes	principle:	rule of action
compliment:	to praise or flatter	stationary:	immovable
conscience:	regard for fairness	stationery:	writing material
conscious:	aware	than:	conjunction showing comparison
council:	governing body		
counsel:	to give advice; advice	then:	adverb meaning "at that time"
desert:	arid land; to abandon		
dessert:	sweet food	their:	possessive form of they
device:	invention or mechanism	there:	at that place or point
devise:	to design or arrange	they're:	contraction of they are
disburse:	to pay out	to:	a preposition; the sign of the infinitive
disperse:	to scatter widely		

too:	an adverb meaning "also" or "to an excessive extent"	*waiver:*	abandonment of a claim
two:	a number	*waver:*	to shake or fluctuate

160 FREQUENTLY MISSPELLED WORDS

absence	desirable	independent	prominent
accommodate	destroy	indispensable	qualify
achieve	development	interrupt	quantity
acknowledgment	disappoint	irrelevant	questionnaire
across	dissatisfied	itinerary	receipt
adequate	division	judgment	receive
advisable	efficient	knowledge	recognize
analyze	embarrass	legitimate	recommendation
annually	emphasis	library	referred
appointment	emphasize	license	regarding
argument	employee	maintenance	remittance
automatically	envelope	manageable	representative
bankruptcy	equipped	manufacturer	restaurant
becoming	especially	mileage	schedule
beneficial	evidently	miscellaneous	secretary
budget	exaggerate	mortgage	separate
business	excellent	necessary	similar
calendar	exempt	nevertheless	sincerely
canceled	existence	ninety	software
catalog	extraordinary	ninth	succeed
changeable	familiar	noticeable	sufficient
column	fascinate	occasionally	supervisor
committee	feasible	occurred	surprise
congratulate	February	offered	tenant
conscience	fiscal	omission	therefore
conscious	foreign	omitted	thorough
consecutive	forty	opportunity	though
consensus	fourth	opposite	through
consistent	friend	ordinarily	truly
control	genuine	paid	undoubtedly
convenient	government	pamphlet	unnecessarily
correspondence	grammar	permanent	usable
courteous	grateful	permitted	usage
criticize	guarantee	pleasant	using
decision	harass	practical	usually
deductible	height	prevalent	valuable
defendant	hoping	privilege	volume
definitely	immediate	probably	weekday
dependent	incidentally	procedure	writing
describe	incredible	profited	yield

Key to Grammar/Mechanics Checkups

Chapter 1

1. attorneys (1.05d)   **2.** Saturdays (1.05a)   **3.** cities (1.05e)
4. turkeys (1.05d)   **5.** inventories (1.05e)   **6.** Nashes (1.05b)
7. 1990s (1.05g)   **8.** editors in chief (1.05f)   **9.** complexes (1.05b)
10. counties (1.05e)   **11.** Jennifers (1.05a)   **12.** C (1.05d)
13. liabilities (1.05e)   **14.** C (1.05h)   **15.** runners-up (1.05f)

Chapter 2

1. he (1.08b)   **2.** his car (1.09b)   **3.** him (1.08c)   **4.** whom
(1.08j)   **5.** hers (1.08d)   **6.** me (1.08c)   **7.** I (1.08a)   **8.** yours
(1.08d)   **9.** whoever (1.08j)   **10.** me (1.08i)   **11.** he (1.08f)
12. us (1.08g)   **13.** her (1.09c)   **14.** its (1.09g)   **15.** his or her
(1.09b)

Chapter 3

1. *are* for *is* (1.10e)   **2.** *has* for *have* (1.10c)   **3.** *offers* for *offer*
(1.10d)   **4.** *is* for *are* (1.10g)   **5.** C (1.10f)   **6.** *is* for *are* (1.10i)
7. C (1.10h)   **8.** *chosen* (1.15)   **9.** *lain* for *laid* (1.15)   **10.** *were* for
was (1.12)   **11.** *is* for *are* (1.10c)   **12.** b (1.15c)   **13.** b (1.15c)
14. a (1.15c)   **15.** b (1.15c)

Chapter 4

1. long-time (1.17e)   **2.** $50-per-year (1.17e)   **3.** C (1.17e)
4. quickly (1.17d)   **5.** had only (1.17f)   **6.** double-digit (1.17e)
7. once-in-a-lifetime (1.17e)   **8.** C (1.17e)   **9.** better (1.17a)
10. well-known (1.17e)   **11.** up-to-the-minute (1.17e)   **12.** after-
tax (1.17e)   **13.** couldn't have been clearer (1.17b)   **14.** fifty-
fifty (1.17e)   **15.** feel bad (1.17c)

Chapter 5

1. b (1.19d)   **2.** a (1.19c)   **3.** b (1.18e)   **4.** b (1.19c)   **5.** a (1.19a)
6. b (1.18a)   **7.** b (1.18b)   **8.** a (1.18c)   **9.** b (1.18b)   **10.** a
(1.19c)   **11.** b (1.19a)   **12.** b (1.19b)   **13.** a (1.19c)   **14.** b (1.18c)
15. b (1.19c)

Chapter 6

1. (2)   not, as a rule, (2.03)   **2.** (2) sure, Mrs. Schwartz, (2.02)
3. (2) reliable, conscientious, (2.01)   **4.** (0)   **5.** (1) fact, (2.03)

Chapter 6 (continued)

6. (3) Memphis, Tennessee, Des Moines, (2.04c)   **7.** (1) meantime, (2.03)   **8.** February 4, 2002, (2.04a)   **9.** (2) Mr. Tran, Mrs.
Adams, (2.01)   **10.** (4) Holmes, Lane, San Diego, CA 92110,
(2.04b)   **11.** (2) feels, needless to say, (2.03)   **12.** (2) supplies,
replacing inventories, (2.01)   **13.** (1) business, (2.02)   **14.** (2)
feels, however, (2.03)   **15.** 0

Chapter 7

1. (1) warranty, (2.06a)   **2.** (1) market, (2.05)   **3.** (0) (2.05)
4. (2) manufacturer, nameless, (2.06c)   **5.** (1) imaginative,
(2.08)   **6.** (0) (2.06c)   **7.** (2) Wilson, area, (2.09)   **8.** (1) buyers,
(2.05)   **9.** (1) quality, (2.06a)   **10.** (1) buyers, (2.07)   **11.** (2) application, Monday, (2.06a, 2.04a)   **12.** (2) hand, hard-working,
(2.03, 2.08)   **13.** (1) Concord, (2.06c)   **14.** (3) telephone, Thursday, June 9, (2.06a, 2.04a)   **15.** (1) classes, (2.05)

Chapter 8

1. (2) name," Zajdel," (2.14a)   **2.** Cox, Ph.D., Merrikin, M.B.A.,
(2.10)   **3.** (1) Monday, (2.14b)   **4.** (0) (2.15)   **5.** (1) investment,
(2.12)   **6.** (3) requested, cartridges, folders, (2.06a, 2.01)   **7.** (2)
think, however, (2.03)   **8.** (2) period, Woodward, (2.07, 2.06c)
9. (2) Diego, Monterey, (2.01, 2.15)   **10.** (1) interviewed, (2.06a,
2.06c)   **11.** (2) years, individuals, (2.07, 2.09)   **12.** (2) Wall,
week, (2.05c, 2.15)   **13.** (0) (2.06c)   **14.** (2) companies, robots,
(2.01)   **15.** (2) fact, unprotected, (2.03, 2.08)

Chapter 9

1. (3) one year; long-term financing, hand, (2.03, 2.16b)
2. (2) December; therefore, (2.16a)   **3.** (3) months: September,
October, (2.01, 2.17a)   **4.** (1) are [omit comma] (2.17b)   **5.** (1)
money, (2.06a, 2.16b)   **6.** (3) short-term credit; manufacturer,
however, (2.03, 2.16a)   **7.** (3) credit: accounts, promissory
notes, (2.01, 2.17a)   **8.** (9) businesspeople: Mary Ann Mahan,
financial manager, Holmes Industries; Terry L. Buchanan,
comptroller, Metropolitan Bank; and Mark Kendall, (2.16d,
2.17)   **9.** (1) largest banks, (2.05)   **10.** (5) customers; for example, retailers, service companies, manufacturers, (2.16e, 2.01)
11. (2) rating, loan; (2.06c, 2.16c)   **12.** (2) Federal, applications
to [omit colon] (2.06a, 2.17b)   **13.** (2) high; therefore, (2.16)
14. (2) 18 percent, prohibitive; (2.06a, 2.16c)   **15.** (1) resources;
(2.16b)

Chapter 10

1. Mr. Wilson's (2.20a, 2.21)   **2.** year's (2.20a)   **3.** weeks' (2.20b)
4. Ms. Lanham's (2.21)   **5.** boss's (2.20b)   **6.** waitress's (2.20b)
7. Kevin's (2.22)   **8.** months' (2.20b)   **9.** companies' (2.20b)
10. month's (2.20a)   **11.** lady's (2.20a)   **12.** secretary's (2.20b)
13. sellers' (2.20b)   **14.** Mark's, David's (2.20a)   **15.** Lisa's (2.20a)

Chapter 11

1. (2) committee—Jim Wong— (2.26a, 2.27)   **2.** (3) please, Miss Sanchez, totals? (2.02, 2.23a)   **3.** (2) variables (see Figure 13 on page 432) (2.27)   **4.** (3) "recommendation" misspelled, (2.06a, 2.28c)   **5.** (1) training— (2.26c)   **6.** (2) said, "Who cartridges?" (2.28f)   **7.** (3) "How You"? (2.28e, 2.28f)   **8.** (2) states—Texas, California, and Alaska— (2.26a)   **9.** (4) Mr. Ronald E. Harris, Miss Michelle Hale, and Ms. Sylvia (2.23b, 2.24)   **10.** (3) "Trading Market" *Securities Markets* (2.28e)   **11.** (2) over"; however, (2.16, 2.28f)   **12.** (3) *liability* defined as "any future." (2.28d)   **13.** (1) June 10; (2.06)   **14.** (4) c.o.d. today? (2.23b, 2.24)   **15.** (3) Hooray! checkup, haven't I? (2.24, 2.25)

Chapter 12

1. (5) American customs inspection International Airport (3.01, 3.02, 3.07)   **2.** (6) Japanese international Japanese economics professor University (3.01, 3.02, 3.04, 3.06d)   **3.** (4) business consumer business consumption (3.01, 3.13)   **4.** (4) history sociology computer science (3.05)   **5.** (5) Horticulture Are Nothing Sneeze At (3.12)   **6.** (2) diskettes diskettes (3.11)   **7.** (4) federal government state county (3.10)   **8.** (4) United States This foreign (3.01, 3.06c, 3.13)   **9.** (8) comptroller president board directors Internal Revenue Service company (3.01, 3.04, 3.06c)   **10.** (2) mother sun's (3.03, 3.06g, 3.08, 3.14)   **11.** (5) managing editor   manager ad campaign (3.01, 3.06d, 3.06e, 3.09)   **12.** (3) Austrian German Italian (3.02, 3.06a, 3.16)   **13.** (4) Park island River Bridge (3.01, 3.03)   **14.** (3) Computer Science Department (3.05, 3.07, 3.09)   **15.** (5) Figure Chapter Census Bureau English (3.02, 3.04, 3.07)

Chapter 13

1. b (4.01a)   **2.** a (4.05b)   **3.** a (4.01a)   **4.** b (4.03)   **5.** b (4.02)
6. a (4.03)   **7.** b (4.04)   **8.** b (4.07)   **9.** b (4.08)   **10.** b (4.10)
11. b (4.02)   **12.** b (4.08)   **13.** b (4.12)   **14.** a (4.06)   **15.** a (4.06)

Chapter 14

1. c (2.05)   **2.** b (2.06)   **3.** a (2.16a)   **4.** c (2.15)   **5.** b (2.16b)
6. b (2.17a)   **7.** a (2.20)   **8.** c (2.16d)   **9.** b (2.04a)   **10.** c (2.03)
11. a (2.08)   **12.** a (2.12)   **13.** a (2.01)   **14.** c (2.07)   **15.** b (2.16)

Notes

Chapter 1

1. Mary L. Tucker and Anne M. McCarthy, "Presentation Self-Efficacy: Increasing Communication Skills Through Service-Learning," *Journal of Managerial Issues*, Summer 2001, 227–244. See also A. Cohen, "The Right Stuff," *Sales and Marketing Management* 151, 1999, 15; and Max Messmer, "Skills for a New Millennium," *Strategic Finance*, August 1999, 10–12.

2. W. J. Wilhelm, "A Delphi Study of Entry-Level Workplace Skills, Competencies, and Proof-of-Achievement Products," *The Delta Pi Epsilon Journal*, 1999, 41, 105–122.; "The Challenges Facing Workers in the Future," *HR Focus*, August 1999, 6; and Vanessa Dean Arnold, "The Communication Competencies Listed in Job Descriptions," *The Bulletin of the Association for Business Communication*, June 1992, 16.

3. Janette Moody, Brent Stewart, and Cynthia Bolt-Lee, "Showcasing the Skilled Business Graduate: Expanding the Tool Kit," *Business Communication Quarterly*, March 2002, 23.

4. "Wanted: Leaders Who Can Lead and Write," *Workforce*, December 1997, 21.

5. Max Messmer, "Enhancing Your Writing Skills," *Strategic Finance*, January 2001, 8–10.

6. Paula Jacobs, "Strong Writing Skills Essential for Success, Even in IT," *InfoWorld*, 6 July 1998, 86.

7. Susan J. Wells, "Making Telecommuting Work," *HRMagazine*, October 2001, 34–46.

8. Hal Buell and Amy Zuckerman, "Information, Please," *Journal for Quality and Participation*, May/June 1999, 52–55.

9. J. Burgoon, D. Coker, and R. Coker, "Communicative Explanations," *Human Communication Research* 12, 1986, 463–494.

10. Ray Birdwhistell, *Kinesics and Context* (Philadelphia: University of Pennsylvania Press, 1970).

11. William E. Nolen, "Reading People," *Internal Auditor*, April 1995, 48–51.

12. E. T. Hall, *The Hidden Dimension* (Garden City, NY: Doubleday, 1966), 107–122.

13. Anne Russell, "Fine Tuning Your Corporate Image," *Black Enterprise*, May 1992, 80.

14. Anthony Patrick Carnevale and Susan Carol Stone, *The American Mosaic* (New York: McGraw-Hill, 1995), 160.

15. Lennie Copeland and Lewis Griggs, *Going International* (New York: Penguin Books, 1985), 12.

16. Nancy Rivera Brooks, "Exports Boom Softens Blow of Recession," *Los Angeles Times*, 29 May 1991, D1.

17. Figures compiled by Janice Hamilton Outtz, using *Outlook 1990–2005*, Bureau of Labor Statistics Bulletin 2402, p. 39, appearing in Carnevale and Stone, *The American Mosaic*, 36.

18. U.S. Department of Labor, Bureau of Labor Statistics, *Outlook 1990–2005*, 35.

19. Joel Makower, "Managing Diversity in the Workplace," *Business and Society Review*, Winter 1995.

20. Carnevale and Stone, *The American Mosaic*, 60.

21. Genevieve Capowski, "Managing Diversity," *Management Review*, June 1996, 13.

22. Makower, "Managing Diversity in the Workplace." See also Terry Lefton, "Bok in the Saddle Again," *Brandweek*, 8 February 1999, 26–31.

23. George Simons and Darlene Dunham, "Making Inclusion Happen," *Managing Diversity*, December 1995 <http://www.jalmc.org/mk-incl.htm> (Retrieved 9 August 1996).

24. John H. Bryan, CEO, Sara Lee Corporation, speech before the Corporate Affairs Communications Conference, 21 May 1990, Chicago.

25. "What's the Universal Hand Sign for 'I Goofed'?" *Santa Barbara News-Press*, 16 December 1996, D2.

26. Pete Engardio, "Hmm. Could Use a Little More Snake," *Business Week*, 15 March 1993, 53.

27. Makower, "Managing Diversity in the Workplace," 48–54.

Chapter 2

1. John Berlau, "Ebony's John H. Johnson," *Investor's Business Daily*, 26 March 1999, A1, A7 .

2. Hugh Hay-Roe, "The Secret of Excess," *Executive Excellence*, January 1995, 20.

3. Earl N. Harbert, "Knowing Your Audience," in *The Handbook of Executive Communication*, ed. John L. Digaetani (Homewood, IL: Dow Jones/Irwin, 1986), 17.

4. Vanessa Dean Arnold, "Benjamin Franklin on Writing Well," *Personnel Journal*, August 1986, 17.

5. Mark Bacon, quoted in "Business Writing: One-on-One Speaks Best to the Masses," *Training*, April 1988, 95. See also Elizabeth Danziger, "Communicate Up," *Journal of Accountancy*, February 1998, 67.

6. Paula J. Pomerenke, "A Short Introduction to the Plain English Movement," *Issues in Writing* 10:1, 1999, 30.

Chapter 3

1. Max Messmer, "Enhancing Your Writing Skills," *Strategic Finance*, January 2001, 8–10.

2. Robert W. Goddard, "Communication: Use Language Effectively," *Personnel Journal*, April 1989, 32.

3. Andrew Fluegelman and Jeremy Joan Hewes, "The Word Processor and the Writing Process," in *Strategies for Business and Technical Writing*, 3rd ed., Kevin J. Harty, ed. (San Diego: Harcourt Brace Jovanovich, 1989), 43. See also Lynn Quitman Troyka, *Simon & Schuster Handbook for Writers*, 4th ed. (Upper Saddle River, NJ: Prentice Hall, 1996), 49.

4. Maryann V. Piotrowski, *Effective Business Writing* (New York: HarperPerennial, 1996), 12.

5. Adapted from Roger N. Conaway and Thomas L. Fernandez, "Ethical Preferences Among Business Leaders: Impli-

cations for Business Schools," *Business Communication Quarterly*, March 2000, 23–38.

Chapter 4

1. John S. Fielden, "What Do You Mean You Don't Like My Style?" *Harvard Business Review*, May/June 1982, 128.
2. W. H. Weiss, "Writing Clearly and Forcefully," *Supervision*, December 2001, 14.
3. Louise Lague, *People* Magazine editor, interview with Mary Ellen Guffey, 5 February 1992.
4. Joe Markoff, "New Economy: A Computer Scientist's Lament: Grammar Has Lost Its Technological Edge," *The New York Times*, 15 April 2002.

Chapter 5

1. Michael D. Eisner, "Enlightened Communication," *Vital Speeches*, 15 July 2000, 593.
2. Ruth Davidhizar, Ruth Shearer, and Becky Castro, "A Dilemma of Modern Technology: Managing E-Mail Overload," *Hospital Materiel Management Quarterly*, February 2000, 42–47.
3. Sana Reynolds, "Composing Effective E-Mail Messages," *Communication World*, July 1997, 8–9.
4. Paula Jacobs, "Strong Writing Skills Essentials for Success, Even in IT," *InfoWorld*, 6 July 1998, 86.
5. Leslie Helm, "The Digital Smoking Gun," *Los Angeles Times*, 16 June 1994, El.
6. Carole O'Blenes, "How to Protect Your Company From Misuse of Electronic Communications," *HR Focus*, April 2000, 7; Linda Himelstein, "Exhibit A: The Telltale Computer Tape," *Business Week*, 15 August 1994, 8; and Lawrence Dietz, "E-Mail Is Wonderful But It Has Risks," *Bottom Line/Business* (published by Boardroom, Inc.), 15 June 1995, 3–4; Jenny C. McCune, "Get the Message," *Management Review*, January 1997, 42–44.
7. Peter H. Lewis, "What's on Your Hard Drive?" *The New York Times*, 8 October 1998, G1.
8. "Employers Urged to be Wary of Workplace E-Mail," *Best's Review*, November 2001, 104.
9. Nan DeMars, "Confidentiality Maintenance," *OfficePro*, February 2001, 22–23.
10. Eleena de Lisser, "One-Click Commerce: What People Do Now to Goof Off at Work," *The Wall Street Journal*, 24 September 1999, B1.
11. Michael J. McCarthy, "Virtual Morality: A New Workplace Quandary," *The Wall Street Journal*, 21 October 1999, B1, B4.

Chapter 6

1. Malcolm Forbes, "How to Write a Business Letter," International Paper Company, reprinted in *Strategies for Business and Technical Writing*, 4th ed., ed. Kevin Harty (Boston: Allyn and Bacon, 1999), 108.
2. Marcia Mascolini, "Another Look at Teaching the External Negative Message," *The Bulletin of the Association of Business Communication*, June 1994, 46.
3. Pamela Gilbert, "Two Words That Can Help a Business Thrive," *The Wall Street Journal*, 30 December 1996, A12.
4. "Whole Foods Harvests a Partner in PeopleWise," *Workforce*, December 2001, 64; Mark McLaughlin, "Healthy Profits," *Kiplinger's Personal Finance*, May 2002, 78.; "Nexis Acquires PeopleWise to Create Dominant Force in Preemployment Screening," News Release at PeopleWise

<http://www.peoplewise.com/press6-1-2000.html> (Retrieved 20 May 2002).
5. Based on Mark J. Scarp, "Hotel to Cease Pigeon Poisoning," *Scottsdale Tribune*, 28 October 1995.

Chapter 7

1. René Nourse, vice president, Investments, Prudential Securities Incorporated, interview with author, 16 January 1995.
2. "How to Ask For—And Get—What You Want!" *Supervision*, February 1990, 11.
3. Dean Rieck, "Great Letters and Why They Work," *Direct Marketing*, June 1998, 20–24. See also John R. Graham, "Improving Direct Mail," *Agency Sales*, January 2002, 47–50.
4. Ernest W. Nicastro, "Deadly Sales Letter Mistakes," *Agency Sales*, March 2000, 41–43.
5. Dennis Chambers, *The Agile Manager's Guide to Writing to Get Action* (Bristol, VT: Velocity Press, 1998), 86.
6. Kevin McLaughlin, "Words of Wisdom," *Entrepreneur*, October 1990, 101.
7. Rob Yogel, "Sending Your Message Electronically," *Target Marketing*, June 1998, 77–78. See also Steven C. Bursten, "E-Mail Marketing: Is It on Your Radar Screen?" *Franchising World*, July/August 2001, 60–61.
8. Pat Friesen, "How to Develop an Effective E-Mail Creative Strategy," *Target Marketing*, February 2002, 46–50.
9. Friesen, "How to Develop an Effective E-Mail Creative Strategy," 46–50.
10. Edward O. Welles, "The Diva of Retail," *Inc.*, October 1999, 36–40.
11. Edward O. Welles, "Turf Wars," *Inc.*, February 2000, 90+.
12. Lin Grensing-Pophal, "Training Employees to Telecommute: A Recipe for Success," *HRMagazine*, December 1998, 76; Jeffery D. Zbar, "Training to Telework," *Home Office Computing*, March 2001, 72.
13. Diana Booher, "Resolving Conflict," *Executive Excellence*, May 1999, 5.
14. Gerald L. Wilson, *Groups in Context*, 4e (New York: McGraw-Hill, 1996), 299–300.
15. Deborah DeVoe, "Don't Let Conflict Get You Off Course," *InfoWorld*, 9 August 1999, 69.
16. Devoe, "Don't Let Conflict," 70.
17. Nora Wood, "Singled Out," *Incentive*, July 1998, 20–23.

Chapter 8

1. Cathy Dial, manager, Consumer Affairs, Frito-Lay, interview with author, 26 November 1996.
2. Mohan R. Limaye, "Further Conceptualization of Explanations in Negative Messages," *Business Communication Quarterly*, June 1997, 46.
3. Elizabeth M. Dorn, "Case Method Instruction in the Business Writing Classroom," *Business Communication Quarterly*, March 1999, 51–52.
4. Marcia Mascolini, "Another Look at Teaching the External Negative Message," *The Bulletin of the Association for Business Communication*, June 1994, 47.
5. "Letters to Lands' End," *February 1991 Catalog* (Dodgeville, WI: Lands' End, 1991), 100.
6. Robyn D. Clarke, "The Bearer of Bad News," *Black Enterprise*, July 2000, 61.
7. Michael Granberry, "Lingerie Chain Fined $100,000 for Gift Certificates," *Los Angeles Times*, 14 November 1992, D3.
8. Elizabeth M. Dorn, "Case Method Instruction," 51–52.

9. Based on Gene Sloan, "Under 21? Carnival Says Cruise Is Off," *USA Today*, 29 November 1996; Jill Jordan Sieder, "Full Steam Ahead: Carnival Cruise Line Makes Boatloads of Money by Selling Fun," *U.S. News & World Report*, 16 October 1995, 72; "What to Expect on Carnival Cruises," Bon Vivant Travel <http://www.bvt-usa.com/cruises/c-expect.html> (Retrieved 2 December 1996).

10. Andrew Ross Sorkin, "J. Crew Web Goof Results in Discount," *The New York Times*, 11 November 1999, D3.

11. Allison Linn, "Starbucks Apologizes for Charging NYC Rescue Workers for Water," Associated Press, 25 September, 2001, and "Statement Re: Bottled Water Incident During the September 11, 2001 Tragedy," press release appearing at <http://www.starbucks.com> (Retrieved 13 October 2001).

12. Based on Oren Harari, "The POWER of Complaints," *Management Review*, July–August, 1999, 31.

13. Elizabeth Douglass and Karen Kaplan, "GTE Admits Releasing Unlisted Numbers," *Los Angeles Times*, 17 April 1998, A1, A24.

14. Jeanette W. Gilsdorf, "Metacommunication Effects on International Business Negotiating in China," *Business Communication Quarterly*, June 1997, 27.

Chapter 9

1. "Quotations from Chairman Powell: A Leadership Primer," *Management Review*, December, 1996, 36.

Chapter 10

1. Thomas Sant, *Persuasive Business Proposals: Writing to Win Customers, Clients, and Contracts* (New York: American Management Association, 1992), vii.

2. Herman Holtz, *The Consultant's Guide to Proposal Writing* (New York: John Wiley, 1990), 188.

3. Leslie Brooks Suzukamo, "Search Engines Become Popular for Fact-Finding, Game Playing," *Knight-Ridder/Tribune News Service*, 3 July 2002, pK 6110.

4. H. B. Koplowitz, "The Nature of Search Engines," *Link-Up*, September/October 1998, 28.

5. Moira Allen, "On a Fact-Finding Mission: Search Engines Make It Easy; Just Follow These Basic Rules," *The Writer*, June 2002, 18.

6. Gerald J. Alred, Walter E. Olin, and Charles T. Brusaw, *The Professional Writer* (New York: St. Martin's Press, 1992), 78.

7. Based on Karen S. Sterkel, "Integrating Intercultural Communication and Report Writing in the Communication Class," *The Bulletin of the Association for Business Communication*, September 1988, 14–16.

Chapter 11

1. Rebecca Dudley, "Effective Telephone Skills as Easy as 123-456-7890," *Wenatchee Business Journal*, February 2001, C3.

2. Shearlean Duke, "E-Mail: Essential in Media Relations, But No Replacement for Face-to-Face Communication," *Public Relations Quarterly*, Winter 2001, 19; Lisa M. Flaherty, Kevin J. Pearce, and Rebecca B. Rubin, "Internet and Face-to-Face Communication: Not Functional Alternatives," *Communication Quarterly*, Summer 1998, 250.

3. Aimee L. Drolet and Michael W. Morris, "Rapport in Conflict Resolution: Accounting for How Face-to-Face Contact Fosters Mutual Cooperation in Mixed-Motive Conflicts," *Journal of Experimental Social Psychology*, January 2000, 26.

4. Jean Miculka, *Speaking for Success* (Cincinnati: South-Western, 1999), 19.

5. Cheryl Hamilton with Cordell Parker, *Communicating for Success*, 6e (Belmont, CA: Wadsworth, 2001), 100–104.

6. Miculka, Speaking, 127.

7. "Fire Up Your Phone Skills," *Successful Meetings*, November 2000, 30.

8. Winston Fletcher, "How to Make Sure It's a Good Call," *Management Today*, February 2000, 34.

9. "Did You know That . . .," *Boardroom Reports*, 15 August 1992, 15.

10. Elizabeth Guilday, "Voicemail Like a Pro," *Training & Development*, October 2000, 68.

11. Hal Lancaster, "Learning Some Ways to Make Meetings Slightly Less Awful," *The Wall Street Journal*, 26 May 1998, B1.

12. Tom McDonald, "Minimizing Meetings," *Successful Meetings*, June 1996, 24.

13. Lancaster, "Learning Some Ways," B1.

14. John C. Bruening, "There's Good News About Meetings," *Managing Office Technology*, July 1996, 24–25.

15. Kirsten Schabacker, "A Short, Snappy Guide to Meaningful Meetings," *Working Women*, June 1991, 73.

16. J. Keith Cook, "Try These Eight Guidelines for More Effective Meetings," *Communication Briefings* Bonus Item, April 1995, 8a. See also Morey Stettner, "How to Manage a Corporate Motormouth, *Investor's Business Daily*, 8 October 1998, A1.

17. Hamilton and Parker, *Communicating*, 311–312.

Chapter 12

1. Hal Lancaster, "Practice and Coaching Can Help You Improve Um, Y'Know, Speeches," *The Wall Street Journal*, 9 January 1996, B1.

2. Jeff Olson, *The Agile Manager's Guide to Giving Great Presentations* (Bristol, VT: Velocity Printing, 1999), 8.

3. Dianna Booher, *Executive's Portfolio of Model Speeches for All Occasions* (Upper Saddle River, NJ: Prentice Hall, 1991), 260.

4. Wharton Applied Research Center, "A Study of the Effects of the Use of Overhead Transparencies on Business Meetings, Final Report" cited in "Short, Snappy Guide to Meaningful Presentations," *Working Woman*, June 1991, 73.

5. "On That Next Business Trip, Leave the Laptop Behind . . . And Do It All on Your PDA, New Mobile Software," *Internet Wire*, 18 June 2002, p1008169u4447. See also "PowerPoint Presentations From Your Pocket PC," *PC Magazine*, 9 April 2002, p. NA.

6. Stanford communications professor Clifford Nass quoted in Tad Simons, "When Was the Last Time PowerPoint Made You Sing?" *Presentations*, July 2001, 6. See also "Geoffrey Nunberg, "The Trouble With PowerPoint," *Fortune*, 20 December 1999, 330–334.

7. Simons, "When Was the Last Time," 6.

8. Jennifer Rotondo, "Customized PowerPoint Templates Make Life Easier," *Presentations*, July 2001, 25–26.

9. Jim Endicott, "It Always Pays to Have a Clean, Professional Package," *Presentations*, June 2002, 26–28.

10. Jim Endicott, "For Better Presentations, Avoid PowerPoint Pitfalls," *Presentations*, June 1998, 36–37.

11. Robert J. Boeri, "Fear of Flying? Or the Mail? Try the Web Conferencing Cure," *Emedia Magazine*, March 2002, 49.

12. Victoria Hall Smith, "Gigs by the Gigabyte," *Working Woman*, May 1998, 115.

13. Joan Lloyd, "Engage Your Audience @ Work," *Baltimore Business Journal*, 14 December 2001, 35.
14. Booher, *Executive's Portfolio*, 259.
15. Peter Schneider, "Scenes From a Marriage: Observations on the Daimler-Chrysler Merger From a German Living in America," *The New York Times Magazine*, 12 August, 2001, 47.
16. Ronald E. Dulek, John S. Fielden, and John S. Hill, "International Communication: An Executive Primer," *Business Horizons*, January/February 1991, 23. See also Susan J. Marks, "Nurturing Global Workplace Connections," *Workforce*, September 2001, 76+.
17. Dulek, Fielden, and Hill, "International Communication," 22.
18. Michael Jackson, quoted in "Garbage In, Garbage Out," *Consumer Reports*, December 1992, 755.

Chapter 13

1. Cynthia A. Wagner, "The New Meaning of Work," *Futurist*, September/October 2002, 16–17; Caitlin P. Williams, "The End of the Job As We Know It," *Training & Development*, January 1999, 52–54. See also John A. Challenger, "The Changing Workforce: Workplace Rules in the New Millennium," *Vital Speeches of the Day*, 15 September 2001, 721–728; Manuel London, "Redeployment and Continuous Learning in the 21st Century: Hard Lessons and Positive Examples From the Downsizing Era," *Academy of Management Executive*, November 1996, 67–79.
2. Maarten Mittner, "The Brave New World of Work," *Finance Week*, 30 October 1998, 77.
3. Cary L. Cooper, "The 1998 Crystal Lecture: The Future of Work—A Strategy for Managing the Pressures," *Journal of Applied Management Studies*, December 1998, 275–281.
4. George B. Weathersby, "Responding to Change," *Management Review*, October 1998, 5.
5. Anne Kates Smith, "Charting Your Own Course," *U.S. News & World Report*, 6 November 2000, 56.
6. Smith, "Charting," 57.
7. Michele Pepe, "ResumeMaker Turns a Complete Circle," *Computer Reseller News*, 29 September 1997, 173.
8. Professor Mark Granovetter, quoted in Susan J. Wells, "Many Jobs on Web," *The New York Times*, 12 March 1998, A12.
9. George Crosby of the Human Resources Network, as quoted in Hal Lancaster, "When Taking a Tip From a Job Network, Proceed With Caution," *The Wall Street Journal*, 7 February 1995, B1.
10. Dan Moreau, "Write a Résumé That Works," *Changing Times*, June 1990, 91. See also Natalie Bortoli, "Resumes in the Right: New Rules Make Writing a Winner Easy," *Manage*, August 1997, 20–21.
11. Elizabeth Blackburn-Brockman and Kelly Belanger, "One Page or Two?: A National Study of CPA Recruiters' Preferences for Résumé Length," *The Journal of Business Communication*, January 2001, 29–57.
12. Bortoli, "Resumes in the Right," 20.
13. H. B. Crandall, quoted in Jacqueline Trace, "Teaching Résumé Writing the Functional Way," *The Bulletin of the Association for Business Communication*, June 1985, 41.
14. Bortoli, "Resumes in the Right," 20.
15. Tom Washington, "Improve Your Résumé 100 Percent" <http://www.nbew.com/archive/961001-001.html> (Retrieved 27 September 1998).
16. Robert Lorentz, James W. Carland, and Jo Ann Carland, "The Résumé: What Value Is There in References?" *Journal of Technical Writing and Communication*, Fall 1993, 371.
17. "As Graduation Approaches . . .," *Personnel*, June 1991, 14.
18. Joyce Lain Kennedy and Thomas J. Morrow, *Electronic Résumé Revolution* (New York: John Wiley & Sons, 1994), Chapter 3.
19. Diane Cole, "Ethics: Companies Crack Down on Dishonesty," *The Wall Street Journal, Managing Your Career* supplement, Spring 1991, 8.
20. "Managing Your Career," *National Business Employment Weekly*, Fall 1989, 29.
21. Joan E. Rigdon, "Deceptive Resumes Can Be Door-Openers But Can Become an Employee's Undoing," *The Wall Street Journal*, 17 June 1992, B1. See also Barbara Solomon, "Too Good to Be True?" *Management Review*, April 1998, 28.
22. Marc Silver, "Selling the Perfect You," *U.S. News & World Report*, 5 February 1990, 70–72.
23. Rhonda D. Findling, "The Résumé Fax-periment," *Résumé Pro Newsletter*, Fall 1994, 10.
24. Harriett M. Augustin, "The Written Job Search: A Comparison of the Traditional and a Nontraditional Approach," *The Bulletin of the Association for Business Communication*, September 1991, 13.
25. Judith Schroer, "Seek a Job With a Little Help From Your Friends," *USA Today*, 19 November 1990, B1.

Chapter 14

1. John D. Shingleton, *Successful Interviewing for College Seniors* (Lincolnwood, IL: VGM Career Horizons, 1992), x.
2. Brad Bigham, Sherrie Ilg, and Neil Davidson, "Great Candidates Fast: On-line Job Application and Electronic Processing," *Public Personnel Management*, Spring 2002, 53–64; "Telephone Instrumental in Screening Job Candidates," *HR Focus*, March 1999, 5; Scott Hays, "Kinko's Dials Into Automated Applicant Screening," *Workforce*, November 1999, 71–72.
3. Steve Alexander, "The Interview Spotlight," *InfoWorld*, 10 May 1999, 111–112.
4. Matt Richtel, "Online Revolution's Latest Twist: Job Interviews With a Computer," *The New York Times*, 6 February 2000, 1.
5. Linda Thornburg, "Computer-Aided Interviewing Shortens Hiring Cycle," *HR Magazine*, February 1998, 73–79.
6. Grant Faulkner, "Be Ready for Group Questioning," *InfoWorld*, 4 August 1997, 95.
7. Ron Fry, *Your First Interview* (Hawthorne, NJ: The Career Press, 1991), 16.
8. Caryl Rae Krannich and Ronald L. Krannich, *Dynamite Answers to Interview Questions* (Manassas Park, VA: Impact Publications, 1994) 46.
9. Julia Lawlor, "Networking Opens More Doors to Jobs," *USA Today*, 19 November 1990, B7.
10. J. Michael Farr, *The Very Quick Job Search* (Indianapolis: Jist Works, Inc., 1991), 177–178.

Index

Channels of communication
    choosing, 32–33
    process, 5
Circle chart, *281*
Citations
    of electronic sources, 274, 448
    for a formal report, 294
    of sources, 243, 443–448
Claims
    refusal, 212-*213*
    request, 138–139, *140, 180*
Clarity, 38, 114–115
Classified ads, using for job searches,
    368
Clauses
    dependent, 60, 473
    independent, 60, 473, 478–479
Clichés, 86, 109
Clip art, 43
Closing
    of an e-mail message, *110*–111
    of e-mail messages and memos, *112,*
    113–114
Coherence, of paragraphs, 67–68
Collaboration
    as a conflict response pattern, 315
    team writing, 260–262
Collaborative software, 43
Colons, 479
Color, use in electronic presentations,
    346
Commas, 451–452, 471–476
Committees, capitalization of, 489
Communication
    by cell phone, 318–319
    channels of, *32*
    cross-cultural, 12–15
    definition of, 5
    diversity and, 15–18
    face-to-face, 308–314
    importance of, 2–4
    internal, 100–101
    in job interviews, 402–416
    listening and, 6–8
    in meetings, 320–324
    nonverbal, 8–12, 406–407
    and oral presentations, 334–355
    process of, 4–6, *5*
    telephone, 314–318
    voice mail, 319–320
Company records
    as data for interview preparation,
        404–405
    as data for reports, 240
Compass points, capitalization of, 489
Competition/forcing, as a conflict re-
    sponse pattern, 315
Complaint letter, *180*
Composing, 31, 68–69
Compromise, as a conflict response pat-
    tern, 315

Computers. *See also* Electronic presenta-
    tions; Internet; Technology;
    World Wide Web
    screening interviews on, 403
    visuals for oral presentations, 345
Conciseness
    in business writing, 29
    of e-mails, 102, 107
    of memos, 102
Conclusions, of a formal report,
    293–294
Conflict resolution, 201–202, 314–316
Confusing words, 497–498
Conjunctions, 61, 451, 454, 468–469
Conjunctive adverbs, 61, 478
Content notes, 443
Contracts, legal, 263
Conversation, and positive workplace
    relations, 311
Coordinating conjunction, 61
Correction symbols, 440–442
Cover letters, for job applications,
    388–393
Critical thinking, 52–53
Criticism
    constructive, 313–314
    responding to, 314
Culture
    comparison of U.S., Japanese, Arab, *13*
    diversity and, 15–18
    effect on communication, 12–15
    e-mail and, 109
    in international and cross-cultural au-
        diences, 354–355
    and miscommunication, 6
    and nonverbal cues, 11
    North American, 12–13
Customer claim response, 144–149, *145*
Customer order response, 142–144

D

Dangling modifiers, 66–67
Dashes, 62, 483–484
Data. *See also* Research
    documenting, 274
    illustrating, 277–282
    for job interviews, 404–405
    organizing and outlining, 274–276,
        275, 276
    primary, 272
        interviews, 272
        observation and experimentation,
            273
    for reports, 240
    secondary, 268
        electronic databases, 269–270
        the Internet, 270–271
        print resources, 269
Databases, 55

Dates
    commas in, 471–472
    style for, 493
Decimals, style for, 495
Decision making, 52–53
Decoding, 5–6, 11
Deemphasis, 63–64
Definitions, quotation marks and, 485
Degrees (academic), commas and, 475
Delivery methods, for oral presenta-
    tions, 351–354
Dependent clauses, 60, 473
Dial, Cathy, 203
Diction, levels of, *37*
Direct address, 471
Direct mail marketing, 181–187
Directness, 12
Direct pattern, *58, 59,* 216, 235
Discussion section, of a formal report, 293
Distractions, nonverbal, 7
Diversity. *See* Culture; Workforce diver-
    sity
Divisions, capitalization of, 489
Documentation. *See* Data, documenting
Documents, formats for, 425–437. *See
    also* individual types

E

Eisner, Michael, 100, *104,* 106
Electronic databases, 269–270
Electronic presentations
    build capability in, 348
    bullet points in, 345
    color in, *346,* 347
    handouts with, 349
    hyperlinks in, 348
    PowerPoint for, 345, *349*
    and the Rule of Seven, 348
    speakers' notes for, 349-*350*
    templates for, 345–346
Electronic sources. *See* Citations, of elec-
    tronic sources
E-mail
    addresses, 106
    bad news in, 107
    conciseness, 102
    conversational tone in, 37
    describing procedures, *114–115*
    effective use of, 106–109
    formatting, 109–111, *110*
    frontloading and, 59
    graphic highlighting in, 102–103
    making requests in, *116*
    netiquette of, 108
    parts of, 437–439
    personal use of, 108
    replying to, 108, 116
    résumés sent by, 388
    sample, *438*

determining purpose and audience, 335–337

frontloading and, 59

good organization for, 337–341

and types of visual aids, 343–345

Order requests, 137–138

Orders/acknowledgments, frontloading and, 59

Organization

formal reports, 274–276

headings for, *277*

outlining, *276*

patterns of, *275–276*

oral presentations, 30

for international and cross-cultural audiences, 354–355

using a word processor, 42, 335–341

résumés, 373, 375–379

Organizations

downsizing in, 100

global competition and, 4

hierarchies in, 4, 100

information and, 4, 100

participatory, 4

team, 4, 100

and technology, 4

and work environments, 4

Outdated expressions, 82–83

Outlining, 42, *57*

for formal reports, *276*

of oral presentations, *339*

Overhead transparencies, 344–345

P

Paragraphs

coherence of, 67–68

length of, 68

Parallel construction, 64–65, 115, 241

Paraphrasing, 274

Parentheses, 484

Parenthetical elements, 471, 483

Parliamentary procedure, 322

Parts of speech, 453. *See also* specific parts of speech

Passive voice, 36, 64, 208

Patterns

for organizing oral presentations, 340

for organizing written reports, *58*

Percentages, style for, 495

Periodicals, as secondary sources, 269

Periods (punctuation), 483

Personal appearance, 11, 406

Personalization, for oral presentations, 341–342

Personal space, 10, *11*

Persuasion

indirect pattern for, 59

informal proposals and, 264

in letters and memos, 174–187

Phrases, 60, 474

Pie chart, *281*

Pitch, 310

Plagiarism, 274

Plain English, *39*

Plural nouns, 450, 455

Polls, 184

Positive language, 38

Possessive nouns, 450

Posture, 9, 11

Powell, Colin, 234

PowerPoint, 345, *349*

Prepositional phrases, 82

Prepositions, 271, 451, 454, 467

Presentation software, 345

Prewriting, for business messages and oral presentations, 29–30

Primary data, 272–273

Print resources, 269

Problem solving, 52–53

Problem-solving, as a conflict response pattern, 315

Product names, capitalization of, 489

Professional organizations, using for job searches, 368

Progress reports. *See* Reports, informal

Pronouns, 67–68, 450–451, 456–459

Pronunciation, 310

Proofreading, 31

of complex documents, 89

e-mails and memos, 105

marks, *89, 442*

process of, 87–88

of routine documents, 88

Proper nouns, 454, 487

Proposals

description of, 263

formal (*See* Reports, formal)

informal, 264–266, *267*

request for proposal (RFP), 263

when to use, 32

Punctuation

proofreading for, 88

styles of, 433

Purpose

for an informal proposal, 264

identifying, 31–32

of messages, 29

of oral presentations, 335

of reports, 239, 268

Q

Question marks, 483

Questionnaires, as data for reports, 240

Questions, commas and, 476

Quotation marks, 271, 484–485

Quotations

colon and, 479

commas and, 476

within quotations, 484

R

Rate, of speech, 311

Readers, comprehension by, 61–62

Readers' Guide to Periodical Literature, 269

Receiver, 5

Recommendation, letters of, 148–149, *150*

Recommendations, of a formal report, 293–294

Redundancy, 83–84

References. *See* Citations

Refusals

claims, 212–*213*

requests, 209–*211*

Repetition, 83

Reports, 33

analytical, 235

conversational tone in, 37

designing, *242*

formal

documenting data for, 274

generating primary data for, 272–274

illustrating data for, 277–282

organizing and outlining data for, 274–276

parts of, 283, *284–293*, 294

preparing to write, 268

researching secondary data for, 268–271

formal, writing style for, *241*

frontloading and, 59

informal, 234

audience analysis and report organization, *236*

developing, 239–243

direct and indirect patterns of, 235–236

feasibility, 244, 247, *249*

formats, 236, 238

functions, 235

informational, *235–236*, 243, 244

justification/recommendation, 244, 245, 246, *248*

minutes of meetings, 244, 249–*250*, 324

progress, 244, 245, *246*

proposals, 264–266, *267*

summaries, 244, 251, *252*

writing style for, 240–242, *241*

Request for proposal (RFP), 263

Request/response

of e-mails and memos, 116–118

frontloading and, 59

Research

formal and informal methods, 55–57

as part of the writing process, 30

of primary data, 272–274

of secondary data, 268–271

using the Web for, 42